The NIV STANDARD LESSON COMMENTARY 2002-2003

edited by

RONALD G. DAVIS, RONALD L. NICKELSON,
AND JONATHAN UNDERWOOD

published by
Standard Publishing

Jonathan Underwood, Senior Editor
Cheryl Frey, Associate Editor
Mark A. Taylor, Vice President, Church Resources
Paul D. Learned, Managing Director
Carla J. Crane, Production Manager

Ninth Annual Volume

Standard
PUBLISHING

CINCINNATI, OHIO

CD-ROM AVAILABLE

The *Standard Lesson Commentary* is available in an electronic format in special editions of the *Standard Lesson Commentary* (King James edition) and *The NIV® Standard Lesson Commentary.* These editions (order #20003 for KJV and 30003 for NIV®) contain a compact disk for use with Windows®-based computers.

The Libronix Digital Library System is the technology that powers the electronic version of the *Standard Lesson Commentary.* In addition to the electronic version of the Commentary, other compatible Bibles and Bible reference books are available on the CD-ROM for purchase. The Libronix DLS is from the makers of the Logos Library System (LLS). All LLS books, including previously released LLS versions of the *Standard Lesson Commentary work with the Libronix DLS.*

SYSTEM REQUIREMENTS
Computer/Processor: Pentium 133MHz (300MHz processor recommended)
CD-ROM Drive: 2x or better
Operating System: Microsoft Windows 95 or later (Will run on Windows 98/98SE/Me/NT 4.0 (SP3)/2000/XP)
Memory: Windows 95/98/Me/NT: 64 MB; Windows 2000/XP: 64 MB (128 MB recommended)
Hard Drive Space: 60 MB Minimum
Screen Resolution: 800x600 or larger

If you have any questions regarding the use of this CD-ROM, please contact Technical Support by telephone at (360) 679-4496, by E-mail at tech@logos.com, or online at www.logos.com/support.

© 2002
STANDARD PUBLISHING
a division of STANDEX INTERNATIONAL Corporation
8121 Hamilton Avenue, Cincinnati, Ohio 45231
Printed in U.S.A.

In This Volume

Special Features

Fall Quarter, 2002
Judgment and Exile

Writers

Lesson Development ....Orrin Root	Discovery Learning ....Ronald L. Oakes
Verbal Illustrations.................Charles R. Boatman	What Do You Think? ....Kenneth Goble
Why Teach This Lesson? ....Ronald L. Nickelson	

Winter Quarter, 2002-2003
Portraits of Faith

Writers

Lesson Development ....Thomas Friskney (1-5), Terry A. Clark (6-9), Michael Shannon (10-13)	Verbal Illustrations ....Robert C. Shannon (1-7), ...Victor Knowles (8-13)
Discovery Learning............................Alan Weber	What Do You Think? ....Richard A. Koffarnus
Why Teach This Lesson? ....Ronald L. Nickelson	

Spring Quarter, 2003
Jesus: God's Power in Action

Writers

Lesson Development ....Dennis Gaertner (1-5), John W. Wade (6-8), Marshall Hayden (9-13)	Discovery Learning.....................Rick Shonkwiler
	What Do You Think?.........................Phil Roberts
Verbal Illustrations.................Charles R. Boatman	Why Teach This Lesson? ....Ronald L. Nickelson

Summer Quarter, 2003
God Restores a Remnant

Writers

Lesson Development...............Lloyd Pelfrey (1-5), Orrin Root (6-11), Douglas Redford (12-14)	Discovery Learning....................Virginia Beddow, ...Greg Delort
Verbal Illustrations ....Jeffrey Metzger, ...Ronald L. Nickelson	What Do You Think? ....David Baynes (1-7), ...Simon J. Dahlman (8-14)
Why Teach This Lesson? ....Ronald L. Nickelson	

Index of Printed Texts, 2002-2003

The printed texts for 2002-2003 are arranged here in the order in which they appear in the Bible. Opposite each reference is the page number on which the lesson that treats the passage begins in this volume.

Cumulative Index of Printed Texts

A cumulative index for the Scripture passages used in *The NIV Standard Lesson Commentary* for September, 1998—August, 2003 is presented here for your convenience.

Fall Quarter, 2002

Judgment and Exile

Special Features

Lessons

Unit 1: Urgent Plea

Unit 2: Limited Hope

Unit 3: Final Defeat

About These Lessons

The lessons of the present quarter chronicle the sad decline of the kingdom of Judah until the fall of Jerusalem in 586 B.C. We then pick up the story of the exiles as they look in hope to their eventual return to their homeland. It is a tale of lessons taught but not learned. May we learn from the failure of God's people so that we might enjoy the blessings of the Lord.

Sep 1
Sep 8
Sep 15
Sep 22
Sep 29
Oct 6
Oct 13
Oct 20
Oct 27
Nov 3
Nov 10
Nov 17
Nov 24

Disaster and Hope

by Orrin Root

In the fall of 1998 we began our six-year cycle of Sunday school lessons with a swift survey of the Old Testament. (See the chart below.) This provided a framework in which later Old Testament lessons can be placed. In the fall of 1999 we traced the escape of God's people from Egypt, their wandering in the desert, and their conquest of the promised land. In the fall of 2000 we considered the time of the judges who followed Joshua, and then the reigns of Israel's first three kings, Saul, David, and Solomon. In the summer of 2001 we saw how Israel was divided into two separate kingdoms, and we followed the fortunes of the two until the northern kingdom was overwhelmed by Assyria and its people were scattered abroad. Now in the fall of 2002 we turn to the southern kingdom, usually called Judah. We shall follow it through good times and bad until we see it conquered by Babylon and taken into captivity. Here are short previews of our thirteen lessons.

International Sunday School Lesson Cycle
September, 1998—August, 2004

YEAR	FALL QUARTER (Sept., Oct., Nov.)	WINTER QUARTER (Dec., Jan., Feb.)	SPRING QUARTER (Mar., Apr., May)	SUMMER QUARTER (June, July, Aug.)
1998-1999	God Calls a People to Faithful Living (Old Testament Survey)	God Calls Anew in Jesus Christ (New Testament Survey)	That You May Believe (John)	Genesis: Beginnings (Genesis)
1999-2000	From Slavery to Conquest (Exodus, Leviticus, Numbers, Deuteronomy, Joshua)	Immanuel: God With Us (Matthew)	Helping a Church Confront Crisis (1 and 2 Corinthians)	New Life in Christ (Ephesians, Philippians, Colossians, Philemon)
2000-2001	Rulers of Israel (Judges, 1 and 2 Samuel, 1 Kings 1-11)	Good News of Jesus (Luke)	Continuing Jesus' Work (Acts)	Division and Decline (1 Kings 12-22, 2 Kings 1-17, Isaiah 1-39, Hosea, Amos, Micah)
2001-2002	Jesus' Ministry (Parables, Miracles, Sermon on the Mount)	Light for All People (Isaiah 9:1-7; 11:1-9; 40-66; Ruth, Jonah, Nahum)	The Power of the Gospel (Romans, Galatians)	Worship and Wisdom for Living (Psalms, Proverbs)
2002-2003	Judgment and Exile (2 Kings 18-25, Jeremiah, Lamentations, Ezekiel, Habakkuk, Zephaniah)	Portraits of Faith (Personalities in the New Testament)	Jesus: God's Power in Action (Mark)	God Restores a Remnant (Ezra, Nehemiah, Daniel, Joel, Obadiah, Haggai, Zechariah, Malachi)
2003-2004	Faith Faces the World (James, 1 and 2 Peter, 1, 2, 3 John, Jude)	A Child Is Given (Samuel, John the Baptist, Jesus) / Lessons From Life (Esther, Job, Ecclesiastes, Song of Solomon)	Jesus Fulfills His Mission (Death, Burial, and Resurrection Texts) / Living Expectantly (1, 2 Thessalonians, Revelation)	Hold Fast to the Faith (Hebrews) / Guidelines for the Church's Ministry (1, 2 Timothy, Titus)

Unit 1. Urgent Plea

September

Judah, the south part of divided Israel, did not fall into idolatry and kindred sins as rapidly as the north kingdom did. The temple was in Judah, and there were faithful priests to lead in God's way. But Judah wavered between true worship and idolatry, swayed by the wish of each new king. Jeremiah was God's outstanding prophet then. Through him God pleaded with the people to be true; but when a king preferred idolatry, some people were all too ready to accept it.

Lesson 1. King Ahaz led the country far into idol worship, but King Hezekiah turned it around. He restored the Passover feast that had been long neglected.

Lesson 2. When Hezekiah died, his son Manasseh became king and did great evil. Very late in life he tried to undo the harm he had done.

Lesson 3. Manasseh's son Amon rejected his father's reforms. After Amon was murdered, his young son Josiah became king and began to seek God.

Lesson 4. In the long reign of Manasseh and the short reign of Amon, places of idol worship were built all over Judah. King Josiah ordered them destroyed.

Lesson 5. After King Josiah died, Judah had no more good kings. The people insisted on ignoring God's law, and punishment drew ever nearer.

Unit 2. Limited Hope

October

Through Jeremiah and other prophets, the Lord kept on warning that evil living would surely bring disaster. But the people did not have to go on with their evil living. They could repent; they could obey God; they could avoid disaster. But the people preferred to believe lying prophets who said no disaster was coming.

Lesson 6. Through many years God's warnings had been ignored. Now came a definite promise: an enemy army was about to strike from the north.

Lesson 7. God's warning came with increased intensity. But the people liked their lawlessness and continued with their evil ways.

Lesson 8. Without withdrawing one word from the promise of captivity, the Lord looked beyond the disaster to a better time and a New Covenant.

Lesson 9. Habakkuk was one of the true prophets of that time when Israel's sins were monstrous and continuous. He asked some important questions.

Unit 3. Final Defeat

November

"The Lord is merciful and gracious, slow to anger, and plenteous in mercy" (Psalm 103:8). But persistent sinners find there is a time when His mercy gives place to wrath.

Lesson 10. The Babylonian army came three times, eventually leveling Jerusalem and the temple. They took most of the survivors to captivity in Babylon.

Lesson 11. The rebellious people of Judah were in captivity. Their grief and hope found expression in the book of Lamentations.

Lesson 12. The prophet Ezekiel was a captive in Babylon. There he rebuked his fellow captives for denying their guilt and for accusing God of being unfair.

Lesson 13. The final lesson of this series brings a promise bright enough to dry all the tears of the long captivity. God was going to take the homesick captives back again—back to the well-loved hills of home. More importantly, the people would be cleansed, purified, made fit to be God's people.

And then comes a surprise. The Lord would not do that for the sake of the people of Israel, who would benefit from it. Stay around and learn why He promised to do such a wonderful thing.

Then stay with us till we return to Old Testament study in the summer of 2003. At that time we shall see how fifty thousand captives led the move from Babylon back to the homeland.

Lesson Planning Page

List the aims here, either directly from the lesson or revised to suit your individual needs.

LESSON AIMS

Begin with an opening activity like the illustration from the beginning of the lesson, "Into the Lesson" from the Discovery Learning page, a discussion question, or some other appropriate opener.

GETTING STARTED

List in order the activities you will use. These include discussion questions, activities from the discovery learning page and the reproducible page—as well as key points from the commentary section.

LESSON DEVELOPMENT

I.

II.

III.

How will you bring the lesson to a climax, stressing the key point and desired action steps?

CONCLUSION & APPLICATION

Dismiss the class with an activity that reinforces the Bible lesson.

CLOSING ACTIVITY

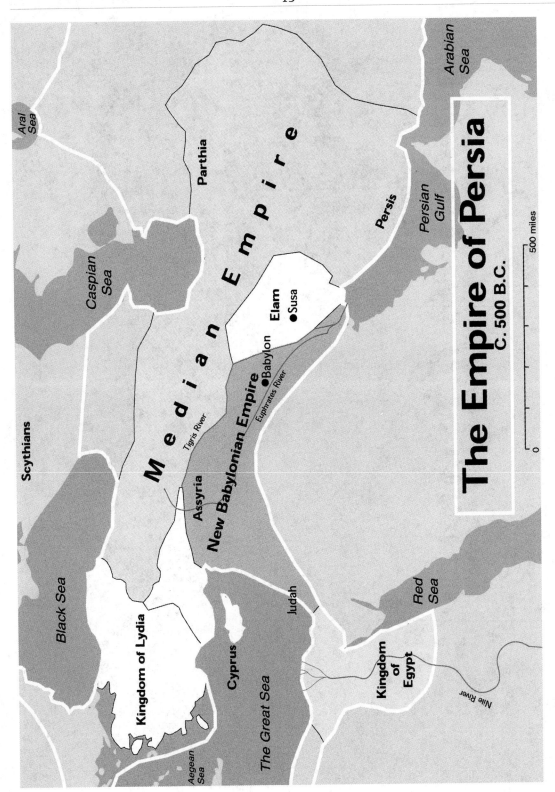

The Empire of Persia
C. 500 B.C.

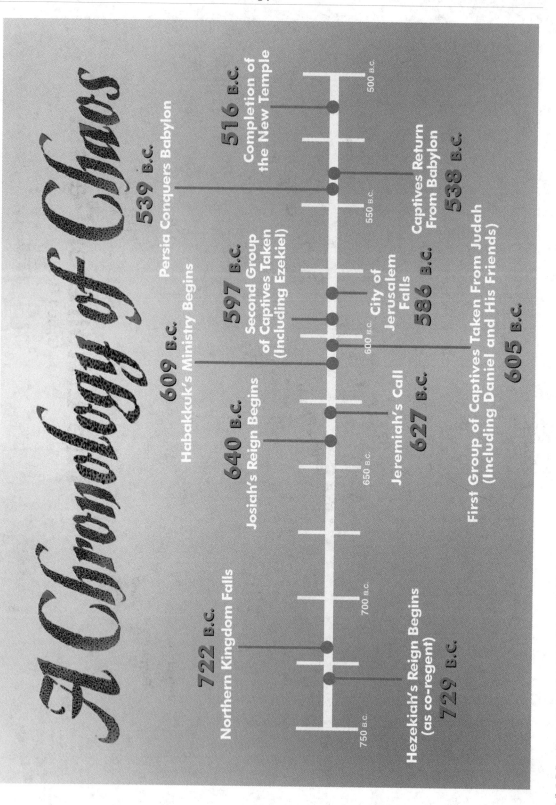

A Chronology of Chaos

REPENTANCE AND RENEWAL

LESSON 1

WHY TEACH THIS LESSON?

Anyone who has ever tried selling something knows the exasperation of having the sales pitch repeatedly rejected. Back when I was in Cub Scouts, I went door-to-door trying to sell tickets to a certain scouting event. I sold exactly zero. (Actually, I think my father bought two out of sympathy!) Later in 4-H Club, I went door-to-door selling miniature first-aid kits for people to keep in their cars. Again, I sold exactly zero. I don't remember ever trying to sell much after those experiences!

Today's lesson is about a godly king who realizes that the "product" he has to offer—renewal of proper worship—is desperately needed by all the Jewish people. So he dispatches his "sales force" throughout the land with the message, only to have them repeatedly rejected and scorned. But he presses ahead with his plans nonetheless, and many are spiritually blessed. Today's lesson will help your learners keep in mind that the majority do not accept the call to true godliness (Matthew 7:13, 14). Of those who do, some will drift away and will reject a call to return (Matthew 13:1-22). Even so, we do not lose heart because Christ has overcome the world (John 16:33).

INTRODUCTION

A. LIKE AND UNLIKE

"Like father, like son." That old adage is so often repeated and so often true that we may forget it can be false. I am the son of an Arizona farmer, but here I am writing lessons at a desk two thousand miles from the old home farm. Dad never wrote a Sunday school lesson. But yesterday on a downtown sidewalk I faced my reflection in a store window, and it was like coming face to face with Dad, who died many years ago. The hat, the face, the coat and tie, the shoulders stooped a little—it was Dad as I remember him. So am I like my father? In occupation, no. We could hardly be more different. But in physical appearance, I am a photocopy. On a deeper level, my father's faith is my faith, and shall be till I die.

When we look at the kings of ancient Judah, we see them alike in ancestry and occupation. They are descendants of David and kings of Judah. Sometimes we see a king duplicating his father's faith and course of action as well. But sometimes we see a king forsaking his father's faith and deliberately revising his father's way of living and ruling.

B. LESSON BACKGROUND

Students of Old Testament history remember that Solomon's magnificent empire was split when that king died (about 931 B.C.). It became two feeble little nations. Ten tribes, mostly in the north, kept the name of Israel. The tribes of Judah and Benjamin, with Jerusalem on the border between them, were known as Judah.

In Israel to the north, King Jeroboam I (reigned 931–910 B.C.) did not want his people to go to Jerusalem and worship with the people of Judah. He was afraid that the two nations would reunite and he would no longer be king. So he established centers of worship in his own domain, with golden calves as idols (1 Kings 12:26-33). In declaring them to be "your gods, O Israel, who brought

DEVOTIONAL READING:
PSALM 122
BACKGROUND SCRIPTURE:
2 CHRONICLES 29, 30; 2 KINGS 18-20
PRINTED TEXT:
2 CHRONICLES 30:1-12

LESSON AIMS

After participating in this lesson, each student will be able to:

1. Tell how Hezekiah attempted to restore the Passover celebration for all Israel and the result of his efforts.

2. Explain why one's efforts to do the right thing are not always appreciated.

3. Commit to do this week something to share the gospel or otherwise honor the Lord even though unbelievers may oppose the effort.

KEY VERSE

The LORD your God is gracious and compassionate. He will not turn his face from you if you return to him.
—2 Chronicles 30:9

you up out of Egypt" (v. 28), King Jeroboam used words startlingly similar to those used by Aaron about five hundred years before! (See Exodus 32:4.) That northern kingdom sank deeper into idolatry and other sins.

Judah, for her part, wavered between the Lord and idols because different kings led in different ways. King Jotham was like his father, Uzziah (790–739 B.C.). Both "did what was right in the eyes of the Lord" (2 Chronicles 26:4; 27:2). But Jotham's son, Ahaz, was different. He did not do right; he made and worshiped idols; he killed his own children in sacrifice to an imaginary god (2 Chronicles 28:1-4).

When Ahaz died, his son Hezekiah (727–695 B.C.) became king and promptly reversed the wicked policies of his father. He reopened the Lord's temple that Ahaz had closed, having it cleaned and repaired. He gave no worship to idols, but restored worship of the Lord with abundant sacrifices and great rejoicing (2 Chronicles 29). This brings us to our printed text.

I. PASSOVER RENEWED (2 CHRONICLES 30:1-4)

The Passover might be called the Jews' independence celebration, since it marks the anniversary of their release from slavery in Egypt. Having been in existence for over seven hundred years, this feast has been ignored during the sixteen-year reign of Ahaz because of that king's devotion to the imaginary gods of the pagans. Now Hezekiah intends to restore the Passover to its proper place in the life of the nation.

A. PASSOVER CALLED (v. 1)

1. Hezekiah sent word to all Israel and Judah and also wrote letters to Ephraim and Manasseh, inviting them to come to the temple of the LORD in Jerusalem and celebrate the Passover to the LORD, the God of Israel.

Roughly two hundred years have passed since ten of Israel's twelve tribes have stopped coming to *Jerusalem* to worship (1 Kings 12:26-33). By 732 B.C., the Assyrians have conquered "Gilead and Galilee, including all the land of Naphtali, and deported the people to Assyria" (2 Kings 15:29). It is within this framework of religious decay and foreign threat that Hezekiah sends *to all Israel and Judah* an invitation to *celebrate the Passover* feast at Jerusalem. Hezekiah longs to see old enmity forgotten, as all Israel once again worships *the Lord, the God of Israel* together.

B. PASSOVER DELAYED (vv. 2-4)

2. The king and his officials and the whole assembly in Jerusalem decided to celebrate the Passover in the second month.

Hezekiah shows a great deal of prudence with his plan. In consulting *his officials and the whole assembly in Jerusalem* (at least the heads of the families in that city), *the king* acts neither hastily nor unilaterally. His consultations undoubtedly reveal that the regular, appointed time of the Passover is to be the fourteenth day of "the first month" (late March or early April to us), and is the beginning of the weeklong Feast of Unleavened Bread (Leviticus 23:5, 6). The law further provided for an alternative date *in the second month*. If anyone is "unclean" at Passover time, or is far away on a long journey, that person may celebrate the Passover in the second month instead of the first (Numbers 9:9-11).

3, 4. They had not been able to celebrate it at the regular time because not enough priests had consecrated themselves and the people had not assembled in Jerusalem. The plan seemed right both to the king and to the whole assembly.

Thus the celebration was delayed a month, first of all, *because not enough priests had consecrated themselves.* When the cleansed temple is rededicated, there are not enough sanctified priests to offer the sacrifices (2 Chronicles 29:34).

WHAT DO YOU THINK?

How much power or influence would a person need in order to inspire our nation to come back to God? Would this person likely be an elected official? A religious leader? A leader of some kind of grassroots movement? Why?

Visual for lesson 1. Use this timeline from the Adult Visuals packet to help your students sort out the chronology of this quarter's studies.

Hezekiah's respect for the holiness of God is such that it seems best to postpone the Passover until the priests are sanctified. After the reign of Hezekiah's wicked father, most of the people as well as many of the priests are undoubtedly unclean in some way, and time will be required for them to sanctify themselves.

Second, the Passover cannot be celebrated at the regular time because *the people had not assembled in Jerusalem.* The decision *to celebrate* this feast must have been made while the temple was being cleaned in the first month of the first year of Hezekiah's reign (2 Chronicles 29:3-5). At that time, it was too late for invitations to be sent to all Israel and for the people to assemble at Jerusalem for a Passover in the first month. Delaying the Passover until the second month will provide time to "get the message out" regarding this upcoming celebration.

II. PEOPLE INVITED (2 CHRONICLES 30:5-9)

As noted above, the Passover celebration is part of the Feast of Unleavened Bread (cf. Matthew 26:17). According to the law of Moses, all adult male Israelites must be invited (cf. Deuteronomy 16:16). The godly Hezekiah makes sure this happens.

A. EXTENT OF THE INVITATION (v. 5)

5. *They decided to send a proclamation throughout Israel, from Beersheba to Dan, calling the people to come to Jerusalem and celebrate the Passover to the LORD, the God of Israel. It had not been celebrated in large numbers according to what was written.*

Beersheba in the south and *Dan* in the north—about 150 miles apart—marked the limits of all *Israel* before the division of 931 B.C. The expression "from Dan to Beersheba" is familiar as a designation for the entire Israelite people (e.g., 2 Samuel 3:10; 17:11; 24:2). The invitation is to be sent to all that territory, which now includes the two separate nations of *Israel* and Judah. *In large numbers* indicates only sporadic (at best) Passover observances over the past two hundred years. We wonder how much of any part of the *written* Word of God has been taught to the people during that period!

B. SPEED OF THE INVITATION (v. 6a)

6a. *At the king's command, couriers went throughout Israel and Judah with letters from the king and from his officials,*

The *couriers* are swift runners (cf. Job 9:25) who carry the *letters from the king and from his officials* to every part of *Israel and Judah*, reading them in the streets and marketplaces of all the towns. There must be a great many of them to reach all the towns quickly, for hardly a month remains until the Passover time in the second month. In Judah, the king invites his own people to come to the Passover. In Israel, Hezekiah bypasses the feeble king and makes his appeal directly to the people.

NEW METHODS, TIMELESS MESSAGE

"Neither snow nor rain nor gloom of night stays these couriers from the swift completion of their appointed rounds." These words, inscribed on the New York City General Post Office building, are those of Herodotus, the ancient Greek. They describe the fidelity of the mounted postal carriers that served the Persian empire under Cyrus, about 500 B.C. Mounted couriers, trains, trucks, and planes have all been used to carry personal mail, government information, newspapers, magazines, and news of every sort. Now, with the advent of speed-of-light E-mail, these methods have all become "snail mail."

WHAT DO YOU THINK?

In 2 Chronicles 30:5 we read that for a long time the Israelites had not observed the Passover "according to what was written." In other words, they had not followed the Scriptures in their practice. How would you go about "speaking the truth in love" to change a long-standing tradition in your church if you became convinced the practice was not in harmony with the Word of God?

WHAT DO YOU THINK?

If you could write a letter to the younger generation in your country to urge them to turn to the Lord, what would you write?

DAILY BIBLE READINGS

Monday, Aug. 26—*Hezekiah Calls for Renewal (2 Chronicles 29:1-11)*

Tuesday, Aug. 27—*Purify and Consecrate (2 Chronicles 29:15-24)*

Wednesday, Aug. 28—*The People Worship (2 Chronicles 29:25-30)*

Thursday, Aug. 29—*Sing to the Lord (Psalm 149:1-9)*

Friday, Aug. 30—*The People Bring Thank Offerings (2 Chronicles 29:31-36)*

Saturday, Aug. 31—*The People Celebrate Passover (2 Chronicles 30:1-12)*

Sunday, Sept. 1—*God Hears the People's Prayer (2 Chronicles 30:21-27)*

WHAT DO YOU THINK?

Spiritually, Hezekiah was unlike his father but more like his faithful grandfather and great-grandfather. Name some people who have influenced you to choose God's way. Thinking of ways that people are influenced both inside and outside the family, how can we help people—especially young people—to choose to follow the positive role models in their lives and not the negative ones? Use 2 Timothy 1:5 to inform your answer.

No longer do missionaries have to wrestle with the vagaries of international phone service or wait days and weeks for mail from their prayer partners and supporters. E-mail lets them communicate almost instantaneously.

There is a downside to this: anyone can send out any kind of message he wants. E-mail hoaxes are legion. Our penchant for speed tempts us to pay less attention to truth than we ought.

The message brought by Hezekiah's couriers wasn't as fast as E-mail, but it was true. In keeping with God's plea to his people in every age they said, "Return to God" in order that "he may return to you." Methods of communicating God's Word may change, but the message is timeless.   —C. R. B.

C. CONTENT OF THE INVITATION (vv. 6b-9)

6b. . . . which read:

"People of Israel, return to the LORD, the God of Abraham, Isaac and Israel, that he may return to you who are left, who have escaped from the hand of the kings of Assyria.

This is more than an invitation to a feast. It is nothing less than a call to forsake idolatry and *return to the Lord, the God of* their ancestors. Already *the kings of Assyria* have conquered a substantial part of Israel's territory, taking captive many Israelites (2 Kings 15:29). In making a promise to the remnant Israelites that God would *return* to them if they would *return* to him, Hezekiah sets a theme that will be echoed frequently by the prophets (cf. Isaiah 31:6; Jeremiah 3:12; Joel 2:13; and others).

7. "Do not be like your fathers and brothers, who were unfaithful to the LORD, the God of their fathers, so that he made them an object of horror, as you see.

The Israelites who have escaped capture so far can *see* with their own eyes the desolation that has come at the hand of the Assyrians. This has come about because the Israelites have been *unfaithful to the Lord, the God of their fathers.* Will the remaining Israelites heed this "visual aid" and not repeat the sin that has brought it about?

8. "Do not be stiff-necked, as your fathers were; submit to the LORD. Come to the sanctuary, which he has consecrated forever. Serve the LORD your God, so that his fierce anger will turn away from you.

The Old Testament refers to the Israelite people as *stiff-necked,* stubborn, or obstinate more than thirty times (also cf. Acts 7:51). This type of attitude toward God always leads to destruction.

The only way to prevent the pending destruction will be for the Israelites to *submit* themselves *to the Lord.* The starting point on this road back to God is to *come* to the Passover and enter into his *sanctuary,* the temple in Jerusalem. The Passover was one of three pilgrimage feasts adult Israelite males were to keep each year. (The Feast of Weeks, later known as Pentecost, and the Feast of Tabernacles were the others; Deuteronomy 16:1-17). To go to all the trouble to make the pilgrimage to observe the Passover will demonstrate action coupled with repentant faith.

9. "If you return to the LORD, then your brothers and your children will be shown compassion by their captors and will come back to this land, for the LORD your God is gracious and compassionate. He will not turn his face from you if you return to him."

The letter now returns to the promise of verse 6b. Since *the Lord your God is gracious and compassionate,* he would rather bless than punish. He will not turn away from the Israelites if they *return to him* with genuine worship and faithful obedience. If they will do that, even those already in captivity will be set free again.

III. PEOPLE RESPOND (2 CHRONICLES 30:10-12)

Drastic proposals can draw mixed responses—and it is certainly a drastic change that Hezekiah advocates. The people now living to the north in Israel have never attended a Passover celebration in Jerusalem. For generations, their government has promoted a state religion with worship centers at Bethel and Dan (1 Kings 12:26-33). Besides that, pagan worship has increased rapidly, especially during the infamous reign of Ahab (1 Kings 16:30-33).

A. SOME WITH SCORN (v. 10)

10. The couriers went from town to town in Ephraim and Manasseh, as far as Zebulun, but the people scorned and ridiculed them.

As *the couriers* travel from *Ephraim* to *Manasseh* to *Zebulun*, they are moving extensively throughout Israel, progressively northward. Asher (v. 11) is the northernmost of the tribal territories. King Hezekiah is serious that all Israelites be invited.

But in Israel the usual response to the invitation is scorn and ridicule. That is not surprising, for people of that area regard Judah as an enemy. They remember the bloody war in the time of King Ahaz. Israel and Syria had formed an alliance to oppose the growing might of Assyria and had tried to conquer Judah to add her to their coalition. They had failed, and that had made them hate Judah all the more. Now they howl in derision when they hear the king of Judah's invitation to come and join his people in worship.

If we take our stand for God and his Word, for Christ and the church, for right instead of wrong, we too can expect to be *scorned and ridiculed.* People who like the drift away from God will despise us.

SATISFIED WITH SUBSTITUTES

Since 1933, the community of Laguna Beach, California, has held an annual *Pageant of the Masters,* an art festival that uses live mannequins to recreate the great paintings and sculptures of the Western world. The subjects appear motionless in life-size reproductions of the art works, and are otherwise indistinguishable from the originals.

Hundreds of works have been presented, ranging from Leonardo da Vinci's *Last Supper* to Seurat's famous *A Sunday on La Grand Jatte* and even the familiar World War II photograph of the American flag being raised on Iwo Jima.

At each presentation from early in July to Labor Day, forty living reproductions are displayed at two-minute intervals. In recent summers, as many as 150,000 people have attended, many of whom probably would decline the opportunity to see the real art works!

For two centuries the people of the northern kingdom of Israel had forsaken worship of the true God. Now they were invited to attend the real thing, but their response was mixed. In worship and in art, apparently the imitation may seem more interesting than the genuine article. Does our worship indicate that we prefer religious substitutes just as ancient Israel did? Or do we continually seek for a more genuine relationship with our God? —C. R. B.

B. OTHERS WITH ACCEPTANCE (vv. 11, 12)

11. Nevertheless, some men of Asher, Manasseh and Zebulun humbled themselves and went to Jerusalem.

Apparently, the history of the nation has been passed from father to son through the generations in at least some of the households of the northern kingdom. Such households, in remaining loyal to the one true God, welcome the revival of the Passover and humbly go *to Jerusalem* to join in the worship of the Lord.

WHAT DO YOU THINK?

What does it take for a group to be spiritually faithful, maintain quality worship, and continue to reach out when their neighbors are responding with scorn and ridicule? How can the church teach members to stand strong today?

WHAT DO YOU THINK?

Hezekiah gave the people enough time to prepare themselves for acceptable worship. What preparation should Christians make in order to be ready for worship?

Considering 1 Chronicles 29:3, Psalm 27:4; John 4:24; 1 Corinthians 11:23-30, what is the difference between "attending" and "worshiping"?

HOW TO SAY IT

Ahaz. AY-haz.

Assyria. Uh-SEAR-ee-uh.

Beer-sheba. Beer-SHE-buh.

Cyrus. SIGH-russ.

Ephraim. EE-fray-im.

Galilee. GAL-uh-lee.

Gilead. GIL-ee-ud.

Herodotus. Heh-ROD-uh-tus.

Hezekiah. Hez-ih-KYE-uh.

Jeroboam. Jair-uh-BOE-um.

Jotham. JO-thum.

Manasseh. Muh-NASS-uh.

Naphtali. Naf-TUH-lye.

Seurat. Suh-RAW.

Uzziah. Uh-ZYE-uh.

Zebulun. ZEB-you-lun.

PRAYER

Forgive us, Father, if we have been drifting. Give us vigor of heart and boldness of spirit to hold forth the word of life to those who are lost in the way of death. In Jesus' name, amen.

THOUGHT TO REMEMBER

"We must pay more careful attention, therefore, to what we have heard, so that we do not drift away" (Hebrews 2:1).

If we take our stand for God and against the drift away from him, we shall not be surprised by the contemptuous hoots of the drifters; but we may be surprised to see how many quiet, thoughtful people will join us!

12. Also in Judah the hand of God was on the people to give them unity of mind to carry out what the king and his officials had ordered, following the word of the LORD.

Now the focus shifts to the southern kingdom. Although the call to observe the Passover is issued by *the king and his officials*, it is ultimately according to *the word of the Lord.* Guided by *the hand of God*, the people of *Judah* are more unanimous in answering that call than those of the northern kingdom. And so they pour into Jerusalem at the appointed time in the second month. They are so delighted to have the Passover back that they continue the celebration for fourteen days instead of the legal seven (2 Chronicles 30:13-26). There is a precedent for such an extension in King Solomon's dedication of the temple, held in conjunction with the Feast of Tabernacles (7:9).

CONCLUSION

"History repeats itself." How many times that old adage has been verified by actual events! In Old Testament history, nothing is plainer than the repeated drift of God's people away from him—and every drift brings disaster (cf. Judges 2:6-19). No less plain are the times when God's drifting people turn back to him, and every return brings spiritual peace. How much better it is never to drift in the first place!

A. TODAY'S DRIFT

Our time is seeing a drift away from God in the European and American nations that once were called Christian. Don't you know some people who proudly run their own lives without any help from God, the Bible, or the church? The drift is seen in increasing tolerance for foul language, pornography, and promiscuous sex. It is seen in churches run by men with no respect for God and his Word. It is seen in people you see as you drive to church on Sunday morning—people raking leaves in their yards, people working on their cars, people leaving home with picnic baskets. It is seen in the removal of the Ten Commandments from public places where they were posted. It is seen in the clever theories that are invented to explain the origin and development of the world and the living things in it—theories that try to discredit the Genesis record.

B. TODAY'S NEED

The solution to this drift is an army of modern-day Hezekiahs to turn people and nations back to God. We need millions of Christians who make no secret of their distaste for what is obscene and evil. But more than opposition to evil, we need adherence to good. We need millions of Christians to proclaim, by word and deed, the goodness of God, the truth of the Bible, and the glory of doing right.

Perhaps your congregation already has a group that can spearhead a drive to bring more people to the Lord, to his church, and to doing right. It may be the elders or the elders and deacons. It may be called the committee on evangelism or the ministry of outreach. If such a group is really committed to the task of evangelism and actively working at it, others can be enlisted in the effort.

When a Christian is asked to become a winner of souls, a frequent answer is "I don't know how." And it's true; he or she doesn't know how. Would your minister like to collect a few eager learners and conduct an intensive course on personal evangelism, meeting every evening for a week or two weeks?

It is (again) time for the church to be serious about turning people from darkness to light, and from the power of Satan unto God (Acts 26:18).

Discovery Learning

*This page contains an alternative lesson plan emphasizing learning activities. Classes
desiring such student involvement will find these suggestions helpful. The next page
is a reproducible activity page to further enhance discovery learning.*

LEARNING GOALS

After participating in this lesson, each student will be able to:

1. Tell how Hezekiah attempted to restore the Passover celebration for all Israel and the result of his efforts.

2. Explain why one's efforts to do the right thing are not always appreciated.

3. Commit this week to do something to share the gospel or otherwise honor the Lord even though unbelievers may oppose the effort.

INTO THE LESSON

Prior to this week's lesson, ask a class member to prepare a five-minute presentation on the contrasting religious practices under King Ahaz and King Hezekiah. Copy the reproducible activity, "Contrasting Religious Practices," from the next page to prepare the presentation. Also, think about some item that has been restored: a broken chair, a broken clock, or even a tarnished silverware set.

Begin this week's lesson by stating, "Today we are starting class with a short background presentation by _____ on the religious practices of two kings, father and son." Give each a copy of the reproducible page activity to write down the information presented. Afterwards thank the student for making the presentation, and state, "Several of us have experienced taking a broken item or old piece of furniture and restoring it. Today, we find King Hezekiah attempting to restore a broken practice in Israel and Judah. Turn to 2 Chronicles 30:1-12, and let's discover how the practice ended up in the sad condition and what was needed to restore it."

INTO THE WORD

Ask one of the students to read the lesson text aloud. Prior to class prepare a worksheet with questions to answer, and make a copy for each student. After reading the lesson text, give a copy of the worksheet to each student. Ask the class to work in groups of twos to answer:

1. What two reasons prohibited the Passover from being celebrated during the first month? (*Not enough priests had consecrated themselves; the people had not assembled in Jerusalem, v. 3.*)

2. How was the decision to celebrate the Passover made? (*King Hezekiah, his officials, and the whole assembly in Jerusalem decided together, vv. 2, 5.*)

3. How was the invitation to come to Jerusalem for the Passover communicated to Israel and Judah? (*Letters were written with the King's proclamation; couriers carried the letters and proclaimed the call, vv. 1, 6.*)

4. How had their fathers responded to the Lord, which led to desolation and captivity by the Assyrians? (*They were unfaithful, v. 7; they were stiff-necked, v. 8.*)

5. What did the proclamation call the people to do to restore the Passover? (*Return to the Lord, v. 6; submit to the Lord, come to his sanctuary, and serve him, v. 8.*)

6. What was the people's response to the couriers giving the King's proclamation? (*In Israel, they scorned and ridiculed them; yet some humbled themselves and came, vv. 10, 11; In Judah, the people had unity of mind to do the commandment of the king, v. 12.*)

After giving the class time to answer the questions, ask for their responses. State: "Here was a neglected religious practice. Even though people knew what to do and when to do it, they failed to celebrate Passover and trespassed against the Lord. In the same way, there are religious practices that people still neglect, even people within the church." Ask the following questions:

1. What practices do religious people often neglect today? (*Possible answers: prayer before meals at home and in public; personal prayer and devotional times; weekly attendance in worship or Bible study; fasting.*)

2. Why do people neglect these practices? (*Lack of time; don't see the value; lack commitment; pride.*)

3. Why are one's efforts to do the right thing not always appreciated by others? (*Possible answers: others don't want to change; they ridicule because of guilt.*)

INTO LIFE

State: "Now, let's see how this passage applies to us. This proclamation by King Hezekiah was a call to repentance and renewal, a call to restore a broken relationship with and personal worship of God. Think of a practice that has become neglected in your life. Verse 9 reminds us that the Lord our God is gracious and compassionate and if we humble ourselves and seek to restore our relationship with God, he will not turn his face from us." Make a copy of the reproducible page activity, "Commitment to Personal Repentance and Renewal," from the next page, and give it to each person. Ask each learner to select a neglected practice and complete the prayer of commitment to renew the practice this week.

Contrasting Religious Practices
of Father and Son

Directions: Read the specific passages listed under each king. Draw from the texts the religious practices that were performed under each king. Write those practices in the space provided.

<table>
<tr><td align="center">KING AHAZ
2 Chronicles 28:1-4, 22-25</td><td align="center">KING HEZEKIAH
2 Chronicles 29:1-5, 18, 19, 25-31, 35</td></tr>
</table>

Commitment to Personal Repentance
and Renewal

Consider filling in the following prayer of commitment. Identify something you have been negligent about toward God. Name one thing you will do in repentance.

PRAYER OF COMMITMENT:

Father in Heaven, after studying this lesson text I am reminded of how easily we tend to neglect many religious practices that keep us close to you. One area I've neglected that has affected my walk with you is _____

_____.

Father, please forgive my negligence and accept my request for forgiveness. In this area I seek to return to you, to submit to your lordship in my life, and desire to serve you this week in a renewed and committed way. I will this week demonstrate my love and commitment to you by _____

_____

_____.

In Jesus' name I pray and make this commitment, amen.

GOD RESTORES A SINNER

LESSON 2

WHY TEACH THIS LESSON?

A few years ago, I was making "cold calls" on hospital patients in my role as a hospital chaplain. In one particular room, the patient had stepped out for a few minutes, so I chatted with his wife instead. It turned out that she wanted to talk about her husband's spiritual condition rather than his physical problems. Both were Christians, but her husband had come to Christ rather late in life and he carried guilt over the fact that he had "wasted fifty years of his life." Shortly, the husband himself (who had not overheard our conversation) returned to the room. One of the first things he said to me was, "Chaplain, I'm a Christian now, but I wasted fifty years of my life before I accepted the Lord!"

For the rest of our conversation we rejoiced in the fact that he did indeed have the assurance of eternal life, while not denying the sobering reality of the years he had spent in rebellion to God. Today we read about a person who also comes to the Lord later in life: King Manasseh of Judah. When he finally turns to God after committing incredible evil, God is right there—ready to accept his repentance! This lesson will help those who see a bit of Manasseh in their own lives (1 John 1:9).

INTRODUCTION

A. QUICK SWITCHES AND FLIP-FLOPS

Last week we began by considering the timeworn maxim, "Like father, like son." It is often true, but not always. The history of ancient Judah presents a number of quick switches from good to bad or bad to good when the crown passed from father to son. Jotham had been a good king (2 Chronicles 27:1, 2), but his son Ahaz was bad (28:1, 2). Then Ahaz's son Hezekiah switched as quickly to good (29:1, 2). Today we see yet another quick switch.

In addition to such quick switches, there are some notable flip-flops. For many years Uzziah was one of the best of kings (26:3, 4). But success went to his head to the point that he became unfaithful and tried to usurp the role of the priests (26:16). For that the Lord struck him with leprosy so that he had to live in isolation the rest of his days (26:17-21). What a flip-flop!

B. LESSON BACKGROUND

Last week we saw the godliness of Hezekiah. Although he suffered the temporary failings of poor judgment (2 Kings 20:12-18) and pride (2 Chronicles 32:24-26), he never faltered in his devotion to God (2 Kings 18:5, 6). His son Manasseh, at the age of twelve, quickly switched the policy of the government from good to evil. But as we shall discover in today's lesson, certain events in Manasseh's life led to a tremendous flip-flop from evil to good toward the end.

I. ACCESSION OF THE KING (2 CHRONICLES 33:1, 2)

When an ancient kingship passed from father to son, sometimes it fell to a minor child quite unprepared to rule a nation. Manasseh inherits the crown when he is only twelve, and his grandson Josiah receives it when he is only eight (2 Chronicles 34:1). Such children do not rule without powerful help.

DEVOTIONAL READING:
2 CHRONICLES 6:36-42
BACKGROUND SCRIPTURE:
2 CHRONICLES 33:1-20; 2 KINGS 21
PRINTED TEXT:
2 CHRONICLES 33:1-13

LESSON AIMS

After participating in this lesson, each student will be able to:

1. Summarize the evil reign of Manasseh and how he finally came to repentance.

2. Compare the turnaround in Manasseh's life with similar changes in the lives of others.

3. Identify a co-worker, family member, neighbor, or other acquaintance who has no interest in God, Christ, or the church, and commit to praying for that person to come to repentance.

KEY VERSE

When he prayed to him, the LORD was moved by his entreaty and listened to his plea; so he brought him back to Jerusalem and to his kingdom. Then Manasseh knew that the LORD is God.   —2 Chronicles 33:13

LESSON 2 NOTES

A. A BOY KING (v. 1)

1. Manasseh was twelve years old when he became king, and he reigned in Jerusalem fifty-five years.

Manasseh begins his reign in about 695 B.C. This is about seventeen years after the northern kingdom of Israel was taken into exile by the Assyrians, and about one hundred and ten years before his own people will be carried off by the Babylonians. Beginning so early in life, he has a long time to rule. Unfortunately, he rules badly (sinfully) for much of that time.

B. A BAD KING (v. 2)

2. He did evil in the eyes of the LORD, following the detestable practices of the nations the LORD had driven out before the Israelites.

Who is the "power behind the throne" that guides the twelve-year-old boy as he sets the course of his kingdom? Perhaps Manasseh is tutored by corrupt priests left over from the time of his evil grandfather Ahaz (2 Chronicles 28:1, 2). Perhaps evil politicians from that same time cleverly manage to win the confidence of the growing boy. Ultimately, we simply do not know. But surely Manasseh is not guided by the best advisers of his godly father, King Hezekiah.

"GOING ZOOM!"

A three-year-old boy in Florida took the family car for a "joyride" a few years ago, and authorities remain puzzled as to how he managed it. The boy was only two-and-a-half feet tall, so how he was able to reach the gas pedal and still steer the car is a mystery.

Well, it must be admitted that his steering wasn't so good: on a journey that lasted less than a half-mile, he ran into three cars. Fortunately, no one was hurt.

In the middle of the night, he had climbed up on top of a five-foot-high dresser in his parents' bedroom without waking them. He then took the car keys and went on his little excursion. Perhaps we should give him high marks for creativity and ambition, at least. When he was caught, his explanation of what happened was, "I go zoom!"

Manasseh was a few years older than the Florida youngster was when he became king. He took Judah on a wild ride, leaving a trail of wreckage—both spiritual and moral—in his path. His immaturity kept him from understanding the consequences of "zooming" off on such a dangerous course. His adult advisors probably bear some blame for this. Good advice might have prevented this "accident." How can we exert a positive influence over the young people whom God has entrusted to our care?

—C. R. B.

II. SINS OF THE KING (2 CHRONICLES 33:3-9)

Seven of the thirteen verses in our text detail the extent and magnitude of the evil practices of King Manasseh and the nation he ruled. What a breathtaking turnaround from the godly rule of his father, Hezekiah! (See 2 Chronicles 29:1, 2.)

A. IDOLATRY (v. 3)

3. He rebuilt the high places his father Hezekiah had demolished; he also erected altars to the Baals and made Asherah poles. He bowed down to all the starry hosts and worshiped them.

The high places are places of worship, usually on hilltops. At times, people had worshiped the Lord in such places, but King Ahaz and his followers had worshiped idols there. King *Hezekiah*, for his part, had destroyed their altars and other furnishings, making them unfit for any kind of worship (2 Kings 18:4).

WHAT DO YOU THINK?

It has been suggested that evil advisers encouraged Manasseh toward evil. Others might assume Manasseh himself is more to blame, behaving as a rebellious teenager. Whether by poor advisers or their own rebelliousness, teens can find themselves in a great many evil situations. What can the church and parents do to help teenagers through the maze of evil present in the world today?

Know That the Lord is God

Lesson	Know That
1	The Lord is gracious and merciful.
2	The Lord hears sincere prayer.
3	The Lord is dependably righteous.
4	The Lord accepts repentance.
5	The Lord will give rest to the faithful.
6	The Lord will punish evil.
7	The Lord demands justice.
8	The Lord offers hope in a new covenant.
9	The Lord is strength in our troubles.
10	The Lord is persistently compassionate.
11	The Lord loves in faithfulness.
12	The Lord requires personal responsibility.
13	The Lord can redeem and renew.

Know the Lord!

Use this chart from the Adult Visuals packet to summarize the theme of each lesson this quarter.

Now Manasseh rebuilds the things his father had destroyed, and he devotes them to the worship of *the Baals*, idols representing an imaginary god called Baal (meaning "lord"). Most Christian scholars believe that simple *poles* were erected beside the *altars* that were dedicated to Baal. Those poles represented an imaginary goddess, *Asherah*, who was associated with Baal. He also encourages the worship of stars and other celestial bodies—*the starry hosts*—which many centuries before Moses had specifically forbidden (Deuteronomy 4:19). By Manasseh's time, the northern kingdom of Israel has already been carried away into captivity for committing such evil (2 Kings 17:16), but the Judean king somehow "misses the message" there.

B. DESECRATION OF THE TEMPLE (vv. 4, 5)

4. He built altars in the temple of the LORD, of which the LORD had said, "My Name will remain in Jerusalem forever."

The temple of the Lord is the magnificent edifice Solomon had built *in Jerusalem* centuries earlier. The Lord had accepted it and had promised to put his *name* there forever (1 Kings 9:3). One of its main features was a massive altar where sacrifices had been offered to the Lord (2 Chronicles 4:1). But now Manasseh adds other *altars* for sacrifices to imaginary gods.

5. In both courts of the temple of the LORD, he built altars to all the starry hosts.

The temple has a big courtyard where anyone, Jew or pagan, could enter. It also features a smaller courtyard where only Jews are admitted. Manasseh puts *altars* for star worshipers *in both* of those *courts*.

C. HUMAN SACRIFICE (v. 6a)

6a. He sacrificed his sons in the fire in the Valley of Ben Hinnom,

The valley of Ben Hinnom (or "son of Hinnom") is the ravine outside the south wall of Jerusalem that serves as part of the boundary between two tribes (Joshua 15:8). The valley also serves as a center for worship of the imaginary god called Molech, a favorite idol of the Ammonites (cf. 1 Kings 11:7). A feature of their worship is the gruesome sacrifice of their own children, whom they burn with *fire*. The Lord, in speaking to Moses, had condemned this hideous practice vigorously (Leviticus 18:21; 20:1-5); but now Manasseh not only encourages it, he even sacrifices some of *his* own *sons*.

Later, the Lord declares that this infamous valley will come to be known as "the valley of slaughter" when the Babylonians come to sack Jerusalem (Jeremiah 19:5, 6). In New Testament Greek, "Ben Hinnom" becomes "gehenna," and is used by Jesus as a description for Hell (Matthew 5:29, 30).

D. SUPERSTITION AND WITCHCRAFT (v. 6b)

6b. . . . practiced sorcery, divination and witchcraft, and consulted mediums and spiritists. He did much evil in the eyes of the LORD, provoking him to anger.

All these terms taken together tell us that Manasseh practices the superstitions and magical arts the pagans use to contact the spirit world in order to predict or control future events. These activities included *sorcery, divination and witchcraft,* as well as consulting *mediums and spiritists.*

Saul, Israel's first king, had banished such practitioners from Israel hundreds of years before (cf. 1 Samuel 28); but they did not disappear. Saul himself was able to find one on the eve of the battle that cost him his life.

All these pagan practices are forbidden to God's people (Deuteronomy 18:9-13). Practicing that which the Lord specifically forbids is a sure way to arouse his *anger!*

HOW TO SAY IT

Ahaz. AY-haz.
Ammonites. AM-un-ites.
Asherah. Uh-SHE-ruh.
Assyria. Uh-SEAR-ee-uh.
Baal. BAY-ul.
Canaan. KAY-nun.
Gehenna. Geh-HEN-uh (G as in GET).
Hezekiah. Hez-ih-KYE-uh.
Hinnom. HIN-um.
Josiah. Jo-SIGH-uh.
Jotham. JO-thum.
Manasseh. Muh-NASS-uh.
Molech. MO-lek.
Pharaoh Neco. FAY-ro NEE-ko.
Uzziah. Uh-ZYE-uh.
Wiccan. WIH-kun.

WHAT DO YOU THINK?

No one is sacrificing children to the god Molech today. How does our culture today "sacrifice" children to modern "gods"? How can the church work to destroy these "gods"?

ANYONE FOR WITCHCRAFT?

Have you ever been caught in traffic when you were in a rush and it seemed the traffic signals stayed red a lot longer than they should have? Dorothy Morrison says a little "white magic" witchcraft can help! In her book *Everyday Magic,* Morrison (a so-called "Third Degree Wiccan High Priestess") suggests that you "focus on the red color of the light and inhale deeply, pulling the color in with your breath. Then exhale fully in green, directing your breath at the bottom globe of the traffic light. The light will change to green." She also suggests trying this chant:

> Gods of Movement and of flow
> Ease this mess that causes woe.
> Move these cars along their way
> And keep traffic moving through the day.
> Do this quickly—hurry, please—
> By winds of change, this traffic ease.

The book also has chants and herbal potions for a good marriage, getting a friend to forgive you, and even for making your car get better fuel mileage. It lists dozens of deities and their specific areas of expertise (e.g., the book claims that there are nine gods that specialize in computers and peripherals).

Most of us probably are tempted to think that Manasseh's sin of dabbling in idolatry, witchcraft, and sorcery was a quaint relic of a much less enlightened age than ours. But this book of modern witchcraft is just one of a multitude to which modern Westerners are turning for spiritual assistance. It is no less a sin in our time than it was in Manasseh's.
—C. R. B.

E. MORE DESECRATION OF THE TEMPLE (vv. 7, 8)

7. He took the carved image he had made and put it in God's temple, of which God had said to David and to his son Solomon, "In this temple and in Jerusalem, which I have chosen out of all the tribes of Israel, I will put my Name forever.

Manasseh wants the Lord to accept an idol—a dead lump of stone or wood or clay—as a housemate. What an insult to the living God! It implies that he is no better than that lump. Manasseh has forgotten the uniqueness of the *temple* and of the God who sanctified it. When *Solomon* completed the construction of the temple, "the glory of the Lord filled the temple" (2 Chronicles 7:1). Later the Lord appeared to Solomon at night and told him that he had "chosen and consecrated this temple so that my Name may be there forever. My eyes and my heart will always be there" (2 Chronicles 7:12, 16).

8. "I will not again make the feet of the Israelites leave the land I assigned to your forefathers, if only they will be careful to do everything I commanded them concerning all the laws, decrees and ordinances given through Moses."

This is not the first time that God promises to keep *the Israelites* in *the land* he has given them (cf. Deuteronomy 28). But God does not say he will do that regardless of what the people do. God promises to keep his people in the land he has given them *if only they will* obey him (1 Kings 9:1-9; 2 Chronicles 7:19-22). However, if God's people continue in the way Manasseh is leading, they surely will be removed from their homeland.

F. SUMMARY OF EVIL (v. 9)

9. But Manasseh led Judah and the people of Jerusalem astray, so that they did more evil than the nations the LORD had destroyed before the Israelites.

King Manasseh's activities are about as sinful as they can possibly be. But even worse is the example he sets as a leader for people to follow (cf. Luke 17:1, 2). How incredible to read that God's own people are actually *more evil than the pa*gans! Several small nations had lived in the land of Canaan before Israel had come there from Egypt. Those nations had been too wicked to be allowed to live any longer. Israel had been God's tool to destroy them. Now *Judah and the people of Jerusalem* have become worse than the nations that had lived there before. How, then, can *the Israelites* live?

III. REFORMS OF THE KING (2 CHRONICLES 33:10-13)

The Lord does not want to destroy the last remaining fragment of the people of Abraham. He wants to preserve them as a separate and easily identifiable group until they bring a blessing to the whole world as God had promised Abraham (Genesis 22:18). Even in the depth of their depravity, he sets about to reform them.

A. WARNING TO THE KING (v. 10)

10. *The LORD spoke to Manasseh and his people, but they paid no attention.*

First God tries to reason with the sinners, to help them see that what they are doing will bring destruction. We are not told how he speaks, and it does not appear that any of the prophets known to us are active at that time. But God has had many prophets of which we know nothing. Perhaps some of them are giving God's warning. But king and people *paid no attention.*

B. CAPTURE OF THE KING (v. 11)

11. *So the LORD brought against them the army commanders of the king of Assyria, who took Manasseh prisoner, put a hook in his nose, bound him with bronze shackles and took him to Babylon.*

Often the Lord accomplishes his purposes by using people who do not believe in him, people who do not want to help him, people who have no idea they are helping him. Before this time, he used the Assyrians to destroy the northern nation of Israel (2 Kings 17:6-23). He had defended the southern kingdom, Judah, because good King Hezekiah was leading it in righteousness (2 Kings 19:35, 36). But now he does not stop the Assyrians from invading Judah and capturing King *Manasseh* and making an example of him. The *hook in his nose* and the *bronze shackles* were used by the Assyrians to humiliate and torture Manasseh.

C. REPENTANCE OF THE KING (v. 12)

12. *In his distress he sought the favor of the LORD his God and humbled himself greatly before the God of his fathers.*

Manasseh the king had been an evil tyrant; Manasseh the prisoner is a humble worshiper of *God.* What a flip-flop—and what an improvement! But how much better it would have been for everyone if Manasseh could have learned such humility without the hard lesson of capture.

D. RELEASE OF THE KING (v. 13)

13. *And when he prayed to him, the LORD was moved by his entreaty and listened to his plea; so he brought him back to Jerusalem and to his kingdom. Then Manasseh knew that the LORD is God.*

The Lord hears Manasseh's prayer and answers it. Somehow—we are not told the details—he secures this captive's release and brings *him back to* his home and to his throne. Assyrian inscriptions mention *Manasseh* by name and also reveal a parallel case where they sent Pharaoh Neco back to his own throne in Egypt.

Undoubtedly, Manasseh pledges some cooperation with the Assyrians and agrees to pay tribute as part of his release agreement. Regardless of that, the king is a changed man spiritually. He knows *that the Lord is God* and that idols are

WHAT DO YOU THINK?

How is it possible that one person in leadership can influence an entire nation to change so radically in just one generation? What psychological, sociological, and spiritual factors make it easier to move away from God when the top leader dishonors God? In order to influence the climate within the culture, how important is it for Christians to be involved in the political arena?

WHAT DO YOU THINK?

In this text, God held the main leader responsible and punished him specifically. Would you expect that God always would respond in this way? Or might God hold all the people responsible? Support your position, using Ezekiel 33:1-9; Hebrews 13:17; James 3:1; and/or other verses.

WHAT DO YOU THINK?

Should the church pray for God to act swiftly and strongly to humble our nation so people will be more receptive to the gospel? How do our comforts and possessions keep Christians from praying this way? How much change would people have to suffer before they turn to God?

worthless. The king demonstrates the change by material and spiritual rebuilding projects (vv. 14-17). In so doing, he tries to correct the evil he has done and to make the people of Judah again the people of God.

Manasseh's repentance, however, is ultimately a case of "too little, too late" in terms of the sobering results that his earlier, sinful actions continue to have on the nation of Judah. As events in Judah and Jerusalem unfold, the evil that Manasseh has done will outweigh any correction that he tries to bring about (see 2 Kings 24:3, 4 and Jeremiah 15:4).

CONCLUSION

Manasseh's capture is ultimately the best thing that ever happened to him. It makes him into the man God wants him to be. More than that, it puts the nation of Judah back on the path where God wants her to be, even if only temporarily.

A. BUSINESS DISASTER

Prosperity was high in Milltown. About half of its employed people worked for the mill, the town's only industry. There was plenty of overtime work for as many employees as wanted it. Business was also booming at Murphy's little hardware store, and Murphy built a fine new home for his family.

Then the mill moved to an area where labor was cheaper, taxes were lower, and electric power was almost free. Some employees went with it; the rest were unemployed. Milltown's prosperity turned to poverty. Without customers, Murphy's store went into bankruptcy. The mortgage holder took his new home.

Murphy had no money, but he had friends. One of them found him a job as maintenance man with the high school. The pay was low, but it provided a frugal living for the Murphy family. Another friend rented them a house for half of what it had earned in the prosperous time.

Murphy is unhappy. He has turned his back on God and the church. "What is God doing for me?" he grumbles. "My friends are helping me, but God isn't."

Is Murphy right? Is God doing nothing for him, or is he doing what he did for Manasseh?

B. MARRIAGE DISASTER

Steve and Jean were the happiest honeymooners in town—until that frightful crash on the highway. Steve was not badly hurt, but Jean was paralyzed from the neck down. Motionless on her bed, she could smile or she could cry, but she could not speak. She could eat if food was put in her mouth, but she could not lift a spoon.

In her presence Steve was quiet and moody. Outside it he was furious. "I'm out of here!" he vowed often and loudly. He snarled at the minister who came to call, "Preacher, tell me about your God. What a monster! Does he really enjoy seeing Jean like that?"

The minister was irritated. "Maybe God is trying to make a man out of you," he snapped. "You have a contract, Steve. In the presence of God and a houseful of people, you promised to love, cherish, and keep Jean as long as you both would live. Men keep their promises, but you keep talking about getting out of here."

"Nuts!" Steve's voice dripped disgust. "I married a woman. I'm not going to spend the rest of my life with a houseplant."

So Steve drew his money out of the bank and vanished into the night. Jean's parents gave her tender, loving care until she died a year later.

What do you do with your disasters—and what do they do to you?

Discovery Learning

This page contains an alternative lesson plan emphasizing learning activities. Classes desiring such student involvement will find these suggestions helpful. The next page is a reproducible activity page to further enhance discovery learning.

LEARNING GOALS

After participating in this lesson, each student will be able to:

1. Summarize the evil reign of Manasseh and how he finally came to repentance.

2. Compare the turn-around in Manasseh's life with similar changes in the lives of others.

3. Identify a co-worker, family member, neighbor, or other acquaintance who has no interest in God, Christ, or the church, and commit to praying for that person to come to repentance.

INTO THE LESSON

For class this week, prepare a transparency or a poster with the following statement: "A person can become so evil that God will not save!" In addition, prepare four signs with the following words: "Strongly Agree" "Mildly Agree," "Mildly Disagree," "Strongly Disagree." Prior to class hang the four signs in the four corners of the room. Place the "strongly" signs in opposite corners diagonally.

To start the class session, say: "We are going to begin class with an agree/disagree statement. By now you have probably noticed the signs in the four corners. I am going to reveal a statement for you to consider. I want you all to stand, and after I read the statement, you have thirty seconds to decide whether you strongly agree, mildly agree, mildly disagree, or strongly disagree with the statement. Then I want you to go stand in the corner under the sign that best represents your opinion."

Reveal the statement to the class; read it audibly. After the class has moved to the various corners of the room, ask each group to explain its particular opinion. (*Agree: God will not save because the evil person does not want to be saved; Disagree: God will save because the evil person turns to him.*) After each group has shared its reasoning, ask all to return to their seats. State: "It is not the amount of evil in one's life, but the response to God that matters. God will save when one turns to him, regardless of how wicked one has been. Today we study a man so evil he was described as worse than the pagans. Turn to 2 Chronicles 33:1-13 to see how God restores a sinner."

INTO THE WORD

Prior to class make copies of the reproducible activity, "Manasseh and the Depth of Evil," from the next page. Ask the class to move into groups of three. Give a copy of the activity to each person and go over the directions. Give the students several minutes to unscramble the words, fill in the blanks, and determine the way Manasseh escaped evil. Briefly review the exercise.

State: "I want one person in each group to read the lesson text to the others. Then I want each group to answer the questions that I will display. After several minutes, we will hear answers from each group." Prior to class, prepare the following questions on a transparency or poster. While the students are reading the text, reveal these questions:

1. Why was Judah's behavior described as more evil than the nations the Lord had destroyed? (*The depth of evil was extensive: idolatry led to the sacrificing of children; witchcraft; divination; mediums, vv. 6, 9.*)

2. How was the temple of the Lord desecrated by Manasseh? (*Altars were built in the house of the Lord to all the starry hosts, and idols were worshiped, vv. 4, 5.*)

3. Describe the circumstances that led Manasseh to turn to the Lord. (*He was taken prisoner by Assyria to Babylon, bound with shackles, and in distress, vv. 11, 12.*)

4. What did Manasseh do to turn to the Lord? (*Sought the Lord, humbled himself, prayed, vv. 12, 13.*)

5. What was the "turning point" in his life? (*Distress and imprisonment, v. 12.*)

After several minutes, review the questions with the class, asking each group its answer. While the class is still in groups of three, ask each group to develop a single answer to the following question: "What one principle is this passage teaching us?" Give each group a large sheet of paper (flip-chart size) and a marker. Ask each group to write the one principle this passage is teaching them. Then, providing some masking tape, have each group tape their paper on the wall for all to see. (*There will be several possible answers. Among those should be: God restores a sinner who turns to him!*)

INTO LIFE

State: "Regardless of how evil a person becomes, God can restore him!" Distribute copies of the reproducible activity, "Memo," from page 30, and ask each student to identify someone he or she knows who has fallen into evil: a family member, a co-worker, a neighbor—someone who cares little for God. State: "Write a memo to yourself to remind you to pray for this person every day." After a few minutes, end the class in a prayer of commitment.

Manasseh and the Depth of Evil

Unscramble each of the words on the left and write the word on the space provided to the right. After unscrambling all the words, copy the letters in the circles to the designated circles in "The Way out of Evil" section below. For example, the number 5 circle represents the letter in the circle in the number 5 unscrambled word.

D U M M I E S
(2 Chronicles 33:6)

1. __ __ __ __ ◯◯ __

I I I N N D T O V A
(2 Chronicles 33:6)

2. ◯ __ __ __ __ __ __ __ __ __

T A D I L R Y O
(2 Chronicles 33:3 implied)

3. __ __ __ ◯ __ __ __ __

R O C S Y E R
(2 Chronicles 33:6)

4. __ __ __ __ ◯ __ __

F A W C T I H T C R
(2 Chronicles 33:6)

5. __ __ __ __ ◯ __ __ __ __

A B S A L
(2 Chronicles 33:3)

6. ◯ __ __ __ __

THE WAY OUT OF EVIL

◯◯◯◯◯◯◯
5 1 1 6 3 4 2

MEMO

TO: Me
FROM: Me
RE: Commitment to Pray for Repentance

Even though Manasseh was in the depths of evil, he came to that point in his life where he sought the Lord, humbled himself, and prayed to God. In the same way, _____ is in the depths of evil. I commit myself to pray every day for a repentant heart and a desire to seek the Lord. I will share this commitment with a classmate who will hold me accountable next week.

Signed _____

Date ____/____/2002

THE LORD PROMISES FUTURE GLORY

LESSON 3

Sep
15

WHY TEACH THIS LESSON?

Psychologist Irving L. Janis has noticed that under certain conditions people in groups will stop thinking for themselves. The result is mindless conformity to the group—or "group-think." Groups that fall into this trap are recognized by (1) an illusion of invulnerability, (2) a belief in the inherent rightness of their cause, (3) an unquestioning atmosphere, (4) stereotyping of "outsiders" to discredit their ideas, (5) self-censorship to eliminate disagreement, (6) an illusion of unanimity because of that self-censorship, (7) direct pressure on dissenters, and (8) existence of self-appointed "mindguards" that protect a leader from troublesome ideas.

Group-Think happens everywhere. Perhaps you even have noticed this problem in your church. We will see this problem today (though not necessarily every one of the symptoms) in God's condemnation of the evil complacency of Jerusalem's leaders. Today's lesson will help your learners recognize the warning signs of spiritual group-think, and avoid its eternal consequences.

INTRODUCTION

A. OBEDIENCE BECOMES COMPLICATED

Obedience to God was simple when the world was young. "You may eat from all the trees except that one. If you eat from it, you die." Adam and Eve violated the only prohibition in the world, and they paid the price.

In later centuries obedience became more complicated. God gave commandments and prohibitions by the dozens through Moses, but his people seemed intent on breaking them all. Even so, a simple principle remained: obedience brought spiritual prosperity; disobedience brought disaster. Why were God's people so slow to learn that? And why haven't people in general, with all their knowledge and sophistication, learned it yet?

B. LESSON BACKGROUND

In the two previous lessons we have seen bewildering changes in the government of Judah. Godly King Hezekiah was followed by evil King Manasseh—who did a thorough flip-flop and finished his reign in noble style. When his son Amon became king, he promptly switched back to his father's earlier style. After Amon was murdered by his servants, "the people of the land" executed the killers and put Amon's son Josiah on the throne (2 Kings 21:19-26). Josiah's thirty-one year reign was marked by a gradual progression from bad to excellent.

Josiah was only eight years old when he became king (2 Chronicles 34:1). In the eighth year of his reign he began to seek God (34:3a). In the eighteenth year Josiah ordered his men to clean and repair the temple as his great-grandfather Hezekiah had done about a century earlier (29:3; 34:8). Perhaps this work was spurred on by the preaching of Jeremiah, who by that time had been at work for about five years

DEVOTIONAL READING:
ISAIAH 55:6-11
BACKGROUND SCRIPTURE:
ZEPHANIAH
PRINTED TEXT:
ZEPHANIAH 1:12; 3:1-7, 11-15

LESSON AIMS

After participating in this lesson, each student will be able to:

1. Describe the situation in Jerusalem when Zephaniah prophesied and why it warranted the prophet's stern warning, and tell of the future hope he described.

2. Compare the Jerusalem of Zephaniah's day with his or her own community and suggest some spiritual and social changes that need to be made.

3. Plan a specific project that can make a difference in the community, turning hearts to God.

KEY VERSE

The LORD within her is righteous; he does no wrong. Morning by morning he dispenses his justice, and every new day he does not fail, yet the unrighteous know no shame. —Zephaniah 3:5

(Jeremiah 1:2). As that was being done, the long-lost book of God's law was found (2 Chronicles 34:14). Apparently it had been totally forgotten during the evil years of Manasseh's reign. Now the king and the people renewed the nation's promise to obey that law (34:31, 32). So true worship and obedience to the Lord were restored (35:1-19). This week we take our lesson from the prophecies of Zephaniah, which were given while Josiah ruled (Zephaniah 1:1).

I. THE LORD AND HIS THREAT (ZEPHANIAH 1:12)

Zephaniah 1 is devoted to the Lord's threat to Judah, a threat of destruction (vv. 2, 3). Our text takes a single verse as a sample.

A. THOROUGH SEARCH (v. 12a)

12a. At that time I will search Jerusalem with lamps

That time is "the day of the Lord" (v. 7), a common theme in Zephaniah. It is the time when God's lordship will be evident, the time when his enemies will be defeated. No enemy can hide in that day, since every dark corner in Jerusalem will be searched figuratively *with lamps*. The meaning is clear: there will be no place to hide, and there will be no escape (cf. Jeremiah 5:1; Revelation 6:15-17).

B. JUST PUNISHMENT (v. 12b)

12b. . . . and punish those who are complacent,
   who are like wine left on its dregs,
 who think, "The LORD will do nothing,
   either good or bad.

Dregs are the worthless and offensive bits of sediment that settle in *wine* as it is fermented and aged. The clear, sparkling wine is carefully removed from that sediment; but the men of Judah are quite content to remain with their dregs of sin. They are not afraid of punishment, for they think that *the Lord will* not intervene in worldly affairs, either to bless the faithful or to punish the wicked. But he will indeed intervene, and people who are content with their sins will be punished.

WHAT DO YOU THINK?

The people of Jerusalem believed the Lord would not do anything, either good or bad. In today's culture, what wrong beliefs about God are held and taught? How can we address these wrong views and help people know the truth?

II. THE SINNERS AND THEIR SINS (ZEPHANIAH 3:1-7)

In Zephaniah 1 we considered the promise of punishment to those who were content to keep on sinning. Now we pause to take note of some of the sinners and their sins.

A. FILTHY CITY (vv. 1, 2)

1. Woe to the city of oppressors, rebellious and defiled!

Zephaniah is not talking about a sanitation issue or a problem with Jerusalem's air quality. It is her morals that are *defiled*. She is a *city of oppressors*—that is, the rich and powerful that trample the rights of the poor and helpless. This, of course, is not a new problem!

2. She obeys no one,
   she accepts no correction.
 She does not trust in the Lord,
   she does not draw near to her God.

Jerusalem cannot plead ignorance. God has been speaking to her through the voices of Zephaniah and other prophets, but *she obeys no one*. God is eager to correct her wrongdoing, but she refuses *correction*. The Lord is ready to bless and help the city where he has put his name, but *she does not trust in the Lord*. God longs for closer fellowship with his people, but Jerusalem chooses to go her own unclean way.

B. Officials and Rulers (v. 3)

3. Her officials are roaring lions,
   her rulers are evening wolves,
   who leave nothing for the morning.

The city's *officials* ought to be servants of its people, managing the city for the common good. Instead, they are beasts of prey, enriching themselves by corruption.

Jerusalem's *rulers* (who often serve as judges) are the same kind of people, dispensing injustice rather than justice. *Evening wolves* are ravenous. After lying hidden all day, they cannot wait to get their teeth into some prey. The phrase *leave nothing for the morning* is a bit difficult. It seems to mean that the rulers make quick work of exploiting their victims. Where a beast might chew leisurely on the bones of its prey days after the meat has been eaten, these wicked rulers take everything at their first opportunity. There are no "bones" left to chew on by the morning.

C. Prophets and Priests (v. 4)

4. Her prophets are arrogant;
   they are treacherous men.
   Her priests profane the sanctuary
   and do violence to the law.

This verse does not speak of God's prophets, such as Zephaniah and his contemporary Jeremiah. Jerusalem's *prophets*, the ones she actually listens to, are like her officials and rulers. They care nothing for truth and right, but only for what they can get for themselves. They *are arrogant,* and no doubt it was their arrogance that produced the wanton recklessness and treachery they displayed.

Jerusalem's *priests* are like her officials, rulers, and prophets: their interest is in what they can get for themselves. Many people like to make sacrifices and offerings to the idols and imaginary gods promoted by King Manasseh at his worst (2 Chronicles 33:1-5). So with appropriate ceremony, the priests accept every offering that is brought, and happily keep the priests' part of it for themselves. In so doing, they *profane the sanctuary* with pagan idolatry.

Zephaniah's words seem to fall on deaf ears, however. Some forty years later, as Jerusalem's collapse approaches, the prophet Ezekiel offers similar descriptions of the ungodly prophets, priests, and princes (Ezekiel 22:23-29).

"Something Really Stupid"

"Every once in a while you want to do something really stupid." With these words John Quincy, a Texas "catapulteer," explains his hobby.

Catapults were first used as weapons of ancient warfare. "Greek fire"—a sort of early-day napalm—was hurled over city walls. In medieval times, dead horses infected with the plague and baskets of snakes and scorpions were catapulted into besieged castles.

Catapulteers today choose from a variety of missiles. Hew Kennedy, who lives near London, England, has a sixty-foot catapult that has thrown grand pianos (in two and one-half seconds they are moving at ninety miles per hour), cars, and dead livestock of various kinds. Caskets, bowling balls, and toilets are also favored today, tossed into empty fields or lakes.

Zephaniah's description of the leaders of Jerusalem makes it seem as if they had decided collectively to "do something stupid!" The priests polluted the temple, the rich and powerful extorted and stole from the poor, and the prophets were arrogant in their treachery, thinking not at all of the consequences. Eagerly and actively they flouted God's laws and values, "catapulting" them over the city wall, from the inside out! Sin is the ultimate stupidity. Not even Christians are immune to participating in it.

—C. R. B.

Daily Bible Readings

Monday, Sept. 9—Seek the Lord (Zephaniah 1:12–2:3)

Tuesday, Sept. 10—Wait for the Lord to Work (Zephaniah 3:1-10)

Wednesday, Sept. 11—The Remnant Will Find Refuge (Zephaniah 3:11-20)

Thursday, Sept. 12—Plans for a Future (Jeremiah 29:10-14)

Friday, Sept. 13—Surely There Is a Future (Proverbs 23:15-23)

Saturday, Sept. 14—A New Thing (Isaiah 43:14-21)

Sunday, Sept. 15—Hope in the Lord (Psalm 130:1-8)

What Do You Think?

Read verses 1-4 again. From this list of sins, which ones are common in our community today? What can we do to address these issues? Could it be that the sins of church leaders are more parallel to this list than those of political leaders?

D. WARNINGS IGNORED (vv. 5-7)

5. The LORD within her is righteous;
   he does no wrong.
   Morning by morning he dispenses his justice,
      and every new day he does not fail,
      yet the unrighteous know no shame.

The *righteous* Lord has not abandoned unjust Jerusalem; he is right there in the middle of it, but having no part in its wrongdoing. On the contrary, every *morning*, through his faithful prophets, he *dispenses his justice* against those who fill the city with iniquity. But *the unrighteous* ignore that unfailing warning. Despite periodic reforms (see 2 Chronicles 29:1–31:21; 33:15-17; 34:1–35:19), the city on the whole continues its shameless rush to destruction.

6. "I have cut off nations;
      their strongholds are demolished.
   I have left their streets deserted,
      with no one passing through.
   Their cities are destroyed;
      no one will be left—no one at all.

Already God has brought about the destruction of some wicked *nations*. These judgments, particularly that against the northern kingdom of Israel, should have been a plain warning to the wicked in the kingdom of Judah.

7. "I said to the city,
      'Surely you will fear me
      and accept correction!'
   Then her dwelling would not be cut off,
      nor all my punishments come upon her.
   But they were still eager
      to act corruptly in all they did."

No doubt God knows from the beginning what the result will be, but he pictures himself reasoning as a man reasons. The people of Judah have eyes and minds. They have seen how God has punished the wicked nations. Isn't it reasonable to suppose that they will get the message that wickedness is intolerable to God? Shouldn't they realize that Judah, too, will be destroyed if it continues in wickedness? The people of Judah should have drawn that conclusion from their own observation. In case they missed it, God confirmed it by his written law and his speaking prophets. But still they failed to take the warning, to reform their lives, and to enjoy God's blessing.

One reason for this seems to be that the unrepentant officials, rulers, false prophets, and priests of Jerusalem count on the presence of the temple as something of a "good luck charm." Less than a hundred years previously, the Assyrians had threatened the southern kingdom of Judah with annihilation. But in 701 B.C., God destroyed the Assyrian army and rescued Jerusalem. This rescue had more to do with the Assyrians' own sin than Jerusalem's goodness—see 2 Kings 19. But the Judeans apparently believed that it was the presence of the temple that had saved them (Jeremiah 7:4, 14; cf. 21:2). So they continued in their sin, pursuing it eagerly.

III. THE FUTURE AND ITS DELIGHT (ZEPHANIAH 3:11-15)

Now the Lord looks beyond all the turmoil of sin and punishment to the time when his people will offer genuine worship, serving him with one heart and one voice. With that holy time in view, the Lord's word on the lips of Zephaniah rises to a hymn of triumph and delight.

WHAT DO YOU THINK?

Words of "doom and gloom" bring feelings of fear and depression. Rescue and salvation words soothe those feelings. But how much comfort do you think the people of Judah took from the prophet's words of hope while witnessing the pruning hand of God chopping everything around them? Could this happen again in our lifetime? Why or why not?

WHAT DO YOU THINK?

Many of the people in today's lesson do not seem to be listening to a spiritual message. Is there any way to phrase the message so people will listen to it even when their lives seem to be going smoothly?

A. FAREWELL TO SHAME (v. 11)

11. *"On that day you will not be put to shame*
    for all the wrongs you have done to me,
because I will remove from this city
    those who rejoice in their pride.
Never again will you be haughty
    on my holy hill.

While "the unrighteous know no shame" (v. 5), there must be a few in Jerusalem who are ashamed of what is happening. They themselves do right, but they are ashamed of the sins of their city. But there is coming a *day* when these will *not be put to shame* anymore.

The phrase *on that day* reflects the word "then" of verse 9. It refers to the future time when people will call upon the name of the Lord. In that day of the Lord's triumph, the Lord will have taken away the shameless sinners and their sins. At that time, there will be no *haughty* people in Jerusalem—only the humble and godly. God's *holy hill* is Mount Zion, where Jerusalem stands. His holy nature is intolerant of any sin (cf. 1 Peter 1:15, 16).

B. WELCOME OF SURVIVORS (vv. 12, 13)

12. *"But I will leave within you*
    the meek and humble,
    who trust in the name of the LORD.

When the arrogant sinners are taken away with their sins, the people left in Jerusalem will be *meek* and destitute of power and prestige. Instead, they will be rich in *trust*, for their trust will be *in the name of the Lord*. The kingdom of God consists of such as these (cf. Matthew 5:1-12).

13. *"The remnant of Israel will do no wrong;*
    they will speak no lies,
    nor will deceit be found in their mouths.
They will eat and lie down
    and no one will make them afraid."

What a change! After the sinners described in verses 1-7 are seen no more, the holy *remnant of Israel*, the survivors, will do right and not *wrong*. Like sheep feeding in abundant green pastures, this remnant will find every want supplied (cf. Psalm 23:1). Tormented Jerusalem at last will be at peace, and from spiritual prosperity will flow physical prosperity (cf. Micah 4:4).

A BLESSING FOR THE REMNANT

The blame for the European portion of World War II may be placed on the leaders of the Axis powers—Germany and Italy. These deluded men translated their own selfish ambition into the language of nationalistic pride, resulting in the deception of countless numbers of their citizens. The results were horrific. One-sixth of Poland's pre-war population had died by the time the war was over. Russia lost fourteen million people, equally divided between military personnel and civilians. And, of course, six million Jews were slaughtered in the Holocaust.

However, the Allied victory proved the Axis' nationalistic pride was both evil and misplaced. There was a brighter side: for most of Europe, the years following the war brought greater prosperity than before. In large part, this was due to the benevolence of the Allied conquerors, who offered aid to both the conquered nations and their victims.

God destroyed Judah's wicked leaders. When the nation had been purged of its misplaced pride, those who remained would find their judgments removed and replaced with the blessings of their benevolent God. We who are Christians may take

WHAT DO YOU THINK?

The meek and humble, often the poorest people, frequently seem to have a closer relationship with God than the wealthy. Why? Do spiritual riches really compensate for the material riches they are missing? Would today's Christians be willing to give up material riches in order to have a better spiritual connection with God? If they tried it, do you think they would be happy? Why or why not?

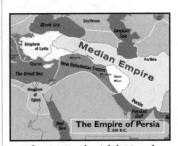

The Empire of Persia

The map in the Adult Visuals packet will be helpful today and throughout the quarter. See page 17 for ordering information.

HOW TO SAY IT

Amon. AY-mun.

Assyrians. Uh-SEAR-e-unz.

Ezekiel. Ee-ZEEK-ee-ul or Ee-ZEEK-yul.

Hezekiah. Hez-ih-KYE-uh.

Jeremiah. Jair-uh-MY-uh.

Jerusalem. Juh-ROO-suh-lem.

Josiah. Jo-SIGH-uh.

Judeans. Joo-DEE-unz.

Manasseh. Muh-NASS-uh.

Zephaniah. Zef-uh-NYE-uh.

PRAYER

How gracious you are, gentle Father! How gracious is Jesus, who died for our sins! By your grace and his we are your people and the sheep of your pasture. By grace we feed on your bounty, and by grace we lie down with none to make us afraid. Thank you, Lord. In Jesus' name, amen.

THOUGHT TO REMEMBER

Our names are written in the book of life!

hope in the promise that better days are ahead—if not soon, then in the ultimate future God is preparing for us at the return of Christ.   —C. R. B.

C. SONG OF JOY (v. 14)

14. Sing, O Daughter of Zion;
    shout aloud, O Israel!
Be glad and rejoice with all your heart,
    O Daughter of Jerusalem!

In that ultimate, *glad* day when all is well, what can the survivors do but burst into song? From grateful hearts that have been relieved of stress will rise a ringing hymn of pure delight. Those survivors, free from sin and free from fear, will be the true progeny of *Zion*, which is also called *Jerusalem*. This remnant will be the real Israel, for they will be what Israel was called originally to be—a people in harmony with the Lord (cf. Romans 11:5).

D. KING OF KINGS (v. 15)

15. The LORD has taken away your punishment,
    he has turned back your enemy.
The LORD, the King of Israel, is with you;
    never again will you fear any harm.

Now we see the reason for that anticipated season of pure delight: it is the presence of *the King of Israel*, even *the Lord*, who is to dwell with them (see also vv. 5, 17). Kings Hezekiah and Josiah tried earnestly to usher in such a season, but their efforts were undone by others. But in a time to come, the greater *King of Israel* ultimately will do what those righteous kings could not: *he has turned back the enemy*.

CONCLUSION

A. NOT IN OLD JERUSALEM

The prophet Zephaniah did not live to see the fulfillment of the bright promise he recorded. Neither did good King Josiah, though he labored earnestly to bring in such a time. Throughout her history, Jerusalem has known times of great sorrow and times of great joy. Sorrow and agony are seen when she is reduced to rubble in 586 B.C., and her people are taken captive to Babylon. Return from the Babylonian exile, in 538, is a time of great joy (Nehemiah 8:17). But in A.D. 70, her citizens are again scattered among many countries. And since the time of Zephaniah, Jerusalem has never reached the zenith of delight promised in our text. Even today, the inhabitants of Jerusalem do not enjoy perfect safety, with none to make them afraid (cf. Zephaniah 3:13). Indeed, fear is common.

B. IN THE NEW JERUSALEM

But think of the New Jerusalem, which John the apostle saw "coming down out of heaven from God" (Revelation 21:2; cf. 3:12). What a city this will be! God lives there with his people (21:3), and his Son, the Lamb of God, is enthroned beside him (22:3, 4). God will make sure that there will be no sorrow, pain, or death in that place (21:4). There are three gates in each of the four walls (21:13), and these stand open at all times to welcome God's people (21:25).

However, the presence of those open gates does not mean that all the people of earth are welcome to enter. The unrepentant are permanently shut out. Their place is the lake of eternal fire (21:8). The New Jerusalem is only for those who reject sin and follow God's plan of salvation.

Discovery Learning

This page contains an alternative lesson plan emphasizing learning activities. Classes desiring such student involvement will find these suggestions helpful. The next page is a reproducible activity page to further enhance discovery learning.

LEARNING GOALS

After participating in this lesson, each student will be able to:

1. Describe the situation in Jerusalem when Zephaniah prophesied and why it warranted the prophet's stern warning, and tell of the future hope he described.

2. Compare the Jerusalem of Zephaniah's day with their own community and suggest some spiritual and social changes that need to be made.

3. Plan a specific project that can make a difference in the community, turning hearts to God.

INTO THE LESSON

Prepare the following activity prior to class. On a large poster board, write the words "Complacency is. . . ." Attach this to the door into the classroom with masking tape or sticky-tack. Have several markers available. Prepare also the instructions on a regular sheet of paper and attach it above the poster board. Write on the paper: "Before you sit down, grab one of the markers. Complete the statement below by writing a word or words you believe describe what complacency is." (*Possible answers: contentment, smugness, indifference, being comfortable, unwilling to change.*) As students arrive, make certain they see the sign and write a suggested answer. When it is time to begin class, move the poster to the front for all to see. State: "As you can see by our definitions of *complacency*, it's a word expressing contentment with what is, an indifference, not wanting to change anything. The text today describes the Lord's attitude toward the complacent. Turn to the book of Zephaniah and read of a complacent people."

INTO THE WORD

Ask a class member to read aloud Zephaniah 1:12; 3:1-7, 11-15. After hearing the lesson text, ask the following questions for the class to answer:

1. How are the complacent people described in verse 12? (*Like wine left on its dregs.*)

2. What is the meaning of "wine left on its dregs"? (*It is a metaphor from wine, which coagulates at the bottom; they were content and satisfied, believing the Lord would do nothing.*)

3. What were the four ways God accused Jerusalem for failing? (*Obeys no one; accepts no correction; does not trust in the Lord nor draw near to God, 3:2.*)

4. Which leaders of Judah have failed God? (*Officials, rulers, prophets, priests, 3:3, 4.*)

Prior to class, make three transparencies of the reproducible page activity named "Add a Verse," from the next page. Move the students into three groups and give each group a transparency and a marker. State: "We want to experience the blessings of the Lord's promise of future glory. Each group will be given a focus as to what should comprise a new stanza for the song, 'Jesus Loves Me.' Each stanza has four lines of seven syllables." Group 1: Focus on what God's people need to do and what the Lord promises he will do, vv. 7, 11. Group 2: Focus on characteristics of God's people, vv. 12, 13. Group 3: Focus on the emotions God's people will have and why, vv. 14, 15. Allow ten minutes for each group to complete their task. Show each new stanza and encourage the class to sing them, along with the chorus.

State: "God promises future glory. Yet the complacency described by Zephaniah could very well describe our community." Ask the groups to discuss the following questions: Group 1: What similarities are there between Zephaniah's Jerusalem and our community? Group 2: What spiritual changes need to be made in our community for it to have the future hope described? Group 3: What social changes need to be made in our community?

Give the groups about ten minutes to work. Then, ask for their answers to be reported to the class.

INTO LIFE

State: "As you can see from our answers, both spiritual and social changes need to be made in our community. We may not be able to change everything in the community, but as a class we can make a difference." Prior to class make a copy of the reproducible page activity, "Project: Making a Difference!" for each student. This activity provides the opportunity to answer the five questions down the left-hand column: What? When? Where? How? Who? The last two questions provide three phases for developing this project: Phase 1: Planning; Phase 2: Preparation; and Phase 3: Performance. Decide on a project. (For example: Try organizing a special collection of donated coats or other useful items from the community for a homeless shelter.) Answer the remaining two questions. Close the class session with a prayer circle committing the class to the project and requesting God's blessing.

Add A Verse—Jesus Loves Me

To add a new verse, compose the lyrics by matching the seven syllables of each line. Write the new syllable or word in the space provided under each syllable or word in the original verse. Make certain that the last syllable of the first two lines rhyme, as well as the last syllables of lines three and four. When you are finished, the class can sing the song with the new words.

JE-	SUS	LOVES	ME	THIS	I	KNOW,
FOR	THE	BI-	BLE	TELLS	ME	SO.
LIT-	TLE	ONES	TO	HIM	BE-	LONG;
THEY	ARE	WEAK	BUT	HE	IS	STRONG.

Project: Making a Difference!

If your class does not develop a group project in response to today's study (or even if it does!), develop a service project of your own. Use the planning sheet that follows.

WHAT service do you choose?

WHERE will you do this?

WHEN will it begin and end?

    Planning, Phase 1:

    Preparation, Phase 2:

    Performance, Phase 3:

HOW exactly will it be accomplished?

WHO will you need to help?

JOSIAH MAKES A NEW BEGINNING

LESSON 4

WHY TEACH THIS LESSON?

"It's all good!" is a cultural cliché from a few years ago. However, as you read the Old Testament, you certainly don't get the idea that God thinks that way! He intended the ancient Israelites to "make distinctions"—to be different in thought and behavior from the nations around them (e.g., Leviticus 20:22-26). When they did, they were holy or "set apart" for God and his work. But they often failed.

Today's lesson is about a godly king's efforts to restore those lost distinctions. In destroying idolatry and unholiness, he was no "moderate" as some of his godly predecessors had been (cf. 2 Kings 12:3; 14:4; 15:4, 35; 22:43). Ultimately, God does not want any kind of "moderate" clean-up of our lives, either. He wants—and is entitled to—100 percent. The life of King Josiah will remind your learners of the holy, fully-dedicated service to which they have been called.

INTRODUCTION

A. WHO'S IN CHARGE?

Do you work for a big corporation? If you do, what would you think if a boy from the third grade of your local elementary school were chosen to be CEO of your company?

First of all, you would know that a child was not really going to run the company. If the subordinate officers of the company were the same ones who had worked with the former CEO, they would be shaping the policies and directing the operation and you would not expect much change. But if a group of officers who had been very vocal in opposing the former leader's policies moved into the subordinates' offices, you would be wise to anticipate some drastic changes.

B. LESSON BACKGROUND

In this lesson we are looking at a country rather than a corporation and a king instead of a CEO, but there are parallels. The country is Judah, and the king is Josiah. Last week we briefly noted some facts about Josiah's era (he reigned 640–609 B.C.) because we were studying prophecies that Zephaniah made during that time. Now we will look more closely at the king and what he did, but first we need to review again the background of Josiah's reign.

Josiah's grandfather Manasseh, in embracing and promoting all kinds of pagan practices, was one of the worst of Judah's kings (2 Chronicles 33:1-7). He led his people in these evil ways until they became worse than the pagans around them (33:9). But this evil king changed in his latter years. He supported the real God as vigorously as he had supported the fakes. Earnestly he tried to undo the evil he had done (33:11-16), but was not completely successful (2 Kings 24:3, 4).

The next king was Amon, Manasseh's son and Josiah's father (cf. Matthew 1:10). He liked the riotous religious feasts of the pagans, the things his father

DEVOTIONAL READING:
PSALM 119:1-8

BACKGROUND SCRIPTURE:
2 CHRONICLES 34, 35; 2 KINGS 22, 23

PRINTED TEXT:
2 CHRONICLES 34:1-4, 19-21, 29-33

Sep 22

LESSON AIMS

After participating in this lesson, each student will be able to:

1. Tell how Josiah "walked in the ways of his father David."

2. Suggest some positive benefits that would derive from the efforts of a few key people to walk in the right way.

3. Cite two personal changes to make this week to be God's man or woman in the community.

KEY VERSE

Because your heart was responsive and you humbled yourself before God when you heard what he spoke against this place and its people, and because you humbled yourself before me and tore your robes and wept in my presence, I have heard you, declares the LORD.
—2 Chronicles 34:27

once had promoted. He was not pleased at all with his father's repentance and reformation. So when Amon became king, he promptly reverted to the evil ways of his father's earlier years (2 Chronicles 33:21-23). This continued for only two years, but that was long enough for him to dismiss his father's godly helpers and surround himself, instead, with evil men from Manasseh's early days.

Having no specific information about Josiah's early helpers, we can suppose those same evil men to have been the "cabinet" that he inherited at age eight. If so, then they undoubtedly were the rulers "in fact" during Josiah's early years, continuing Amon's evil policies. But ultimately the boy king was not seduced by them. As the boy became a man, he became God's man.

I. GROWING IN GOODNESS (2 CHRONICLES 34:1-4)

At the age of eight, the king is a "zero" in the government of Judah, but the recorder can hardly mention him without writing of his goodness. As we read, our admiration will grow, too.

A. THE FACTS ARE POSITIVE (vv. 1, 2)

1. Josiah was eight years old when he became king, and he reigned in Jerusalem thirty-one years.

A news writer is taught to include the main facts of a story in the lead paragraph so a hasty reader can get a quick summary of the whole. The writer of Chronicles begins the record of each *king* with just such a summary. This opening verse records the length of Josiah's reign, while the next offers an estimate of its character. With *Josiah* at age *eight*, the year is 640 B.C.

2. He did what was right in the eyes of the LORD and walked in the ways of his father David, not turning aside to the right or to the left.

David, now dead for some three hundred and thirty years, is the patriarch of the royal family in Judah. He is considered to be a role model for all the later kings, even though he fell into terrible sins of his own. Josiah has the good judgment to copy David's right *ways*, but not his sins.

B. THE FACTS BECOME EVEN BETTER (vv. 3, 4)

3. In the eighth year of his reign, while he was still young, he began to seek the God of his father David. In his twelfth year he began to purge Judah and Jerusalem of high places, Asherah poles, carved idols and cast images.

Josiah is about sixteen years old *in the eighth year of his reign* (v. 1)—about 632 B.C. We wonder exactly how he begins *to seek the God of his father David*. He cannot simply sit down with his Bible at home. It seems he has no Bible there, as we shall see later. Though the law requires that the king have a copy of it and read it daily (Deuteronomy 17:18, 19), probably Josiah has never heard of that requirement nor has ever laid eyes on a copy of the law. We wonder whether Manasseh in his evil days had destroyed the king's copy, and perhaps others, but we have no information about that. But some faithful remnant has kept alive the truth of God's Word, and one of them has apparently influenced the king. Or perhaps Josiah has been tutored by Jeremiah, who will begin his own prophetic ministry in about five years (Jeremiah 1:2). However the instruction has come about, Josiah has been able to learn something about God and his will.

In his twelfth year, four years after starting his search for God, twenty-year-old Josiah begins to act on what he has learned. He begins to *purge Judah and Jerusalem*, destroying the places and things used in the worship of idols. The *high places* are worship sites, usually on hilltops. *Asherah* is the fictitious goddess associated with the equally fictitious Baal. *Carved idols* were sculpted from wood or

What Do You Think?

Someone must have had a positive influence on Josiah during his first ten years on the throne. Who in your congregation has a knack for positively influencing teenagers? What makes this person so influential with the youth? What are some ways the church can encourage young people and the people who influence them for good?

stone; *cast images* were idols made by melting metal and pouring it into molds that were usually made of clay.

4. Under his direction the altars of the Baals were torn down; he cut to pieces the incense altars that were above them, and smashed the Asherah poles, the idols and the images. These he broke to pieces and scattered over the graves of those who had sacrificed to them.

King Josiah is there to watch personally as his men destroy the paraphernalia of idol worship. The Baals were various images depicting that imaginary god of the Canaanites. Where our text says that *incense altars* were *above* the altars to Baal, the *King James Version* refers to "images" that were above the altars. While this leaves unclear just exactly what was above the altars, the difference in translation is not really important. Both versions make it plain that everything used in idol worship was destroyed.

As we see Josiah beating the idols into powder and scattering it on *the graves of those who had sacrificed to them*, we recall that graves are regarded as "unclean" in Numbers 19:16. What fitting places for the remnants of the unclean idols! To bring the process "full circle," 2 Kings 23:16 tells us that Josiah also did the opposite: he dug up the bones from those graves and burned them on the idolatrous altars to defile them. Like other religious reforms, Josiah's was violent, even to the point of bloodshed (2 Kings 23:20; cf. 1 Kings 18:40; 2 Kings 10:25-27; 11:18).

King Josiah carries this clean-up beyond the borders of Judah into the territory once occupied by the northern kingdom of Israel (2 Chronicles 34:6, 7), but now claimed by Assyria. By this time Assyria is in a weakened state and does not move to oppose Josiah. Josiah's destruction of the altar at Bethel in this territory fulfills a prophecy that is now about three hundred years old (see 1 Kings 13:2, 31, 32; 2 Kings 23:15-18).

DESTROYING THE SYMBOLS

When James I became king of England in 1603, Roman Catholics were hoping he would be tolerant of their faith. When he was not, some of them vowed to destroy this Protestant king, whom they saw as a symbol of heresy.

A small group of Roman Catholics stashed thirty-six barrels of gunpowder in a cellar under the government buildings in London. They planned to blow them up when the king opened Parliament in November of 1605, killing both the king and members of Parliament. But shortly before it was to happen, Guy Fawkes, one of the dissidents, was arrested. He named his fellow conspirators, and all were executed. November 5 is still celebrated annually as the day when the king and Parliament were saved from death. With typical British whimsy, the day is named after Guy Fawkes.

King Josiah and Guy Fawkes had one thing in common: the desire to destroy the symbols of what each considered to be false religion. But there were two significant differences: first, Josiah was getting rid of a religion that was definitely contrary to God's Word on every level, and second, God guided Josiah in his quest.

When we feel led to stand up for truth (or purge evil from our society), we must be sure we are acting in the spirit of Josiah and not upon our own misguided feelings.

—C. R. B.

II. APPEALING TO THE LORD (2 CHRONICLES 34:19-21)

When King Josiah is about twenty-six years old, he appoints a committee of his officials to repair the temple (2 Chronicles 34:8), as his great-grandfather Hezekiah had done at about the same age (29:1-3). As Josiah's orders are being carried out, a priest finds a book containing the law that God had given to Moses more than

WHAT DO YOU THINK?

If we attempted to tear down pagan or other sinful places in our culture, what would we be allowed to do legally? What strategies or approaches might be effective in eliminating pagan or sinful practices? How difficult would this task be?

Visual for lessons 4 and 5. This poster issues a challenge for all believers. You may want to post it outside the classroom after this quarter.

WHAT DO YOU THINK?

It was a custom in Josiah's day to tear one's clothes when deeply troubled or grieved. In our time, what are some signs that indicate a person is deeply troubled or repentant? Do you think church members should be more open or apparent about such feelings? Why or why not?

WHAT DO YOU THINK?

When Josiah first heard God's Word read, his reaction was, essentially, "It is no wonder we are in this national danger. God warned us, and we did not listen!" Do you think the average Christian reacts the same way upon hearing God's warnings? Why or why not?

eight hundred years before. A scribe takes the book and reads the law to King Josiah (34:14, 15, 18). The next part of our text takes up the account at this point.

A. AN OUTPOURING OF GRIEF (v. 19)

19. When the king heard the words of the Law, he tore his robes.

Tearing one's clothing is a traditional way of expressing extreme grief and dismay. Hearing *the words of the Law,* the *king* knows he has seen it broken continually—all his life and in many ways. Furthermore, the law prescribes terrible punishment, even national destruction. The king is appalled. Are all his reforms in vain? Is Judah still doomed? Must it be destroyed, as northern Israel already has been?

B. A SEARCHING FOR ANSWERS (vv. 20, 21)

20. He gave these orders to Hilkiah, Ahikam son of Shaphan, Abdon son of Micah, Shaphan the secretary and Asaiah the king's attendant:

The king needs answers to the desperate questions that assail him. He has spent years in wiping out idolatry. We do not know how much time and money he has invested in repairing the temple to make it fit for its proper use. But the people still are ignoring God's law because they are ignorant of it, breaking it every day in many ways. Does this mean that Judah is about to be destroyed as the law indicates? The king appoints a committee to find out, a committee as prestigious as the one that he had formed to repair the temple.

21. "Go and inquire of the LORD for me and for the remnant in Israel and Judah about what is written in this book that has been found. Great is the LORD's anger that is poured out on us because our fathers have not kept the word of the LORD; they have not acted in accordance with all that is written in this book."

Only *the Lord* has the answers that are needed by the king and all his people, so the committee must *inquire* of him. They are sent to a prophetess named Huldah, of whom we know no more than what is written in this chapter (v. 22). Apparently she is well-known in Jerusalem, and none of the committee doubts that she really speaks for God.

Huldah's reply is direct. Yes, Judah will be destroyed for her sins, as the law indicates (vv. 23-25). But because Josiah is doing his best to lead the nation in true worship and righteousness, the destruction will not come in his time (vv. 26-28; 2 Kings 22:18-20). The historical record verifies this prophecy. Four kings follow Josiah. All of them are evil, and the sinning of the people is not checked. About a quarter of a century after Josiah's death, the Babylonians destroy Jerusalem and take most of its people captive (2 Chronicles 36:1-21).

CURIOUS? ABOUT WHAT?

Since 1901, the Nobel Prize has been awarded annually to people whose inquiring minds have led them to great accomplishments in the fields of peace, literature, chemistry, physics, and physiology and medicine.

On the other hand, some minds inquire into much less noble matters. To give appropriate jeers to such endeavors, each year the Society for Basic Irreproducible Research presents an Ig Nobel prize in (dis)honor of achievements that "cannot or should not be repeated." Among the winners have been a Harvard University study on the reaction of cats to bearded men, a group of researchers who taught pigeons to distinguish between the paintings of Picasso and Monet, and a Pennsylvania zoologist who tried to make clams happier by feeding them the drug Prozac.

Obviously, many people are curious about things that have no readily apparent significance (or perhaps no significance at all). Not so with Josiah! When he heard the words of the law, his curiosity was aroused, and he commanded that its meaning for him and his kingdom be determined. How *unlike* so many Christians today who are far more interested in sports statistics or soap opera plots or a multitude of other matters than they are in what God has to say about their lives! Are *we* curious about what God has said to us? Does it show in the way we live?   —C. R. B.

III. OBEYING THE LAW (2 CHRONICLES 34:29-33)

Cheered by the promise God sends through his prophetess, Josiah moves promptly to make the whole nation aware of the law that he has heard for the first time. He wants to lead all his people to pledge their allegiance to that law.

A. GATHERING THE PEOPLE (vv. 29, 30)

29. Then the king called together all the elders of Judah and Jerusalem.

The elders are heads of families—highly respected and very influential in their family groups. Apparently *the king* assembles them to explain his plan and secure their help in calling the larger convocation described in the next verse.

30. He went up to the temple of the LORD with the men of Judah, the people of Jerusalem, the priests and the Levites—all the people from the least to the greatest. He read in their hearing all the words of the Book of the Covenant, which had been found in the temple of the LORD.

Now the whole nation gathers in a mass meeting in *the* house *of the Lord,* the *temple* in Jerusalem. There the king reads to his people the book recently found in the temple. As a result, they agree to obey the laws written in that book.

B. RENEWING THE COVENANT (vv. 31, 32)

31. The king stood by his pillar and renewed the covenant in the presence of the LORD—to follow the LORD and keep his commands, regulations and decrees with all his heart and all his soul, and to obey the words of the covenant written in this book.

The king apparently has a certain place to stand (see 2 Chronicles 23:13). After taking that place, he leads the way by embracing *the covenant* Moses had received at Mount Sinai more than eight hundred years before. We need not try to press distinctions among *command, regulations,* and *decrees.* Taken together these terms form "the Book of the Covenant" of verse 30 and *the words of the covenant* here. Josiah's promise to obey *with all his heart and all his soul* is borne out by the events of his life.

32. Then he had everyone in Jerusalem and Benjamin pledge themselves to it; the people of Jerusalem did this in accordance with the covenant of God, the God of their fathers.

The king asks all the people to follow his lead, and they do. The commitment they make is the same made by their forefathers centuries ago (Exodus 24:3).

C. SERVING THE LORD (v. 33)

33. Josiah removed all the detestable idols from all the territory belonging to the Israelites, and he had all who were present in Israel serve the LORD their God. As long as he lived, they did not fail to follow the LORD, the God of their fathers.

This verse presents a quick review, a summary of what Josiah achieved in his reign of thirty-one years. First, he took away all the *detestable idols.* Included would be the idols, the altars, and whatever other things were used in pagan worship. We read about Josiah's campaign against them in verses 3 and 4 of our text. An even longer account is seen in 2 Kings 23:4-20.

Second, King Josiah *had all who were present in Israel serve the Lord their God.* It was not enough to stop the worship of idols. This king did not want a godless or irreligious nation. He wanted everyone to worship and obey the real God. This short summary does not explain how he made them do this, whether by persuasion or

HOW TO SAY IT

Abdon. AB-dahn.
Ahikam. Uh-HIGH-kum.
Amon. AY-mun.
Asaiah. As-uh-HYE-uh.
Asherah. Uh-SHE-ruh.
Assyrians. Uh-SEAR-ee-unz.
Baal. BAY-ul.
Canaanites. KAY-nun-ites.
Hezekiah. Hez-ih-KYE-uh.
Hilkiah. Hill-KYE-uh.
Huldah. HUL-duh.
Josiah. Jo-SIGH-uh.
Levites. LEE-vites.
Manasseh. Muh-NASS-uh.
Shaphan. SHAY-fan.
Zephaniah. Zef-uh-NYE-uh.

DAILY BIBLE READINGS

Monday, Sept. 16—Josiah Does Right (2 Chronicles 34:1-7)

Tuesday, Sept. 17—Hilkiah Finds the Law Book (2 Chronicles 34:8-18)

Wednesday, Sept. 18—The Words Grieve Josiah (2 Chronicles 34:19-28)

Thursday, Sept. 19—Josiah Makes a Covenant (2 Chronicles 34:29-33)

Friday, Sept. 20—Josiah Keeps the Passover (2 Chronicles 35:1-10)

Saturday, Sept. 21—No King Like Him (2 Kings 23:24-30)

Sunday, Sept. 22—Be Renewed (Ephesians 4:17-24)

by coercion. Those people had just heard God's law for the first time. No doubt many of them were enthusiastic about it. They obeyed it gladly, with all their heart and soul, as did their king (v. 31). But many of the people had recently seen their cherished idols destroyed violently. Probably some of them were resentful and angry. We can imagine the police were kept busy enforcing the law among them. Whether gladly or resentfully, the people did serve God as long as King Josiah lived—about thirteen years after the book of the law was found in the temple.

CONCLUSION

As the boy king becomes a man, he becomes God's man. But young Josiah does more than turn his own life away from idolatry. He also turns his idolatrous nation into God's nation. Josiah's faith becomes the nation's faith.

A. GOD'S MAN

Josiah wanted to be God's man. Though he was initially surrounded by people who gave their worship and service to imaginary gods, somehow, at the age of sixteen, he "began to seek the God of his father David" (2 Chronicles 34:3).

Perhaps his initial "instruction" came from creation itself (cf. Psalm 19:1-6; Romans 1:20). Around us and in us is evidence that all creation is planned by one supreme mind. We do not know how much the evidence from creation persuaded Josiah. Most likely he was taught by those who cherished in their memory parts of God's law and parts of Israel's history. If the young king learned even the first of the Ten Commandments, he knew that the idols about him were sinful.

Do you want to be God's man or God's woman? You have a head start. You do have God's written Word in your home, both the law and the gospel. Are you reading them daily, as the king of Israel was required to do? Are you constantly improving your obedience to God's Word? Are you teaching it diligently to your children, discussing the keeping of it both at home and away? This is the way of God's man in ancient times, and now, and as long as the world stands.

B. GOD'S NATION

Recently I heard an American Christian express concern about the drift of the United States away from God. This believer was anxious about God's judgment coming against the country as it had come against Israel. Another Christian tried to reassure the anxious one, replying that the United States is not God's "chosen" nation, and God's dealing with Israel was unique.

That is true, but it is not the whole truth. Israel and Judah were not the only nations that were destroyed because of their wickedness. The nations that lived in the land of Canaan before Israel came out of Egypt were destroyed so Israel could take their land—not because of Israel's goodness, but because the other nations were too evil to be allowed to live (Deuteronomy 9:5).

In addition to those tiny nations we can cite the huge empires of the Assyrians, the Babylonians, the Persians, the Greeks, and the Romans. One by one they became corrupt, and one by one they passed into the dustbin of history. History testifies that nations that become enemies of God do not survive.

C. GOD'S PEOPLE AT WORK

God's people today must protect the holiness of their own lives, even as they hold forth the Word of life to the unbeliever who lives across the street or across the ocean. We share the Word personally, and we support missionaries in every country where spiritual darkness reigns. Jesus instructs us to do this (Matthew 28:19, 20). People of God, get busy!

Discovery Learning

This page contains an alternative lesson plan emphasizing learning activities. Classes desiring such student involvement will find these suggestions helpful. The next page is a reproducible activity page to further enhance discovery learning.

LEARNING GOALS

After this lesson each student will be able to:

1. Tell how Josiah "walked in the ways of his father David."

2. Suggest some positive benefits that would derive from the efforts of a few key people to walk in the right way.

3. Cite two changes he or she can make this week to be God's man or woman in the community.

INTO THE LESSON

For this week's lesson, make a copy for each class member of the acrostic opposites puzzle activity from the reproducible page that follows. Give a copy of the puzzle to each person. Say: "In this puzzle the left column contains the word clues for determining the correct word for each line. The right column gives the blanks for each letter of the correct word. The correct word for each line is the opposite of the capitalized word in the word clue section. This week we begin by introducing a basic theme from our lesson text. Complete this puzzle by writing the letters of the correct word on the spaces provided. When you complete the puzzle, the theme will be obvious." The nine lines of word clues (and answers) are: 1. Not OUT but *IN*; 2. Not EVERYTHING but *NOTHING*; 3. Not PAST but *FUTURE*; 4. Not HATE but *LOVE*; 5. Not OVER but *UNDER*; 6. Not HARD but *EASY*; 7. Not OLD but *NEW*; 8. Not RARE but *COMMON*; 9. Not WEST but *EAST*.

Give the students time to complete the puzzle. State: "The basic theme of this week's lesson is 'influence.' In 2 Chronicles 34 we'll discover the influence one man had on the nation of Israel."

INTO THE WORD

Move the class members into five groups of at least three students each. Smaller classes may have fewer groups. This newspaper article activity on page 46 is designed to help the students understand the events that led to Josiah's new beginning. Each group will be given a slip of paper containing one of the following categories and Scripture passage to read: Josiah interview, 2 Chronicles 34:1-4; Interview of a Baal worship team member, 34:1-4; Article on temple repairs, 34:8-13; Article on ancient discovery, 34:14-21; Article on the town meeting and the influence of reform initiatives, 34:29-33. Give

each group a copy of the reproducible activity *The Jerusalem Gazette* (from page 46) and a pencil. Give the groups about twenty minutes. State: "Imagine that you are a reporter for *The Jerusalem Gazette*, the local newspaper in Jerusalem at the time of our text. You have received information about the reform initiatives that have taken place, and your editor has assigned a topic. Gather the facts from the assigned Scripture and write a newspaper article describing the events at they might have been told in the imaginary *Jerusalem Gazette*. Remember, news stories must answer the who, what, when, where, why, and how questions. Work in your small group and write your article on the paper provided. When all are finished, we will read the stories to the class."

After sufficient time, ask a reporter from each group to read its news article aloud. Say: "These articles reveal how much influence Josiah had on Israel. A number of positive benefits resulted from his influence. Let's list those benefits you saw from the text." After writing on the board the various benefits from Josiah's covenant with the Lord, say: "The greatest benefit is found in verse 33: 'They did not fail to follow the Lord, the God of their fathers.'"

INTO LIFE

State: "In much the same way, we have influence on other people. Imagine what would happen if Christian people in your neighborhood or in your place of employment made a similar covenant with the Lord and did not depart from it for the rest of their lives. What would be some positive benefits from their efforts at walking in the right way for God?" Write suggested answers on the board as they are given. Then ask: "What are two key changes that you believe most Christians need to make to be God's man or woman in the community?" Again write these specific ideas on the board for all to see. "Why do Christians seem to have trouble in these areas?"

Next guide the students to think about their own personal walk with the Lord. Ask: "What two changes do you need to make this week to follow the Lord?" Give each person a sheet of stationery and an envelope and ask them to write a reminder note to themselves to perform those two changes in their life this week. Close the class session with a prayer of dedication to keep God's covenant.

Turning Things Around

Read the clue in the left column. Think what the opposite of the capitalized word should be. Write the letters of the correct word on the spaces in the right column. Copy the vertical word in the highlighted spaces in the blanks below. You'll see what Josiah had.

Not OUT but ___ ___

Not EVERYTHING but ___ ___ ___ ___ ___ ___

Not PAST but ___ ___ ___ ___ ___ ___

Not HATE but ___ ___ ___ ___

Not OVER but ___ ___ ___ ___

Not HARD but ___ ___ ___ ___

Not OLD but ___ ___ ___

Not RARE but ___ ___ ___ ___ ___

Not WEST but ___ ___ ___ ___

Josiah had ___ ___ ___ ___ ___ ___ ___ ___ ___

The Jerusalem Gazette

After being assigned a category and Scripture passage, write a headline and a short "news" article in the spaces below.

Headline

Article:

REBELLION AND JUDGMENT

WHY TEACH THIS LESSON?

I used to teach at a Bible college. This ministry was rewarding in many ways, but the one aspect of teaching that I think I hated most was giving tests. It always seemed like a waste of valuable class time to give tests when I could be using that time to teach new things instead!

But life is full of tests; they cannot be avoided. For instance, every minute you drive a car tests your driving ability. God has spiritual tests that cannot be avoided, either. Today's lesson concerning ancient Judah reminds us that God does not give us an "A" merely for showing up. The test Judah failed is the test we must pass.

INTRODUCTION

We live in a time of "tolerance." Nothing is intolerable, it seems, except intolerance itself. "The right to choose" one's own path and destiny is exalted to the skies.

A. CHOICES HAVE CONSEQUENCES

God does let us choose, but he warns that we must accept the consequences of our choices. Adam and Eve chose to disobey, and they died as God had warned that they would. Instead of learning from that sad experience, humanity continued to disobey so persistently that "every inclination of the thoughts of his heart was only evil all the time" (Genesis 6:5). So most of humanity died in the flood. In the dawn of the Hebrew nation, God said (through Moses), "I set before you today life and prosperity, death and destruction . . . choose life" (Deuteronomy 30:15-19). How disappointing it is to see that Israel chose death! Likewise Jesus set before his disciples the way that leads to destruction and the way that leads to life, and he warned that the popular way is not the best choice (Matthew 7:13, 14). But consider how many are choosing the popular way today.

B. LESSON BACKGROUND

In our two previous lessons, we considered the life of Josiah, Judah's last godly king. After four years of seeking the Lord, in the twelfth year of his reign that young king launched a vigorous campaign to rid his people of idolatry (2 Chronicles 34:3). In the following year the prophet Jeremiah began to proclaim God's word in Judah (Jeremiah 1:1, 2). We can imagine that his eloquent preaching lent power to the king's effort. Jeremiah's laments for Josiah following the king's untimely death were memorable to the people (2 Chronicles 35:25). In the years following that death, Jeremiah's preaching could not prevent a return to idol worship.

Today's text offers us two segments from the sixth chapter of the book of Jeremiah. This prophet's ministry lasted over forty years (from 626 B.C. to beyond the fall of Jerusalem in 586 B.C.). We do not know exactly when Jeremiah delivered these particular messages.

Chapter 6 begins with a warning of hostile forces that would overrun Judah from the north. This prophecy was fulfilled by the Babylonian army. While Babylon is actually east of Judah rather than north, there is a vast, waterless desert between the two. The Babylonians had to go north to get around the desert, so they

DEVOTIONAL READING:
PSALM 16:5-11
BACKGROUND SCRIPTURE:
JEREMIAH 6
PRINTED TEXT:
JEREMIAH 6:16-21, 26-30

Sep
29

LESSON AIMS

After participating in this lesson, each student will be able to:

1. Summarize God's complaint against the people of Judah.

2. Contrast true worship with the worthless worship of the people of Judah.

3. Suggest one specific way to make his or her own worship of God (either personal or corporate) more meaningful.

KEY VERSE

This is what the LORD says: "Stand at the crossroads and look; ask for the ancient paths, ask where the good way is, and walk in it, and you will find rest for your souls." —Jeremiah 6:16

LESSON 5 NOTES

approached Judah from that direction. In Jeremiah 6:1-15, prophecies of disaster mingle with declarations of Judah's sins to be punished by the disaster. This brings us to the first part of today's text.

I. SIN AND PUNISHMENT (JEREMIAH 6:16-21, 26)

The sinners in Judah cannot complain that they have no way of knowing what is right, since God's prophets are constantly among them. But the people refuse to pay attention and repent.

A. PLEA RESISTED (vv. 16, 17)

16. This is what the LORD says:
> "Stand at the crossroads and look;
>   ask for the ancient paths,
> ask where the good way is, and walk in it,
>   and you will find rest for your souls.
> But you said, 'We will not walk in it.'

There are many roads in Judah, many ways of living and acting. Many are bad, but among them are *the ancient paths*, the ways followed by good people and good kings like David and Hezekiah. Such a path can be called *the good way* because it leads to peace with God, to spiritual prosperity and happiness. The result of walking in this ancient path, God promises, is that *you will find rest for your souls*.

But the people refuse to walk in that good way. If a man is getting rich by lending money at exorbitant rates of interest, or by cruelly foreclosing mortgages, or by fraud and deception, or by outright stealing, he might think that is the good way. So the people reject what God is teaching them through Jeremiah. They choose ways that are immoral and illegal, but profitable.

The priests, who should be strongly supporting what Jeremiah says, are no better than the people. There are also false prophets to contradict the true prophets and approve the sins of the people (Jeremiah 2:8). So the sinners can find plenty of so-called teachers to praise them when they rejected the true teaching of Jeremiah. The people should look at the record. The evil ways they are following have brought disaster again and again in Israel's history; the good way that Jeremiah favors has brought success and happiness.

17. "I appointed watchmen over you and said,
>   'Listen to the sound of the trumpet!'
> But you said, 'We will not listen.'

A city that is in danger of attack might post *watchmen* on its highest towers so they can see an approaching enemy from a distance (e.g., 2 Samuel 18:24-27). A watchman is to *sound* a *trumpet* to warn the people of the city to get ready to meet a foe. Likewise the Lord has set prophets as watchmen for his people (cf. Ezekiel 3:17).

By divine inspiration, Jeremiah foresees the attack of the Babylonians while it is still years in the future. But his message of repentance, his trumpet call of warning, ultimately falls on deaf ears. By changing their ways of living, by doing right instead of wrong, Judah can forestall the Babylonian invasion. Tragically, the people reply not with repentance, but with a flat refusal.

UNHEEDED WARNINGS

For decades scientists have warned that Lake Tahoe is in danger, but the warnings have not been heeded. Forty years ago this lake on the California-Nevada state line was so clear that a white disc such as a dinner plate could be seen more than one hundred feet below the surface. Today the disc is visible only as deep as sixty-

Visual for lessons 4 and 5. Use the same visual from the Adult Visuals packet that you used to illustrate last week's lesson.

five feet, and another foot of visibility is lost every year. Experts say the lake is "gravely imperiled."

Steps have been taken to curtail the problem, but there is no prospect of a return to the region's former purity. In 1960, there were only five hundred houses on land surrounding the lake. Now there are some twenty thousand. Silt from construction sites runs into the lake, and ash from wood fires drops into it, as do other airborne pollutants from the increasing number of people who want to live in the Tahoe basin. These pollutants act as nutrients for algae, which continues to grow and cloud the water. So, despite the warnings, a pristine environment is being destroyed by the people who enjoy it.

The people of Judah ignored numerous warnings about the moral pollution that gravely imperiled their society. They were told how to cure it, but they were too busy enjoying life. Sometimes we are like Judah, ignoring warnings until it is too late, thinking, "Surely, it won't happen to *me*." But the Bible says a society can become so polluted that there is no cure. Is that happening to *our* society? —C. R. B.

B. Punishment Promised (vv. 18, 19)

18. "Therefore hear, O nations;
    observe, O witnesses,
    what will happen to them.

Therefore, because the people of Judah refuse to act in God's way and refuse to heed his warnings, he will have all the other *nations* take notice. This verse offers some difficulties to translators, and so the English versions are not all alike. But in any translation the main thought is clear: God wants the whole world to be witness to the fact that rebellion against him will be punished. The following verse tells how.

19. "Hear, O earth:
    I am bringing disaster on this people,
        the fruit of their schemes,
    because they have not listened to my words
        and have rejected my law.

God is going to bring *disaster* to the *people* of Judah—not because he wants to but because *the fruit of their schemes* requires it. For some reason they think that they need not pay attention to God's *words* and *law* as spoken through his genuine prophets. When confronted with those words, they either turn a deaf ear (Jeremiah 5:21; 6:10) or choose to listen to false prophets instead (28:15; cf. 2 Timothy 4:3). In short, they hear only what they want to hear.

Consequences now must follow. The armed invaders, instruments of the Lord's vengeance, will come from "the north"—a notable reference in Jeremiah (1:14, 15; 4:6; 6:1, 22; 10:22; 13:20; 16:15; and others). Later, the prophet specifically identifies this northern invader as Nebuchadnezzar (also spelled "Nebuchadrezzar"), king of Babylon (25:9). His forces will destroy Jerusalem and take most of its survivors into captivity. Interestingly, even the pagan Babylonian commander Nebuzaradan will know why the exile occurs (40:2, 3).

C. Worship Condemned (vv. 20, 21, 26)

20. "What do I care about incense from Sheba
    or sweet calamus from a distant land?
    Your burnt offerings are not acceptable;
    your sacrifices do not please me."

Incense represents the same Hebrew word that is translated "frankincense" in Exodus 30:34-36. In that passage we learn that frankincense is a part of the sacred perfumed incense used in the Lord's tabernacle and later in the temple (cf.

How to Say It

Babylon. BAB-uh-lun.
Babylonian. Bab-ih-LOW-nee-uh.
calamus. KAL-luh-mus.
Ezekiel. Ee-ZEEK-ee-ul or Ee-ZEEK-yul.
frankincense. FRANK-in-sense.
Hezekiah. Hez-ih-KYE-uh.
Jeremiah. Jair-uh-MY-uh.
Josiah. Jo-SIGH-uh.
Nebuchadnezzar. NEB-yuh-kud-NEZ-er.
Nebuchadrezzar. NEB-uh-kad-REZ-er.
Nebuzaradan. NEB-you-zar-AY-dun.
Sheba. SHE-buh.

What Do You Think?

When a car alarm sounds today, people often ignore it. Why? Does the same reaction hold true when spiritual warnings are sounded? For example, how effective are the posters that say, "The end is near"? Recalling the old proverb that "familiarity breeds contempt," are there other, more personal ways to communicate God's warnings? How?

WHAT DO YOU THINK?

The people in the text continued to burn incense and offer sacrifices. They believed they were faithful in their "worship services." So why was God so upset with them? To what extent would God have the same reaction to worship practices today? Why?

DAILY BIBLE READINGS

Monday, Sept. 23—Look for the Good Way (Jeremiah 6:16-21)

Tuesday, Sept. 24—People Tested as Silver (Jeremiah 6:22-30)

Wednesday, Sept. 25—Reform Your Ways (Jeremiah 7:1-7)

Thursday, Sept. 26—People Will Not Listen (Jeremiah 7:16-28)

Friday, Sept. 27—Repentance and Rest (Isaiah 30:15-19)

Saturday, Sept. 28—Those Who Enter God's Rest (Hebrews 4:1-11)

Sunday, Sept. 29—Christ Will Give Rest (Matthew 11:25-30)

Matthew 2:11). Likewise, *calamus* is an aromatic oil extracted from a certain kind of reed. It is a part of the holy oil used in anointing people and things for the service of God (translated as "fragrant cane" in Exodus 30:22-30). The incense is imported *from Sheba,* probably southwest of Arabia. The calamus likewise comes from a *distant land,* perhaps India. Therefore both of these substances are expensive.

Thus the disobedient people in Judah are still "going through the motions" of worship, even at a high cost. Adding to the expense are the *burnt offerings* and other *sacrifices* that require valuable livestock. But all of this pretended worship is worthless because they are wicked in their daily living (cf. Isaiah 1:13-17). Going to church and putting money in the offering plate cannot win God's favor while we are disobedient in the way we live our daily lives.

21. *Therefore this is what the* LORD *says:*
"I will put obstacles before this people.
Fathers and sons alike will stumble over them;
neighbors and friends will perish."

The *obstacles* that *fathers and sons . . . will stumble over* will be the Babylonians that the Lord will use as his instruments to bring about the "physical" downfall of a people that already has collapsed morally. The people of Judah and Jerusalem have rejected the rest that God offers (6:16). The suffering will come upon all—no one will escape.

STUMBLING BLOCKS

A stumbling block might be an issue of morals a spiritually weak person trips over, but more often it is something we seize upon as an excuse for failure. However, sometimes a person comes along who shows us how puny our excuses are for failing to conquer life's obstacles.

Erik Weihenmayer (*VI-en-mai-er*) is one such person. At the age of thirteen, he became totally blind at about the same time his mother was killed in a car accident. But rather than stumbling over this significant impediment, Weihenmayer accepted his blindness as a challenge. After a brief (and understandable) bout with self-pity, he set about to overcome the setback life had given him. He eventually became a schoolteacher, skydiver, skier, marathon runner, and a wrestler with membership in the National Wrestling Hall of Fame. Even more amazing, he is a "world-class" mountain climber, well on his way to his goal of climbing the highest mountain on *every* continent on earth. On May 25, 2001, he reached the summit of Mt. Everest, the world's highest mountain!

Judah no doubt had excuses as to why they could not live by God's will. So God said (in effect), "I will really give them something to trip over." And because of their lack of spiritual will, God's challenge to them to repent turned into a stumbling block. Are the challenges in our lives excuses for failure or stepping-stones to faith?

—C. R. B.

26. *"O my people, put on sackcloth*
and roll in ashes;
mourn with bitter wailing
as for an only son,
for suddenly the destroyer
will come upon us.

O my people is a figurative way of addressing the whole population of Judah. Everyone in Judah should *mourn,* for everyone will suffer in the coming disaster. *Sackcloth* is a rough kind of fabric, uncomfortable to wear and unattractive to look at. Wearing it is a traditional way of indicating the discomfort and ugliness one feels in a time of deep mourning (cf. 4:8; 49:3). Sprinkling oneself with *ashes* is an added way of showing how debased and worthless the mourner feels, but sprinkling is not enough for the mourners of this disaster. They should also *roll in* those ashes (cf. Ezekiel 27:30, 31).

In ancient times it was considered a disgrace to have no children, no one to carry on the family name. Thus, the grief over the loss of *an only son* was the deepest, most inconsolable kind of sorrow. Mourning over the coming disaster should (and will) be like that. *The destroyer* is the army of Babylon. It will *come* in 605 B.C. and take a few captives, but it will not yet plunder the city. It will return in 597 to steal the gold articles of the temple and seize the best and brightest of the people (2 Kings 24:13, 14). It will come yet again in 586 B.C., and the city will be destroyed (2 Kings 25:1-21; Jeremiah 52).

II. TEST AND FAILURE (JEREMIAH 6:27-30)

Now the Lord speaks directly to Jeremiah to describe the prophet's work in another way: Jeremiah is administering a test. The test will demonstrate whether the people of Judah are indeed the people of God. But there can be no grade of "B–" or "C+" here. This test is strictly pass/fail.

A. THE TESTER (v. 27)

27. *"I have made you a tester of metals*
    and my people the ore,
that you may observe
    and test their ways.

In addition to being "a fortified city, an iron pillar and a bronze wall" (1:18), Jeremiah is now also a *a tester of metals*. When the people are tested, will genuine gold be discovered—or something else? The verses to follow provide the answer.

B. THE TESTED (v. 28)

28. *"They are all hardened rebels,*
    going about to slander.
They are bronze and iron;
    they all act corruptly.

The people of Judah are miserable failures when tested against the faultless law of God. As *hardened rebels*, they shamelessly turn away from God's commands to do as they please. Instead of "speaking the truth in love" (Ephesians 4:15), they participate in spreading malicious lies in violation of Leviticus 19:16. They are *bronze and iron*. That does not mean they are strong and durable. It means they are inferior to what God wants of them. God wants his people to be precious metal, gold and silver; but they are made of cheaper stuff. They are corrupters, not only acting *corruptly* themselves, but making others corrupt (cf. Matthew 23:15).

C. THE TEST (v. 29)

29. *"The bellows blow fiercely to burn away the lead with fire, but the refining goes on in vain; the wicked are not purged out.*

Now Jeremiah's testing of Judah is pictured as an assayer's testing of certain metals. In ancient times, a precious metal such as silver would be heated to remove impurities. But before the silver is heated, *lead* is added. Then as both are heated together, the molten lead carries off the impurities from the silver. But the precious silver in this case—the people of Judah—is so thoroughly corrupt that the lead cannot do its job and *the wicked are not purged out*, no matter how hot *the bellows* are burned. The wicked are just too numerous.

WHAT DO YOU THINK?

If God's promise in this passage had been full of positive news of future greatness instead of warnings of punishment, do you think the people would have been more willing to embrace the message? Why or why not? What are the differences in people's perspectives when they hear positive and negative messages? What does that say about the work of the church as it speaks locally and to various cultures around the world?

WHAT DO YOU THINK?

In verse 29 Jeremiah is demanding a major change from the people—and change is necessary for people today as well. For which age group is change the most difficult? Why? What implications does this have in how long a message needs to be taught before results can be expected?

D. THE TEST RESULT (v. 30)

30. *"They are called rejected silver, because the LORD has rejected them."*

The wicked people of Judah go through the motions of worship (v. 20) and pretend to be pure *silver,* the unsullied people of God, but God is not fooled. He has *rejected them* because they are disobedient in their daily living. Soon disaster will come to them, and then everyone will know that they do not really belong to God. They will be known as *rejected silver*—mere pretenders. As the nation rejects God, so God rejects the nation.

CONCLUSION

Those of us who attend Sunday school and worship services regularly: are we really God's people, or are we only silver-plated vessels masquerading as sterling? The answer is not found in our thoughts and actions on Sundays alone.

A. DECISIONS WE MAKE

We face decisions every day. In business, for family activities, for social life, for community service, for fun—in all these areas, we have to make choices. Here are some questions to guide us in our choosing, from least important to most important:

Question 5. What is easiest?

Question 4. What do I like best?

Question 3. What is best for me?

Question 2. What is best for those I do business with, for my family, for friends and neighbors, for the community?

Question 1. What is pleasing to God?

B. LEADERS WE FOLLOW

The false prophets of Judah told the truth sometimes—that's partly what made them so dangerous. They approved the worship of the Lord that was carried on in the temple, even though it was costly. But they didn't speak up to confront idolatry.

False prophets of our time tell the truth sometimes, too. As this lesson is being written—long in advance to allow time for printing and distribution—it happens to be the Thanksgiving season in the United States. Among the soap operas on television, viewers are hard pressed to find one that does *not* center on the theme of Thanksgiving. Here are the main points I remember from one "informative" program.

1. The Pilgrims came to the New World because they wanted to be free.

2. After the Indians taught the Pilgrims how to grow corn, they all celebrated the harvest together.

Point number one is partially true. The Pilgrims did indeed come to the New World because they wanted to be free. But the Pilgrims were not slaves in England. They were free citizens of a magnificent free nation. The freedom they were looking for in the New World was one specific freedom only: they wanted to be free to worship God in the way they thought was right. Why didn't the program say that?

Point number two is true as far as it goes: the Pilgrims and Indians did indeed celebrate the harvest. But this inadequate statement does not mention the thanks the Pilgrims offered to God!

So, shall we listen to modern false prophets or to Jeremiah? Shall this coming Thanksgiving Day be renamed Turkey Day and devoted to football, or shall we truly thank the Lord?

Discovery Learning

This page contains an alternative lesson plan emphasizing learning activities. Classes desiring such student involvement will find these suggestions helpful. The next page is a reproducible activity page to further enhance discovery learning.

LEARNING GOALS

After participating in this lesson, each student will be able to:

1. Summarize God's complaint against the people of Judah.

2. Contrast true worship with the worthless worship of the people of Judah.

3. Suggest one specific way to make his or her own worship of God (either personal or corporate) more meaningful.

INTO THE LESSON

This week's lesson begins with three scrambled words to focus attention on the themes from the lesson text. Prepare either a transparency or a poster with the scrambled words. (You could simply write them on the board.) In big letters write the following scrambled words: ILEREBOLN (rebellion), NGEJTUDM (judgment), and PHOSWRI (worship). For smaller classes (less than fifteen), move the students into three separate groups and assign one scrambled word to each group. For larger classes, move the students into groups of three and assign a word to each group. State: "To begin class this week, I am going to reveal three words that have been scrambled. They represent the basic themes of this week's lesson. You will have three minutes to unscramble the word you have been assigned. If you finish before the time is up, work on the other two words." When time is up, ask the students of each group to reveal their word. Write the unscrambled word on the transparency, poster, or board used earlier. State: "The one word that does not relate with the other two words is *worship*. We think that if people rebel against God, they don't worship him. Yet, the people of Judah worshiped in spite of their rebellion and coming judgment. Turn to Jeremiah 6 and let's see the worthless worship of the people of Judah as they rebelled against God."

INTO THE WORD

For this study activity, use the reproducible crossword puzzle "Rebellion and Judgment" from page 54. Photocopy the activity so that each student will have a copy. Make certain each student also has a Bible. Allow approximately twenty minutes. After the puzzle is completed, ask the class to summarize why God was so displeased with Judah. Write suggested answers on another transparency or on the board. Say: "We've seen now how displeased God was with Judah. But we need to look more closely at Judah's worship. Let's look again at the text and contrast their worthless worship with what we would call true worship." In preparation for this activity make a two-column chart on a transparency or draw it on a regular sheet of paper and photocopy it. Label the left column "Worthless Worship" and the right column "True Worship." Make at least four rows below the title row and write one of the following verse numbers on each row: 16, 17, 20, 20 (again). Ask the class to work with a neighbor to describe the worthless worship in the left column. Give several minutes to complete that section. Say: "Before we look at what constitutes true worship, it would be helpful if we compare those qualities of worthless worship to present-day examples. What are some present-day examples of what you would call worthless worship?" Next, ask the class to describe the qualities and characteristics of true worship and to write them in the right column.

INTO LIFE

For this final section of the lesson, use the reproducible activity "Ways to Have a More Meaningful Worship." Make a transparency of this activity and project it. Say, "We've seen how worship can be perceived by God as worthless. And we've looked at qualities or characteristics of true worship. Let's now consider the specific application of these truths to a Christian's life. What would help a Christian's personal worship and corporate worship to be more meaningful?" As ideas are suggested, write them in the proper column on the transparency.

Say, "Meaningful worship is something we all want to experience. What one suggestion do you see on these lists that would help your personal or corporate worship to be more meaningful? Select at least one suggestion on the personal side and at least one on the corporate side to put into practice today."

Give time for the students to evaluate their own worship and what would be needed to make it more meaningful. Then ask each student to pair up with another class member. Say, "Tell your partner your ideas for more meaningful personal and corporate worship. Then I'll direct you in a closing prayer time." Close the class period by asking the pairs to pray a prayer of commitment to put into practice those suggestions that were shared.

Rebellion and Judgment

Use the clues below, all from Jeremiah 6:16-21, 26-30, to complete this crossword puzzle.

ACROSS

2. O my people . . . roll in _____. v. 26

5. Hardened rebels . . . they are bronze and _____. v. 28

6. O my people, put on _____. v. 26

9. The Lord has _____ them. v. 30

10. To burn away the lead with _____. v. 29

14. Your _____ offerings are not acceptable. v. 20

15. Your _____ do not please me. v. 20

17. The _____ blow fiercely. v. 29

18. You will find _____ for your souls. v. 16

DOWN

1. Ask where the good way is, and _____ in it. v. 16

3. The _____ are not purged out. v. 29

4. I appointed _____ over you. v. 17

7. Your burnt _____ are not acceptable. v. 20

8. Listen to the sound of the _____. v. 17

11. Neighbors and friends will _____. v. 21

12. What do I care about _____ from Sheba? v. 20

13. To burn away the _____ with fire. v. 29

16. They are called rejected _____. v. 30

Ways to Have a More Meaningful Worship

Decide ways both you and your congregation can improve in worship of God. Write your decisions here.

PERSONAL WORSHIP

1.

2.

3.

4.

CORPORATE WORSHIP

1.

2.

3.

4.

Judgment and Exile

Unit 2: Limited Hope
(Lessons 6-9)

GOD ISSUES
A STRONG WARNING

WHY TEACH THIS LESSON?

There's a lot of truth to the old cliché, "Appearances can be deceiving." Consider the hummingbird, for example. Fascinating and beautiful on the surface, these creatures are actually quite *mean*. The problem is their metabolism, which burns calories so fast that a hummingbird must drink twice its weight in nectar each day in order to stay alive. This drive leads to very aggressive behavior in defense of turf while seeking food—even to the point of killing other hummers that represent competition for a limited food supply.

Ancient Judah was a nation satisfied with the outward appearance of her national life. In her own eyes, she seemed beautiful. But inwardly the selfish focus of her people resulted in a meanness of spirit that resulted in an evil, injustice, and idolatry that provoked God's anger. Today's lesson reminds us that there is more to life than mere appearances.

INTRODUCTION

Jeremiah walks where the people of Judah walk, probably in the big court of the temple. But Jeremiah is different from the rest. On his neck he wears a yoke, such as oxen wear to pull a wagon or a plow. You can imagine the comments of careless observers:

"Hey, guy, what's up with the yoke?"

"Are you looking for a donkey?"

"No, a donkey can't get into the temple. He's unclean."

"Maybe this guy is just a donkey in disguise!"

So the banter may have gone on while a curious little crowd gathers. Then Jeremiah lets them have it: "Every one of you will be wearing a yoke soon enough. You'll all be beasts of burden for the king of Babylon."

A. GETTING ATTENTION

The above dialogue is imaginary, but the yoke is real. The Lord told Jeremiah to wear it. He even had the prophet send replicas to the kings of other nations near Judah. You can read about it in chapter 27 of the book of Jeremiah.

That device was useful in calling attention to a message the people did not care to hear. At ease and comfortable, they were inclined to scoff at prophecies of doom and gloom. Some were angry with the prophets. Few took God's messages seriously. Three times in the first eight verses of our text we read, "You have not listened." The people of Judah simply were not paying attention!

B. LESSON BACKGROUND

The book of Jeremiah contains many messages that God gave through that prophet. Some of them are dated and some are not. Last week we considered

DEVOTIONAL READING:
PROVERBS 4:20-27

BACKGROUND SCRIPTURE:
JEREMIAH 25, 26; 2 CHRONICLES 36

PRINTED TEXT:
JEREMIAH 25:1-9; 26:12, 13

Oct
6

LEARNING AIMS

After participating in this lesson, each student will be able to:

1. Tell what God said would happen to Judah and the reasons he gave for this punishment.

2. List some ways our society is like that of Judah in Jeremiah's day.

3. State his or her own commitment to "choose life," following the Lord and his commands.

KEY VERSE

Now reform your ways and your actions and obey the LORD your God. Then the LORD will relent and not bring the disaster he has pronounced against you.

—Jeremiah 26:13

one that was undated, but we suppose it was given while Josiah was king of Judah, and it strongly supported that king's effort to turn Judah back to true worship and obedience to the Lord.

Now let us pause for a quick look at the larger picture of world events. By the time Jeremiah began his prophetic ministry in 626 B.C. (Jeremiah 1:3), the Assyrian empire had been greatly weakened. They had carried the northern kingdom of Israel into exile about a hundred years before (722 B.C.), but about twenty years after that event, God had stopped their invasion of Judah by killing 185,000 of their troops (2 Kings 19:35).

Since then, it seems to have been pretty much downhill for the Assyrians. Nineveh, their capital city, fell to the Babylonians and others in 612 B.C., or about fourteen years after Jeremiah came on the scene. Three years later, Pharaoh Neco II of Egypt led an expedition up the Judean coastline to link up with what was left of the Assyrian army in an attempt to stop the Babylonian expansion.

Josiah, the last godly king of Judah, rashly led his army out to stop Neco's northward march. Perhaps Josiah hoped to curry the friendship of the up and coming Babylonians with this maneuver, but he ended up losing both the battle and his life (2 Chronicles 35:22-24).

After this battle, Pharaoh Neco briefly took charge of Judah. He allowed Josiah's son and successor to rule for only three months. Then he was deposed and taken captive to Egypt. The Egyptians then put his brother on the throne and named him Jehoiakim. He was allowed to rule Judah and was compelled to pay tribute to Egypt.

Josiah's ill-conceived action in intercepting the Egyptian army had another important effect: it delayed the Egyptian army long enough for the Babylonians to defeat the Assyrians thoroughly first. When the Egyptians finally completed their trip up to the Euphrates River to join their Assyrian allies, they were too late. They suffered a devastating defeat at the hands of the Babylonians at the epic battle of Carchemish in 605 B.C.—the very year that Jeremiah delivered the message in our lesson text for today (see 2 Chronicles 35:20; Jeremiah 46:2). From this time onward, the Babylonians were the force to reckon with, as the Assyrians and Egyptians faded away (2 Kings 24:7; Nahum 3:18, 19).

This background sets the stage for a message that God gave to Jeremiah in the fourth year of the new king, Jehoiakim. In the first three years of his reign, that king had shown clearly that he was not interested in the reforms made by his godly father, Josiah. Swiftly he was leading the nation back to idolatry and all the sins associated with it. God and his prophet were not pleased by this turn of events.

I. GOD'S MESSAGE INTRODUCED (JEREMIAH 25:1-3)

This time, Jeremiah tells us a little about the message before delivering it. He specifies the date, identifies the speaker and the hearers, and gives a bit of background.

A. WHEN (v. 1)

1. The word came to Jeremiah concerning all the people of Judah in the fourth year of Jehoiakim son of Josiah king of Judah, which was the first year of Nebuchadnezzar king of Babylon.

The message that follows is spoken by *Jeremiah*, but it is not his own. It *came* to him from the Lord. It is about *all the people of Judah*, both good and wicked together. *The fourth year of Jehoiakim* is 605 B.C., also *the first year of Nebuchadnezzar king of Babylon*. What a monumental change in the course of history has occurred in the short time Jehoiakim has been king.

HOW TO SAY IT

Ahikam. Uh-HIGH-kum.

Ammon. AM-mun.

Amon. AY-mun.

Assyrian. Uh-SEAR-e-un.

Babylonians. Bab-ih-LOW-nee-unz.

Carchemish. KAR-kuh-mish.

Euphrates. You-FRAY-teez.

Ezekiel. Ee-ZEEK-ee-ul or Ee-ZEEK-yul.

Habakkuk. Huh-BACK-kuk.

Hezekiah. Hez-ih-KYE-uh.

Jehoahaz. Jeh-HO-uh-haz.

Jehoiakim. Jeh-HOY-uh-kim.

Jeremiah. Jair-uh-MY-uh.

Josiah. Jo-SIGH-uh.

Judean. Joo-DEE-un.

Nahum. NAY-hum.

Nebuchadnezzar. NEB-yuh-kud-NEZ-er.

Neco (also Necho or Nechoh). NEE-ko.

Nineveh. NIN-uh-vuh.

Pharaoh. FAY-ro.

Phoenicians. Fuh-NISH-unz.

Uriah. You-RYE-uh.

Syrians. SEAR-ee-unz.

Zephaniah. Zef-uh-NYE-uh.

Nebuchadnezzar will come calling on Judah three times over the next nineteen years. The first will be in 605 B.C., an invasion that will take the prophet Daniel into captivity (see Daniel 1:1-6). The second will be about eight years later, in 597 B.C., when the Babylonian king will carry off much more, including much of the temple treasure and probably the prophet Ezekiel (2 Kings 24:10-17). The third will be eleven years after that, as the city and the temple are destroyed and Judah is carried into exile in 586 B.C. (2 Kings 25).

B. WHO (v. 2).
2. So Jeremiah the prophet said to all the people of Judah and to all those living in Jerusalem:

The message is spoken by *Jeremiah*, but again we note that Jeremiah is *the prophet*, the spokesman for the Lord. Jeremiah does not make up the message he speaks. He may have spoken it more than once to reach *to all the people of Judah and to all those living in Jerusalem;* but probably he can address most of them when they gather at the temple for worship. Those people continue their worthless "worship" of the Lord (Jeremiah 6:20).

C. WHAT (v. 3)
3. For twenty-three years—from the thirteenth year of Josiah son of Amon king of Judah until this very day—the word of the LORD has come to me and I have spoken to you again and again, but you have not listened.

Jeremiah is now in "mid-career." He had begun proclaiming God's word in Judah in the thirteenth year of Josiah's reign (Jeremiah 1:1, 2) and has continued through the rest of Josiah's thirty-one year kingship (2 Chronicles 34:1), the three-month reign of Jehoahaz (2 Kings 23:31-35), and on into the fourth year of Jehoiakim's reign. That adds up to a total of *twenty-three years.*

Jeremiah has not been slack in bringing his message but has *spoken* it *again and again*. The people of Judah have had ample opportunity to hear God's messages. But they *have not listened.*

II. GOD'S MESSAGE REVIEWED (JEREMIAH 25:4-7)
Jeremiah is not the only prophet speaking for the Lord during these twenty-three years. We do not know for certain exactly how many others were active then, but we are sure God is not sending any contradictory messages.

A. A MESSAGE FROM MANY (v. 4)
4. And though the LORD has sent all his servants the prophets to you again and again, you have not listened or paid any attention.

The Lord has been diligent in sending his messengers. Also active (or very close to starting their prophetic activities) are Zephaniah, Uriah, Daniel, Habakkuk, and Ezekiel. No one in Judah can complain that he or she does not know what God wants. But the stubborn wrongdoers ultimately turn deaf ears to every message from Heaven.

B. A MESSAGE REPEATED (vv. 5, 6)
5. They said, "Turn now, each of you, from your evil ways and your evil practices, and you can stay in the land the LORD gave to you and your fathers for ever and ever.

Stop doing *evil!* That is the consistent message sounded day by day from uncounted prophets. Why is such preaching still needed? After King Josiah read the law to his people (2 Chronicles 34:29, 30) and everyone pledged to obey it, they

WHAT DO YOU THINK?

Even during the most wicked years, worship in the temple continued for the weekly and annual celebrations. God was displeased because their worship had more form than substance. How can we ensure that our worship is acceptable to God and that we are not merely going through the motions of worship?

WHAT DO YOU THINK?

Jeremiah warned Judah for twenty-three years, but he was ignored by almost everyone. That can be discouraging! Christian leaders may also become discouraged when their ministries seem to show little or no fruit. List specific ways Christians can encourage their leaders to remain faithful in preaching and teaching God's truth.

Use this poster to illustrate Jeremiah 26:13. You will find it in the Adult Visuals packet. (See page 17 for ordering information.)

What Do You Think?

The people in our text preferred prophets using pleasant words and predicting positive outcomes. They rejected messages condemning their actions or warning of impending doom. How can we keep ourselves open to all parts of God's message? Using James 5:19, 20, suggest some methods Christians can use to awaken other Christians who may be becoming complacent in their discipleship.

should have been following it without any prompting. But they ignored the law as easily as they ignored the prophets!

The people are still living in the good *land* that God had promised them long before. They can live there forever if they will obey him. God has promised just that. But just as plainly he has promised that they will lose that good land if they do not obey—in other words, the promise is conditional. The people are claiming the promise, but ignoring the conditions. (See Deuteronomy 8:6-20; 28:36, 37, 63-68; 29:28; 30:1-4, 17, 18.). Each one continues in his or her own *evil practices*—especially in the worship of "other gods" (v. 6, below).

6. *"Do not follow other gods to serve and worship them; do not provoke me to anger with what your hands have made. Then I will not harm you."*

Idols and imaginary *gods* sometimes are worshiped with merry feasting and revelry (cf. Exodus 32:5, 6; Daniel 5:1-4). God knows that the people of Judah will be tempted to join their pagan neighbors at such times, but that will break the very first of the Ten Commandments (Exodus 20:3). Such behavior, worshiping idols that are nothing more than the works of their own *hands,* as well any other evil that they might do, will *provoke* the Lord, stirring him *to anger* (e.g., Jeremiah 32:37; 44:3). If the people of Judah are careful not to disobey God, he will bless them in many ways. Deuteronomy 28 sets forth some of the ways God will bless his people if they are obedient, and some of the ways he will *harm* (punish) them if they are not.

C. A Message Spurned (v. 7)

7. *"But you did not listen to me," declares the Lord, "and you have provoked me with what your hands have made, and you have brought harm to yourselves."*

No doubt the prophets have been calling attention to God's promises and threats, such as those written in Deuteronomy 28, but the people pay no attention. They go right on worshiping their hand-made gods and doing anything else that appeals to them. That kind of behavior will result in *harm to* themselves. They will be punished.

III. GOD'S MESSAGE ENHANCED (JEREMIAH 25:8, 9)

Now God adds another message. It is more specific about the punishment that is hinted at in verses 6 and 7.

A. Reason for Punishment (v. 8)

8. *Therefore the Lord Almighty says this: "Because you have not listened to my words,*

For twenty-three years Jeremiah and other prophets have been delivering God's messages faithfully. For twenty-three years the people of Judah have been ignoring them. For that, punishment is demanded.

B. Method of Punishment (v. 9)

9. *. . . . I will summon all the peoples of the north and my servant Nebuchadnezzar king of Babylon," declares the Lord, "and I will bring them against this land and its inhabitants and against all the surrounding nations. I will completely destroy them and make them an object of horror and scorn, and an everlasting ruin."*

The peoples of the north may include people groups such as the Syrians and Phoenicians, but most likely this phrase refers to the Babylonians, who will eventually attack Judah from the north. *Nebuchadnezzar* the *king of Babylon* is God's *servant* without knowing it (also Jeremiah 27:6; 43:10). He intends to conquer

Judah for his own selfish purposes, but God will use him to punish Judah for ignoring God's leading and doing evil persistently. (Interestingly, this foreign king humbles himself before God toward the end of his own life; see Daniel 4:34-37.)

Also to be punished are the pagan *nations* that surround Judah, such as Ammon, Moab, and Edom. These nations will not submit quietly to Babylonian rule. They will be so stubborn in resistance and rebellion that the Babylonians will find it necessary to *completely destroy them*. That end of once prosperous nations will be an *object of horror and scorn* to all who see it.

The phrase *everlasting ruin* describes the result of the Babylonian conquest. Cities are to become heaps of rubble, and fertile fields will become wasteland or grazing country.

IV. GOD'S MESSENGER DEFENDED (JEREMIAH 26:12, 13)

Added predictions of disaster fill the rest of chapter 25 and continue into the first part of chapter 26. This message is not popular. People who are enjoying their wrongdoing do not want to hear anything against it. The priests, who should be teaching as Jeremiah does, seem content to go along with the new king's lapse into evil (2 Chronicles 36:5). They get their share of an offering whether it is made to the Lord or to Baal, so why not be "tolerant"? Then there are the self-appointed, false prophets who teach what people like to hear (cf. 2 Timothy 4:3). To them, Jeremiah is a real threat to their cozy arrangements.

So corrupt priests and false prophets seize Jeremiah as he teaches in the temple. They are supported by a crowd of the "tolerant" people—people ready to tolerate anything but Jeremiah's intolerance. To them, Jeremiah seems to be taking the side of Judah's enemy (Jeremiah 25:9); he is a traitor and must die! (See 26:8, 9.)

News of this soon reaches the government officials, who come as a body to deal with the disturbance in the temple court. In their presence, the accusers repeat their charge against Jeremiah (26:10, 11). The final verses of our text bring us a bit of Jeremiah's defense against this accusation.

A. JEREMIAH PRESENTS HIS AUTHORITY (v. 12)

12. Then Jeremiah said to all the officials and all the people: "The LORD sent me to prophesy against this house and this city all the things you have heard.

This house is the temple and *this city* is Jerusalem. Jeremiah has indeed spoken *against* both of them. He has said they will be destroyed. But he has said this by the authority of the Lord God Almighty. God's people had better listen!

B. JEREMIAH PRESENTS A WAY OF ESCAPE (v. 13)

13. "Now reform your ways and your actions and obey the LORD your God. Then the LORD will relent and not bring the disaster he has pronounced against you."

In the face of a death sentence, Jeremiah's message does not change: *disaster* is indeed coming, but it's not too late to escape this pending devastation. If the people of Judah will only do right instead of wrong, they will be safe. Wouldn't that be better than killing God's messenger and going on to destruction?

As the rest of the chapter unfolds, we see precedents cited. Back in the time of King Hezekiah, a prophet of disaster had been tolerated and even heeded (v. 18). In the time of King Jehoiakim, a similar prophet had been put to death (vv. 20-23). But a statesman named Ahikam defends Jeremiah and has enough influence to win the argument (v. 24). Jeremiah is allowed to live and continue his preaching until the predicted disaster becomes a fact.

WHAT DO YOU THINK?

When Christians see a street preacher yelling, "The end is near," they often are embarrassed and resolve never to do anything that can be ridiculed. As a result, Christians become fearful and do not even share with their neighbors. What does the church need to do to help members get over this reluctance to speak about their faith?

Perhaps differentiating between method and message will be helpful in this discussion. What dangers exist for those who fail to note this difference? What victories are gained by those who do?

WHAT DO YOU THINK?

The people seemed to hold on to faulty theological beliefs like "We are God's chosen people. Therefore, God will always protect us." Their misbeliefs about God increased their difficulty in recognizing their sin. What methods can Christians employ to protect against letting faulty religious or cultural beliefs distort their walk with God?

PRAYER

Father in Heaven, it is discouraging to read how many people through the ages have chosen death rather than life. But when we recall that your Son died in our place, discouragement vanishes in the glory of your grace. In gratitude, we pledge ourselves to put your will above our own. In Jesus' name, amen.

THOUGHT TO REMEMBER

The choice is yours. Choose life!

CLEAR, UNDERSTANDABLE COMMUNICATION

If you are one of the increasingly large numbers of people who have a computer that is connected to the World Wide Web, you have a ready supply of words available to you in many languages. At www.spanishdict.com, you can find the translation and pronunciation of nearly fifty-five thousand Spanish words. Or check out www.yale.edu/swahili if you're planning a trip to Africa. There you'll find translation and pronunciation of Swahili words and phrases. Various Chinese dialects, Greek, German, and other languages have Web sites dedicated to them.

If you just want to speak English, but need plain-talk explanations of medical terms, go to www.medterms.com. "Surfer"-talk, rap music, computer tech-speak, and various sports all have their Web sites as well.

When it comes to our faith, most of us have some passages of Scripture that are not clear to us. However, most people also have very little difficulty understanding the basics of what God expects. In fact, we probably understand very clearly what God says about the sins that may trouble us the most.

The same was true of Judah in the distant past. Their problem was that Jeremiah was speaking all too plainly (for their comfort) about what God demanded of them. His clear call to repentance made them very uncomfortable, and also made them wish he would go away and leave them alone.   —C. R. B.

CONCLUSION

A parallel between Jeremiah's time and ours is clear in the growing exaltation of people's wills and desires over God's. Those who insist on what the Bible says are likely to be branded as narrow-minded, intolerant, and "out of touch." But God's way is still right—to the exclusion of all others.

A. THAT WAS THEN

When Jeremiah issued his warning, people scoffed. The people of Judah were God's people, they said. God would keep them secure. There was nothing to worry about. After all, Jerusalem was the location of the temple (Jeremiah 7:4, 14; cf. 21:2).

With such contradictory leading, how could the people know who was telling the truth and who was lying? One way to tell was to wait and see whose prophecies actually came true (Jeremiah 28:9). Another way was to compare the messages with God's previously revealed Word. Isaiah, in warning against false fortune-tellers of various kinds, said, "To the law and to the testimony! If they do not speak according to this word, they have no light of dawn" (Isaiah 8: 20).

The law and the testimony! The written Scriptures give all the help that is needed.

B. THIS IS NOW

As Christians, we are not under the law, but under grace (Romans 6:14). But does that mean we are lawless? Not at all. Like the apostle Paul, we are under the law of Christ (1 Corinthians 9:21). The fact that we follow Jesus requires no less goodness in thought, word, and action than lawkeeping does. In fact, it takes more. The law forbade adultery; Jesus warns against even lust (Matthew 5:27, 28). The law required the keeping of oaths; Jesus advocates truth without an oath (5:33-37). The law enjoined love for neighbors; Jesus teaches love for enemies in imitation of the heavenly Father's love (5:43-48). Jesus taught people to do good without any thought of thanks on earth (6:1-4), to pray simply and secretly (6:5-13), and to forgive (6:14, 15). We could give many other examples.

If you were to grade yourself on following Jesus, would it be "pass" or "fail"?

Discovery Learning

This page contains an alternative lesson plan emphasizing learning activities. Classes desiring such student involvement will find these suggestions helpful. The next page is a reproducible activity page to further enhance discovery learning.

LEARNING GOALS

After participating in this lesson, each student will be able to:

1. Tell what God said would happen to Judah and the reasons he gave for this punishment.

2. List some ways our society is like that of Judah in Jeremiah's day.

3. State his or her own commitment to "choose life," following the Lord and his commands.

INTO THE LESSON

As you begin this week's lesson, ask the class to rearrange their chairs into a circle. For classes with more than twelve students, move the class into several circles of six to ten students. When the students are arranged in circles, say, "Today's lesson is called 'God Issues a Strong Warning.' To begin, I want you to think about the ways we receive warnings. Starting with the person in each group who would be listed first if the last names were alphabetized, each of you identify a type of warning device. You may not speak unless it's your turn. See how many warning devices you can name in your circle." (*Possible answers include smoke or radon detectors; ambulance siren; yellow flashing light; messages on prescription medicines; computer virus detector; car or house alarms; lighthouse; fog horn.*) In smaller classes, write the suggested warning devices on an overhead transparency or board for all to see. In larger classes with several circles, ask one person in each circle to record the suggestions. After several minutes, review the many different warning devices and say, "These various warning devices alert us to possible danger. Sometimes these warnings are given by a brilliant light, sometimes by a sound such as a siren, and sometimes by written words. Our lesson text today is likewise a strong warning to God's people. Turn to Jeremiah 25 and let's find out why Judah is receiving this strong warning from God."

INTO THE WORD

In preparation for this week's Bible study section, photocopy the reproducible activity "Quiz of Warning" from the next page. Distribute copies to the students, and ask them to answer the questions by working in pairs. Say, "In preparation for answering the questions on this quiz, read Jeremiah 25:1-9 and Jeremiah 26:12, 13. After reading each statement on the quiz, look in the text for the correct answer. You have only a few minutes." After time is given, review the questions, asking for correct answers. Then ask the following questions:

1. Why was God warning Judah of the coming judgment? (*Judah had not listened to Jeremiah and the prophets, vv. 3, 4; evil ways, evil practices, v. 5; idol worshippers, v. 6*).

2. What will the Babylonians do when they go up against Judah? (*Go against the land, the inhabitants, the surrounding nations, v. 9; Judah will be destroyed, become an object of horror and scorn, and an everlasting ruin, v. 9*).

Say, "Now, let's consider ways this passage relates to our lives."

INTO LIFE

Move the class into groups of three, and ask each group to list ways our society is like that of Judah in Jeremiah's day. Give several minutes. Then ask for suggested answers. As these ways are suggested, write them on the board or overhead transparency for all to see. Say, "Our society is much like that of Judah, isn't it? And just as in Jeremiah's day, it's easy for each of us to fall into those evil ways and reject our Lord's warnings in Scripture. All of us need to rise up and commit ourselves to follow the Lord and to obey his commands. I challenge you to be a Jeremiah and warn people in our society to follow God."

In preparation for this final activity, use the reproducible activity "License Plate: Life Warning" from page 62. Make enough copies of this activity so each student has one. Give both the activity page and markers. Say, "Imagine we are from the state of 'New Church,' and we are designing a new "vanity plate" for our car. We want the license plate to communicate a warning to everyone who sees it. So this is what I want you to do individually: devise a combination of letters and/or numbers to fill the seven spaces. Be creative, and let's see what type of warnings we can design." (*Suggested examples: OBA2LIV = Obey to Live; TRN2HIM = Turn to Him*).

Allow several minutes for the students to create warning messages to write on their license plate activity sheets. When time is up, ask those who want to reveal their warning messages to hold them up for all to see.

Conclude class today by asking each group of three to have a prayer time. Challenge them to commit themselves to obeying God and being as bold and fearless in our evil day as Jeremiah was in his.

Quiz of Warning

Read each statement following and circle the T if Jeremiah 25:1-9; 26:12, 13 reveals it is true; circle the F if that lesson text reveals it is false. You may want to add chapter and verse references at the end of each.

T F 1. Jehoiakim was the grandson of Amon.
T F 2. Judah worshiped other gods and provoked the Lord to anger.
T F 3. Nebuchadnezzar, King of Babylon, started to reign in Josiah's fourth year.
T F 4. Judah's obedience could reverse God's planned punishment for them.
T F 5. Time and again the prophets spoke God's warning to Judah.
T F 6. Jeremiah began speaking the Word from the thirteenth year of Josiah.
T F 7. Jeremiah promised that no harm would come to Jerusalem and the inhabitants of Judah.
T F 8. The Babylonians were coming from the South.
T F 9. Jeremiah and Nebuchadnezzar were both God's servants.
T F10. At this time the Word has come to Jeremiah for a period of twenty-three years.

License Plate: Life Warning

Directions: Use only the seven spaces below to write either characters or numbers to communicate a warning message for choosing life. Example: URB4GOD.

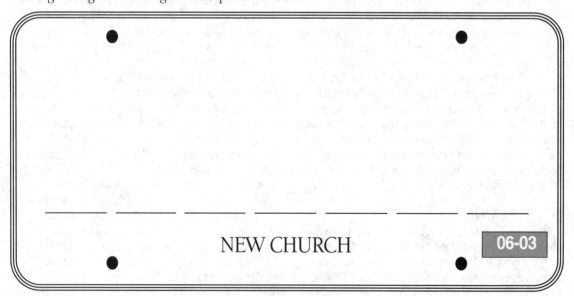

NEW CHURCH

06-03

Judgment and Exile

Unit 2: Limited Hope
(Lessons 6-9)

GOD DEMANDS A JUST SOCIETY

LESSON 7

WHY TEACH THIS LESSON?

The "American Dream" has come to be identified with having more and more possessions and conveniences. There's really nothing "American" about that dream. People have always wanted more. Solomon of old said he had pursued such a course: ""I . . . owned more herds and flocks than anyone . . . before me. I amassed silver and gold for myself. . . . I denied myself nothing my eyes desired" (Ecclesiastes 2:7-10) Wise Solomon learned that the pursuit of such a course was "meaningless, a chasing after the wind" (v. 11).

Unfortunately, not all of Solomon's descendants learned from their ancestor's wisdom. King Jehoiakim thought his position entitled him to all the finest luxuries his culture had to offer. The prophet Jeremiah said God measured kings by a different standard. Today's lesson offers a sobering reminder of what will happen to people who are selfishly enamored with their own prosperity. For all who live in affluent cultures, it is a reminder desperately needed.

INTRODUCTION

Freedom of speech is high among the liberties people cherish. Wise or foolish, right or wrong, true or false, people like to be able to say what they think. There was no such freedom of speech, however, in ancient monarchies where the king's word was law. The prophet Uriah spoke against Judah much as Jeremiah did, and he lost his life as a result. He had hoped that fleeing to Egypt would guarantee his safety, but King Jehoiakim sent men to bring him back and had him killed (Jeremiah 26:20-23). Whether he was extradited legally or simply kidnapped, we do not know.

A. A PROPHET'S TASK

As we saw last week, Jeremiah also came close to being killed (Jeremiah 26:11). With a message similar to Uriah's, Jeremiah may have preferred to speak softly or not at all. But the Lord's prophet does not choose what he will say—or how, when, where, or to whom he will say it. The Lord sent Jeremiah straight to the royal palace with an unwelcome message for the king and his cronies (22:1-9)—and this is the same king who had killed Uriah.

B. LESSON BACKGROUND

Let us review the events in Judah that provide a background for our lesson. Josiah, Judah's last godly king, was defeated and killed in battle with the Egyptians (2 Chronicles 35:20-24). The next king was his son Jehoahaz, also called Shallum. But soon the victorious Egyptians took charge of Judah, carrying this new king to captivity in Egypt, and putting his brother Jehoiakim in his place to rule Judah and to pay tribute (36:1-4).

DEVOTIONAL READING:
EPHESIANS 5:8-17

BACKGROUND SCRIPTURE:
JEREMIAH 22

PRINTED TEXT:
JEREMIAH 22:13-17, 21-23

LESSON AIMS

After participating in this lesson, each student will be able to:

Oct
13

1. Cite some of the ways the king of Judah failed to follow the good example of his father.

2. Tell why the example of a person in leadership is important to those who follow.

3. Suggest some specific way to influence people around him or her with the power of the gospel.

KEY VERSE

I warned you when you felt secure, but you said, "I will not listen!"   —Jeremiah 22:21

LESSON 7 NOTES

Last week, we noted one of the king's advisers defending the prophet Jeremiah, allowing him to escape from the murderous hands of corrupt priests and false prophets. This week we see the Lord sending Jeremiah on a mission even more daring. He must take his message of destruction directly to the king, his officials, and his counselors (Jeremiah 22:1, 2). We take a part of that message for our text.

I. THE KING AND HIS SINS (JEREMIAH 22:13, 14)

Jeremiah's message at the palace sounds much like his message to the common people: Judah must stop doing wrong—she must worship God and obey him. Otherwise, disaster is coming (Jeremiah 22:3-9). The text at hand focuses on the king.

A. INJUSTICE TO THE WORKERS (v. 13)

13. *"Woe to him who builds his palace by unrighteousness,*
*   his upper rooms by injustice,*
* making his countrymen work for nothing,*
*   not paying them for their labor.*

King Jehoahaz, also called Shallum, is now a captive in Egypt (vv. 11, 12; also 2 Kings 23:31-33; 2 Chronicles 36:2-4). This message is for the next king, Jehoiakim, who is named in verse 18. He is noted for his evil in general (2 Chronicles 36:5), but the verse at hand singles out one specific sin: he is building his house *by unrighteousness* and *by injustice*.

It is fitting for a king and his family to have "above average" living quarters. Any monarch needs an impressive throne room where he can hold court and receive ambassadors from foreign countries. A banquet hall for state dinners is also appropriate, as are adequate offices for the government officials. Building such things is not necessarily wrong in and of itself, but the way this king is going about it is highly unethical. He is apparently drafting citizens to do the work without pay.

Perhaps the tribute Jehoiakim has to pay to Egypt is creating a cash-flow problem for the king (2 Kings 23:34, 35). In spite of that, the king will not settle for second best where his comfort or image is concerned. But while the king indulges himself, imagine the dismay of a man who toils in the stone quarry for a month, or makes the long trip to the mountains of Lebanon for cedar, only to receive no payment to provide for his family. There will be *woe* for that worker, of course; but there will be *woe* also for the king who is disobeying a law of God (Leviticus 19:13; Deuteronomy 24:14, 15). This is neither the first nor last time that God notices such exploitation (cf. Isaiah 58:3; Malachi 3:5).

B. LUXURY FOR THE KING (v. 14)

14. *"He says, 'I will build myself a great palace*
*   with spacious upper rooms.'*
* So he makes large windows in it,*
*   panels it with cedar*
*   and decorates it in red.*

This verse lists items of luxury in the king's palace: *spacious upper rooms, large windows,* expensive *cedar* from Lebanon to cover the cold stone walls inside, and costly *red* paint for decoration. Rather than cut back on his own luxury items, the king cuts costs by making the builders work without pay.

II. THE KING AND HIS FATHER (JEREMIAH 22:15-17)

King Jehoiakim's wickedness is inexcusable in light of the fact that his father, King Josiah, "did what was right in the eyes of the Lord" (2 Chronicles 34:1, 2). Jehoiakim had had that noble example before him through all the years of his

WHAT DO YOU THINK?

Some segments of our culture are very suspicious of the rich, believing their wealth must have been gained through unscrupulous means. What must Christians do to ensure they do not develop a prejudice against any group, which in turn might have a negative impact on evangelistic efforts toward that group?

WHAT DO YOU THINK?

Is it wrong to want a bigger house? Using passages such as Proverbs 19:17; 21:13; 29:7; Matthew 25:14-31; Luke 16:19-31; 1 Timothy 6:6-10; and James 1:27; 5:1-7, suggest standards a Christian can use to decide whether his or her desire for a new house or other possessions is excessive. How can a Christian ensure that he or she views possessions from a spiritual perspective?

young adult life. But as king he ignores the good example and turns to his own greedy and godless way. Jeremiah draws a sharp contrast between father and son.

A. A SHARP CONTRAST (v. 15)

15. "Does it make you a king
    to have more and more cedar?
  Did not your father have food and drink?
    He did what was right and just,
    so all went well with him.

What does it take to *make* a *king?* Jehoiakim seems to think that the true marks of a king consist of a *cedar*-lined palace and all the luxury that he can get away with (v. 14). So he oppresses and robs his people to provide such a lifestyle.

By contrast, his father, Josiah, thought the true marks of a king to be doing *right* in providing justice for his people. He had had all he needed of *food and drink* without robbing anyone. Jehoiakim had been about twelve years old when his father initiated his shattering reforms and reinstituted the Passover celebration. So why doesn't Jehoiakim follow the same path?

B. THE FATHER'S WAY (v. 16)

16. "He defended the cause of the poor and needy,
    and so all went well.
  Is that not what it means to know me?"
    declares the LORD.

King Josiah had provided justice for all—*the poor and needy* as well as the rich and powerful. In his court, there was no special treatment for a man who could support him with money and influence: he did what was right. And he paid his workers (2 Chronicles 34:9-11).

The result was that *all went well* with him. More than that, the king's way of judging had shown that he knew God, for God also cares for the poor and needy, and he gives no special favor to the rich just because they are rich. Josiah had included "all the people from the least to the greatest" in his reforms (2 Chronicles 34:30), and he gave freely to the people from his own possessions (35:7). This set a good example that others followed (35:8, 9).

C. THE SON'S WAY (v. 17)

17. "But your eyes and your heart
    are set only on dishonest gain,
  on shedding innocent blood
    and on oppression and extortion."

King Jehoiakim, on the other hand, cares nothing for the poor and needy. What could they do for him? His care is for himself and what he can get. The last of the Ten Commandments says, "You shall not covet" (Exodus 20:17), but this king's covetousness makes him break any command or law that stands in the way of his gain. He resorts to *oppression*, compelling citizens to work without wages (v. 13). He will use violence and shed *innocent blood*. Over two hundred years before, evil Ahab had used perjured testimony to convict and execute a man in order to confiscate his property (1 Kings 21). Perhaps Jehoiakim does the same.

The disgraceful end of this evil king is foretold in verses 18 and 19, which are not included in our printed text. For him there will be no state funeral, with mourners bewailing their loss. His burial will be like that of an unclean animal, which is no burial at all. His dead body will be dragged away from human habitations and left for the buzzards (cf. Jeremiah 36:30).

HOW TO SAY IT

Ahab. AY-hab.
Babylon. BAB-uh-lun.
Babylonian. Bab-ih-LOW-nee-un.
Ezekiel. Ee-ZEEK-ee-ul or Ee-ZEEK-yul.
Jehoahaz. Jeh-HO-uh-haz.
Jehoiachin. Jeh-HOY-uh-kin.
Jehoiakim. Jeh-HOY-uh-kim.
Jeremiah. Jair-uh-MY-uh.
Jezebel. JEZ-uh-bel.
Josiah. Jo-SIGH-uh.
Nebuchadnezzar. NEB-yuh-kud-NEZ-er.
Shallum. SHALL-um.
Uriah. You-RYE-uh.
Zedekiah. Zed-uh-KYE-uh.

WHAT DO YOU THINK?

Verse 17 lists four sins. One is a thought-life sin (coveting) while three are outward-action sins (murder, oppression, and extortion). With which of these four sins is the average Christian most likely to become entangled? Why? What steps can a Christian take to avoid this trap?

"I spake unto thee in thy prosperity; but thou saidst, I will not hear."
Jeremiah 22:2

Use this visual to prompt some application discussion on verse 21. See page 17 for information on ordering visuals.

Jehoiakim dies in 597 B.C. Although historical records do not record the fulfillment of the details of this prophecy, there is no reason to doubt that it is indeed fulfilled. Perhaps King Jehoiakim is killed in some skirmish with the Babylonians or their agents, and when the skirmish is over those invaders perhaps drag his body far from their camp and leave it unburied. He may even have been assassinated by his own people during the Babylonian siege of 597 B.C., with his body being thrown over the wall as a message of surrender. In any case, his death is as dishonorable as that of Jezebel (1 Kings 21:23; 2 Kings 9:30-37).

LIKE FATHER, LIKE SON?

Historically speaking, most national leaders have tried to pass their position on to their offspring. Leaders of many nations in the modern Middle East have passed on power to their sons. It has been so for centuries in England also (although some of these sovereigns were women). In the United States of America, two father-son pairs have been elected as president. George H. W. Bush and his son, George W. Bush—the forty-first and forty-third presidents—follow in the train of John Adams and John Quincy Adams, the second and sixth presidents.

In Judah, it was common for son to follow father to the throne. We have seen this in our earlier studies. Occasionally, this turned out to be good for the kingdom (at least for a time), as in the case of David and Solomon. More often, however, it was to the detriment of the kingdom. This was certainly the case with Josiah and Jehoiakim. Josiah was one of the best kings ever to reign over the Israelites, in large part because of his love for God's law. His son, Jehoiakim, was among the worst of Judah's kings. He disregarded God's concern for judgment and justice for his people. It should have been clear that the nation prospered when God's word was followed. It should also be clear that the principle still holds true. Unfortunately, even Christians sometimes forget the principle when their stomachs and purses are full.

—C. R. B.

III. JUDAH AND HER DESTINY (JEREMIAH 22:21-23)

The prophecy about King Jehoiakim ends with verse 19. The remaining verses of our text are addressed to the nation of Judah, not to the king. We know this because the pronouns *you* and *your* in these remaining verses are feminine in the Hebrew text. In the earlier verses, addressed to the king, those pronouns are masculine in form.

A. THE PROBLEM (v. 21)

21. "I warned you when you felt secure,
    but you said, 'I will not listen!'
This has been your way from your youth;
    you have not obeyed me.

WHAT DO YOU THINK?

How does God speak to us when we feel "secure"? What does he say? What evidence is there, if any, that anyone is listening?

Through the written law and the speaking prophets, God has been speaking to his people through all the centuries from Moses to Jeremiah. But in the history of those centuries, they have turned away from God repeatedly in times of prosperity and security—the times when it seemed that all was well with the nation. From the *youth* of the nation, from its very infancy, its response to God's speaking has been a refusal to listen and obey. For example, when Moses was receiving the law from God on Mount Sinai, the people on the plain below were worshiping a golden calf (Exodus 32:1-6).

B. THE PUNISHMENT (vv. 22, 23)

22. "The wind will drive all your shepherds away,
    and your allies will go into exile.

*Then you will be ashamed and disgraced
   because of all your wickedness.*

Of course Judah has literal *shepherds* taking care of sheep; but those mentioned here are the rulers, leaders, and teachers of the people. They are the king and other officials of government, the corrupt priests, and the false prophets. They should be concerned about the welfare of the people, but they are "shepherds . . . who only take care of themselves" (Ezekiel 34:2; cf. Jude 12)—they are eager for their own gain. All those greedy shepherds will be gone with the *wind.* Like dry leaves in a storm, they will vanish before the Babylonian invaders.

Judah's *allies* are the other little countries of that region. They will join in resisting the Babylonians, but they will be defeated and made captives. Without leaders and without helpers, Judah will be *ashamed, disgraced,* and utterly defeated. She, too, will become captive of Babylon as we see in verses 25 and 26, which are not included in our printed text. All this will be the result of Judah's wickedness.

THE PLACEBO EFFECT

Good medical science requires that new drugs be tested against placebos to determine their effectiveness. Placebos are commonly referred to as "sugar pills" in layman's terms. Doctors have found that even the color of pills—whether placebos or genuine drugs—sometimes can make a difference in their effectiveness.

In one test, one hundred people were told they would be given either a stimulant or a sedative. Actually, all were given identical placebos, except that some were blue in color, some pink. In the group taking the blue pill, 66 percent reported feeling less alert and were sure they had taken the sedative. Only 26 percent of those taking the pink pill felt less alert. The rest of that group was confident they had received the stimulant!

Thus it is obvious that what we may think about our situation is not necessarily the case. In Judah, the people were blindly following their leaders, trusting the neighboring nations, and reveling in their good fortune and luxurious surroundings. All the while, they were thinking—in the terms we are using here—that they must have been taking a wonder drug that brought them a long-lasting dose of the good life. Little did they know that this was merely a placebo. There is no "success pill," and the fake drug they had consumed would soon prove to have no power to save them from the deadly disease of sin that was destroying them.   —C. R. B.

23. *"You who live in 'Lebanon,' who are nestled in cedar buildings, how you will groan when pangs come upon you, pain like that of a woman in labor!"*

For hundreds of years, Lebanon has been famous for its cedar trees (Judges 9:15; 1 Kings 4:33; 5:6; etc.). Even today, the flag of Lebanon displays the image of a cedar tree prominently in its center. Here, Judah is referred to as one who lives *in Lebanon,* not because her people have moved north to that country, but because they have brought so much cedar from Lebanon to build their homes in Judah. They *are nestled in cedar buildings,* their cedar-lined houses in Judah.

Living in such homes was gracious, luxurious living. But soon the people will be groaning in misery—their lovely homes destroyed and the inhabitants dragged away to captivity!

The prediction is clear: the Babylonians will come, and all Judah will experience *pain like that of a woman in labor.* The pain will come because Judah has rejected the Lord's leading and has insisted on doing wrong.

In 597 B.C., the Babylonians will return as the prophet has predicted (Jeremiah 22:25). They will come in overwhelming numbers. They will come because a few years before that time King Jehoiakim will rebel against Babylon (2 Kings 24:1).

Jehoiakim's rebellion will come at a time when the Babylonian army is busy elsewhere. But by then the little nations around Judah will belong to Babylon's

WHAT DO YOU THINK?

If government, business, or even church leaders are responsible for actions that oppress the poor, what responsibility do Christians have to take a stand against the practice? What steps can Christians take when it is apparent these leaders are mistreating people?

DAILY BIBLE READINGS

Monday, Oct. 7—Act With Justice and Righteousness (Jeremiah 22:1-9)

Tuesday, Oct. 8—A House Built by Injustice (Jeremiah 22:13-23)

Wednesday, Oct. 9—The Shepherds Scatter the Sheep (Jeremiah 23:1-6)

Thursday, Oct. 10—Do Justice (Micah 6:3-8)

Friday, Oct. 11—The Faithful Have Disappeared (Micah 7:1-7)

Saturday, Oct. 12—Judge According to Righteousness (Psalm 7:1-11)

Sunday, Oct. 13—Righteousness in Christ (1 John 2:28–3:7)

empire, and Babylon will send them to harass Judah. Raiding parties from those nations probably sweep into Judah to drive off the livestock, steal the grain of harvests, destroy villages, and kill or enslave people (2 Kings 24:2). And when King Nebuchadnezzar of Babylon is able, he will bring his huge army back to subdue Judah as he had in 605 B.C. It is sometime during this troubled period that King Jehoiakim dies (or is killed), and his dead body mistreated as Jeremiah predicts (Jeremiah 22:18, 19).

When Nebuchadnezzar's army comes back in force, the new king of Judah is Jehoiachin, son of Jehoiakim (2 Kings 24:6). Wisely he decides not to resist. He is made prisoner and taken to Babylon, along with his family, the officials of government, the military commanders, and the smiths skilled in making weapons. Thousands of captives are taken, including leaders, skilled artisans, and soldiers. This leaves behind a weakened nation that the captors hope will not be able to revolt again (2 Kings 24:10-17). The conquering Babylonians install Zedekiah, brother of King Jehoiakim, to be king of Judah and pay the tribute (24:17).

For eleven years Zedekiah rules Judah and pays the tribute. Toward the end of that time, Zedekiah seems to forget both the power of Babylon and the weakness of Judah, so he rebels (2 Kings 24:18, 20). For the third time, Nebuchadnezzar comes with his army to subdue Judah, and he does not intend to have to come again. In 586 B.C., his men smash Jerusalem into heaps of rubble and take most of the surviving people to Babylon and captivity (2 Kings 25:1-12).

Already the people of Judah have been subject to Babylon for some twenty years. Now they have to live as captives in Babylon for about fifty more. In addition to the book of Lamentations, Psalm 137 records their homesick wail:

> By the rivers of Babylon we sat and wept,
> when we remembered Zion.

CONCLUSION

People seem to be such slow learners! From the loss of paradise in Eden to the collapse of the Soviet Union and beyond, history itself cries out to all who will listen. It says that obedience to God brings spiritual peace and joy, while disobedience brings distress and disaster. When will we learn?

A. ABOUT NATIONS

In this series of lessons, we have noted that Judah was prosperous and blessed when the people followed King Josiah in obedience to God. But the kings who followed him chose to do evil, so Judah became captive in Babylon. Has anyone learned from this tragedy? As the exile was taking place, the pagan Babylonian commander knew why this disaster was happening even while the Jewish people remained stubborn (compare Jeremiah 40:2, 3 with chapter 44).

The English-speaking countries of Europe and North America grew great when they were known as Christian nations. Now a trend away from God is so evident that ours is a "post-Christian era." Will we learn in time?

B. ABOUT PEOPLE

When the Babylonians took charge of Judah in 605 B.C., they took some of the finest Hebrew young men to be trained in Babylon (Daniel 1:1-7). These young men remained loyal to the Lord in a time when most of the nation had turned away from him. God showed his power by delivering them; other faithful men showed their faith by their martyrdom (Acts 6:8–7:60; 12:1, 2; Hebrews 11:35-38) To them and to us Jesus says, "Be faithful, even to the point of death, and I will give you the crown of life" (Revelation 2:10). Have we learned to trust him?

PRAYER

Our Father, God Almighty and all-merciful, thank you for the long record that tells us it is best for us to obey you. Thank you for all the spiritual heroes who have trusted you and obeyed you even when their promised joy had to wait for the reality of Heaven. Give us wisdom to learn what is taught in history and Scripture, and give us strength to obey you today, tomorrow, and forever. In Jesus' name, amen.

THOUGHT TO REMEMBER

Obeying God is best for me.

Discovery Learning

This page contains an alternative lesson plan emphasizing learning activities. Classes desiring such student involvement will find these suggestions helpful. The next page is a reproducible activity page to further enhance discovery learning.

LEARNING GOALS

After participating in this lesson, each student will be able to:

1. Cite some of the ways the king of Judah failed to follow the good example of his father.

2. Tell why the example of a person in leadership is important to those who follow.

3. Suggest some specific way to influence people around him or her with the power of the gospel.

INTO THE LESSON

Prior to the students' arrival, write on the board the phrase: "The power of . . . example." When it's time for class to begin, state: "Consider the phrase on the board. Think of someone in your past who served as an example for you, either positive or negative. I want some of you to share how you've been influenced by the power of someone's example." Ask for some to share. Then state: "All of us can think of someone who has influenced us by his or her example. To continue, think about people in the Bible who set positive examples."

Prior to class, make photocopies of the reproducible activity, "Examples to Follow," from the next page. See that each student has one, and then move the class into groups of three. Say, "List in the left column up to five Bible characters who set a positive example. In the middle column write the name of the person or group who saw the example. Then, in the right column, describe what the example was about." After giving time, ask each group to give one complete response. State: "Today's lesson from Jeremiah 22 is about a king who failed to follow the good example of his father."

INTO THE WORD

Ask someone to read the lesson text, Jeremiah 22:13-17, 21-23, aloud to the class. State: "Our lesson text skips over verses 18-20, but verse 18 tells us who the good king was and the king who failed to follow his father's example. Who were they? (Josiah and his son Jehoiakim). Ask the following questions:

1. In what ways did Josiah set a good example for Jehoiakim to follow? *(vv. 15, 16, he did what was right and just; he defended the cause of the poor and needy.)*

2. What was Jehoiakim building, according to verses 13, 14? *(Building his palace with spacious upper rooms and large windows.)*

3. What was Jehoiakim doing that was so wrong? *(Not paying his builders for their labor.)*

4. From verses 13-17 identify Jehoiakim's character. *(Unrighteous, unjust, dishonest, murderous, oppressive, given to extortion.)*

5. Describe Jehoiakim's character in light of verse 21. *(Rebellious to God; from youth he did not obey God.)*

6. What does Jeremiah mean by "shepherds" and "allies"? *("Shepherds" were rulers, leaders, and teachers; "allies" were other countries who had sided with them against Babylon.)*

7. Why is Judah called, "You who live in Lebanon" (v. 23)? *(They had brought so much cedar from Lebanon to build their homes.)*

8. How is God's judgment on Judah described in verse 23? *(Painful, like that of a woman in childbirth.)*

9. Why is it important for leaders to be an example for those who follow? *(People tend to follow their leader. Example influences people to act. Josiah led a national repentance and reform, 2 Chronicles 34:31, 32.)*

INTO LIFE

Say, "Jehoiakim's unrighteousness, injustice, dishonest gain, murder, oppression, and extortion were quite a contrast to his father Josiah, who humbled himself before the Lord and did what was just. We need to follow Josiah's example of justice and ministry to the poor and needy." Prior to class photocopy the reproducible activity entitled "Gospel: Power to Influence People" on the next page. Move the class back into the groups used earlier in the lesson. Say, "Josiah knew God and, as a result, he defended the cause of the poor and needy (see Jeremiah 22:16). Answer both of the questions in the activity. In other words, how is the power of the gospel demonstrated to the poor or to the needy by those who are committed to its truth? How is justice demonstrated to influence people with the power of the gospel?" Give about ten minutes for this activity. Then ask class members to tell their ideas. List on the board the various suggestions. Say, "Agree on two or three we can recommend to church leadership. Then select one idea you can begin doing this week, and write that in the space provided." Close the class session by having a prayer of commitment in each group. Suggest that group members pray for one another's individual choices, both for opportunity and for wisdom.

Examples to Follow

Generate a list of Bible people whom you admire for being an example. Write his or her name in the left column. In the middle column, write to whom the example of the person was directed. Finally, record what the example was about.

	PERSON?	TO WHOM?	OF WHAT?
1.			
2.			
3.			
4.			
5.			

Gospel: Power to Influence People

Josiah knew God, and as a result, "he defended the cause of the poor and needy" (Jeremiah 22:16). And God asks the rhetorical question, "Is that not what it means to know me?" The gospel likewise calls us to practice justice and to minister to the poor and needy. Read James 1:27 for one Spirit-led, early church leader's evaluation of "religion that God our Father accepts as pure and faultless."

In your congregation's plan for Christian service, how is it demonstrating that the church knows God and is giving opportunity for the "poor and needy" to glorify God?

What new ideas will you recommend to the leadership of the congregation?

In your personal (and family) plan for Christian service, how are you demonstrating that you know God and are giving opportunity for the "poor and needy" to glorify God?

In what new ministry will you involve yourself on behalf of the poor and needy?

GOD OFFERS HOPE FOR THE FUTURE

LESSON 8

WHY TEACH THIS LESSON?

Members of the armed forces often find themselves "deployed" at various locations around the globe where they really would rather not be. To leave the relative comfort and security of home to be put in harm's way in a foreign land can be quite unsettling. But it is the reality of having faced danger and hardship that makes one anticipate the sweetness of the homecoming all the more.

Such longings are not new. Today we find the prophet Jeremiah anticipating the sweetness of a homecoming as he looks ahead to the end of the Babylonian captivity and the arrival of a New Covenant. As we live today in a world full of evil, we are in a captivity of our own—and the longing for our "eternal homecoming" can become intense! (See Philippians 1:23, 24.) Today's lesson will help your learners realize that the sweetness of their future homecoming is grounded in their present salvation and the holiness of the New Covenant that is written on their hearts.

INTRODUCTION

A. BROKEN PROMISES

Dwight and Mary had to get a divorce. That was the one thing they agreed on. But before calling a lawyer, they decided they would talk with the minister who had married them eight years before.

"Dwight, Mary," the minister said, "you have a contract, a covenant. Let me remind you." He rummaged in his files and found a sheet of paper, from which he read the marriage vows. "Remember what you said to that, Dwight?"

Dwight grunted, "I said, 'I do.'"

"So did I," Mary added.

"Now," the mister said thoughtfully, "do you suppose you can postpone your divorce for a week? Call it a favor to me."

Dwight grunted again, "I can do that."

"So can I," Mary added.

"Here's what I'd like to have you do for a week. Take this home with you." He handed Dwight the sheet with the marriage vows printed on it. "Every evening after the dishes are washed, I want you to sit down together and read this again. Then, Dwight, you are not to say anything about Mary. But if you can remember a time when you broke your promise, make note of that."

"I don't get the point," Dwight complained, "but if it's a favor to you, I'll do it."

"And you, Mary," the minister went on, "not a word about Dwight, remember. But if you can remember a time when you broke your promise, write it down."

"All right," Mary agreed unwillingly, "but I'm not much of a promise breaker."

A week later the two sat facing the minister again. "Well," he began after the greetings, "did either of you remember a time when your promise was broken?"

DEVOTIONAL READING:
HEBREWS 10:11-18
BACKGROUND SCRIPTURE:
JEREMIAH 30, 31
PRINTED TEXT:
JEREMIAH 31:23-34

LESSON AIMS

After participating in this lesson, each student will be able to:

1. Summarize God's promise to restore the exiles and to give a New Covenant.

2. Contrast the Old Covenant with the New.

3. Praise God for the forgiveness of sins available in the New Covenant.

Oct
20

KEY VERSE

"This is the covenant I will make with the house of Israel after that time," declares the LORD. "I will put my law in their minds and write it on their hearts. I will be their God, and they will be my people."

—Jeremiah 31:33

"Did I ever!" Mary burst out sadly, "And you knew it all the time, you old smoothie. I can't believe I've broken my promise as many times as I know I did." She waved her written list and looked at Dwight. "I'm sorry."

"You ain't seen nothin' yet," Dwight grumbled, waving his own list. "Take a look at this. What a scum I turned out to be! I'm sorry, too."

The three sat in silence while long seconds ticked away—five seconds, six, seven, eight, nine, ten. Then the minister spoke softly: "Want to try again?"

"I do," said Dwight.

"I do," said Mary.

This week's lesson is about two marriage covenants of a different kind. According to one, God was a husband to his people (Jeremiah 31:32), but they broke that covenant long ago. According to the other, the holy Jerusalem (the church) is the Lord's bride and wife (Revelation 21:2, 9, 10). That covenant needs to be kept today.

B. LESSON BACKGROUND

In recent lessons, we have considered the sinful actions of Jehoiakim, king of Judah, when Nebuchadnezzar came with his huge Babylonian army to annex that country to his empire. Lacking the strength to resist, Jehoiakim accepted the annexation in 605 B.C. and promised to pay tribute; but after three years, he rebelled and stopped paying the tribute.

Nebuchadnezzar was busy elsewhere at the time. But since the little nations around Judah also belonged to his empire, he sent them to harass Judah until he could come to put down the revolt. In those troubled times, Jehoiakim died.

The next king of Judah was Jehoiachin, also known as Jeconiah and Coniah. He ruled only three months before Nebuchadnezzar took him prisoner and sent him to Babylon. Along with him went ten thousand citizens of Judah, including the civilian and military leaders, plus the blacksmiths who could make weapons of war. It seems plain that Nebuchadnezzar was trying to make Judah incapable of another rebellion. He left Zedekiah to rule that feeble nation and pay tribute. All this is recorded in 2 Kings 23:36–24:17.

Loss of those leaders in 597 B.C. was, of course, a severe blow to Judah. But cheerful false prophets were ready with encouragement. For example, Hananiah promised that the power of Babylon would be broken and the prisoners would be back home within two years (Jeremiah 28:1-4). Jeremiah countered with the Lord's true message. He wrote to the captives (recorded in Jeremiah 29), advising them to settle down for a long stay in Babylon. They would not be released until seventy years were completed (29:10).

Even so, the Lord's true message was a message of hope, a hope better than that brought by the lies of false prophets. The seventy years of Babylonian dominance would end; the captives would be set free. Those who were devoted to the Lord could then return to the homeland with his blessing. This is declared at length in chapters 30 and 31 of Jeremiah, from which we take a few verses for our text.

I. PROMISE OF HOMECOMING (JEREMIAH 31:23-26)

Even those of us who have been terribly homesick probably cannot truly grasp the anguish of the Judeans as they are driven over weary miles to be captives of the most powerful empire in the world. To the sinners in Judah, the voice of Jeremiah has been the voice of doom. But now Jeremiah is the voice of hope. Jeremiah writes from Jerusalem some time after the deportation in 597 B.C., but before the "final" exile of 586 B.C.

How to Say It

Babylon. BAB-uh-lun.

Coniah. Ko-NYE-uh.

Ezekiel. Ee-ZEEK-ee-ul or Ee-ZEEK-yul.

Hananiah. Han-uh-NYE-uh.

Isaiah. Eye-ZAY-uh.

Jeconiah. JEK-o-NYE-uh.

Jehoiachin. Jeh-HOY-uh-kin.

Jehoiakim. Jeh-HOY-uh-kim.

Jeremiah. Jair-uh-MY-uh.

Judah. JOO-duh.

Judeans. Joo-DEE-unz.

levitical. leh-VIT-ih-kul.

Nebuchadnezzar. NEB-yuh-kud-NEZ-er.

Saddam Hussein. Suh-DAHM Hoo-SANE.

Zedekiah. Zed-uh-KYE-uh.

A. SPIRITUAL RENEWAL (v. 23)

23. This is what the LORD Almighty, the God of Israel, says: "When I bring them back from captivity, the people in the land of Judah and in its towns will once again use these words: 'The LORD bless you, O righteous dwelling, O sacred mountain.'

How the homesick hearts must have leaped at these words! They will go *back* to *Judah*. They will again see Jerusalem, the city that is their chief joy (cf. Ezekiel 24:25). More than that, they will not be as they had been, a "sinful nation, a people loaded with guilt" (Isaiah 1:4). Restored Judah, as a *righteous dwelling*, will reflect God's own nature (Psalm 89:14). The *sacred mountain* refers to Jerusalem and its temple (cf. Psalm 2:6; Isaiah 66:20). The people coming back from Babylon will pray for God's blessing on their holy homeland. And it is none other than *the Lord Almighty, the God of Israel* who makes this promise.

B. PHYSICAL RENEWAL (v. 24)

24. "People will live together in Judah and all its towns—farmers and those who move about with their flocks.

People freed from captivity will be happily working in the tilled fields of *Judah*; shepherds no less happily will lead their *flocks* on the unplowed ground of the open range. Before the captivity, many Judeans eagerly had sought unjust gain; when they come back, they will prefer to earn an honest living. At that time, the desolation of Judah's *towns* and cities will be reversed (cf. Jeremiah 10:22).

C. TOTAL RENEWAL (vv. 25, 26)

25. "I will refresh the weary and satisfy the faint."

The spiritual rejuvenation of verse 23 combined with the earthly well being of verse 24 results in the total renewal of the *weary*. Every soul tired of captivity will be rested and refreshed by liberty; every soul that mourns in Babylon will be filled with delight in Judah. God has decreed it. He will supply whatever is needed to make everyone satisfied, content, and blessed.

26. At this I awoke and looked around. My sleep had been pleasant to me.

Apparently, Jeremiah is sleeping when God reveals the message of verses 23-25 to him in a dream. The *sleep* he has just finished seems *pleasant* because the message revealed in it was pleasant: a promise of return and renewal for the captives. We can speculate that Jeremiah especially treasured the blessing of this moment given the harshness of his life as a whole. In the Old Testament, no one suffers more than Jeremiah (see chapters 37, 38, etc.)

COMING HOME TO FREEDOM

Saddam Hussein's Iraqi forces invaded the tiny nation of Kuwait in the late summer of 1990. Acting on a United Nations resolution condemning the invasion, a coalition of Western nations responded on January 17, 1991.

On the second day of Operation Desert Storm, Lieutenant Colonel Cliff Acree, USMC, was on an air mission over Iraq when his plane was hit by a ground-to-air missile. Acree survived and was captured. The war was short, but Acree and other Allied airmen endured weeks of torture and solitary confinement. Finally, on March 10, Freedom One—the plane bringing the captives home—landed at Andrews Air Force Base in Maryland. Acree appeared in the plane's doorway, and his wife burst from the waiting crowd to greet him in an emotional embrace.

Over several months, Colonel Acree's emotions and body would heal, but the real change was seen in his statement about freedom: "Freedom is precious. You don't fully realize its value until it's taken away."

Jeremiah's prediction of Judah's homecoming probably sounded too good to be true, but God's word described it accurately. Weary souls would find the joy of

---

WHAT DO YOU THINK?

When the older people learned that God would take his people back to Jerusalem after the captivity, what stories might they have told the younger captives about their homeland? What hopes might they have shared? Considering Titus 2:1-6, in what ways can older Christians guide and challenge younger Christians today?

WHAT DO YOU THINK?

Suppose a new Christian comes to you for advice. He is facing some chronic health problems that have put him into a financial bind. His marriage is tense, and recently his employer informed him that layoffs are imminent. He asks you, "Where is all this rest for the weary and comfort for the sorrowful?" Without necessarily quoting to him a passage such as Hebrews 12:3, how will you answer?

WHAT DO YOU THINK?

In what ways do people like to blame someone else (spouse, parent, boss, other drivers, etc.) for their sins? How can we learn to inspect our own behavior for needed changes instead of blaming someone else?

[Consider Matthew 7:1-5 in your discussion.]

---

freedom replacing the sorrow of captivity. We *also* are captives—enslaved to sin. But the promise of the gospel is that one day God shall bring us home, and inexpressible joy will replace our sorrow and hurt.   —C. R. B.

II. PROMISE OF PROSPERITY (JEREMIAH 31:27-30)

God is going to restore the captives to their homeland, not as the sinners they are now, but as true worshipers, purified and obedient to God. In their own land they will grow, being built up in the knowledge of God and in their own godly character.

A. GOD'S REPLANTING (v. 27)

27. *"The days are coming," declares the LORD, "when I will plant the house of Israel and the house of Judah with the offspring of men and of animals.*

The overall thought here echoes that of 31:24 above, but now *Israel* is also included (as in 30:3). The ultimate result of God's reuniting and replanting of Israel and *Judah* will be, of course, the coming of Christ (Hosea 1:11).

B. GOD'S REBUILDING (v. 28)

28. *"Just as I watched over them to uproot and tear down, and to overthrow, destroy and bring disaster, so I will watch over them to build and to plant," declares the LORD.*

God would rather *build* and *plant* than *destroy*. Contrary to the people's belief, *the Lord* is indeed watching *over them*, both in the current punishment as well as the coming restoration (cf. 12:4 and 23:24). And when the restoration comes, the people should make no mistake that it is the Lord who is bringing this about, thus putting the lie to the false prophets and their idols.

C. GOD'S JUSTICE (vv. 29, 30)

29, 30. *"In those days people will no longer say,*
    'The fathers have eaten sour grapes,
        and the children's teeth are set on edge.'
Instead, everyone will die for his own sin; whoever eats sour grapes—his own teeth will be set on edge.

Many of us can recall the sharp and very unpleasant sensation felt in our teeth when we bit into a very sour grape. The Jews in captivity know that sensation, and they use it in a popular proverb. In claiming that *the fathers have eaten sour grapes, and the children's teeth are set on edge,* they make the claim that the bitter captivity they suffer is not their own fault, but is due to the sins of former generations.

This false conclusion perhaps is due to a misapplication of Exodus 20:5, 6. But God, speaking through both Jeremiah and Ezekiel (himself among the captives in Babylon), forbids this proverb (cf. Ezekiel 18:1-4). Even so, the Lord's command here is nothing new. It merely brings back the clear precept of Deuteronomy 24:16. The whole of Ezekiel 18 expands on the correction that *everyone will die for his own sin.* (See more discussion of this in lesson 12.) The returning exiles must be ready to face the facts honestly. They must admit that they are suffering for their own sins, and not for the sins of their parents.

III. PROMISE OF COVENANT (JEREMIAH 31:31-34)

Looking more than five hundred years into the future, the Lord promises a New Covenant to replace the old one he had made with Israel more than eight hundred years previously. That New Covenant is the one God has made with all of us who are Christians; it is the same one he offers to non-Christians everywhere.

A. New and Different (vv. 31, 32)

31. *"The time is coming,"* declares the LORD,
      "when I will make a new covenant
   with the house of Israel
      and with the house of Judah.

The houses *of Israel* and *Judah* are the two parts into which the larger nation of Israel was divided after King Solomon's death in 931 B.C. More than a century before Jeremiah's writing, *the house of Israel* had been taken captive (2 Kings 17:6). As Jeremiah writes, *the house of Judah* has been partially taken into captivity in Babylon—with a much more extensive exile to follow in a few years. Yet the *New Covenant* is intended for both of these broken parts, for the whole house of Israel (cf. Romans 9–11)—and for the rest of the world, too (see Isaiah 42:6; 49:6). For this reason, many scholars consider Jeremiah 31:31-34 to be one of the most important sections in the entire Old Testament! (See also discussion of 31:27 above.)

32. *"It will not be like the covenant*
   I made with their forefathers
   when I took them by the hand
      to lead them out of Egypt,
   because they broke my covenant,
      though I was a husband to them,"
         declares the LORD.

The Old Covenant presents a multitude of rules for living. If the Israelites had kept the rules, surely their society would have been the most orderly, the most peaceful, and the most pleasant the world had ever known. But that *covenant* failed to produce such a society because the people *broke* the rules. *I was a husband to them* recalls similar statements in 3:14, 20.

New, Not Just Restored

Most of us have seen an old tractor, its days of usefulness long past, sitting broken and rusting beside a barn. The farmer has replaced it with a new, larger, and more powerful machine. However, some people like old tractors. Don Dahlinghaus, an Ohio farmer, is one such person. His collection of fifty antique tractors contains examples dating back into the 1920s. Photos and descriptions of many of them can be seen at his Web site www.dondatractors.homestead.com. Each winter Dahlinghaus restores another tractor or two. When he is finished with the task, he uses them in parades and occasionally does some token farm work with them.

The Old Covenant was somewhat like these old tractors. It served its purpose for its time, but a "new and better model" was eventually needed—a covenant with "more power," power to meet the needs of the human race in a way the old one never could. The New Covenant that God promised through the prophet would do the job so much better than the old one. The Old Covenant (like the old tractors) had become broken and useless. But rather than attempt to restore what had been broken (as some people still do), God offered a New Covenant that comes with a divine guarantee that it will perform the task it was designed for: to bring us salvation and forgiveness through the blood of Christ, the Son of God.   —C. R. B.

B. Hearts and Minds (v. 33)

33. *"This is the covenant I will make with the house of Israel*
      after that time," declares the LORD.
   "I will put my law in their minds
      and write it on their hearts.
   I will be their God,
      and they will be my people.

What Do You Think?

The New Covenant was to be made with the people of both the northern and southern kingdoms. God wanted all to come together again under his leadership and salvation. Considering the oneness that Jesus desires in John 17:20-23, what can churches do to bring about God's goal of spiritual unity?

What Do You Think?

The New Covenant is to be more than a set of codes and rituals. It is a covenant of the heart, expressed in heartfelt devotion. How can we insure that our class or church is protected from practicing an empty and ceremonial religion? What can fellow Christians do to encourage their brothers and sisters in the Lord to deepen their relationship with God?

"They shall all know me, from the least of them unto the greatest of them," saith the Lord.
Jeremiah 31:34

The visual for today's lesson illustrates verse 34. See page 17 for ordering information.

WHAT DO YOU THINK?

How can the church's teaching ministry maintain an effective balance between imparting facts about God and leading people to know God himself more intimately?

PRAYER

How good you are, our Father, how merciful and gracious! How you loved us to give your Son! How he loved us to give his life! Grateful for your grace, we promise to live daily by the New Covenant you have written in our hearts; and we pray for wisdom and strength to keep our promise. In Jesus' name, amen.

THOUGHT TO REMEMBER

Let God's New Covenant rule your heart and your life.

God's law had been written on stone (Exodus 31:18; 32:19; 34:1) and in a book (Deuteronomy 31:24-26). The people had been told to keep it in their hearts (Deuteronomy 6:6). Even so, they had broken this *covenant* repeatedly through the course of the centuries. The result is captivity.

But now God says that he himself will write his New Covenant in *their minds and . . . on their hearts.* But he will write it only in willing hearts. Those who open their hearts to the New Covenant will be God's *people,* and he *will be their God.*

C. KNOWLEDGE AND FORGIVENESS (v. 34)

34. "No longer will a man teach his neighbor,
    or a man his brother, saying, 'Know the LORD,'
because they will all know me,
    from the least of them to the greatest,"
                        declares the LORD.
"For I will forgive their wickedness
    and will remember their sins no more."

In the time of the New Covenant, *no longer . . . teach* means that people will have direct access to God without needing to go through the human intermediaries—the priests of the levitical system (cf. Isaiah 54:13). Of course, a teaching function still exists in the New Covenant (1 Corinthians 12:28, 29; Ephesians 4:11, 12).

An outstanding feature of this New Covenant is God's forgiveness. Because Christ takes the sin penalty upon himself, God takes away the *sins* of his people. To remind us of these facts, the writer of Hebrews quotes from this section of Jeremiah in Hebrews 8:8-12 and 10:16, 17 (see also Romans 11:27). When Christ returns, *all* Christians will *know* him in the fullest sense of Jeremiah's prophecy.

CONCLUSION

Christians, he is our God, and we are his people according to his New Covenant. Our sins are forgiven because of the death of Christ. Praise the Lord!

A. GOD'S HOLY PEOPLE

Through the blood of animals and the will of God, the Old Covenant was a physical deliverance from earthly oppressors. Through the blood of Christ, the New Covenant is eternal deliverance from the oppression of sin and the wrath of God. With God's New Covenant written in our hearts (2 Corinthians 3:3), we obey God because obeying him is our chief joy. We do not continue in sin (Romans 6:2). But if we do sin—and even God's holy people do—then "if we confess our sins, he is faithful and just and will forgive us our sins and purify us from all unrighteousness" (1 John 1:9). Praise the Lord again!

B. OUR HOLY CALLING

The problem is that God's law is not the only thing in our hearts. Also crowded in there are our daily concerns that result in selfishness, pride, greed, and other impure motives. Even so, God calls us to holiness (1 Peter 1:15, 16). The word *holy* means "set apart," or "dedicated." God calls us to dedicate ourselves to his service, and he has dedicated us, too, in writing his law in our hearts. It is God who empowers us to resist sin and live a holy life (cf. 1 Corinthians 10:13; James 4:7). Although the temptation to sin is inevitable, our surrender to that temptation is not. It is possible to live a life that is not characterized by a pursuit of sin. If you have God's law written in your heart and you use it well, you can defeat Satan every time. And if you do not know the law of Christ that is in your heart well enough to use it properly, whose fault is that?

Discovery Learning

This page contains an alternative lesson plan emphasizing learning activities. Classes desiring such student involvement will find these suggestions helpful. The next page is a reproducible activity page to further enhance discovery learning.

LEARNING GOALS

After participating in this lesson, each student will be able to:

1. Summarize God's promise to restore the exiles and to give a New Covenant.

2. Contrast the Old Covenant with the New.

3. Praise God for the forgiveness of sins available in the New Covenant.

INTO THE LESSON

Begin this week's lesson with a wordfind activity. Prior to the lesson, photocopy the reproducible activity "Wordfind Challenge" from the next page. Give a sheet to each person and make certain each one has a pencil or pen. Say, "We begin today's lesson with a wordfind activity that contains eight hidden words. These words help to focus our thinking on today's lesson from Jeremiah 31:23-34. The words may be spelled forwards or backwards, vertical, horizontal, or diagonal. Circle each of the eight words of three letters or more. Ignore any two-letter words you may find." Give a few minutes for this activity and then have learners identify the hidden words: *covenant, new, old, exile, law, know, forgive,* and *sin.* State: "Under the old covenant of law, the people of Judah sinned and were taken captive to Babylon. But God promised a new covenant. They will know the Lord and receive the forgiveness of sins. Let's read the lesson text and see the hope he gave to them for the future."

INTO THE WORD

Ask a class member to read the lesson text aloud. Prior to class, prepare the following questions on a worksheet and make a copy for each person. Move the class into groups of three to work together.

1. With what groups will the new covenant be made? (v. 31) *(The house of Judah and the house of Israel.)*

2. When the exiles return to Judah, in what two trades will many work? (v. 24) *(Farmers and shepherds.)*

3. Describe how God indicated he would restore them from captivity to their home land. (v. 23) *(They will use these words once again, "The Lord bless you, O righteous dwelling, O sacred mountain.")*

4. Contrast the ways that God had watched over the people with the ways he will watch over them in the future. (v. 28) *(To uproot; to tear down; to overthrow; to destroy; to bring disaster. To build and to plant.)*

5. What is the meaning of, "The fathers have eaten sour grapes, and the children's teeth are set on edge"? (v. 29) *(The people of Judah and Israel have been subjected to captivity in Babylon due to the sins of their fathers.)*

6. In the New Covenant, how will that phrase be changed and properly understood? (v. 30) *(Whoever eats sour grapes—his own teeth will be set on edge; people suffer for their own sins, not their father's sins.)*

7. Why do people in the New Covenant not have to teach one another to know the Lord? (vv. 33, 34) *(Entrance into the new covenant comes with knowing the Lord; they will already know the Lord.)*

8. How will sins of the people be regarded in the New Covenant? (v. 34) *(Forgiven and forgotten by God.)*

9. Contrast the Old Covenant with the New Covenant. *(Old: external, on a stone tablet; New: internal, on the heart. Old: people claimed to be punished for their fathers' sins; New: punishment recognized as for their own sins. Old: sin was punished; New: sin is forgiven.)*

Review the answers with the whole class.

INTO LIFE

Say, "If Jesus is your Lord and Savior, listen to the words of the Lord in verse 34, 'For I will forgive their wickedness and will remember their sins no more.' God has forgiven us our sins and he no longer remembers them. When we truly understand that, what response to God should we make? We should praise him!"

Prior to class, photocopy the "Ways to Demonstrate Praise to God" activity from the next page. Give a copy to each student. Say, "In your group of three, brainstorm some practical ways that we can praise him this week. Write your suggested ways on the activity page in the spaces provided." Give approximately five minutes for each group to generate a list of practical ways to praise God this week. *(Example: select a praise chorus to sing every day.)*

When time is up, say, "Let's see your answers to this activity." Ask one person from each group to go to the board and write their suggestions for all to see. After the suggestions have been placed on the board, say, "Now, I want you to select one of those ways to do this week as an expression of your praise to God for forgiving you of your sins. Tell the others in your group the practical way you have chosen. Close our class time with a prayer of commitment in your groups of three."

Wordfind Challenge

There are eight words hidden in this puzzle. They may be spelled forward or backwards, diagonally, horizontally, or vertically. Circle each word of three letters or more, ignoring any two-letter words that may be found. In the space to the right, write the words that you find.

```
T U S O R G B A
K N O W A W T Z
O W A B E I S E
R I T N J F O Q
H O B A E X T U
I V G X Y V A D
G S I N Q N O G
M L E C U V L C
E P A U B E D O
R O G W D H I Z
E V I G R O F E
```

_____

_____

_____

_____

_____

_____

_____

Ways to Demonstrate Praise to God

The forgiveness of sins is available to those in the New Covenant. What are some specific ways that you can demonstrate your praise to God for forgiving your sins? Write them on the following lines. Then, read the instruction below, and pray to our God.

_____

_____

_____

_____

_____

_____

_____

Select one of those ways listed above, and commit yourself in prayer to demonstrating praise to the Lord.

LIVING IN FAITH

LESSON 9

WHY TEACH THIS LESSON?

"Extreme sports" came into vogue a few years back, as people began to try bungee-jumping, "free climbing" of mountains, and other risky recreational activities. This trend may be the result of modern life's having become so "civilized" that many people find their daily existence offers them little challenge.

In a sense, extreme sports are nothing new. Ancient Judah played a version of this game when it risked its well-being and its very existence with an in-your-face challenge to God's power, authority, and justice. Habakkuk's vision in today's lesson reveals that God will respond in a most severe manner to such a challenge. Today's lesson reminds us how foolish and self-defeating it is to play games with God.

INTRODUCTION

The ideal of the U.S. government is carved in stone on the front of a local courthouse: EQUAL AND EXACT JUSTICE TO EVERY MAN. But everyone in the government or out of it knows that this ideal is far from being reached.

A. HOW IS JUSTICE IN YOUR TOWN?

Do you know someone who has lost money in a scam of some kind? Do you have to pay more for your groceries because your grocer loses thousands of dollars each year to shoplifters? Have you been treated unjustly because you are a "minority"? Did the person who fixed your car overcharge you? Do you suspect that the justice system wrongly sets criminals free on a regular basis? Are you suspicious of political leaders at every level from local to national? Are there unsolved crimes on your local police department's books, so that thieves and murderers are apparently walking around free?

Injustice can work the other way around, too. While most Christians would protest that they never would be guilty of injustice, think about it. When you bump another car in the parking lot, do you volunteer to pay for the damage even if no one knows you did it? Do you ever lie to your spouse? What do you do when the clerk at the checkout counter gives you too much change?

Injustice may be bad in our country today, but it was worse in ancient Judah when Jehoiakim was king (609–597 B.C.). This king took the lead in wrongdoing, and most of his people were glad to follow.

B. LESSON BACKGROUND

Habakkuk had a problem. King Jehoiakim of Judah was leading his people into idolatry, evil, and injustice, and the people were following him. Perhaps some of them were even "running ahead" of him in committing evil. How could a just and holy God let all that go on?

Habakkuk was a prophet. He was used to getting revelations directly from God, so he took his problem directly *to* God. The conversation between the prophet and the Lord fills the first two chapters of Habakkuk's book, but the following condensed paraphrase captures the main points.

DEVOTIONAL READING:
HEBREWS 11:32–12:2
BACKGROUND SCRIPTURE:
HABAKKUK
PRINTED TEXT:
HABAKKUK 3:2-6, 16-19

LESSON AIMS

After participating in this lesson, each student will be able to:

1. Tell what Habakkuk saw in his vision of the destruction of Jerusalem, and how his faith sustained him in the face of disaster.

2. Compare/contrast Habakkuk's response of faith with the responses many people today have toward disaster.

3. State one specific lesson he or she can learn from a current difficulty in life.

Oct
27

KEY VERSE

LORD, I have heard of your fame; I stand in awe of your deeds, O LORD. Renew them in our day, in our time make them known; in wrath remember mercy. —Habakkuk 3:2

Habakkuk: How can you tolerate all this wickedness, Lord? How long must I live in the midst of it?

The Lord: Take it easy, Habakkuk. I'm going to bring the Babylonians to punish evil Judah.

Habakkuk: But Lord, the Babylonians are worse than the people of Judah! How can you let those scoundrels punish people better than they are?

The Lord: Take it easy, Habakkuk. The Babylonians will be punished in their turn. They are going to lose their empire.

I. THE PROPHET'S PRAYER (HABAKKUK 3:2)

Our text this week is from chapter 3 of Habakkuk, which offers a prayer of that prophet. The term *shigionoth* in verse 1 perhaps names a tune to which that prayer is to be sung. When the Babylonian captivity is over and the people of Judah live again in their homeland, perhaps the temple choir will put this inspired composition to music. As such, chapter 3 of Habakkuk can be thought of as a psalm.

A. AWE AT GOD'S WORK (v. 2a)

2a. LORD, *I have heard of your fame;*
   I stand in awe of your deeds, O LORD.

Habakkuk knows about the *deeds* and awe-inspiring power of the Lord. Perhaps the prophet had been taught the history of his people in the time when godly King Josiah was encouraging such teaching. Such teaching would have included instruction on how the Lord freed his people from slavery in Egypt—providing for them through forty years of wandering in the desert, granting them victory in the promised land, and even punishing them when they fell (or "jumped"!) into sin as the prophet now sees them doing again. Habakkuk's *awe* indicates a deep sense of reverence for the Lord.

B. PLEA FOR GOD'S POWER AND MERCY (v. 2b)

2b. *Renew them in our day,*
   in our time make them known;
   in wrath remember mercy.

Habakkuk begs the Lord to show his awe-inspiring power again by doing marvelous things *in our day,* in the very years in which Habakkuk is living. He wants the Lord to make known his power and justice, even if he has to do it by punishing his people in Judah. But he wants the Lord to temper his *wrath* with *mercy:* to limit their punishment and then to grant forgiveness when they repent and obey him again. (Compare with Psalm 77, particularly v. 9.)

Issues of wrath and mercy are expressed together back to the earliest days of the Old Covenant. See Exodus 32:10-12; Deuteronomy 4:31; and 29:20-28.

IN OUR TIME

Neville Chamberlain was the British Prime Minister when Adolf Hitler and Benito Mussolini began their siege of Europe. He signed a treaty accepting Italy's invasion of Ethiopia on the basis of Mussolini's promise to stay out of the Spanish Civil War.

Hitler's invasion of the German-speaking areas of Czechoslovakia brought another crisis. At a conference in Munich, Chamberlain allowed Hitler's claims to those territories in exchange for Hitler's pledge not to take the rest of Czechoslovakia. He came back to Britain with the words that his concession to Hitler had brought "peace in our time," as he phrased it. We now know that he was terribly naïve in compromising with the evil Nazi regime.

We all want things to be right "in our time." It makes life so much easier when we don't have to deal with the evil that surrounds us in society. Habakkuk prayed

The visual for today's lesson suggests one application of Habakkuk's prayer for God to renew his deeds (v. 2).

WHAT DO YOU THINK?

Righteous Habakkuk would suffer along with the wicked of Judah. How can righteous people sustain their faith when they suffer because of the misdeeds of the unrighteous? What can Christians do to keep their faith strong during trying circumstances?

that God would remove the idolatry and wickedness in Judah, and that God would bring righteousness to his people, *within his lifetime*. But Habakkuk had to accept the divine timing rather than his own, just was we do. A line in an old hymn says, "God doesn't always come when we call him, but he always comes on time." And often, when God comes, he comes with a challenge for us to assist him in his work. Haven't you found it to be so in your life?   —C. R. B.

II. THE PROPHET'S VISION (HABAKKUK 3:3-6)

It seems that the Lord answers Habakkuk's prayer with what theologians call a "theophany": a tremendous vision of himself. (Compare his vision with that of Isaiah in Isaiah 6.) Habakkuk sees the Lord coming with visible glory: enough to fill earth and sky; with hidden power, enough to punish Judah as he has promised to do; and with mercy, enough to preserve some of Judah's people and give them another chance to be his people.

A. VISION OF GLORY (v. 3)

3. *God came from Teman,*
   the Holy One from Mount Paran.   Selah
His glory covered the heavens
   and his praise filled the earth.

Teman is a city in the region of Seir (also called Edom). Both the city and *Mount Paran* are south of Judah. Mount Paran is mentioned in the Old Testament only here and in Deuteronomy 33:2. Since the wording of that passage is similar to this one (but with "Seir" instead of "Teman"), we get the idea that Habakkuk is reflecting back to the time of Moses when the Old Covenant had its beginning. The God who guided Moses and the Israelites so many centuries ago is the same God who lives and guides now!

Selah appears seventy-one times in Psalms and three times in Habakkuk (3:3, 9, 13). Many students believe it to be a musical direction. Perhaps it calls for an interlude on the instruments. When the choir announces the coming of the Lord (v. 3a), can't you imagine that the singers will be interrupted by a great flourish of trumpets?

The words *glory* and *praise* are not always synonymous, but sometimes they are. For example, giving glory to God is the same as giving him praise. If the two words have the same meaning here, they tell us that the light of God's glory flooded both earth and sky as God came "from Teman." Again noting the similarity to Deuteronomy 33:2, we see Habakkuk looking to the future by connecting with the past.

B. VISION OF POWER (v. 4)

4. *His splendor was like the sunrise;*
   rays flashed from his hand,
   where his power was hidden.

His splendor was like the sunrise emphasizes the brilliance of the glory of God. It must have been truly dazzling (cf. Acts 26:13).

Coupled with that splendor is God's *power*. But as Habakkuk looks on, that power is *hidden*—it is not visibly at work. God's *hand* is the hiding place of power, but in Habakkuk's time this limitless power is not evident in some tremendous work. Interestingly, where the *New International Version* has *rays flashed from his hand*, the *King James Version* has "horns coming out of his hand." The Hebrew word in question here can be translated either as *rays* or *horns*, and the Old Testament uses horns as a symbol of power (cf. Jeremiah 48:25). As with verse 3 above, the connection with Deuteronomy 33:2 is important.

HOW TO SAY IT

Babylon. BAB-uh-lun.
Babylonians. Bab-ih-LOW-nee-unz.
Habakkuk. Huh-BACK-kuk.
Jehoiakim. Jeh-HOY-uh-kim.
Jeremiah. Jair-uh-MY-uh.
Josiah. Jo-SIGH-uh.
Paran. PAIR-un.
Seir. SEE-ir.
Selah (Hebrew). SEE-luh.
Septuagint. Sep-TOO-uh-jint.
shigionoth (Hebrew). shig-eh-OH-noth.
Teman. TEE-mun.
theophany. thee-AHF-uh-nee.

WHAT DO YOU THINK?

Many in Judah would not have connected their trouble with their sin. But the prophet Habakkuk declared the one to be a result of the other. Is every tragedy a judgment from God? If some unfortunate circumstance falls on a group of people today, is there any way to know whether the action was an example of God's punishing that group for their wickedness? Explain.

[Consider Luke 13:1-5 in your discussion.]

WHAT DO YOU THINK?

Today's church seems to prefer happy messages of God's love. Not too many years ago, some churches served a constant menu of "hellfire and brimstone." How can today's church accurately represent both sides of God's nature—his mercy and his justice—as Habakkuk did?

C. VISION OF DESTRUCTION (vv. 5, 6)
5. Plague went before him;
   pestilence followed his steps.

Now we are reminded that God is coming in judgment to punish the wicked people of Judah. The Babylonian army will be his instrument to do that. At the final onslaught of that army, the people of Judah will take refuge behind the strong walls of Jerusalem, to be besieged for a year and a half. Undoubtedly, certain diseases will become rampant as bodily immune systems are compromised because of starvation and declining sanitary conditions. These diseases could very well include various kinds of *plague* and *pestilence*.

The word for *pestilence* in this verse presents a challenge to translators. The Hebrew word at issue has the primary meaning of "something burning." Probably the translators of the *New International Version* used *pestilence* here (as in Deuteronomy 32:24) as a synonym for *plague,* as Hebrew poetry very frequently uses a second line to repeat a first line, using slightly different words. Other versions maintain the word's primary sense. As such, it may very well be a prediction that, when the city eventually falls, everything combustible will be burned (2 Kings 25:1-10).

6. He stood, and shook the earth;
   he looked, and made the nations tremble.
   The ancient mountains crumbled
      and the age-old hills collapsed.
   His ways are eternal.

Before, God's tremendous power had been "hidden" (v. 4). Now it is dramatically demonstrated. The word for *shook* in the first line can be translated either as it is here or as "measured." While some versions follow the alternative, our text here matches the Septuagint, a Greek translation of the Old Testament, which was made about 200 B.C. "Shook the earth" also seems to be more in accord with the rest of the verse, which says the *mountains* and *hills*—supposed to be everlasting—crumble and collapse as the result of a glance from God.

In contrast with those changeable things, God's own *ways* really *are eternal.* Verses 7-15, which are not included in our printed text, continue with the demonstration of God's tremendous power. Judah is indeed to be punished severely by that power; but God's ultimate purpose is actually the salvation of his people, not their destruction. "You came out to deliver your people, to save your anointed one" (Habakkuk 3:13).

III. THE PROPHET'S RESPONSE (HABAKKUK 3:16-19)

Who could be unmoved by such an imposing vision of God coming with earth-shattering power, especially when he is coming with punishment on his mind? Certainly Habakkuk is moved, and the next verses of our text reveal his reaction.

A. FEAR (v. 16a)
16a. I heard and my heart pounded,
   my lips quivered at the sound;
   decay crept into my bones,
      and my legs trembled.

Now it appears that the prophet has *heard* a *sound* in connection with the vision, and he is terrified. Sometimes fear brings a flow of adrenaline and rouses a person to fight or flee, but obviously no human can either oppose or escape the all-powerful God when he comes in wrath to punish his people. Habakkuk is paralyzed. He can only wait and tremble.

B. FAITH (v. 16b)

**16b. Yet I will wait patiently for the day of calamity
to come on the nation invading us.**

Habakkuk's fear is for his people rather than himself. Personally, he expects to *wait patiently for the day of calamity*. He trusts God; he is confident God will do right. Judah has been deep in sin for a long time, so God is coming with *the nation invading us*—the Babylonian army. There will be a terrible siege; Jerusalem will be taken and destroyed; most of the surviving people will become captives.

Even so, Habakkuk's faith is bright and clear. The captivity will end; God's people will be liberated; and God's prophet will be secure through it all. The Babylonians trust in their own strength as "god" (Habakkuk 1:11). But the prophet knows better. It is the one true God who is in control, whether we are talking about his pending judgment against Judah, or the judgment against Babylon that will follow.

C. JOY (vv. 17, 18)

**17. Though the fig tree does not bud
and there are no grapes on the vines,
though the olive crop fails
and the fields produce no food,
though there are no sheep in the pen
and no cattle in the stalls,**

This picture is of Judah's total desolation as a result of the Babylonian invasion (cf. Jeremiah 5:15-17). The *fruit* trees and *vines* and *fields* will *produce no food* because they have been trampled and destroyed by the invaders. (And even if they did yield their fruit, the people of Judah would not enjoy them, because they would be far away, captives in Babylon.) But nothing can destroy the joy of God's prophet. See the next verse.

HOLDING ON TO OUR "STUFF"

Nearly every person or family has something stored away in the basement, attic, or garage that they do not need. But most of us aren't like Ann Jones (as we'll call her), who has a real problem with holding on to her "stuff."

Ann's home is piled so high with junk mail, unread newspapers, broken appliances, empty food containers, and dirty dishes, that the place is nearly uninhabitable. The front door can hardly be opened. Even her bed is piled with junk except for the narrow patch on which she sleeps.

Ann is an intelligent, clean, outgoing, active person, involved in community and church work. She has many friends. But her hoarding disorder is out of control. It has made her home a dysfunctional place; its systems don't work for her. Only a regimen of radical therapy might possibly release her from her pathology.

Judah's inability to rid itself of its hoard of stuff—its religious and moral perversion—was making the nation a dysfunctional place. Habakkuk saw that even the food supplies on which the nation relied would wither away, and its support systems would no longer work for it. Judah was suffering from a pathological spiritual condition. The only solution was the radical "therapy" God would provide when Babylon took Judah away into captivity. What kind of moral or spiritual "stuff" are we holding on to that keeps us from living life as God intended?

—C. R. B.

WHAT DO YOU THINK?

When the average Christian gets a real sense of the majesty and power of God, can we expect him or her to tremble in awe as Habakkuk did? Can you tell of a time when you or someone you know has been significantly influenced by coming to a better understanding of the awesomeness of God?

DAILY BIBLE READINGS

Monday, Oct. 21—I Stand in Awe (Habakkuk 3:2-6)

Tuesday, Oct. 22—The Lord Is My Strength (Habakkuk 3:8-19)

Wednesday, Oct. 23—My Heart Trusts in God (Psalm 28:1-9)

Thursday, Oct. 24—I Will Trust in God (Isaiah 12:1-6)

Friday, Oct. 25—Trust in God (Isaiah 26:1-6)

Saturday, Oct. 26—Acknowledge God's Plan (Isaiah 26:7-13)

Sunday, Oct. 27—The Fight of Faith (1 Timothy 6:11-16)

18. . . . *yet I will rejoice in the* LORD,
    I will be joyful in God my Savior.

The Lord is in control, and his prophet is glad. The mighty God who comes in majesty to punish his people is not only the God of disaster to the wicked; he is the *God of salvation* to his prophet and to all who will repent and obey him. Perhaps Habakkuk recalls the ancient promise of restoration as well (see Deuteronomy 30:1-10; 32:34-43).

D. STRENGTH (v. 19)

19. *The Sovereign* LORD *is my strength;*
    he makes my feet like the feet of a deer,
    he enables me to go on the heights.

Those who follow God do not depend on their own *strength*. Such a person—whether an ancient prophet or a modern Christian—does God's will and depends on God to supply whatever spiritual strength, wisdom, or ability is needed to keep on doing that will. *Deer* are gifted with *feet* that seem to have a magical ability to cling to the ground in places that are steep and dangerous. Likewise, God's man or woman seems to have a miraculous ability to survive whatever difficulties and dangers are encountered in service to God. With God on our side, who can be against us? (See Romans 8:31.)

CONCLUSION

Habakkuk knew the worst. His beloved country was going to be destroyed, and he was scared. But he knew the best, too. After the destruction, Judah would emerge as a smaller but godlier nation. So Habakkuk rejoiced in the Lord.

A. DISASTER NOW

Disasters did not cease when ancient times were past. These lines are being written in the closing months of a year that has brought a record number of forest fires in North America. Hurricanes are more numerous than usual, too. Lightning and tornadoes seem to take a relentless toll. Japan experienced a typhoon, and India is suffering a lengthy monsoon. Europe and Africa continue to suffer small wars of extreme savagery. AIDS threatens to decimate the entire African continent.

Are such tragedies to be seen as God's punishment on people all around the world? We do not have inspired prophets today such as Habakkuk and Jeremiah to provide a direct answer from God to this question. A much more useful question is, "How should I react?"

B. OUR REACTION

Jesus commented on two minor disasters of his own time in Luke 13:1-5. In the first, Pilate apparently had had some Galileans put to death unjustly. In the second, eighteen people "died when the tower of Siloam fell on them." In both cases Jesus cautioned against concluding that the victims were worse sinners because of their suffering. He drew his audience to a different conclusion: unless they repented, they would all perish as well.

Jesus' words and this year's deadly disasters remind us that life is uncertain, and the time to repent is now. Death is our destiny (Hebrews 9:27), but whether it will come by an earthquake tomorrow or by old age in later years, we cannot say. The important question is, have I repented? The choice is ours, and the time to choose is now.

Discovery Learning

*This page contains an alternative lesson plan emphasizing learning activities. Classes
desiring such student involvement will find these suggestions helpful. The next page
is a reproducible activity page to further enhance discovery learning.*

LEARNING GOALS

After this lesson each student will be able to:

1. Tell what Habakkuk saw in his vision of the destruction of Jerusalem, and how his faith sustained him in the face of disaster.

2. Compare/contrast Habakkuk's response of faith with the responses many people today have toward disaster.

3. State one specific lesson he or she can learn from a current difficulty in life.

INTO THE LESSON

Begin this week's lesson with an art activity to focus attention and to introduce the subject of disaster. If possible, provide a variety of colored felt-tip markers and paper or poster board cut to four and one-fourth inches high by eleven inches wide for the students to use in making "bumper stickers. Provide masking tape for students to tape their bumper stickers to the wall. Prior to class time, write on the chalkboard the following message: "Take paper and felt pens to create a 'bumper sticker' that focuses on the non-Christian's response to personal disaster. When you complete the sticker, tape it on the wall." (*Sample responses might be* "Why me? It's not fair!" *or* "I'm gonna sue" *or* "I get even!") If you cannot supply the materials mentioned above, photocopy the reproducible activity "Bumper Sticker: 'Disaster Response'" from the next page and adjust the directions as needed.

When students arrive, direct their attention to the message on the board and encourage them to participate. After the "bumper stickers" have been taped to the wall, state: "Disasters come in different forms. There are weather-related disasters such as tornadoes or hurricanes, mechanical failure disasters such as plane crashes, accidental disasters such as automobile crashes, and intentional disasters such as terrorist bombings. People respond to disasters in different ways. Non-Christians may respond in these ways." At this point, review the various ideas the class prepared. State: "Today, we focus on disaster and—in particular—the way God's people react when they face disaster. Turn to Habakkuk 3, and let's read verses 2-6, Habbakuk's description of God and the impending disaster."

INTO THE WORD

Ask a class member to read Habakkuk 3:2-6 aloud to the class. Briefly review the lesson background, pointing out the two impending disasters: one coming on Israel and the other coming on the Babylonians. Prior to class time, photocopy the reproducible activity "In the Face of Disaster" from the next page. Make enough copies so that each learner may have a copy. Move the class into three equal-sized groups of no more than ten. If you have more than thirty students, move the class into six equal-sized groups. Give a copy of the chart to each person.

Assign one Scripture passage in the column headings to each group. Ask the group to appoint someone to read the passage aloud. Then, ask each group to identify from the passage the personal disaster, the faith response, and the personal principles to apply. Allow approximately fifteen minutes. When sufficient time has elapsed, ask each group to report their answers from the personal disaster row. Ask the class the following: "The disasters that these people of God faced were quite different, but what was the common element in these three events?" (*Their belief and faith in God to protect and deliver them.*)

Now ask the groups to tell both the faith response and the personal principles to apply to life today. Make a transparency of the chart; as each group shares an answer, write the answer in the appropriate space.

INTO LIFE

Say, "We may not face an impending disaster like what Habakkuk or Shadrach, Meshach, and Abednego or the apostle Paul faced, but we may be facing personal difficulties and struggles. Think about a current difficulty that you face. In consideration of the godly responses to personal disaster that we have just studied, what one specific principle can you take from today's lesson and apply to a personal difficulty that you face?"

Give several minutes for each to select a difficulty and a personal principle to apply. Then ask each student to write on a three-inch-by-five-inch card anonymously the difficulty that is faced and the Scriptural principle to apply. Collect all the cards and shuffle them. Read the difficulties and principles aloud as time permits.

Say, "We all face difficulties and struggles. Yet, I want you to remember that faith overrides despair. We don't have to respond as non-Christians do. We can respond as people of faith." Then ask for several students to lead the class in a prayer of commitment to applying those principles to their personal lives.

Bumper Sticker: "Disaster Response"

Using the box below to represent a "bumper sticker," use felt-tip pens to write a message that describes the non-Christian's response to a personal disaster.

In the Face of Disaster

For the three occasions represented in the Bible texts in the following chart, identify what each person's personal disaster was and what each did in the face of disaster. Write a godly principle of dealing with such life circumstances based on each biblical incident.

	HABAKKUK 3:2-19	DANIEL 2:47-3:29	ACTS 27:13-44
PERSONAL DISASTER			
FAITH RESPONSE			
GODLY PRINCIPLES TO APPLY			

JERUSALEM FALLS

LESSON 10

WHY TEACH THIS LESSON?

When volcanoes are about to erupt, they often give advance warning in the form of seismic activity and preliminary "venting." Modern devices can monitor those indicators. Even so, there are documented cases of people who pointedly ignore the warnings at the cost of their lives. We can only shake our heads at such incredible foolishness. In today's lesson, ancient Jerusalem is about to experience the volcanic eruption of God's wrath. But it didn't have to be that way—the warning signs were all there! The people had it in their power to abandon their sinful ways and put a stop to the eruption altogether.

In visiting the year 586 B.C. today, your learners will be sobered by this reality. Christians live in the shadow of God's love; but since evil still exists, we also live in the shadow of his wrath. This fact will motivate your learners to lead others to abandon evil and become Christians, perhaps helping avoid a repeat of 586 B.C.

INTRODUCTION

A. THE NAMING GAME

In certain times and cultures, babies receive meaningful names. This was especially true in antiquity. When Eve's first child was born, she named him Cain, which means gotten or brought forth (Genesis 4:1). We may suppose the birth of her next boy was easy, for she named this one Abel, which means a breath, a puff of air, a mere trifle (Genesis 4:2).

Of special interest are names that are changed. In Ur, a baby was named Abram, which usually is translated "exalted father." At age ninety-nine, the Lord changed his name to Abraham, which means father of many (Genesis 17:4, 5). The current series of lessons calls our attention to two kings of Judah whose names were changed, not by the Lord, but by victorious enemies who made the changes for political reasons.

When Pharaoh Neco II of Egypt defeated Judah and took charge of it, the king he appointed was Eliakim, which means God (Elohim) will establish. But Neco changed that name to Jehoiakim, The Lord (Yahweh) will establish (2 Kings 23:34). Although seemingly a slight change, Neco's ability to control the king's name demonstrates his ability to control Judah as well—a sign of vassalage.

A little later, Nebuchadnezzar, king of Babylon, conquered Judah. The king he appointed to rule Judah was Mattaniah, whose name means gift from the Lord. Nebuchadnezzar changed it to Zedekiah, meaning the Lord is righteous (2 Kings 24:17). Again, the name change appears harmless on the surface, but Nebuchadnezzar's ability to do this shows that he was in control (cf. Daniel 1:6, 7).

B. LESSON BACKGROUND

In previous lessons, we have seen bits of the teaching of three prophets: Zephaniah, Jeremiah, and Habakkuk. We have seen their repeated rebukes of the evil that was widespread and persistent in Judah about six hundred years before Christ. We have seen their repeated predictions of disaster because of the continuing evil.

DEVOTIONAL READING:
PSALM 75

BACKGROUND SCRIPTURE:
2 CHRONICLES 36:9-21; 2 KINGS 24:8-25; 26

PRINTED TEXT:
2 CHRONICLES 36:11-21

LESSON AIMS

After participating in this lesson, each student will be able to:

1. Tell how Judah "drifted" toward its sad end and how thorough was that end.

2. Compare Judah's "drift" with the changing morality evident in modern culture.

3. Suggest a specific way to confront society's "drift" with the gospel.

Nov
3

KEY VERSE

The LORD, the God of their fathers, sent word to them through his messengers again and again, because he had pity on his people and on his dwelling place. But they mocked God's messengers, despised his words and scoffed at his prophets.
—2 Chronicles 36:15, 16

Apparently, few people of Judah took the predictions seriously. Happy with idol worship and sinful living, the people preferred to listen to false prophets who assured them that all was well—telling them what they wanted to hear. Judah was God's own nation, the false prophets said, and God would always protect it.

So Jeremiah and other prophets continued their predictions of disaster until they saw those predictions proven true. See 2 Kings 24:18–25:21 and Jeremiah 52:1-30 for parallel accounts to today's text.

I. PERSISTENT EVIL (2 CHRONICLES 36:11-16)

When we last visited 2 Chronicles six weeks ago, we saw King Josiah trying earnestly and successfully to restore exclusive worship of the Lord and obedience to his law (chapter 34). But Josiah is the last godly king that Judah will have. The kings who follow ignore God's law and prophets, and most of the people follow right along. We now return to 2 Chronicles for a summary of the prevalent evils in Judah and the disaster that God sends as punishment and correction.

A. STUBBORN DEFIANCE (vv. 11, 12)

11. Zedekiah was twenty-one years old when he became king, and he reigned in Jerusalem eleven years.

Zedekiah begins to reign when Nebuchadnezzar removes the previous king, Jehoiachin, and takes him prisoner to Babylon (vv. 9, 10). Judah is now a tiny part of Nebuchadnezzar's great Babylonian Empire, but Jehoiakim (Jehoiachin's father) had rebelled against Babylonian rule (2 Kings 24:1). Jehoiakim died before Nebuchadnezzar arrived to punish the rebellious king, so it was Jehoiachin whom Nebuchadnezzar took, along with ten thousand leading citizens and the treasures of the king's house and the temple (2 Kings 24:10-16).

12. He did evil in the eyes of the LORD his God and did not humble himself before Jeremiah the prophet, who spoke the word of the LORD.

Zedekiah cannot claim ignorance of the difference between good and *evil* since *Jeremiah the prophet* has been giving him instructions straight from *the Lord*. As king, Zedekiah apparently thinks he is entitled to do as he pleases, so he defies both the prophet and the Lord. So Zedekiah continues in the sins of his predecessors (Jeremiah 52:2), for which the Lord already had delivered ten thousand leaders of Judah into captivity (2 Kings 24:14).

B. REPEATED REBELLION (v. 13)

13. He also rebelled against King Nebuchadnezzar, who had made him take an oath in God's name. He became stiff-necked and hardened his heart and would not turn to the LORD, the God of Israel.

Zedekiah has defied God, and apparently (by earthly standards) he has gotten away with it. Now he goes on to defy *Nebuchadnezzar*, the Lord's instrument (Jeremiah 21:4-7). Zedekiah had sworn allegiance to that king, but he breaks his *oath* (cf. Ezekiel 17:13-15). Arrogantly he turns away from Nebuchadnezzar, but in the process does not turn to *the Lord, the God of Israel*. With a stiffened *neck* and a *hardened heart*, he simply goes his own way. This type of attitude is, of course, nothing new—either then or now (cf. Proverbs 14:12; 16:25). But for a king, the consequences are more serious because he leads others by example down the same path (e.g., Jeremiah 44:15-17).

DO YOU REALLY KNOW WHAT TIME IT IS?

Is your life just out of control when you don't know the time to the exact minute? Relax! Now there is hope for you. The National Institute of Standards and

WHAT DO YOU THINK?

Jeremiah the prophet confronted King Zedekiah about his evil behavior. If a Christian knows of solid evidence of an official's corrupt behavior in office, what should he or she do?

Technology (Time and Frequency Division) for several years has had a clock that measures each second of time as 9,192,631,770 vibrations of a cesium-133 atom in a vacuum. It's accurate to within one second in a *million* years!

But here's the really good news for everyone who worries about being on time: for less than $200, you can buy a wristwatch that "listens" to a radio signal broadcast. At 1:00 A.M. each day, the watch corrects itself to a millisecond, thus assuring that when you arise in the morning you will know exactly what time it is.

King Zedekiah didn't know what time it was. He didn't know that Judah's time as a free nation was drawing short, or that it was time to yield to King Nebuchadnezzar, or that it was time to turn back to the God of Israel. The reason for his ignorance was not due to the inaccuracy of his clock (or sundial), but because he would not "tune in" to God and listen to what his prophets had been saying. There is a lesson here for us, if we will only hear it.   —C. R. B.

C. INCREASING IDOLATRY (v. 14)

14. Furthermore, all the leaders of the priests and the people became more and more unfaithful, following all the detestable practices of the nations and defiling the temple of the LORD, which he had consecrated in Jerusalem.

Priests in earlier times were dedicated to the service of the Lord; but in Zedekiah's time it seems that the priestly leaders are devoted to "freedom of religion." If someone wants to worship Baal, Ashtoreth, or Molech, these priests do not discriminate in helping out. Apparently, they will conduct whatever unholy pagan ceremony the worshiper asks. In today's politically correct language we would say the priests were "tolerant" of other religions.

So priests and people together *became more and more unfaithful, following all the detestable practices of the* pagans. *The temple* had been built by Solomon for the one true God—the God of Israel. God had *consecrated* it by accepting it as his (2 Chronicles 7:16). Now the priests and people have defiled that sacred place with the worship of idols and imaginary gods. (See Ezekiel 8.)

LOOKING FOR ANSWERS IN ALL THE WRONG PLACES

In October 1347, the worst mass killer in history started on its awful (and awe-inspiring) course. In less than four years, twenty-five million people in Europe—one-third of the population—had died from the Black Death. Most of its victims died within a week, their skin bearing the black blotches that gave the plague its name.

Some physicians blamed an unfortunate alignment of the planets; others said the plague came from poisonous fumes released by earthquakes. Not knowing that being bitten by fleas (which transmitted the disease from infected rats) was the source of the disease, doctors recommended various avoidance regimens, such as eating figs and filberts in the morning or not sleeping on one's back so "evil airs" would not run down the nose into the lungs. The doctors were looking in all the wrong places. Religious leaders were no better: to avoid the Black Death, Pope Clement VI isolated himself and rubbed an emerald ring.

In Zedekiah's time, the priests and the people together practiced the idolatrous and immoral follies of their neighbors rather than looking to God for answers to the troubles their nation was having. We do the same today: after each news-making tragedy, we pass more laws or sanction some rogue dictator or take some other external action. What we need is a moral regeneration that only God can provide.   —C. R. B.

D. MOCKED MESSENGERS (vv. 15, 16)

15. The LORD, the God of their fathers, sent word to them through his messengers again and again, because he had pity on his people and on his dwelling place.

WHAT DO YOU THINK?

It is politically correct to speak with tolerance and even be supportive of the varied beliefs of all people. Teaching anything as "absolute" truth is considered bigotry. What methods can the church and average Christians use to overcome cultural barriers that work against the freedom to openly teach the truth of God's Word?

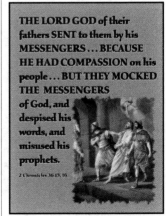

THE LORD GOD of their fathers SENT to them by his MESSENGERS...BECAUSE HE HAD COMPASSION on his people...BUT THEY MOCKED THE MESSENGERS of God, and despised his words, and misused his prophets.

2 Chronicles 36:15, 16

The visual for today's lesson illustrates the tragic truth of verses 15 and 16.

WHAT DO YOU THINK?

The text points out that God's condemnation of Judah's sin was an act of his compassion. But when Christians point out how different groups either tolerate or subtly embrace progressive evil, they are accused of being too restrictive, even hateful. How can the church continue its work when it is being unfairly characterized in the community?

[Consider Acts 4:23-29.]

WHAT DO YOU THINK?

The people mocked God's prophets, but the prophets continued to proclaim the sacred message. Today's church is ridiculed in the media, at school and in the workplace, and even in the neighborhood. Which is the greatest threat—direct or indirect ridicule? Why? What can the church do to help young people stand strong in their belief in the face of ridicule?

HOW TO SAY IT

Abram. AY-brum.
Abraham. AY-bruh-ham.
Ashtoreth. ASH-toe-reth.
Baal. BAY-ul.
Babylon. BAB-uh-lun.
Babylonian. Bab-ih-LOW-nee-un.
Cyrus. SIGH-rus.
Eliakim. Ee-LYE-uh-kim.
Elohim (Hebrew). El-o-HEEM.
Ezekiel. Ee-ZEEK-ee-ul or Ee-ZEEK-yul.
Habakkuk. Huh-BACK-kuk.
Jehoiachin. Jeh-HOY-uh-kin.

(continued on p. 91.)

God has not accepted silently the worship of imaginary gods and the polluting of his house. He has sent *his messengers,* Jeremiah and other prophets, to protest the wrongs that were done. *Again and again* God's prophets have been there to warn the *people.* The prophets have protested continually against the idolatry, have reminded the people that the Lord is the only real God, and have exhorted them to worship and obey him only.

God has kept such messages before Judah because of his *pity* or compassion. He wants to save *his people* from the punishment that their wrongdoing demands. God also has compassion on *his dwelling place,* the temple. He is hurt when that holy place is polluted by pagan ceremonies. He wants his people to stop that pollution before it is too late to avert their just punishment.

16. But they mocked God's messengers, despised his words and scoffed at his prophets until the wrath of the LORD was aroused against his people and there was no remedy.

The people of Judah have no regard for God's message or his *messengers.* In fact, just the opposite is true! The *prophets* are misused in various ways (cf. Hebrews 11:32-38), and Jeremiah himself notes how he has been *mocked* (Jeremiah 20:7). In an earlier lesson, we noted that corrupt priests and false prophets wanted Jeremiah put to death for delivering God's message (Jeremiah 26:8-24). They also tortured him with imprisonment and starvation (Jeremiah 37:16; 38:6). In the Old Testament no one suffers more than Jeremiah. But in the end it will be the mockers who will be mocked (Ezekiel 22:5).

II. JERUSALEM FALLS (2 CHRONICLES 36:17-19)

Let us very briefly review the three phases of Babylon's dominion over Judah.

Phase One. Judah surrenders without a fight when Nebuchadnezzar first comes. A few young Hebrews are taken to be trained in Babylon and to become advisers to Nebuchadnezzar (Daniel 1:1-7). Jehoiakim is left to be king in Judah and pay tribute. The year is 605 B.C.

Phase Two. While Nebuchadnezzar and his army are busy elsewhere, Jehoiakim rebels, refusing to pay tribute. When the Babylonians finally come, Jehoiakim is dead and Jehoiachin is king. The new king is taken to Babylon along with ten thousand leading citizens of Judah. Zedekiah is left to be king of Judah and pay the tribute (2 Kings 24:8-17). The year is 597 B.C.

Phase Three. In the ninth year of his eleven-year reign, Zedekiah refuses to pay the tribute (2 Kings 24:18-20). The king and his people take refuge behind the strong walls of Jerusalem when Nebuchadnezzar and his army return. For a year and a half, the Babylonians camp around the city so no food can be brought in. In 586 B.C. the Babylonians break through the wall to take the starving city (2 Kings 25:1-3; Ezekiel 4:16, 17). Our text relates what happens next.

A. THE PEOPLE KILLED (v. 17)

17. He brought up against them the king of the Babylonians, who killed their young men with the sword in the sanctuary, and spared neither young man nor young woman, old man or aged. God handed all of them over to Nebuchadnezzar.

A quick look back at verse 16 informs us the *He* is the Lord. *The king of the Babylonians* is Nebuchadnezzar. In coming to Jerusalem, Nebuchadnezzar thinks he is acting in his own interest, but actually the Lord is using him to punish the sinful people of Judah. The Lord *handed all* the people of Judah *over to Nebuchadnezzar* and gave him power over them. When at last his troops break into Jerusalem, they kill all who get in their way, and some who do not. *Young* people, *old* people, men, women, and children are slaughtered without mercy.

B. THE TREASURES LOOTED (v. 18)

18. He carried to Babylon all the articles from the temple of God, both large and small, and the treasures of the LORD's temple and the treasures of the king and his officials.

The invaders loot the *temple*, the king's palace, and the houses of the subordinate *officials*. Some of *the articles* from the temple are made of gold and silver, but most of the stuff taken as booty is made of less valuable bronze (2 Kings 25:13-17; Jeremiah 52:17-23). Nebuchadnezzar had taken all the gold items in 597 B.C. (2 Kings 24:13), so most of the gold items taken now must have been made only within the previous ten years. The Babylonians keep these items as trophies of victory, eventually using them in their own drunken, idolatrous feasts (Daniel 5:1-4). The exiles who return several decades later will be able to bring some of these items back (Ezra 1:7-11).

Besides the sacred vessels, the looters take money from the temple treasury and from the homes of the king and his subordinate officials. In leaving nothing of value in the hands of those rebellious leaders of Judah, the chance of a future rebellion is diminished.

C. THE CITY DESTROYED (v. 19)

19. They set fire to God's temple and broke down the wall of Jerusalem; they burned all the palaces and destroyed everything of value there.

No city will remain where *Jerusalem* now is. Everything combustible is *burned*. With much effort, the massive stone walls around the city are broken down. Probably the walls of the temple and palaces also are reduced to rubble. No rebellious citizen of Judah will find shelter in Jerusalem. Even after the exiles return, the walls will not be rebuilt for quite some time (Ezra 4:6-23). About one hundred and forty years will have to pass after their return before the Judean people once again feel the security of walls (Nehemiah 1–4).

III. UNHAPPY ENDING (2 CHRONICLES 36:20, 21)

This account is one of tragedy. The end of Jerusalem brings no joy to anyone in Judah. Nor does it bring joy to God, who has decreed this punishment (cf. Ezekiel 18:32; 33:11).

A. THE REMNANT IN EXILE (v. 20)

20. He carried into exile to Babylon the remnant, who escaped from the sword, and they became servants to him and his sons until the kingdom of Persia came to power.

If the record of Jerusalem's fall had ended with verse 17, we might think that everyone in the city has been killed. Now, however, we see that there are many survivors. Perhaps the killers have spared the unarmed people who surrendered humbly without trying to fight or to run away (cf. Jeremiah 39:9). We can only guess how many survivors there are. Some of these are left in the land of Judah (39:10), but many thousands are driven over the miles *to Babylon*. Interestingly, Jeremiah himself receives better treatment by the Babylonians than by his own people (see 39:11-13; 40:1-5).

The subjugation of the people is total, as they become servants to Nebuchadnezzar. Earlier prophecies are graphic in predicting that members of the royal line will become eunuchs in the service of the king of Babylon (2 Kings 20:16-18; Isaiah 39:5-7). The subjugation will last until the kingdom of Persia conquers Babylon in 539 B.C., and Cyrus issues his decree allowing the exiles to return (2 Chronicles 36:22, 23; Ezra 1:1-4).

HOW TO SAY IT (continued)

Jehoiakim. Jeh-HOY-uh-kim.
Jeremiah. Jair-uh-MY-uh.
Josiah. Jo-SIGH-uh.
Judean. Joo-DEE-un.
Leviticus. Leh-VIT-ih-kus.
Mattaniah. Mat-uh-NYE-uh.
Molech. MO-lek.
Nebuchadnezzar. NEB-yuh-kud-NEZ-er.
Neco. NEE-ko.
Pharaoh. FAY-ro.
Ur. Er.
Yahweh (Hebrew). YAH-weh.
Zedekiah. Zed-uh-KYE-uh.
Zephaniah. Zef-uh-NYE-uh.

WHAT DO YOU THINK?

When all of the items of the temple were carried off, it would have been very hard for the few people who remained to continue with their regular worship routine. Recently a Christian college in Myanmar was seized and bulldozed to the ground. If that happened to our church, what would the members do to survive and thrive?

PRAYER

Almighty God, ruler of people and of nations, with gratitude we cherish the privilege of being your children. Help us to be faithful; and help us also to reach out to win others to the same precious faith we hold. In Jesus' name, amen.

THOUGHT TO REMEMBER

Take the gospel to all nations.

B. THE LAND AT REST (v. 21)

21. The land enjoyed its sabbath rests; all the time of its desolation it rested, until the seventy years were completed in fulfillment of the word of the LORD spoken by Jeremiah.

Not only is the destruction and captivity a *fulfillment* of the prophecy of Jeremiah (25:11, 12; 29:10; cf. Daniel 9:2), it also fulfills Leviticus 26:34, 35. God's law had provided that one year of seven should be a *sabbath* for the land. The ground was not to be plowed or planted that year; grapevines were not to be pruned (Leviticus 25:1-5). Harvesters in the sixth year would accidentally drop some seed in the field, and a bit of wheat or barley would grow from that. Grapevines produce some fruit even if they are not pruned. Those bits of produce in the seventh year were to be for the poor of the land, not for the owners of the field (Exodus 23:10, 11). Greedy landholders had been breaking that law for a long time, planting and reaping in the seventh year as in the other six. This was part of the injustice of which the Judeans were guilty. Now the farmers were taken away. To make up for all the Sabbaths that had been missed, every year will now be a Sabbath for the land until the exiles return.

CONCLUSION

Captivity in Babylon was a climax in the history of Israel. It was the culmination of what the Israelites had been doing for eight hundred years. They had been drifting.

A. THE DRIFTERS THEN

The people of Israel were not drifters when they entered the promised land and took possession of it. They were dynamic, aggressive, determined, powerful. Better still, they trusted God. They knew he gave them victory over the wicked pagans. Happily and obediently, they settled down to enjoy the land.

Years went by. Joshua and the heroes who had fought with him died. They were replaced by a generation who had grown up in times of peace. They did not suddenly rebel against the Lord; they just began to drift away from him. They began to ignore his law; they began to deceive and cheat and mistreat each other for gain. In the pursuit of pleasure, they began to eat and drink in pagan feasts. Drifting further, they actually participated in pagan worship.

Then suddenly their peace, prosperity, and pleasure were gone. Armed bands invaded their land to steal livestock and harvests, killing anyone who stood in their way. Then the people prayed, imploring God to help them. They worshiped in sincerity and truth. They respected God's law and obeyed it. So God raised up from among the people a leader to rally them to defeat the invaders. Peace and prosperity returned. But the next generation began another drift away from God.

The same cycle was repeated over and over in the history of Israel. Honoring God and obeying him brought success; drifting away from him was drifting into disaster. Still Israel drifted till the nation was split, until Israel in the north was destroyed by the Assyrians, until Judah in the south was captive in Babylon.

B. THE DRIFTERS NOW

In previous lessons, we noted a drift away from God in the countries of Europe and North America. The only way to reverse this drift is for Christians to take the gospel to every creature (Mark 16:15). We must make disciples, baptizing them in the name of the Father, and of the Son, and of the Holy Ghost, and teach them to do all that Jesus has commanded (Matthew 28:19, 20). It's the only way—for a nation or for an individual.

Discovery Learning

This page contains an alternative lesson plan emphasizing learning activities. Classes desiring such student involvement will find these suggestions helpful. The next page is a reproducible activity page to further enhance discovery learning.

LEARNING GOALS

After participating in this lesson, each student will be able to:

1. Tell how Judah "drifted" toward its sad end and how thorough was that end.

2. Compare Judah's "drift" with the changing morality evident in modern culture.

3. Suggest a specific way to confront society's "drift" with the gospel.

INTO THE LESSON

Prepare a worksheet by photocopying the reproducible activity "Simile Completion" on the next page. As you distribute the worksheet, say, "We begin with a Simile Completion. Read the statement and then write how the two items are similar." (*Possible answers include "They are not connected to a standard"; "They both keep drifting farther away."*)

After a few minutes, ask volunteers to share their completed statements with the class. State: "Just as a rowboat that is not tied to a mooring post drifts out to sea, present-day morality that is not tied to a standard drifts farther from God. Our lesson text today describes how Judah drifted away from God and how erosion of morality eventually led to Jerusalem's destruction. In 2 Chronicles 36:11-21 we read how they drifted away."

INTO THE WORD

Ask a class member to read the lesson text aloud to the class. Say, "First, let's review a number of basic facts from our passage. As I ask the questions, if you know an answer, call it out, along with the verse where that answer is found":

1. How old was Zedekiah when he became king, and how long did he reign? (*Twenty-one years old, and he reigned for eleven years, v. 11.*)

2. What words describe Zedekiah's movement away from God? (*Did evil; did not humble himself, v. 12; rebelled, became stiff-necked, hardened his heart, v. 13.*)

3. What did King Nebuchadnezzar get Zedekiah to do so he would obey him? (*He made Zedekiah take an oath in God's name, v. 13.*)

4. How did King Zedekiah's behavior affect the leaders of the priests and the people? (*They became more and more unfaithful, following the detestable practices of nations and defiling the temple of the Lord, v. 14.*)

5. Why did God send messengers again and again? (*Love for his people and his dwelling place, v. 15.*)

6. What did the people do to God's messengers? (*Mocked and scoffed; despised God's words, v. 16.*)

7. How was Jerusalem destroyed by the king of the Babylonians? (*Killed male and female, old and young, v. 17; carried away all the articles and treasures of the temple and the king, v. 18; set fire to God's temple, destroyed the wall of Jerusalem, burned the palaces, v. 19.*)

8. What was done to those who escaped the sword? (*Carried into exile to Babylon to become servants, v. 20.*)

9. How long did the land remain in desolation? (*Seventy years, v. 21.*)

INTO LIFE

Say, "Just like a rowboat loosed from its mooring post, Judah drifted farther and farther from God—even to the point of 'no remedy' (v. 16). This 'drifting' has also occurred in our society and in Christian people. Let's see how this passage relates to us." Move the class into groups of three. Prepare the following questions on an overhead transparency:

1. In what specific ways has the morality of society eroded or drifted away from God? (*Accepting improper sexual relationships, increased violence, and others.*)

2. What would help Christians not to drift away from God? See Ephesians 4:13, 14 and Hebrews 2:1-3. (*Not being influenced by "every wind of teaching," by "cunning and craftiness of men," and because of growing "to the whole measure of the fullness of Christ"; give heed to "what we have heard."*)

3. What can Christians do specifically to confront society's drift with the gospel? (*Grow strong in faith; share Christ and our faith with people around us; become an active participant in voting for God-serving individuals running for public office.*)

Project the questions and give several minutes for the groups to discuss them. Then, go over the questions and have the groups share their answers. Write their answers on the transparency so all students can see them.

Photocopy the reproducible activity "Confronting Society's 'Drift'" from page 94. Give a copy to every student, and ask each one to select one specific way he or she can confront society's "drift" and to write it on the lines provided. Ask the students to keep these in their Bibles as reminders. End the class in a prayer of commitment.

Simile Completion

Read the following statement. Describe on the lines provided how you think the rowboat and morality are similar.

"A free-floating rowboat and present-day morality are similar in that . . ."

_____

_____

_____

_____

_____

_____

Confronting Society's "Drift"

On the side of the picture of the rowboat "Society," write specific ways you can confront society's "Drift" away from God.

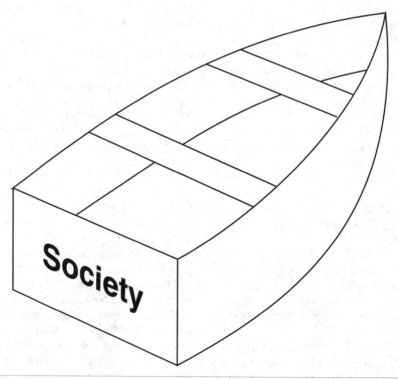

GRIEF AND HOPE

LESSON 11

WHY TEACH THIS LESSON?

At times we all sink into the miry pit of despair. When we do, we always ask, "Now what?" Up to a point, everyone can seek relief in the same ways: seeking counseling, acknowledging personal responsibility, getting a medical evaluation for depression, etc. The point where the Christian and non-Christian part company is in recognizing God's ultimate control over all of life's situations. Only the Christian can wait and pray with a confident expectation that God will reveal his will and his solution in his own time—and his timing is always perfect!

Few if any of your students today will have ever experienced anything as bad as the Babylonian captivity. But if the folks who suffered through the horror of that ancient distress could continue to look to God in hope, so can we! This lesson is for those who need to experience God's presence in all of life's situations.

INTRODUCTION

The titles of books may be chosen for various reasons. The title *Robert Kennedy and his Times*, for example, seems designed to tell me what the book is about. On the other hand, *Gone With the Wind* gives me scarcely a hint of the book's contents; but it makes me want to read the book and see what it is about.

No such purpose is seen in the titles of the books in the Hebrew Scriptures. Instead, the first word of a book becomes its title. Looking at the first word of the first book of the Hebrew Bible and trying to put the sound of it in English letters instead of Hebrew, we have *bereshith*. That same word appears as the title of the book. It means "In the Beginning." Centuries later the Greek translators titled that book *Genesis*, which means "Origin." That, too, is an excellent name for the first part of the book, and the Greek word *Genesis* is brought into our English translation.

A. HOW

This week we take our text from a book whose original title is the Hebrew word for *How*, because that is the first word of the book. The ancient Hebrews used that word as a cry, wail, or lament at funerals. From this fact, the ancient Greek translators gave this book the title *The Lamentations of Jeremiah*. We see this same title in the *King James Version*, although other versions, including the *New International Version*, shorten it simply to *Lamentations*.

That book is a collection of sorrowful songs arising from the end of Jerusalem, the tragic death of many of her people, and the sad captivity of others in Babylon. Jeremiah himself was not one of those captives. He stayed in Judah and soon went to Egypt with the others who did not go to Babylon. So he, too, was an exile from his beloved homeland. For years he had tried earnestly to turn his people back to God and so to save them from defeat and captivity. No one mourned more deeply and sincerely than he did when that effort failed.

B. LESSON BACKGROUND

The background of this lesson lies in the destruction of Jerusalem that we read about last week. Through many years God's people had done wrong. They had

DEVOTIONAL READING:
PSALM 42:5-11
BACKGROUND SCRIPTURE:
LAMENTATIONS
PRINTED TEXT:
LAMENTATIONS 1:12-16; 3:22-26, 31-33, 40

LESSON AIMS

After participating in this lesson, each student will be able to:

1. Summarize the dismay of fallen Jerusalem and the hope that God still gave her for the future.

2. Explain how disaster or hardship can sometimes help turn a people to the Lord.

3. Suggest one or two ways to put into practice the message of Lamentations 3:26.

Nov
10

KEY VERSE

Because of the Lord's great love we are not consumed, for his compassions never fail. They are new every morning; great is your faithfulness.
—Lamentations 3:22, 23

ignored God's will, disobeyed his laws, and scorned his prophets. At last God sent the mighty army of Babylon to punish his heedless people.

The first time that army came, Judah surrendered, promising to pay tribute. But after a time Judah rebelled and refused to pay until that army came back. After a period of submission Judah rebelled again, and the army came yet a third time and laid siege to the city for a year and a half. Inside the walls many died of disease and starvation. The rest were weak with hunger when the invaders finally broke into the city. Anyone who stood against them was cut down; some surrendered abjectly enough to be made prisoners. The temple and palaces and homes of Jerusalem were burned. Stone walls were torn apart and scattered over the landscape. The captives were marched a thousand weary miles to Babylon.

Imagine the sorrow over loved ones who had died. Imagine the grief over Jerusalem, lovely and beloved, now only a field of rubble. Imagine the horror of captivity in a strange and cruel land. All of these find expression in *Lamentations*. These lamentations are lyric poetry, poetry designed to be sung. Perhaps they were sung by mourning captives "by the rivers of Babylon" (Psalm 137:1). When the captivity was over, perhaps in restored Jerusalem they were sung in memory.

In this disaster everyone in Judah could see the cruel face of captivity and death. But God's prophet could see another face of disaster, a kindly one. God did not design this horrible event to destroy his people, but to help them. Some thoughtful people now would listen to God's prophets. Some would see that the disaster was the result of their own wrongdoing. Some would repent. They would worship God in truth. They would obey him. Then they and their children could return to rebuild Jerusalem and be what God wanted them to be—his chosen people.

In the brief sample of the lamentation before us, we shall catch a glimpse of that kindly face along with the more obvious face of horror and death.

I. THE CRUEL FACE (LAMENTATIONS 1:12-16)

The siege of Jerusalem is now past. Those who had been trapped within her walls had died slowly of hunger and disease. When the enemy finally had broken into the city, many had died quickly by the edge of the sword (Jeremiah 21:9).

A. SORROW AND HELPLESSNESS (vv. 12, 13)

12. "Is it nothing to you, all you who pass by?
     Look around and see.
   Is any suffering like my suffering
        that was inflicted on me,
     that the LORD brought on me
        in the day of his fierce anger?

The "singer" of this doleful song is Jerusalem herself, not Jeremiah. The prophet puts into words and music the feeling of that crushed city, the feeling of her people driven over the weary miles to an uncertain future in Babylon. With one voice those people call every observer to testify. In the entire world, is there *any suffering like* the suffering of desolate Jerusalem?

And with divine insight, the prophet puts into the song more than all of the people yet realize: it is not just Babylon that is inflicting this monstrous sorrow, it is *the Lord*. The reality of *the day of his fierce anger* reflects the prediction of Jeremiah 4:26. That anger is just, and so is the sorrow inflicted on the captive people.

IS IT NOTHING TO YOU?

The most famous photograph from the Vietnam War may well be that of Kim Phuc, a child running naked and badly burned down the street after her village had

WHAT DO YOU THINK?

"Is it nothing to you?" cries Jerusalem over her sad condition. Sometimes people in grief feel that no one cares about their situation. What can we do to express support for our brothers and sisters in grief and hardship? Is it enough to say, "If you need anything, just call"? Why or why not?

been napalmed. After shooting the picture, the American photographer took Kim to a hospital for treatment—a series of ordeals that would go on for many years.

The picture of Kim pained the hearts of many who saw it. One man, especially, was touched by it. Chuck Colson, a White House aide at the time, says, "No person can look at such a picture and not be deeply moved. And because I was part of the administration prosecuting this war, there was no escaping a sense of personal responsibility, which made my agony deeper."

Years later, Kim—by then a grown woman—married a Christian man and became a Christian herself. They wanted to go to Bible college but lacked the means to do so. Colson heard of their plight, told her story, and solicited help for them on his daily radio broadcast. Several colleges immediately offered them scholarships. The actions of both the photographer and Colson said, in effect, "Yes, it does mean something to me that I was in some way involved in Kim's tragedy, and I will do what I can to change things for the better." This is the task of all who have been touched by the gospel: to feel the pain of those who suffer and do what we can to redeem their situation.   —C. R. B.

13. *"From on high he sent fire,*
    sent it down into my bones.
He spread a net for my feet
    and turned me back.
He made me desolate,
    faint all the day long.

Bones give shape and firmness to a person's body. Without them we would sink into shapeless and helpless lumps of flesh. Now the bones of Jerusalem are gone as if destroyed by *fire* from *on high*—fire from the Lord himself. He has made his people helpless before the might of Babylon.

The rest of the verse pictures that helplessness in different ways. *A net,* cleverly spread and weighted, will enclose and capture small animals that touch it. In turning Jerusalem *back,* the Lord had stopped her mad course of sinning. The image of being *desolate* and *faint* indicates that the Lord has made Jerusalem weak and helpless, as if from being inflicted with a serious disease. Often a person in such a condition can do little but lie on a sickbed—and think.

B. Bondage and Trampling (vv. 14, 15)

14. *"My sins have been bound into a yoke;*
    by his hands they were woven together.
They have come upon my neck
    and the Lord has sapped my strength.
He has handed me over
    to those I cannot withstand.

In the book that bears his name, Jeremiah uses *yoke* imagery more than a dozen times. Jerusalem's *sins,* the reason for her captivity, have become a yoke for her *neck.* In plainer language, the Lord has taken away Jerusalem's *strength* and has *handed* her *over* into the power of the Babylonians. In describing Jerusalem as not being able to *withstand* her enemies, the text gives no hope for the future. This distress seems to be "open ended," with no relief in sight.

15. *"The Lord has rejected*
    all the warriors in my midst;
he has summoned an army against me
    to crush my young men.
In his winepress the Lord has trampled
    the Virgin Daughter of Judah.

How to Say It

Babylon. BAB-uh-lun.
Babylonian. Bab-ih-LOW-nee-un.
bereshith (Hebrew). beh-reh-SHEET.
Ezekiel. Ee-ZEEK-ee-ul or Ee-ZEEK-yul.
Jeremiah. Jair-uh-MY-uh.
Judah. JOO-duh.
Judeans. Joo-DEE-unz.
Kim Phuc. Kim FOOK.
Lamentation. Lam-en-TAY-shun.
Noriaki Yamashita. Nor-ee-AH-kee Yahm-ah-SHEE-tah.

WHAT DO YOU THINK?

Jerusalem rightly saw its troubles as sent by God as discipline. Considering passages such as John 9:1-3 and Hebrews 12:4-11, should we see our difficulties as God-sent? Why or why not? Perhaps some are and some aren't—how do we know the difference?

WHAT DO YOU THINK?

"Survivor guilt" often happens to individuals who have lived through a very tragic situation in which others were severely hurt or killed. How can Christians keep their spiritual equilibrium when things just do not seem to be fair—either to themselves or for others? Why is it not wise to think things should be "fair"? How can we be sure not to fall into that kind of thinking?

WHAT DO YOU THINK?

God used strong measures to punish Jerusalem, but because of his mercy he tempered that punishment. Many parents, knowing the necessity of punishing their children, are emotionally torn by their desire that their children not have to experience pain from the punishment. How can parents use the times when they have to administer corrective measures as a means to teach their children about the nature of God and his reaction to punishment?

Jerusalem is still speaking or singing this mournful song. She recognizes that it is *the Lord* himself who *has rejected all* her *warriors*. Once her protection is crushed, then the city itself is open to being *trampled*. However, the Lord has not done that all without the help of human feet. The Babylonian *army* he has called has squeezed out the very lifeblood of the city and its people, as if in a *winepress*.

C. TEARS AND DESOLATION (v. 16)

16. *"This is why I weep*
and my eyes overflow with tears.
No one is near to comfort me,
no one to restore my spirit.
My children are destitute
because the enemy has prevailed."

Jerusalem is weeping uncontrollably. After the people return from exile, they will *weep* tears of repentance over what they had done (Ezra 3:13; 10:1; Nehemiah 8:9). But right now, there seems to be *no one* anywhere nearby to give *comfort* to her or *to restore* her *spirit*, not even God. Her *children*, her people, *are destitute because the enemy has prevailed*: the army of Babylon broke into the fortified city and crushed all the people who were there. About six centuries later, Jesus will weep over Jerusalem as he foresees another destruction of the city, this time at the hands of the Romans (Luke 19:41-44).

II. THE KINDLY FACE (LAMENTATIONS 3:22-26)

In chapter 3 we no longer hear the voice of Jerusalem. It is now the voice of a man who has suffered much (3:1). Are we hearing Jeremiah himself? For years he has faithfully delivered God's message, and his payment has been cruel persecution.

Most of the people of Jerusalem can see only the cruel face of the monstrous calamity that has crushed Jerusalem and transported her people to an enemy land. But Jeremiah is God's prophet. He can see a kindly face in that same calamity. He writes it into his song so that we can see it, as well.

A. SURVIVAL AND COMFORT (vv. 22, 23)

22. *Because of the* LORD'S *great love we are not consumed,*
for his compassions never fail.

The captives fretting in captivity are still alive. That is more than they deserve. In simple justice, God could have wiped them out for their long years of stubborn sinning. It is God's *great love*, not his justice, that keeps them alive. The captives can see this for themselves if they can set aside their emotions and think reasonably. God's *compassions* have not failed in the disaster just past. He is grieved with their grief; he will be glad when again their obedience will be such that he can give them gladness. Then they can be a blessing to "all peoples on earth" (Genesis 12:3). For the sake of his own purpose, the Lord will preserve the descendants of Abraham until they bring into the world the Christ who will offer the salvation to all.

23. *They are new every morning;*
great is your faithfulness.

God's great love and compassions (v. 22)—deserved or not—are as sure as the dawning of each *new* day. The Lord is faithful to his people even when they are not faithful to him. He is faithful enough to punish them when nothing else will work.

GOD STILL LOVES US

Most golfers think of a hole-in-one as a marvelous stroke of good luck. Not so in Japan, however! Noriaki Yamashita described his feelings when he shot a hole-in-one with these words: "I knew something terrible had happened." What was terrible was that, according to Japanese custom, he had to buy drinks, dinner, and other gifts for club members and friends when he got his hole-in-one. It is a custom that cost him almost $10,000!

To prevent such "good luck," Japan's four million golfers spend considerably more than $200 million annually to insure themselves against hole-in-one expenses as well as damages or injuries caused by shots that go astray. Yamashita was carrying only $5,000 on that day, so he immediately doubled his coverage. It was a wise decision: a year later he hit another hole-in-one, and this time he was covered fully.

When "bad luck" or "misfortune" (or whatever we want to call life's calamities) strikes us, we don't have to worry about the need to "pay off" our best friend—our heavenly Father. On the contrary, even when (or if) calamity comes as part of God's judgment on sin, God is standing by, offering us the compassion, love, and support that we need to survive and overcome the sins that have beset us. As our text says, "[God's] compassions never fail. They are new every morning."   —C. R. B.

The visual for today's lesson, with its lovely picture of a desert sunrise, illustrates the daily newness of God's blessings.

B. HOPING AND WAITING (vv. 24-26)

24. I say to myself, "The LORD is my portion;
    therefore I will wait for him."

Like other people of Judah, this solemn singer has lost possessions, friends, and the city he loved. All he has left is his *portion* in *the Lord*. And so he has hope. Fallen Jerusalem will rise again; the captives will walk free; God's people will worship him and obey him; Judah will live to fulfill her destiny, to bring a blessing to all the world.

25. The LORD is good to those whose hope is in him,
    to the one who seeks him;

The nightmare that keeps replaying in their heads won't go away. Weeping in captivity, the people find it hard to believe that *the Lord is good*. The Babylonians have leveled Jerusalem, slaughtered thousands of its people, dragged other thousands away—and *the Lord* sent them to do that.

But *wait*. The Lord has not finished. After this horrible captivity brings the Judeans to their senses, the Lord will send them back to rebuild Jerusalem. When he does, they will move on toward the purpose for which the Lord has made them his people—to bring a blessing to the whole world. That is the *good!*

26. . . . it is good to wait quietly
    for the salvation of the LORD.

The captives are not to give way to despair. The prophets who foretold the captivity also foretold also the end of it. The captives should not try to escape from their captivity by flight or rebellion. The Lord has brought them into subjection and has promised that it will last for seventy years (cf. Jeremiah 29:4-14). He will rescue them when that time is up. In the meantime, their task is to *wait quietly for the salvation of the Lord*. This is not the "wishful thinking" kind of hope. This kind of hope has a definite object and basis.

III. SUMMARY (LAMENTATIONS 3:31-33, 40)

In a few words, the final verses of our text sum up the teaching of this lesson for the captives.

A. GOD'S REPRIEVE (vv. 31, 32)

31. For men are not cast off
    by the Lord forever.

As the years of captivity roll by, the unhappy captives may think that *the Lord* has abandoned them. They would have a hard time praying that, "God is our

WHAT DO YOU THINK?

Some people have difficulty experiencing the daily newness of God's compassion. Others tend to become cynical or pessimistic and lose hope. How can a Christian learn to recognize God's daily blessings while also quietly waiting on the Lord for another deeply desired blessing? What does "wait quietly for the salvation of the Lord" mean, anyway? Surely it's not sitting in a rocking chair doing nothing! But what is it?

PRAYER

Whatever happens, Father, we know that you are good. We trust you. In every time of trouble, help us to work and wait for what we hope for, secure in the confidence that you will do all things well. In Jesus' name, amen.

THOUGHT TO REMEMBER

God knows best.

refuge and strength, an ever-present help in trouble" (Psalm 46:1). In their present trouble he actually has been on the side of the enemy. But that is only temporary.

32. Though he brings grief, he will show compassion,
    so great is his unfailing love.

The *grief* the Lord has caused matches the greatness of their transgression. But that grief will accomplish its purpose in bringing the people to repent and obey God. Their God then will have *compassion* to match the greatness of his mercies. The Lord will end their grief by leading them back to Jerusalem in joy (cf. Ezra 1:11).

B. GOD'S WISH (v. 33)

33. For he does not willingly bring affliction
    or grief to the children of men.

The Lord finds no pleasure in afflicting his people (Ezekiel 18:23, 32; 33:11). He does it with regret, not *willingly*. He is driven to it by their persistent wrongdoing and his own holiness. He has tried milder ways of guiding them: his law given centuries earlier and the voices of his prophets in recent times. But his people have ignored those. Now disastrous *affliction* will stop their mad rush. God's wish for his people is that they glorify him and enjoy his goodness. He afflicts them because at this point there is no other way to bring this about.

C. OUR DUTY (v. 40)

40. Let us examine our ways and test them,
    and let us return to the LORD.

The people have been living in *ways* that have brought them to loss and captivity. They need to *examine* those ways, to *test* them by God's written law and the teaching of his living prophets. That examination will show clearly that it is their own actions that have brought on the calamity (cf. Jeremiah 31:29, 30; Ezekiel 18), although those born while in captivity can make a good case for their own innocence (Lamentations 5:7).

CONCLUSION

The twofold message of this lesson is as clear to us as it was to the people of Judah long ago. First, don't drift away from God. That way leads to disaster. Second, if disaster strikes, "it is good to wait quietly for the salvation of the Lord" (3:26).

A. DON'T DRIFT

We avoid drifting by spending time in his Word and by doing what we find God says there (James 1:22). Drifting seems so harmless at first. Telling a dirty joke here, looking at a pornographic Web site there—what's the big deal? The drift of the Jewish people occurred over decades and centuries. But finally God showed them that sin certainly was—as it still is—a big deal! (Compare Hebrews 2:1-3.)

B. HOPE AND WAIT

Sometimes we, like the people of Judah, can see that disaster is the result of our own mistakes or misconduct. Then we work to repair the damage while we hope and wait for better times. We can pray while we work, and find that God is "faithful and just and will forgive us our sins" (1 John 1:9). Praise the Lord!

Sometimes disaster comes because of circumstances beyond our control. If what is lost can be replaced, our grief is lightened as we work, pray, hope, and wait. If what is lost cannot be replaced, then we work to adjust ourselves to the loss realizing that God himself is our ultimate "portion" (Lamentations 3:24). Either way, we find ourselves growing stronger spiritually. Praise the Lord!

Discovery Learning

*This page contains an alternative lesson plan emphasizing learning activities. Classes
desiring such student involvement will find these suggestions helpful. The next page
is a reproducible activity page to further enhance discovery learning.*

LEARNING GOALS

After participating in this lesson, each student will be
able to:

1. Summarize the dismay of fallen Jerusalem and the
hope that God still gave her for the future.

2. Explain how disaster or hardship can sometimes
help turn a people to the Lord.

3. Suggest one or two ways to put into practice the
message of Lamentations 3:26.

INTO THE LESSON

Begin class this week by writing the words *waiting for*
on the board or an overhead transparency for all to see.
Say, "Think about the various situations in which people
find themselves waiting for someone or something. As
you think of those situations, call them out, and I'll
write them on the board." (*Possible situations may include
birth of a baby; company coming to your house; doctor's appointment; stuck in a traffic jam; buying tickets for a popular show.*) Say, "Now, think about what people do when
they are waiting in these situations. Once again, call
them out, and I'll write them on the board." (*Possible
actions include pacing, looking out the window, glancing
through magazines, continually looking at the clock, blowing
the horn, worrying about not getting tickets.*) Say, "People
often find themselves waiting for someone or something. And they engage in all kinds of behaviors while
they are waiting. In today's lesson, God instructs Judah
to 'wait quietly.' Turn to the book of Lamentations and
let's read about the situation they were in when they
were told to wait."

INTO THE WORD

Prior to class, photocopy the reproducible activity
"Making Sense From the Senses" from the next page.
Make enough copies that each student may have one.
Distribute these to the class and move the learners into
groups of four. Then appoint someone to read the first
passage of Scripture aloud to the class. Say, "I want each
of you to describe the situation in this passage of Scripture
in terms of your five senses. In other words, what color do
you see in this situation? what texture? and so forth. Write
your answers in the spaces provided. Then tell your answers and your reasons tot he others in your group."

Allow about twelve minutes. Then briefly review the
activity, asking for answers. Say, "Now have someone in
your small group read the Scripture from the third column aloud. Once again, describe the situation in terms
of your five senses and share those with your group."
Allow another twelve minutes for this section, and then
call both for answers and the reasons for their answers.

Prior to class, ask four members to serve on a panel.
Assign one of the following texts to each: Luke 8:43-48;
Mark 5:2-15; Mark 9:15-27; and Luke 17:12-19. State:
"At this time we are going to have a panel tell us some
biblical examples of people who turned to the Lord
when they were in hardship or trouble." Ask the four to
sit at a table in front of the class and present two-minute
summaries of their texts to illustrate how people in disaster or hardship turn to the Lord.

INTO LIFE

Say, "God's message to Judah, and to us as well, is
to 'wait quietly for the salvation of the Lord,' Lamentations 3:26. What are some ways God expects people to
put into practice the message of Lamentations 3:26?"
Ask class members to discuss possible ideas with the
students sitting next to them. Then ask for volunteers
to report their answers to the class. As ideas are given,
write them either on the chalkboard or on an overhead
transparency so everyone can see them. (*Possible answers include the following: trust God to take care of you;
remember that God is faithful; stop worrying about your
hardship.*)

Prior to class time, make copies of the reproducible
activity "Wait Quietly for the Salvation of the Lord" from
page 102. Hand a copy of this activity to each person.
State: "Today we've seen both the grief and the hope of
Judah. In spite of God's judgment, God gave them encouragement for their future. But they were told in
Lamentations 3:26 to 'wait quietly for the salvation of
the Lord.' We've suggested several ways for people to
put this message into practice. Now, I'd like you to suggest one or two specific ways that you will put this message of Lamentations into practice in your life. Write
them on the lines provided." After several minutes have
passed, ask the class to share their suggestions with
someone sitting next to them or with the whole class.
Then, end the class time with a prayer of commitment, a
personal dedication to waiting quietly for the salvation
of the Lord, and a petition for God to help develop patience in our lives.

Making Sense From the Senses

Directions: Read the lesson text in the center column. Then try to express the sense of the passage by selecting a word or words that best describes it from the perspective of each of the five senses. Write the word(s) in the space provided. Next, read the text in the right column and try to express the sense of that passage by choosing words that best represent it.

Senses	Lamentations 1:12-16	Lamentations 3:22-26, 31-33, 40
Color		
Texture		
Sound		
Taste		
Smell		

"Wait Quietly for the Salvation of the Lord"
—Lamentations 3:26

Identify one or two ways you can put the message of today's lesson into practice in your life.

1. _____

_____

_____

2. _____

_____

_____

TURN AND LIVE

WHY TEACH THIS LESSON?

A high school freshman brings home his report card, and the news is not good. When asked to explain the low grades, the teenager thinks for a moment then replies, "Gee, Dad, I'm not sure. It could be either heredity or environment—what do you think?"

Blame-shifting is not a new problem. But when it comes to our relationship with God and our sin, blame-shifting is can have eternal consequences; it needs to be purged from our tendencies. Today's lesson shows why and how.

INTRODUCTION

"It's not fair!" Perhaps you recall that plaintive cry from childhood, uttered by someone who had lost a game, was intimidated by a bigger child, or found himself in a minority overruled by a majority. Or perhaps you remember uttering that cry yourself when a teacher imposed some rule that you found oppressive.

A. VARIED VOICES OF COMPLAINT

Adults have the same complaint when misfortune strikes, but they voice it in various ways. The favorite cry, "Why me?" means, "I don't deserve this misfortune—it's not fair." Another way of protesting is, "It's not my fault." The implication of this one is that someone else should bear the blame.

In the opening verses of our text we see the victims of a disaster trying to blame their parents and grandparents. Perhaps they fooled themselves with that deception, but they could not fool God or his prophet. Even worse is the self-deception when we tell ourselves that God is at fault. In the last part of our text today we shall hear people of Judah doing just that.

But God certainly knows something about what is "unfair." Remember that his own Son suffered and died in the most unfair act ever done by human beings against another. Even in spite of that, God is always fair—or better than fair—toward us. Think about his forgiveness of our sins even though we are unworthy. He is generous. He gives us more than we deserve. In time of distress or disaster, we must not let our discomfort put an end to our straight thinking in this regard. God is good, just, right, and fair. "Righteousness and justice are the foundation of your throne; love and faithfulness go before you" (Psalm 89:14; cf. 97:2). Whenever we doubt that, we are wrong.

B. LESSON BACKGROUND

For this lesson and the next, we take our text from the book of Ezekiel, who may be called "the captive prophet." These studies will be helped by a review of what we already know about the Babylonian captivity and by learning a little about Ezekiel's book. You might find it helpful at this point to review the three phases of the Babylonian captivity discussed on page 90 in lesson 10 (also see the lesson background to lesson 11, pages 95 and 96).

Two prophets are outstanding during the Babylonian captivity. Ezekiel is among the ten thousand taken to Babylon in the second phase of the captivity. In

DEVOTIONAL READING:
ROMANS 6:17-23
BACKGROUND SCRIPTURE:
EZEKIEL 18
PRINTED TEXT:
EZEKIEL 18:1-4, 20, 21, 25-32

LESSON AIMS

After this lesson each student will be able to:

1. Explain the principles of justice and personal responsibility as illustrated in Ezekiel's message to the exiles of Judah.

2. Tell how repentance can avert the condemnation that one's actions might otherwise merit.

3. Express repentance for some action or attitude that he or she needs to eliminate from his or her life.

KEY VERSE

For every living soul belongs to me, the father as well as the son—both alike belong to me. The soul who sins is the one who will die.
—Ezekiel 18:4

Nov
17

the fifth year of that captivity (about 593 B.C.), he began to proclaim God's word among the captives (Ezekiel 1:2, 3). Meanwhile, Jeremiah was carrying on a similar ministry back in Jerusalem (and, later, in Egypt). Thus the two prophets were speaking to two segments of Judah in the same time of peril. Their messages are similar, although the life situations of the two segments are different. Past lessons have brought us Jeremiah's blunt warning of disaster (lesson 6) and his bright gleam of hope (lesson 8). This week's lesson brings us Ezekiel's own blunt warning of personal guilt. Next week's lesson will bring us Ezekiel's gleam of hope.

I. MISTAKEN PROVERB (EZEKIEL 18:1-4)

We cherish the God-inspired wisdom in the book of Proverbs. But we should not assume that every proverb is inspired by God. Ungodly people can make up proverbs, too, and use them to deceive. We come now to a proverb devised to make people believe a lie. The Lord quotes that proverb only to denounce it.

A. THE PROVERB QUOTED (vv. 1, 2)

1. *The word of the LORD came to me:*

This statement or a similar one occurs more than four dozen times in the book of Ezekiel (e.g., 6:1; 13:1). The prophet wants us to be sure that what follows is not his own *word*, but God's.

2. *"What do you people mean by quoting this proverb about the land of Israel:*
   "'The fathers eat sour grapes,
   and the children's teeth are set on edge'?

What the captives *mean* by the *proverb* is plain enough. They mean to say, "This captivity is not our fault. Our fathers and grandfathers did wrong, and we are being punished for their sins." God did say he would punish all Judah for the sins of Manasseh, and he said it long after Manasseh was dead (Jeremiah 15:4).

But God did not mean Manasseh's descendants would be punished because Manasseh himself sinned. It meant they would be punished because they were continuing Manasseh's sins in their own time and in their own lives. If God punishes a sinner, it is for his or her own sins, not the sins of parents or anyone else. That will be made abundantly clear in the latter part of our text. But the sinners of Judah are trying to blame their ancestors. That is true in the homeland as well as among the captives in Babylon. (Consider again Jeremiah 31:29, 30 from lesson 8, where we found the same mistaken proverb mentioned of those in Jerusalem.) Both groups could be misusing Exodus 20:5 (discussed below).

Now, thousands of years later, sinners still try to blame their parents or their teachers or someone. And the effort is still futile. All of us are sinners, responsible for our own sin (Romans 3:23; 1 John 1:8). Let us confess our sins, stop our sinning, and beg God to forgive us (1 John 1:9).

B. THE PROVERB DENOUNCED (vv. 3, 4)

3. *"As surely as I live, declares the Sovereign LORD, you will no longer quote this proverb in Israel.*

What God is saying might best be explained in this expanded way: it will not be appropriate, it will not be just or proper or right, for the captives to keep on repeating *this proverb*. It simply is not true. When the captives get their thinking straightened out, they no longer will promote that falsehood. God makes this emphatic by the preface *as I live*. God's own life is no more certain than the assurance that the misleading proverb *will no longer* be used *in Israel*.

4. *"For every living soul belongs to me, the father as well as the son—both alike belong to me. The soul who sins is the one who will die."*

WHAT DO YOU THINK?

Some of the captives in Babylon could have perceived of God as a big bully because they (with their "little" sins) were being punished for the big and repeated sins of their ancestors. How can the church teach so people will understand that any sin is big enough to deserve the full punishment for disobedience?

[Consider such passages as Romans 3:9-12, 23 in the course of your discussion.]

God created all the people of the world; the lives of all the people of all generations are in his hand. He is not squeamish about taking the lives of those who are guilty. Consider the countless sinners who drowned in the great flood (Genesis 6–8), the many people of Judah who die by the sword when Jerusalem falls (2 Chronicles 36:17), and the false prophet who dies for his own falsehood (Jeremiah 28:15-17). The God who gives us all the breath of life in the first place is the same One who has the right to take that life back whenever he so chooses (e.g., Numbers 31:17; Deuteronomy 2:34).

But the Lord does not kill one soul unjustly. A *son* does not die for the sins of his *father* unless the son also commits those sins. This truth is reaffirmed at length in verses 5-18, which are not included in our printed text. Still the people were not convinced, and still the Lord repeated the truth (Ezekiel 18:19).

WHOSE RESPONSIBILITY?

Talk about life's ironies! The house in Braunau (*brow-now*), Austria where Adolf Hitler was born is now the home and workplace of about forty Austrians with mental and physical handicaps who make handicrafts for sale. The chief propagator of the "master race" philosophy would have had such people exterminated (along with the six million other "undesirables" killed by his regime) if his Nazis had won World War II.

Hitler's family moved from the house when he was only two years old, but more than 110 years later, it still carries the stigma of his residence. It is a run-down eyesore, referred to by local people as the "Hitler house."

Leaders in the city of Braunau want to do something about "the burden," as they refer to this awful reminder of the past. They are trying to raise funds to turn the building into a "House of Responsibility" to teach visitors about atrocities in wars past with hope of deterring them in the future. They are hoping to remind the citizens of Austria that each person bears some responsibility for the prevention of evil in the community.

It is a lesson the citizens of Judah had to learn. God was not punishing them because of what their ancestors had done; his wrath was coming upon them because they did not accept responsibility for their own sins. It is a timeless principle we all must learn.   —C. R. B.

II. SOUND TEACHING (EZEKIEL 18:20, 21)

These two verses are chosen for our text because they summarize the teaching of the chapter. The two truths they present are repeated emphatically because Ezekiel's hearers were not willing to accept them.

A. RESPONSIBILITY STRESSED (v. 20)

20. *"The soul who sins is the one who will die. The son will not share the guilt of the father, nor will the father share the guilt of the son. The righteousness of the righteous man will be credited to him, and the wickedness of the wicked will be charged against him.*

The Bible repeatedly stresses personal responsibility (e.g., Genesis 2:17; 4:7; Deuteronomy 24:16; 2 Kings 14:6). But the captives in Babylon are resisting this truth. Trying to believe a lie and deny the truth, they claim they are innocent—suffering unjustly for the sins of their ancestors.

Perhaps they are looking to Exodus 20:5 and its parallel Deuteronomy 5:9 to bolster their belief. Those passages warn that God extends his punishment for a father's sin to the children down to "the third and fourth generation." But when harmonized with other Scripture, these passages simply indicate that God's wrath on the fathers is bound to have some indirect or "collateral" effect on their children.

WHAT DO YOU THINK?

God's answer ("I made them; I can kill them") seems to bother some today. They want a God who will act in a manner that does not disturb their own sense of justice. How important is it for every believer to carry a firm picture that God is sovereign and has the right to do whatever pleases him? Why?

[Consider Romans 9:20, 21.]

WHAT DO YOU THINK?

People in every culture have a way of inventing their own "truth." How can the church help believers not to fall for these self-deceiving conclusions?

The captives find help in the fact that sons do often suffer for their fathers' sins. For example, children may suffer poverty because their father is in jail and cannot provide the necessities of life. Such hardships are a natural result of the father's sin, but they are not God's punishment on the child. This fact also applies, of course, to the innocent children who are later born to the captives in Babylon (cf. Lamentations 5:7). Jesus dealt with a similar question in His day (John 9:1-3).

B. REPENTANCE REQUIRED (v. 21)

21. "But if a wicked man turns away from all the sins he has committed and keeps all my decrees and does what is just and right, he will surely live; he will not die.

Here is the second great truth of this chapter, and it is good news indeed. Even the sinner does not have to *die*. He or she can repent, can stop sinning and become devoted to doing right. Then he or she will be treated as righteous. (The reverse can also happen; see v. 26 below.)

The phrase *he will surely live* may be a reflection of Leviticus 18:5, but the world would have to wait several centuries for the full explanation. Now we understand that a sinner can escape his or her just punishment because Jesus the Savior has taken that punishment in his place. What is revealed to Ezekiel is only a dim preview of the Christian gospel, but it gives encouragement to sinners who are honest enough to see their sin and concerned enough to stop it.

III. ANTICIPATED OBJECTION (EZEKIEL 18:25-32)

Ezekiel presents God's truth to people who are addicted to their own lie. They want to continue thinking that they are innocent victims of their fathers' sins. But God is not willing for any to perish. He wants all sinners to repent (Ezekiel 18:23; 1 Timothy 2:4; 2 Peter 3:9). So God continues to reason with the sinners.

A. COMPLAINT AND ANSWER (v. 25)

25. "Yet you say, 'The way of the Lord is not just.' Hear, O house of Israel: Is my way unjust? Is it not your ways that are unjust?

Despite what the Lord has just said, he now anticipates that the captives will raise an objection concerning his justice. They will continue to say that he is not fair in punishing them for their fathers' sins. God's answer is a challenge for them to look again at the facts. Wouldn't an honest examination show that it is God's *way* that is fair, and it is their *ways* that are unfair?

WHAT IS FAIR?

Alvin Cullum York has been called "the most celebrated G.I. in America's military history." York was drafted for service in World War I and sent to Europe. His actions in just four hours on October 8, 1918, gained him the fame that lives today. In that one battle, he is credited with leading about a half-dozen men in killing 25 German soldiers, neutralizing numerous machine-gun batteries, and capturing 132 German soldiers! For his efforts that day, York received the Medal of Honor and a hero's welcome back home. His story was made into a 1941 movie starring Gary Cooper in an Academy Award-winning role. For the rights to his story, York received $150,000. He gave it all away, but he was still hit with a bill for $172,000 in taxes and interest!

Few people would argue that it was fair for a patriot like York to be treated in such a manner. But fairness is not necessarily a common quality in the workings of governmental bureaucracy. God, on the other hand, is fairness personified. Twice in our text today, Ezekiel challenges us to acknowledge God's fairness in dealing with our sins on a personal basis. He holds us all accountable only for our own sins, and not for the sins of others. Who can argue with that?   —C. R. B.

WHAT DO YOU THINK?

Some Christians have been heard to say, when "a very sinful person" comes to Christ, that "it won't stick." How can the church help its members mature so they realize they are responsible to help every new convert to remain faithful to his or her commitment?

HOW TO SAY IT

Babylon. BAB-uh-lun.

Babylonian. Bab-ih-LOW-nee-un.

Ezekiel. Ee-ZEEK-ee-ul or Ee-ZEEK-yul.

Haggai. HAG-eye or HAG-ay-eye.

Jeremiah. Jair-uh-MY-uh.

Lamentations. Lam-en-TAY-shunz.

Manasseh. Muh-NASS-uh.

B. CHANGE AND RESULTS (vv. 26-28)

26. "If a righteous man turns from his righteousness and commits sin, he will die for it; because of the sin he has committed he will die.

The first step in exposing the weakness of their arguments is to state an obvious truth: when a *righteous man* becomes evil, he will be held accountable for that evil. What's wrong with that?

27. "But if a wicked man turns away from the wickedness he has committed and does what is just and right, he will save his life.

If *a wicked man* repents and turns to the good, God grants him *life*. What's wrong with that?

This, of course, is not to say that living a righteous life "earns" eternal life. That would be inconsistent with what Scripture has to say elsewhere. Under the Old Covenant, a righteous life is characteristic of one whose faith looks ahead to the coming of God's Messiah (John 8:56).

28. "Because he considers all the offenses he has committed and turns away from them, he will surely live; he will not die.

Because he considers is the key to turning away from the wrong and to the right. God's law is very plain with promises of blessing for obedience and punishment for disobedience (Deuteronomy 4:1-40). The history of Israel shows that God always has kept the law's promises. Anyone who considers that fact should know that he will continue to keep them. The captives are far from obedience to God's law, and they have been so for years. Anyone who stops to consider his or her own lifestyle would know that.

But those captives are not considering, not thinking. They find pleasure in doing wrong and apply a silly proverb to excuse their behavior. The people treasure that proverb and keep repeating it to comfort themselves. Even after the people return from exile, the Lord will find it necessary to challenge their thinking processes to get them to reconsider what they are doing (Haggai 1:5, 7; 2:15, 18).

C. COMPLAINT AND ANSWER REPEATED (v. 29)

29. "Yet the house of Israel says, 'The way of the Lord is not just.' Are my ways unjust, O house of Israel? Is it not your ways that are unjust?

Again, God anticipates that the people will be unconvinced. Even after the arguments of verses 26-28, they will repeat the complaint we just saw in verse 25. This demonstrates the stubbornness of their hearts (see Ezekiel 3:7; 18:31 [below]; and 36:26). A little reasonable thinking will show that they deserve all the punishment they are getting.

D. JUST JUDGMENT (v. 30a)

30a. "Therefore, O house of Israel, I will judge you, each one according to his ways, declares the Sovereign LORD.

Even while in exile, there is more judgment to come upon the *house of Israel.* God's judgment will be fair, just, and right, whether the people choose to see it that way or not. Judging *each one according to his ways* means that no one will be held guilty or innocent because someone else has done wrong or right.

E. REPENT AND LIVE (vv. 30b-32)

30b. "Repent! Turn away from all your offenses; then sin will not be your downfall.

Sin indeed has been their *downfall* up to this point. But it need not continue to be this way. Although the people must now obey their captors, it seems that the treatment in captivity is not as severe as it could be. From this point on, they could be reduced to poverty and hunger, treated with extreme cruelty, or killed

DAILY BIBLE READINGS

Monday, Nov. 11—The Righteous Will Live (Ezekiel 18:1-9)

Tuesday, Nov. 12—The Person Who Sins Will Die (Ezekiel 18:19-24)

Wednesday, Nov. 13—Turn and Live (Ezekiel 18:25-32)

Thursday, Nov. 14—Why Will You Die, Israel? (Ezekiel 33:7-11)

Friday, Nov. 15—Without Excuse (Romans 1:16-25)

Saturday, Nov. 16—God Will Repay (Romans 2:1-8)

Sunday, Nov. 17—Belief in the Son Brings Life (John 3:16-21)

WHAT DO YOU THINK?

The sign says, "Repent! The end is near!" Do most people even know what that means? How can the church help people understand the need to repent and turn from their sinful ways?

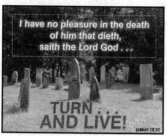

Today's visual is a stark image that speaks to our need for repentance. Use it to illustrate verse 32.

outright, as many of their countrymen will be when Jerusalem is razed (Ezekiel 33:21-29). To avoid further ruin themselves, they had better *repent*. They should settle down to productive and holy living. While in captivity, they should do all they can for the welfare of Babylon because the Lord promised them, "if [Babylon] prospers, you too will prosper" (Jeremiah 29:4-7).

31. "Rid yourselves of all the offenses you have committed, and get a new heart and a new spirit. Why will you die, O house of Israel?

The call to repentance goes on. Disobedient for many years, these people now must obey God. Ezekiel in the midst of the captives is speaking the very words of God. Jeremiah in Jerusalem is writing God's will and sending it across the miles (Jeremiah 29:1). God is exhorting the people to throw their *offenses* on the garbage heap of discarded evil, to set their hearts on doing God's will to cultivate *a new spirit* of obedience. *Why will you die?* This is a matter of life and death, and you can choose. Will you choose to die? What insanity!

32. "For I take no pleasure in the death of anyone, declares the Sovereign LORD. Repent and live!"

If God could do the choosing, he would choose life for all those captive people; but they themselves must make the choice. They can obey God and live, or disobey him and die. Why is it so hard to choose life?

CONCLUSION

God's standards of right and wrong have been plain for centuries. Jesus reinforces those standards when he teaches us to control our thoughts, motives, and wishes as well as our actions. With eternity at stake, how can anyone ignore these standards and substitute others?

A. POPULAR STANDARDS AND PROVERBS

I like it; therefore it is good. Ancient Hebrews enjoyed themselves at pagan festivals (Numbers 25:1-3), so they thought there was nothing wrong in such activities. People today think the same way. The modern proverb might be, "It can't be so wrong if it feels so right."

Everybody does it; therefore it is good. You're driving along the interstate highway. The speed limit is sixty-five, but everyone seems to be going seventy-five or more. So you speed up, too, in violation of the law. The proverb here is, "You have to go with the flow or you'll get run over."

It is bad; therefore it is good. There is something attractive about doing what is forbidden. It shows you are independent enough to do as you please. So people take up smoking, drug use, and immorality. Being bad makes them feel so good! The proverb here might be, "It's important to live life on your own terms."

I need it; therefore it is good. Why do workers in shops and offices go outside in midwinter to smoke? Because they need it—they're addicted. Without it they will be nervous, irritable, unable to do their best work. If they work better, that's good, isn't it? The proverb here might be, "It works for me."

B. GOD'S STANDARDS

An old story tells of a man who is examining yesterday's shirt, hoping to find it clean enough for one more day. Not quite sure, he appeals to his wife: "Honey, is this shirt dirty?"

The wife tosses it into the laundry hamper without a second glance. She says, "If it's doubtful, it's dirty."

Undergirded by the Word of God, perhaps that would be a safe principle to apply to any number of practices that are popular today!

Discovery Learning

This page contains an alternative lesson plan emphasizing learning activities. Classes desiring such student involvement will find these suggestions helpful. The next page is a reproducible activity page to further enhance discovery learning.

LEARNING GOALS

After participating in this lesson, each student will be able to:

1. Explain the principles of justice and personal responsibility as illustrated in Ezekiel's message to the exiles of Judah.

2. Tell how repentance can avert the condemnation that one's actions might otherwise merit.

3. Express repentance for some action or attitude that he or she needs to eliminate from his or her life.

INTO THE LESSON

Prior to class time, write on the board: "That's Not Fair!" Begin this week's lesson by stating: "All of us have heard the phrase on the board. You probably have said it yourself. I'd like to start by asking you to think about the different situations in which you have heard this phrase. Then I would like groups to prepare skits to present to the class to illustrate that phrase." (*Possible scenario: a whole class punished for one person's action, or the like.*)

Move the class into groups of four or five. Give them seven to ten minutes to develop a skit that illustrates the phrase, "That's Not Fair!" When the groups appear to be ready, ask them to give their skits one at a time.

Say, "We all understand this phrase and different situations in which it's said. But what is interesting to me is that the people of Israel said it to God. They thought he was being completely unfair! Let's turn to Ezekiel 18 and read their challenge to God's integrity."

INTO THE WORD

Ask a class member to read the lesson text aloud. Then, ask the following questions:

1. What is meant by the proverb, "The fathers eat sour grapes, and the children's teeth are set on edge"? (*The children inherit the sins of their parents and are suffering because of them; v. 2.*)

2. Why does God reject that proverb for Israel? (*Every soul is God's. The soul who sins will die; vv. 3, 4.*)

3. Describe the principle of justice seen in verse 20. (*People bear their own sin and guilt, not those of the son or of the father.*)

4. Describe the principle of personal responsibility as seen in verse 20. (*Each person's righteousness or wickedness will be upon him. Each is accountable for his/her own actions.*)

5. What is required for the wicked to live and not die? (*He turns away from his sins, keeps God's decrees, does what is just and right; v. 21.*)

6. On what basis will God judge the house of Israel? (*Each one according to his ways; v. 30.*)

7. What did God want the house of Israel to do? (*Repent and turn away from their offenses; 30.*)

8. What is meant by, "Then sin will not be your downfall"? (*The downfall would be their own cruel treatment and death by the Babylonians; v. 30.*)

9. Describe the inner transformation God requires (*A new heart and a new spirit of obedience to God; v. 31.*)

After answering those questions, say, "Repentance and inner transformation are required not only of the house of Israel, but of all who have committed sin. Even people who have experienced salvation by God's grace need to repent of actions or attitudes that should not be a part of their lives." Prior to class, make copies of the reproducible activity "Actions and Attitudes: Laying Them at the Cross" from the next page. Distribute the worksheets and ask the class to move into their previous groups. Say, "In your groups, make a list of actions and a list of attitudes Christians need to eliminate from their lives. Write them on the lines provided."

After several minutes, ask groups to report their answers. Write the answers on the board or overhead transparency for all to see. (*Possible actions include lying, gossip, stealing, judging. Possible attitudes include prejudice, hate, greed, lack of forgiveness.*)

INTO LIFE

Say, "Possibly, some of these actions and attitudes need to be eliminated from your lives as well." Distribute copies of the reproducible activity "Repentance Response," also on page 110.

Ask each student to complete the prayer privately, listing at least one action or attitude of which he or she needs to repent. After a few minutes, ask each one to join one other person and to share the action or attitude that needs to be eliminated from his or her life. Say, "By sharing your action or attitude with a classmate, you are asking each other to hold you accountable in the near future for this commitment to turn away from this behavior. Agree on a time and place to review your decisions."

Close the session with a prayer of commitment and surrender to God.

Actions & Attitudes:
Laying Them at the Cross

Under the respective arms of the cross, make a list of attitudes and actions Christians need to eliminate from their lives.

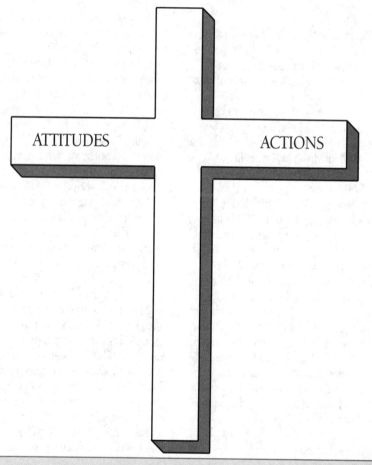

ATTITUDES   ACTIONS

Repentance Response

Dear Father in Heaven,

Today's lesson has helped me to understand your principles of justice and personal responsibility. I am responsible for my own sins, and I am responsible for turning away from them. Father, I still have an attitude/action that needs to be eliminated from my life. Today, I want to "Turn and Live." I confess to you my sin of

After considering it during this lesson, I want to turn away from it; I want to keep your decrees, and I want to do what is just and right. Strengthen me by your Spirit, O God, so that its temptation no longer has a hold on me. Create within me a new heart and a new spirit of devotion to you.

In Jesus' name I pray, Amen.

LOOK TO THE FUTURE

LESSON 13

WHY TEACH THIS LESSON?

This Old House is one of the most enduring television programs on the Public Broadcasting System. In each show, viewers see an older house being remodeled in some way. Many of these renovations are quite drastic, with seemingly very little of the original house remaining after the work is completed. God's renovation of ancient Judah was just as drastic. The spiritual structure of that house had deteriorated so badly that nothing less than a total restoration would do. This restoration would be painful, but the pain would be temporary. And God made clear how beautiful the house would look when his work was finished.

Some of your students undoubtedly are feeling discomfort as God's Holy Spirit works to clean up various areas of their lives. This lesson will show them that, just as God's cleansing of ancient Judah was for her ultimate good, so is his clean up of our own sinful lives. What a cause for thanksgiving!

INTRODUCTION

A. EVIDENCE

Charlie was a friendly man, but he never went to church. Cheerfully, he explained his skepticism to the preacher. "If God is up there," he said, pointing a bony finger toward the sky, "He's got to let me know. Me personally. Understand?"

The preacher pointed to the first verse in the Bible. "God created the heaven and the earth. Doesn't that prove he is up there?"

"Maybe," Charlie replied. "But how do I know he did it?"

Charlie had time on his hands, and he really did think about God. He was lost in thought as he drove home one day—so lost that he didn't hear the train whistle. His car rolled onto the track just in time to be hit broadside by the powerful locomotive. The car's passenger side was mangled, and the car was crushed to half its width. In that condition it rode the cowcatcher for a few seconds. As the train slowed, the car finally broke free and rolled over and over, battering the left side. Finally it came to rest on its roof, leaning against a pole, with Charlie dangling upside down in his seat belt.

In time, help arrived. When someone pried open a mangled door, Charlie stepped out jauntily, apparently unhurt. Declining to be taken to the doctor, he was taken home instead.

The next day was Sunday. When Charlie stepped through the church door, the preacher was speechless, but Charlie was not. "He let me know," said Charlie, pointing a finger skyward. "He's up there all right."

It took a remarkable escape from death to convince old Charlie. What makes you sure God really is "up there"?

B. LESSON BACKGROUND

In the sixth chapter of Ezekiel, we hear the Lord shouting to the mountains of Israel. He has tried talking to the people, to little avail. In Jerusalem, some people want Jeremiah killed for bringing the Lord's message (Jeremiah 38:4), but it seems that no one thinks seriously about doing right instead of wrong. Over in Babylon,

DEVOTIONAL READING:
JEREMIAH 32:36-41
BACKGROUND SCRIPTURE:
EZEKIEL 36, 37
PRINTED TEXT:
EZEKIEL 36:22-32

LESSON AIMS

After participating in this lesson, each student will be able to:

1. Cite the kinds of restoration God promised to the exiles for the sake of his own name.

2. Cite some ways the restoration of the exiles—in purity as well as in residence in their homeland—would honor the Lord.

3. Suggest ways we today can honor the Lord by our lifestyles.

KEY VERSE

I will give you a new heart and put a new spirit in you; I will remove from you your heart of stone and give you a heart of flesh.
—Ezekiel 36:26

Nov
24

the captive Israelites listen to Ezekiel as they might listen to an entertainer. They, too, have no thought of changing their way of living (Ezekiel 33:30-32). So the Lord calls to the mountains, which were no more unresponsive than the people.

The mountains of Israel were not like the Asian Himalayas or the Rockies of North America. Compared with those majestic mountain ranges, we would refer to the mountains of Israel as "hills." Wheat grew in the valleys between them; grapevines and olive trees grew on their slopes. But God said those hills would be deserted and desolate (Ezekiel 6:1-7). There would be no one to plant wheat or prune grapevines.

That is exactly what happened, as we have seen in earlier lessons. Jerusalem was destroyed with a great slaughter, most of the survivors were taken to Babylon; the rest fled to Egypt (2 Kings 25:1-26). The hills of Israel were deserted and desolate.

In chapter 36 of Ezekiel we hear the Lord shouting again to the mountains of Israel (v. 1). Those hills would be inhabited again, and recovered from those who had taken possession of them illegitimately (vv. 2-7). They would be cultivated; they would be fruitful (vv. 8-12).

I. GOD'S OWN HONOR (EZEKIEL 36:22-24)

Our text begins by explaining why God is going to return the people of Israel to their promised land and make that land fruitful again. The promised restoration goes beyond a reclaiming of land, however. Cleansing from sin, empowerment by the Holy Spirit, and renewal and prosperity are included. Some commentators suggest that the last three of these ultimately are fulfilled in Jesus' shedding of his blood, the outpouring of the Spirit on the Day of Pentecost (Acts 2), and our future life in Heaven.

A. GOD'S NAME PROFANED (v. 22)

22. *"Therefore say to the house of Israel, 'This is what the Sovereign LORD says: It is not for your sake, O house of Israel, that I am going to do these things, but for the sake of my holy name, which you have profaned among the nations where you have gone.*

God is not going to end the captivity for the *sake* of the captives. They deserved nothing less. But God had his own *holy name* to think about.

From the time of Abraham, and more notably from the time they left Egypt to become a nation among nations (Deuteronomy 28:9, 10), the people of Israel were God's people. God gave his people his laws to guide them. He gave them a good land, abundant crops, and healthy livestock. In this relationship with the Lord, the people of Israel had a unique opportunity and duty. They ought to be completely obedient to the Lord who blessed them so abundantly. Thus they could show to the whole world that it is good and wise and profitable to obey the Lord.

In that duty the people of Israel failed miserably. In the midst of the Lord's blessings they disobeyed him. Through centuries they disobeyed more and more, until they were actually worse than the surrounding nations (2 Chronicles 33:9). Thus the people not only disgraced themselves; they also dishonored God. They made it seem that he was giving rich blessings to gross sinners, and therefore that he was no better than Baal or Molech or any of the imaginary gods of the pagans. "The Lord is compassionate and gracious, slow to anger, abounding in love" (Psalm 103:8); but he could not let his people go on enjoying his blessings while they disgraced both themselves and him. So he punished them with captivity in Babylon.

That punishment let them know that their disobedience was not acceptable, but it did not renew respect for God's name among the pagans. Now the pagans merely suppose the Lord to be a feeble deity, unable to protect his people. To correct that

HOW TO SAY IT

Baal. BAY-ul.
Babylon. BAB-uh-lun.
Barnabas. BAR-nuh-bus.
Deuteronomy. Due-ter-AHN-uh-me.
Ezekiel. Ee-ZEEK-ee-ul or Ee-ZEEK-yul.
Levite. LEE-vite.
Molech. MO-lek.
Pentecost. PENT-ih-kost.

WHAT DO YOU THINK?

An unbeliever reading today's text might accuse God of being selfish or conceited because he says he redeems people for the sake of his "holy name." How would you respond? How can Christians make sure they are giving God all the honor he deserves?

(Consider such passages as Exodus 20; Matthew 6:9, 10; and Colossians 3:17 in the course of your discussion.)

false notion, the Lord is going to crush mighty Babylon and take the people of Israel back to their homeland. Then who will be able to doubt his power?

B. GOD'S NAME SANCTIFIED (vv. 23, 24)

23. "'I will show the holiness of my great name, which has been profaned among the nations, the name you have profaned among them. Then the nations will know that I am the LORD, declares the Sovereign LORD, when I show myself holy through you before their eyes.

Names were important in the Old Testament, since they usually had a particular meaning and significance. God is so concerned about the significance of his own *name* that he explicitly forbids its misuse (Exodus 20:7; Deuteronomy 5:11). God is *holy*. That means he is separated, "set apart," from all that is evil, and even from what is common or ordinary. Since his identity cannot be separated from his *name*, it, too, is holy.

But God's holy name has been *profaned*, made to seem unholy, common, or ordinary. In their own country, God's people had profaned God's name by their wickedness—by child sacrifice (Leviticus 18:21), by swearing falsely (19:12), in their dress and appearance (21:5, 6), and in their disobedience (22:31-33). They have profaned God's name in their idol worship (Ezekiel 20:39) and sexual immorality (Amos 2:7). Now God promises to sanctify his name by making it holy, to make observers see that the Lord is different from all of the make-believe gods.

24. "'For I will take you out of the nations; I will gather you from all the countries and bring you back into your own land.

And here's how he is going to make his name holy: God is going to crush Babylon and take his people *back* home. Won't that convince every observer that the Lord is supreme in power? As our next verses show, the Lord will offer other evidence to demonstrate his goodness in addition to that power.

II. GOD'S HOLY PEOPLE (EZEKIEL 36:25-28)

Obviously, the captivity will be useless if the people who come back to the homeland are no better than those taken into captivity. But the Lord promises to restore his people to godliness as well as to the land of Israel.

A. PURITY RENEWED (v. 25)

25. "'I will sprinkle clean water on you, and you will be clean; I will cleanse you from all your impurities and from all your idols.

Sprinkling with blood or *water* is frequent in Old Testament ceremonial cleansings (e.g., Leviticus 14:7, 16, 27, 51; Numbers 8:7; 19:18-21). This is so well known that even in New Testament times "sprinkled" is used figuratively to mean "cleansed" (Hebrews 10:22).

Literally, of course, neither a sprinkling nor a deluge of water can wash away the kind of *impurities* the captives have wallowed in for years. The primary instrument of God's cleansing is the captivity itself. Homesick in Babylon, perhaps a few of them begin to think seriously when they hear the same kind of preaching from Ezekiel that they had heard in Jerusalem from Jeremiah. Where the pagan practices of their neighbors had seemed enticing in Judah, the pagan practices of their captors are repulsive. They learn to cleanse themselves of such practices.

"STUFF WASHES OFF"

What is the dirtiest, most loathsome job you can imagine? Please pardon the repulsive suggestion, but have you thought of cleaning out a city's sewer lines? Whatever goes down the toilet, the sink, and the storm drains (including such things as

WHAT DO YOU THINK?

God says Israel had "profaned [his holy name] among the nations" but that he would once again "show the holiness of" his name. How has the church profaned God's name among the pagans of today? What can we do to show the holiness of his name?

WHAT DO YOU THINK?

God said, "I will cleanse you." What must believers do to allow God to complete his work of cleansing? Don't we sometimes hang on to some favorite sins—"guilty pleasures," as some have termed them? How do get those removed?

(See James 5:16; 1 John 1:9.)

A new heart also will I give you, and a new spirit will I put within you.

Ezekiel 36:26

The visual for today's lesson illustrates verse 26 of the printed text. Display it as you begin to discuss that verse.

bicycles and hypodermic needles) ends up in the city's lines. And sometimes, they get plugged up.

Roy Parrino has cleaned out sewer lines for more than a dozen years, and he does it for $25 per hour. His work uniform consists of hip waders, rubber gloves, a hard hat, and goggles. He braves the dangers of rancid water, bacteria, disease, toxic fumes and, of course, *the smell!* As Parrino says, "You really have to psych yourself up for it. It's about as dirty as you can get. You've got to look at it one way: 'Stuff washes off.'"

Yes, stuff washes off, but the kind of pollution in which ancient Israel had immersed herself took more than a simple bath to remove. The spiritually toxic environment of idolatry and immorality had nearly killed Israel as a nation, but God used their captivity in Babylon as the cleansing agent that restored them to life. Even today, God sometimes allows us to wallow in the depths of our chosen "sewer" in order to make us seek his cleansing power.   —C. R. B.

B. HEART REPLACED (v. 26)

26. "'I will give you a new heart and put a new spirit in you; I will remove from you your heart of stone and give you a heart of flesh.

For years, Jeremiah had been delivering God's message back in the homeland. Those who heard with their ears but not their hearts wanted that prophet killed (Jeremiah 26:8, 9). The hearts of those people are like *stone*, hard as flint. God's teaching does not penetrate them (cf. Mark 3:5).

Now God promises to give the captives *a new heart*, and as history unfolds we see God doing exactly that. That softer heart receives God's teaching through Ezekiel, and the people respond with obedience. God gives also *a new spirit* to replace their spirit of stubborn rebellion. God's people are ready to go home.

C. SPIRIT RECEIVED (v. 27)

27. "'And I will put my Spirit in you and move you to follow my decrees and be careful to keep my laws.

When the captives receive their new hearts and willing spirits, God will complete their transformation by putting his own *Spirit in* them (also Ezekiel 37:14; 39:27-29). With that Spirit to guide them, they will have a renewed commitment to obey God's law. They will worship God in spirit and in truth, as God always wants his people to do (John 4:23, 24).

D. RELATIONSHIP RESTORED (v. 28)

28. "'You will live in the land I gave your forefathers; you will be my people, and I will be your God.

Beginning with Abraham in about 2000 B.C., God repeatedly made known his wish for the children of Abraham to become a nation and to possess the country at the east end of the Mediterranean Sea. From the time of Joshua in about 1400 B.C. to the fall of Jerusalem in 586 B.C., they actually did possess that land. They lost this homeland in the time of Jeremiah, Ezekiel, and Daniel, however, because of their long and constant disobedience to God—especially with regard to idolatry. By means of their captivity in Babylon, God makes them ready to go back home and to be restored to their proper relationship with him. Back in the homeland they will be his *people*, knowing his will and taking delight in doing it.

III. GOD'S RENEWED BLESSINGS (EZEKIEL 36:29-32)

The final verses of our text reveal that God is ready to give his restored people even more than they need. Long after they return home, he will ask them again to obey him and receive his blessing. "Test me in this," he will add, "and see if I will not throw open the floodgates of heaven and pour out so much blessing that you will not have room enough for it" (Malachi 3:10).

A. BOUNTIFUL HARVESTS (vv. 29, 30)

29. *"I will save you from all your uncleanness. I will call for the grain and make it plentiful and will not bring famine upon you.*

The mention of *famine* must have stirred painful memories in the minds of the captives. They had suffered through famine just before their captivity (Ezekiel 5:16). A quick death by the sword is certainly preferable to the slow death of starvation! (See Lamentations 4:9.) Famine can be a result of drought, diseased crops, insects, or, as in this case, an enemy invasion that stole the crops and ravaged the land (cf. Deuteronomy 28:49-51).

But captives restored to their homeland are made spiritually pure (Ezekiel 36:25); they will no longer need this type of punishment. Instead, God will give them abundant harvests of *grain* for their food. We should remember in passing that as bad as a "physical" famine is, a "spiritual" famine is worse (Amos 8:11, 12).

30. *"I will increase the fruit of the trees and the crops of the field, so that you will no longer suffer disgrace among the nations because of famine.*

The *increase* of *the crops of the field* was the abundant grain harvest (v. 29). Now God promised that the fruit *trees* also would have abundant *fruit*. If the people who returned to the homeland would be faithful and obedient, never again could the pagan people around them look down on them—or on their God—because they were suffering from a *famine*.

B. SOBERING REMEMBRANCE (vv. 31, 32)

31. *"Then you will remember your evil ways and wicked deeds, and you will loathe yourselves for your sins and detestable practices.*

The captives are going back—back to the dear familiar hills of home. Fields long desolate will be planted and will yield tremendous harvests. Fig and olive trees will bow down with the weight of their fruit. What joy! And yet the homecomers will find a shadow on their bliss. They will have to *remember*. Those fruitful fields have been ravaged by invaders and have long lain desolate; and that is due to the *evil ways and wicked deeds* of many of these very ones returning home.

Lovely Jerusalem is gone. It will have to be rebuilt, along with its magnificent temple; that destruction, too, is due to the sins of the very people who will participate in the rebuilding. When this happens, many of those folks will weep aloud (Ezra 3:12). Hundreds of their countrymen had died in the fall of Jerusalem, and the *sins* of these now returning—those not born in captivity—had contributed to that debacle. Many of us know what it means to *loathe* ourselves for what we have been and what we have done.

PAINFUL REMINDERS

The image of the "suffering artist" is a staple of modern folklore: actors, singers, painters, or sculptors whose work goes unnoticed by critics and public alike, who struggle for years before being "discovered" and gaining fame and fortune.

Now the new health discipline of "arts medicine" is treating artists for more tangible forms of suffering. Violinists can develop a form of dermatitis called "fiddler's neck" from friction of the violin on their skin. Bagpipers may get lung infections from the mold and bacteria that grow in the bagpipe skins. Ballerinas get stress fractures and foot deformations from standing on their toes. (As one wag put it, "Why don't they just get taller girls?") And, of course, athletes—"artists" of another sort—live with painful reminders of their sports injuries long after their careers come to an end.

WHAT DO YOU THINK?

Some people are counseled just to forget the past and go on. The advice assumes that focusing on past sins will poison the soul. How does remembering one's past, as God advises in today's text, help a person to become more righteous? When should a person forget and when should he or she remember?

[Consider 2 Corinthians 7:8-11 and Philippians 3:13.]

DAILY BIBLE READINGS

Monday, Nov. 18—Israel Shall Soon Come Home (Ezekiel 36:8-12)

Tuesday, Nov. 19—The Lord's Holiness (Ezekiel 36:16-23)

Wednesday, Nov. 20—A New Heart (Ezekiel 36:24-28)

Thursday, Nov. 21—God Will Save From Uncleanness (Ezekiel 36:29-33)

Friday, Nov. 22—They Shall Know Who God Is (Ezekiel 36:34-38)

Saturday, Nov. 23—Can Dry Bones Live? (Ezekiel 37:1-6)

Sunday, Nov. 24—God's Spirit Within (Ezekiel 37:7-14)

Israel was "healed" of its spiritual diseases by the captivity in Babylon. God sent them back to their land with the promise of bountiful yields from their fields. However, he also pronounced a statement of fact: they would never be able to forget the sins that had brought them so low. It is a timeless truth: even after forgiveness and restoration have come, we still must live with the effects of what we have done and who we have been.

—C. R. B.

32. "'I want you to know that I am not doing this for your sake, declares the Sovereign Lord. Be ashamed and disgraced for your conduct, O house of Israel!'"

Our text ends as it began (v. 22): God is not freeing the captives for their own sakes. Rather, the Lord is giving them and the pagans around them a demonstration of his own power, his own mercy, his own goodness. He is the Lord, the only true God (v. 23).

CONCLUSION

There has been much sadness in the series of lessons that we are completing. But the series ends with a bright gleam of hope in the promise of return—return to godliness and to the homeland. When we return to Old Testament study in June, we shall see fifty thousand captives lead the return to the land of Israel. The Babylonian exile and return will become one of the truly watershed events in Israelite history (cf. Matthew 1:11, 12, 17).

A. LARGER HOMECOMING

After the initial return of the fifty thousand (Ezra 2), smaller groups will move back to the ancient homeland as the years pass. In the New Testament we read that Anna is of the tribe of Asher (Luke 2:36) and Barnabas is a Levite (Acts 4:36). Paul says "our twelve tribes" are serving God "day and night" (Acts 26:7). The return of captives from Babylon is only the beginning of the restoration that the Lord promises.

B. DANGEROUS DRIFTING

The people of Israel were defeated and taken captive because they rebelled against God, but they did not plan out that rebellion in any systematic way. They did not intend to rebel. When they were prosperous and comfortable, they just drifted into wrongdoing—drifted so slowly that they gave hardly a thought to the change taking place (cf. Judges 2:10, 11).

At several points in this lesson series we have taken note of a similar drift away from God in the post-Christian countries of Europe and North America. A thoughtful student can hardly fail to see the drift that has occurred in the prosperous years since World War II.

So again we ask, are you drifting? Consider the week just past. Did you have a definite plan to have a part in God's work? Or have you simply been floating along—taking everything "one day at a time"?

Is your congregation drifting? Is it too easily satisfied with itself as it is? Is it failing to keep its members growing "in the grace and knowledge of our Lord and Savior Jesus Christ" (2 Peter 3:18)? Are its members growing spiritually as well as in number? (See Matthew 28:19, 20; Ephesians 4:15.) As these lines are being written, one church in the outskirts of a certain city is making definite plans not only to stop its drift, but to turn it into fervent and continuing activity for the glory of God and the salvation of people on earth. Prayer will be fervent, plans will be made, tasks will be assigned, and God will grant the increase (cf. 1 Corinthians 3:6). Does your church need something like that?

PRAYER

Lord, grant us clear sight to see ourselves as you see us, and the will and wisdom to do what you want us to do. In Jesus' name, amen.

THOUGHT TO REMEMBER

"Do not merely listen to the word, and so deceive yourselves. Do what it says" (James 1:22).

Discovery Learning

This page contains an alternative lesson plan emphasizing learning activities. Classes desiring such student involvement will find these suggestions helpful. The next page is a reproducible activity page to further enhance discovery learning.

LEARNING GOALS

After participating in this lesson, each student will be able to:

1. Cite the kinds of restoration God promised to the exiles for the sake of his own Name.

2. Cite some ways the restoration of the exiles—in purity as well as in residence in their homeland—would honor the Lord.

3. Suggest ways we today can honor the Lord by our lifestyles.

INTO THE LESSON

Prior to class time, prepare this opening activity: photocopy the reproducible activity "Shield of Promises" from the next page so that each person in class can have a copy. Also make an overhead transparency of the activity to project.

Give a copy to each person. Say, "This morning we want to start by focusing upon the topic of promises. Move into groups of three, and for the next several minutes generate some characteristics and/or qualities of promises. Write them in the blank areas of the shield. Then we'll share our answers."

While they are working on this activity, project the image of the shield on the screen or wall. After several minutes, ask the class to tell their answers. As they are given, write them on the transparency. (*Possible answers may include expectation, inheritance, assurance, commitment, pledge, and vow.*) Once the answers have been listed, say, "Promises—we've all experienced them, in making promises or in getting the benefits. Today's lesson text focuses on the promises that God made to Israel. Turn to Ezekiel 36:22-32 and let's identify the promises that Israel received from God."

INTO THE WORD

Ask a class member to read the lesson text aloud to the class. Say, "In your groups, identify the promises God gave to Israel in this text. You have a few minutes."

After a short time, ask a reporter from each group to tell what the group came up with. As answers are given, write them on the chalkboard or overhead transparency. (*Answers may include the following: to restore them to their land; to cleanse them from sin and idolatry; to give them a new heart and a new spirit; to give them abundant harvests.*) Then ask the following questions:

1. For whose sake was God going to restore Israel and fulfill all his promises to them? (*Not for their sakes, but for the sake of God's holy name; v. 22.*)

2. What did Israel do to God's name among the nations? (*Profaned his name among them; v. 23.*)

3. How was God going to show the holiness of his great name? (*Gather them together from all the countries and bring them back to their own land; v. 24.*)

4. What would be the practical benefits to the people of Israel in God's showing the holiness of his name? (*Cleansed from impurity and idols; they will follow his decrees and keep his laws; the grain will be plentiful and there will be no famine; fruit of the trees and the crops of the field will be increased; vv. 25-30.*)

5. What did God know would happen to Israel after they become so abundantly blessed in their own land? (*They will remember their evil ways and wicked deeds, loathe themselves for their own sins and detestable practices, and become ashamed; vv. 31, 32.*)

Say, "These promises God made to Israel were in the context of sanctifying his great name. And, we've seen how Israel benefited from the fulfillment. In the same way, giving honor to God is something Christians need to do. What are some ways Christians today can honor the Lord?" (*Possible answers include the following: regular worship; setting a sterling example; sharing Christ with non-Christians; respecting God and his Word; obeying God; loving God and loving people.*)

INTO LIFE

State: "Christians can honor the Lord by their lifestyles. How can you honor the Lord in your life today?" Prior to class, photocopy the activity at the bottom of the reproducible page ("How Can I Honor the Lord?") so that each student can have one. Distribute it to the students, and say, "I want each of you to reflect on your lifestyle before God. Think about areas you know you need to honor God more than you do. Then decide one way that you will honor the Lord with your body this week. Write it on the banner on the worksheet and take it home to remind you to honor the Lord in a specific way this week."

After everyone has completed this activity, ask for volunteers to tell the class of their commitment. Then ask the class to stand together in a circle and have a prayer of commitment to give the Lord the honor that is due him.

Shield of Promises

In the sections of the shield following, write in characteristics and qualities of promises.

How Can I Honor the Lord?

God expects us to honor him! Today we have looked at a number of ways that Christians can honor our Lord. But what can you do specifically, even this week, to honor him? Think about it, and then write it on the banner and take this home as a reminder.

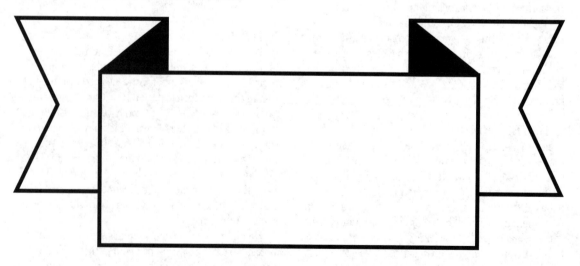

Winter Quarter, 2002–2003

Portraits of Faith
(New Testament Personalities)

Special Features

Lessons

About These Lessons

How much better to have a guide than a map! In the present quarter, we have real people portrayed before us to act as guides. Their faith and their failures alike serve to point the way for us to follow. If you and your students will follow closely, they will take you nearer to the Master!

Dec 1

Dec 8

Dec 15

Dec 22

Dec 29

Jan 5

Jan 12

Jan 19

Jan 26

Feb 2

Feb 9

Feb 16

Feb 23

Portraits of Real People

by Thomas E. Friskney

Portraits are pictures with such details that the viewer sees or conceives the dimensions that show life and character, times, places, and events. Such pictures can be graphically presented in words. The Scriptures have more than enough detail to enable us to comprehend the real persons and the roles God has entrusted to them. It is our responsibility to form these properly and to imitate the models in a way that is pleasing to God: faith and obedience. This quarter's lessons give us ample opportunity to identify with several real people as we examine their responses in the portraits presented in the New Testament.

DECEMBER

When we open God's picture album in this series, we find a devoted husband and wife—devoted to one another and to God. They are Elizabeth and Zechariah, and both understood the promises of God found even though they did not anticipate what their personal involvement would be.

Two lessons allow us to glance at portraits of Mary. Her beauty attracts us as in humble servant-faith she yields herself as the handmaid of the Lord. We have the privilege to place that portrait alongside that of Elizabeth to see how the faith of these two beautiful women reinforce one another.

We find it easy to place the next portrait with that of Mary, for it is that of Joseph her husband. Joseph's faith, too, was put to the test.

We can connect the portrait of John the Baptist to the first portrait of Elizabeth and Zechariah, for they were his parents. As the forerunner of the Messiah, John introduced Jesus as the one who takes away the sins of the world.

JANUARY

Our eyes look upon the portrait of the rich young ruler with mixed emotions. Jesus loved him; yet we see the young man go away sorrowful because he did not want to part with his possessions.

The portrait of Mary and Martha of Bethany comes alive as we consider them when Jesus and the disciples are in their home. They fulfill roles as hosts, even though there was difficulty in balancing being hostesses and in being listeners, especially for Martha. We also see the test of their brother Lazarus' death.

The portrait of Pontius Pilate is most thought provoking. Who is on trial, Jesus or Pilate? Pilate tries to displays his authority only to have his words come back to taunt him.

Among the twelve apostles, one who rises to the forefront often in the final days of Jesus' ministry on earth is Peter. His portrait at the last supper is attractive yet foreboding. We like the picture in John 21 better as we see Jesus restore him.

FEBRUARY

After the beginning of the church we are privileged to see the personality of Barnabas. He was genuine in his giving, and was trustworthy in his presentation of Saul of Tarsus to the apostles.

A convert on Paul's first missionary journey was Timothy. His real portrait takes form as we see him joining with Paul and Silas on the second missionary journey. This was the beginning of his role as a trusted helper of Paul.

Another welcome portrait we find among Paul's companions and helpers is a husband and wife team, Aquila and Priscilla. Wherever Priscilla and Aquila were, the church was "in their house." From time to time and place to place they were always helpers to Paul and the work of the gospel.

We learn from these role models and we give thanks. We also reflect on the fact that there may be those who look to us as models. May people see in our own portraits real people who demonstrate faith and obedience.

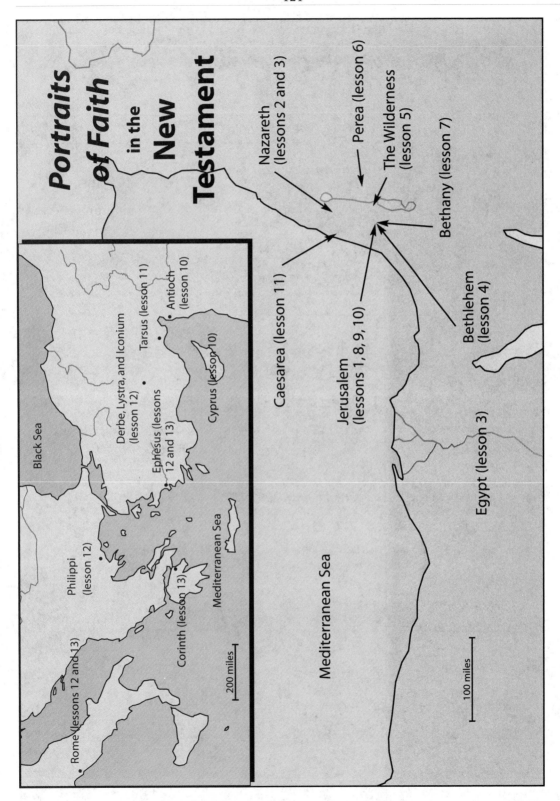

Portraits
of Faith
in the
New
Testament

Nazareth
(lessons 2 and 3)

Perea (lesson 6)

The Wilderness
(lesson 5)

Bethany (lesson 7)

Caesarea (lesson 11)

Jerusalem
(lessons 1, 8, 9, 10)

Bethlehem
(lesson 4)

Egypt (lesson 3)

Mediterranean Sea

100 miles

Black Sea

Tarsus (lesson 11)

Antioch
(lesson 10)

Derbe, Lystra, and Iconium
(lesson 12)

Ephesus (lessons
12 and 13)

Cyprus (lesson 10)

Philippi
(lesson 12)

Corinth (lesson 13)

Mediterranean Sea

Rome (lessons 12 and 13)

200 miles

Portraits of Faith

Person	Challenges to Faith	Level of Response
Elizabeth & Zechariah	Advanced Age and Unanswered Prayer	Compliance, With Some Temporary Doubt
Mary	Youth and Humble Circumstances	Complete Submission
Joseph	Sense of Justice and Unique Circumstance	Full Obedience
John the Baptist	Personal Popularity and Political Consequences	Early Belief and Later Doubt
The Rich Man	Dependence on Wealth; Self-confidence	Sad Refusal
Mary and Martha	Human Familiarity With Jesus; Personal Jealousies	Devoted Service and Acquiescence
Pilate	Political Correctness and Egotism	Capitulation and Rejection
Peter	Rashness and Overconfidence	Repentant Recommitment and Enthusiasm
Barnabas	Family Loyalties and National Pride	Christlike Generosity and Persistence
Paul	Legalism and Intellectualism	Total Surrender
Timothy	Family Background and Youth	Lifelong Self-Denial
Aquila & Priscilla	Roman/Greek Culture and Mobility	Contentment in Service

ELIZABETH AND ZECHARIAH

LESSON 1

WHY TEACH THIS LESSON?

Cover up the rest of this paragraph so you won't see the answer to the following question: Where in the Bible does it say, "God moves in a mysterious way, His wonders to perform"? The answer: Nowhere! That line is actually from the poet William Cowper (1731–1800). What fools many people is the fact that God often does work in ways that are mysterious to us, so that little saying seems like it should be in the Bible—somewhere.

Today's lesson features an elderly couple who felt an emptiness in their lives because they were childless. They must have asked dozens of times why God had not granted their request for a son, an heir. Years passed, and yet there was still no son and no answer to their questions—until one special day when their prayer was finally answered. Today's lesson will remind your learners that life's struggles may actually result in a greater good somewhere down the road when God chooses to reveal his plan—in his own time.

INTRODUCTION

A. PORTRAIT OF ELIZABETH AND ZECHARIAH

Elizabeth and Zechariah knew the Old Testament, for that was the Word of God there was at that time. They knew the requirements of the law of Moses. They knew what it meant to minister for God. We do not know all the aspects of Zechariah's particular ministry, but the window that is opened for us in Luke 1 enables us to go with him into the temple for a once-in-a-lifetime experience. This experience also enables us to connect a religious act with a circumstance in their own home. Elizabeth was unable to bear children, a role she wanted very much. In fact, both Elizabeth and Zechariah had desired to be parents for years to the point that they knew only God could make it possible. (Childless couples today can empathize very well with their anxiety.)

In our mind's eye we see the people, and we recreate the time and place for the important events in their lives. But more importantly, our thoughts move to consider their son John, the supernatural events in the lives of his parents, and John's ministry in introducing the Messiah. John is the one to preach repentance so that the hearts of the people of Israel would be prepared for the coming of the Messiah and his kingdom.

B. LESSON BACKGROUND

We need to stretch our imaginations back some two thousand years to place ourselves into the setting in which Elizabeth and Zechariah rose to the forefront. With the close of the book of Malachi, it had been about four hundred years since there had been a direct revelation from God. Devout Jewish people used whatever opportunity was theirs to hear Old Testament messages, especially as those messages nourished their hope for the coming of the Messiah. Elizabeth and Zechariah had an advantage in this regard, since they both were of priestly family lines.

They did not squander the benefit of their heritage. They responded positively to the personal roles with which God had entrusted them. God had chosen this

DEVOTIONAL READING:
ISAIAH 40:3-11

BACKGROUND SCRIPTURE:
LUKE 1:5-66

PRINTED TEXT:
LUKE 1:5-14, 39-45, 57, 58

LESSON AIMS

After participating in this lesson, each student will be able to:

1. Describe the character of Elizabeth and Zechariah as seen in today's lesson texts.

2. Tell how submission to God's will was critical for Elizabeth and Zechariah and remains so today.

3. Express a commitment born of faith and hope to do what God is wanting to accomplish in his or her life.

KEY VERSE

The angel said to him: "Do not be afraid, Zechariah; your prayer has been heard. Your wife Elizabeth will bear you a son, and you are to give him the name John."   —Luke 1:13

couple to play a significant part in preparing the way for the Messiah. Their son John would be the one to introduce the Messiah. At the time they did not comprehend what all this meant.

From the lesson, we have opportunity to examine the kind of people God uses. The time frame of Elizabeth and Zechariah was that of the Old Covenant. They knew and kept the laws and regulations of that Covenant, but their relationship with God also was limited by these same statutes. Zechariah's ministry in the temple with his particular duties was central in their lives. We may consider Elizabeth to be a homemaker, taking care of the priestly vestments of her husband and helping with his needs pertaining to his service as she was able. It is easy for us to note that God challenges people to serve "where they are."

How much Elizabeth and Zechariah were aware of the prophecy in Isaiah 40, we don't know. What did they think when they heard, "See, the Sovereign Lord comes with power" (Isaiah 40:10)? However, we can be sure it would take on greater dimension after the birth of their son, for they would then be involved personally with what God was doing in the blessing that would come with the Messiah.

I. GOD'S CALL OF ZECHARIAH (LUKE 1:5-14)

In writing his account of the life of Christ, Luke gives Elizabeth and Zechariah an honored role in introducing his Gospel. The portrait of their faith is real, and a model for us today.

A. CHARACTER AND OPPORTUNITY (vv. 5-9)

5. In the time of Herod king of Judea there was a priest named Zechariah, who belonged to the priestly division of Abijah; his wife Elizabeth was also a descendant of Aaron.

Herod the Great was *king* over *Judea* from 37 to 4 B.C. He is Jewish in background, but his faith is nil. His place of power in the Roman Empire allows him to be as selfish, ruthless, and corrupt as he desires (cf. Matthew 2:16). But *Zechariah* and *Elizabeth* are two people with different roles and very different qualities from those of the evil king. The impact of their lives on history ultimately is greater than that of Herod.

Zechariah (whose name means "God remembers") is a *priest* descended from *Abijah,* one of the grandsons *of Aaron.* There are twenty-four divisions, or courses, of the priesthood, based on the families of Aaron's descendants (cf. 1 Chronicles 24). Each division serves twice a year for one week, and the priests consider their ancestral positions as trusts from God. All of us can learn from this example and be more aware of the trusts we have from God—our family backgrounds, our abilities, and the time and place in which we live.

6. Both of them were upright in the sight of God, observing all the Lord's commandments and regulations blamelessly.

The lifestyle of this couple is pleasing to *God;* they are the kind of people he can use to have an impact on human affairs. If God uses people to the extent that they have prepared themselves to be used by him, then Elizabeth and Zechariah have prepared well.

This passage reminds us that "real people" are participating in bringing about God's plan of redemption. Their response to God's law is exemplary, but is not complete. Their obedience to Old Testament law and Zechariah's ministry as a priest are central in their lives. They anticipate the time when sin will be forgiven. Only then will their relationship with God be complete. They expect the Messiah to provide this blessing. These two apparently have some spiritual insight into God's coming redemptive work.

WHAT DO YOU THINK?

In what ways are Christian role models important to the ministry of the church?

[Consider the significance of the term disciple or discipleship in your discussion.]

WHAT DO YOU THINK?

Since all people sin, we might be surprised to read that Elizabeth and Zechariah kept God's law "blamelessly." This term obviously is not absolute, then, but describes the couple's lifestyle. They pursued a course of righteousness even though they were not perfect. Of whom would you apply the term blameless today? Why? What can you learn from their example?

So Elizabeth and Zechariah watch, learn, and serve as they wait for that plan to unfold. Faith and patience are necessary companions for servants of God. As we look forward to the second coming of Christ, we too faithfully watch, learn, and serve.

7. But they had no children, because Elizabeth was barren; and they were both well along in years.

Having *no children* is heartbreaking to would-be parents today. To an ancient Jewish family, it was even more so. In fact, it was often viewed as a judgment of God (cf. Genesis 20:18; Hosea 9:14).

For *Elizabeth* and Zechariah, what may have seemed "unfair" actually becomes the occasion for demonstrating the power and purposes of God. Their situation demonstrates that God's people can be his servants regardless of age. God gives Elizabeth and Zechariah the chance for their faith and patience to develop.

Various situations in Scripture awaken us to occasions where human limitations serve as God's time to bring together the human and the divine. Think of the testimonies that Sarah and Abraham (Genesis 17:15-19), as well as Hannah and Elkanah (1 Samuel 1:1-20), give us concerning their own childless states.

8. Once when Zechariah's division was on duty and he was serving as priest before God.

Each member of the *division* takes his turn at serving in the temple, where God had revealed his presence among the people in the past. For Zechariah, ministering *before God* on behalf of the people is a high and holy service. It is a time of being close to God, of sensing his presence.

We may do well to consider if we ever have trouble worshiping or serving Christ, our problem could be solved by an awareness of the presence of Christ. This matter is a central feature in the book of Revelation as John pictures Christ in the center position of the seven churches of Asia, knowing their situations and ready to be their provider and protector. We live in the presence of Christ! Our relationship is even greater than what Zechariah had; so there ought to be even a greater response. "From the one who has been entrusted with much, much more will be asked" (Luke 12:48).

A SENSE OF TIMING

The baseball player describes his success by saying, "It's all in the timing." The one who invests in stocks or real estate says, "It's all in the timing." We are impressed with the timing of the angel's visit in today's lesson. Of course, in the Bible angels brought messages at various times, and they appeared in various places. Sometimes they delivered their message through dreams while people slept, sometimes as people walked along the way, and sometimes when they were at work. Still, it is instructive to read that the message came to Zechariah when he was serving! Many have received their greatest blessings when they were serving. Many have received insights into life when they were serving. Many have found a fresh spiritual joy when they were serving.

There is something about serving God that clears the mind, opens the heart, and softens the will. God could have delivered his message to Zechariah at any time, but he chose to do it when Zechariah was serving—and serving in the temple.

Today, we do not regard any place as truly a holy place. We speak of holy places only because there is no other way to describe them. We believe that any place becomes a holy place when we meet God there. Church conventions used to appoint a time-and-place committee for the next convention. Such a committee could not have improved on the choice God made. Those who forget to serve, or will not serve, may miss out on a very special blessing that God has for them. We do not serve in order to receive, but when we serve we often do receive.   —R. C. S.

WHAT DO YOU THINK?

What are some ways that the church can use the talents and experience of senior members to enhance its ministries?

DAILY BIBLE READINGS

Monday, Nov. 25—An Angel Visits Zechariah (Luke 1:5-13)

Tuesday, Nov. 26—Zechariah Questions the Promise (Luke 1:14-20)

Wednesday, Nov. 27—Elizabeth Conceives (Luke 1:21-25)

Thursday, Nov. 28—His Name Is John (Luke 1:57-66)

Friday, Nov. 29—Zechariah Prophesies (Luke 1:67-75)

Saturday, Nov. 30—John Will Go Before the Lord (Luke 1:76-80)

Sunday, Dec. 1—Prepare the Way of the Lord (Isaiah 40:3-11)

Portraits of Faith

Person	Challenges to Faith	Level of Response
Elizabeth & Zechariah	Advancing Age and Unanswered Prayer	Compliance, With Some Temporary Doubt
Mary	Youth and Climactic Circumstances	Complete Submission
Joseph	Sense of Justice and Unclear Circumstance	Full Obedience
John the Baptist	Personal Popularity and Political Consequences	Early Belief and Later Doubt
The Rich Man	Dependence on Wealth, Self-confidence	Sad Refusal
Mary and Martha	Human Familiarity With Jesus; Personal Jealousies	Devoted Service and Acquiescence
Pilate	Political Correctness and Egotism	Capitulation and Rejection
Peter	Rashness and Overconfidence	Repentant Recommitment and Enthusiasm
Barnabas	Tenacity, Loyalties and National Pride	Christlike Generosity and Persistence
Paul	Legalism and Intellectualism	Total Surrender
Timothy	Family Background and Youth	Lifelong Self-Denial
Aquila & Priscilla	Roman/Greek Culture and Mobility	Contentment in Service

The first visual gives an overview of the personalities to be studied this quarter.

HOW TO SAY IT

Abijah. Uh-BYE-juh.

Abraham. AY-bruh-ham.

Elizabeth. Ih-LIH-zuh-beth.

Elkanah. EL-kuh-nuh or
  El-KAY-nuh.

Gabriel. GAY-bree-ul.

Hannah. HAN-uh.

Hebron. HEE-brun or HEB-run.

Herod. HAIR-ud.

Judea. Joo-DEE-uh.

Messiah. Meh-SIGH-uh.

Zechariah. ZEK-uh-RYE-uh.

9. . . . he was chosen by lot, according to the custom of the priesthood, to go into the temple of the Lord and burn incense.

The opportunity to minister at the altar is determined by drawing lots. Moreover, this occasion to offer *incense* ordinarily is allowed once in a lifetime because of the large number of priests. So for Zechariah, this is "his hour"—long awaited and long desired. But Zechariah cannot anticipate all that is in store. How can anyone know the full mind of God or what the future will hold as God's will is being accomplished?

B. CONVERSATION WITH AN ANGEL (vv. 10-14)

10. And when the time for the burning of incense came, all the assembled worshipers were praying outside.

Under the Old Covenant, priests are considered to be "go betweens" in bringing the peoples' sacrifices to God. The worshipers, on behalf of whom Zechariah is ministering, are assembled outside the temple and are *praying* silently. (The rising smoke of the *incense* signifies those prayers.) Incense is burned twice a day in the temple, in the morning and in the evening—Luke does not tell us the time of day here. It is certainly appropriate for Zechariah to pray at this once-in-a-lifetime service, especially since it is a time when he must be feeling closer to God than at any other time. Surely he prays for various needs of the *worshipers,* and we would be surprised if he did not petition God for the desire of his own heart, as well. But does he ask for a child? Has he long since given up hope, or does he still pray?

11. Then an angel of the Lord appeared to him, standing at the right side of the altar of incense.

What a distinct privilege this is to Zechariah that *an angel of the Lord* should appear *to him!* It has been four centuries since any heavenly messenger has walked the earth. The Word does not tell us what the angel looks like. (Whenever angels appeared on earth, they took a form appropriate for their mission.) For Zechariah there is no mistaking who he is. And the important thing is his message. The angel appears *at the right side of the altar of incense* between the altar and the golden lampstand. Being in a situation where God's communication is so personal is a real test to one's faith.

12. When Zechariah saw him, he was startled and was gripped with fear.

Zechariah thinks he is alone, but to his amazement someone else is there, representing God with a personal communication. This is the angel Gabriel, as verse 19 tells us (see also Daniel 8:16; 9:21). Will this be judgment or blessing? Awe surrounds Zechariah as one in the presence of God. His *fear* is a godly fear. But what will be next?

13. But the angel said to him: "Do not be afraid, Zechariah; your prayer has been heard. Your wife Elizabeth will bear you a son, and you are to give him the name John.

This answer to his *prayer* is probably not what *Zechariah* expects! The announcement of the birth of John is very similar to the announcement given to the parents of Samson in Judges 13:3-5. The child to be born in each situation is empowered from birth for a special task. *John* means "the Lord's gift" or "the Lord is gracious." And so he is!

14. "He will be a joy and delight to you, and many will rejoice because of his birth."

Truly the child's *birth* will be a time for rejoicing by his parents; yet, what is implied by *many?* The angel tantalizes Zechariah's hope and faith with the additional assurance that the child "will be great in the sight of the Lord" (v. 15). What does that mean? Zechariah can only wait for more of the divine message—and the unfolding events of history—for his answer!

II. GOD'S MISSION FOR ELIZABETH (LUKE 1:39-45)

The angel Gabriel appears to Mary about six months later (v. 26). He tells her that she will give birth to Jesus. Quickly Mary goes to see Elizabeth.

A. MARY'S VISIT TO ELIZABETH (vv. 39, 40)

39. At that time Mary got ready and hurried to a town in the hill country of Judea.

Elizabeth and Zechariah live in *the hill country of Judea*, probably in the city of Hebron, the city of priests (Joshua 21:11). This is about forty miles from Jerusalem and seventy miles—a four- or five-day journey—from Nazareth. The visit will be an occasion to strengthen the faith of both *Mary* and Elizabeth and to heighten their hope concerning the Messiah. Again we note that God does not always reveal all details quickly. He does it in ways that develop faith, patience, and hope.

40. . . . where she entered Zechariah's home and greeted Elizabeth.

The meeting of the two women is surely special. A unique spirit of joy and expectation fills the heart of each one, for each has a significant ministry in the work God is doing. For each of them, it is important to share some time together. We all know what comfort it brings when we can share our blessings, sorrows, or hopes with those who understand us and our circumstances.

B. ELIZABETH'S MESSAGE TO MARY (vv. 41-45)

41. When Elizabeth heard Mary's greeting, the baby leaped in her womb, and Elizabeth was filled with the Holy Spirit.

In so many ways we are reminded of the quality of individual that *Elizabeth* is for the role that is hers. On this meeting with *Mary* God divinely equips her by the power of the *Holy* Spirit to speak even more than she understands. Even the movement of her unborn child communicates to encourage her in her poetic proclamation.

42. In a loud voice she exclaimed: "Blessed are you among women, and blessed is the child you will bear!

Mary is greatly honored as the chosen of God. Elizabeth's words strengthen Mary and challenge her faith as well. It will be a message to reflect upon later as she ponders her role and that of her unborn son. What will it mean to be the earthly mother of God's child? What responsibility, what trust from God!

43. "But why am I so favored, that the mother of my Lord should come to me?

To what extent Elizabeth understands that Mary's son will be the Messiah is hard to know. But God has revealed some semblance of that fact through Elizabeth to reassure both women. Her use of the phrase *my Lord* is similar to David's calling the Messiah "my Lord" in Psalm 110:1 (quoted numerous times in the New Testament). What confidence this is for them that God is fulfilling his promises! Perhaps Elizabeth reflects on the meaning of her own name, "God is an oath." His word will come to pass!

44. "As soon as the sound of your greeting reached my ears, the baby in my womb leaped for joy.

Elizabeth testifies to Mary the personal witness of her unborn son concerning Mary's arrival with her own unborn son—both sons are from the promise and power of Almighty God. Although the two women cannot anticipate what is ahead for each, they can patiently trust God.

45. "Blessed is she who has believed that what the Lord has said to her will be accomplished!"

Faith is the foundation of hope and happiness. Whatever God promises, he intends to accomplish in his time. Sometimes we get in a hurry, only to find it is not yet the fullness of time (cf. Galatians 4:4). Whenever we try to "push" God's

VISUALS FOR THESE LESSONS

The small visual pictured in each lesson (e.g., page 126) is a small reproduction of a large, full-color poster included in the Adult Visuals packet for the Winter Quarter. The packet is available from your supplier. Order No. 292.

WHAT DO YOU THINK?

How has an older believer challenged and/or encouraged you in your walk with Christ? How have you done the same for a younger believer?

timetable, we run a big risk! God's own authority is sufficient reason that we should believe his promises. We see models in the portraits of Mary and Elizabeth. Even though we do not have the roles of these two women today, God provides us with happenings that both test and develop our faith.

STANDING ON THE PROMISES

All of life is built on promises. Marriage begins with promises. And before those vows are said, sometimes someone sings that lovely song "Oh, Promise Me!" Business is built on promises, as everyone who has ever signed a promissory note knows. It begins with, "I promise to pay." People who enter the military must first make promises. Elected officials are inducted into office with promises. And in recent years large numbers of men have come together with a group called Promise Keepers to strengthen their resolve to be faithful husbands and fathers.

God, of course, is the ultimate promise keeper. You can see his track record in the Old Testament and mark it in the New Testament. You can observe it in the lives of others, and you can experience it in your own life. God keeps his promises. He always has and he always will. Many products are advertised on the basis of their performance, from automobiles to kitchen devices. God's performance record is perfect.

Elizabeth believed this. Mary believed this. The whole history of the church is the record of men and women who believed this. It is the kind of faith that will cheer you on your worst day and calm you on your best day. The old song is right: we are standing on the promises. In truth there is no other place to stand. We who serve a promise-keeping God must respond by keeping our own promises—to him, to others, and to the world. —R. C. S.

III. GOD'S FULFILLMENT OF THE PROMISE (LUKE 1:57, 58)

Mary stays with Elizabeth about three months (v. 56), probably long enough to see John born.

A. BIRTH OF JOHN THE BAPTIST (v. 57)

57. When it was time for Elizabeth to have her baby, she gave birth to a son.

During the three months that Mary is there, the two women undoubtedly share the burdens and the joys on their hearts. The common experience of approaching motherhood is not a time to talk of age difference, but to praise God and pray that they will have the faith to fulfill their roles in God's plan. These are days of preparation.

B. OCCASION FOR REJOICING (v. 58)

58. Her neighbors and relatives heard that the Lord had shown her great mercy, and they shared her joy.

What a time for rejoicing! Many of the relatives and friends present would think, "God has taken away her disgrace" (compare Luke 1:25). However, the event has much more meaning than that. Here is a great demonstration of God's mercy. Here is divine evidence that the Messianic hope is still alive in this baby. Even greater things are ahead! It is noteworthy that Zechariah's first words after the return of his speech are to praise the Lord (v. 64). Is there a better way to rejoice?

CONCLUSION

We no longer are the same if we are able to identify with the faith of these real people. Our faith is stronger because of their models. We look forward with desire to the work God is doing, and we offer ourselves ready to serve him, knowing he trusts real people to do his work, regardless of their ages or the eras in which they live. There is always a place for faith and patience the promises of God.

Discovery Learning

This page contains an alternative lesson plan emphasizing learning activities. Classes desiring such student involvement will find these suggestions helpful. The next page is a reproducible activity page to further enhance discovery learning.

LEARNING GOALS

After this lesson the student will be able to:

1. Describe the character of Elizabeth and Zechariah as seen in today's lesson texts.

2. Tell how submission to God's will was critical for Zechariah and Elizabeth and remains so today.

3. Express a commitment born of faith and hope to do what God is wanting to accomplish in his or her life.

INTO THE LESSON

VERBAL PORTRAITS. Ask each student to identify a person who was (1) influential in the development of his or her spiritual life, or (2) who serves as a good model of faith in today's world. Ask students to create a "verbal portrait" of this person, answering the following questions:

• What was the person's name and occupation?

• How was faith or faithfulness to God demonstrated in this person's life?

• How did this person serve in the life of the church?

• If you were to describe this person's spiritual life in just three words, what three words would you choose?

Allow each student to share his or her "verbal portrait" with at least one other person. Make the transition to Bible study by reminding the class that godly lives and experiences of real persons often serve as models for our lives. We are embarking on a new study of New Testament models for life today. These verbal portraits in the Scripture are intended to inspire and give confidence to today's follower of Jesus Christ.

INTO THE WORD

Early in the week ask a class member to prepare a brief report on the Jewish priesthood. This person should identify the primary tasks of the priests and tell how they were divided or organized. Give this person a copy of the lesson commentary and a copy of an article on priests from a Bible dictionary or encyclopedia.

Begin the class by reading the printed text. Tell the class there are many questions we could ask of Zechariah and Elizabeth. Say, "We are going to prepare some interview questions we might like to ask this couple. For example: 'What emotions did you feel when it became apparent you were not going to have children?'" As class members offer questions for the interview, have a class member be the "scribe" and write the questions

on the board. After several questions are listed, have small groups discuss potential answers.

Tell the class that it is often encouraging to discover characteristics of persons who are effective servants of God. Ask them to look for verbal clues to the character of Zachariah and Elizabeth from today's text. (*Examples: "Priest," "Upright in the sight of God," "Observed all the Lord's commandments."*) Have the "scribe" list these on the board. The reproducible activity "Now I Know My ABC's" on the next page could be useful as this is done.

Have the report on the tasks and organization of priests given at this time.

INTO LIFE

State: "Even though Zechariah was a priest, God often uses people from ordinary walks of life as his special servants." Make two columns on the board. One should be titled "Priests or Religious Leaders"; the other, "Laymen."

Ask "Who were some other religious leaders God used to accomplish his will in the Old and New Testaments?" (*Examples may include Eli, Saul/Paul, and others.*) Then tell them that God used many more people as his servants that were not priests or religious officers. Ask for names and list them on the chalkboard in the second column. (*Examples include Moses, Abraham, Jacob, Peter, Andrew, Priscilla, and others.*) Discuss how those in both groups were useful to God only as they submitted to his will.

Give each student a piece of paper with a picture frame on it. (You can generate this from a computer program or clip art, or refer the students to the appropriate page in the *NIV Bible Student* workbook.) Near the bottom of that frame write, "Dear Lord, help me to learn to be always ready to accept responsibilities and opportunities you provide in my life. Signed _____."

Say, "We are going to create another 'Verbal Portrait.' We want to list as many characteristics of great and humble servants of God as possible and to learn from this model. Brainstorm names of some of God's servants and the characteristics that made these people great servants." Ask the learners to write the characteristics of these servants in the open part of the picture frame.

After reviewing these characteristics, ask them if they would be willing to sign the prayer at the bottom of the page. Or you might choose the prayer activity atop the reproducible page that follows.

God Answers Prayer

The angel said to the priest, "Do not be afraid, Zechariah; your prayer has been heard." God has promised that the prayer of a righteous man is powerful and effective (James 5:16).

Jot a few notes about what the incident in today's study has taught you about prayer.

Now I Know My ABC's . . .

Use the "ABC's" to unfold today's story of faith, joy, and surprise from Luke 1:5-14, 39-45, 57, 58. (All words are taken from the *New International Version*®.)

Elizabeth was a descendent of A _ _ _ _ _. (v. 5)

Elizabeth was B _ _ _ _ _ _. (v. 7)

Elizabeth and Zechariah observed God's C _ _ _ _ _ _ _ _ _ _ _. (v. 6)

Zechariah was a priest before _ _ D. (v. 8)

Zechariah was the husband of E _ _ _ _ _ _ _ _ _. (v. 5)

Zechariah's reaction to the heavenly messenger: F _ _ _ _. (v. 12)

Who appeared to Zechariah? _ _ G _ _ _. (v. 11)

The King of Judea at this time: H _ _ _ _ _. (v. 5)

Zechariah burned this: I _ _ _ _ _ _ _. (v. 9)

Zechariah's priestly division: _ _ _ _ J _ _. (v. 5)

Herod's title: K _ _ _. (v. 5)

How Zechariah was chosen to serve: by L _ _. (v. 9)

Where Zechariah was confronted by an angel: _ _ M _ _ _ _. (v. 9)

Mary was blessed among _ _ _ _ _ N. (v. 42)

Elizabeth's baby's name was to be _ O _ _ _. (v. 13)

What worshipers were doing during Zechariah's service: P _ _ _ _ _ _ _. (v. 10)

Q: A Free Space!

Both Elizabeth and Zechariah were _ _ _ R _ _ _ _ _. (v. 6)

Elizabeth was filled with the _ _ _ _ _ S _ _ _ _ _ _ _. (v. 41)

The angel stood near this: _ _ T _ _ _. (v. 11)

How Mary came to see Elizabeth: _ U _ _ _ _ _ _. (v. 39)

Zechariah's team was called a _ _ _ V _ _ _ _ _ _. (v. 8)

A leaping place for the baby! W _ _ _ _. (v. 41)

"In a loud voice she . . . _ X _ _ _ _ _ _ _ _." (v. 42)

A clue to Zechariah's and Elizabeth's age: Y _ _ _ _ _. (v. 7)

The priest at the center of this incident: Z _ _ _ _ _ _ _ _ _. (v. 1)

MARY:
HANDMAID OF THE LORD

LESSON 2

Dec
8

WHY TEACH THIS LESSON?

Should private conduct have any bearing on suitability for a public leadership role? Does "character count"? Unfortunately, those who think that character does indeed count seem to be in the minority, as most people base their votes on party labels, campaign promises, and sound bites rather than issues of private virtue.

This certainly isn't the way God operates. In the Scriptures we see him selecting leaders based on what's in the heart (e.g., 1 Samuel 16:7). At times this results in what seems to be some rather astonishing choices. Think of the one whom God chose to be the mother of the Messiah: a lowly peasant girl, from a town of little account, located in a backwater province on the fringe of the Roman Empire. Today's lesson will challenge us to look past our own external circumstances to see what truly lies in the depths of our hearts. When we examine own character, do we see the type of person God can use for service?

INTRODUCTION

A. PORTRAIT OF MARY

When I was in my teens, I corresponded with a cousin of my sister-in-law in New Orleans, Louisiana. I never met her. I did not talk to her on the telephone—and that was long before the computer age and E-mail. She sent me her picture and wrote me several letters. Still it was possible, with what evidence I had, to know that she was a pretty, young woman. She was real.

Sometimes it is hard to think of people in the Bible as being real. Like the evidence that my correspondent was real, the Holy Spirit-inspired Word removes all doubt of the reality of Mary. With the details recorded in the Scriptures, Mary the mother of Jesus can come to life in our understanding. We all can form a portrait of Mary as we bring those details together.

B. LESSON BACKGROUND

The Lesson Background dovetails with last week's lesson. As we continue reflecting on New Testament personalities involved in the Messiah's coming, some of these have common connections. Luke 1:24 tells us that Elizabeth has conceived a child and hidden herself for five months. Our attention then is focused quickly on a betrothed virgin, Mary, living in Nazareth in Galilee. The text leads us to consider the type of person she is and the role she has in God's plan in sending the Messiah as Savior.

I. MARY VISITED (LUKE 1:26-33)

Gabriel is mentioned by name four times in the Bible (Daniel 8:16; 9:21; Luke 1:19, 26). He is one of only two angels mentioned by name at all. Apparently, his role is very significant. Certainly, his announcement to Mary is!

DEVOTIONAL READING:
PSALM 146
BACKGROUND SCRIPTURE:
LUKE 1:26-56
PRINTED TEXT:
LUKE 1:26-38, 46-49

LESSON AIMS

After participating in this lesson, each student will be able to:

1. Cite the details concerning God's call of Mary and her significant response.

2. Express confidence that seemingly impossible tasks undertaken in submission to God's will are possible.

3. Express a commitment born of faith and hope to do what God is wanting to accomplish in his or her life.

KEY VERSES

"Do not be afraid, Mary, you have found favor with God. You will be with child and give birth to a son, and you are to give him the name Jesus."—Luke 1:30, 31

Display this visual at the beginning of your session. Leave it on display until after lesson 4.

A. MARY INTRODUCED (vv. 26, 27)

26. In the sixth month, God sent the angel Gabriel to Nazareth, a town in Galilee.

It is one thing to have an unexpected visit from a friend or a neighbor. It is quite another thing to be visited by an *angel* that was *sent* from *God*. What an occasion this visit of the angel *Gabriel* is to Mary! The meaning of the name *Gabriel*, "man of God," may have come to her mind. Here in her very presence is the "man of God," God's messenger.

The visit of the angel to Mary is about six months after the appearance to Zechariah (see last week's lesson). One might expect an angel to appear to a priest in glorious Jerusalem. But to have Gabriel appear in *Nazareth*—and to a young peasant woman (cf. Luke 1:48)—is most surprising. In Mary's time Nazareth is an insignificant village of fewer than two thousand inhabitants. Though we know little of her past, it is Mary's future role that is now at issue.

27. . . . to a virgin pledged to be married to a man named Joseph, a descendant of David. The virgin's name was Mary.

For a Jewish family in Bible times, the parents normally arrange the marriages for their children. Such marriages have three segments. Mary is in the first part: she has been *pledged* to *Joseph*. This betrothal agreement is as binding as we think of marriage itself. It requires divorce to break it. The next segment is a time of testing. During this period the groom or his representative will negotiate the dowry with the bride's father, and the dowry money will then be paid. Then, finally, comes the marriage feast, which is a public recognition of the agreement that already has been established. The couple does not live together until then. The betrothal usually precedes the wedding by about a year.

The groom, Joseph, can claim King *David* as an ancestor. Thus the child to be born of *Mary* will have by adoptive right the legal connection with the royal heritage of the house of David. (Next week's lesson will focus on Joseph and his role.)

Finally, this verse emphasizes that Mary is a virgin. From a distance of two thousand years, we may think first of the purity of her life as she looks forward to her marriage. We may also reflect on the fact that God knows the quality of the one he is calling to be his handmaid. Most importantly, we recall the prophecy of Isaiah 7:14, "The virgin will be with child . . . and will call him Immanuel."

B. MARY GREETED (vv. 28-30)

28. The angel went to her and said, "Greetings, you who are highly favored! The Lord is with you."

The divine communication becomes real and clear with the greeting to Mary. This is the heavenly greeting to the noble virgin who is to become the mother of the Messiah, Jesus. What is about to be offered is by the grace and favor of God. She is chosen in preference to all other women on earth at the time.

It means something to be chosen. Do you not recall those times as children when the group you were a part of was going to play ball? The teacher appointed two to choose their teams. What a thrill it was if you were the first one to be chosen! But that thrill was by no means to be compared with the favor that God displays in choosing Mary. Nor does it compare with the blessing that we Christians have as the chosen people of God. Being "chosen" brings with it the important responsibility of personal response. This point for Mary will come later in our text.

29. Mary was greatly troubled at his words and wondered what kind of greeting this might be.

Mary's full emotional mind-set is impossible to know. Nothing like this has ever happened to her, nor has she heard of anything like it for anyone of her acquaintance. Mary finds herself on center stage, but she definitely has not asked for

WHAT DO YOU THINK?

Our lesson writer notes that "it means something to be chosen." It means someone thinks highly of you for some reason. It means you must respond in some way. What do you find most significant about being among the "chosen people of God"?

such an honor. Mary knows that with blessing comes responsibility. What will be the responsibility expected of her? Such honor she cannot immediately grasp.

"WE'LL UNDERSTAND IT BETTER BY AND BY"

Some years ago, a teenage girl went to church camp. She was asked to sing a solo for the vesper service. The campers and the counselors knew that her father had died a few months before, suddenly and unexpectedly. So they were greatly moved when she sang a song of assurance that God would someday make everything plain to her.

Mary could have sung such a song. She was perplexed at the visit of the angel. She was perplexed at the visit of the shepherds in Bethlehem (Luke 2:19). She was perplexed at the wisdom of the boy Jesus when he was in the temple at age twelve (Luke 2:42, 51). No doubt she was perplexed often during his ministry and certainly at his crucifixion. Eventually, however, she did understand. The disciples also were sometimes perplexed, but later they came to understand as well (John 12:16).

Often, we are like Mary and the disciples. We do not understand things that happen to us or to someone whom we love. Sometimes, years later perhaps, we come to understand. In other cases we will not understand until we get to Heaven. But still we believe that the old songs are correct. We believe that we will understand it better by and by, and we believe that someday he will make it plain to us. Until then we live simply by trusting him.

We live in an age when people want to understand everything fully. It takes faith, and a lot of patience to wait for the answer to our perplexity. But such faith and patience will be rewarded. If it is not at some time later in this life, then certainly it will be in the life to come. —R. C. S.

30. But the angel said to her, "Do not be afraid, Mary, you have found favor with God.

The additional greeting does not resolve the entire puzzle, but it does bring some assurance. Some kind of assurance to be unafraid is common in Old Testament revelations (e.g., Joshua 1:9; Judges 6:23; Jeremiah 1:8; cf. Luke 1:13). Mary joins the list of those in the Bible who have received the *favor* of God in connection with the roles he has given them. These people of faith become models for us.

C. MARY INSTRUCTED (vv. 31-33)

31. "You will be with child and give birth to a son, and you are to give him the name Jesus.

Here the angel reveals a new and more amazing dimension. Mary, a virgin (vv. 27, 34), is to conceive a *child!* To Mary's Aramaic ears, the name *Jesus* is the equivalent of "Joshua." This Old Testament name means "the Lord is salvation" or "the one who saves."

The full import of this *name* probably is more than young Mary can grasp. The message of the Old Testament has brought the knowledge of sin but not of the means by which God will solve that problem. Bringing together the concepts of the Messiah, his kingdom, and the forgiveness of sin is more than Mary or any of her contemporaries can do at the time. Therefore, it is necessary for Mary to receive this revelation with some amplification (cf. Matthew 1:21). God gives as much information as he deems sufficient at the time, enough to strengthen Mary's faith as his special servant.

32. "He will be great and will be called the Son of the Most High. The Lord God will give him the throne of his father David.

From her training in the home, Mary knows that there had been a continuous line of kings descended from *David*—first for the united kingdom and then for

WHAT DO YOU THINK?

What honor or position have you received that created a sobering responsibility? How did your faith help you to handle both the honor and the responsibility in a successful manner? Be as specific as you can.

WHAT DO YOU THINK?

Mary probably did not grasp the full significance of Jesus as Savior—at least, not right away. Many people today do not grasp the significance, either. In a culture that rejects the idea of moral absolutes, the concept of sin is foreign to many today—so people do not realize their need to be saved from sin.

How can we impress on people the need for salvation and the truth that Jesus is the only one who can provide it? Since "story" seems especially important today, how may "personal testimonies" play a part? How can you tell your "story" in such a way as to lead another to Christ?

HOW TO SAY IT

Aramaic. AIR-uh-MAY-ik.
Elizabeth. Ih-LIH-zuh-beth.
Gabriel. GAY-bree-ul.
Galilee. GAL-uh-lee.
Isaiah. Eye-ZAY-uh.
Jeremiah. Jair-uh-MY-uh.
Joshua. JOSH-yew-uh.
Magnificat. Mag-NIF-ih-cot.
Messiah. Meh-SYE-uh.
Nazareth. NAZ-uh-reth.
Zechariah. ZEK-uh-RYE-uh.

Judah after the kingdom was divided—until the Babylonian captivity in 586 B.C. Perhaps Mary can see the angel's message as a prediction that this *Son* will complete that succession, and bring the kingdom to a climax! Somehow, this one will uniquely be *the Son of the Most High.* (See Jeremiah 23:5, 6.)

33. . . . and he will reign over the house of Jacob forever; his kingdom will never end."

The hard part for Mary and others at that time is catching the spiritual meaning. It is a spiritual *kingdom* that is envisioned for the Messiah and his people, the true Israel of God (cf. Galatians 6:16). (Even after Jesus spends more than three years with his disciples, this overriding spiritual element will be hard to grasp; see Acts 1:6.) The concept of an everlasting kingdom is hard to fathom. Again, here is where faith steps into the picture.

KINGDOMS RISE AND WANE

Those of us who grew up singing four-stanza hymns may remember that we often skipped the third one. However, the third stanza of the hymn "Onward Christian Soldiers" may be the most important of the entire song. Part of it says, "Crowns and thrones may perish, Kingdoms rise and wane. . . ." History bears out that truth. The kingdom won by Alexander the Great did not last as long as it took him to win it. The Roman Empire is gone.

In the heyday of the Austro-Hungarian Empire, the design for the Hofburg Palace in Vienna featured the letters a, e, i, o, and u. Not only are they our vowels, they also stood for a phrase that translates as "Austria Will Live Forever." But that great empire is no more, and today Austria is one of the smaller countries in Europe. Once it was said that the sun never set on the British Empire, but that empire is gone as well. Hitler's "Third Reich" is only a bad memory. The mighty Soviet Union fell apart in the late 1980s.

Against the background of these fleeting earthly kingdoms stands the promise of today's lesson: "his kingdom will never end." It began with 120 people (Acts 1:15) and now numbers millions. It speaks a thousand languages, is seen on every continent, and includes people of "every tribe and tongue and nation." No movement has ever spread so far, or grown so fast—and no kingdom will endure except his kingdom. So it is good to set Luke 1:33 of today's lesson alongside the entirety of the third stanza of that old hymn:

> Crowns and thrones may perish,
>   Kingdoms rise and wane,
> But the church of Jesus
>   Constant will remain;
> Gates of hell can never
>   'Gainst that Church prevail;
> We have Christ's own promise,
> And that cannot fail.

—Sabine Baring-Gould (1834–1924)

—R. C. S.

II. MARY'S RESPONSE (LUKE 1:34-38)

Some people in the Bible were speechless in the face of heavenly messages—or nearly so. (See Isaiah 6:5; Daniel 5:6; 10:15-17; Acts 9:7.) Zechariah became speechless as a result of a heavenly message (Luke 1:20). Neither is true of Mary!

A. THE QUESTION (v. 34)

34. "How will this be," Mary asked the angel, "since I am a virgin?"

Mary's question confirms the statement that she is *a virgin* (v. 27). There has been the contractual agreement (a "betrothal"), but she and Joseph have not yet completed the marriage process. Nor have they had relations outside the marriage bond. She knows that no conception of a child could have taken place yet—it is not humanly possible. Such a reaction from Mary is very understandable. Thus, she needs further explanation before she can give the angel her full reply.

B. THE ANSWER (vv. 35-37)
35. The angel answered, "The Holy Spirit will come upon you, and the power of the Most High will overshadow you. So the holy one to be born will be called the Son of God.

Gabriel answers Mary's "how?" by telling "Who." *The Holy Spirit* will bring this about. Mary knows there have been occasions when God has equipped his people for special tasks by the power of his Spirit (Exodus 31:3; Numbers 11:17, 25; Judges 6:34; 1 Samuel 10:6, 10). By enabling Mary to conceive a child while she is still a virgin, God's Spirit brings together the physical and the spiritual means to cause what we call "the incarnation": God in the flesh (John 1:14). The whole matter is another way of God's demonstration of his presence among his people (Matthew 1:23).

All of this helps us as readers to know that this *Son of God* has his beginning now only in the sense that this is a unique manifestation of God as Son. He has existed from all eternity (John 1:1). He becomes flesh (John 1:14) in Mary's womb to be a unique manifestation of God as Son (1 Timothy 3:16). There never has been a greater communication of who God is and of his care for us. The divine and the human will now be teamed together to accomplish God's purposes. Praise God!

36. "Even Elizabeth your relative is going to have a child in her old age, and she who was said to be barren is in her sixth month.

To help Mary understand this whole setting, the angel Gabriel gives additional revelation concerning the status of her *relative* Elizabeth. Their exact relationship is not clear by the term in the text. Since *Elizabeth* and Mary are of the tribes of Levi and Judah, respectively, their kinship is on the mother's side for at least one of the women. Perhaps Elizabeth is Mary's mother's aunt or some other, more distant, relative.

The important thing is not the human aspect, but the divine. God has acted for Elizabeth; he has nullified that which had been impossible for her. He can still do anything, even something greater. He can cause a virgin to conceive a child!

37. "For nothing is impossible with God."

Words with the very same impact are given to Sarah in Genesis 18:14. Even though Mary probably knows that passage, it must be hard for her to think of having such a place of favor with God. In the next verse Mary demonstrates greater faith than either her ancestor Sarah or her contemporary Zechariah (Luke 1:18-20).

C. THE COMMITMENT (v. 38)
38. "I am the Lord's servant," Mary answered. "May it be to me as you have said." Then the angel left her.

Mary submits to the Lord's will with words similar to those found in some Old Testament settings. (See the responses of Hannah in 1 Samuel 1:18 and Abigail in 1 Samuel 25:41.) In place of potential shame over a premarital pregnancy stands faith and submission. She has been God's *servant* in the past, and she is ready for God's role for her in the future. Mary surrenders her whole being to God's will.

III. MARY'S MESSAGE (LUKE 1:46-49)
After Mary accepted the angel's announcement with faith and commitment to God's will, she went to visit Elizabeth. Knowing what the angel had told her about Elizabeth's pregnancy, this would be an occasion to strengthen her faith. Still, she did not know how all this revelation would fit together in God's plan.

WHAT DO YOU THINK?

Mary's obedience and submission challenge us. What risks are we willing to take in order to comply with God's commands to live the gospel and to take the gospel to others?

PRAYER

Almighty God, your workings are beyond our comprehension. Yet help us, through the model of Mary, to see how you can work through us in accomplishing your purposes in your kingdom. In Jesus' name, amen.

OPTION

Use the reproducible activity "Mary's Song—and Mine" on page 138 to explore the full text of Mary's song and to help your students make a similar expression of praise.

THOUGHT TO REMEMBER

God does his work today through willing hearts and hands.

WHAT DO YOU THINK?

As the mother of the Messiah, Mary stands apart from all other women in history. Even so, the details about her are amazingly brief. God's regard for her shows she has his approval. With that approval there is the understanding that she will be remembered beyond her death because of the part she has in his plan to bring salvation to the world. What encouragement does that offer us today in our service?

[Consider 1 Corinthians 15: 58; Galatians 6:9; and Hebrews 6:10 in your discussion.]

When she arrived, she was further amazed at the special greeting given by Elizabeth (cf. last week's lesson).

A. HER PRAISE (vv. 46, 47)

46, 47. And Mary said:
   "My soul glorifies the Lord
     and my spirit rejoices in God my Savior.

Just as Elizabeth has delivered a message by a power more than her own, Mary responds with a declaration that shows that her thoughts and longings are ever directed toward God (Luke 1:46-55). This hymn of praise—often called "the Magnificat" from the first word in the Latin translation—shows us a wide range of spiritual comprehension. There are elements here that reflect thoughts presented in the Psalms and in the song of Hannah (1 Samuel 2:1-10).

Verses 46 and 47 show the Hebrew parallelism that is common in the Psalms. Notice how the second line (v. 47) essentially repeats the first line (v. 46) in different words.

B. HER STATUS (v. 48)

48. . . . for he has been mindful
   of the humble state of his servant.
 From now on all generations will call me blessed.

Mary sees herself as a nobody whom God has made into a somebody by his grace. Her faith, reflected in her utterance, gives her the courage to accept her role. So sure is she of God's promises she speaks as if everything is already completed. (In that way her statement is like the messages of the Old Testament prophets.) God's plan is in motion!

Mary knows she is blessed, and that results in obvious joy. But this joy is not the type that is connected with entertainment or social events that delight one's ego. It is a deeper satisfaction, for it is the Spirit of God that brings true joy: "The Spirit himself testifies with our spirit that we are God's children" (Romans 8:16).

C. HIS POWER (v. 49)

49. . . . for the Mighty One has done great things for me—
   holy is his name.

Mary knows the reality of God's goodness and greatness. She knows the message of Psalm 103:17, "But from everlasting to everlasting the Lord's love is with those who fear him, and his righteousness with their children's children." In spite of human frailty, God's servant can know God's greatness as she yields herself to his power. Thinking on her own insignificance, she acknowledges that God alone is all in all. His name, reflecting his whole character, is beyond expression! The spiritual insight in the Magnificat reassures us today of the power of the Almighty.

CONCLUSION

When Mary responds to God's call with willingness, the result is a means for God to accomplish his purposes. Mary is a great model as a servant of the Lord.

In that respect, this event in the life of Mary is not an end in itself. We are made aware that there is an enduring principle involved because the Word of God confronts us, too. This Word contains a personal message for us. Our response to that message will reflect our commitment to Christ and his purposes for the church. As with Mary's life as a whole, there may be both joy and sorrow connected with our willing response. Each of us has a unique part to play in God's plan as we prepare ourselves for "any good work" (2 Timothy 2:21).

Discovery Learning

This page contains an alternative lesson plan emphasizing learning activities. Classes desiring such student involvement will find these suggestions helpful. The next page is a reproducible activity page to further enhance discovery learning.

LEARNING GOALS

After this lesson each student will be able to:

1. Cite the details concerning God's call of Mary and her significant response.

2. Express confidence that seemingly impossible tasks undertaken in submission to God's will are possible.

3. Express a commitment born of faith and hope to do what God is wanting to accomplish in his or her life.

INTO THE LESSON

Prepare a visual with the following open-ended sentences. (Or refer students to the appropriate page in the student handbook, *NIV Bible Student*.)

1. A very difficult time for me to be submissive to God is when _____.

2. A person who models a submissive spirit to God is _____ (name) because _____.

3. Being submissive to God's will is easier to talk about than to do because _____.

4. It is easier/harder (choose one) for me to be submissive to God today than ten years ago because _____.

Ask class members to work in groups of three or four. Each person in the group may respond to any of the statements except number 1. Allow about six to eight minutes for these responses. Then ask everyone to identify an answer to statement 1. (Students do not need to share these with their groups.) Make the transition to Bible study by saying, "We all have areas of our lives that we may find difficult to submit to God. However, as we glimpse Mary's spirit, we may find encouragement and help in learning this godly trait."

INTO THE WORD

Give each of three readers a copy of today's text (Luke 1:26-38, 46-49). Have each copy marked to highlight the part of a narrator, the angel, or Mary. Ask these students to read the text by reading the highlighted parts.

Explain how this lesson relates to last week's study.

Lead a discussion of the following questions. (Those with an asterisk [*] are also in the student book.)

*1. The lesson commentary says, "One might expect an angel to appear to a priest in glorious Jerusalem. But to have Gabriel appear in *Nazareth*—and to a young peasant woman (cf. Luke 1:48)—is most surprising." What do you think the writer meant by this distinction? What does this say to you?

2. Verse 27 speaks of Mary's engagement. What can you tell us about the process of engagement and marriage in this culture? How did this cause concern for Mary and Joseph? (Use the lesson commentary to clarify answers.)

*3. It was prophesied that the Messiah was to be born of a virgin. (Write Isaiah 7:14 on a poster and display it). Why do you think God decided to make Jesus' birth supernatural?

Ask the class to put themselves in Mary's place. Mary must have been surprised, puzzled, honored, humbled, and frightened. Read Luke 1:28-37. Then, in pairs or small groups, jot notes on the questions you imagine in Mary's mind. Allow groups to share their answers.

Remind them of Mary's response: "I am the Lord's servant." Ask what Mary was implying by calling herself that. After their responses, identify two Old Testament women who used that title for themselves: Hannah (1 Samuel 1:18) and Abigail (1 Samuel 25:41).

Ask the class, "How did Mary's willingness to be God's servant make it possible for the 'impossible' to happen—the virgin birth?" Ask also, "Why does God not work apart from the will of the person he chooses as his servant?"

INTO LIFE

Prepare and display two posters. The first should say "God's Angel+Willing Women=Means for God to Accomplish His Purpose." Explain the meaning of this statement as you display the poster. Then put up the second poster, reading "God's Word+Committed Christian=Vessel for God to Use." Use the commentary for ideas to emphasize how Mary's experience reveals this principle for life today. Then remind the class of the opening exercise where they identified times when they have a hard time submitting to God's will. The final activity on the reproducible page (138), "My Journey in Submission," will work well at this point.

Ask small groups to pray together. Give three pieces of paper to each, asking for one person in each group to pray about one of the suggestions on the papers: #1: thank God for speaking to us through his Word, the Bible; thank him for his wisdom; #2: offer God your promise to try to trust him and his wisdom more and more in your daily life; #3: ask God to work in our lives, helping us to learn to be submissive to him and willing to do his will.

Mary's Song—and Mine!

Mary's "Magnificat" or song is a wonderful expression of her joy, submission, and faith. It is a grand prayer expressing how Mary reacts to what God has done. Use Luke 1:46-55 to record Mary's beautiful words of praise and submission. Write these in the first column below.

You also have reason to praise God. Use some of the lines of Mary's song to create your own expression of worship. Use the second column to fill in the blanks a second time from your own experience with God.

	MARY'S SONG	*MY SONG*
My soul		
And my spirit		
For he has		
His mercy		
He has performed		
He has brought down		
But has lifted up		
He has filled		
He has helped his servant		

My Journey in Submission

Most of us do not learn complete submission to the will of God immediately. We begin to turn over more and more of our lives as we journey with him. Look back on your walk with Christ. Try to remember areas of your life and practices that you've learned to submit to him. Jot these down as you think of them. Then go back and try to number them in the order (as much as possible) you learned to give them over to God. Finally, note one area you are presently working on (or should be working on) surrendering to our Savior.

JOSEPH: A RIGHTEOUS MAN

LESSON 3

DEVOTIONAL READING:
ISAIAH 11:1-5

BACKGROUND SCRIPTURE:
MATTHEW 1:18-25; 2:13-23

PRINTED TEXT:
MATTHEW 1:18-21, 24, 25; 2:13-15, 19-21, 23

Dec
15

WHY TEACH THIS LESSON?

The well-known hymn "Trust and Obey" by John H. Sammis (1846–1919) enjoys enduring popularity. Its five stanzas speak of the many blessings that come from the twin responses of trust and obedience, two words that sum up the life of Joseph of Nazareth. As you read today's lesson, you will see one or the other of those responses in every verse. In some verses you see both at once.

Like Joseph, we need both qualities. Like Joseph, we trust God even when we do not understand fully, even when we cannot see every detail of what lies ahead. Like Joseph, our obedience is the proof of our trust. When we are convinced that God does all things for our good and that God is the one in charge of history, then we will trust and obey without trying to second-guess him. We all need help in this area from time-to-time, and Joseph is just the model for us.

INTRODUCTION

A. PORTRAIT OF JOSEPH

Getting to know Joseph, the carpenter of Nazareth, is important. The portrait given us in the Scriptures may seem sketchy. It lacks many of the details that our twenty-first-century minds might desire. But the picture presented is clear in that he is the proper man to be Mary's husband and the guardian of her child Jesus. His genealogy emphasizes that he is descended from the line of King David. Such lineage is very important to the Jewish people because of their heritage and their hope. Their redemption lies in this promised one, even though for the most part they think in terms of a political, earthly deliverance (cf. Acts 1:6).

Who is the person you have as the model of a righteous person? What woman? What man? Since we desire to be righteous before God, we need to seek out models in whose lives we see that the gospel really produces desired results. If we have had God-fearing parents, they were our first models. As we grew, our experiences have resulted in contacts with many others who have become important as we admired their lifestyles. Today's lesson offers us another role model. It is Joseph, a "just" or righteous man. His responses toward God's message for him challenge us to be righteous as well.

B. LESSON BACKGROUND

Flesh-and-blood people, with all their strengths and weaknesses, are important to God in achieving his plans for humanity. In fact, it is impressive to observe that Matthew begins his account of the life of Christ with due consideration for the role of Joseph. We are not told his age, his education, the details of his parents and home life, or other matters that our curiosity might desire. Those issues are not significant to Matthew's purpose.

What Matthew wants to bring to our attention is the quality of man that Joseph is. That quality is revealed by the way he deals with issues that call for decisions on his part. In these matters, Matthew lets us know that God trusts Joseph with divine direction. Such direction does not always take the same form,

LESSON AIMS

After participating in this lesson, each student will be able to:

1. Recall the details of God's call to Joseph and his significant response.

2. Tell how the responses Joseph made to divine direction typify how modern believers should respond to the will of God.

3. State one way he or she can view the challenge to one's faith to follow the model of Joseph.

KEY VERSES

Joseph . . . did what the angel of the Lord had commanded him and took Mary home as his wife. But he had no union with her until she gave birth to a son. And he gave him the name Jesus.
—Matthew 1:24, 25.

Post this visual at the beginning of the session. Note how Joseph's life demonstrates righteousness.

WHAT DO YOU THINK?

In our day, pregnancy outside of marriage is all too common. Often there is little disgrace or stigma with the situation. How should the church deal with this situation today? How can we, like Joseph, blend compassion with taking a stand for morality?

[Use Acts 15:20; 1 Corinthians 5:1-11; 6:9-20; 2 Corinthians 2:6-11; and Galatians 5:19 to guide your discussion.]

but in each circumstance Joseph shows himself to be a man after God's own heart. By his responses, Joseph's portrait is that of a righteous man.

I. JOSEPH'S CRUCIAL DECISION (MATTHEW 1:18-21, 24, 25)

Living in a fallen world as we do, we are sometimes forced to choose between uncomfortable alternatives. Joseph seems to face just such a sobering choice.

A. PONDERING A SOBER REALITY (vv. 18, 19)

18. This is how the birth of Jesus Christ came about: His mother Mary was pledged to be married to Joseph, but before they came together, she was found to be with child through the Holy Spirit.

Mary was pledged to be married to Joseph. This pledging is much more than what we commonly think of as an "engagement." For the ancient Jew marriage vows are exchanged at the time of the betrothal, and divorce is required to break them. There is usually about a year until the bride takes residence at the husband's house. During this time, her purity is established and the dowry paid. Residency with the husband—and physical union that consummates the marriage—does not take place until after the wedding feast.

During this interval Mary is found to be *with child*. We know from Luke's account how this has come to be. (See last week's lesson.) But Matthew delays explanation, and the reader puts him- or herself in Joseph's place to wonder how it has happened.

19. Because Joseph her husband was a righteous man and did not want to expose her to public disgrace, he had in mind to divorce her quietly.

Joseph evidently believes that Mary has been with another man. This would be adultery under the laws of betrothal. Has Mary not explained the situation to Joseph? Has she explained but Joseph found the story incredible? These are questions we cannot answer. Either way, at this point Mary can do nothing but trust God to ensure her safety and well-being.

While adultery carries the death penalty under the law of Moses (Deuteronomy 22:23, 24), such a penalty is rarely invoked in Joseph's day. As the New Testament era dawns, Joseph is freer in his options and can give Mary either a *public* or a private *divorce*. By choosing a private, quiet divorce, Joseph will be conforming to the law while being compassionate at the same time.

Joseph's compassion in not wanting *to expose* Mary to *public disgrace* is now at odds with the fact that he is *a righteous man*. On the one hand, he wants to make the situation as easy for her as possible because of his concern for her well-being. But on the other hand, the fact that he is righteous (or just) makes him unwilling to go ahead with the marriage, because then others would logically (but wrongly) conclude that he is the other guilty party in this out-of-wedlock pregnancy.

Surely Joseph prays much about all this before he acts. As his son James will later write, "The prayer of a righteous man is powerful and effective" (James 5:16). God's answer follows.

B. RECEIVING DIVINE DIRECTION (vv. 20, 21)

20. But after he had considered this, an angel of the Lord appeared to him in a dream and said, "Joseph son of David, do not be afraid to take Mary home as your wife, because what is conceived in her is from the Holy Spirit.

Joseph has decided already on his course of action (v. 19) when *an angel* intervenes with a message from God. There are several elements in that message that catch his attention. First, the angel addresses him as *Joseph son of David*. This reminder of his lineage to King David perhaps will bring to Joseph's mind (after he awakens from the sleep and its dream) the ancient promise of a Messiah to solve Israel's despair—a Messiah from David's line (Isaiah 16:5; 55:3; Jeremiah 33:14-17). But he undoubtedly does not yet have the comprehension to put all the circumstances together in a way that results in a clear understanding for him in his dilemma with *Mary*.

Joseph must clearly see, however, that this divine announcement is a means to reinforce his faith and to help him to act with confidence in doing God's will. Perhaps Joseph's faith will be strengthened after he awakens and recalls the accounts of divine messengers that God has sent to others in times long past (cf. Genesis 16:7-12; 22:11-18; Exodus 3:1–4:17). His fear of what other people might say will not be as important as what God communicates. God reassures him that Mary is pure, even if she is pregnant. He is to take her as his *wife*. He is to provide for and protect her as her husband. He is to accept the fact that God is the one who has brought about this conception.

21. *"She will give birth to a son, and you are to give him the name Jesus, because he will save his people from their sins."*

The unfolding revelation provides Joseph with greater insight regarding his role in God's plan. Joseph is to have parental responsibility as reflected in the instruction on naming the Child *Jesus*. Joseph knows, of course, that this name means "the Lord is salvation." But how will it be possible for this Child to *save his people from their sins*? The divine messenger doesn't say. Only God knows how it will all be resolved. He gives Joseph only what he needs to know at this point in the unfolding life of Christ.

In the verses not included in the printed text, Matthew reminds the reader of the Messianic promise in Isaiah 7:14 concerning the virgin birth. God provided deliverance from enemies in Isaiah's time. Such a deliverance becomes a "type" of the deliverance God provides in sending Jesus as Savior. He is also Immanuel, "God with us" (Matthew 1:23).

C. RESPONDING WITH HUMBLE OBEDIENCE (vv. 24, 25)

24. *When Joseph woke up, he did what the angel of the Lord had commanded him and took Mary home as his wife.*

As Mary obeys in Luke 1:38, so *Joseph* responds in faith based on a message from God. The betrothal period ends, and Joseph takes Mary to live with him in his home. Jesus will thus be the legitimate son and heir to the throne of David (Matthew 1:1, 16; cf. Deuteronomy 23:2).

Joseph's actions are like those of other men and women of the Old Testament who obeyed God's call. Such responses may seem out of harmony with common sense. But Matthew wants his readers to catch a clear portrait of Joseph, an obedient and righteous man, as evidenced by his response to God's call.

Joseph thus serves as a model for us in how we can respond properly to God's message. Our roles are not the same as his, and today God communicates his will for us in the pages of Scripture rather than dreams. Even so, we also have a place in God's plan to bring his saving gospel to all the world today. People are still the instruments to accomplish God's saving work.

OUT OF THE SCRIPT

A little church was having the final rehearsal for the Christmas pageant. Then distressing news came to the director. The little boy who was to play the part of Joseph was sick and would not be able to be in the pageant. The director said, "I guess we'll just have to write Joseph out of the script."

WHAT DO YOU THINK?

How many names and titles of Jesus can you recall? What is significant about each name?

WHAT DO YOU THINK?

Have you ever had to choose between obedience and "common sense"? How did you handle the situation? What did you learn from it?

Sometimes that is what we do. We focus entirely on the other "players" in the drama and fail to pay attention to Joseph. If God chose Mary with care, we may be certain that he took into consideration the man to be her husband. After all, he would be the man who would fill the role of father through the years of Jesus' childhood. If the character of Mary was the first consideration in God's choice, the character of Joseph must have been the close second. So we do well today to pay attention to Joseph. What a great example he provides for a Father's Day sermon! What a great role model! What a great example for family life and for the godly home! What a great example he is for anyone, father or not.

All of us face situations where we need to show kindness, where we must trust even when we cannot understand. We all face situations where we must take the first step without knowing what the next step is going to be. We know so little about this carpenter from Nazareth, but what we do know warms our hearts, and encourages us to be better than we are. —R. C. S.

25. But he had no union with her until she gave birth to a son. And he gave him the name Jesus.

The phrase *had no union with her* makes clear that Joseph did not have any sexual relations with Mary until after the birth of *Jesus*. The phrase that begins with the word *until* lets us safely assume that Mary and Joseph enjoyed a normal husband and wife relationship after Jesus' birth. (Jesus' siblings are mentioned in Mark 6:3.) Joseph "officially" gives Jesus his *name* eight days after his birth (Luke 2:21).

II. JOSEPH'S PARENTAL ROLE (MATTHEW 2:13-15, 19-21, 23)

The birth of Jesus now draws the ire of a petty tyrant. Although this threat is a deadly challenge to the young family, it is also an occasion for a new father to demonstrate his obedience to God once again.

A. SECOND DIVINE DIRECTION (vv. 13-15)

13. When they had gone, an angel of the Lord appeared to Joseph in a dream. "Get up," he said, "take the child and his mother and escape to Egypt. Stay there until I tell you, for Herod is going to search for the child to kill him."

They refers to the wise men (or "Magi") of Matthew 2:1-12. After these men conclude their visit to see *the child*, the one who is "King of the Jews" (2:2), Joseph receives a second divine direction. *Herod* the Great has interviewed the wise men about their quest, and he is greatly troubled (2:3). When Herod is upset, everyone knows that someone will pay. Herod is a ruthless ruler, caring for no one but himself. His position of power is paramount. If that is threatened, not even his wives or his sons are safe.

God providentially directs the wise men not to return to Herod, but to go to their own country another way (2:12). Failing in his attempt to get the information he desires through the wise men, Herod is furious. To "play it safe," he decides to get rid of any baby who could be a future threat to his throne: he orders the death of all infants two years old and younger in Bethlehem and the surrounding area (2:16).

Yet there is a power in place greater than that of Herod. God takes care of his Son by sending an *angel* to Joseph *in a dream* with specific instructions. The border of *Egypt* is about sixty miles from Bethlehem, or a three-day journey. At this time a colony of about a million Jews lives there. They may be descendants of those who settled there in Jeremiah's time and at other periods (1 Kings 11:40; Jeremiah 26:21-23; 43:7).

Egypt, once a place of refuge (Genesis 46), became a place of oppression for God's people prior to Moses' day. But for Joseph and his family, it is once again a safe haven. God is making sure of that, but it is still important for Joseph to carry out his parental role as family protector and provider.

14. So he got up, took the child and his mother during the night and left for Egypt.

Having received the instruction, Joseph knows he must react immediately. They begin their journey at *night* because delay can mean the death of *the child*, for whose care he is responsible. Providentially, the gifts from the wise men will provide for their needs in the days ahead. Sometimes it is only "after the fact" that we have the insight to recognize the providential hand of God in meeting our needs and in providing wisdom. The importance of this Child is seen in the fact that he is mentioned before *his mother* (also in 2:13, 20, 21).

15. . . . where he stayed until the death of Herod. And so was fulfilled what the Lord had said through the prophet: "Out of Egypt I called my son."

The Jewish settlement in *Egypt* will welcome Joseph and his family, but that place is not to be a permanent residence for them. Just how long they will stay we cannot tell. *The death of Herod* can be dated as March of 4 B.C., probably within just a few months of Jesus' birth. We do not know how many months or years Joseph waited after that before the Lord told him to return to the land of Israel.

Matthew reminds his readers that Joseph's response to the divine direction makes the exodus of the children of Israel a "type" of this event: "Out of Egypt I called my son" (Hosea 11:1). The deliverance from bondage in Egypt through the leadership of Moses over fourteen centuries previously will be overshadowed by the deliverance for the Christ child, and, more significantly, the deliverance from eternal death through the Christ as Savior from sin.

B. THIRD DIVINE DIRECTION (vv. 19, 20)

19. After Herod died, an angel of the Lord appeared in a dream to Joseph in Egypt.

This is now the fourth *dream* mentioned in the book of Matthew (see 1:20; 2:12, 13), and the third dream noting an *angel of the Lord* (see 1:20; 2:13). Even though *Herod* the Great has *died*, Herod Archelaus, the worst of his sons, is now ruling in Judea (2:22). Returning to Bethlehem would not be the safest thing for this young family to do. But whatever the direction God has for *Joseph*, we will see him ready to obey.

20. . . . and said, "Get up, take the child and his mother and go to the land of Israel, for those who were trying to take the child's life are dead."

Exactly who *are dead* (other than Herod himself) is hard to determine. The plural *those* may be a tie-in to Exodus 4:19 where we see Moses being directed to return *to* Egypt after threats against his life disappear. On the other hand, they may include Herod's oldest son Antipater, whom Herod had executed shortly before his own death. (A saying that circulated stated that it was better to be one of Herod's pigs than one of his sons.) In any case, we will continue to see Joseph trusting God's direction.

C. PARENTAL RESPONSE AND DIVINE CONFIRMATION (vv. 21, 23)

21. So he got up, took the child and his mother and went to the land of Israel.

Again, we are not given the details connected with this journey. The main point that presents itself is Joseph's responsible reaction. Joseph trusts the all-knowing God. God has directed him in the past, and he knows that God will not fail him in whatever tests are ahead as he fulfills his parental role. Verse 22

WHAT DO YOU THINK?

When have you looked back on a situation and believed God's providence had been at work— even if you did not recognize it at the time?

DAILY BIBLE READINGS

Monday, Dec. 9—You Have Found Favor (Luke 1:26-33)

Tuesday, Dec. 10—I Am the Lord's Servant (Luke 1:34-38)

Wednesday, Dec. 11—Elizabeth Greets Mary (Luke 1:39-45)

Thursday, Dec. 12—Mary's Song of Praise (Luke 1:46-56)

Friday, Dec. 13—I Praise God's Mighty Deeds (Psalm 71:15-21)

Saturday, Dec. 14—Great Are God's Works (Psalm 111:1-6)

Sunday, Dec. 15—Magnify the Lord With Me (Psalm 34:1-5)

WHAT DO YOU THINK?

The lesson writer says Joseph's home was a type of "greenhouse" for the kind of Child who would have an impact on the world. What characterizes a home today that is a "greenhouse" for people destined to have an impact on the world for the sake of Christ?

THOUGHT TO REMEMBER

Emulate godly role models so others will emulate you!

informs us that God further warns Joseph of the continuing danger in Judea, and as a result the young family ends up in Galilee.

23. . . . *and he went and lived in a town called Nazareth. So was fulfilled what was said through the prophets: "He will be called a Nazarene."*

Nazareth, about seventy miles north of Bethlehem, is a safe place for Joseph to take Jesus and Mary to live. Nazareth is Joseph and Mary's former home (Luke 1:26, 27; 2:4, 39). With family ties and familiar surroundings, Joseph will support his family there by working as a carpenter.

Nazareth may seem to be an unlikely place as the home of the one to be the Messiah. Being *called a Nazarene* is not a compliment (see John 1:46). There may be a reference here to various Old Testament prophecies that allude to the Messiah as being despised (cf. Isaiah 53:3; Psalm 22:6; Daniel 9:26). The word *Nazarene* also sounds like the Hebrew word that is translated as "branch" in Isaiah 11:1.

CONCLUSION

From Matthew's narrative we catch a welcome portrait of Joseph in his role as the earthly stepfather to Jesus of Nazareth. We have examined with interest those occasions where Joseph receives divine direction when crucial decisions have to be made with regard to the Child and his mother, Mary. Joseph accepts with faith and obedience his parental role and all directions from God.

It can be interesting to let our "sanctified imaginations" ponder what the home in Nazareth might have been like. The house probably was one story with a center room and other rooms adjoining. There would have been simple furniture, beds rolled up during the day, an oven, and water pots in place. Jesus, with his brothers and sisters, would have shared household duties. They would have attended the synagogue school, and they would have been taught the Law of Moses at home. Joseph may even have owned a copy of some portions of the Old Testament. Members of the household speak Aramaic and Greek, and they probably can read Hebrew. In the home Joseph is an upright man and Mary is one of the rarest of all women. Such a home would be a type of "greenhouse" for the Child who will have an impact upon generations to come—indeed, upon all of history.

The life of Joseph invites us to view his decisions against an Old Testament backdrop. Joseph's reaction to divine direction can result in judgment or blessing—it all depends on the responses that follow the messages. If there is obedience to the divine direction, then there can be blessing. But if disobedience, there is penalty and due judgment. Righteousness results from obedience, and unrighteousness is the alternative—doom, separation from God. God provides the opportunity. We make the choices.

We all are (or should be) continually concerned about doing God's will. Each new day brings life situations that call for choices. We as Christians want to make the right choices, to do what is pleasing to God. It would be easy, we think, if God would give us direct revelation as he did Joseph in this context. Or perhaps Gideon's request regarding the fleece in Judges 6:36-40 is our reason for expecting God to do the same thing for us. But remember that all do not have the same roles before God. Gideon's role as judge is one thing, and Joseph's role in caring for Jesus and Mary is another. Although none of us have such roles today, we do have the direction provided by God's Word, as well as the guiding presence of his Spirit in our lives. As we study his Word and submit our will to His, we will have the guidance we need in all choices. May Joseph serve as a model and example of obedience and righteousness to us all!

Discovery Learning

This page contains an alternative lesson plan emphasizing learning activities. Classes desiring such student involvement will find these suggestions helpful. The next page is a reproducible activity page to further enhance discovery learning.

LEARNING GOALS

After this lesson each student will be able to:

1. Recall the details of God's call to Joseph and his significant response.

2. Tell how the responses Joseph made to divine direction typify how modern believers should respond to the will of God.

3. State one way he or she can view the challenge to one's faith to follow the model of Joseph.

INTO THE LESSON

This lesson will emphasize making godly choices. As class members arrive, offer them two choices of snacks: healthful fruit (bananas, apples, oranges) and tasty (but not-so-good-for-you) pastries. Coffee and juice will also be appropriate. Do not comment on their choices.

As you begin the lesson, write or post the word *Choices* at the front of the room. Ask class members to tell about choices they have had to make recently. These may be tough choices and significant decisions, or the choices may be simple, everyday choices like whether to work late or to eat dinner with the family, or whether or not to break a diet. Allow several minutes.

Make the transition to Bible study by reminding them that life is filled with choices. Some are seemingly small and insignificant, like whether to choose healthful fruit for breakfast or tasty and fattening pastries. Other choices may be hard. One thing is certain: we are all called upon to make choices that may or may not reflect a healthy relationship with God. For those choices, however, we do have some help. Today, our help is in the form of a model. Our model could have said, "You've got to be kidding. I won't do it!" Instead, he chose to obey, and so he became an encouraging model of righteousness.

INTO THE WORD

Use the crossword puzzle from the reproducible page that follows to survey the facts of today's text.

Give each student a printed copy of Matthew 1:18-21, 24, 25; 2:13-15, 19-21, 23. Leave a margin on one side of the text for the student to make notes. Use the following exercises to explore the Word.

Background on Joseph. Use the Lesson Background to prepare remarks about the setting for Joseph's adventure. Include comments about Matthew's choice to emphasize the qualities of Joseph's character and his obedience. Also remind the class of the process of betrothal and marriage in first-century Israel. (See last week's lesson.) Explain that Joseph is called upon to make several tough choices critical to God's plan.

Clues to Joseph's Character. Ask class members (in teams or small groups) to read Matthew 1:18-21, 24, 25 and circle phrases or sentences that give clues to Joseph's character. (*Answers may include "was a righteous man," "did not want to expose her to public disgrace," "had in mind to divorce her quietly," and "took Mary home as his wife."*) Ask what character trait each phrase exemplifies (*e.g., considerate, merciful, intelligent, obedient*).

Tough Choices. Ask the groups to number the choices Joseph had to make as they read the text. Then in the margin they are to write a note on what the issue or choice was that he had to make. (*These will include verse 19, whether or not to humiliate Mary; verse 20, whether or not to obey the angel; verse 21, whether to name the baby as instructed; verse 25, whether to have sexual intercourse with Mary; 2:13, whether or not to go to Egypt; 2:20, whether or not to go back to Israel.*)

Discussion. As groups report, list these decisions on the board. Highlight the more difficult choices Joseph made by asking these questions:

Matthew 1:24: Why would this be a particularly tough choice? What are some of the issues Joseph had to face in order to make this choice?

Matthew 1:25: Why do you suppose Joseph chose not to have sexual contact with Mary until Jesus was born? Did they have intimate relations after Jesus was born? Did they have other children? (*See Matthew 13:55, 56.*)

Matthew 2:13: How is this a particularly tough choice? (*Economics, travel safety, home.*)

Matthew 2:21: Was this one of the easier choices for Joseph? Why or why not?

INTO LIFE

Display four posters. Each is to have one of the following headings: "Parents," "Work/Career," "Husband and Wife," and "Personal." Tell the class, "We are called upon to make tough choices that affect our spiritual health or the spiritual health of those around us. Brainstorm the tough choices that affect our relationship with the Lord." Note the responses on the appropriate posters. Following the exercise, ask for prayer that we, like Joseph, will be found righteous in God's eyes.

Puzzling Dreams and Guests!

It was not only Joseph of the Old Testament that found angels appearing to him in dreams. Joseph, the husband of Mary, found himself in similar circumstances many years later. Read Matthew 1:18-26; 2:13-23 and discover God's mysterious communications with a New Testament role model of obedience and trust.

ACROSS

4. Jesus would be called a _____ (2:23)
5. Herod's son (2:22)
8. Who spoke through the prophets? (1:22)
10. Joseph and family were to _____ to a far land (2:13)
11. Means "God with us" (1:23)
12. He will save people from their sins (1:21)
13. Reaction to the loss of children (2:18)
15. The prophet quoted about Bethlehem's sorrow (2:17)
16. Great weeping is heard here (2:18)
18. The wise men did this to Herod (2:16)
19. Another name for the wise men who visited Jesus (2:16)
20. Not "concocted," but " _____ " (1:20)
25. A person through whom the Lord spoke (1:22)
28. Joseph intended to do this to Mary (1:19)
29. The family's destination after leaving Egypt (2:20)

DOWN

1. Herod's intent for the Christ child (2:13)
2. Joseph had no _____ with Mary (1:25)
3. Herod's reaction to being out-smarted (2:16)
4. The final hometown for the family of Joseph (2:23)
6. The grieving woman named in prophecy (2:18)
7. A city of great joy that turned to great sorrow (2:16)
9. Joseph wished to avoid _____ for Mary (1:19)
14. Another name for "engaged" (1:18)
16. A wonderful quality of Joseph's life (1:19)
17. The source of Mary's pregnancy was the ____ _____ (1:18)
21. The refuge country for the fleeing family (2:13)
22. Another dream; another destination. This time to _____ (2:22)
23. A vehicle for an angelic message (1:20)
24. The king seeking Jesus' death (2:15)
26. Joseph was addressed as "son of _____ " (1:20)
27. Wow! Supernatural! The mother was a _____ (1:23)

MARY:
MOTHER OF THE MESSIAH

LESSON 4

WHY TEACH THIS LESSON?

Businesses compete for customers in various ways. One method is price cutting—trying to undersell the competition. And when companies try to outdo one another with such a strategy, we consumers certainly enjoy the results! But several years ago I saw a chain of pizza restaurants avoid this technique by stressing that their product was worth its higher price. Their marketing slogan was, "We have no quarrel with those who sell for less. They know what their product is worth!"

This lesson brings us to that unique time of year when we are reminded of our own true worth in the eyes of God. God doesn't use any "lowest bidder" strategy to save us from our sin. Instead, he sends his only Son into the world to pay sin's price. The Son's ministry on earth begins when the Father entrusts his care to fallible human parents. In fully surrendering their wills to God, those parents are models for us. Once we come to terms with God's efforts to rescue us from eternal destruction, we will learn to surrender our wills to him as well.

INTRODUCTION

A. PORTRAIT OF MESSIANIC MOTHERHOOD

If you were to enter our country home, built in 1969, from the entry hall you might be ushered straight ahead into the parlor or to the left to the family living area. *Parlor* may sound a bit old-fashioned to some, but I designed it to be a very functional room. At the time the house was built, I was preaching in a local church and teaching at a Bible college. There were various times when we needed that separated room for counseling, meetings, or marriage planning. Our home was always very much alive with six children and their activities; but the parlor was always in good array, ready to receive visitors.

In the center of that room is the library table, and a part of the display on it is an antique photo album, keeping with the old-time decor of the whole room. In the album are pictures of family members of generations past. Life stories can accompany those portraits. In this lesson from Luke 2, we are invited into "Luke's parlor" and given the opportunity again to see the portraits on display. This one is a favorite—Mary: Mother of the Messiah. No other woman in all history has had such a ministry in motherhood.

B. LESSON BACKGROUND

The portraits we have been examining in Luke 1 and Matthew 1 and 2 have given us opportunities to reexamine the lives of those chosen by God to fill certain roles in the advent of the Messiah. The common element that brings them together is the "fullness of the time" in God's plan to provide salvation (Galatians 4:4, 5). We note the places both men and women had. Our purpose in viewing each one has not been to take the spotlight off the Messiah, but rather to see the

DEVOTIONAL READING:
ISAIAH 9:1-7

BACKGROUND SCRIPTURE:
LUKE 2:1-20

PRINTED TEXT:
LUKE 2:1, 4-20

Dec 22

LESSON AIMS

After participating in this lesson, each student will be able to:

1. Tell how Mary—and the shepherds—acted in faith to fulfill God's plan at the birth of Jesus.

2. Describe the way God's providence was at work in the unusual decree of Caesar and the routine work of the shepherds.

3. Express confidence that God has a work for him or her.

KEY VERSE

[Mary] *gave birth to her firstborn, a son. She wrapped him in cloths and placed him in a manger, because there was no room for them in the inn.*

—Luke 2:7

ways these people and their ministries are necessary in God's plan. We want to see how these complement the ministry of the Messiah, God's anointed. Each has his or her particular importance in the overall picture. These people bring life to geographical settings. Whether it is Jerusalem, Bethlehem, Nazareth, the hill country of Judah, or even somewhere in Egypt, the places become very real as we recall the events and their characters.

All of these take on fuller dimensions when we awaken to their connections with us and to God's meeting our need in the Messiah. The coming of the Messiah was a turning point in history, as our calendars remind us. Thus, this lesson presents a climax as we view the portrait of Mary: mother of the Messiah. The prophets predicted his coming, the world awaited it, and Mary gave birth! The angels and the shepherds worshiped. All meditated on its meaning, and many became evangels. Their examples are for us to emulate.

I. GOING TO BETHLEHEM (LUKE 2:1, 4, 5)

A. TAXATION DECREE (v. 1)

1. In those days Caesar Augustus issued a decree that a census should be taken of the entire Roman world.

Luke is the only Gospel writer who dates his account by this taxation. The registration or *census* for the taxation is done every fourteen years by *Caesar Augustus*, who lives from 63 B.C. to A.D. 14. For this census each man is required to go back to the city of his ancestors.

B. BETHLEHEM REGISTRATION (vv. 4, 5)

4. So Joseph also went up from the town of Nazareth in Galilee to Judea, to Bethlehem the town of David, because he belonged to the house and line of David.

Galilee is the region around the Sea of Galilee. *Nazareth* in this area is located on the trade route that connects the coastal plain to Damascus and other points east. South of *Galilee* is Samaria, and south of that, bounded on the west by the Mediterranean Sea and on the east by the Jordan River and the Dead Sea, is *Judea*.

Bethlehem, located five miles south of Jerusalem, is the original home of King David. It was here that young David kept sheep and received Samuel's anointing about a thousand years before the birth of Christ (1 Samuel 16:4, 13). Joseph is a descendant of David, so he must return to Bethlehem to register. (Locate these sites on the map on page 121.)

This verse brings to mind two passages from the Old Testament prophets. One is Isaiah 9:1, 2. Light to dispel the darkness of the land is brought from "Galilee of the Gentiles." The other is Micah 5:2, which foretells a "ruler over Israel" to come from Bethlehem. The events we are considering in our text are reminders that these did not just happen to fulfill prophecy; but when they happened, prophecy was fulfilled.

5. He went there to register with Mary, who was pledged to be married to him and was expecting a child.

Since Mary is far along in her pregnancy, we might think that such a trip would be too strenuous for her. She is not legally required to go along, so there must be other considerations. No doubt Joseph is acting as a protective husband by keeping Mary with him, even under these circumstances. Jewish law permits midwives to travel long distances, even on the Sabbath Day, to assist delivery. So even though none is mentioned in the text, it is possible that Mary and Joseph have a midwife with them. Whatever preparations they make, Joseph and Mary cannot anticipate all that is ahead for them. We know they are not alone, for the Heavenly Father is present and ready to supply.

"Mary, you have found favor with God."

"Mary treasured up all these things and pondered them in her heart." —Luke 1:30, 2:19, NIV

Post today's visual at the beginning of the session. It is the same visual as you used for lesson 2.

II. GIVING BIRTH TO THE SAVIOR (LUKE 2:6-17)

A. IN THE FULLNESS OF TIME (vv. 6, 7)

6. While they were there, the time came for the baby to be born.

It is the "fullness of time" for the birth of the Messiah. What the Holy Spirit has equipped Mary to do is greater than the skills provided the artisans in the building of the tabernacle and all the articles of furniture for it. Yet, this is the same Holy Spirit that indwells each Christian today. The same Spirit is there but not the same manifestation because the role is different.

7. . . . and she gave birth to her firstborn, a son. She wrapped him in cloths and placed him in a manger, because there was no room for them in the inn.

We do not know the actual date of Jesus' birth. The traditional observance of December 25 cannot be traced back earlier than the fourth century A.D. However, this issue is not nearly as important as other concerns.

One important issue is that of being *firstborn*. Other children will be born to Mary, with Joseph as their natural father (cf. Matthew 13:55, 56; Galatians 1:19). James and Jude will be two of these, and they will write the two New Testament books that bear their names.

There is another factor to bear in mind with regard to the Son of Mary as *firstborn*. Not only does he have the role of firstborn in the family with the responsibilities therein, but he also is "firstborn" among many. He is the "firstborn from the dead" never to die again! As Adam headed up the human family, so does Christ head up the spiritual family as the "second Adam." (See Romans 5 and 1 Corinthians 15.) The hour of anguish for Mary in childbirth is also her hour of glory as mother of the Messiah.

The baby is cared for properly. The expression *wrapped . . . in cloths* is just one word in Greek, the original language of the text. This denotes the action of giving proper care for a newborn child. From the poor to the palace the same word can be used. The baby's crib is unusual since it is a feeding *manger* for animals, as well as the place—likely some kind of stable behind *the inn*. As early as the second century A.D. tradition designated it a cave. But again, such a detail is unimportant. Since so many have come to Bethlehem for the registration, the city is crowded; sleeping rooms are occupied. Mary and Joseph content themselves with the protection of the stable and the comfort of a manger. And all the while God is watching over them.

B. ANNOUNCED BY ANGELS (vv. 8-14)

8. And there were shepherds living out in the fields nearby, keeping watch over their flocks at night.

This is the time of year that *shepherds* watch their flocks day and *night*. In this situation, there is not the security of a sheepfold, a protected walled area. Being a shepherd is a common occupation. Shepherds are despised by many religious people at the time, since they are considered ceremonially unclean, and thus are not permitted to participate in the religious activities of the community. However, God does not judge by outward appearances, but by what is in the heart (1 Samuel 16:7).

9. An angel of the Lord appeared to them, and the glory of the Lord shone around them, and they were terrified.

The shepherds are familiar with the usual scenes in the sky at night, but the appearance of an *angel* is too great for them. It is not only the appearance of the angel that causes their fear, but also *the glory of the Lord*. In being privileged to view this glory, the shepherds are seeing something not revealed to either Zechariah or Mary when an angel appeared to them. In their fright, the shepherds must be

WHAT DO YOU THINK?

Does it bother you that we cannot confirm December 25—or some other specific date—as the day Jesus was born? Why or why not? What do you find significant about the date of Christ's birth?

WHAT DO YOU THINK?

What group in our community is shunned or despised because of some "outward appearance"? How can the church demonstrate God's love for such people?

wondering if this appearance means blessing or judgment. They get their answer quickly.

10. But the angel said to them, "Do not be afraid. I bring you good news of great joy that will be for all the people.

It is a blessing! Though they are inexperienced in such a glorious event, they know God is acting at this time, as at other times in history, in a special way. The greeting calms their spirits, yet they have had no idea that they are the first people on earth to receive this news. They know now it is *good news*, but all the dimensions of this goodness cannot dawn on them so soon. The fear in their hearts (v. 9) is giving way to *joy*. But what this joy will mean for *all the people* is still unknown to them.

How wonderful it is that God can take the commonplace and make it an occasion for awakening people to who he is, what his purposes are, and how those purposes include us! If we will let it, such a scene as this with the shepherds becomes personal for us. Even "nobodies" are important to God, and through them he may reach out to others.

FREEDOM FROM FEAR

Several years ago in central Florida, a man was charged with the crime of frightening another man to death. A young man broke into the trailer home of sixty-seven-year-old Walter Schultz. He was armed with a knife and, according to the indictment, caused such fear as to result in the death of Schultz. He died of a heart attack that was brought on by the assault.

Fear is commonplace, though it is seldom deadly. The fear the shepherds experienced was more awe and reverence than it was terror. Still, the appearance of an angel in the Bible often causes fear. And yet Christ came to take away our fears! When U.S. President Franklin D. Roosevelt listed the four freedoms, one of them was freedom from fear. But no government on earth can give you freedom from fear. Only the Lord Jesus Christ can do that. He does it by forgiving our sins. He does it by comforting our hearts. He does it by assuring us of his presence.

While there are many legitimate fears in the world, most of our fears are phantom fears with no basis in reality. But faith drives out fear, whether real or imaginary. Certainly we still view God with awe and come into his presence with reverence. Certainly we fear sin enough to respect it and avoid it. But the fears that paralyze people, the fears that keep them awake at night and distracted by day, are taken away when faith comes in. The phrase *fear not* appears over sixty times in the *King James Version* of the Bible—that's more than once for every week of the year!

—R. C. S.

11. "Today in the town of David a Savior has been born to you; he is Christ the Lord.

Angels are the first to know of Jesus' birth, and they are privileged to share it first with the shepherds. Identifying specifics are given. The place of the birth is *the town of David*, which the shepherds know to be Bethlehem. The Child is *Savior*. The shepherds are aware that the Roman emperors are hailed as "Savior" and "Lord." However, another title links these terms for the shepherds: *Christ* or "Messiah"—God's anointed, promised Deliverer (cf. John 1:41; 4:25). He is the hope of all Israel! The shepherds understand this good news is not about a Roman ruler, for it means real deity—Almighty God!

12. "This will be a sign to you: You will find a baby wrapped in cloths and lying in a manger."

Proof for the shepherds is awaiting them at the *manger*. The *sign* is the evidence of the reality of what has been said concerning this birth. The lowly

How to Say It

Bethlehem. BETH-lih-hem.

Caesar Augustus. SEE-zer Aw-GUS-tus.

Damascus. Duh-MASS-kus.

Elizabeth. Ih-LIH-zuh-beth.

Galatians. Guh-LAY-shunz.

Galilee. GAL-uh-lee.

Judea. Joo-DEE-uh.

Mediterranean. MED-uh-tuh-RAY-nee-un.

Messiah. Meh-SIGH-uh.

Messianic. Mess-ee-AN-ick.

Nazareth. NAZ-uh-reth.

Samaria. Suh-MARE-ee-uh.

Zechariah. ZEK-uh-RYE-uh

manger will distinguish this One from a Roman emperor. Their hearts undoubtedly are open to learn even more!

13. Suddenly a great company of the heavenly host appeared with the angel, praising God and saying,

This *heavenly* choir is in contrast with Roman choirs that are used in the worship of the emperor. *Host* is the Greek word for "army," though how many angels are present we do not know. But this host makes the shepherds aware that this is an occasion for *praising God*. The presence of God calls forth worship! Therefore, if there are occasions when we have difficulty in worshiping or in serving, we need to get a real sense of the presence of God. Then we won't have to be told to worship and to serve. We can do nothing else!

14. "Glory to God in the highest,
    and on earth peace to men on whom his favor rests."

The angels conclude their message to the shepherds with a doxology (a praise). Hebrews 1:14 tells us that angels are "ministering spirits," sent on our behalf. In ministering to these shepherds, the message is one of *peace*. Undoubtedly, the shepherds relate that to the Old Testament concept that God saves his people from their earthly enemies. But in Christ this message is superseded by the idea that God saves his people from the "sin enemy." This is the type of salvation that results in peace between God and people, and it is Christ who will bring this peace about by dying to pay sin's penalty.

Some today have challenged the angel's message. Where is this peace *on earth* to the *men on whom his favor rests?* Of course, the whole context of the New Testament shows this peace is not for everyone, but only those who accept God's grace or good will.

C. VISITED BY SHEPHERDS (vv. 15-17)

15. When the angels had left them and gone into heaven, the shepherds said to one another, "Let's go to Bethlehem and see this thing that has happened, which the Lord has told us about."

How much checking will be necessary for *the shepherds* to find the right stable behind a dwelling or an inn? Fortunately, *Bethlehem* is not a large city. Whatever the challenge, the shepherds handle it with confidence, knowing the source of their information concerning the child's birth. The response of these devoted shepherds is a model for us all: every message from the Lord—messages that today come through the pages of Scripture—requires our response and action.

16. So they hurried off and found Mary and Joseph, and the baby, who was lying in the manger.

The scene is just as the Lord had said it would be. The dominant figures, of course, are the Messiah's mother, *Mary*, the protective *Joseph*, and *the baby*, properly cared for and *lying in the* feed *manger*. The lowly shepherds have accepted the message at face value and have acted on it. In so doing, they show more faith than the well-educated priest Zechariah! (See Luke 1:18.)

17. When they had seen him, they spread the word concerning what had been told them about this child.

The shepherds become the world's first evangelists of this good news. Luke leaves to our imagination the direction and the destiny of their ministry. Shepherding remains their livelihood, but sharing this thrilling message sets their feet on fire and their hearts ablaze. As Billy Sunday, the preacher of a couple of generations past, said of his own ministry: "It is surprising what a straight blow God can strike with a crooked stick."

DAILY BIBLE READINGS

Monday, Dec. 16—Jesus Is Born (Luke 2:1-7)

Tuesday, Dec. 17—Shepherds Hear the Good News (Luke 2:8-14)

Wednesday, Dec. 18—Mary Ponders the Shepherds' Words (Luke 2:15-20)

Thursday, Dec. 19—A Sword Will Pierce Your Soul (Luke 2:21-35)

Friday, Dec. 20—Anna Sees and Believes (Luke 2:36-40)

Saturday, Dec. 21—Mary Treasures All These Things (Luke 2:41-51)

Sunday, Dec. 22—A Child Has Been Born (Isaiah 9:1-7)

WHAT DO YOU THINK?

Many preachers, teachers, and other such leaders have been role models for us. Who, like the shepherds, has been a role model for you even though he or she was not a religious leader by profession? How can you be such a model to someone else?

[Use 1 Corinthians 11:1 to frame your answer.]

PRAYER

Our loving Father, thank you for the wisdom in your plans as you have made forgiveness of sin a reality for us through your Son, the Messiah. We thank you today for the witness of Joseph and the shepherds, but especially for the portrait of Mary, the earthly mother of the Messiah, and the faith she models to us. In Jesus' name, amen.

WHAT DO YOU THINK?

When have you had an experience of being confronted with the presence and power of God? What change did it make in your life?

THOUGHT TO REMEMBER

With the evidence we have, there is no substitute for faith, submission, and commitment to Jesus.

III. REACTIONS TO THE BIRTH (LUKE 2:18-20)

A. BY THOSE AROUND (v. 18)

18. . . . and all who heard it were amazed at what the shepherds said to them.

Now the ball is in other people's courts. What will they do with the message? Wonder or amazement can work in one of two ways. Either there will be acceptance of the divine nature of it all that calls for obedient response, or one may be hardened in unbelief. Preaching and teaching the gospel work that way. All is not done by the speaker. People must respond.

B. BY MARY (v. 19)

19. But Mary treasured up all these things and pondered them in her heart.

Mary is a new mother. Motherhood in itself is a grand blessing of God. But then there are all the other factors: the astounding pronouncement from her relative Elizabeth, the message of the angel to Joseph, Joseph's own caring response, and then the coming of the shepherds with their news. God is so great! And what will be next? Mary's faith grows as she continues to be the Lord's trusting servant. She will defer to her son at his first miracle (John 2:5). She will meet with others in prayer after Jesus ascends into Heaven (Acts 1:14). May our own faith demonstrate a similar commitment and growth.

C. BY THE SHEPHERDS (v. 20)

20. The shepherds returned, glorifying and praising God for all the things they had heard and seen, which were just as they had been told.

It is good when the pieces of a puzzle fit together, and the desired picture is complete. The result is worth the effort. What a night this has been for *the shepherds!* When they return to their flocks, they are not the same people they were before. When confronted with the presence and power of God, praise is the proper response (Luke 5:25, 26; 7:16; 13:13; etc.), and praise indeed fills their being.

The response of the shepherds is based on satisfactory evidence of the truth of the good news of the Messiah. As with Mary, what the future holds for them they do not know. But they know the meaning of believing God. They know what it means to be instruments in God's hand. Again, submission and commitment are key in our being shepherds ready to serve. Being in the presence of the glory of God brings one first to praise, and then to service.

CONCLUSION

Mary surrenders her whole being to God's will. The promise, the conception, the nine months' waiting, and the birth—but it is more than even all that. Mary knows that the One born of her is the promised Messiah. He is hers and he is God's. The miracle of the virgin birth is a part of the divine framework of God's redemption of sinful man. Each new aspect of life with Jesus and Joseph will bring more occasions for pondering the meaning of it all (cf. Luke 2:25-33, 41-52, etc.).

God does not reveal his entire plan to Mary all at once. She must have faith that whatever plan God has in mind, he is the One who is in charge, and he is the One who will bring that plan to fruition. Mary's mission of being the earthly mother of the Son of God never falters from the manger to the cross. There are times she is tested, but we see no regrets for submitting herself as she does.

Mary's mission does not end with the resurrection of Christ, nor should ours. In Acts 1:14, she is mentioned one last time as she meets with other believers after the ascension of Christ. The group is praying with the apostles and anticipating what will be next. Mary typifies the noble qualities of both motherhood and servanthood; thus, we too say, "Blessed are you among women."

Discovery Learning

This page contains an alternative lesson plan emphasizing learning activities. Classes
desiring such student involvement will find these suggestions helpful. The next page
is a reproducible activity page to further enhance discovery learning.

LEARNING GOALS

After this lesson each student will be able to:

1. Tell how Mary—and the shepherds—acted in faith to fulfill God's plan at the birth of Jesus.

2. Describe the way God's providence was at work in the unusual decree of Caesar and the routine work of the shepherds.

3. Express confidence that God has a work for him or her.

INTO THE LESSON

"*Precious Memories!*" Ask class members to pull out their imaginary videos of Christmases past and briefly tell the class or a small group about a favorite Christmas memory. Consider using the "Nativity Awards" activity from the reproducible page that follows.

Make the transition to Bible study by telling the class that Mary's favorite imaginary video shot may be of some of the traditional manger scenes: baby Jesus in the manger, shepherds crowding into the small stable or the like. However, there is another wonderful scene in which she realizes she is being asked to do an extraordinary task by the Lord. She was an ordinary Jewish girl with an extraordinary faith. And she was asked to be a part of something supernatural.

INTO THE WORD

Read aloud today's printed text from Luke 2:1, 4-20. Then divide the class into groups of four to six. Each group is to work on one of the three following tasks. Give each group a written copy of their task, a large piece of poster board, and a marker. If there are more than eighteen in your class, have more than one group working on the same assignment.

Task #1: Make two columns on your poster board. Head the first column "Sweet Memories" and the second column "Sweet Songs." After reading today's text, in the first column list all the words or phrases that may become the foundation of a "sweet memory" for this new mother. In the second column list a line or a phrase of a Christmas carol (or other song) that has helped to preserve these sweet memories. Not all of these memories, of course, have been captured in song.

Task #2: Read today's text. Then on the poster board provided summarize your understandings and feelings about each of the following questions or assignments.

1. Describe how you see God's providence at work in the unusual decree from Caesar. Tell how the occupational routine of the shepherds made them available to be used by God.

2. How was it special that the shepherds were among the first to visit Mary?

Task #3: Please read today's text. Focus on Luke 2:19. Use your imagination and put yourself in Mary's place. Think how God has worked through the life of an unknown girl. On the poster board make a detailed list of all the wonderful and frightening things Mary may have chosen to note in her mental diary. You may choose to list them as questions. For example: "Did Mary think about God's use of a far-off Roman emperor's decree to accomplish his will in her life?"

INTO LIFE

Use any or all of these discussion questions to apply the lesson to life today.

1. Mary was both an ordinary girl and an extraordinary girl. In what way would you say she was ordinary? In what way would you say she was extraordinary?

2. Let's talk about whom God chooses to use to accomplish his tasks. Who are some other "ordinary" people in Scripture God has called? Or even some unlikely people he has used for his purpose? As you make the list, ask, "Why do I consider this person to be ordinary, unlikely?" You may want to ask, "What do I have in common with these ordinary, unlikely people?"

3. Cite examples of persons you know who are in ordinary walks of life but whom you think God is working through in an extraordinary way to accomplish the purposes of his church.

4. What sets these Christian servants apart and makes them special? What lessons do you learn?

Close by asking the class to repeat the lines of this prayer as you read it sentence by sentence: "Dear Lord, thank you for Mary. Thank you for her submissive and adventurous spirit. I know you will give me opportunities to be your servant. I have one request—teach me to watch and listen for these opportunities. And I make this promise—I will use these opportunities and will look for at least one special skill I can develop for you. Amen." Sing the chorus of "I Surrender All."

Recommend that each learner respond to the "Personal for Me" activity on the reproducible page that follows.

Nativity Awards!

The Christmas story has a special place in our hearts. Its touching scenes are memorable. Allow yourself to give awards for the following that have captured your eye:

Most Memorable Character: _____   Best Supporting Actor: _____
Most Touching Speech: _____   Most Memorable Scene: _____
Best Song: _____   Best Stage Set: _____

Of course, this was not a make-believe drama. It is a real event in history. All praise and honor goes to the "author" of our salvation!

Personal for Mary

Mary provides a model for the key word in this exercise. Find the words for each box. Then write the letters in the highlighted boxes in the grid at the bottom to discover a key to Mary's relationship with God.

Mary willingly gave this to Jesus in spite of the threat of backlash from society (v. 7).

Mary had been _____ to marry a man by the name of Joseph (v. 5).

Mary's child was called this, among other names and titles (v. 11).

Mary's submissive spirit enabled this to come to the world (v. 14).

Mary had to be amazed as she _____ what had happened (v. 19)

Lacking a proper crib, Mary laid her newborn baby in this (vv. 7, 12).

These folk came to see Jesus (vv. 8, 16).

A key word in Mary's relationship with God is

Personal for Me

Mary was responsive to God's will and the task for her life. While you will never be called to this same task, God does have a place for you to serve him. Use this exercise to stretch your vision and discover places of service.

1. What gift or skills do you see in yourself that you may give to the Lord?

2. What have you been asked to do in Christian service that you've not accepted? Why did you decline?

3. Where do you think the Lord is calling or stretching you to serve in the near future? In what way do you think he'd like to use you? Mary's key word should be yours, too!

Unit 1: *Personalities Involved in the Messiah's Coming*
(Lessons 1-5)

JOHN THE BAPTIST: MESSIAH'S FORERUNNER

LESSON 5

WHY TEACH THIS LESSON?

Extremists make people nervous. Candidates for public office can often win by depicting their opponents as extremists, while offering themselves as moderates. No one wants to be known as an extremist—not in politics, and not in religion.

But extremists are also the ones who change the course of human events. John the Baptist was an extremist. Yes, he made people nervous. His bold preaching and his austere appearance were upsetting to many. But those who sincerely listened to his message were changed, and the way was prepared for the Christ to come.

If your students voice their convictions about Jesus, about morality, about judgment to come, then they have probably been called extremists more than once. This lesson will reassure them that they are in good company!

INTRODUCTION

A. PORTRAIT OF JOHN, PREACHER AND BAPTIZER

Many people today want to get back to nature. Natural food products sound the note for those who want a healthy diet—low cholesterol and low fat. They want dietary supplements that are "natural." That word *natural* sells. People want quality lives, disease free. *Free* is another buzzword. Many like to be free to do as they please, free from obligations. Sometimes being free is good and sometimes it is not.

At first glance John the Baptist, the Messiah's forerunner, may appear to be "natural and free." He makes his living in a wilderness environment and eats a Spartan, but completely natural, diet. But when we study his portrait carefully, we find the divine artist sets forth a personality that has greater and more meaningful dimensions. The Bible introduces John the Baptist in all four Gospels. (John the Baptist is not to be confused, of course, with the apostle John.) Bringing the details of those gospels accounts together gives us our portrait. Part of that portrait is the godliness of his parents, Zechariah and Elizabeth, whose portraits we viewed in the first lesson of this series.

Beyond the miraculous nature of his conception, we know nothing of John's childhood. Then suddenly he appears on the scene as a bold preacher of repentance and a baptizer of the penitent. His appearance is rugged—characteristic of one living in the wilderness. he is important enough to be the one sought out by Jesus for his own baptism (Matthew 3:13-15). John is the one who introduces Jesus as the Messiah, directing his disciples to follow Jesus instead, noting that, "He must become greater; I must become less" (John 3:30).

B. LESSON BACKGROUND

Since John's parents were of the priestly line of Aaron (Luke 1:5), so was he—though he himself did not become a priest. Instead, he became much more! Undoubtedly, his parents helped to mold him to be the unique person he became.

DEVOTIONAL READING:
JOHN 1:1-15
BACKGROUND SCRIPTURE:
MATTHEW 3; 11:2-19; 14:1-12
PRINTED TEXT:
MATTHEW 3:1-11; 11:7-10

Dec 29

LESSON AIMS

After participating in this lesson, each student will be able to:

1. List features that characterized the lifestyle and ministry of John the Baptist.

2. Compare the nature of John's ministry as forerunner of Jesus with the church's ministry of telling people of Jesus.

3. Suggest a specific way the student or church can perform this ministry.

KEY VERSE

This is the one about whom it is written:

"I will send my messenger ahead of you, who will prepare your way before you."

—Matthew 11:10

Dedicated to God's service from birth, he was to drink no wine or strong drink. He would be filled with the Holy Spirit from birth (Luke 1:15). The parents were promised that John would be called "a prophet of the Most High" and that he would "go on before the Lord to prepare the way for him" (Luke 1:76).

John lived in the wilderness area of Judea until he appeared in his special role to prepare the hearts of the people for the Messiah and his kingdom. John's whole personality and his vocabulary reflected the desert lifestyle. He was fully equipped for his ministry and drew many of his preaching illustrations from desert experience.

I. JOHN'S MINISTRY (MATTHEW 3:1-11)

The ministry of John the Baptist prefaces the public ministry of Jesus. It is fair to refer to John's ministry as the "beginning" of the gospel (cf. Mark 1:1; Acts 1:22).

A. HIS BEGINNING (v. 1)

1. In those days John the Baptist came, preaching in the Desert of Judea.

Luke is more specific than Matthew in designating *in those days* to be "in the fifteenth year of the reign of Tiberius Caesar" (Luke 3:1). This would be late A.D. 26 or early A.D. 27. John's parents, Zechariah and Elizabeth, had lived in the hills of *Judea*, perhaps at Hebron. *John* probably spent his youth in this same area. John is very familiar with this *desert* area, which constitutes about one-third of Judea proper. This area is mostly uninhabited, and is arid and hot except for the Jordan Valley just north of the Dead Sea. But here is where John lives "until he appeared publicly to Israel" (Luke 1:80).

What was life like for John here? What did he do? Did he have any portions of the Old Testament prophets? We do not know the day-by-day details, but he could have spent time reflecting on Old Testament prophecies he had learned from his parents. He could meditate and commune with God even as he took care of his daily needs.

B. HIS THEME (v. 2)

2. . . . and saying, "Repent, for the kingdom of heaven is near."

As he begins his public ministry, this thirty-something preacher has a ready message that seems to dovetail with the message of Old Testament prophets (see Ezekiel 18:30-32; Matthew 11:13). Those prophets had a message of judgment. But if there is repentance, then there can be blessing. If we had been in the audience, we may have heard John begin with the prophet Malachi (see especially Malachi 3:2; 4:1).

John's theme included a call to repentance from sin and an announcement that *the kingdom of heaven is near.* He urged them to repent—to prepare their hearts for the coming Messiah and his kingdom. They wanted change, and that change must begin with their change of heart.

RATING THE SERMON

The British statesman William Lamb, Lord Melbourne who lived from 1779 until 1848, once remarked, "Things have come to a pretty pass when religion is allowed to invade the sphere of private life!" Was he serious or was he joking? True religion always invades the sphere of private life. And good sermons are the means by which it does so. In fact, Lord Melbourne made that remark after listening to an evangelical sermon!

Someone has said that we ought to devise a rating system for sermons like the rating system for movies and television. Some sermons could be rated G. They are

Aaron. AIR-un.

Abraham. AY-bruh-ham.

Antipas. AN-tih-pus.

Elijah. Ee-LYE-juh.

Elizabeth. Ih-LIH-zuh-beth.

Ezekiel. Ee-ZEEK-ee-ul or Ee-ZEEK-yul.

Hebron. HEE-brun or HEB-run.

Herod. HAIR-ud.

Isaiah. Eye-ZAY-uh.

Judea. Joo-DEE-uh.

Leviticus. Leh-VIT-ih-kus.

Machaerus. Muh-KEY-rus or Muh-KYE-rus.

Malachi. MAL-uh-kye.

Messiah. Meh-SYE-uh.

Messianic. Mess-ee-AN-ick.

Pharisees. FAIR-ih-seez.

Sadducees. SAD-you-seez.

Tiberius Caesar. Tie-BEER-ee-us SEE-zur.

Zechariah. ZEK-uh-RYE-uh.

generally acceptable. There is nothing disturbing in them. They do not invade our private lives!

Sermons for the spiritually mature would get different ratings. Some could be rated R. These sermons need to be restricted to those who are not upset by the truth and who recognize that sometimes preaching must be controversial. And some sermons could be rated X. This is not because of offensive language but because they contain explosive ideas.

That is the rating we would have to give to John the Baptist—and to many who went before him. This kind of preaching caused Jeremiah to be dropped into a well, Amos to be run out of town, and Stephen to be stoned. Certainly no preacher needs to be unkind, but every sermon should invade the sphere of private life.   —R. C. S.

C. HIS PERSON (vv. 3, 4)

3. This is he who was spoken of through the prophet Isaiah:
   "A voice of one calling in the desert,
    'Prepare the way for the Lord,
       make straight paths for him.'"

Matthew quotes Isaiah 40:3 to describe John as *a voice*. But a voice needs an audience. John attracts an audience *in the desert* because his message ties in to the expectations of the day, and word spreads. The simplicity of his personal dress and lifestyle undoubtedly become part of the message that attracts (see vv. 4, 5, below). There has not been preaching (or a preacher) like this since the Old Testament prophets!

John's preaching has as its goal the removal of obstacles that might impede the Messiah and his message. This is what is meant by *make straight paths for him.* It is like clearing the way with "God's bulldozer." The biggest obstacle is hardness of heart. When that is removed, people are prepared to accept Jesus when he begins his own ministry (see John 10:40-42).

4. John's clothes were made of camel's hair, and he had a leather belt around his waist. His food was locusts and wild honey.

John's appearance and lifestyle reflect the desert area where he lives. Rough clothing made from *camel's hair* and held in place by a heavy *leather belt* covers his strong frame. This is the clothing of a poor person. It surely is not comfortable by any standard. His garb is similar to that of the prophets, like Elijah (2 Kings 1:8; cf. Malachi 4:5; Matthew 17:10-13). His diet is simple and sufficient, but few of us would want to try to survive on *locusts* (large grasshoppers) and *honey*, especially if we had to gather them ourselves! The severity of his message and lifestyle witnesses against the spiritual and physical indolence of the time.

D. HIS AUDIENCE (vv. 5, 6)

5. People went out to him from Jerusalem and all Judea and the whole region of the Jordan.

John's pulpit is surcharged with Messianic expectation. Many people like that and respond. John's message and manner are not those of a pretender. It does not make any difference whether the hearers were Jews or non-Jews. The people were excited and enthusiastic, ready to respond (see also John 3:23).

6. Confessing their sins, they were baptized by him in the Jordan River.

John is the one who introduces baptism to the New Testament era. In John's baptism, both Jew and non-Jew are yielding to God's will in *confessing their sins.* John's baptism differs from Christian baptism, which does not come until the Day of Pentecost after Christ's resurrection (Acts 2:38). (Those who receive John's baptism will later need to be rebaptized; see Acts 19:1-5.)

WHAT DO YOU THINK?

   What effect do you think John's lifestyle and appearance had on the way his message was received? How would a character like John be received today? What kind of preacher might have an impact today similar to John's impact on his hearers? Be specific.

E. HIS CHALLENGE (vv. 7-11)

7. But when he saw many of the Pharisees and Sadducees coming to where he was baptizing, he said to them: "You brood of vipers! Who warned you to flee from the coming wrath?

The *Pharisees* are a strict religious party of the Jews, priding themselves in their fastidious adherence to the law of Moses. The *Sadducees*, on the other hand, are a liberal party, who do not believe in angels or resurrection (Acts 23:8). It is said that "nothing makes better friends than a common enemy," and for these two groups to join forces like this to investigate what John is doing is quite remarkable!

The fact that these two groups are *coming to where he was baptizing* does not mean they are coming to *be* baptized (see Luke 7:29, 30). As they approach, John denounces them for their hypocrisy for not showing signs of true repentance. They do not want the wrath or judgment of God, but are not willing to have the change of heart necessary to be ready for the Messiah and his spiritual kingdom.

John is unafraid and unthreatened by those in high stations. He is a faithful forerunner, not afraid to use his wilderness vocabulary in calling deceitful people *vipers* (cf. Isaiah 14:29). Vipers are known for eating their parents and escaping fires. What snakes they are, wanting to *flee* the fire of judgment in their own way!

8. "Produce fruit in keeping with repentance.

John is separate from the mainline religious system. He calls for people to come away from empty religion. *Fruits* is a good agricultural concept for them to understand. The kind of plant or tree is seen by the fruit borne. If they are going to do God's will, their penitent hearts will be evident in their lifestyles. The religious leaders who come forth make a display, but there is no spiritual change.

9. "And do not think you can say to yourselves, 'We have Abraham as our father.' I tell you that out of these stones God can raise up children for Abraham.

The Jews of John's era often grab hold of their biological descent from *Abraham* as their security blanket. They feel their heritage insures them against judgment. They fail to see that God has no obligation to them as a nation because of their biological connection. When John looks at the common *stones* around his feet, he emphasizes his point by saying that if God wanted to he could make his *children* from them. To do so, it would be no more difficult than when God created Adam from dust. As Jesus and Paul will stress later, the true children of Abraham are those who have Abraham's deeds and faith (John 8:31-41; Romans 4:16).

10. "The ax is already at the root of the trees, and every tree that does not produce good fruit will be cut down and thrown into the fire.

John uses a dramatic analogy to strike home his point. The *trees* have been marked. The tree cutter has his *ax* ready to come down with a mighty blow. Unless there is a change of heart soon, destruction is ahead. They will become firewood. There is not a moment to spare.

It is too easy to have a false sense of security, thinking nothing so bad can happen. Many people put off making a decision, thinking they have plenty of time. But it may be later than they think. God is patient and long-suffering, not wanting any to perish. But if that is the course they choose, he can do nothing except bring due penalty.

THE COMING JUDGMENT

Charlemagne (A.D. 742–814) was the first European ruler known as the Holy Roman Emperor. He was crowned by the Pope himself on Christmas Day of the year 800. Charlemagne subdued various invaders and imposed order on the quarreling princes and wild tribes of central Europe. When he died, his body was embalmed in a sitting position—sitting on a golden chair, with a golden sword at

---

WHAT DO YOU THINK?

Who are the powerful people today whom some are afraid to offend? How should we address such people?

[Use Ephesians 4:15 and 1 Corinthians 9:19-22 in your discussion.]

WHAT DO YOU THINK?

Today, what constitutes good "fruit" for the Christian?

[Consider such passages as Matthew 7:20; Galatians 5:22-25; and Colossians 1:10.]

WHAT DO YOU THINK?

The Jews were proud to include Abraham in their heritage. What is it about our own national or family heritage that may keep us from embracing the future God has for us?

his side, a gold chain about his neck, and a golden volume of the four Gospels on his knees.

But all that will mean nothing when Charlemagne comes to the final judgment. He will not go to the head of the line. When small and great stand before God, he will stand alongside the poorest peasant from an unmarked grave in potter's field. "God is no respecter of persons."

No one will escape that judgment. We don't often hear that these days. But it is a theme we need to hear, and it is a theme that always has been needed. So you find it in the Psalms (see 58:11 and 62:12). You find it in the prophets (e.g., Jeremiah 17:10). It was a part of the preaching of the apostles (Acts 10:42; 17:31). It was a part of the preaching of Jesus (Matthew 11:22; 25:32; Luke 12:48). God is described as the judge of all in the first book of the Bible (Genesis 18:25) and in the last (Revelation 20:12).

The warning John the Baptist gave so long ago is as relevant today as it ever was. We would be wise to heed that warning. —R. C. S.

Use this visual to illustrate the Key Verse. Discuss how we, too, can be the Lord's messengers.

11. *"I baptize you with water for repentance. But after me will come one who is more powerful than I, whose sandals I am not fit to carry. He will baptize you with the Holy Spirit and with fire."*

John's baptism is not an end in itself, but it looks to the future. He is the Messiah's forerunner. Greater things are coming. John's baptism will be followed by Jesus' baptism (i.e., Christian baptism). John does not have revelation of all the details; so he preaches his sermon as an Old Testament prophet would.

There are two aspects ahead. There is blessing. That blessing will come on the Day of Pentecost after Jesus' resurrection, when Peter and the other apostles will preach the first gospel messages: "Repent, and be baptized, every one of you, in the name of Jesus Christ for the forgiveness of your sins. And you will receive the gift of the Holy Spirit" (Acts 2:38). The other half of the message presents the alternative: *fire*. This is judgment. For the obedient there is blessing; for the disobedient, judgment. It's the individual's choice.

The one who will make such a blessing possible is the Messiah. John, as a lowly servant, says he is not worthy to *carry* his *sandals* (cf. Matthew 3:13-15 and John 1:29, 30). Jesus' ministry will be greater than John's. We today can testify to that fact since we are on this side of the cross and the empty tomb. We know forgiveness of sin and the abiding presence of the Holy Spirit. As Paul reassures in Romans 8:1, "Therefore, there is now no condemnation for those who are in Christ Jesus."

II. JESUS' EVALUATION OF JOHN (MATTHEW 11:7-10)

Early in Jesus' public ministry, Herod Antipas (a son of Herod the Great) threw John into prison (Matthew 4:12; 14:3, 4). John had denounced Herod for taking Herodias, his brother's wife, to be his wife. Of course, Herodias was the power behind the throne that brought about this situation for John—and later his beheading. Dark, dank Machaerus prison was in stark contrast with the fresh air and sunlight of the Judean hills and the Jordan River. But more than the prison, John was struggling to put all the things together about the Messiah and his kingdom. "If Jesus is setting up his kingdom, I should not be here," John could have thought. In fact, John sent word to Jesus and asked, "Are you the one who was to come, or should we expect someone else?" (11:3). He said this even though he had introduced Jesus as the Lamb of God that takes away the sin of the world. Jesus sent back word to John to remind him of the miracles he was doing and the good news he was preaching. In other words, "John, don't forget; it is a spiritual kingdom I am setting up. Don't stumble."

WHAT DO YOU THINK?

Jesus, in essence, told John not to lose sight of the spiritual nature of the kingdom and thus to stumble. What causes us to lose sight of the spiritual nature of the kingdom and to stumble?

PRAYER

Almighty God, today we have learned how you have been able to work through people like John, people yielded to your will. Give us courage to introduce others to the Lamb of God, who alone can forgive sin and provide the Holy Spirit. In Jesus' name, amen.

THOUGHT TO REMEMBER

Have the courage of your convictions.

A. STRENGTH AND COURAGE (v. 7)

7. As John's disciples were leaving, Jesus began to speak to the crowd about John: "What did you go out into the desert to see? A reed swayed by the wind?

The arrival and departure of *John's disciples* provides Jesus with an opportunity to deliver a ringing declaration of John's greatness. John's question (11:2, 3) did not arise out of a lack of faith, because Jesus' role is still veiled at this point in time. John's courage and commitment means that he is no spindly *reed* of grass!

B. OUTWARD VS. INWARD (v. 8)

8. "If not, what did you go out to see? A man dressed in fine clothes? No, those who wear fine clothes are in kings' palaces.

What John's outward appearance suggests is not the full story or the complete portrait of the man. His rough, wilderness garb does not make him come across as being important, unless we think that is the way an Old Testament prophet would be. John introduces the King of kings, but he does not wear royal attire to do so. *Clothes* don't really "make the man"! What matters is Lord's commendation. In fact, those people *in kings' palaces*, wearing their *fine clothes*, are the very ones who now hold John prisoner unjustly!

C. PROPHET AND MORE (vv. 9, 10)

9. "Then what did you go out to see? A prophet? Yes, I tell you, and more than a prophet.

In a way John is the last of the Old Testament prophets. But what makes him *more than a prophet* is the fact that he was the Messiah's immediate forerunner. John ties together the thread of hope in the messages of the prophets with the Messiah, who makes righteousness a reality. John brings the role of a *prophet* to a climax.

10. This is the one about whom it is written:
    "'I will send my messenger ahead of you,
    who will prepare your way before you.'"

John is the direct announcer of the Messiah. In this he fulfills the message in Malachi 3:1, a fact that Jesus affirms. John came in the spirit and power of Elijah, and Jesus further affirms this in verse 14. (See also Matthew 17:10-13; Luke 1:17.) John's whole ministry has been a flaming prediction and testimony concerning the Christ who was coming to take away the sins of the world. Many have misunderstood the God-designed nature of the Messiah's kingdom and have tried to make it something different. Their forceful efforts will not change its spiritual design.

John does not become a part of that kingdom; he died before its beginning. Thus Jesus said, "He who is least in the kingdom of heaven is greater than he" (Matthew 11:11). We have the privilege of serving in the kingdom that John could not. Let us be as faithful to our opportunity as John was to his.

CONCLUSION

John plows and prepares the soil for Jesus to sow the seed of the kingdom of Heaven. John announces a new era even before he knows the Messiah. He has faith in God's messages to him and acts accordingly.

John is a solitary figure. No person pictured in the Bible is alone more than he, but he is not lonely, knowing Whom he serves. John heralds the Dayspring, the Sun of Righteousness, with healing in his wings (Malachi 4:2)—healing for sin sickness. John revives people's faith in the ancient promises. John is great in the message he preaches, and great in his courage in preaching it. John is the Messiah's forerunner. Yet John does not promote himself, for he says of Jesus, "He must increase, but I must decrease" (John 3:30).

Discovery Learning

This page contains an alternative lesson plan emphasizing learning activities. Classes desiring such student involvement will find these suggestions helpful. The next page is a reproducible activity page to further enhance discovery learning.

LEARNING GOALS

After this lesson each student will be able to:

1. List features that characterized the lifestyle and ministry of John the Baptist.

2. Compare the nature of John's ministry as forerunner of Jesus with the church's ministry of telling people of Jesus.

3. Suggest a specific way the student or church can perform this ministry.

INTO THE LESSON

Option 1: Ask, "What are some of the highest paying careers today?" List these on a board. Then ask, "What are some of the lower-paying careers?" Also list these.

Then ask, "Do salaries necessarily reflect how much good a career contributes to mankind?" Make the transition to Bible study by stating: "Today a very poorly paid prophet calls to the rich and the poor to make a difference—to bear fruit. The theme of God's followers' bearing fruit laces the Old and New Testaments. This is an important theme for our Master—and an important lesson for his followers. Today, we will hear that theme again from one of the Bible's most colorful characters."

Option 2: Make an acrostic of the word *Fruitful.* Print the letters of the word vertically on poster board. Ask students to volunteer words that describe a believer's fruitful life. Each word must begin or end with one of the letters on the poster. Make the transition to Bible study by telling the class today's study will give encouragement and ideas on how to honor God by being fruitful.

INTO THE WORD

Say, "Today we are going to share the teaching responsibilities. We will work in small teams, make our preparations, and report our findings or conclusions with each other."

Divide the class into groups of four to six, and assign each group one of the following tasks. Give group 1 a photocopy of an article about John the Baptist from a Bible dictionary and a copy of the the Lesson Introduction and Lesson Background from the lesson commentary.

Group 2 will need a copy of the lesson commentary on Matthew 3:6, 11, also a Bible dictionary article on John's baptism (often found under "baptism"). Group 3 should be given a copy of the lesson commentary on Matthew 11:7-10. Group 4 will need a concordance.

Distribute the following written instructions to the appropriate groups.

Group 1. Use the attached article and notes on today's text to gather information about John and his ministry. One person should report on John's unusual birth story and childhood years. Another team member should report on his personal life and the purpose of his ministry. A third person should report on the circumstances of John's imprisonment and terrible death.

Group 2. Read the attached article and lesson commentary on Matthew 3:6, 11. Report on the purpose of John's baptism and its similarities to, and distinctions from, Christian baptism.

Group 3. Reread Jesus' evaluation of John in Matthew 11:7-10. After reading notes in the lesson commentary, write a paraphrase of Jesus' remarks so today's listener can understand.

Group 4. Look up the word *fruit* in the Bible concordance. Find at least four prophetic calls to bear good fruit in the Old Testament. Psalm 1 and Psalm 92 may be helpful. Find definitions or descriptions of good fruit and bad fruit in the New Testament. The words *fruit of the Spirit* are a clue.

Encourage groups to work quickly (about ten minutes). Allow groups to report their findings and summations to the class.

INTO LIFE

Use the commentary on Matthew 11:7, 8 to remind the class of the heart of today's lesson: John's comments on bearing fruit. Use the following questions to stimulate application.

1. The idea of bearing good fruit was a frequent illustration by Bible speakers. Why do you think they used this terminology so often? If you were going to use a similar analogy in today's urban life, what would be an appropriate illustration? (*Dividends, yields, productivity.*)

2. Point out words in the opening activity that deal with bearing fruit in the various stages of life. Ask, "What are practical ways people can bear fruit in these different seasons of life? In youth? Parenting years? Old age?"

Stress that bearing good fruit is an important concept in the Bible, repeated over and over. Have learners respond to the two activities on the reproducible page that follows. After some discussion, ask for a volunteer to word a prayer of commitment to bear good fruit.

Picking Fruit!

John the Baptist and a host of others in the Old and New Testaments keep hammering home the point that believers are to be fruitful. Just what is this good "fruit"? For a partial definition read Galatians 5:22, 23. Write these nine delicious fruits in the grapes on the cluster below.

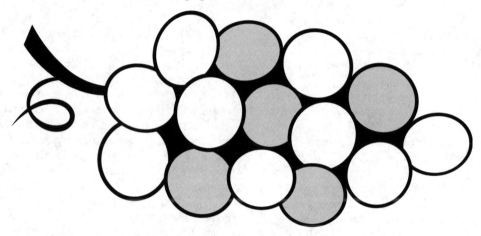

After discovering these fruits, identify the one that is best seen in your own life. Circle it.

Now comes the tough part. What fruit needs to be "sweetened up" a bit in your life? Draw a box around the one you believe God would like to be more evident in your life.

Destroying Bad Fruit

Followers of Jesus also need to know what kind of fruit is not to be present in their lives. Read Galatians 5:19-21 and identify some of the acts that believers are to avoid. Write the names of these bad fruits in the "flames of destruction" pictured.

THE RICH MAN: WRONG PRIORITIES

LESSON 6

WHY TEACH THIS LESSON?

Some of your learners have made a habit of ignoring the account of the rich young ruler. "It doesn't apply to me," they say, "because I'm not rich." But material wealth is a relative thing! Thomas Sowell, in an article of January 5, 2000, entitled "Revolutionary Century," notes that, "By 1970, virtually all [American] families living in poverty had refrigerators. By 1994, most American households below the poverty line had a microwave oven and a videocassette recorder—things that less than 1 percent of all American households had in 1971." Surely the richest person of two thousand (or even two hundred) years ago would have looked upon such conveniences as unbelievable luxuries!

So, in a sense, most of us are indeed rich. Further, the temptation to try to accumulate greater wealth and more possessions is always with us. God will challenge our attitudes toward such things in today's lesson.

INTRODUCTION

A. YOU ASK TOO MUCH

Before you step onto the lot of your local new car dealer, be ready for "sticker shock." People of retirement age spend more for cars today than they paid for their first homes! The price of almost everything seems ridiculously high. Candy bars cost a dollar, and a day in the hospital may cost a thousand. Professional ballplayers are paid millions of dollars. Perhaps the fans need to go to the ticket window at their favorite team's stadium and simply say, "You ask too much!" But that probably wouldn't get anyone's attention since boycotts have a poor track record.

With this week's lesson, we begin a new unit of study that focuses on some of the personalities in Jesus' life and ministry. Jesus' encounter with the rich man is probably one of the saddest moments in that ministry. Jesus had much to offer, but the rich man was unwilling to rearrange his priorities in order to gain that which he said he wanted. We do not read of him again in the New Testament. Did he ever change his mind, return to Jesus, and do what Jesus asked? We simply do not know. In essence, this man said to Jesus, "You ask too much." May his rejection of the Lord's instruction remind us that Jesus knows our hearts and demands that nothing and no one take his position in our lives.

B. LESSON BACKGROUND

Parallel accounts of this incident are found in Matthew 19 and Luke 18. Those accounts give us a few more details about the rich man. Matthew tells that he was "young" (19:20), while Luke adds that he was a "ruler" (18:18). From all three Gospels together we have come to call this the account of "the rich, young ruler." There is no elaboration on the title "ruler," so we do not know whether the man was a local official or part of the Jewish aristocracy.

DEVOTIONAL READING:
1 TIMOTHY 6:6-19
BACKGROUND SCRIPTURE:
MARK 10:17-27
PRINTED TEXT:
MARK 10:17-27

Jan
5

LESSON AIMS

After this lesson each student will be able to:

1. Recount the details of the encounter between Jesus and the rich man.

2. Express the difference between morality and a commitment to giving God first place in one's life.

3. Examine his or her priorities, and yield to God if there is anything that he or she has been unwilling to surrender in order to please and honor God.

KEY VERSE

Jesus looked at him and loved him. "One thing you lack," he said. "Go, sell everything you have and give to the poor, and you will have treasure in heaven. Then come, follow me."
—Mark 10:21

In any case, he found Jesus and asked him the right question. Before you can get the right answer, you have to know what question to ask! But right questions also must be asked with right motives and attitudes. Jesus, who knows us better than we know ourselves, went right to the heart of the young man's problem.

I. AN IMPORTANT QUESTION (MARK 10:17, 18)

As the tenth chapter of Mark opens, Jesus goes "into the region of Judea and across the Jordan" (v. 1). This is the east side of the Jordan River, labeled "Perea" on most Bible maps and part of the modern nation of Jordan. There he is thronged by eager crowds, crafty religious leaders, and little children (vv. 1-16).

A. "WHAT SHALL I DO?" (v. 17)

17. As Jesus started on his way, a man ran up to him and fell on his knees before him. "Good teacher," he asked, "what must I do to inherit eternal life?"

After blessing the children (Mark 10:13-16), Jesus resumes his journey to Jerusalem (10:32). Along the way a certain man interrupts the journey. What does he actually know of Jesus? The fact that the man kneels indicates that he has some sense of respect for Jesus. Jesus certainly has no financial superiority over this man (cf. Luke 9:58). And Jesus is not a "ruler" in any earthly sense (cf. John 6:15). Perhaps the rich man has heard of Jesus as a miracle-worker or a great teacher. In any case, something he has heard compels him to kneel before Jesus and ask a very important question about obtaining *eternal life*.

The rich man calls Jesus *good teacher*. Whatever the rich man means when he addresses Jesus in the way he does, it is obvious that he believes there is something extraordinary about Jesus. The man seems to believe that Jesus, above all other Jewish rabbis, can tell him how to have eternal life.

B. ASKING THE RIGHT PERSON (v. 18)

18. "Why do you call me good?" Jesus answered. "No one is good—except God alone.

Even though the rich man's final response to *Jesus* will be disappointing, as we shall see, we have to give him credit for addressing that important question to the right person. Jesus seems to want to know more about what the rich man believes about him, so he asks him why he calls him *good*. A Jewish man would be reluctant to call any human being "good." Only *God* is good! (See Psalms 106:1; 118:1; 1 Chronicles 16:34; 2 Chronicles 5:13.) Is the rich man acknowledging that Jesus is God? That seems to be what Jesus is asking. Whatever the rich man thought about Jesus, he clearly felt that Jesus alone could answer the question that plagued his mind.

II. AN IMPRESSIVE RESPONSE (MARK 10:19, 20)

A. THE EASY ANSWER (v. 19)

19. "You know the commandments: 'Do not murder, do not commit adultery, do not steal, do not give false testimony, do not defraud, honor your father and mother.'"

Mark records no answer to Jesus' question, "Why do you call me good?" (v. 18). Was it a rhetorical question, posed to make the rich man think but not to be answered? Or did Jesus pause until the silence became awkward, but the rich man could voice no answer? We can only speculate, but it's easy to imagine the rich man's relief when Jesus resumes speaking.

Jesus' preliminary response to the rich man's question seems too simple. The man obviously knows the tenets of the law of Moses, especially the Ten Commandments (see the next verse).

What are some things people do to try to earn their way to Heaven? Why does this notion of earning one's salvation by good works and by being a "good person" persist in the minds of so many? What can we do to change that perception?

Jesus refers to the last six of the *commandments*. These are God's instructions on how people are to deal with one another. (The first four Commandments, not cited by Jesus, are God's instructions for our relationship with him.) The command to *not defraud* may be a synopsis of the Tenth Commandment. It probably also refers to the teaching of Deuteronomy 24:14, 15. This is particularly appropriate to remind a rich man that wealth should not come at the expense of the poor. Jesus eventually will confront the rich man with the heart of his problem, which is his relationship with God. Although Jesus begins with the easy answer, he will not stop there.

TABLETS OF STONE

The Ten Commandments were not written on papyrus, which was in common use but only about as durable as paper. They were not written on clay tablets, also in common use then. Clay tablets could break or crack easily. They were written in stone! Surely there is a lesson in that. These Commandments were meant to endure. Every one of the Ten Commandments of the Old Testament is repeated in some form in the New, except for the one governing the Sabbath Day. You can find a parallel to the other nine in the teachings of Jesus and the apostles. These basic laws are the enduring foundation of a moral and civil society.

It is surprising, and alarming, that in many places people are objecting to the display of the Ten Commandments in public buildings such as courthouses and schools. What is there in those Commandments that is offensive? Nothing. Even more troublesome than removing them is the fact that there are organized groups so zealously devoted to removing them. There can be no civil or moral society that ignores the principles behind them. They are basic to civilization as we know it.

In Babylon three or four centuries before Moses, the ruler Hammurabi developed a code of laws. They do not compare to the Ten Commandments. The Ten Commandments are sharper in focus, briefer yet more comprehensive. They will never be out of date. If we fail to keep them, we make a very large mistake.   —R. C. S.

B. THE ARROGANT ANSWER (v. 20)

20. "Teacher," he declared, "all these I have kept since I was a boy."

Does the rich man really believe that he has kept the law perfectly? This answer reminds us of Paul's description of himself prior to his conversion (see Philippians 3:6). Maybe this man, like Paul, claims only to be blameless according to the law—even if not actually perfect. Either way, however, in the presence of the "Good teacher" his answer is quite arrogant!

Many people are like the rich man—they think their morality is enough. As long as you don't kick your dog or bother anyone, what's to worry about? The rich man views himself as perfect in the sight of the law. In other words, he is as moral as moral can get. Yet he has the wisdom to know there is more than that to gain eternal life.

Most people today do not have that wisdom. If they think about judgment at all, they view it as a review of life in which they will be found to have been "nice" enough to get into Heaven. The rich man has in his favor a gnawing suspicion that "nice" is not going to be enough.

III. A LOVING REQUIREMENT (MARK 10:21, 22)

A. SEEING THE HEART (v. 21)

21. Jesus looked at him and loved him. "One thing you lack," he said. "Go, sell everything you have and give to the poor, and you will have treasure in heaven. Then come, follow me."

Jesus looks beyond the rich man's appraisal of himself and sees his heart. Of course, Jesus loves everyone, so Mark's notation that Jesus *loved him* must indicate

HOW TO SAY IT

Abraham. AY-bruh-ham.

Assisi. Uh-SEE-see.

Deuteronomy. Due-ter-AHN-uh-me.

Ezekiel. Ee-ZEEK-ee-ul or Ee-ZEEK-yul.

Hammurabi. HAM-muh-RAH-bee.

Lyons (France). Lee-OWN.

Perea. Peh-REE-uh.

Philippians. Fih-LIP-ee-unz.

rabbi. RAB-eye.

rabbinical. ruh-BIN-ih-kul.

Thessalonians. THESS-uh-LO-nee-unz.

DAILY BIBLE READINGS

Monday, Dec. 30—The Rich Man Goes Away Sorry (Mark 10:17-22)

Tuesday, Dec. 31—Hard for the Rich to Enter (Mark 10:23-31)

Wednesday, Jan. 1—Simon Wants to Buy Power (Acts 8:14-24)

Thursday, Jan. 2—I Will Follow You, But . . . (Luke 9:57-62)

Friday, Jan. 3—You Are Lukewarm (Revelation 3:14-20)

Saturday, Jan. 4—What Tomorrow Will Bring (James 4:13-17)

Sunday, Jan. 5—Save Your Life and Lose It (Matthew 16:24-28)

WHAT DO YOU THINK?

Jesus' response to the rich young ruler was based on his love for the man (v. 21). When have you had to issue a strong challenge or even a rebuke to another because of your love for him or her? What happened?

WHAT DO YOU THINK?

What is involved in following Jesus? What does it require us to give up? (Is there anything that competes with his authority in our lives?) What does following Jesus require us to do? (Are there things we do because we are disciples that we would not do otherwise? Are there things we do for Jesus that we would not do for anyone else?) Be specific.

Use this visual to call attention to the rich man's expression of grief at Jesus' words (verses 21, 22).

a special feeling for this man. Perhaps it is love like that of a parent when a child has said something exceedingly immature. The immaturity is an indicator of a continuing need for parental love.

Jesus sees the rich man's heart and knows that a barrier exists between him and God. He has another god—his wealth. Jesus loves him and does not want him to be alienated from the Father because of his wealth. The solution to the problem is radical: *sell* all he has and *give* the proceeds *to the poor.* Is Jesus serious? Apparently so!

Does divesting one's earthly wealth and assisting the poor gain eternal life for anyone willing to take such a radical step? No. Altruism is fine, but it does not save us—no good work can do that (Ephesians 2:8-10). In this instance, Jesus senses that the rich man's desire for God is genuine, but it is superseded by his desire for wealth. God does not have first place in the man's heart. His first love is his money! That is the problem. Jesus' solution is painfully honest.

Jesus does not leave the rich man reeling in his thoughts about the proposed solution. Jesus immediately goes on to assure the rich man that he will be making a better investment by having *treasure in heaven.* This call is not exclusive to the rich man. Jesus calls on all who *follow* him to divest themselves of earthly restraints in seeking God's kingdom (Luke 12:29-34).

Consider what it would mean if we really believe what Jesus said. Obviously, we are not to give away all we have and then become a burden for others to care for (cf. 2 Thessalonians 3:7-10). Jesus challenges us, rather, to consider where our hearts truly are (Matthew 6:19-21; 1 Timothy 6:17-19). Anything we put before God in our heart is an idol (Ezekiel 14:3, 4; Ephesians 5:5; Colossians 3:5).

SELL AND GIVE

Francis of Assisi (c. 1181–1226) was the son of a wealthy Italian cloth merchant. He took literally what Jesus said to the twelve whom he sent out as recorded in Matthew 10:7-10. The instruction was similar to that given to the young man in today's lesson. Francis thought all the family wealth should be given to the poor. His father was angry over this application of the words of Jesus, so Francis left home wearing a ragged cloak and a belt taken from the rope around the waist of a scarecrow. He begged from the rich. He gave to the poor. And he preached. His followers became known as the Franciscans and history knows him as Francis of Assisi.

In 1173, Peter Waldo, a wealthy merchant in Lyons, France, had the same idea, so he gave away all his worldly goods and led a life of poverty and preaching. His followers became known as Waldensians. Though fiercely persecuted, they survive to this day, and their views of a simpler Christianity have affected many streams of Christian thought.

These are only two of many who through the centuries have taken the words of today's lesson literally. Certainly we applaud such sacrifice, even though we understand the command to be specific to the young ruler's personal problem, not general instruction for everyone's life. Whatever it is that comes between you and Christ must be given up. Perhaps only you and Christ know what that is. Whether it is wealth or power or pleasure or some other thing, if it keeps you from Christ, it must be sacrificed.

—R. C. S.

B. REJECTING THE COMMAND (v. 22)

22. At this the man's face fell. He went away sad, because he had great wealth.

Mark records no words from the rich man. (Neither do Matthew or Luke, who also write of this event.) The man just walks away, looking *sad.* His desire for eternal life is genuine, and he thought he had come to the right person to answer his question. But Jesus simply asked too much. It is in this verse that we first learn that the man is rich—*he had great wealth*. The greater sadness, however, is in the heart of Jesus.

The rich man had the right desire, but was unwilling to make the right investment. Ultimately, his problem is traced to an unwillingness to become a disciple of Jesus. That is where salvation lies. The rich man is unwilling to carry his cross and follow Jesus.

Even though Jesus loves this man, he does not chase after him. He does not offer to change the terms of his command. Jesus could have called out, "Okay, how about half?" This man could have financed much of Jesus' ministry. Is it prudent to offend him? How many preachers have avoided specific topics in sermons fearing that they would alienate some of their more generous contributors?

So the rich man leaves, and Jesus lets him go. We do not hear of this man again in the New Testament. Even so, the question remains, "What does God require of us?" The answer is given by the apostle Paul, who notes that we have only one thing that matters to God. If we put him first, and offer our lives as "living" sacrifices to him in becoming his disciples, we will gain what the rich man was looking for (Romans 12:1, 2).

IV. AN ASTONISHING LESSON (MARK 10:23-27)
A. IT ISN'T EASY! (vv. 23-25)
23. Jesus looked around and said to his disciples, "How hard it is for the rich to enter the kingdom of God!"

We can only imagine the reactions of Jesus' *disciples* at this turn of events. They are probably ashen-faced and speechless. How could Jesus ask so much? How could he have let the rich man just walk away? Have they given all their assets to the poor in order to follow Jesus? Will he ask that of them at some point?

Jesus recognized their lack of understanding. He summarized the whole incident in very simple terms. It isn't easy for rich people to *enter* his *kingdom*.
24. The disciples were amazed at his words. But Jesus said again, "Children, how hard it is to enter the kingdom of God!

Jesus' words further astonish his followers. Is this some new teaching? Many of the great figures in Israel's history were men of great wealth—Abraham, David, and Solomon, for example. Have things changed? Is it now wrong to be wealthy?

There is nothing wrong with wealth in and of itself. The problem is that riches often keep people from following God's instruction to trust in him and follow Jesus. This goes to the heart of the rich man's misunderstanding. It isn't easy to let go of self-sufficiency and learn to trust in God. It is easier to trust in riches. (See 1 Timothy 6:10.)
25. "It is easier for a camel to go through the eye of a needle than for a rich man to enter the kingdom of God."

Jesus now illustrates the difficulty of rich people entering his kingdom with an analogy that seems ridiculous. He uses what is called "hyperbole"—extreme exaggeration to achieve a certain teaching effect.

You may have heard a lesson or sermon from this text that claimed that there was a small gate in the wall around Jerusalem known as *the eye of* the *needle*. This gate supposedly was so low that no *camel* could pass through it loaded with cargo. The camel first had to be unloaded and then forced to kneel in order to crawl through the gate. Under this theory, Jesus is saying that in order to be a part of his *kingdom*, we have to unload our earthly "cargo" and humble ourselves. The problem is that there is no evidence that such gate ever actually existed!

WHAT DO YOU THINK?

Why is wealth so often a stumbling block to faith in Christ? How can we use our possessions for God without becoming enslaved by them?

[See Psalm 50:10; Luke 16:11; and 1 Timothy 6:17.]

PRAYER

Heavenly Father, help us be honest in assessing our priorities. If some idol exists in our hearts, help us remove it and place you on the throne as King of kings in our lives. Help us offer ourselves to you as living sacrifices. Grant us your peace and blessing. In Jesus' powerful name, amen.

THOUGHT TO REMEMBER

In light of what Jesus has done for us, is it possible for him to ask too much of us?

WHAT DO YOU THINK?

How have you found the "cost" of discipleship to be "worth it"?

[Include a look at Romans 8:18 and 2 Corinthians 4:16-18 in your discussion.]

B. IT'S IMPOSSIBLE! (v. 26)

26. The disciples were even more amazed, and said to each other, "Who then can be saved?"

The disciples' response is the key to understanding that there was no gate in the wall called "the eye of the needle." If they were familiar with such a gate, they would understand Jesus to be saying that it is difficult to get into the kingdom. They would understand the implicit illustrations of unloading earthly "cargo" and humbling oneself. These thoughts apparently never occur to them. They are incredulous! They know that what Jesus is talking about is impossible.

In response, Jesus' disciples pose an interesting question: *Who then can be saved?* Why do they ask that? Everyone isn't rich. Jesus has not said anything about the poor. Why do the disciples view Jesus' statement about rich people as applying to all people? There are many who live in Jesus' time who consider wealth to be a sign of God's blessing. Logically, then, poverty is a sign of God's disapproval and disdain. If the rich can't get into Heaven, then who can?

The disciples' astonishment might also be the response of people who understand human nature. Rich or poor, everyone can get attached to his or her possessions! Even if our earthly possessions are of little value to others, they may well be of great value to us. Bill Gates might not want my house, but I'm sure glad I have it!

The disciples are having great difficulty accepting the interaction Jesus has just had with the rich man and his subsequent teachings about earthly riches. It seems as though Jesus is saying that true discipleship must be characterized by abject poverty. Such a connection reveals that the disciples have missed Jesus' point.

C. GOD'S SPECIALTY (v. 27)

27. Jesus looked at them and said, "With man this is impossible, but not with God; all things are possible with God."

Jesus has to remind his followers that God specializes in the *impossible!* (See Genesis 18:14; Job 42:2; and Luke 1:37.) Making a camel go through the eye of a needle is no more difficult than dividing the Red Sea or causing fire to consume Elijah's offering on Mount Carmel. Jesus—the one who can calm the wind and waves; the one who can walk on water; the one who can feed thousands with a little boy's lunch; the one who can make the blind see and the lame walk; the one who can stop a funeral procession to bring a son back to life and restore him to his mother—can put a camel through the eye of a needle and save a rich man. Jesus' very presence before them is a reminder that God can do things we cannot comprehend, imagine, or duplicate. Jesus is reminding his followers that he is there to do things humans cannot do, and no one, rich or poor, can save himself and gain eternal life.

CONCLUSION

Peter's follow-up response in verse 28 (not in our text) shows that the disciples still didn't understand that God's favor is not to be earned or deserved. Jesus' conversation with the rich man concerning that man's expectations and ultimate loyalty should have been getting through to the disciples, but it wasn't. Is it getting through to you? If not, you might be caught in the eye of the needle. Placing first loyalty or trust in your own effort or wealth puts you in an impossible situation with God. He cannot save you any more than you yourself can shove a camel through the eye of a sewing needle. God, however, offers the solution to your dilemma: make him your first priority! Put him in first place in your heart. Jesus talked about the cost and conditions of discipleship in other places (e.g., Luke 14:25-27). In the end, though, the cost will be worth it (Mark 10:29-31).

Discovery Learning

This page contains an alternative lesson plan emphasizing learning activities. Classes desiring such student involvement will find these suggestions helpful. The next page is a reproducible activity page to further enhance discovery learning.

LEARNING GOALS

After this lesson each student will be able to:

1. Recount the details of the encounter between Jesus and the rich man.

2. Express the difference between morality and committing oneself to giving God first place in one's life.

3. Examine his or her priorities, and yield to God if there is anything that he or she has been unwilling to surrender in order to please and honor God.

INTO THE LESSON

Give students a piece of paper and time to consider and write down their personal financial goals for the next one to three years. Ask what they would like to accomplish financially in that period of time. Allow three to five minutes. Then ask people to make a mental check mark if their goals include each of the following:

____ Paying down a debt, such as a credit card

____ Saving for or purchasing a car or house

____ Investing for children's college education

____ Helping someone financially (parents, friend, needy family, or other)

____ Increasing financial support for the Lord's work

Make the transition to Bible study by reminding the class that our attitude toward, and use of, money give hints to our priorities in life.

INTO THE WORD

Give a brief lecture on the background for this study by using the Introduction on page 163. Then divide the class into three groups. Give the students a handout with the following outline and questions (or the appropriate page in *NIV Bible Student.*) Assign one point to each group.

A. The Request.

1. What words in Mark 10:17, 18 indicate the rich man's respect for Jesus? How or why does this indicate respect? (*"fell on his knees," v. 17*)

2. What words indicate he knew or suspected that Jesus was deity? (*"Good teacher, what must I do to inherit eternal life?" v. 17*)

3. Why did Jesus reminded the ruler, "No one is good—except God alone"? (*v. 18*)

B. The Response.

1. Read Mark 10:19. Why did Jesus quote the last six of the Ten Commandments and not the first four? See also Exodus 20:1-7.

2. Was the rich man's response in verse 20 honest, arrogant, or self-deceiving? Why?

3. The rich man obviously thought that "nice" was not good enough to get one into Heaven. Yet when told what to do, he didn't do it. What does his experience say about God's expectations?

C. The Requirements.

1. Is Jesus saying (Mark 10:21) that using all of one's earthly wealth and assisting the poor will assure us of Heaven? If not, what is he saying?

2. What lessons do you learn from this event about personal priorities? wealth? trusting God?

Allow the groups to work for about ten minutes. Then ask for persons from Groups A and B to share their findings. Use the lesson commentary to supplement and summarize the answers.

INTO LIFE

Make the transition to application by saying, "Group C has been wrestling with how to apply these teachings of Jesus to our lives today." Allow Group C to report.

Direct the class to the reproducible activity "Money Matters" on the next page. Say, "Jesus spoke the principle 'Where your treasure is, there your heart will be also' during his famous 'Sermon on the Mount' (Matthew 6:21). His teaching then, as in today's text, was that our view and use of possessions affects and reflects our relationship with him. Let's list some different ways we can use our material goods to honor Christ." Ask for a volunteer to write these suggestions on a poster as the class suggests ideas. You may need to stimulate the students' thinking by asking how we can honor Christ in the following areas:

1. Fulfilling family financial responsibilities.

2. Acts of kindness or benevolence.

3. Our gifts or tithes to the Lord's work.

4. Accumulating wealth.

5. Saving for retirement or financial crisis.

6. Our spending habits.

Have the class respond to the "Treasure Chests" activity on the reproducible page. Ask, "Where would God like to be honored more in your material wealth?" Like the rich man, we must make a choice about what we are going to do. Recommend that each adult answer the final question on the reproducible page. Close with prayer, asking God for help as we grow in this area of our spiritual lives.

Money Matters

Jesus makes it clear that our attitude toward money and how we use it matters to God. He even goes so far as to point out how difficult it is for the wealthy to enter the kingdom of God. Answer the questions below and discover important truths about our attitudes toward money.

What are some of the reasons the wealthy may find it so difficult to go to Heaven?

Do you consider yourself wealthy as compared to your acquaintances? Why or why not?

How do you see this principle pertaining to the spiritual health of our nation?

Do you consider yourself wealthy as compared to the rest of the world? Why or why not?

Treasure Chests

Jesus taught "Where your treasure is, there your heart will be also" (Matthew 6:21).

He also emphasized storing up treasures in Heaven rather than treasures on earth. Look back over the past year and try to remember a few deposits you may have made "in your heavenly treasure chest." Note a specific incident beside any of the following acts that you may have done in the past year.

Contributions to a humanitarian organization

Anonymous gift to meet someone's need

Gift with a note to encourage someone

Special gift to a missionary

Regular support of a missionary

Regular support to my church

What commitment will you make to improve your "treasure-storing" behavior in the next year?

MARY AND MARTHA: FRIENDS OF JESUS

LESSON 7

WHY TEACH THIS LESSON?

Christians use the word *service* in two ways. We use it to mean what happens inside the church building on Sunday, but also we use it to mean what happens outside the church building between Sundays. The former involves a "worship service" (cf. Hebrews 10:25), while the latter is service in the sense of work and ministry for God (cf. Romans 12:1). A problem we have here is that there is always the temptation to do one of these to the neglect of the other. Clearly, we need some sort of balance.

Today's lesson will help you and your learners to maintain that balance. As you and they listen to Jesus teach, look to see whether there may a bit too much "Martha" where a little more "Mary" is called for.

INTRODUCTION

A. "'TIS BETTER TO HAVE LOVED"

The young man sat forlornly on the front steps of an apartment building. In his hands were a rose, a box of candy, and a Valentine card. The look on his face revealed the disappointment in his heart. The girl he so longed to impress had, alas, been more impressed by another. Expressing both the agony of the heartbroken and the optimism of youth, he said, "'Tis better to have loved and lost than never to have loved at all."

One might be impressed with the young man's handling of a difficult situation, but we should not be impressed with his literary knowledge. He quoted Alfred Tennyson (1809–1892) correctly, but sadly out of context. Tennyson wrote that aching lament not over a romantic loss but because of the death of a friend. Tennyson had become best friends with Arthur Henry Hallum when they attended Trinity College at Cambridge University. When Hallum died of a stroke at age twenty-two in 1833, Tennyson was devastated. He wrote the poem *In Memoriam A. H. H.* in tribute to his dear friend. He had loved him and lost him. His heart ached, but he rejoiced that he had shared his friend's life for those few brief years. Such is the nature of true friendship.

B. LESSON BACKGROUND

We have been taught that God loves all people (John 3:16) and that God doesn't show favoritism (Deuteronomy 10:17; Acts 10:34). It is obvious, however, that while on earth Jesus was personally closer to some people than to others. Among the Twelve, he had an "inner circle" of Peter, James, and John. Even within that small group, John was especially close to Jesus (see John 13:23; 19:26; 20:2; 21:7, 20, 24). Jesus also developed close personal friendships with others. Mary and Martha, as well as their brother Lazarus, are examples. This week's lesson reveals the depth of Jesus' friendship with these sisters.

DEVOTIONAL READING:
JOHN 15:12-17
BACKGROUND SCRIPTURE:
LUKE 10:38-42; JOHN 11:20-32
PRINTED TEXT:
LUKE 10:38-42; JOHN 11:20-32

LESSON AIMS

After participating in this lesson, each student will be able to:

Jan 12

1. Characterize friendship, as based on Jesus' interactions with Martha and her sister Mary on his two visits to Bethany.

2. Explain how friendship leads to particular behaviors in both routine and extreme life experiences.

3. Affirm personal appreciation for a brother or sister in Christ in a tangible way.

KEY VERSES

"Martha, Martha," the Lord answered, "you are worried and upset about many things, but only one thing is needed. Mary has chosen what is better, and it will not be taken away from her."
—Luke 10:41, 42

LESSON 7 NOTES

I. IMPROMPTU VISIT (LUKE 10:38-42)

A. DISCERNING DISCIPLE (vv. 38, 39)

38. As Jesus and his disciples were on their way, he came to a village where a woman named Martha opened her home to him.

It is the third year of Jesus' ministry. Sometime during the two-month interval between the Feast of Tabernacles (John 7:2) and the Feast of Dedication (10:22), Jesus makes an impromptu visit to the home of his friends Mary and *Martha* in the little *village* of Bethany. It is an easy stopover anytime Jesus is near Jerusalem. Bethany is just about two miles southeast of that major city (cf. 11:18).

Martha welcomes Jesus. The fact that it is *her home* probably indicates that she is a widow. If the house were an inheritance from parents, it would be referred to as her brother Lazarus's house (cf. Ruth 1:8). Lazarus is not even mentioned in this text, however. He probably has a separate residence. A fuller description of this household is found in John 11:1-44; 12:2 (see below).

39. She had a sister called Mary, who sat at the Lord's feet listening to what he said.

Mary is probably younger than Martha. When Jesus arrives at their house, she immediately stops whatever she is doing and devotes her complete attention to Jesus. Sitting at his *feet* is the custom for someone who is in the presence of a teacher. Paul, for example, was taught "at the feet of Gamaliel" (Acts 22:3, *King James Version*). Even though Mary is a friend of Jesus, he is the teacher, and she takes the customary position of a student. What privilege this is for Mary!

B. DISTRACTED DISCIPLE (vv. 40-42)

40. But Martha was distracted by all the preparations that had to be made. She came to him and asked, "Lord, don't you care that my sister has left me to do the work by myself? Tell her to help me!"

As soon as company arrives, *Martha* throws herself into *all the preparations* of appropriate hospitality. Preparing food for guests is the highest priority in any Middle Eastern home of that era (see Genesis 14:17-20; 18:1-8; Judges 13:15; 2 Kings 4:8). Failure to feed a guest would be an unthinkable affront.

One cannot help but visualize Martha scurrying about the house and occasionally shooting a "Why-aren't-you-in-here-helping-me?" glance at her *sister*. Mary, it seems, never gives a thought to hospitality. Instead, she is perfectly content to sit at Jesus' feet and listen or converse with him. Burdened with unexpected company and a none-too-helpful sister, Martha finally explodes.

Using a tactic familiar to any parent of siblings, Martha does not directly confront Mary. Instead, she tells Jesus to tell Mary what to do. In fact, she almost scolds Jesus. Doesn't he *care* about Martha's being stuck to do all the *work* alone?

41. "Martha, Martha," the Lord answered, "you are worried and upset about many things.

Jesus is not oblivious to Martha's distractions. He knows she is busy, most likely preparing a meal for him. He calls her by name and repeats it, perhaps indicating a slight annoyance with her immaturity. She is *worried and upset* about relatively inconsequential matters. Jesus had once gone without food for forty days (Matthew 4:2)! Will a couple of hours without a meal really make that much difference? Rather than enjoying Jesus' company and taking advantage of the opportunity to learn from him, *Martha* is getting upset about household chores. She should know better.

42. " . . . but only one thing is needed. Mary has chosen what is better, and it will not be taken away from her."

There is some disagreement about what *one thing* Jesus means. It may mean that Martha is trying to make many dishes for a full meal, and Jesus is telling her

---

"Careful and troubled about many things: but **one thing is needful.**" —Luke 10:41, 42

Use today's visual to spark discussion on how to focus on that "one thing [that] is needed."

to simplify things and make just one dish. More likely, Jesus is saying that the one thing necessary is what *Mary* is doing: learning from him. What Martha is doing is not unimportant, but it can wait. A special opportunity is present, and Mary has chosen not to miss it.

Jesus does not rebuke Martha for her kindness. He is not unappreciative of her hospitality. He simply is trying to get her to understand a basic truth about the kingdom of God. "The kingdom of God is not a matter of eating and drinking, but of righteousness, peace and joy in the Holy Spirit" (Romans 14:17). Martha just has her priorities mixed up!

II. INDIGNANT FAITH (JOHN 11:20-24)

A. GENTLE CONFRONTATION (vv. 20, 21)

20. When Martha heard that Jesus was coming, she went out to meet him, but Mary stayed at home.

We cannot tell how much time elapses between the events of Luke 10:38-42 and John 11:20-24. It may be no more than a few weeks. After the impromptu visit with *Martha* and *Mary* of Luke 10, Jesus attends the Feast of Dedication in late December (John 10:22, 23). That high profile visit results in threats to his life (10:31, 39), so he retreats across the Jordan River to the east, where it is safer (10:40).

But after being there a short time (11:8), Jesus hears that Lazarus is near death. Jesus does not, however, rush right back to Bethany (11:1-6). In his own time, he finally begins his journey back into Judea, where his enemies are planning to have him seized and killed. Jesus probably sends someone ahead to Bethany to let the two sisters know he is nearing the village.

Martha leaves her *home*, which is filled with mourners, to go *out* and *meet* Jesus. She probably understands his desire to meet privately instead of in a houseful of people. Mary, meanwhile, stays in the house. This may be her desire, or it may be to keep people from accompanying Martha to meet Jesus.

21. "Lord," Martha said to Jesus, "if you had been here, my brother would not have died.

Martha seems to be scolding Jesus again. Surely greater haste on his part would have spared the life of Lazarus! But we must not be too hard on Martha. Words spoken in grief often seem harsh or indignant. She is emotionally distraught. This is not just a case of distress over a death, however. It is distress over a preventable death.

But notice Martha's belief in Jesus' power to heal. This belief combined with her scolding results in an odd mixture of faith and indignation. Martha does not understand why Jesus has delayed his trip to Bethany. She is hurt and disappointed. Jesus understands her disappointment. He knows our hearts and shares our burdens (Matthew 11:28-30). But, as John 11:40-44 will show (not in our text for today), Jesus has a plan that transcends the desires of the two sisters. Martha will find out that God's ways and thoughts are not the same as ours (Isaiah 55:8, 9).

PAYING THE DEBT

Someone asked a Hollywood producer what he thought about death. He replied, "Out here we don't care for it." Except in the most extreme cases, none of us cares for it. Dying used to be called paying the debt of nature. The great English preacher Charles Spurgeon (1834–1892) said that it was more like taking in a paper note and getting gold in exchange. American paper money used to be called "silver certificate." You could actually exchange that piece of paper for silver. That is no longer the case, but the illustration still holds true. When we die we exchange the paper for the real thing.

WHAT DO YOU THINK?

Martha was "distracted by all the preparations." We, too, have many things calling for our attention. How can we balance these and still choose "what is better" as Mary chose?

Ask volunteers to tell how they keep "first things first."

WHAT DO YOU THINK?

The lesson writer notes Martha's "odd mixture of faith and indignation." How can we be sensitive to the conflicting emotions of those who grieve? How can we share hopeful passages of Scripture without being preachy or condescending? In short, how can we best minister to them?

A man said that once he was walking through a cemetery and saw some distance ahead a stone that said, "DEATH IS ETERNAL." He thought it was an awful epitaph. Then he got closer and saw that one word had been obscured by another stone. It really said, "DEATH IS ETERNAL LIFE."

When the Egyptians decorated their tombs they carved figures of people as they were in death. The English did the same. London's Westminster Abbey is filled with these figures lying, hands folded, as they lay in death. The Greeks, however, memorialized people by carving them as they were in life. The Austrians did even better. On the tomb of the Empress Maria Theresa and her husband, the two figures are carved sitting up—as if just awakening on the morning of the resurrection. We may have to pay the debt of nature, but we will be richly repaid!   —R. C. S.

B. MUSTARD-SEED MOMENT (v. 22)

22. "But I know that even now God will give you whatever you ask."

It is difficult to imagine what is in Martha's mind as she speaks these words. Does she regret the tone in her voice of her previous sentence? Is this a "backing off" to express some sort of apology? Or is Martha grasping at straws? It is difficult to believe that Martha has not heard about two previous miracles in which Jesus brought dead people back to life (Luke 7:11-15; 8:41, 42, 49-55). Is Martha hinting to Jesus that perhaps he should resurrect Lazarus? Does she have that much faith? Jesus has taught that it takes only a little faith to prompt God to do miraculous things (Matthew 17:20). Is this a "mustard-seed moment" for Martha? The use of the phrase *even now* suggests that it might well be.

C. FINE-TUNED FAITH (vv. 23, 24)

23. Jesus said to her, "Your brother will rise again."

The Jewish people are not unified in what they believe about resurrection. The concept of resurrection is mentioned clearly in only a few places in the Old Testament (e.g., Daniel 12:2, 3). The Sadducees—the "liberal" party of the Jews—do not believe in resurrection, and Jesus addresses their error in Mark 12:18-27. At this point in the text, Jesus' statement to Martha could be taken as a reference to the miracle that is imminent (John 11:43), or it may have been a general reference to the Old Testament concept of resurrection.

24. Martha answered, "I know he will rise again in the resurrection at the last day."

Martha obviously thinks that Jesus is referring to *the resurrection at the last day* of all who are in the grave. Jesus, however, is interested in fine-tuning her faith. Does she truly believe that the dead *will rise again?* More importantly, does she truly believe that Jesus has miraculous power over death "even now" (v. 22)? Exactly what does Martha believe? What is the genuine nature of her faith in God?

III. INCREDIBLE PROFESSION (JOHN 11:25-27)

A. JESUS' TEACHING (vv. 25, 26)

25. Jesus said to her, "I am the resurrection and the life. He who believes in me will live, even though he dies.

Jesus' profession to be *the resurrection and the life* is astonishing! What does he mean? What is he claiming? We have a clearer understanding of his meaning because of our historical perspective, living after Jesus' own resurrection. What, however, does Martha understand him to mean? Does she believe that Jesus possesses the power to defeat death—even four days after it happens (see v. 39)?

26. ". . . and whoever lives and believes in me will never die. Do you believe this?"

Jesus asks the point-blank question! What does Martha truly believe? What is the nature of her belief in him? That is life's ultimate question. What do you truly believe about Jesus? How does that belief affect your life? How does it change the way you live? When you stand at the grave of a loved one, do you feel hopeless or hopeful? The words of Jesus echo down the halls of time to whisper to each of us today, *Do you believe this?*

B. MARTHA'S CONFESSION (v. 27)

27. *"Yes, Lord," she told him, "I believe that you are the Christ, the Son of God, who was to come into the world."*

Martha's confession of faith reminds us of that of Peter (Matthew 16:16). Martha believes that Jesus is the Messiah, God's Anointed One. She believes he is *the Son of God*. But what do those terms mean to Martha? Andrew told Peter that Jesus was the Messiah (*the Christ*, or "Anointed One"), and Nathaniel called Jesus the Son of God (John 1:40-49; cf. 4:25). Was there common acceptance of Jesus as a divine being? We today speak of Jesus as fully human and fully divine. Is that how his contemporaries viewed him?

Martha's confession of faith, like that of Peter, must be taken at face value. We today can read of Jesus' life and conclude that he was truly God's Son. Surely those who actually saw him perform miracles also could have held correct beliefs about his identity!

IV. UNALTERED AFFECTION (JOHN 11:28-32)

A. THE OTHER SISTER (vv. 28, 29)

28. *And after she had said this, she went back and called her sister Mary aside. "The Teacher is here," she said, "and is asking for you."*

Jesus apparently asks about *Mary*, so Martha returns home to get her. Martha converses with Mary out of earshot of the mourners gathered at her house so that they will not intrude on Jesus' fellowship with them at this sobering time. But her plan is not successful, as we see from verse 31 below. Martha's designation of Jesus as *the Teacher* (or Master) is a common way to refer to someone who is considered to be a rabbi. (See Mark 10:17 and comments on page 164 above.)

29. *When Mary heard this, she got up quickly and went to him.*

Filled with the same mixed emotions as Martha, Mary rushes to see Jesus. She is eager to hear his comforting words and experience again the depth of their friendship. Those feelings are probably tinged with disappointment at Jesus' late arrival. Mary is greeting an old friend, but a friend who, in her mind, has let her down.

B. ANOTHER MEETING (vv. 30, 31)

30. *Now Jesus had not yet entered the village, but was still at the place where Martha had met him.*

Jesus does not accompany *Martha* into Bethany. Perhaps he doesn't want another argument with his enemies to flare up (cf. v. 8). Or Martha may have suggested he remain at their meeting place so that he can avoid the crowd of mourners gathered at their home. In any case, Mary is expected to go to Jesus.

31. *When the Jews who had been with Mary in the house, comforting her, noticed how quickly she got up and went out, they followed her, supposing she was going to the tomb to mourn there.*

Martha's apparent desire to get *Mary* out of *the house* without being *noticed* goes unfulfilled. In that time and culture, family tombs were often nearby, and it was customary for families to continue to go *to the tomb* for days after a person's death. Continuing to visit the tomb was a way of paying homage to the deceased.

Mourners are quick to follow to share the grief. Were it not for the pathos of the moment, this scene would be almost comical. Martha tries to get Mary out

---

DAILY BIBLE READINGS

Monday, Jan. 6—Jesus Visits Mary and Martha (Luke 10:38-42)

Tuesday, Jan. 7—The Sisters Send Jesus a Message (John 11:1-6)

Wednesday, Jan. 8—Lazarus Dies (John 11:7-16)

Thursday, Jan. 9—Lord, If You Had Been Here (John 11:17-27)

Friday, Jan. 10—Jesus Weeps (John 11:28-37)

Saturday, Jan. 11—Lazarus, Come Out (John 11:38-44)

Sunday, Jan. 12—Mary Anoints Jesus (John 12:1-8)

PRAYER

Father, thank you for loving us and giving us your Son as our eternal friend. May we draw near to him, constantly seeking to deepen the bonds of that friendship. May our lives give consistent testimony of that friendship. In name of our Friend—and King—Jesus, amen.

WHAT DO YOU THINK?

Martha and Mary both commented on what would have been if only Jesus had been there. Of course, when Jesus did arrive, things turned out even better than the sisters could have imagined. How can that help us when we start thinking "if only"? How can you use this text to help someone else who is thinking "if only"?

[Note Romans 8:28 in the course of your discussion.]

secretly to meet Jesus when they discover they are being followed by a train of wailing mourners! Like many folks, the mourners mean well, but in this instance they are hurting rather than helping. Martha and Mary want to meet their friend Jesus in private. They do not want to be in the midst of a great throng of people.

C. ANOTHER BROKEN HEART (v. 32)

32. When Mary reached the place where Jesus was and saw him, she fell at his feet and said, "Lord, if you had been here, my brother would not have died."

There is a sweetness to this moment. Despite her disappointment in Jesus' late arrival, Mary still falls at his feet. Whenever we read of Mary of Bethany in the New Testament, she is said to be at Jesus' feet (cf. Luke 10:39; John 12:3). We also know that she is weeping (John 11:33). This is a moment of overwhelming emotion. When Mary is finally able to speak, she echoes the words of her sister.

These two women probably have spoken again and again of the *"if only."* It may be that in each hour of Lazarus's deepening illness these sisters had whispered constantly to one another, "If only Jesus were *here.*" Just as they had kept a vigil at Lazarus's bedside, they probably also kept a vigil at a window, constantly scanning the horizon to see whether Jesus were finally arriving in Bethany. Mary's disappointment, like that of Martha, is expressed openly. Such is the nature of true friendship. Martha and Mary probably do not think Jesus will bring Lazarus back to life; when Jesus asks for the stone at the entrance to the tomb to be removed, Martha seems hesitant rather than expectant (John 11:39). Despite their disappointment and despair, Martha and Mary appreciate Jesus' presence in their time of grief. He is their friend, and they need his love. And the lesson they will learn about God's greater plan will far outweigh any grief they suffer now (John 11:40-44).

WORDS AND DEEDS

Today's printed text stops too soon. That's obvious to anyone familiar with this account. Jesus' words about resurrection are followed by the actual raising of Lazarus. Imagine that you are a preacher and you are preaching on this text. Suddenly you realize that there sits before you a family that has just experienced the death of a loved one. Jesus is not going to come physically to your town as he came to Bethany. He is not going to engage that family in conversation. He is not going to walk with them out to the village cemetery. He is not going to call the name of their loved one and bring that person back to life again. How would you relate the raising of Lazarus to their situation?

There are at least two possibilities. When you read closely today's lesson, you cannot escape the feeling that Martha and Mary found comfort in the presence of Jesus, even though they didn't know he would bring Lazarus back from the dead. You cannot escape the feeling that they found comfort in the *words* of Jesus even though they did not know what he would do. So grieving people in any place and at any time can find comfort in the presence and in the words of Jesus.

But this is also true: if the one who died was a believer, then Jesus *is* going to do for that person what he did for Lazarus. He is not going to do it immediately, but he is going to do it eventually. The only difference is a matter of time!   —R. C. S.

CONCLUSION

A true friend will do for us what we *need* in the long run rather than what we *want* in the short run. Such a friend will also lovingly confront us with our blind spots and problem areas. Jesus is just such a friend, as Mary and Martha discovered. But Jesus, as the Son of God, is unlike any earthly friend we might have because of his death on the cross. Jesus' friendship is expressed not only in his life of love, but also in his death for us while we were still sinners (Romans 5:6-8).

THOUGHT TO REMEMBER

Jesus is the Friend who never fails us.

Discovery Learning

This page contains an alternative lesson plan emphasizing learning activities. Classes desiring such student involvement will find these suggestions helpful. The next page is a reproducible activity page to further enhance discovery learning.

LEARNING GOALS

After participating in this lesson, each student will be able to:

1. Characterize friendship, as based on Jesus' interactions with Martha and her sister Mary on his two visits to Bethany.

2. Explain how friendship leads to particular behaviors in both routine and extreme life experiences.

3. Affirm personal appreciation for a brother or sister in Christ in a tangible way.

INTO THE LESSON

Before class begins write one of each of the letters of the word *friendship* on ten pieces of lightly colored construction paper. Mix up the letters. To begin class, give one of the scrambled letters to ten students. Ask them to unscramble the word and stand in the correct order to display it when finished. Note: if your class is smaller, use the word *friend* instead of *friendship*.

State: "Friendships are an important part of our daily lives." Draw three concentric circles on the board. Pointing to the outer circle, tell the class we have some people in our lives we might call "acquaintances." The next circle can represent "friends." The inner circle represents one or two "very close friends." Write the words in as you identify them.

Ask each class member to identify a person he or she calls a very close friend. Ask volunteers to tell what makes their friends special to them.

Make the transition to Bible study by telling them we will glimpse the wonderful friendships of Mary and Martha with Jesus. From them we will learn how to appreciate, understand, and encourage our friendships.

INTO THE WORD

Using the Lesson Background (page 171) and the circle of friends illustration from above, remind the class that Mary and Martha (and Lazarus) fall into the very close personal friendship category. Read aloud the printed texts, telling the class that these are two very different incidents in the lives of these friends. One incident has a touch of humor; the other is a sharing of grief.

Use the reproducible word-find puzzle on the next page to review the incidents and look for hints to qualities of healthy friendships. What characteristics of friends are demonstrated here? Ask one class member to be a "scribe" and write answers on the board. (*Answers may include hospitality, listening, enjoying the company of the other person, openness, kindness, and others.*)

Then do the same thing with the other incident. (*Answers may include sympathy, compassion, empathy, honesty, understanding.*)

Display a poster with the words "Jesus did something for Lazarus that no other friend could do." Mention to the class that we cannot overlook the supernatural side to this event. Jesus raised his friend, Lazarus, from the dead (v. 44). Ask, "What did Jesus do for you that no other friend could do?" (*He died for me!*) Ask, "Is it presumptuous to consider Jesus, the Son of God, our friend? Is there Scriptural foundation for considering him our friend?" (See John 15:13-15.) Consider using the "What a Friend" section of the reproducible page that follows here.

INTO LIFE

Ask the class to refocus on the qualities that make good friendships. Ask for other qualities that have made their friendships strong. List these with the others already posted.

Then tell the class you are going to provide an opportunity to prepare a note to send to a friend expressing appreciation or offering encouragement. Give each person a piece of paper with three columns. The heading of the first column is to be "Precious Memories"; the second, "Treasured Items"; the third, "Special Qualities." Ask each student to write the name of a friend at the top of his or her paper. Then ask the students to think of special experiences they have had with their friends and note those in the first column. If time permits, after a few moments, ask for a few volunteers to share what they wrote. The second column is to list possessions that come from that relationship. It may be photographs, gifts, or something special from their experiences together. The third column is an opportunity to list the special qualities of that person. They may mention their friend's persistence, faith, laughter, sensitivity. Again, if time permits, allow a few people to share their notes and thoughts after completing columns two and three.

Ask the class to use these notes as a foundation for letters of appreciation or affirmation to their friends within the next two days. (This activity is included in the student book, *NIV Bible Student.*)

Good Friends

Having good friends is one of God's blessings in life. In today's text we discover that Jesus enjoyed a special friendship with Mary, Martha, and Lazarus. Find qualities of good friends in the "word-search" grid puzzle and list them to the right.

```
M F K G E C O M P A S S I O N E
D K Q H O S P I T A B L E Q U M
F A I T H F U L I S T E N S E P
X G E N T L E N E S S I B P W A
U E N G D R V O N X I D E N U T
D N C P D N J F I N X O B N V H
G E O Z L U E L L H O N E S T Y
T R U N D E R S T A N D I N G P
L O R O M B P U S N T J B M Z N
L U A R C E T A R E D I S N O C
A S G H Y U H A K V J J T S D A
L A I C I F I R C A S X S X O F
R O N W R Q W J F U T U U O E F
T H G U X K L G U Y F U U L S X
```

_____

_____

_____

_____

_____

_____

_____

_____

_____

_____

_____

_____

_____

_____

Bad Friends

The friends we choose make a great deal of difference in our lives (Psalm 1:1). What risks do Christians encounter when we choose ungodly friends?

What a Friend . . .

We sing of Jesus' friendship in songs like "What a Friend We Have in Jesus." Another song testifies "No One Ever Cared for Me Like Jesus." Jot a few notes to him expressing appreciation for his friendship and what he has done for you.

PILATE: JUDGE ON TRIAL

LESSON 8

WHAT DO YOU THINK?

Political correctness is a phrase that became popular in the United States in the early 1980s. Throughout that decade and the one following, this phrase underwent various changes in meaning. Today it refers to the insistence that a person's thoughts and actions be brought in line with popular opinion.

Probably your students have been pressured more than once to conform to political correctness. Sometimes they have handled the pressure well, and sometimes they haven't. Today's lesson provides something of a negative example, a look at one who gave in to the pressure. Pontius Pilate was the Roman governor who heard Jesus' case. Convinced of Jesus' innocence, still Pilate handed him over for execution. That way he would satisfy the political demands and expediency of the moment. Pilate stands as a sobering warning for your learners to maintain their witness at all times, in all circumstances, lest they crucify "the Son of God all over again . . . subjecting him to public disgrace" (Hebrews 6:6).

INTRODUCTION

A. GETTING A BAD RAP

In the early morning hours of April 15, 1865, a man with a broken leg knocked on the door of Dr. Samuel A. Mudd. The doctor set the man's leg, put a splint on it, and let him stay in his house for a few hours to recuperate. The man with the broken leg was John Wilkes Booth, who had just assassinated U.S. President Abraham Lincoln. Dr. Mudd was accused of complicity in that crime and sentenced to life in prison. President Andrew Johnson pardoned Dr. Mudd in 1869.

Some historians are convinced that Dr. Mudd was one of the conspirators in the Lincoln assassination. Others believe that Dr. Mudd got a "bad rap"—that he had no idea who Booth was or what he had done. Whatever the case, almost everyone knows the saying, "His name is Mudd." Long after his death, Dr. Mudd's name is still an epithet—fairly or unfairly.

Pontius Pilate is an enigmatic figure. People automatically associate him with history's greatest injustice. Pilate, not a particularly sympathetic character, was a man caught in the midst of political intrigue. Several times he tried to do what was right regarding Jesus. In the end, however, he capitulated to pressure from the Jews and had Jesus executed. Did Pilate get a bad rap? Ask yourself that question at the end of this week's lesson.

B. LESSON BACKGROUND

Palestine was, at the time of Jesus' life, an imperial province of Rome. The Jews had a figurehead king on the throne, but the true power in Palestine was in the hands of the Roman governor. He was considered a personal servant of the emperor. Pilate had control over all civil, military, and criminal matters.

Pilate governed Palestine from A.D. 26 or 27 to 37. Historians of his time have little to say about him. The Roman historian Tacitus barely mentions Pilate. Jewish historians Josephus and Philo of Alexandria give more information, but even their descriptions are sketchy. The most revealing source of information about

DEVOTIONAL READING:
1 TIMOTHY 6:11-16

BACKGROUND SCRIPTURE:
JOHN 18:28–19:16

PRINTED TEXT:
JOHN 18:31-38; 19:12-16

LESSON AIMS

After this lesson each student will be able to:

1. Tell how Pilate was pressured into convicting and sentencing Jesus against his better judgment.

2. Compare Pilate's predicament with the situation of people today who are pressured to compromise principles.

3. Suggest a specific means of reaffirming one's commitment to Christ and resisting pressure to compromise.

Jan
19

KEY VERSES

[Jesus said,] "Everyone on the side of truth listens to me."

"What is truth?" Pilate asked.
—John 18:37, 38

LESSON 8 NOTES

Pilate is the New Testament. The reference in Luke 13:1 to Pilate's brutality poses many questions, all of which remain unanswered.

Pilate's place in history is marked by his dealings with one man. His record as governor is undistinguished. Pilate could easily have been totally unrecognized in the annals of history—a petty ruler of an obscure province. His name, however, always will be associated with one cowardly act of capitulation. He is the judge whom history, in turn, has put on trial.

I. PROTECTING A KINGDOM (JOHN 18:31-35)

A. AN UNWANTED SITUATION (vv. 31, 32)

31. Pilate said, "Take him yourselves and judge him by your own law."

"But we have no right to execute anyone," the Jews objected.

After his arrest in Gethsemane, Jesus is subjected to a series of "interviews" with the Jewish high priest Caiaphas and his father-in-law, Annas. Without doubt, Caiaphas wants Jesus to be executed. But Caiaphas knows that the Jewish Sanhedrin no longer has the power to carry out a death sentence. It lost that power when Rome changed the nature of its rule over the area in A.D. 6. So Caiaphas follows the proper political channels and sends Jesus to *Pilate*.

Jesus appears before Pilate in the very early hours of Friday morning. It seems that Pilate is not eager to deal with Jesus (John 18:28-30). Pilate, like most governors in the Roman Empire, wants to stay off Rome's radar screen, but the political infighting in Palestine makes that difficult. He may have heard some of the rumors about Jesus, but we can be sure Pilate wants to avoid political intrigue. It is not surprising, then, that Pilate tells *the Jews* to deal with the problem internally. He wants no part of the matter! The proconsul Gallio will take much the same attitude a few years later when dealing with the apostle Paul (Acts 18:12-15).

32. This happened so that the words Jesus had spoken indicating the kind of death he was going to die would be fulfilled.

Jesus has prophesied that he will be crucified (Matthew 20:19; John 3:14; 12:32, 33). But the Jews do not execute by crucifixion. They normally execute by stoning (Deuteronomy 21:18-23), but even that cannot be done without the Romans' permission. The stoning of Stephen in Acts 7 is not sanctioned by the Romans, but that is not a formal, court-ordered execution. Stephen's death is the impulsive act of an angry mob.

B. A TRICKY QUESTION (v. 33)

33. Pilate then went back inside the palace, summoned Jesus and asked him, "Are you the king of the Jews?"

Despite his desire to be left out of this matter, *Pilate* knows that he has a kingdom to protect. Rome will not tolerate insurrection in any of its provinces, and will deal harshly with any governor who does not investigate quickly rumors of sedition. So protecting Rome's interests is a way of protecting Pilate's own job!

Pilate undoubtedly has heard rumors of the man from Nazareth who some claim to be a *king*. (After meeting Jesus once, Nathanael had declared him to be "the Son of God" and "the King of Israel"; John 1:49. And in Jesus' appearance before Caiaphas, the high priest had pointedly asked Jesus if he was the Christ—the Messiah—and Jesus had answered, "I am"; Mark 14:61, 62. To the Jewish people, the promised Messiah is to be *the king of the Jews*.) Pilate may have chosen to ignore it, but Jesus' triumphal entry into Jerusalem probably piqued his interest. He may desire to stay out of Jewish inner-circle politics, but he also does not want Rome breathing down his neck. So when the Sanhedrin brings Jesus before him, he knows he has no choice but to examine the case.

Pilate asks what at first glance seems to be a simple question. It is, however, a very tricky question. Is Jesus the king of the Jews? A "yes" answer will take the proceedings down one path, while a "no" answer would take it down another. Jesus eventually will answer "yes," but not just yet.

THE GREAT ONE

The Honeymooners became one of the most popular television "situation comedies" in the 1950s. All America became well acquainted with the antics of blustery Ralph Cramden (played by the rotund one, Jackie Gleason), his patient and long-suffering wife (played by Audrey Meadows), and their upstairs neighbors—a zany free spirit who worked in the sewers of Brooklyn (Art Carney) and his equally long-suffering wife (Joyce Randolph).

Nearly every episode featured two famous lines by Gleason: "One of these days, Alice!" and "Baby, you're the greatest!" But the greatest, at least in Gleason's mind, was Gleason himself. Actors have egos and Gleason was no exception. He went on in show business to be billed as "The Great One." Jackie Gleason was the undisputed king of comedy at a time when black and white television ruled the night.

History establishes that Jesus Christ was indeed the King of the Jews, the King of Israel. More than that, the book of Revelation calls Jesus "King of kings and Lord of lords." All kings have egos, but Jesus had none. He did not have to bluster his way through life as did "The Great One." He did not have to climb up on the prow of a ship, as did Leonardo DiCaprio in *Titanic*, and shout into the wind, "I'm the king of the world!"

Was Jesus a king—*the* King? Oh, yes, he was (and is) the King. But he lived like a servant. He was God, but he died as a man. Part of his greatness is in his humility.
—V. K.

C. A STINGING RESPONSE (vv. 34, 35)

34. "Is that your own idea," Jesus asked, "or did others talk to you about me?"

Pilate certainly does not expect to be questioned by a prisoner, especially this lowly peasant from the hill country of Galilee. But Jesus is not intimidated! He responds with a stinging rebuke. Is Pilate speaking from his own initiative and curiosity, or is he merely parroting the charge of the Sanhedrin? Jesus always cuts to the heart of the matter. There is no pretense with him. He knows what Pilate is doing and what kingdom Pilate is protecting.

35. "Am I a Jew?" Pilate replied. "It was your people and your chief priests who handed you over to me. What is it you have done?"

What is the tone of Pilate's voice? Is it defensive or contemptuous? No doubt he is caught off-guard by Jesus' question. Some believe he is pleading ignorance: he isn't *a Jew*, so how can he understand what is going on? He did not initiate Jesus' arrest. Jesus' problem is with his own people! They are the ones who are making the accusations against him.

Others see Pilate as more hostile. Who does Jesus think he is, questioning the Roman governor? Jesus might be able to baffle and outwit those Jewish leaders, but Pilate is not a Jew! Now that the leaders have brought Jesus to him, Jesus had better start answering the charges. What has *he done?*

II. PROCLAIMING THE KINGDOM (JOHN 18:36-38)

A. THE RIGHT METHOD (v. 36)

36. Jesus said, "My kingdom is not of this world. If it were, my servants would fight to prevent my arrest by the Jews. But now my kingdom is from another place."

Jesus acknowledges that he has a *kingdom*, but it is not an earthly kingdom. It therefore poses no threat to the Roman Empire. Earthly kings come to power by

HOW TO SAY IT

Alexandria. Al-iks-AN-dree-uh.
Annas. AN-nus.
Antonia. An-TOE-nee-uh or An-TOE-nyuh.
Caesar. SEE-zur.
Caiaphas. KAY-uh-fus or KYE-uh-fus.
Corinthians. Kor-IN-thee-unz.
Deuteronomy. Due-ter-AHN-uh-me.
Gabbatha (Hebrew). GAB-buh-thuh.
Galilee. GAL-uh-lee.
Gallio. GAL-ee-o.
Gethsemane. Geth-SEM-uh-nee.
Josephus. Jo-SEE-fus.
Nathanael. Nuh-THAN-yull.
Nazareth. NAZ-uh-reth.
Philo. FIE-low.
Pontius Pilate. PON-shus or PON-ti-us PIE-lut.
Sanhedrin. SAN-huh-drun or San-HEED-run.
Tacitus. TASS-ih-tus.

might. They have great armies, powerful weapons, and military strategy. They conquer, terrorize, and kill without conscience in order to attain land and people. Jesus' kingdom is different. He does not subjugate people by might but by love. He does not conquer by power of the sword, but by an appeal to the heart. If his were an earthly kingdom, then his followers would have fought to keep him from being arrested. In fact, Peter had tried to do just that! (See John 18:10.)

Think about what kind of threat Jesus could have posed to his enemies. If Jesus had been interested in an earthly kingdom, what a military leader he would have been! His army would have been invincible! Think of the possibilities. He had the power to calm the wind and the waves (Mark 4:37-41). Power over nature could come in very handy in the midst of a battle. Jesus could feed thousands of people with miniscule amounts of food (Luke 9:12-17). No need to worry about feeding the troops! Jesus could heal the sick. If a man were wounded in battle, Jesus could heal him immediately and have him rejoin the battle. The ultimate power would have been that of resurrection. If a man were killed in battle, Jesus could raise him to fight again and again! The powers at Jesus' disposal are awe-inspiring. No military force on earth could have stopped him.

Jesus, however, is not interested in an earthly kingdom or in any form of earthly power. The true enemy is not the Roman Empire, but Satan and death (Luke 10:18, 19; 1 Corinthians 15:26). Jesus will have a kingdom, but it will not be attained by the methods used by sinful men or expected by the Jewish leaders. His method is entirely different. He will love his enemies and do good to those who hate him (Matthew 5:44). He will not merely proclaim these as vaunted principles, he will practice them. He will die to pay sin's price. He will rise again to defeat the true enemies.

In the twentieth century, a chancellor came to power in Germany. Accepting the philosophy "might makes right," he began to bully all of Europe. He proclaimed a rule that would last a thousand years. It lasted less than twelve. Hitler's "Third Reich" was responsible for the deaths of millions of innocent people. His method was wrong and his reign was short. Jesus' method is right, and his reign, in the hearts of men and women throughout the world and throughout the ages, is endless!

THE WIZARD OF AHS

In Frank L. Baum's timeless tale, *The Wonderful Wizard of Oz*, Dorothy and her little dog Toto are transported via a furious cyclone from their humble home on the plains of Kansas to the fantastic and sometimes frightening kingdom of Oz. Dorothy's breathtaking adventures and misadventures with the tin man, scarecrow, and cowardly lion regale the reader and lead him or her into a mystifying kingdom that truly is not of this world.

The power behind this eerie kingdom is an anonymous figure who is "pulling the strings," so to speak. He holds sway over everyone by pretending to be someone he is not. "Oohs and ahs" are extracted from those he is fooling. When the curtain is finally pulled back, he is exposed for all to see. The "wonderful wizard of Oz" is nothing more than a crafty charlatan.

How often we are fooled by the ruler of this world! Like Dorothy and her traveling companions, we are taken in by the tantalizing tinsel or tough-talking tactics of the enemy. Scripture depicts Satan as a deceiver (cf. 2 Corinthians 11:14). Christians must be wary of his devious schemes, lest they be drawn into his counterfeit kingdom.

Jesus firmly declared that his kingdom was not of this world—that his kingdom was not from here. His is a *spiritual* kingdom first and foremost. And to that we can say, with a measure of relief, "Ah-men!"   —V. K.

WHAT DO YOU THINK?

Jesus was not interested in earthly power. To what extent, if at all, is it proper for Christians to seek earthly power? What does this signify for Christians participating in their country's political process?

DAILY BIBLE READINGS

Monday, Jan. 13—When You Have Turned Back (Luke 22:24-34)

Tuesday, Jan. 14—Peter Denies Jesus (Luke 22:54-62)

Wednesday, Jan. 15—Peter Goes Fishing (John 21:1-6)

Thursday, Jan. 16—It Is the Lord (John 21:7-14)

Friday, Jan. 17—Simon, Do You Love Me? (John 21:15-19)

Saturday, Jan. 18—Repent and Be Baptized (Acts 2:37-42)

Sunday, Jan. 19—In Jesus' Name, Walk (Acts 3:1-7)

B. THE RIGHT CONCLUSION (v. 37)

37. "You are a king, then!" said Pilate.

Jesus answered, "You are right in saying I am a king. In fact, for this reason I was born, and for this I came into the world, to testify to the truth. Everyone on the side of truth listens to me."

Jesus' response has left *Pilate* reeling. Pilate had not expected a philosophical debate with this itinerant rabbi from Nazareth. What is this talk about a kingdom not of this world? Pilate wants Jesus to get to the point—is he saying that he is *king* or not?

Jesus affirms that Pilate is *right in saying* that he is *a king*. But Jesus needs to offer further clarification: his is a kingdom of *truth*. Only those *on the side of truth* will listen to him (cf. 10:3, 16, 27).

C. THE RIGHT QUESTION (v. 38)

38. "What is truth?" Pilate asked. With this he went out again to the Jews and said, "I find no basis for a charge against him."

Pilate has no idea what Jesus is talking about. Nor does he care! To the pragmatic politician, truth is whatever he needs it to be at the moment. Like many today, Pilate has abandoned the idea of absolute *truth*. He walks away before Jesus can answer his question.

Yet, there standing before Pilate was *Truth!* Jesus is not a man who merely tells the truth; he is the living truth (John 14:6). Knowing him means knowing truth and freedom (John 8:32). Jesus makes freedom available to us by the power of his own life, death, and resurrection. And the one who is the truth also teaches truth. Despite what men may say, there are absolute truths that are immutable. And there is the absolute *Truth*, who lives and reigns in the hearts of his followers. Jesus came to proclaim a kingdom and to proclaim himself as the King!

Pilate has indeed asked the right questions. Even though he does not acknowledge Jesus as any kind of king except sarcastically (19:14, 15, 19), Pilate at least recognizes that Jesus is no criminal. He can find *no basis for a charge against him.*

III. PLACATING THE CROWD (JOHN 19:12-16)

A. THE REJECTION (vv. 12, 13)

12. From then on, Pilate tried to set Jesus free, but the Jews kept shouting, "If you let this man go, you are no friend of Caesar. Anyone who claims to be a king opposes Caesar."

Much has happened in the intervening text not included in our lesson (John 18:39–19:11). *Pilate* has squirmed this way and that, trying to get Jesus released. He knows the charge against Jesus is without legal foundation, but that the Jewish leaders have brought Jesus to him out of envy (Matthew 27:18). He knows Jesus poses no threat to Rome, so he wants *to set Jesus free.*

The leaders of *the Jews* are livid. They are also cunning politicians. They know the power of rumor and innuendo. Their threat is not veiled as they switch their argument from theology (John 19:7) to politics: *Caesar* will not be pleased to hear that his governor in Palestine has failed to deal with one who claims to be a king. As is often the case, hardball politics wins the day.

13. When Pilate heard this, he brought Jesus out and sat down on the judge's seat at a place known as the Stone Pavement (which in Aramaic is Gabbatha).

There is some debate among scholars about the location John describes. It may be part of the Roman fortress, the Antonia, which is adjacent to the northwest

WHAT DO YOU THINK?

In a "postmodern" culture that believes that truth and moral values are relative, how important to the Christian faith is belief in absolute and objective truth? Why?

[Consider John 14:6 in your discussion.]

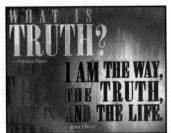

Display this poster from the Adult Visuals packet as you discuss verse 38. Note the irony of Pilate's question, asked in the presence of the one who is Truth.

WHAT DO YOU THINK?

The Jews pressured Pilate into doing what he did not really want to do by invoking the name of Caesar. What are some techniques that people use today to pressure Christians into doing what they know they shouldn't? How can we resist such pressure?

PRAYER

Father, give us wisdom and courage. May we make Jesus our King. May he reign in our hearts with supreme authority. In his holy and majestic name we pray, amen.

WHAT DO YOU THINK?

The Jewish leaders committed blasphemy even as they pushed to have Jesus executed for "blasphemy." Have you ever been condemned by someone for something you knew your accuser to be guilty of? Have you ever found yourself guilty of the very thing you condemned in another? How do you deal with such situations?

[See Matthew 7:1 and Galatians 6:1, 2.]

THOUGHT TO REMEMBER

Jesus is the King. Let him reign in your heart.

corner of the temple grounds. In any case, Pilate brings Jesus to a public *place* to pronounce his judgment and dispatch the matter. The one to whom all judgment ultimately is trusted (John 5:22) is now to be judged himself.

B. THE REPUDIATION (vv. 14, 15)

14. It was the day of Preparation of Passover Week, about the sixth hour.
 "Here is your king," Pilate said to the Jews.

Although some have argued that these events took place on Thursday, or even Wednesday, most Bible scholars agree that John spoke of the sixth day of the week, Friday. There also has been some controversy about John's notation of time. If the trial was still in progress at *the sixth hour*, then how could Jesus have been crucified at the third hour, as Mark 15:25 records? The simple solution is that John was using Roman time, which places these events at about 6 a.m. (Other time references in John's Gospel are consistent with a use of Roman time.) Mark used Jewish time, which would place the crucifixion at 9 a.m., three hours after these events.

Pilate's sarcasm and taunting of his Jewish opponents is revealed in his statement, *Here is your King*. Even though Pilate rejects their charge against Jesus, he bows to their wishes and gives in to their threats. The great irony is that the King of the universe is indeed standing in their midst, and no one recognizes it. The blindness noted in John 12:37-41 is complete.

15. But they shouted, "Take him away! Take him away! Crucify him!"
 "Shall I crucify your king?" Pilate asked.
 "We have no king but Caesar," the chief priests answered.

The Jewish authorities lead the charge to have Jesus crucified. Victory is within their grasp. Again, *Pilate* sarcastically refers to Jesus as their *king*. The reply, *We have no king but Caesar* is blasphemous (cf. Judges 8:23; 1 Samuel 8:7). God has sent his own dear Son to reign over them, but they reject him and claim allegiance to the pagan in Rome instead. Even that claim is drenched in hypocrisy because they hate Caesar—they just hate Jesus more.

C. THE RESULT (v. 16)

16. Finally Pilate handed him over to them to be crucified.
 So the soldiers took charge of Jesus.

This pathetic drama moves toward its final act as Pilate gives in to political extortion. Rome will hardly note the crucifixion of a peasant from Galilee who has no friends in high places. The Jewish leaders, on the other hand, could create a political firestorm. Pilate does not need that kind of complication. Pilate wants to do the right thing, but he is a pragmatic governor. History has judged Pilate an evil man. In reality, he is a coward and a political opportunist.

So the King of kings is led down the dusty streets of Jerusalem to be nailed to a cross. The Son of God will hang suspended between Heaven and earth to pay the penalty for our sin, to be God's sacrificial Lamb.

CONCLUSION

God sent his Son to earth. The people who had waited for the Messiah for centuries did not understand the nature of his kingdom and rejected Jesus. Pilate deserves our disdain for his cowardice. The Jews deserve our disdain for they, in one of history's most ironic judgments, rejected Jesus and claimed Caesar as their king. But we must reserve some disdain for ourselves because our sin made Jesus' crucifixion necessary. But today God still gives us the opportunity to make Jesus our King.

Discovery Learning

This page contains an alternative lesson plan emphasizing learning activities. Classes desiring such student involvement will find these suggestions helpful. The next page is a reproducible activity page to further enhance discovery learning.

LEARNING GOALS

After participating in this lesson, each student will be able to:

1. Tell how Pilate was pressured into convicting and sentencing Jesus against his better judgment.

2. Compare Pilate's predicament with the situation of people today who are pressured to compromise principles.

3. Suggest a specific means of reaffirming one's commitment to Christ and resisting pressure to compromise.

INTO THE LESSON

Before class write "His name is mud" on the chalkboard. Also prepare two pieces of paper with one of these names on each, *Mudd* and *Pilate*.

Begin by asking what the saying means. Then ask if any one knows the source of the saying. Use the lesson Introduction (page 179) to tell the story. Do not use Dr. Mudd's name until the end when you attach the paper with his name on it over the word *mud*.

Make the transition to Bible study by saying, "Fairly or unfairly, long after his death, Dr. Mudd's name is still an epithet. In today's study, we glimpse another figure whose name, fairly or unfairly, has been associated with history's greatest injustice. His name is Pilate." At this time place Pilate's name over Mudd's.

INTO THE WORD

Prepare a handout for the class. On one side include the printed Scripture from John 18:28-38, 19:1-16. (The back side is described in the group discussion activity.) Highlight the reading parts for a narrator, Pilate, Jesus, two chief priests, and two soldiers on their individual handouts. Ask the narrator, Pilate, and Jesus to stand at the front of the class for the reading. All others will read the part of the crowd from where they are seated.

Use the Lesson Background to prepare a brief lecture on the setting for this occasion. Prepare visual cards you can attach to the wall as an outline during this brief lecture. The cards should have one of the following words on each: *Palestine, Province, Power, Procurator,* and *Pilate*.

The following activities may be done in small groups or by the entire class. Both tasks should be printed on the back side of the handout.

Pilate's Problem: Pilate was a man caught in political intrigue. He appeared to try to do what was right. But in the end he capitulated to pressure and had Jesus executed. Does Pilate get a "bad rap"? Read the following texts for a closer look. Beside each text, write a phrase that describes his character or actions.

John 18:28, 29   _____

John 18:31-33   _____

John 18:33-38   _____

John 19:1   _____

John 19:4, 5   _____

John 19:8   _____

John 19:9-12   _____

John 19:16   _____

Luke 13:1   _____

What conclusions do you draw about Pilate's character and circumstance? How does Pilate's dilemma compare to those in situations today that tempt them to compromise?

(After allowing class members to share their answers, say, "Jesus shares something wonderful with Pilate that helps us understand our future. The next activity will focus on Jesus' teachings about the kingdom of God.")

Jesus' Kingdom: Re-read Jesus' private interview with Pilate (John 18:33-38). Answer these questions:

1. Why did Pilate have to know whether Jesus was King of the Jews?

2. Why—if his kingdom were of this world—would Jesus' servants fight (v. 36)? What is Jesus teaching about his kingdom here?

3. Jesus gave a reason for his coming to this world in verse 37. What does he mean "to testify to the truth"?

4. Jesus also said, "I am the way and the truth and the life" (John 14:6). Notice he didn't say he "told the truth." He said "I am the . . . truth!" What is the difference?

(After a time, allow the groups to respond.)

INTO LIFE

The reproducible page that follows has a series of activities designed to get learners to think about the kingdom of Christ, both in its present reality and in its future glory. Use that page to encourage the group to read and think "heavenly thoughts."

Ask class members to think about what they are looking forward to most in Heaven. Ask the class to share their hopes in groups of two or three. Those small groups then can pray together, thanking God for their hope in the kingdom.

Living in and for the Kingdom of God!

GLIMPSES OF THE KINGDOM

There are so many snapshots of the kingdom of God in the Gospels. Matthew, especially, has filled his book with kingdom sayings and kingdom parables. Some have clear meanings, while others require thought and research. Read selected passages below and note what you learn about the kingdom of God by each. You will discover rich promises and blessings!

Matthew 4:17 _____   6:33 _____

4:23 _____   7:21 _____

5:3 _____   10:7 _____

5:10 _____   11:11 _____

5:19 _____   12:28 _____

5:20 _____

LIVING IN THE KINGDOM

As a part of God's family, you are part of his present kingdom. What does this wonderful assurance mean to you about your life's purpose? Your possessions? Consider the following texts.

Matthew 13:11, 19 _____   18:1-4 _____

13:24, 38 _____   18:23-35 _____

13:31 _____   19:14 _____

13:33 _____   19:23, 24 _____

13:44 _____   20:1-16 _____

13:47 _____

LOOKING FORWARD TO THE KINGDOM

The kingdom of God is not only present in us. It is also a future world beyond imagination. But imagine as best you can.

What do you look forward to leaving behind when you enter the eternal kingdom of God?

What skill, job, or opportunity would you like to have in Heaven that you do not have here?

PETER: RESTORED LEADER

LESSON 9

WHY TEACH THIS LESSON?

Our church recently created a new pictorial directory. You know how it works: a photography company comes in, takes the pictures, creates a "free" directory for each family, and hopes people will buy enough portraits that the company can make a profit. While listening to the sales pitch, I was quite amused by the option to purchase a "touch up" service to erase wrinkles. The photographer was offering to make me look better than I really do! Taking my cue from Oliver Cromwell, Lord Protector of England from 1653 to 1658, I declined the offer. In sitting for his own portrait, Cromwell instructed the artist to use all his skill "to paint my picture truly like me, and not flatter me at all; but remark all these roughnesses, pimples, warts, and everything as you see me, otherwise I will never pay a farthing for it."

The Bible is this way, too. Its heroes are presented with "warts and everything"—nothing is glossed over. Since your learners—like everyone else—are all flawed people as well, today's lesson reminds them that God can use them in his service despite their shortcomings. He uses you in just the same way!

INTRODUCTION

A. FLAWED PEOPLE

Occasionally you will hear someone use the phrase "revisionist history." That expression refers to a retelling of history with a different slant on things. Sometimes revisionist history makes things sound a little better than they really were, and sometimes it makes things sound a little worse. It depends on the way a person wants to slant things!

One of the great strengths of the Bible is that it is not "revisionist history." If the Bible were, as some claim, a collection of myths or fables, why would we so consistently see the foibles and failures of its heroic figures?

Abraham was a great man of God, but his faith sometimes wavered in the face of danger, leading him to lie to protect himself. Moses was God's chosen servant to deliver his people out of bondage and to deliver to those people the law of God. But Moses was also a man with a temper—a temper that once erupted so violently that he killed someone!

Elijah was the great Old Testament prophet who called down fire from Heaven to defeat the prophets of Baal on Mount Carmel. He appeared on the Mount of Transfiguration with Moses and Jesus. Yet Elijah had such severe moments of doubt that he once wished he were dead. David is the only person in Scripture who is characterized as a man after God's own heart (1 Samuel 13:14; Acts 13:22). But we know also that David was a man guilty of lust, deception, and murder.

In the New Testament, the two most prominent Christian leaders are Paul and Peter. But remember that Paul had been an ardent persecutor of the church. He was responsible for the imprisonment and death of many believers. Peter, the focus of this week's lesson, was also a man deeply flawed.

The Bible's honesty about its heroes adds to its credibility. No revisionist history here! The Bible does not hedge about the flaws of its main characters. The Bible never flinches at the truth.

DEVOTIONAL READING:
ACTS 4:1-13

BACKGROUND SCRIPTURE:
LUKE 22:31-34, 54-62; JOHN 21

PRINTED TEXT:
LUKE 22:31-34, 54-62; JOHN 21:17

LESSON AIMS

After participating in this lesson, each student will be able to:

1. Cite the events surrounding Peter's denial of Jesus and his eventual restoration.

2. Explain why one who confidently asserts devotion can yield to denial in the heat of opposition.

3. Recall a time when he or she has denied (in word or in deed) the Lord, and express repentance and renewed love for him.

Jan 26

KEY VERSE

Jesus said to Simon Peter, "Simon son of John, do you truly love me more than these?"

"Yes, Lord," he said, "you know that I love you."

Jesus said, "Feed my lambs."
—John 21:15

B. LESSON BACKGROUND

This week's lesson begins at the Passover meal on Thursday evening. After Jesus instituted the Lord's Supper, he sat talking with his disciples. He had a lot to say. He knew what would happen the next day. Imagine that you knew you had only a few hours to live. Wouldn't you have a lot to say to the people you love? That's probably how Jesus felt. He talked to the disciples about the nature of greatness in God's eyes and about their place in his kingdom. Then he turned to Peter.

I. THE DECLARATION (LUKE 22:31-34)

Imagine what might be in Peter's heart when Jesus turns to him. Jesus has been talking about being great and about ruling in his kingdom. Peter has been waiting for this moment for almost three years. He is the one who had proclaimed Jesus to be the Christ, the Son of God (Matthew 16:16). He is the bold one, the fearless leader of the band of disciples. Surely his moment has come!

A. THE ENEMY'S REQUEST (v. 31)

31. "Simon, Simon, Satan has asked to sift you as wheat.

Simon Peter might not be surprised to hear Jesus say, "The Father and I have been talking about you." Instead, imagine Peter's confusion when he hears Jesus tell him that he and *Satan* have been talking about him!

But Peter is not alone, since the Greek pronoun translated *you* is plural. Jesus is addressing Peter, but speaking of the entire group of disciples. Satan wants to test all of them! Winnowing or sifting of *wheat* is a common event in agricultural Palestine. The disciples understand what Jesus is talking about, but they must wonder why. At the last supper, they undoubtedly are thinking about Jesus' being recognized as the Ruler of Israel and setting up his kingdom. But he is talking about Satan's testing them. Peter is not the only one who is confused!

B. THE SAVIOR'S PRAYER (v. 32)

32. "But I have prayed for you, Simon, that your faith may not fail. And when you have turned back, strengthen your brothers."

Jesus addresses Peter personally in this verse (the word translated *you* is singular). Jesus has asked the Father to bind them together so that Peter will not feel alone and his *faith* will not waver.

But Jesus knows what is about to happen. He knows that Peter will experience a moment of utter failure. But when Peter recovers from this failure—has *turned back*—the darkness of his denials will be transformed into a light that burns brightly for Christ. Jesus knows that Peter's post-resurrection boldness can invigorate his fellow apostles in their mission of proclamation.

C. AN APOSTLE'S AFFIRMATION (v. 33)

33. But he replied, "Lord, I am ready to go with you to prison and to death."

We often think of Peter as having "foot in mouth" disease because of his apparent tendency to pop off at times. Not this time! Peter means what he says. At this moment, he truly counts himself as *ready* to die for Jesus. And when the mob comes for Jesus in the garden, Peter will draw his sword and prepare to kill or be killed! It is easy to criticize Peter for his failures, but do not characterize him as a coward.

INTO PRISON, AND TO DEATH

Ivan S. Prokhanoff (1869–1935) was the dynamic leader of the evangelical Christian movement in Russia before and after the Bolshevik Revolution of 1917. Twice he was put in prison for his faith. Arrested by the Cheka, the political police

WHAT DO YOU THINK?

Satan wants to enslave every Christian, just as he wanted Peter and the other apostles. (See 2 Timothy 2:26; 1 Peter 5:8; Revelation 2:10.) How does knowing this help you? How can Christians be more sensitive to spiritual forces at work?

[Consider 1 Corinthians 10:12 and Galatians 6:3 in your discussion.]

WHAT DO YOU THINK?

How do experiences of testing equip us to strengthen the faith of other Christians? How can the church cultivate an environment where we encourage other people to do that?

[Use 2 Corinthians 1:4 to frame your answer.]

of the revolution, Prokhanoff and his followers (known simply as "Gospel Christians") joyfully witnessed in their cells. "We sang, read the Word of God, and prayed. The red soldiers, militiamen, and even the Cheka came and listened to us. . . . Many people gathered in the street outside to listen to our singing. Was there ever such a testimony?" (*In the Cauldron of Russia*, 1933).

Richard Wurmbrand was a Romanian Jew who converted to Christianity. He spent fourteen years in prison for leading an underground church and smuggling Bibles into Russia. After his release he wrote a best-selling book *Tortured for Christ* (Spire, 1962; reprinted 1998), and in 1966 testified in Washington, D.C. before the Senate Internal Security Subcommittee about what believers like himself were enduring in prisons behind the Iron Curtain. He stripped to the waist to convince skeptical politicians with his "scars and stripes" that torture in Communist prisons was real. But many of his fellow prisoners never came out of the prisons alive. They were terribly "tortured and refused to be released, so that they might gain a better resurrection" (Hebrews 11:35).

> Must I be carried to the skies
>   On flow'ry beds of ease,
> While others fought to win the prize
>   And sailed through bloody seas?   —Isaac Watts (1674–1748)

—V. K.

D. THE MASTER'S REPLY (v. 34)

34. Jesus answered, "I tell you, Peter, before the rooster crows today, you will deny three times that you know me."

If words can pierce the human heart, *Peter* is wounded. What is Jesus saying? Has Peter not just declared his loyalty to the point of imprisonment and death? How, then, can Jesus be saying that Peter will shrink back at simply being accused of knowing Jesus? In Peter's mind, there is no conceivable scenario in which he *will deny* knowing Jesus. That simply is never going to happen. And to think it will happen *three times* before the dawn of the next morning is absurd. In his heart, Peter knows that he would rather die than deny!

II. THE DENIALS (LUKE 22:54-62)

In order to understand the subsequent denials of Peter, certain events must be placed in context. Jesus and his followers have gone to Gethsemane after celebrating the Passover and instituting the Lord's Supper. There Jesus prayed. His weary disciples succumbed to their exhaustion and slept.

Sometime during the early morning hours on Friday, Judas and the members of the temple guard came to Gethsemane to get Jesus. Jesus accepted the ironic kiss from the traitorous Judas. Then, when the members of the temple guard stepped forward to seize Jesus, Peter drew his sword and tried to defend Jesus by attacking the high priest's servant (John 18:10), slicing off the man's ear. Let's give Peter credit for his courage. He was ready to defend Jesus with his life! How many of us have such courage?

But with adrenaline pumping and muscles tensed for further battle, Peter sees Jesus reach for something on the ground. It is the severed ear of Malchus. Jesus turns to Peter and tells him to put away his sword (John 18:11). Then Jesus miraculously restores Malchus's ear to its proper place on the side of his head (Luke 22:51). Imagine the confusion in Peter's mind! Jesus had just said, in effect, "Peter, that just isn't the way we do things!"

Peter does not understand just how God is going to do things. He is no coward, but he is very much confused. He is also embarrassed and hurt. Jesus' healing of Malchus probably humiliated Peter. He is probably asking himself, "What

HOW TO SAY IT

Abraham. AY-bruh-ham.
Annas. AN-nus.
Baal. BAY-ul.
Caiaphas. KAY-uh-fus or KYE-
   uh-fus.
Elijah. Ee-LYE-juh.
Galilean. Gal-uh-LEE-un.
Galilee. GAL-uh-lee.
Gethsemane. Geth-SEM-uh-nee.
Judas. JOO-dus.
Malchus. MAL-kus.

am I supposed to do, anyway?" He stands there perplexed as the soldiers lead Jesus away.

A. INTERESTED PARTY (v. 54)

54. Then seizing him, they led him away and took him into the house of the high priest. Peter followed at a distance.

Perhaps because of the early hour, Jesus is taken to the high priest's home rather than to any official site. Annas, the father-in-law of the high priest, will interrogate Jesus. Caiaphas, the high priest himself, also will ask questions (John 18:12, 13). Luke's focus at this point, however, is upon *Peter*. When Jesus is taken from the garden, Peter probably does not move for a moment. When he does move, he does not run off and hide in a cave. He follows the mob—but from a safe *distance*.

The stunning sequence of events in Gethsemane has unnerved a very confused Peter. He does not walk away from the situation because he wants to know how events will unfold from that point on. Perhaps Gethsemane was the wrong place, and Jesus is waiting to get inside the walls of Jerusalem before effecting some miraculous escape. Perhaps Peter will have an even better opportunity for heroic action in defense of Jesus. Peter does not know what is going to happen, but he is an interested party. Whatever is about to happen, Peter apparently wants to be close by.

B. THREE DENIALS (vv. 55-60)

55. But when they had kindled a fire in the middle of the courtyard and had sat down together, Peter sat down with them.

The high priest's house is actually a palace. Like most palaces of the time, it includes open courtyards. Some people in the palace complex know the apostle John. He accompanies *Peter* into the city, and they are allowed onto the palace grounds (John 18:15-17). It is not yet dawn and it is cold, so it is normal to build *a fire*. After first standing beside the fire, Peter sits *down* with others who are warming themselves there (John 18:18).

56. A servant girl saw him seated there in the firelight. She looked closely at him and said, "This man was with him."

The people gathered beside the fire obviously are aware of some of the events that have taken place. They know that something is going on between Jesus and someone in the high priest's palace. Such a hubbub at this hour of the morning is unusual. People are curious!

If anyone ever wanted to go unnoticed in a crowd, it is Peter at that moment. But a young woman staring at Peter recognizes him as an associate of Jesus.

57. But he denied it. "Woman, I don't know him," he said.

Peter suddenly hears himself saying that he does not even *know* Jesus. This is not a reasoned response—it is an adrenaline rush into self-preservation. Peter is in the wrong place, at the wrong time, associated with the wrong person. He does not have time to think about the past or the future. He lives only in that moment, and in that moment he does something he never dreamed he would do.

58. A little later someone else saw him and said, "You also are one of them."

"Man, I am not!" Peter replied.

Peter's first denial has bought him a *little* time, but it also causes people to look at him more closely. Then someone else speaks up and claims that Peter is a part of the group that followed Jesus. We must remember that Jesus often has been the center of attention in Jerusalem, and Peter is no shrinking violet. So it is not unreasonable to think people would recognize him. But Peter again denies that association.

Peter is like an animal caught in a trap. He is acting out of fear and not from logic. It is not just that Peter fears for his life—he is confused about why Jesus is acting the way he is. All the solid ground has fallen away from under Peter, and he isn't sure of anything except his own desire to survive.

59. About an hour later another asserted, "Certainly this fellow was with him, for he is a Galilean."

Peter's second denial bought him more time, but it also has given someone time to look more closely at him and to listen to him talk. It is Peter's *Galilean* accent that gives him away (Matthew 26:73). Everyone knows that Jesus is from Galilee and most of the men in his band of close associates are also Galileans. The man who spoke was confident that he is correct about Peter. Peter feels he must appear equally confident that the man is wrong.

60. Peter replied, "Man, I don't know what you're talking about!" Just as he was speaking, the rooster crowed.

Peter vehemently denies any knowledge of what his accuser was talking about—even invoking a curse (an oath; Matthew 26:74; Mark 14:71). His life is at stake. He cannot afford to be ambiguous. He has to be forceful and persuasive. The words fly from his mouth. Then, with the final syllables of Peter's denial still hanging in midair, *the rooster* crows to welcome the morning and fulfill Jesus' prophecy.

C. JESUS' EYES (v. 61)

61. The Lord turned and looked straight at Peter. Then Peter remembered the word the Lord had spoken to him: "Before the rooster crows today, you will disown me three times."

This is surely one of the most poignant moments in the Bible. Perhaps Jesus has been brought into the courtyard or is passing by a window. Now close enough to see and hear *Peter,* Jesus turns just long enough to make direct eye contact.

What Peter suddenly feels is more than a lump in the throat. It far transcends embarrassment or humiliation. This is one of those moments when the whole world changes. Having *remembered* the words of Jesus, Peter is abruptly reminded of Jesus' identity. He is the one who can foretell future events. He is God in the flesh. And Peter has just denied any association, much less loyalty, to him.

Jesus' look does not merely remind Peter of his identity and power; it is the look of one friend into the eyes of another. It is almost impossible to fathom the sense of betrayal, hurt, and at the same time love in those eyes. If the events of the preceding hours had confused Peter's mind, the eyes of his friend surely break his heart.

D. PETER'S SORROW (v. 62)

62. And he went outside and wept bitterly.

With his mind reeling and his heart aching, Peter flees. He doesn't just tear up or get reddened eyes. His weeping is the kind that must have left him unable to catch his breath. Jesus' look has penetrated Peter's soul, and he feels an anguish he has never known before. Peter has promised to die for Jesus, and then, during the span of a very short time, denies even knowing him. And Jesus has heard those terrible words spew from Peter's mouth. For the rest of Peter's life, will the sound of a rooster crowing bring back those tears again and again?

RECANTING A RECANTATION

On a visit to England some years ago, I had the privilege to stand in the pulpit where Thomas Cranmer once preached. As I stood in the pulpit, placing my hands on the very wood where he once had placed his hands, I recalled his bittersweet story.

Cranmer (1489–1556) was a Cambridge-educated preacher who had come under the influence of Martin Luther during travels on the continent. Cranmer was glad when Henry VIII brought an end to the rule of the Pope over the Church of England.

WHAT DO YOU THINK?

How was it possible for Peter to deny Christ? What factors contributed to his failing? What danger signs can we see in his experience that we should watch for in our own lives?

WHAT DO YOU THINK?

Peter had promised to die for Jesus, but he was not willing even to admit he knew him. How can Christians avoid committing Peter's sin of denial when their faith is severely tested?

[Passages such as 1 Corinthians 10:13; Hebrews 12:1, 2; and James 1:2, 3 may help in your discussion.]

PRAYER

Father, help us remember that no matter what we have done, we can be restored to fellowship with you and to usefulness in your kingdom. In Jesus' name, amen.

Display this visual as you set the scene for the last verse of the text.

WHAT DO YOU THINK?

What comfort can we take from the fact that Jesus forgave Peter for his earlier denials? [See 1 John 1:7, 9.]

THOUGHT TO REMEMBER

God is in the restoration business!

In 1532, Henry VIII appointed Cranmer as the first Protestant archbishop of Canterbury. After Henry VIII died, Cranmer became the prime "mover and shaker" in the English Reformation. *The Book of Common Prayer,* still used by the Anglican Church today, and the Forty-Two Articles (which was made the official creed of the Anglican Church in 1553) were largely the work of Cranmer. He was the hero of the day.

But when Edward VI died of tuberculosis in 1553, his sister "Bloody Mary" took the throne and did her best to return England to the fold of Roman Catholicism. By the end of 1556, seventy-five people had been burned at the stake, among them Thomas Cranmer. In a moment of weakness the acknowledged hero of English Protestantism recanted, signing a statement in which he denied the cause for which he had labored. Then, realizing the shock waves that would result from what he had done, he recanted his recantation. On March 21, 1556, at Oxford, by a great act of the will he held his hand that had signed the denial in the flames until the flesh dropped from the bones.

If Peter could have burned out his tongue and thus erased his denial, he would have done it. But no act of the will could undo what Peter had done. There was only one solution. Nothing but the grace of God could take away Peter's shame.

God's grace is greater than our disgrace.   —V. K.

III. THE DUTY (JOHN 21:17)

The final verse of this week's lesson provides what Paul Harvey calls "the rest of the story." After Peter flees the courtyard, Jesus goes through other appearances before officials and is finally crucified. Then, on Sunday morning, he rises from the dead. He appears before his disciples a number of times before his final ascension into Heaven. John 21:17 relates a portion of one of those appearances.

A. PIERCING QUESTION (v. 17a)

17a. The third time he said to him, "Simon son of John, do you love me?" Peter was hurt because Jesus asked him the third time, "Do you love me?"

Jesus has a job for *Peter* to do, but the Lord has to ask some questions to be sure Peter is up to the task. The most important question centers on the degree of Peter's devotion to him. Just as Peter has given voice to three denials, Jesus poses his question three times. Peter is anguished that such a repetition is necessary.

B. COMPLETE RESTORATION (v. 17b)

17b. He said, "Lord, you know all things; you know that I love you." Jesus said, "Feed my sheep."

Peter is a changed man. He had been transformed by his own anguish and by seeing Jesus alive again. Too much has been made of the different words for *love* (in the Greek) that Jesus and Peter use. Much more important is that Peter's earlier, three-fold denial is now replaced by a three-fold affirmation of love.

Jesus knows that Peter is a changed man, and he knows that Peter is up to the job of proclaiming the gospel and caring for the body of believers who will be the church, as are the other disciples. Jesus' complete restoration of Peter is expressed in the simple words, *Feed my sheep*.

CONCLUSION

Perhaps of all the imperfect people who appear in the pages of the Bible, none is more striking than Peter—the man who denied even knowing Jesus after following him for over three years. But God is in the restoration business! He is the great Potter, and we are his clay. He takes the shattered pieces of our imperfect lives and not only restores our fellowship with him, he makes us useful in his kingdom. What a mighty God we serve!

Discovery Learning

*This page contains an alternative lesson plan emphasizing learning activities. Classes
desiring such student involvement will find these suggestions helpful. The next page
is a reproducible activity page to further enhance discovery learning.*

LEARNING GOALS

After this lesson each student will be able to:

1. Cite the events surrounding Peter's denial of Jesus and his eventual restoration.

2. Explain why one who confidently asserts devotion can yield to denial in the heat of opposition.

3. Recall a time when he or she has denied (in word or in deed) the Lord and express repentance and renewed love for him.

INTO THE LESSON

Remind the class that this series of character studies has made the point that God uses imperfect people to accomplish his will. Ask people to identify Old or New Testament heroes of faith who failed God, disappointed God, or resisted God's will. Ask people to stand and identify the person by speaking in the first person: have them say the name, some action of faith for which the person is noted, and what the person did to hurt, disappoint, or flee from the Lord. Post a visual with the opening and closing lines of their presentation:

Opening: "My name is _____, and. . . ."

Closing: "I blew it, and I'm not proud of that."

Give this example: "My name is Elijah. God used me on Mount Carmel to call down fire from Heaven and defeat the prophets of Baal. But I confess that there were times I doubted the Lord so much that I actually said, 'I wish I were dead.' I blew it, and I'm not proud of it."

As volunteers do so, write the names they mention on the board. Make the transition to Bible study by drawing a circle around Peter's name or by adding his name. State: "Peter is another good example of how God can work through people with foibles and failures."

INTO THE WORD

Have the class fill in the reproducible activity from the next page and then do the following clusters of activities in small groups or as a whole class. If done in small groups, write the instructions below for each group. Give group 1 a piece of poster board and marker pen.

Activity 1: "Exercise in Chronology." Scan all of Luke 22:31-62. On your poster board make three major headings of the places where events occurred in this passage. Under each place, list a summary of the events.

Activity 2: "In Peter's Shoes: Denial." Imagine what was in Peter's heart when he had this experience.

1. Did Peter deny Jesus because he was a coward, or was he simply overconfident with bravado (v. 33)? Why do you say so?

2. Why did he deny Jesus? Why would he do such a thing? What does his action teach us?

Activity 3: "In Peter's Shoes: Restoration." Peter made confident statements of determined faithfulness. But he blew it! He denied Jesus. However, after the resurrection, Peter changed and was restored. After reading John 21:17, answer these questions.

1. Why did Jesus ask Peter the same question three times?

2. What was Jesus asking of Peter by saying "Feed my sheep"? What would the image of the shepherd mean to Peter? (See also John 10:15.)

INTO LIFE

Remind the class that God uses imperfect people and that he is in the restoration business for those who disappoint him but choose to return to him. Give each student a handout of the following activity. It should have the heading "Chapter Titles for My Book" and read as follows:

"If you were writing a book about your walk with Christ, what would you use as chapter titles for the following chapters?

"Chapter 1. A chapter describing how you came to know and accept Jesus. (If you are not yet a Christian, this chapter can describe how God is working in your heart today.)

"Chapter 2. A chapter describing an event(s) when you blew it and disappointed the Lord.

"Chapter 3. A chapter describing the healing of the event(s) described in chapter two, if such healing has already occurred.

"Chapter 4. A chapter detailing what you think God is calling you to do or try right now."

Give students five minutes to write chapter titles to as many of the above as possible. Then, in small groups (or with the whole class), ask them to share their chosen titles for chapter two. They do not need to share the events of that chapter if they do not choose to.

Remind the class that we, like Peter, blow it, sadly disappointing God. But God still calls imperfect people like us to serve. Remind them to "complete" chapter four by saying "yes" to God's call.

Do You Love Me?

Peter seemed so confident as he said, "I am ready to go to prison with you and to death!" What a disappointment when he failed Jesus by denying he knew his Lord. It is good to hear of Peter's change after the resurrection.

Fill in the blanks below from Luke 22:31-34, 54-62 and John 21:17. Fill in each word on the corresponding line below. You will find a challenge for each of us today. Are you ready for such a challenge?

1. Jesus said to Simon Peter that _____ has attacked his faith (Luke 22:31).

2. Jesus told Simon Peter that he had _____ for Him (Luke 22:32).

3. Peter told Jesus he was ready to go with him to prison and to _____ (Luke 22:33).

4. Jesus' prophecy: Peter would _____ that he knew Jesus (Luke 22:34).

5. Jesus was arrested and taken to the home of the High _____ (Luke 22:54).

6. and 7. A _____ had been kindled in the middle of the _____ (Luke 22:55).

8. A _____ girl was the first to accuse Peter (Luke 22:56).

9. The gender of the second accuser is revealed when Peter says, "_____, I am not!" (Luke 22:58).

10. Peter was hurt when Jesus asked the third time, "Do you _____ me?" (John 21:17).

11. Jesus' third command to Peter was, "_____ my sheep" (John 21:17).

From the letters in the shaded boxes complete this statement of challenge:

Like Peter, I am to be ⬜⬜⬜⬜⬜⬜⬜⬜⬜⬜⬜

Key: 1. Satan, 2. Prayed, 3. Death, 4. Deny, 5. Priest, 6. Fire, 7. Courtyard, 8. Servant, 9. Man, 10. Love, 11. Feed.
Key word: Transformed

BARNABAS: ENCOURAGER AND ENABLER

WHY TEACH THIS LESSON?

In just a little more than a month "March Madness" will be upon us. That's the nickname for the media attention and hype given to the NCAA basketball tournament. If you have basketball fans in your class, they probably are already speculating about which teams will get the top seeds, which ones will be left out, and which ones have the potential to go all the way.

The more avid fans can quote statistics. They can tell you who has scored the most points, who has the most rebounds, and who does best at the free-throw line. Ask your statisticians about assists—who has the most of them? That's a statistic that fans often overlook, but coaches don't. They know it takes someone to feed the ball to that hot shooter to win ball games. It's not as glamorous as scoring, but it's just as important.

Some of your learners don't feel as if they "score" well in the Christian life. They have no big "accomplishments" to point to. Today's lesson will reassure them that not everyone scores, but everyone can assist!

INTRODUCTION

A. "I BELIEVE IN YOU"

Was there a person who changed your life because he or she believed in you? Perhaps it was a coach or a teacher. There are millions who can see our flaws, but how many will notice our potential? It is only natural that you would be drawn to people like those.

The problem is there are not enough such people. Add up the criticism others give us and the criticism we give ourselves, and it is a heavy burden. What a treasure are those who see our best qualities and spur us on to become even more than we are! The man who occupies our attention in this lesson was clearly a person who believed in people.

B. LESSON BACKGROUND

Today's lesson is drawn from several passages in the book of Acts. These passages form a series of snapshots of a man called Barnabas, also known as Joseph. Admittedly he is not as well known as some of the other characters in the New Testament. He is surely at the top of the list of the second rank.

Barnabas is best known as the supporter, mentor, and traveling companion of the apostle Paul. F. F. Bruce notes that one might question "whether Barnabas belonged to the Pauline circle or . . . Paul belonged rather to the circle of Barnabas." In his early work with Saul (Paul's previous name), Barnabas is clearly preeminent. The book of Acts initially refers to this team as Barnabas and Saul (11:25; 12:25). Later, it becomes Paul and Barnabas (13:42, 43), but there is no hint that there was ever any jealousy about this.

DEVOTIONAL READING:
HEBREWS 10:19-25

BACKGROUND SCRIPTURE:
ACTS 4:32-37; 9:26, 27; 11:19-30; 15:36-41

PRINTED TEXT:
ACTS 4:36, 37; 9:26, 27; 11:22-26; 15:36-41

LESSON AIMS

After participating in this lesson, each student will be able to:

1. Tell how Barnabas lived up to his name as an encourager to the early church, to Saul of Tarsus, and to John Mark.

2. Explain why encouragement is so needed in ministry.

3. Suggest a specific means of encouraging a Christian worker.

Feb
2

KEY VERSES

When he [Barnabas] arrived and saw the evidence of the grace of God, he was glad. . . . He was a good man, full of the Holy Spirit and faith.
—Acts 11:23, 24.

We know nothing factual of Barnabas's physical qualities, although we have one tantalizing clue. On one occasion, some villagers who saw Barnabas and Paul do miracles called Barnabas "Zeus" and Paul "Hermes" (Acts 14:12). Zeus was the king of the gods of the mythical Greek pantheon, and Hermes was his messenger. We might infer by their identification that Barnabas was the more physically impressive while Paul, "the chief speaker," was the more talkative.

We do not know when Barnabas became a Christian. The historian Eusebius claims that he was one of the seventy disciples Jesus commissioned to preach in Luke 10:1, but we have no reliable evidence of this.

Let us proceed now to the events that give us insight into Barnabas and his positive character qualities.

I. GENEROSITY (ACTS 4:36, 37)

In our lesson today, we'll be jumping around through the text in Acts to sketch our portrait of Barnabas. As we begin, the events of the Day of Pentecost are still fresh in people's minds.

A. BARNABAS'S BACKGROUND (v. 36)

36. Joseph, a Levite from Cyprus, whom the apostles called Barnabas (which means Son of Encouragement),

Although Barnabas's proper name is *Joseph*, he comes to be known almost exclusively by his nickname, *which means* "son of consolation," *"son of encouragement,"* or "son of exhortation." Many people in the Bible take on new names or become known by some nickname. In the Old Testament the list includes Abraham and Jacob. In the New Testament it includes Simon Peter and Paul.

Barnabas, as a *Levite*, is of the ancient priestly tribe of Israel. *Cyprus*, his home, is a large island about one hundred miles off the coast. John Mark, whom we will meet later, is a relative (Colossians 4:10).

B. BARNABAS'S GIFT (v. 37)

37. . . . sold a field he owned and brought the money and put it at the apostles' feet.

The early church is noted for its extraordinary generosity—in its willingness to have a common treasury through which to care for the needs of its members. Barnabas serves as an illustration of that generosity. He also serves as a backdrop for the mistaken and tragic decision of Ananias and Sapphira (Acts 5:1-11).

Some have compared this shared treasury to modern Communism. This comparison is not warranted, since this generosity is always voluntary. The purpose of relating this account is not to develop an economic model, but to illustrate a spiritual dynamic of the early church.

Levites, descendants of Levi, had no tribal land in Israel except for the forty-eight Levitical cities designated in Joshua 21. Was this land that Barnabas owned near one of those? Was it in his native land of Cyprus? We simply don't know. Wherever it was, selling the land and giving all *the money* is a significant sacrifice. Laying the money *at the apostles' feet* is the method of sharing this offering.

II. DISCIPLING (ACTS 9:26, 27)

As we move from Acts 4 to Acts 9, at least three years have passed. Stephen has been stoned, and Saul of Tarsus stood by holding the coats of those who stoned him (Acts 7:58). The gospel is spreading as the church is persecuted and scattered. But then Saul, the chief persecutor, is converted. Later he returns to Jerusalem.

A. AN UNLIKELY DISCIPLE (v. 26)

26. When he came to Jerusalem, he tried to join the disciples, but they were all afraid of him, not believing that he really was a disciple.

Galatians 1:18 tells us that Saul's arrival is about three years after his conversion. The disciples' suspicion, given Saul's record, is understandable (cf. Acts 8:3). We have the benefit of hindsight to know that his conversion is genuine.

The church in *Jerusalem* will not soon forget the image of Saul holding the coats of those who stoned Stephen to death. This puts Saul in an awkward situation. He cannot go back to his old friends, for they will not embrace his conversion. The church is not yet ready to accept him, either. This must be a lonely time for him.

Into that void of loneliness steps Barnabas. Vouching for someone always involves risk. People frequently let us down. Vouching for a person like Saul, with his history, is a great risk, indeed.

B. A RISKY ENDORSEMENT (v. 27)

27. But Barnabas took him and brought him to the apostles. He told them how Saul on his journey had seen the Lord and that the Lord had spoken to him, and how in Damascus he had preached fearlessly in the name of Jesus.

Barnabas is the one willing to take this former enemy of the church and introduce him to the leaders. No doubt there is some lingering resentment and suspicion about Saul. When one's chief persecutor becomes an ally, there are bound to be some who doubt the sincerity of the conversion. That is only human nature.

The apostles mentioned here do not include all (or only) the Twelve. Paul notes in Galatians 1:18, 19 that he visited only Peter and James the Lord's brother. Barnabas tells them about Saul's vision and courageous preaching in the days after his conversion. Mentioning Saul's boldness is perhaps a way to underscore to the apostles that Saul has put his own life at risk. Indeed, Saul only recently had escaped death *in Damascus* (Acts 9:22-25). Anyone risking life and limb for the gospel would not be some kind of spy.

STANDING SPONSOR

I am convinced that Acts 9:27 is the pivotal passage in the book of Acts. Were it not for that single adversative conjunction *but* at the beginning of verse 27, the book of Acts might well have ended with verse 26 on an extremely negative note. Here is the Jerusalem church, "the mother of us all," about to reject one of her sons—a son who, if given a chance, will do more for her and the world than any other of her illustrious children in all history.

Don DeWelt said of Barnabas, "He believed when others doubted; he loved while others were suspicious." Do we really believe that God's grace is greater than man's disgrace?

On May 10, 1993, convicted serial killer Jeffrey Dahmer repented and was baptized in a maximum-security prison in Portage, Wisconsin. A personal friend of mine, Roy Ratcliff, a minister in nearby Madison, made the initial contact, did the teaching, baptizing, and follow-up work with Dahmer until he was brutally bludgeoned to death by a fellow inmate on November 28, 1994. *Newsweek* magazine, December 12, 1994, later reported that Ratcliff was Dahmer's only regular visitor.

Roy testified, "Since the baptism, the most frequent question I have been asked is if I believe that all of Jeffrey Dahmer's sins have been forgiven. . . . 'Aren't there some sins too evil to be forgiven?' All such questions reflect a poor understanding of the grace of God and the complete forgiveness that is available in Christ Jesus" (*One Body*, Autumn 1994).

Thank God for brave souls who dare to stand sponsor for those converted from a life of sin and shame! —V. K.

Post this visual at the beginning of the session. It sets the stage for application of this lesson.

HOW TO SAY IT

Ananias. An-uh-NYE-us.
Antioch. AN-tee-ock.
Barnabas. BAR-nuh-bus.
Cilicia. Sih-LISH-i-uh.
Cyprus. SIGH-prus.
Eusebius. You-SEE-be-us.
Galatians. Guh-LAY-shunz.
Gethsemane. GETH-sem-uh-nee.
Hermes. HER-meez.
Levi. LEE-vye.
Levite. LEE-vite.
Levitical. Leh-VIT-ih-kul.
Pamphylia. Pam-FILL-ee-uh.
Sapphira. Suh-FYE-ruh.
Silas. SIGH-luss.
Silvanus. Sil-VAY-nus.
Tarsus. TAR-sus.
Zeus. Zoose.

WHAT DO YOU THINK?

Acts 11:24 summarizes the character of Barnabas. What characteristics (from this verse or others) do you especially appreciate about him as a good role model for Christians today?

III. MENTORING (ACTS 11:22-26)

Barnabas's efforts on Saul's behalf were successful. Saul was accepted by the church, and he "stayed with them and moved about freely in Jerusalem" (Acts 9:28). His bold preaching soon got him in trouble with some of the enemies of the church, however, so he was sent to his hometown of Tarsus for safety (9:29, 30). When we next hear of Saul, it is Barnabas once again who is encouraging his ministry.

A. A MINISTRY (vv. 22-24)

22. *News of this reached the ears of the church at Jerusalem, and they sent Barnabas to Antioch.*

Antioch in Syria is a major commercial center, the third largest city in the Roman Empire. And something wonderful is happening there: the church is growing! (See Acts 11:19-21.) This growth is coming in part from the conversion of Gentiles (v. 20). The mother *church* in *Jerusalem* is understandably concerned about the ramifications. It is a tribute to his character that Barnabas is selected to investigate. Being from Cyprus, Barnabas understands the Gentiles. (Some men from Cyprus are in Antioch preaching; see 11:20.) Being a Levite, Barnabas is trusted by the Jewish believers.

23. *When he arrived and saw the evidence of the grace of God, he was glad and encouraged them all to remain true to the Lord with all their hearts.*

The encouragement Barnabas receives in Antioch leads him to encourage others there in turn. He is certain that these conversions are genuine, and evidently he does much preaching and teaching for this church. He encourages them to build on the great beginning they have made and to continue *to remain true to the Lord.*

24. *He was a good man, full of the Holy Spirit and faith, and a great number of people were brought to the Lord.*

What a summary of a man's character! Every Christian would be glad to be considered *full of the Holy Spirit* and full of *faith.* In addition, it is no small thing to be labeled *a good man.* Being called "good" does not mean perfect. It is not an exaltation of human goodness, but rather a description of how the goodness of the Lord is exemplified in Barnabas. The result of his ministry is more converts *to the Lord.*

B. AN ASSISTANT (vv. 25, 26)

25. *Then Barnabas went to Tarsus to look for Saul.*

The success of the endeavor prompts *Barnabas* to *look for* an associate in ministry. The particular nature of the church in Antioch somehow makes Barnabas think of *Saul.* Perhaps it is the Gentile involvement. Even though Saul is Jewish and thoroughly trained in the law, he has grown up in the Gentile world and understands Gentiles. As his Greek name Paul becomes more dominant (Acts 13:9), he will become known as the apostle to the Gentiles (18:6).

What Saul has been doing in *Tarsus,* his hometown (21:39), is not known. He may well have been there for several years. But those years were not wasted; they are undoubtedly a period of preparation.

26. *. . . and when he found him, he brought him to Antioch. So for a whole year Barnabas and Saul met with the church and taught great numbers of people. The disciples were called Christians first at Antioch.*

The work of *Barnabas and Saul* continues for a *year* with great success. This verse also gives us an interesting detail in that it is in *Antioch* that the followers of Jesus are first called *Christians.* The Greek word used here has been understood in various ways. Some say it signifies "follower of Christ." Others favor "member of the household of Christ."

We do not know who coined the term *Christians*. Some argue that it is God himself, but there is no strong evidence for that. Others propose that it is the citizens of Antioch—perhaps in some kind of derogatory sense. In any case, it has become the term of choice for disciples of Jesus, even in our own time. Previously, Christians were simply known as disciples (6:1), brothers (9:30), or members of "the Way" (9:2).

IV. CONFLICT MANAGEMENT (ACTS 15:36-41)

Much has happened between chapters 11 and 15 of Acts. Barnabas and Saul have completed a missionary journey and returned to Antioch (13:1–14:28). From there they traveled to Jerusalem to participate in the Jerusalem Conference (15:1-29). Saul, now known as Paul, returns with Barnabas, Silas, and some others to resume the ministry in Antioch—for a while (15:30-35).

A. A PROBLEM (vv. 36-38)

36. Some time later Paul said to Barnabas, "Let us go back and visit the brothers in all the towns where we preached the word of the Lord and see how they are doing."

We don't know exactly how long the phrase *some time later* signifies, but the year is now about A.D. 50. Paul wants to go back to the churches he and Barnabas had planted on their first missionary journey and to encourage them. This is a sensible plan, and Barnabas is eager to go along. But the agreement between them ends there.

37, 38. Barnabas wanted to take John, also called Mark, with them, but Paul did not think it wise to take him, because he had deserted them in Pamphylia and had not continued with them in the work.

Barnabas wants to take along his relative *John* Mark, who had accompanied them part-way on the first missionary journey (Acts 12:25; 13:5). John *Mark* is most likely the author of the book of Mark. Many believe he also was the young man whose presence in the Garden of Gethsemane is reported only by Mark (Mark 14:51, 52). We don't know why, but Mark had left them during that journey (13:13). Paul sees this as a desertion and believes that this disqualifies him for this trip.

B. A SOLUTION (vv. 39-41)

39. They had such a sharp disagreement that they parted company. Barnabas took Mark and sailed for Cyprus.

Fresh from a great victory at Jerusalem where they had stood together for including the Gentiles in the church (15:2), these two giants of the faith now split over an issue of procedure! They are great men, but men nonetheless. The Bible does not gloss over their weaknesses. We sometimes live under the illusion that the great heroes of the faith never had disagreements. This text dismisses that notion. Some see a subtext here because Paul and *Barnabas* have had a previous *disagreement.* (See Galatians 2:13.) However, while we do not minimize the incident, we dare not make too much of it, either.

Nothing more is ever said about this trip without Paul to Cyprus. Barnabas and Mark are, however, mentioned in complimentary terms in Paul's letters (1 Corinthians 9:6; Colossians 4:10; 2 Timothy 4:11; Philemon 24), so there must have been some kind of reconciliation. In his decision to part company, Barnabas is actually doing what he once did for Paul: he is being a sponsor and mentor for a promising servant of the Lord.

WHAT DO YOU THINK?

Paul and Barnabas disagreed over the issue of John Mark's failure. How should the church deal with those who fail in some ministry and then want to participate again? Would the concept of "probation" play a role?

[Include a look at 1 Corinthians 5 and 2 Corinthians 2:5-11 in this discussion.]

PRAYER

Dear Father, help me to find ways to encourage those with whom I come in contact. Help me to see the best in people, and help me to bring out the best in people. In doing so, I hope to bring glory to your name and success to your cause. In the name of Jesus I pray, amen.

Some have asked, "Who was right—Paul or Barnabas?" Evidence can be presented on both sides, and it probably doesn't matter. Some think the fact that Mark later proved himself (Paul even asked for John Mark to come to him) proves that Barnabas was right. Perhaps, however, it was the combination of Paul's toughness and Barnabas's gentleness that helped develop Mark into the helpful servant he became.

CONTENDING WITHOUT CONTENTION

A Christian minister once wrote a wonderful little tract called "Come to Jesus." The piece was instrumental in bringing many lost people to the Lord. But some years later the author had a falling out with a Christian brother. He became a merchant of venom and wrote a bitter broadside, consigning to Hell the man with whom he disagreed. When he asked another Christian friend what title he should give to his new tract he was told, "Why don't you call it 'Go to the Devil' by the author of 'Come to Jesus'?"

General Stonewall Jackson once overheard some of his troops arguing with each other over which strategy should be used in battle. In the heat of discussion some of them began making personal attacks on each other. Jackson, pointing to the battlefield, wisely reminded them, "Remember, gentlemen, the enemy is over there."

We do not have the luxury of fighting with each other. We do not wrestle against flesh and blood but against spiritual powers. Satan is our real enemy. Each of us must make every effort to keep the unity of the Spirit in the bond of peace. God wants us to contend for the faith without being contentious with one another. A house divided against itself cannot win the war.   —V. K.

40, 41. . . . but Paul chose Silas and left, commended by the brothers to the grace of the Lord. He went through Syria and Cilicia, strengthening the churches.

Silas, also known as Silvanus, takes Barnabas's place as Paul's traveling companion. We don't know where Paul first met Silas. But we do know that when the Jerusalem church council decided that Gentiles did not have to become Jews before they could be Christians, Silas was one of the men who accompanied Paul and Barnabas to Antioch to deliver the report and encourage the new believers (Acts 15:22).

Was it God's intention that Paul and Barnabas split up? Probably not. But God in his grace makes good come from bad, and this parting of ways is no different. Perhaps without this opportunity Silas never would have become as involved in missionary work as he did. Without Barnabas's continued mentoring, perhaps John Mark would have been "lost" to continued work for the kingdom of God.

WHAT DO YOU THINK?

How should Christians handle serious disagreements between themselves?

[Notice how Paul was able to be complimentary to both Barnabas and John Mark later in 1 Corinthians 9:6; Colossians 4:10; 2 Timothy 4:11; and Philemon 24.]

CONCLUSION

Perhaps you have heard the story of the little boy who said to his dad, "Let's play darts. I'll throw the darts, and you stand there and say, 'Good shot.'" This little story illustrates how even at an early age we need encouragers in our lives. One Bible teacher says that we should institute a new office in the church. He says that we need "cheerleaders," people who have the spiritual gift of encouragement.

Leslie Flynn notes that even though Barnabas left no epistle or gospel, he did influence much of our New Testament because of his significant impact on both Paul and John Mark. Adding Barnabas's indirect influence on Luke, through Paul, the impact becomes staggering.

As to what becomes of Barnabas, we have no reliable information. One ancient tradition says he was stoned to death, and another says he moved to Cyprus, served the Lord for many years, died, and was buried there. While we may be curious, it doesn't really matter. We have enough information about "the encourager" that can inspire us to be encouragers as well.

THOUGHT TO REMEMBER

People who encourage others are the most blessed people in the world.

Discovery Learning

This page contains an alternative lesson plan emphasizing learning activities. Classes desiring such student involvement will find these suggestions helpful. The next page is a reproducible activity page to further enhance discovery learning.

LEARNING GOALS

After participating in this lesson, each student will be able to:

1. Tell how Barnabas lived up to his name as an encourager to the early church, to Saul of Tarsus, and to John Mark.

2. Explain why encouragement is so needed in ministry.

3. Suggest a specific means of encouraging a Christian worker.

INTO THE LESSON

Remind the class that we have been discovering models for living as Christians. Today's model is Joseph, better known by his nickname, Barnabas (see the notes on Acts 4:36). "Barnabas" means "son of encouragement" or "son of exhortation." Ask, "If people were to give you a nickname about your service to Christ, what might it be? You may be known as 'Mr. Sunday School,' 'church handyman,' 'the elder's elder,' 'model mom,' 'Mr. Sound Man,' 'the nursery specialist,' or some other." Then have groups of about four people assign positive "nicknames" to each other that the group believes would be appropriate to each person's service to Christ. Allow a representative from each group to introduce the nicknames to the class. Make the transition to Bible study saying, "It is good to be recognized for what you do. Barnabas will teach us one quality that we desperately need in the church: the ability to encourage one another."

INTO THE WORD

Make copies of the reproducible activity "Exploring God's Word" from the following page. Have the class complete this activity to prepare for the following one.

During the week before class, recruit four people to give a brief "eyewitness report" on Barnabas's activities. Each person will be given: (a) one of the Scripture texts for today's lesson, (b) a copy of the lesson commentary for the text assigned, and (c) this note: "Imagine you were a witness to the events described in this Scripture text. Read the lesson commentary. Then plan a brief testimony to share with the class about what you witnessed, the circumstances shaping this event, and how Barnabas fulfilled his nickname 'son of encouragement' in this incident. Also, say how this event touched or impressed you." Take to class a staff, prayer shawl, or scroll to give each person prior to his or her presentation as a way to identify the person giving the testimony.

Follow this procedure for each witness. First, give the person the staff, shawl, or scroll to identify who will speak. After this witness tells his or her story, read the text (see below) and discuss it, using the questions found below. Also, write the heading "Encourager" on the chalkboard. List the means used by Barnabas to encourage another as the class discusses the questions.

Speaker #1 (Acts 4:36, 37): What way did Barnabas use to be an encourager in this incident? (*Generosity.*) What is different between the way the early church shared their possessions and communism. (*The church shared voluntarily, without compulsion; in communism the "sharing" is imposed by the state.*)

Speaker #2 (Acts 9:26, 27): How did Barnabas become an encourager in this text? (*He was an enabler of Saul's ministry.*) Who was encouraged? Why might this attempt to enable Saul (Paul) be risky for Barnabas?

Speaker #3 (Acts 11:22-26): What ways did Barnabas use to encourage the Antioch church? (*Exhortation, mentoring, teamwork.*) What clues to his character do you see in this text?

Speaker #4 (Acts 15:36-41): This part of the story shows a human side to Barnabas in a conflict. Do you see qualities here that serve as models, either good or bad? (*Conflict management.*)

INTO LIFE

Make the transition to application by reminding the class that "Barnabas" was a nickname describing a wonderful quality of his life. We can be encouragers in many ways. Ask the class to add to the board a list of other ways to encourage. Add these to the list.

Remind the class that Barnabas was especially encouraging to church leaders. He laid a generous offering at the apostles' feet, endorsed and encouraged Paul when he was a new disciple, and more. Let's focus on how we may be encouragers to church leaders, such as teachers, ministers, elders, and youth leaders. Distribute copies of the "Living God's Word" activity from the following page. Ask each learner to fill in the blanks after considering the initial three questions. Remind the class of the list you have on the board, and encourage each person to select one or more of those encouragement activities for his or her personal commitment

Exploring God's Word

Read Acts 4:36, 37; 9:26, 27; 11:22-26; 15:36-41; then fill in the blanks below.

1. The name *Barnabas* means _____ _____ _____.

2. Barnabas put the money from a real-estate sale at the _____ _____.

3. When Saul came to Jerusalem, the disciples did not believe he had really become a _____.

4. Barnabas testified to the disciples that Saul had _____ _____ in the name of Jesus.

5. The church at Jerusalem sent Barnabas to _____, after hearing of all the conversions there.

6. Barnabas' role in Antioch was to encourage believers to _____ _____ to the Lord.

7. Barnabas was described as a _____ man, full of the Holy Spirit and _____.

8. The disciples were called _____ first at Antioch.

9. Barnabas and Paul eventually had a _____ _____ and parted company, each selecting another traveling partner in ministry.

Key: 1. Son of Encouragement; 2. apostles' feet; 3. disciple; 4. preached fearlessly; 5. Antioch; 6. remain true; 7. good; faith; 8. Christians; 9. sharp disagreement

Living God's Word

Barnabas sets an example of one who knows how to encourage and enable other people and their ministries. Most of us would like to be an encourager of other people, but it takes time to learn this skill.

1. Name two or three people in your church whom you consider to be "encouragers." If possible, cite specific acts they have done that encouraged other people.

2. Barnabas was especially helpful and encouraging to Christian leaders. Why do Christian leaders in today's church need a special word of encouragement?

Clip the box that follows, fill it in, and carry it until you accomplish your commitment.

From among our church leaders, I will encourage _____.

I appreciate this person because . . .

I will do the following to encourage this person:

PAUL: OBEDIENT MESSENGER

LESSON 11

WHY TEACH THIS LESSON?

Years ago, I took a tour of an aircraft assembly plant. One sign posted in a work area caught my eye. It said, "Either conform exactly to the standard, or cause the standard to be changed." How important that directive was to those workers! As they labored to assemble those jet airliners, they must follow all blueprints and procedures to the letter. If anyone thought a blueprint or a procedure to be in error, then he or she could submit a suggestion to get it changed. But there was to be no tolerance for anyone just "doing their own thing" and making changes as they saw fit.

Such concrete examples put the lie to the prevailing mindset that says nothing is absolute. If those aircraft builders do not believe in an absolute standard, lives will be in jeopardy. And failing to abide by God's absolute standards has put our culture in jeopardy as well. If your students are feeling pressure from the world to abandon the clear and absolute standards of God, today's lesson will be a good reminder for them. Paul, the apostle of grace, still believed in faithful obedience.

INTRODUCTION

A. WHERE WOULD WE BE WITHOUT HIM?

Who can understand Christianity without understanding Paul? In modern times he has frequently been criticized, yet where would the church be without his influence? Of course, Jesus was the founder of Christianity, but it was Paul who became its intellectual center and its pre-eminent missionary and church planter. And ultimately we can understand Paul only if we first understand his conversion. This lesson centers on one of Paul's explanations of that conversion.

The book of Acts tells us much about Paul's life, and his epistles reveal much of his thinking. We know little to nothing, however, about his physical appearance. Second Corinthians 10:10 suggests that people thought him to be physically unimpressive. An ancient tradition says Paul was bald-headed, bowlegged, small but muscular, with eyebrows that met in the middle, and a prominent nose. He may have had some persistent physical problem, which is what many assume to be the "thorn in [his] flesh" he wrote of in 2 Corinthians 12:7. Some believe this "thorn" involved some kind of eye problem that may have made it difficult to look him in the face.

We know a lot about Paul's hometown of Tarsus. Tarsus was a river city near the northeast corner of the Mediterranean Sea, and it saw many name changes through the years. The Roman general Mark Antony (c. 83–31 B.C.) became quite fond of the city during his military campaigns. It was at Tarsus that he first met Queen Cleopatra of Egypt. Paul was right when he said it was "no ordinary city" (Acts 21:39).

Still, there is much we don't know and we will never know about Paul (at least in this life). But what we do know is enough to develop an appreciation of the man and his influence. Some have said that as Shakespeare is to literature, Paul is to theology. Frederick Buechner calls him the "Johnny Appleseed" of church planting.

DEVOTIONAL READING:
EPHESIANS 3:1-13
BACKGROUND SCRIPTURE:
ACTS 25:23—26:32
PRINTED TEXT:
ACTS 26:12-23, 27-29

LESSON AIMS

After participating in this lesson, each student will be able to:

1. Recite the details of Paul's experience on the road to Damascus and his response to it.

2. Explain why Paul's conversion and call are significant to the spread of the gospel.

3. Assess his or her own response to God's call and determine to take one specific step to conform to God's call more closely.

Feb
9

KEY VERSE

So then, King Agrippa, I was not disobedient to the vision from heaven.   —Acts 26:19

B. LESSON BACKGROUND

The incident we examine today is Paul's defense before King Agrippa in about A.D. 60. Officially named Marcus Julius Agrippa II, this ruler is known more simply as Herod Agrippa II. He was the great-grandson of Herod the Great, who was the ruler when Jesus was born. Since Herod was a family name, there were several in the dynasty who bore that designation, so some confusion of identity is natural.

Agrippa had been reared in Rome and was a court favorite during the reign of Emperor Claudius, who ruled A.D. 41–54. Agrippa oversaw a small piece of his family's original kingdom. He was frequently in the company of his sister Bernice, as he was in this incident. Rumors abounded that their relationship had become incestuous. Bernice later became the mistress of General (later Emperor) Titus. As the mistress of the general, Bernice eventually moved with him to Rome. Later, however, he sent her away because she was not accepted by Roman society. Herod Agrippa II was the last king descended from Herod the Great.

Paul's defense before Agrippa takes place in the city of Caesarea, a port city by the Mediterranean Sea. (This is not Caesarea Philippi, where Peter made the Good Confession—Matthew 16:13-20. That city is located some seventy miles to the northeast.) The city in our lesson is often called Caesarea by the sea. It was considered a more hospitable town for the Romans than Jerusalem, so Roman governors spent most of their time there. It was built by Herod the Great (reigned 37–4 B.C.) and was named in honor of Caesar Augustus (reigned 27 B.C.–A.D. 14). It was here that Peter first preached to the Gentiles (Acts 10).

Festus, the Roman provincial governor, set up the meeting between Paul and Agrippa. New in his position, Festus evidently wanted to dispose of the troublesome cases and was determined to come to some kind of resolution about Paul. After all, Paul had been in prison for two years. We know much less about Festus than we do about his predecessor. The Jewish historian Josephus mentions Festus, and we can suppose from what is recorded that the rule of Festus was fairly brief. It was also a stormy period. All indications are that during the entire reign, Festus sided with Herod Agrippa and they became good friends.

I. PAUL'S COMPELLING VISION (ACTS 26:12-18)

A. THE "WHERE" OF THE VISION (v. 12)

12. "On one of these journeys I was going to Damascus with the authority and commission of the chief priests.

The account Paul relates to Agrippa appears three times in the book of Acts: here and in chapters 9 and 22. This repetition illustrates how crucial the account is, not only to Paul, but also to the church as a whole. There are variations in the three accounts, depending on what needs to be emphasized.

Damascus is a Gentile city, but it has a strong Jewish population. Some have claimed Damascus to be the oldest continuously inhabited city in the history of the world. Indeed, its more than fifty references in the Bible go back as early as the days of Abraham (Genesis 14:15).

The two previous accounts of Paul's conversion in Acts tell that he carried letters (9:2; 22:5). No doubt these "letters" spelled out *the authority and commission* which Paul received from *the chief priests.*

B. THE "WHAT" OF THE VISION (vv. 13-15)

13. "About noon, O king, as I was on the road, I saw a light from heaven, brighter than the sun, blazing around me and my companions.

Here, Paul adds a bit more detail than that found in the earlier two accounts. This event happened at approximately noontime. This detail is significant because

HOW TO SAY IT

Agrippa. Uh-GRIP-puh.

Ananias. An-uh-NYE-us.

Aramaic. AIR-uh-MAY-ik.

Armenia. Ar-MEE-nee-uh.

Augustus. Aw-GUS-tus.

Basil. BAY-zul.

Bernice. Ber-NYE-see.

Buechner. BEEK-ner.

Caesarea. Sess-uh-REE-uh.

Claudius. CLAW-dee-us.

Cleopatra. Clee-oh-PAT-ruh.

Damascus. Duh-MASS-kus.

Festus. FES-tus.

Herod. HAIR-ud.

Isaiah. Eye-ZAY-uh.

Josephus. Jo-SEE-fus.

Licinius. Luh-SIH-nee-us.

Mediterranean. MED-uh-tuh-RAY-nee-un.

Sebaste. Seh-BAS-tee.

Tarsus. TAR-sus.

it shows that the light that surrounded him was even brighter than the noonday sun. The light could not be lightning, for there was no indication of storm conditions. Acts 9:8 and 22:11 mention Paul's being blinded by this light. Clearly, this was a supernatural occurrence; there is no natural explanation for it.

14. "We all fell to the ground, and I heard a voice saying to me in Aramaic, 'Saul, Saul, why do you persecute me? It is hard for you to kick against the goads.'

God is conversant in all human languages, and he chose what the translators here call *Aramaic* to make an impact on Paul. The terms used could refer either to Aramaic (which was at that time the language of the Hebrew people) or to what we might call "classic Hebrew." It is hard to say which was actually used. If it was classic Hebrew, the impact on Paul would be that of quoting the ancient tongue of his ancestors, the language of the Scriptures—seldom heard except in the synagogue in Paul's day. If it was Aramaic, then the impact would be that of speaking in his native language. Paul probably heard and spoke Greek, the common trade language of the day, more than his native language (cf. Acts 21:37).

This is the only place where Paul quotes Jesus as saying, "*It is hard for you to kick against the goads.*" Scholars point out that this was a common expression that described being in opposition to a deity or perhaps being in opposition to one's destiny. A "goad" is a cattle prod. It is used to get an animal to go in a certain direction. A compliant animal will feel the pricking of the goad and turn in the desired direction. A more stubborn one will resist, even kicking at the goad (and the person wielding it). Invariably this just creates more trouble for the animal.

In Paul's case, such "goads" perhaps include the example of Stephen and the courage of those Saul was persecuting at the time. That Paul was kicking against this prompting suggests he was troubled by them. They had caused him to doubt his own position and consider that of "the Way."

15. "Then I asked, 'Who are you, Lord?'

"'I am Jesus, whom you are persecuting,' the Lord replied.

Even though Paul referred to the person who appeared to him as *Lord*, he may not have had anything particularly religious in mind at this point (cf. Acts 9:5; 22:8). The Greek behind this word could be used in the sense of calling someone "sir," but Paul most certainly did accept the lordship of Christ in short order.

There is a word of encouragement to the church in Jesus' words. Notice that Jesus regards persecution against the church as something personal. It is persecution against him. He does not take it lightly.

THE FORTY MARTYRS OF SEBASTE

Persecution of the church (which, in reality, is persecution against Christ) has continued without ceasing since the establishment of the church. Those who wear the name of Christ must be prepared to bear the sufferings of Christ. One of the most stirring and enduring stories of persecution is that of the forty martyrs of Sebaste.

The account of their heroic martyrdom, according to Basil of Caesarea, goes something like this. Forty men, all Roman soldiers of the Twelfth "Thundering" Legion, serving during the reign of Licinius, were stationed near Sebaste in Lesser Armenia. The year was about A.D. 320. Refusing orders to sacrifice to the gods and renounce Christ, they were condemned to a cruel death.

The forty soldiers were stripped of their clothing and were forced to stand on the ice of a frozen lake until they either recanted or died. Bonfires, warm baths, and hot food tempted them on the shores of the frozen lake. One soldier, in a moment of weakness, broke ranks and left his companions. The remaining thirty-nine soldiers held fast.

Then something wonderful happened. One of the soldiers standing guard, who was not a believer, was deeply affected by the witness of the persecuted Christian

WHAT DO YOU THINK?

Why do some people, like Saul, resist the gospel so strenuously? What "goads" point people to Christ today, even if they "kick against" such prodding?

soldiers. He threw off his clothing and joined his comrades on the lake. The next morning there were forty frozen bodies. They died as one, the tortured but triumphant body of Christ.

—V. K.

C. THE "WHY" OF THE VISION (vv. 16-18)

16. "'Now get up and stand on your feet. I have appeared to you to appoint you as a servant and as a witness of what you have seen of me and what I will show you.

This is a brief summary of what Jesus communicated to Paul personally some twenty-five years previously. It also summarizes what Jesus communicated to Paul through God's messenger, a man named Ananias (see Acts 22:14, 15). This vision was not just for Paul's conversion, but also for receiving his divine orders of apostleship.

17. "'I will rescue you from your own people and from the Gentiles. I am sending you to them.

Paul now relates the commission he received for his lifework: he was to be a special envoy to the Gentile world. This meant double trouble for him since he would then face opposition from both Jews and *Gentiles*. But Jesus promised to see him through those trials.

18. "'. . . to open their eyes and turn them from darkness to light, and from the power of Satan to God, so that they may receive forgiveness of sins and a place among those who are sanctified by faith in me.'

Paul's mission is dramatic. He will open spiritually blinded eyes, take people to the light, turn them away from Satan, help them find forgiveness, and prepare them for their place in Heaven. (The church's ongoing commission is the same as Paul's, although worded a bit differently; Matthew 28:19, 20.)

Much of the gospel is summarized in these brief words. Many of these concepts also appear in the preaching of Jesus. Jesus compared sinfulness to spiritual blindness (e.g., Matthew 23:16-19). The Gospels frequently make use of the imagery of light and *darkness* (e.g., Matthew 4:16). Jesus also warned us about the strategy of the evil one (Mark 4:15).

Parenthetically, the word *satan* means "adversary." Sometimes the word *satan* is used for any kind of adversary. When it is used as a proper name, *Satan*, it refers to the ultimate adversary, the devil.

FROM DARKNESS TO LIGHT

Perhaps no world is darker than the world that imitates light. Ben Alexander was born a Jew on Christmas Day, 1920, in London's notorious East End. He went to Hebrew school and learned the Ten Commandments, but that was about the extent of his spiritual upbringing. Young Ben was terrified when his father died screaming one dark night. From that time forward, nights became micro-eternities.

Ben came to seek solace in the practice of spiritualism, which involves communicating with the spirit world. He attended séances. He became a practicing "medium." His unholy fascination with the occult world grew deeper and darker year by year.

Eventually Ben set sail for America to found a spiritualist society. Instead, in God's providence, he found Christ. Someone loved him enough to introduce him to Jesus Christ, "the light of the world." Ben's night turned to day. All the answers he had been desperately seeking for he found in Christ. He had been turned from darkness to light, from the power of Satan to God.

Not long after his conversion, Ben began a special ministry called *ESP Ministries*. ESP stands for "Exposing Satan's Powers." Ben's unique ministry, headquartered in St. Petersburg, Florida, has helped untold thousands of people

---

WHAT DO YOU THINK?

Jesus said he would make Saul "a servant and a witness" What can congregations do to channel young people into ministry today?

WHAT DO YOU THINK?

Why is it important to realize that our real enemy is Satan, not the people under his power?

[Use Luke 4:18; 1 Corinthians 15:50-57; Ephesians 4:8; 6:12; 1 John 3:8; and Revelation 12:9 to frame your answer.]

worldwide to escape the darkness of Satan's kingdom and come into the glorious kingdom of Christ's light. —V. K.

II. PAUL'S COMPLETE OBEDIENCE (ACTS 26:19-21)

A. IMMEDIATE OBEDIENCE (vv. 19, 20)

19. "So then, King Agrippa, I was not disobedient to the vision from heaven.

Even before Paul became a Christian, he was zealous for God. Whatever else one might say about him, Paul always obeyed what he thought God wanted him to do. When the high priest gave him instructions, he carried them out (Acts 9:1, 2; 22:5; 26:10). When Paul received different orders from Jesus, he carried them out, too. This is what Paul wants *King Agrippa* to know: he is under authority and is following orders.

20. "First to those in Damascus, then to those in Jerusalem and in all Judea, and to the Gentiles also, I preached that they should repent and turn to God and prove their repentance by their deeds.

Paul gives a general summary of the territory he has covered in his ministry up to this point. This is not a chronological list, but more of a spatial list. (See Acts 1:8; Romans 15:19.)

Paul stresses the substance of his message by informing the king that he told his listeners to *repent and turn to God*—ideas that are virtually synonymous. He also mentions that he has urged them to do deeds that are consistent with their *repentance*. There is no incompatibility between faith and works in the Bible as long as one doesn't try to "earn" salvation by those works (cf. Romans 3:28; 4:1-25; Ephesians 2:8, 9; James 2:14-26).

B. COSTLY OBEDIENCE (v. 21)

21. "That is why the Jews seized me in the temple courts and tried to kill me.

At the end of his third missionary journey, Paul had returned to Jerusalem and *the temple courts* (Acts 21:17-26). The Roman authorities had stepped in and saved Paul's life when a lynch mob tried to seize him (21:27-36). When a plot to kill Paul was uncovered in Jerusalem, Paul was transferred to Caesarea (23:12-35). When Governor Festus tried to transfer Paul's case back to Jerusalem to appease the Jews, Paul felt compelled to appeal to Caesar (25:9-12), and that appeal eventually brought him to this point before Agrippa. The appeal to Caesar is the right of a Roman citizen, and the book of Acts makes clear that Paul is indeed such a citizen (22:25-29). This fact gives him more civil rights than *Jews* would ordinarily have.

III. PAUL'S CHALLENGING MISSION (ACTS 26:22, 23, 27-29)

A. THE GOSPEL MADE ACCESSIBLE (vv. 22, 23)

22. "But I have had God's help to this very day, and so I stand here and testify to small and great alike. I am saying nothing beyond what the prophets and Moses said would happen—

Paul is comfortable in all kinds of settings and with all kinds of people. When he says he witnessed both to *small and great*, he means those who are considered as such by society. Paul preaches to whoever will listen, regardless of social class. (See Romans 12:16; James 2:1-7.)

Paul defends his message as being completely consistent with what was taught by *the prophets and Moses*. This is first a legal defense, since the Jews have accused him of violating Jewish law. But Paul has more in mind than a legal defense. He is laying the foundation to preach the resurrection, as we see in the next verse.

"*Whereupon, O king Agrippa, I was not disobedient unto the heavenly vision.*" Acts 26:19

Today's visual pictures Paul before Agrippa. The quotation is from verse 19.

WHAT DO YOU THINK?

What can we learn from Paul's pattern of evangelism as outlined in verse 20? How can we follow his example? (See also Acts 1:8.)

DAILY BIBLE READINGS

Monday, Feb. 3—Paul Stands Before Festus (Acts 25:1-12)

Tuesday, Feb. 4—Festus Explains Paul's Case (Acts 25:13-22)

Wednesday, Feb. 5—Paul Comes Before Agrippa (Acts 25:23-27)

Thursday, Feb. 6—Paul Begins His Defense (Acts 26:1-8)

Friday, Feb. 7—Paul Tells of His Conversion (Acts 26:9-18)

Saturday, Feb. 8—I Was Not Disobedient (Acts 26:19-23)

Sunday, Feb. 9—Paul's Appeal to Agrippa (Acts 26:24-32)

23. *". . . that the Christ would suffer and, as the first to rise from the dead, would proclaim light to his own people and to the Gentiles."*

When a Christian presents the gospel to an unbeliever, the point can come when the listener refuses to hear any more (cf. Acts 17:32; 22:22). For the Roman governor Festus, this is that point, as verse 24 shows. The idea of a suffering Messiah is somewhat of a stumbling block to those who first hear the gospel. Paul mentions it here as part of the substance of his preaching, and he is well aware that this concept was prophesied by the prophet Isaiah (chapter 53) over seven hundred years before.

Not only is the Messiah's suffering a major theme for Paul, but so is the Lord's resurrection. Paul further stresses that the message is not just for Jews, but also for *the Gentiles.* This is consistent with his teaching in many other places.

B. THE GOSPEL MADE PERSONAL (vv. 27-29)

27. *"King Agrippa, do you believe the prophets? I know you do."*

After responding to Festus's interruption (vv. 24-26), Paul turns his attention back to *King Agrippa.* Paul gives him the benefit of the doubt in noting the king's belief in *the prophets.* Agrippa has a reputation for being knowledgeable about the Scriptures and the customs of Judaism (Acts 26:3).

28. *Then Agrippa said to Paul, "Do you think that in such a short time you can persuade me to be a Christian?"*

Agrippa's response might literally be rendered, "In a little you persuade me to be a Christian." If the king says this matter-of-factly or pensively, then the *King James Version* accurately captures the thought with, "Almost thou persuadest me to be a Christian." That would mean that Agrippa is on the verge of accepting Paul's message and, thus, accepting Christ. This wording has given us the old gospel invitation song, "Almost Persuaded." However, if Agrippa is speaking sarcastically, then his intent is better reflected in the way the translators of the *New International Version* have rendered it.

29. *Paul replied, "Short time or long—I pray God that not only you but all who are listening to me today may become what I am, except for these chains."*

If Agrippa is sarcastic, Paul is undaunted. He presses the invitation. No doubt, Paul expresses this sentiment while gesturing to his *chains.* Paul certainly doesn't like being a prisoner, but he could wish that other than that, Agrippa would be as he is. It is his desire that *all who* listen to him will become Christians.

CONCLUSION

Paul eventually went to Rome, which had been his dream for some time (Acts 19:21). But it was not in the manner he had originally planned. The book of Acts ends with the apostle Paul under house arrest there, evidently waiting for his appeal to be heard. Even so, he is relatively free to share the gospel from his place of detainment.

We know Paul still had other hopes for the gospel. Among them was his dream to visit Spain (Romans 15:24). While we don't have any biblical accounts about this period in his life, a persistent legend holds that Paul was released from prison and that he did go to Spain, and that later he was arrested again and beheaded about A.D. 66 or 67.

Paul, who once had caused persecution, became a victim of it himself through much of his ministry. He who once watched with approval as Stephen was stoned to death ultimately faced his own martyrdom (2 Timothy 4:6). Whatever the circumstances of that martyrdom, there is no doubt that he considered it a great honor.

Discovery Learning

This page contains an alternative lesson plan emphasizing learning activities. Classes desiring such student involvement will find these suggestions helpful. The next page is a reproducible activity page to further enhance discovery learning.

LEARNING GOALS

After this lesson each student will be able to:

1. Recite the details of Paul's experience on the road to Damascus and his response to it.

2. Explain why Paul's conversion and call are significant to the spread of the gospel.

3. Assess his or her own response to God's call and determine to take one specific step to conform to God's call more closely.

INTO THE LESSON

Before class hang three signs from the ceiling in different areas of the room. One sign is to read "Big Mistakes: Social." Another will read "Big Mistakes: Spiritual." The third will read "Big Mistakes: Financial." Have five to seven chairs under each sign. On each chair have a copy of the reproducible activity "Big Mistake" from the next page. (For larger classes, put up additional signs with the same headings.)

As people enter, tell them to be seated under a sign that represents a big mistake they have made in life. (Reassure them they won't have to tell what the mistake was unless they choose to.)

To begin, have the learners fill in the "Big Mistake" acrostic. Then introduce the lesson by saying, "Everyone makes mistakes—and most of us at some time make a big mistake. We make mistakes in relationships, behavior, finances, and in religious decisions or activities."

Ask those willing to share with their small groups brief summaries of a big mistakes they have made. Ask a volunteer from each group to share his or her mistake with the entire class.

Make the transition to Bible study by reminding them that we all make mistakes—and sometimes they are truly significant. Saul (Paul) also made mistakes. He made a major mistake in his religious life. His error and how he changed will teach us much.

INTO THE WORD

"Teamwork!" Ask each person to select a partner to answer the following questions on a handout. Before they begin, however, give a brief lecture on the setting for this study by using the Lesson Introduction and Background from the lesson commentary (pages 203, 204). Prepare the following small posters to attach to the wall during your lecture as an outline: "Paul's Appearance,"

"Tarsus," "Johnny Appleseed of Church Planting," "King Agrippa and Bernice," "Caesarea," and "Festus."

Then ask the teams to read Acts 26:12-23, 27-29, and answer the following questions on the handout you have prepared and distributed:

1. What does verse 12 reveal about Saul's commitment to the Lord before his conversion?

2. What clues do you find in verse 13 that this was a supernatural event?

3. Why did God speak in Aramaic (or Hebrew) to Saul?

4. What did Jesus mean when he said, "It is hard for you to kick against the goads" (v. 14)?

5. What is the purpose of Saul's vision? What did the Lord want of Saul?

6. What was the cost of Paul's obedience to his commission (v. 21)?

7. What was the focus or heart of Paul's message throughout his ministry (v. 23)?

8. "What if . . . ?" Suppose Saul had refused to accept Jesus. Recall some of Saul's experiences and the lives that he touched. Note some of the consequences if he had failed to accept his task.

Allow about fifteen minutes for this team project. Then allow people to report conclusions or answers to each question. Use your lesson commentary to supplement answers. List answers to question 8 on a visual.

INTO LIFE

"Lessons Learned!" Distribute copies of the reproducible activity "And Victories" from the next page. Have students complete these and then allow volunteers to report their victories within the small groups formed earlier.

Point out that believers today, like Paul, have been called to share the gospel. If we do not do our job, there will be negative consequences. First, ask class members to suggest categories or groups of people with whom most Christians have opportunity to share the gospel (children, grandchildren, spouses, neighbors, work associates). List these on the board or a poster.

Second, ask "What are the potentially negative consequences of not completing our mission?" List answers.

Third, use the last section of the reproducible page. Ask people to identify one person with whom they will share the gospel this week and write that name on the line.

Lead a prayer for help in keeping this commitment.

Big Mistakes!

Saul made a big mistake in persecuting Christians, even though he thought he was doing God's will. We also make big mistakes in our Christian life. Use each of the letters in the word "MISTAKES" to form another word that describes categories of some of the errors believers make in their Christian life and behavior. The categories may start, end, or merely appear in the new words. An example has been done for you.

M _____

I _____

S _____

T _____

FIN*ANCES*_____

K _____

E _____

S _____

And Victories

Use the space below to write a brief note about how God has blessed you as you overcame a big mistake in living your Christian life. You may choose to mention how this has changed you, given you maturity, helped you have an impact on others, or other results.

My Mistake:

My Blessings:

And Lessons Learned!

Paul learned that the mission of the Christian's life includes sharing the good news about Jesus. Note below the name of one person with whom you have opportunity to complete this mission. Do so with a commitment to accomplish this task this week.

"I will tell this person about Jesus this week: _____."

TIMOTHY: VALUED HELPER

LESSON 12

WHY TEACH THIS LESSON?

While aircraft were used some in World War I, it was not until World War II that the airplane came into its own as a fighting machine. Those who are interested in such things will immediately recognize the "P-51 Mustang," "Spitfire," and "Me-109" as some of the best fighter aircraft of World War II. But how many would also recognize "P-40 Warhawk"? Historians have dubbed the Warhawk "the best second-best fighter aircraft" of that war. If a pilot couldn't fly one of the best planes, the Warhawk was his "best second-best" choice.

Like the Warhawk, Timothy could be called the "best second-best" of the disciples because of the supporting role he played. In the life of the church, some people are up front and some are in the back. Some are leaders and some are helpers. And many more are helpers than leaders. It's not really "best" and "second-best," but sometimes it seems that way. Your class surely includes many helpers. Today's lesson will encourage them to become like Timothy, willing to accept whatever role God chooses for them, and eager to do their best at it!

INTRODUCTION

A. BEST SUPPORTING ACTOR

Would an actor prefer to be nominated for an Oscar for "Best Actor" or for "Best Supporting Actor"? From all the publicity, the "Best Supporting" Oscar is seen as less prestigious.

But every great endeavor needs people who can serve in supporting roles. Young actors are frequently told, "There are no small parts—only small actors." Plays, movies, and television programs are greatly enhanced by the work of supporting actors and actresses. No great story can be told without them.

Timothy had no problem with playing a supporting role in the work of the kingdom. As often happens with actors who play the supporting role well, Timothy later moved into a leading role.

B. LESSON BACKGROUND

In some respects they may have seemed like the odd couple. Paul was probably middle-aged, and Timothy likely was a teenager. While Timothy knew the Scriptures (2 Timothy 3:15), he probably was not formally schooled in religion. Paul, on the other hand, possessed the best theological education available in his day (Acts 22:3). Paul was bold, but Timothy may have been somewhat timid (1 Corinthians 16:10). Nevertheless, they became inseparable—in spirit even if often separated by space.

Timothy's name is mentioned in ten of Paul's letters, and Timothy may have played a small role in writing some of those. Paul addresses two letters directly to him, and we will look at some references from those epistles as part of this lesson.

I. TIMOTHY, THE TEAMMATE (ACTS 16:1-5)

The year is about A.D. 50 or 51, and Paul is in the early stages of his second missionary journey. Paul and Silas are revisiting the cities in Galatia where Paul

---

DEVOTIONAL READING:
2 TIMOTHY 2:1-7

BACKGROUND SCRIPTURE:
ACTS 16:1-5; 17:13-15; 18:5;
PHILIPPIANS 2:19-24;
1, 2 TIMOTHY

PRINTED TEXT:
ACTS 16:1-5; PHILIPPIANS 2:19-24; 1 TIMOTHY 1:1-3; 2 TIMOTHY 1:3-6

LESSON AIMS

After this lesson each student will be able to:

1. Describe Timothy's background and character as revealed in today's lesson texts.

2. Tell why a supporting role in ministry is vital to the ministry's success.

3. Identify a young person whom he or she can encourage to get involved in ministry in the church.

Feb
16

KEY VERSE

Make my joy complete by being like-minded, having the same love, being one in spirit and purpose.
—Philippians 2:2

and Barnabas had planted churches earlier. Paul's first visit to this area had not been pleasant; it was stressful and unusual. While in Lystra, he and Barnabas had been taken to be Greek gods by the local populace (Acts 14:11-13). But then the crowd was swayed and Paul barely escaped with his life, having been stoned and left for dead (14:19). Still, it is obvious that good things had happened in the ministry when they were there the first time. Sometime during this visit, Paul must have come into contact with Timothy's family and led them to conversion.

A. FAMILY BACKGROUND (vv. 1, 2)

1, 2. He came to Derbe and then to Lystra, where a disciple named Timothy lived, whose mother was a Jewess and a believer, but whose father was a Greek. The brothers at Lystra and Iconium spoke well of him.

This is the first of six references to *Timothy* in the book of Acts. Timothy is already *a disciple*. No doubt Timothy was converted, or at least his *mother* and/or grandmother were (2 Timothy 1:5), during Paul's first visit. (Paul's reference to Timothy as his "son" in 1 Corinthians 4:17 implies that he is a convert of Paul.) In time he will become invaluable to the apostle. He knows both the *Greek* world and the Jewish world. He understands both worlds and is comfortable in either one.

The Jewish population around *Derbe, Lystra,* and *Iconium* is very small at the time, so mixed marriages are more common here than in Judea. It also appears from the way this is worded that Timothy's father is probably dead.

The fact that Timothy is spoken *well of* indicates that he is already involved in serving the church. Perhaps he is involved even in preaching and teaching.

B. RELIGIOUS BACKGROUND (v. 3)

3. Paul wanted to take him along on the journey, so he circumcised him because of the Jews who lived in that area, for they all knew that his father was a Greek.

In passages such as Acts 15:1, 2; Romans 2:25-29; and 1 Corinthians 7:18, Paul makes it clear that circumcision is no longer necessary under the New Covenant. Some students find it startling, then, to read here that he had Timothy *circumcised.*

But the issue at hand is not one of doctrinal necessity, but practical expediency. Paul realizes that for Timothy to remain uncircumcised will be a hindrance to bringing the gospel message to *the Jews who lived in that area.* As F. F. Bruce notes, the Jews in the area would consider Timothy to be a Gentile, and the Gentiles would consider him to be a Jew.

Some question Paul's judgment here. They say it seems inconsistent with his views on circumcision. They point out that, in another case, Paul had decided not to circumcise Titus (Galatians 2:1-5). But these critics forget that while Paul thought circumcision unnecessary for Gentiles, Jewish practices were still appropriate for Jews. Paul continued to practice those customs the rest of his life. Titus was in no way considered to be Jewish, and Paul did not want to appear to be demanding obedience to the law as a condition of salvation (Acts 15:1-11). Attempting to be justified by law-keeping was a major problem with certain churches, and circumcision had become a flashpoint in this doctrinal struggle (Galatians 5:1-6). So Paul's differing treatments of Timothy and Titus is completely consistent with his stated views on the issue.

C. EARLY LABORS (vv. 4, 5)

4. As they traveled from town to town, they delivered the decisions reached by the apostles and elders in Jerusalem for the people to obey.

Paul, Silas, and Timothy undertake a trip to the cities that Paul had visited on his first missionary journey with Barnabas. They take with them the letter written by the leaders *in Jerusalem* concerned with allowing Gentiles to become Christians with few restrictions (Acts 15:22-29). The so-called "Jerusalem Conference" had been made up primarily of *the apostles and elders* of the Jerusalem church (Acts 15:6), which could now be regarded as the "mother" church. It is impossible to overestimate the importance of this conference's decision for the Gentile believers and the church at large. There is no question that the church already had made inroads into predominantly Gentile areas, but would the Gentiles be accepted, and on what basis?

James the brother of Jesus, who had become a prominent leader in the Jerusalem church, apparently chaired this conference (Acts 15:13-21). Interestingly, Peter was the most vocal advocate for the Gentiles (Acts 15:7-11). Barnabas and Paul also made a report. After all the debate and discussion, little was asked of the Gentiles in terms of adherence to Jewish custom. They were asked to abstain from idolatry, the drinking of blood, meat from strangled animals, and sexual immorality. This letter was seen as an official welcome to the Gentiles. Interestingly, just as Silas replaces Barnabas, it seems that Timothy replaces John Mark in Paul's heart and strategies.

5. So the churches were strengthened in the faith and grew daily in numbers.

This verse provides a summary statement of all the progress on this part of the journey through the territory of Galatia. The mention of both spiritual growth and numerical growth recognizes the importance of each.

II. TIMOTHY, THE SERVANT (PHILIPPIANS 2:19-24)

Probably ten years have now passed. After Paul's trial before Agrippa (see last week's lesson), Paul was sent to Rome. There he was incarcerated for two years (Acts 28:30). During this time he wrote several of his epistles, including the one to the Philippians (Philippians 1:13, 14).

A. AFFINITY WITH PAUL (vv. 19, 20)

19. I hope in the Lord Jesus to send Timothy to you soon, that I also may be cheered when I receive news about you.

Paul wants to know how things are going with the church at Philippi, a church that Paul and his companions had established on the second missionary journey (Acts 16:11-40). To find out, he will have to send a personal representative to gain the information he desires. We do not know when *Timothy* went to Rome or why. Perhaps Paul summoned him for this very mission.

20. I have no one else like him, who takes a genuine interest in your welfare.

There is *no one else* Paul can think of who is as ready for this task as is Timothy. The Philippians do not need an introduction to Timothy, for they already know him. Still, Paul wants them to appreciate how in tune Timothy is with the mind of Paul. Not only is Timothy in tune with Paul, but he also has a *genuine* concern for the church.

B. CONCERN FOR THE CHURCH (vv. 21-24)

21, 22. For everyone looks out for his own interests, not those of Jesus Christ. But you know that Timothy has proved himself, because as a son with his father he has served with me in the work of the gospel.

Unfortunately, some who preach the gospel do so from wrong motives (Philippians 1:15, 16). Not *Timothy!* He stands as an example of a person who clearly and unambiguously seeks the things which are Jesus Christ's. Paul, we presume, has no son in the flesh, but Timothy is his *son* in the faith. It is certainly true that some people who labor together in *the gospel* are as close or closer than blood relatives.

WHAT DO YOU THINK?

We note in the lesson that both spiritual and numerical growth are important in the church. What emphasis should we put on each? How should we balance the two?

WHAT DO YOU THINK?

How can you tell when people will "look out for their own interests" and when they will take "a genuine interest in your welfare"?

HOW TO SAY IT

Agrippa. Uh-GRIP-puh.

Artemis. AR-teh-miss.

Barnabas. BAR-nuh-bus.

charis (Greek). KAH-riss.

Corinthians. Kor-IN-thee-unz.

Derbe. DER-be.

Ephesus. EF-uh-sus.

Eunice. U-NYE-see or U-nis.

Galatia. Guh-LAY-shuh.

Galatians. Guh-LAY-shunz.

Gentiles. JEN-tyles.

Gnosticism. NAHSS-tih-SIZZ-um.

Iconium. Eye-KO-nee-um.

Lystra. LISS-truh.

Philippi. Fih-LIP-pie or FIL-ih-pie.

shalom (Hebrew). shah-LOME.

Silas. SIGH-luss.

Titus. TIE-tus.

Welshimer. WEL-shuh-mer.

John Wilson preached for many years in Springfield, Ohio, and encouraged many "Timothys" to join him in ministry. Today's visual features Brother Wilson and some of the young people he recruited to vocational ministry.

23. I hope, therefore, to send him as soon as I see how things go with me.

Paul urges patience on the Philippian church. He does not want to let Timothy go until his own fate is determined. Paul may have had some upcoming legal decision in mind. He not only needs Timothy with him at this crucial time, but if he waits Timothy will have some fresh news to pass on.

24. And I am confident in the Lord that I myself will come soon.

Paul decides to be content no matter what the outcome for himself. He has no special revelation, but he is optimistic that he will be released from this particular imprisonment. The book of Acts ends with Paul still incarcerated, but church tradition indicates that he was released.

III. TIMOTHY, THE TEACHER (1 TIMOTHY 1:1-3)

This part of our text comes from one of the letters that bear Timothy's name. It is now about A.D. 65; Paul and Timothy have known each other for fifteen years or so.

A. TAUGHT BY PAUL (vv. 1, 2)

1. Paul, an apostle of Christ Jesus by the command of God our Savior and of Christ Jesus our hope.

The conventional way to begin a letter in the ancient world is to affix the signature first. In the opening of the letter, *Paul* identifies himself as *an apostle . . . by the commandment of God*. In a general sense, all of the apostles served at the commandment of God. Paul may be referring specifically to his commission on the road to Damascus. He may also be responding to critics who think that he is not a genuine apostle. Paul feels the need to affirm and defend his apostleship in other places as well (1 Corinthians 9:1, 2; 2 Corinthians 12:11, 12; Galatians 1:1).

He mentions Jesus as Lord here also. Jewish Christians understand Jesus to be the Messiah. As the gospel spreads to Gentiles, the concept of *Messiah* is not as significant, as Gentiles have little understanding of that. As the gospel proceeds, *Lord* becomes a more significant title, since both Jew and Gentile can understand it.

HOPE NEVER DIES

The 1994 movie *The Shawshank Redemption* is a story about hope. The two central characters, Andy and "Red," are serving time in a prison notorious for corruption. Both men are in for murder: Andy, for a murder he did not commit; "Red," for one he did commit when he was young.

The warden is nothing more than a bully and a thief. He and many of the crooked prison guards use Andy's banking skills to salt away laundered money. But Andy outsmarts them all. For twenty years he piles up evidence. Then he uses a small rock hammer to tunnel his way to freedom.

After Andy's daring escape, shocking exposure of the evils at Shawshank, and the warden's suicide, Red is finally paroled. He has spent forty years at Shawshank. In a previously agreed upon place, Red finds a note from Andy. It is in a tin box along with some money to help Red on his way. The note reads: "Hope is a good thing . . . and no good thing ever dies."

The Christmas hymn, "O Little Town of Bethlehem" tells us that Jesus personifies "the hopes and fears of all the years." Indeed, he is our hope—"a living hope," "the hope of glory," "the blessed hope." And that is a hope rooted in more than the clever scheming of a movie character; it is based on the infinite power of God himself.

My hope is built on nothing less
Than Jesus' blood and righteousness;
I dare not trust the sweetest frame,
But wholly lean on Jesus' name.   —Edward Mote (1797–1874)

—V. K.

2. To Timothy my true son in the faith:
   Grace, mercy and peace from God the Father and Christ Jesus our Lord.

Interestingly, the two letters addressed to *Timothy*, along with the letter to Titus, have come to be known as "the Pastoral Epistles." Timothy certainly has a pastoral concern for the churches, as we saw hinted at in Philippians 2:20 above. But the phrase "Pastoral Epistles" deals more with the concerns of Paul as the author of these works rather than Timothy as the recipient.

As we have already noted, Paul sees Timothy as a son—not a son of the flesh, but a *son in the faith*. As the years have passed, there has been no lessening of Paul's appreciation for Timothy in this regard (cf. 1 Corinthians 4:17).

The greeting we see here is typical of Paul in that grace and peace appear in the salutation of all thirteen of his letters. Many commentators note that in this greeting is a hint of the union between Jew and Gentile since *grace* (the Greek word *charis*) is a typical Gentile greeting while *peace* (the Hebrew word *shalom*) is a typical Jewish greeting. Added to Paul's traditional greeting is the word *mercy*. Since there is a special personal dimension to this letter, Paul adds a personal blessing.

B. Trusted by Paul (v. 3)
3. As I urged you when I went into Macedonia, stay there in Ephesus so that you may command certain men not to teach false doctrines any longer.

In Philippians 2 (above), it is Paul who "stays put" while Timothy travels. Now the reverse is true. *Ephesus* (which means "desirable") is one of the most fascinating cities of its time, and its ruins are a worthwhile visit even today. Ephesus is the location of one of the seven wonders of the ancient word, the temple of Artemis. Paul had set off a riot in this city in the process of establishing one of the most noteworthy churches in biblical times (Acts 19).

The primary thing Timothy is to do at Ephesus is teach. One of the most difficult challenges for a Christian teacher is to deal with matters of doctrine. Doctrinal disputes can produce very sharp disagreements. Teaching doctrine is always a challenge, particularly when *false* doctrine is making its way around. Paul entrusts to Timothy the challenging task of helping the fledgling church sort out true from false doctrine, and silence those teaching falsehood. (See also 1 Timothy 6:3-5.)

What doctrinal problems does the church at Ephesus face? If you continue reading through verse 7, you get a hint. In verse 4, Paul refers to people's devoting themselves to fables (or myths) and genealogies. (Paul repeats this concern, in part, in Titus 1:14.) This statement probably refers to one of two possibilities. It may refer to Jewish myths and Old Testament genealogies.

Another possibility is that it refers to what will later become known as Gnosticism. One of the Gnostic beliefs was that there were a good god and an evil god. The evil god, who they believed created the world, was the result of countless emanations from the good god. (These emanations could be considered a genealogy of the evil god.) Either of these concepts would have been damaging to the church and needed correction.

IV. TIMOTHY, THE LEADER (2 TIMOTHY 1:3-6)

We now move to Paul's second letter to Timothy, probably written just before Paul's execution in A.D. 66 or 67.

A. Prayer for Leadership (vv. 3, 4)
3. I thank God, whom I serve, as my forefathers did, with a clear conscience, as night and day I constantly remember you in my prayers.

What Do You Think?
Who might refer to you as a son or daughter in the faith? Why? How do you show your appreciation to this person? And whom might you call a son or daughter in the faith? Why? (If no one, why not?)

Daily Bible Readings
Monday, Feb. 10—Paul Takes Timothy With Him (Acts 16:1-5)

Tuesday, Feb. 11—I Have No One Like Him (Philippians 2:19-24)

Wednesday, Feb. 12—A Loyal Child in the Faith (1 Timothy 1:1-5)

Thursday, Feb. 13—A Man of Sincere Faith (2 Timothy 1:1-7)

Friday, Feb. 14—Timothy and Silas Stay in Berea (Acts 17:10-15)

Saturday, Feb. 15—Paul Sends Timothy to Encourage (1 Thessalonians 3:1-6)

Sunday, Feb. 16—Come to Me Soon (2 Timothy 4:9-15)

WHAT DO YOU THINK?

What do you think Paul prayed about in Timothy's behalf? Why?

[Perhaps there are hints in 1 Timothy 1:3, 18; 3:15; 4:6, 12.]

PRAYER

Help us, Father, to value those who mentor us. Help us to be willing to mentor others that your Word may go forth from generation to generation. In the name of our Redeemer we pray, amen.

THOUGHT TO REMEMBER

Everyone needs both a Paul and a Timothy in his or her life.

In mentioning his *forefathers*, Paul reflects on his religious heritage. Even though he is the apostle to the Gentiles, Paul appreciates his Jewish heritage. It is as important to him now in the waning days of his life as it had been earlier (Acts 22:3; 24:14).

Paul's claim of a pure *conscience* does not mean that he is perfect, but that he is satisfied with the sincerity of his service (cf. Acts 23:1). Perhaps these references to his heritage and his conscience are both hints to Timothy as a church leader that he, too, should embrace and pass on a sound heritage while maintaining a good conscience. Timothy may be encouraged to do both as he experiences the reality of Paul's continual *prayers*.

4. Recalling your tears, I long to see you, so that I may be filled with joy.

Paul probably recalls the last time he and Timothy parted, when probably they both shed *tears*. (See the tearful parting of Paul and the Ephesian elders in Acts 20:36-38.) We do not know when this parting was, but Paul certainly desires *to see* Timothy one last time (2 Timothy 4:9, 21).

B. PREPARATION FOR LEADERSHIP (v. 5)

5. I have been reminded of your sincere faith, which first lived in your grandmother Lois and in your mother Eunice and, I am persuaded, now lives in you also.

After recalling his own religious heritage in verse 3, Paul now reminds Timothy of his. Timothy is an example of what can happen when the *faith* is passed down in a family. Both his *mother* and *grandmother* were well versed in the Scriptures and shared that knowledge with Timothy.

Even though *Eunice* and *Lois* are Jewish, their names are distinctly Greek. Since they live in the Greek world, this is not really so unusual. The name Eunice means "good victory." Timothy's name, interestingly enough, means "friend of God."

C. EMPOWERMENT FOR LEADERSHIP (v. 6)

6. For this reason I remind you to fan into flame the gift of God, which is in you through the laying on of my hands.

Our ability to fulfill the call of God in our lives comes from the Holy Sprit. Paul undoubtedly has in mind a particular spiritual gift that was given, in Timothy's case, by a prophecy and the laying on of hands of Paul and a body of elders (1 Timothy 4:14). Even spiritual gifts given by an apostle must be put to use if they are to be effective. That is the reason Timothy is told to stir up this *gift*.

CONCLUSION

P. H. Welshimer (1873–1957) advised preachers, "If you have to be a second-rater, then be a first-rate second-rater." Surely Timothy is at least a first-rate second-rater!

What ultimately becomes of Timothy, we do not know. We do know that he was imprisoned later, but eventually released (Hebrews 13:23). There are very few reliable traditions that give us any hint about how Timothy lived the rest of his life or about his death.

But what we do know of Timothy's life is enough to encourage us to follow his example. A famous conductor purportedly was asked what was the most difficult instrument in the orchestra to play. With a twinkle in his eye he is said to have replied, "Second fiddle!" Someone has to play it, and Timothy played it like a virtuoso.

Discovery Learning

This page contains an alternative lesson plan emphasizing learning activities. Classes desiring such student involvement will find these suggestions helpful. The next page is a reproducible activity page to further enhance discovery learning.

LEARNING GOALS

After this lesson each student will be able to:

1. Describe Timothy's background and character as revealed in today's lesson texts.

2. Tell why a supporting role in ministry is vital to the ministry's success.

3. Identify a young person whom he or she can encourage to get involved in ministry in the church.

INTO THE LESSON

Distribute copies of the reproducible activity "Great Second Fiddlers" from the next page. Begin this session by asking class members to identify ministry teams in your church. "Teams" may be groups such as financial teams, care-building teams, elders, church staff, teaching teams, or others. If possible, include the names of people of the smaller teams. List these team categories on a board or poster. Then ask class members to identify the ones who fill support roles in those teams. Have the students write the names on the reproducible activity page.

Make the transition to Bible study by using the lesson introduction in the lesson commentary to emphasize the value of talented people who play a supporting role in the church's ministry teams.

INTO THE WORD

Distribute copies of the second activity on the reproducible page. Have the class examine today's texts, complete the activity, and then do the following.

INTERVIEW WITH PAUL. Play the part of Paul (or recruit a class member) for an interview. Use a prop (staff, beard, robe, shawl) that identifies you as an actor in this role. Prepare the following list of questions to be asked of you by class members. Also ask different people to read today's printed text at the appropriate times. Use your lesson commentary to prepare your responses. As you put on your clothing or prop, explain to the class what you are staging and that the focus of this interview is about your young assistant, Timothy.

Sample questions include the following:

1. (Have a class member read Acts 16:1-5.) "Paul, before you came to this area and met Timothy, you had been here before. I know your first trip was not pleasant. Tell us what happened."

2. "One of the great results of that visit, of course, is that you eventually got acquainted with Timothy. Tell us a little bit about his background and what drew you to him."

3. "Paul, the record says that you circumcised Timothy. Why did you do that?"

4. "When you, Timothy, and Silas made your trip back through cities you had visited before, the record says you gave them decrees to keep that were from the apostles and elders and Jerusalem. Explain what this was all about."

5. (Have someone read Philippians 2:19-24.) "Tell us why you sent Timothy to Philippi, Paul."

6. (Have 1 Timothy 1:1-3 read.) "Paul, you are giving more and more responsibility to Timothy. When you went to Macedonia, you asked Timothy to stay in Ephesus. Why was it important for him to be there?"

7. "There is one more text I'd like to ask about." (Have someone read 2 Timothy 1:3-6.) "You pay tribute to Timothy's home life. How did his background shape him into such a valuable teammate?"

INTO LIFE

As you slip out of your stage props or garb, explain that Timothy was a great teammate or "supporting actor." Ask the following discussion questions to encourage application.

1. What qualities or characteristics help to make great support persons in ministry teams? (List answers.)

2. Why are supporting roles valuable in ministry today? (Ask people to illustrate their answers.)

3. Paul encouraged Timothy to "fan into flame the gift of God" (2 Timothy 1:6). Even Timothy needed to be encouraged to develop and use gifts God had given. What ways can we encourage young people in our church to develop their leadership skills and their spiritual lives? (List these ideas on a poster or chalkboard.)

Distribute copies of the reproducible activity "Young Timothy/Timothyettes" from the next page. Ask each student to write the name of one teenager or young adult in the church he or she will encourage to be more involved in the church's ministry.

Identify a way to allow the skill or gift of that young person to be used. Call attention to the list from discussion question 3 for ideas on how to encourage that young person. Class members may even need to contact a church leader, asking that person to help find a way to use the young person in ministry or service.

Great Second Fiddlers!

A conductor was asked what was the most difficult instrument to play in the orchestra. With a twinkle in his eye, he said, "Second fiddle." But the support role is vital in music and in church leadership. Name some people who play great support roles in your church's ministry. You may discover them in teaching teams, youth leaders, paid staff, ministry teams, or simply as individuals. List their names below.

Affirming _ _ _ M _ _ _ _

Find the words in today's Scripture text to fill in the boxes of the statement or phrases <u>below</u>. You will discover wonderful qualities in young Timothy's life that allowed him to play a first-class second fiddle in ministry. Then use the highlighted letters in order of appearance to fill in the blanks in the title <u>above</u>.

"A disciple named [   ]" (Acts 16:1).

"He has [   ] with me in the work of the gospel" (Philippians 2:22).

"I have been reminded of your sincere [   ]" (2 Timothy 1:5).

"So the churches . . . [   ] daily" (Acts 16:5).

"Timothy has [   ] himself" (Philippians 2:22).

"Who takes a genuine [   ] in your welfare" (Philippians 2:20).

"The brothers at Lystra and Iconium [   ] well of him" (Acts 16:2).

ANSWERS: Timothy, served, faith, grew, proved, interest, spoke. Key word: Teamwork

Young Timothy/Timothyettes

Identify one or more teens or young adults in your congregation in whom you see a real gift for ministry that needs to be developed in service. Choose one and write her or his name in the box below along with your plan for facilitating an opportunity for that experience.

PRISCILLA AND AQUILA

LESSON 13

WHY TEACH THIS LESSON?

Combat forces go to war with various supporting units backing them up. Sometimes a support unit is called a "force multiplier." According to the U.S. Department of Defense, a force multiplier is "a capability that, when added to and employed by a combat force, significantly increases the combat potential of that force and thus enhances the probability of successful mission accomplishment."

In his spiritual battle against Satan and the forces of darkness, the apostle Paul had a force multiplier: the husband and wife team of Aquila and Priscilla. Today's lesson will help your learners see how they, too, can be force multipliers for God's kingdom. Does a couple in your class frequently open their home for church functions? They are helping to multiply the effectiveness of your church's outreach. Does one lead a home Bible study? That one, too, is multiplying the effectiveness of your church's ministry. May your students never again minimize the importance of their ministries. They are God's force multipliers!

INTRODUCTION

A. GREAT TEAMS

Some names are always thought of together. Names like Fred and Ginger, Lucy and Desi, and George and Gracie. In the Bible one particular couple stands out, for they are always mentioned together. They are Priscilla and Aquila.

Priscilla and Aquila are mentioned six times in the New Testament. In four of those references Priscilla (sometimes designated by the more formal *Prisca*) is named first, an indication of her importance among Christians.

B. LESSON BACKGROUND

While the Bible exalts marriage, we find few detailed examples of solid marriages in its pages. No doubt there were many such marriages among God's people, but we just don't have the details necessary to examine them closely. We know, for instance, that Peter had a wife and that she traveled with him on at least some of his journeys, but we know nothing else about that marriage (see Matthew 8:14; 1 Corinthians 9:5). Today we learn about a wonderful Christian couple by the name of Priscilla and Aquila.

This lesson also highlights the important part that both men and women played in the church of the first century. Today, some Bible passages are hotly debated in how they do or do not speak to the issue of gender roles in the church. This lesson does not address those issues. Instead, we will adopt a focused look at a particular man and woman—a married couple—who played a crucial part in growth of the infant church.

I. THE TEAM INTRODUCED (ACTS 18:1-4, 18, 19a)

As we pick up the narrative here, the year is about A.D. 51. Paul is on his second missionary journey. Having traveled through Galatia, he had hoped to visit Asia Minor, but that will have to wait (Acts 16:6). Instead, he and his party arrive in Troas, where Paul receives a vision compelling him to minister in Macedonia

DEVOTIONAL READING:
EPHESIANS 4:1-13

BACKGROUND SCRIPTURE:
ACTS 18:1-4, 18-26; ROMANS 16:3-5a; 1 CORINTHIANS 16:19; 2 TIMOTHY 4:19

PRINTED TEXT:
ACTS 18:1-4, 18, 19a, 24-26; ROMANS 16:3-5a; 1 CORINTHIANS 16:19; 2 TIMOTHY 4:19

LESSON AIMS

After participating in this lesson, each student will be able to:

1. List three cities where Priscilla and Aquila labored for the Lord, and note something of their work in each.

2. Explain how Priscilla and Aquila's style of hospitality and teaching can be used to help the church today.

3. Express appreciation to a person or couple who help to facilitate the ministry in his or her church.

KEY VERSES

Greet Priscilla and Aquila, my fellow workers in Christ Jesus. They risked their lives for me. Not only I but all the churches of the Gentiles are grateful to them.
—Romans 16:3, 4

(vv. 7-10). The remainder of Acts 16 and 17 tell of what happened in Macedonia and in Athens, Greece. During this part of the trip Paul sometimes sends his coworkers on separate missions while he continues on his own (Acts 17:14; 1 Thessalonians 3:1-5). So as our text begins, Paul is traveling alone from Athens to Corinth.

A. MEETING PAUL (vv. 1-4)

1. After this, Paul left Athens and went to Corinth.

Paul's association with Priscilla and Aquila begins when Paul travels from *Athens* to *Corinth*, a distance of about forty miles. Athens is named in honor of the mythical Greek goddess Athena, and at the time it is a city of great philosophical ferment. Perhaps a bit discouraged from the lukewarm response to his preaching in that city (Acts 17:16-34), Paul has decided to move on.

As Paul enters Corinth in southern Greece, he finds a military outpost and a crossroads for commerce. This city has all the advantages and disadvantages that such a setting brings. Corinthians are particularly fond of the Greek god Apollo and the goddess Aphrodite, and the city is known for its immorality. Massive stone columns still stand today on the site where the temple of Apollo stood in Corinth. Just outside the city on a high hill called the Acrocorinth are the remains of the temple of Aphrodite, where a thousand temple prostitutes served the goddess.

2. There he met a Jew named Aquila, a native of Pontus, who had recently come from Italy with his wife Priscilla, because Claudius had ordered all the Jews to leave Rome. Paul went to see them.

Aquila is specifically called *a Jew* even though he has a distinctly Roman name, a name that means "eagle." He is originally from the territory of *Pontus*, near the Black Sea. Pontus is adjacent to Bithynia, a territory the Holy Spirit did not allow *Paul* to enter (Acts 16:7). There must have been a strong Jewish presence in Pontus since residents of that area are mentioned as being in Jerusalem on the Day of Pentecost (Acts 2:9).

Aquila and *Priscilla* probably had made their home in Rome. No doubt they had conducted business in that city just as they are doing in Corinth when Paul meets them. Since Priscilla is not specifically called a Jew, some believe that she is a Gentile who married into the Jewish faith. Whether she was from Pontus or Rome or some other place is unknown.

Since nothing is said of Paul's converting Priscilla and Aquila, it is generally assumed that they already had become Christians before meeting Paul in Corinth. Was Aquila one of the Jews from Pontus in Jerusalem at that momentous Pentecost? (See Acts 2:8, 9.)

Claudius ruled the Roman Empire from A.D. 41 to 54. Because of an edict by that emperor in A.D. 49 or 50, Aquila and Priscilla had *to leave Rome.* (Historical references outside the Bible also mention this edict.) The historian Suetonius discusses the eviction and even mentions a leader named "Chrestus." Probably Suetonius had the name slightly wrong—it should be "Christus" or "Christ." If so, then the unrest in Rome that prompted the eviction probably was related to tensions within Judaism regarding Jesus. To the Roman authorities, Christianity is just a sect of Judaism. So even if Aquila and Priscilla were Christians in Rome, they would still be evicted because of Aquila's Jewish heritage.

All this suggests that the first group of Christians in Rome may have been a predominantly Jewish group rather than a Gentile group. With the Jews evicted, those of Gentile background began to be the majority of Christians in Rome (Romans 1:5, 6). We know that when Paul wrote the book of Romans in about A.D. 57, he had not yet had an opportunity to visit this church. By that time, however,

HOW TO SAY IT

Antioch. AN-tee-ock.

Aphrodite. Af-ruh-DITE-ee.

Apollo. Uh-PAH-low.

Apollos. Uh-PAHL-us.

Aquila. ACK-wih-luh.

Athens. ATH-unz.

Bithynia. Bih-THIN-ee-uh.

Cenchrea. SEN-kree-uh.

Claudius. CLAW-dee-us.

Corinth. KOR-inth.

Corinthians. Kor-IN-thee-unz.

Chrestus. CREST-us.

Christus. CRISS-tus.

Ephesians. Ee-FEE-zhunz.

Ephesus. EF-uh-sus.

Judaism. JOO-duh-izz-um or JOO-day-izz-um.

Messiah. Meh-SIGH-uh.

Nazirite. NAZ-ih-rite.

Onesiphorus. AHN-uh-SIF-oh-ruhs.

Pontus. PON-tuss.

Priscilla. Prih-SIL-uh.

Septuagint. Sep-TOO-ih-jent.

Suetonius. Soo-TOE-nee-us.

synagogue. SIN-uh-gog.

Syria. SEAR-ee-uh.

Troas. TRO-az.

the edict of Claudius was no longer in force and Aquila and Priscilla had returned to their home in the capital city (Romans 16:3, below).

3. . . . and because he was a tentmaker as they were, he stayed and worked with them.

Paul, in a strange pagan city, is no doubt glad to meet this hospitable couple as he looks for a place to ply his trade or craft. All Jewish boys are expected to learn some kind of trade, and Paul's is tent-making. (The term probably refers to something that includes more than making tents; we might call such a one a "leather worker.") It seems that Paul frequently uses his trade skills to support himself on his missionary journeys rather than accept support from churches (cf. Acts 20:34; 1 Corinthians 9:3-6; 1 Thessalonians 2:6-9; 2 Thessalonians 3:6-10; however, also see 2 Corinthians 11:7-9). What a joy it must have been to Paul to find that this couple, with whom he shared job skills, also shared his faith in Jesus.

Paul, Aquila, and Priscilla have given us a name for a certain kind of missionary or preacher. We use the term *tentmakers* to refer to Christian workers who earn their livelihood in a secular occupation while also preaching and teaching the gospel.

4. Every Sabbath he reasoned in the synagogue, trying to persuade Jews and Greeks.

With the help of this hospitable couple, Paul begins preaching in the local *synagogue, trying to* convince his fellow *Jews* about Christ. It was customary in the ancient world to ask a visiting rabbi to address the assembly on the *Sabbath* (cf. Luke 4:16). If there were ten male Jews in a community, they could have a synagogue.

Paul normally begins his evangelistic efforts in such gatherings. This practice makes sense given the fact that Christianity has Old Testament Judaism as its foundation (John 4:22). The worshipers are familiar with the Old Testament and its prophecies of the Messiah. Thus it is a good, practical place to find a ready-made audience. Apparently some *Greeks* (Gentiles) attend these Sabbath assemblies as well.

B. ENTRUSTED BY PAUL (v. 18, 19a)

18. Paul stayed on in Corinth for some time. Then he left the brothers and sailed for Syria, accompanied by Priscilla and Aquila. Before he sailed, he had his hair cut off at Cenchrea because of a vow he had taken.

The ministry *in Corinth* is very fruitful, but Paul decides to travel back to *Syria* where his home base of Antioch is located. Paul now has been in Corinth at least eighteen months (Acts 18:11), and it's time to move on. When he goes, *Priscilla and Aquila* begin the journey with him. Theirs is the kind of business that easily moves from place to place. It is possible that they turn over their Corinth operation to someone else and prepare to open a new business elsewhere.

Priscilla and Aquila's willingness to uproot and accompany Paul for an uncertain future speaks to their devotion and faith. Did they volunteer, or did Paul ask them to accompany him? There is no way to know, but one easily imagines the idea springing almost spontaneously as the three discussed Paul's future labors.

Luke reveals an interesting detail about Paul here. He has finished—or initiated—*a vow*. It seems to be what was called the Nazirite vow or something akin to it (Numbers 6:1-21). Such a vow includes letting one's *hair* grow. We remember that Samson was a Nazirite, and he let his hair grow by decree of an angel of the Lord (Judges 13:5). Now that Paul's vow is completed, he cuts his hair. (Some students believe the hair was shaved at the initiation of the vow as well as at the completion—so this may be the beginning of a vow.)

WHAT DO YOU THINK?

Suppose another member of your church says, "I think preachers should work secular jobs as Paul did—and not be paid by the church." How would you respond? When may such a practice be helpful to the church or the preacher? Why might it not be helpful?

[You might find Acts 18:5; 1 Corinthians 9:7-11, 14; and 1 Timothy 5:17, 18 useful in this discussion.]

WHAT DO YOU THINK?

Paul regularly went into synagogues to find an audience for his preaching. Where can we go or what can we do to get a hearing for the gospel? What methods can we employ to determine where we may find a receptive audience?

Even though Paul is increasingly comfortable in the Gentile world, he is still a Jew and takes his Jewish obligations seriously. Eventually he will go to Jerusalem, where he will be asked to sponsor four others who have completed vows (Acts 21:17-26). Many believe it is at that time that Paul completes the terms of his own vow mentioned here. This type of witness could be important to Aquila, who is also a Jew (v. 2, above).

19a. They arrived at Ephesus, where Paul left Priscilla and Aquila.

Now the travelers spend some time in the great city of *Ephesus*. When Paul leaves this place, he turns over the ministry there to *Priscilla and Aquila*. This was probably Paul's intent from the time they left Corinth.

As was mentioned in last week's lesson, Ephesus is a significant city in the Roman Empire. It is significant in church history as well. On his third missionary journey, Paul will spend the better part of three years here (Acts 20:31). The church in Ephesus was one of seven to receive a special message from Christ (Revelation 2:1-7). There is also a book to the Ephesians in the New Testament. These facts speak highly of Priscilla and Aquila's ministry there.

II. THE TEAM INSTRUCTS (ACTS 18:24-26)

As we move to our next section of text, Paul has said farewell to Priscilla and Aquila (Acts 18:21), has completed his second missionary journey (18:22), and has begun his third (18:23). Priscilla and Aquila are prominent in the ministry at Ephesus while Paul is away.

A. WHOM THEY TEACH (vv. 24, 25)

24. Meanwhile a Jew named Apollos, a native of Alexandria, came to Ephesus. He was a learned man, with a thorough knowledge of the Scriptures.

While in *Ephesus*, Priscilla and Aquila meet a Jewish scholar and orator named *Apollos*. The fact that he has *a thorough knowledge of the Scriptures* tells us what kind of scholar he is.

Apollos's scholarly abilities undoubtedly have been honed in his hometown *of Alexandria* in northern Egypt. This city was founded by, and named for, Alexander the Great in 332 B.C. It is an important seat of learning at the time. The scholars of the large Jewish colony in that city had produced the Septuagint (the Greek version of the Old Testament) about 250 years before Christ.

Apollos becomes very prominent in early Christianity. One of the factions that eventually develops in the church at Corinth even claims to follow him (1 Corinthians 3:4), although Apollos himself is surely not to blame for that problem. Other passages that establish his prominence are Acts 18:27, 28; 19:1; 1 Corinthians 3:22; 4:6; 16:12; and Titus 3:13.

25. He had been instructed in the way of the Lord, and he spoke with great fervor and taught about Jesus accurately, though he knew only the baptism of John.

We don't know exactly how Apollos received his first instruction in *the way of the Lord*. Since he knows *only the baptism of John*, his incomplete information about Jesus likely comes from disciples of John the Baptist.

B. HOW AND WHAT THEY TEACH (v. 26)

26. He began to speak boldly in the synagogue. When Priscilla and Aquila heard him, they invited him to their home and explained to him the way of God more adequately.

To encourage this great preacher, this gentle couple does not confront him publicly but invites *him to their home* instead. There they privately point out to him where his knowledge of *the way of God* is incomplete. To his credit, Apollos

---

WHAT DO YOU THINK?

Paul left Priscilla and Aquila in Ephesus to prepare for planting a church in that city. How can Christians today determine the best places to plant new congregations?

WHAT DO YOU THINK?

Paul seems to have had a special interest in planting city churches. What is the advantage of planting a church in the city? What can our church do to reach the major urban centers of our country?

DAILY BIBLE READINGS

Monday, Feb. 17—They Were Tent-makers (Acts 18:1-10)

Tuesday, Feb. 18—Aquila and Priscilla Teach Apollos (Acts 18:24-28)

Wednesday, Feb. 19—They Risked Their Lives (Romans 16:1-5)

Thursday, Feb. 20—The Church in Their Home (1 Corinthians 16:13-24)

Friday, Feb. 21—Greet Priscilla and Aquila (2 Timothy 4:16-22)

Saturday, Feb. 22—Maintain the Unity of the Spirit (Ephesians 4:1-8)

Sunday, Feb. 23—Gifts for Equipping the Saints (Ephesians 4:9-16)

accepts this instruction readily and becomes one of the most influential preachers of the apostolic age. The prominence of Apollos in the writings of Luke and Paul speaks also of the importance of Apollos's instruction by Aquila and Priscilla.

Priscilla and Aquila serve as a model of Christian hospitality for us today. Not only do they open their home to an itinerant preacher, later they also will allow the church to meet in their house. We will see this in the next section.

HOW TO REACH A ROCKER

In their book *When God Builds a Church*, authors Bob and Rusty Russell tell the remarkable story of the Southeast Christian Church in Louisville, Kentucky. Evangelism is the primary mission at Southeast, one of America's largest and fastest growing congregations.

Before she moved to Louisville, Liz Curtis was billed as "Detroit's number one lady of rock 'n' roll." Her lifestyle was so bad that even shock jock Howard Stern told her, "Liz, you've got to clean up your act!"

In Louisville, Liz ran into Evelyn and Tim Kelly, new Christians at Southeast, who hosted a morning talk show at her new radio station. They invited her to church. Bob Russell was preaching from Ephesians 5 on how husbands should be like Christ in being willing to die for their wives. Liz whispered to Evelyn, "If I ever met a man who'd die for me, I'd marry him in a minute!"

Evelyn whispered back, "Liz, a Man has already died for you."

Several Sundays later, Liz gave her life to Christ. "I was delivered, body and soul, from one location to another—from the gates of Hell to the gates of Heaven."

Today Liz Curtis Higgs is one of the most popular speakers in America. She is a member of the National Speakers Association's Hall of Fame. Her books include *Bad Girls of the Bible*. She, like Apollos, is reaching many for Christ because Evelyn and Tim Kelly, like Priscilla and Aquila, reached out to her.   —V. K.

III. THE TEAM REMEMBERED (ROMANS 16:3-5a; 1 CORINTHIANS 16:19; 2 TIMOTHY 4:19)

As Paul moves into the latter stages of his missionary journeys, eventually to face execution, he remembers Priscilla and Aquila with fondness.

A. ROMAN CONNECTION (ROMANS 16:3-5a)

3. Greet Priscilla and Aquila, my fellow workers in Christ Jesus.

As he writes to the church at Rome, Paul is probably back in Corinth, and the year is about A.D. 57. With the death of Emperor Claudius in 54 his edict (see Acts 18:2) had expired. *Priscilla and Aquila* eventually, then, moved back to Rome. Paul mention both as his *fellow workers*, indicating that women as well as men played an important part in the life and work of the early church.

4. They risked their lives for me. Not only I but all the churches of the Gentiles are grateful to them.

Paul indicates that this noble couple *risked their lives for* him. We don't know any specific incident Paul had in mind. Perhaps the riot in Ephesus (probably A.D. 53; cf. Acts 19:23-41) was the occasion. The *King James Version* renders this more literally as "laid down their own necks." Some believe this phrase to be more than a figure of speech; they suggest the couple was in danger of suffering a beheading!

RISKING YOUR LIFE FOR OTHERS

Would you put your own life on the line for someone else? Would you risk the life of your mate or your children to save someone who is not even a member of your family? That was the choice that many Gentiles made in Nazi-occupied Europe

WHAT DO YOU THINK?

What if an eloquent speaker visited your church but taught error? Who should correct him? How? What would you *do*?

[Use Acts 20:28-31; Galatians 6:1, 2; and Titus 1:9 in the course of your discussion.]

"My fellow workers in Christ Jesus . . . [who] risked their lives for" the gospel!
—from Romans 16:3 NIV

The photos on today's visual are from actual mission fields showing some of the risks that must be endured for the spread of the gospel.

PRAYER

Thank you, Lord, for Christian homes, Christian couples, and Christian hospitality. We thank you for those who can stand for truth without sacrificing kindness and civility. Help us to learn from their example. In Jesus' name we pray, amen.

WHAT DO YOU THINK?

Some people believe the New Testament allows only for "house churches" and that erecting church buildings is wrong. Considering biblical, financial, parking, fellowship, and visibility issues, how would you answer such a claim?

OPTION

Use the reproducible activity on page 226 to facilitate this discussion of the advantages and disadvantages of a house church.

THOUGHT TO REMEMBER

Two can make a big difference in the work of the Lord if they are one in spirit.

during World War II. Some, without even thinking twice, put all at risk to hide Jewish people from those who were seeking them.

In her best-selling book *The Hiding Place,* Corrie ten Boom relates how her parents took compassion on Jews and hid them in a secret room above their tiny clock shop in Haarlem, Holland. Father ten Boom would tell them, "In this household God's children are always welcome."

But the ten Boom family paid a high price for caring. On February 28, 1944, the dreaded Gestapo raided their home. The hiding place went undiscovered, but the ten Booms were arrested anyway. Father ten Boom died in The Hague and Corrie's sister, Betsie, died in the notorious Ravensbrück concentration camp. In God's providence, Corrie was released due to a clerical error. One week later, all women her age who were still at the camp were marched to the gas chambers. Ninety-six thousand women perished at Ravensbrück.

Although we do not know how Priscilla and Aquila risked their necks for Paul, we know that compassion for others is always the right thing to do.   —V. K.

5a. Greet also the church that meets at their house.

Many of the congregations in the first century meet in private homes. Evidently Priscilla and Aquila open their home to *the church* in Rome as a place of worship. For this couple to have a home large enough for this purpose indicates that they are somewhat wealthy.

B. CORINTHIAN CONNECTION (1 CORINTHIANS 16:19)

19. The churches in the province of Asia send you greetings. Aquila and Priscilla greet you warmly in the Lord, and so does the church that meets at their house.

This passage comes after Romans in the New Testament, but was written earlier. Paul is back in Ephesus on his third missionary journey as he writes (1 Corinthians 16:8, 9). The year is probably early A.D. 56. Naturally, the Corinthians to whom Paul writes still remember *Aquila and Priscilla* with great fondness from their previous time there (Acts 18:1-3). Again their house is open to the church. This is obviously a pattern in the lives of this couple.

C. EPHESIAN CONNECTION (2 TIMOTHY 4:19)

19. Greet Priscilla and Aquila and the household of Onesiphorus.

This writing comes much later, from what is probably Paul's final correspondence. Paul is now a prisoner in Rome, and the year is about A.D. 65. As he writes to Timothy, that young preacher is laboring back in the great city of Ephesus. Evidently, *Priscilla and Aquila* have left Rome to return once again to Ephesus, and are in some way assisting Timothy in his ministry there. As Paul's martyrdom approaches, his greeting list here (vv. 19-21) is much shorter than the one in Romans 16. But Priscilla and Aquila are still on the list, and they are still at its top!

We know little about *Onesiphorus.* We know he risked much trying to find Paul in Rome (2 Timothy 1:16-18). He probably gave Paul some financial support. Some deduce that since Paul speaks only of his *household* that Onesiphorus is either absent or has passed away.

CONCLUSION

In our wedding ceremonies, we speak of two becoming one. If any couple is a model for that relationship, it is Aquila and Priscilla. Their unity is not, however, a unity of flesh only. These two are so connected spiritually that for the rest of history Christians cannot think of one without the other. What a model for Christian husbands and wives today!

Discovery Learning

*This page contains an alternative lesson plan emphasizing learning activities. Classes
desiring such student involvement will find these suggestions helpful. The next page
is a reproducible activity page to further enhance discovery learning.*

LEARNING GOALS

After participating in this lesson, each student will be able to:

1. List three cities where Priscilla and Aquila labored for the Lord, and note something of their work in each.

2. Explain how Priscilla and Aquila's style of hospitality and teaching can be used to help the church today.

3. Express appreciation to a person or couple who helps to facilitate the ministry in your church.

INTO THE LESSON

Distribute copies of the reproducible activity "Spending Time in a House Church" from the following page. Explain that house churches were very common in the New Testament culture, even as they are in some countries today. House churches offer some wonderful opportunities and blessings. But they also have unique problems. Ask the class to cite what they think would be blessings or challenges unique to these churches. Members can add notes as they are suggested.

Make the transition to Bible study by saying, "Our focus today is not so much on the house church as it is upon the kind of person who could host or start this kind of church. In the lives of these people we will find qualities that should be attractive to believers today."

INTO THE WORD

Using the lesson commentary Introduction and Background, prepare a brief lecture to introduce Priscilla and Aquila. (See page 219.) Have a map available to locate Pontus, Corinth, Ephesus, and Rome.

Also, tell the class that two familiar expressions that are used in the church or even in society at large today have their roots in today's text: *Tent-making Preachers* (or *Missionaries*) and *risked their necks.*

Before class mount three pieces of poster board around the room. One should be labeled "Rome," one, "Corinth," and one, "Ephesus." Ask class members to cluster in three groups, each near a poster. Give the groups these written assignments, along with photocopies of the lesson commentary on their assigned texts.

CORINTH: Read Acts 18:1-4 and 1 Corinthians 16:19. Then answer the following and put notes on the poster board that will help the rest of the class understand what happened in that city.

1. What was the city of Corinth like?

2. Tell about the national roots of Priscilla and Aquila and why they had come to Corinth.

3. What occupation did this couple have in common with Paul? Explain the term *tent-making preachers.* Describe the leadership of this couple in Corinth.

EPHESUS: Read Acts 18:18, 19, 24-26 and 2 Timothy 4:19. Answer the following questions and put notes on the poster that will help the class identify what happened in Ephesus.

1. What was Priscilla's more formal name? (See 2 Timothy 4:19 footnote.)

2. Tell what happened through the ministry of Priscilla and Aquila in Ephesus. (Lesson commentary notes on vv. 24-26 will be especially helpful. Note the remarks about a house church.)

3. Explain why Paul cut his hair.

ROME: Read Acts 18:2 and Romans 16:3-5a. Answer the following questions and write notes on the poster that will help the class understand what happened in Rome.

1. Explain Paul's term *risked their lives for me.* (Note that the expression is literally *risked their necks.*)

2. What service to Christ did this couple give in Rome?

3. This text compliments the ministry of a woman in the New Testament church. Who were some other women noted for their leadership and service to the early church? Acts 16:14, 15 and Romans 16:1, 2 will be helpful.

INTO LIFE

Say, "While not many churches meet in homes today, there are many lessons about how to live life as we observe this couple." Write three leadership headings at the top of the board with these words: "Christian Marriage," "Christian Hospitality," and "Christian Teaching." Ask the class to brainstorm lessons we learn from this couple for these.

After this exercise, tell the class, "There is one more very important lesson to learn from this study. But this lesson comes from Paul. Notice how often and how lavishly he encourages the ministry of Priscilla and Aquila." Distribute "thank you" cards and ask class members to write a note to a "tent-making" minister (volunteer), encouraging and thanking that person (or couple) for the ministry and service given. Consider granting a "Priscilla and Aquila Award" as described at the bottom of the reproducible page.

Spending Time in a House Church!

Many of the churches in the New Testament met in homes, such as that of Priscilla and Aquila. Even today there are many "house churches," especially in some cultures and countries. These churches enjoy some special blessings and opportunities—and face special challenges and handicaps. Let's face some of these issues right now. What are some of the special blessings and opportunities one might find in a house church?

_____   _____

_____   _____

_____   _____

What are some of the special challenges or handicaps facing these house churches?

_____   _____

_____   _____

_____   _____

Paul and his colleagues, Priscilla and Aquila, were "tent-making" leaders. Like leaders for small churches and house churches, they had careers that provided their material needs while they worked in their ministries.

What may be some of the special blessings for these leaders?

_____   _____

_____   _____

_____   _____

What may be some of the unique hardships and challenges these leaders face?

_____   _____

_____   _____

_____   _____

If you know a "tent-making" minister or missionary or a small church with a "tent-making" leader, write a note of encouragement and appreciation to that person or congregation. If you choose, select a couple out of your own local church to honor in some way; call it a "Priscilla and Aquila Award."(This could also be a class project and include a special gift for that congregation, minister., or couple.)

Spring Quarter, 2003

Jesus: *God's Power in Action*
(*Mark*)

Special Features

Lessons

About These Lessons

As Christians, we wear the name of Christ. He is the Head of the church. His teachings and His actions comprise the foundation of our faith. Therefore, it is important to study the life of Christ with some regularity. This quarter's study comes from the Gospel of Mark, a fast-paced account of the life of Jesus well-suited to Mark's readers of the first century—and the twenty-first!

Mar 2
Mar 9
Mar 16
Mar 23
Mar 30
Apr 6
Apr 13
Apr 20
Apr 27
May 4
May 11
May 18
May 25

Jesus and Unchanging Truth

by Ronald L. Nickelson

The concept of "truth" keeps changing! For most of history, truth was understood to be something that was *revealed* by God. We found meaning in the truth by listening to it. Our duty after listening to the truth was to obey.

But this understanding of truth changed in the 1780s with the birth of the "scientific method." After that time, truth became something *discovered* by science. Our duty after discovering truth was not to obey, but to learn more.

In the latter part of the twentieth century, truth for many people became something to be *experienced* by each individual. No longer was there one path to truth, whether revealed by God or discovered by science. Each person was to figure out "what works for me." With such an understanding, the duty of humanity then is not obedience or learning, but survival.

What a challenge it is for Christians to break through such a mind-set! But despite these sobering changes, the message of Christianity is unbending: God has acted and spoken through his Son, Jesus Christ, and those actions and words *reveal* truth. This truth is objective fact.

This quarter's lessons present truth about God's power at work in Jesus to change people's lives. The truth of those changes leads us to faith in him and eternal life.

March: Unit 1 **Lesson 1: Jesus Begins His Ministry.** Jesus chooses some unlikely men to be his first disciples. But through them God changes human history. Truth!

Lesson 2: The Conflict Begins. The historical facts of Jesus' miracles are designed to lead us to faith. That was truth in Jesus' day, and is still truth now.

Lesson 3: Jesus Displays His Authority. The facts of history establish Jesus' power and authority. Those truths should strengthen our faith anew each day.

Lesson 4: Rejection and Mission. Jesus put his mission ahead of his own well-being despite rejection. He expects us to do so as well. This also is truth.

Lesson 5: What Really Defiles. Jesus pointed out wrong beliefs when He came to earth, and He still does so today. Will we accept his Word as truth?

April: Unit 2 **Lesson 6: The Messiah Challenges the Corrupt.** Sometimes Jesus uses only words to speak truth. At other times he adds sharp actions.

Lesson 7: Jesus Gives Passover New Meaning. After many centuries the Passover gives way to the Lord's Supper. This, too, is a truth of history.

Lesson 8: Jesus Dies and Lives Again. The focal point of Jesus' earthly ministry is his death and resurrection. Christianity depends on this truth.

Lesson 9: Faith Conquers Fear. A person who has faith in the power of God does not fear. He or she knows that God will handle all problems in his own way.

May: Unit 3 **Lesson 10: Jesus Honors Bold Faith.** Great things that are possible when people approach God with boldness combined with right motives!

Lesson 11: Putting Faith in Jesus Alone. When it comes to a person's eternal destiny, one must put faith in Jesus alone! Eternal truth lies only in him.

Lesson 12: Expressing Honest Faith. Sometimes we all have doubts, and we wrestle with unbelief. This is a sobering truth, but Jesus knows how to help.

Lesson 13: Faith Becomes Sight. Jesus granted eyesight to blind men because of their faith. But much more importantly, Jesus can heal spiritual blindness!

The Gospel of Mark is sometimes called the "Gospel of Action." But your study will not be complete until this Gospel *of* action is translated into the gospel *in* action—as you and your students put into practice the bold faith that Jesus inspires.

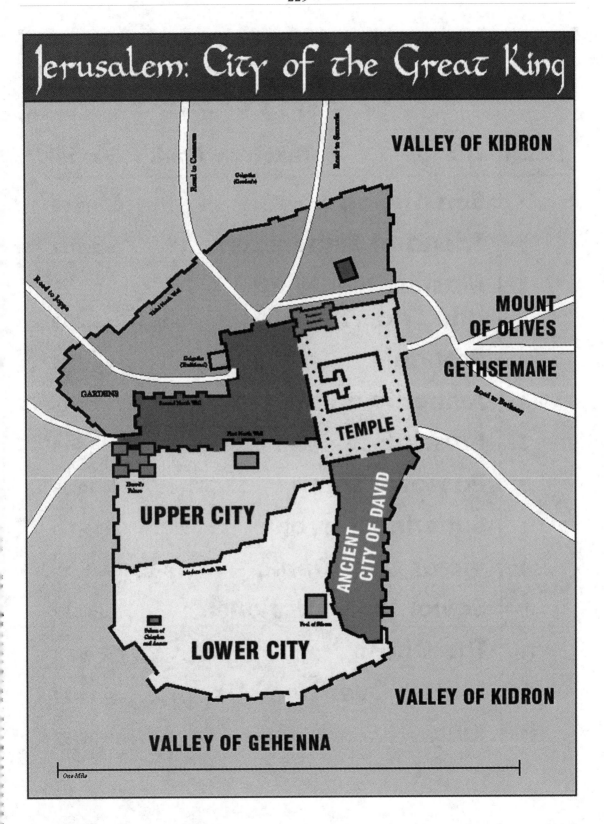

Who Is Jesus?

Lesson	He is	Text from Mark's Gospel
1	Son of God	1:9-26
2	Friend of Sinners	2:3-17
3	Master Over Wind and Sea	4:36-41; 5:2-13
4	Prophet	6:1-13
5	Authority on the Law	7:1-15
6	Messiah	11:1-9, 15-18
7	Passover Lamb	14:12-25
8	Suffering Servant	15:21-25, 33-37; 16:1-8
9	Victor Over Death	5:22-36, 41, 42
10	Savior for All Nations	7:24-37
11	The Christ	8:27-36; 9:2-8
12	Master Over Demons	9:14-29
13	King	10:35-52

Jesus: God's Power in Action

Unit 1: Jesus' Early Ministry
(Lessons 1-5)

JESUS BEGINS HIS MINISTRY

LESSON 1

WHY TEACH THIS LESSON?

The hallmark of a postmodern culture is uncertainty. Today's postmodern gurus tell us that people are not supposed to be sure about anything. After all, if you're sure of something—if you believe that a certain fact or principle applies to everyone—then that means that you are not being tolerant of folks who are not as sure as you are. And shame on you for your intolerance—your intolerance is something not to be tolerated!

The God of the universe, however, is not postmodern. There are things he is very sure of. People are sinners. People will spend eternity in Hell for their sins. Jesus is the only one who can solve this problem and keep people out of Hell.

More and more, your learners are coming face-to-face with the intolerance of postmodernism. Perhaps they are beginning to question in their own minds those things of which they have been certain in the past. Today's lesson will give them certainty. God himself is certain about his Son. (Interestingly enough, so are the demons!) You and your students can be certain about Jesus, too, and certain that his kingdom is for you!

INTRODUCTION

A. URGENT MISSION

Leighton Ford knows what it means to be frightened when a child wanders off. He describes the day his daughter came up lost: "During the nearly two hours that Debbie Jean was missing, nothing else mattered. In my study were books to read, letters to be answered, articles to be written, planning to be done—but it all was forgotten. I could think of only one thing: my little girl was lost. I had only one prayer, and I prayed it a thousand times. 'Oh, God, help me to find her.' How often, I asked myself later, had I felt such a terrible urgency about people who were lost from God?"

Mark begins his Gospel with a record of how Jesus began his ministry. The word *urgent* marks everything Jesus did. Time was short. The moments could not be wasted. The kingdom of God could not wait for trivial concerns.

B. LESSON BACKGROUND

The Gospel of Mark is second in order among the Gospels of the New Testament. The shortest of the four Gospels, Mark presents a compact but powerful account of Jesus' words and, especially, his actions. Readers notice from the first lines some of the obvious differences between this Gospel and the other three. The Gospel of John begins with a reflection on the existence of Christ before the creation of the world. Matthew and Luke begin with details of Jesus' birth. Mark skips past this information to go directly to Jesus' baptism as the beginning point of his presentation.

This difference should not be misunderstood. Mark does not imply that the origin of Jesus is unimportant. As a matter of fact, Mark's Gospel opens with an identification of Jesus as "Jesus Christ, the Son of God" (1:1). In this way Mark emphasizes that Jesus came from God in order to announce God's kingdom.

DEVOTIONAL READING:
LUKE 4:14-21

BACKGROUND SCRIPTURE:
MARK 1:1-45

PRINTED TEXT:
MARK 1:9-26

LESSON AIMS

After participating in this lesson, each student will be able to:

1. Cite the significant details of Jesus' early ministry, including his baptism and teaching.

2. Explain the urgency of Jesus' ministry, both in his day and in ours.

3. Express a commitment to speak the good news of God's kingdom with boldness, knowing that Christ's own authority empowers us.

KEY VERSE

A voice came from heaven: "You are my Son, whom I love; with you I am well pleased."
—Mark 1:11

LESSON 1 NOTES

Mark establishes that this Jesus began his ministry by submitting to the baptism of another servant sent by God, John the Baptist (1:1-9).

After describing Jesus' baptism, Mark focuses (from 1:14 to 3:6) on the early stages of Jesus' Galilean ministry. There Jesus calls his first disciples (1:16-20) and establishes his authority in his teaching. He also demonstrates his power to drive out demons (1:21-28).

I. THE BAPTISM OF JESUS (MARK 1:9-11)

A. SUBMISSION (v. 9)

9. At that time Jesus came from Nazareth in Galilee and was baptized by John in the Jordan.

At that time refers to the time of John the Baptist's ministry around the Jordan River. This is an area remote enough from Jerusalem and Jericho that Mark can refer to it in verse 4 as "the wilderness." To the north is the territory of Galilee, some fifty miles distant. Jesus comes from the village of *Nazareth,* located in the hills of lower *Galilee.* The time is about A.D. 27, and Jesus is about thirty years old (Luke 3:23).

Mark reports in a matter-of-fact way that Jesus is baptized by *John* the Baptist. He does not report any of the conversation that Matthew includes—an exchange related to why Jesus would consent to baptism by a preacher who is proclaiming the need for repentance from sin. Matthew's expanded account explains that Jesus submits to this baptism, not because he is in need of forgiveness, but because he is determined to "fulfill all righteousness" (Matthew 3:15).

B. AFFIRMATION (vv. 10, 11)

10. As Jesus was coming up out of the water, he saw heaven being torn open and the Spirit descending on him like a dove.

There is no other example in the Bible of someone's baptism being accompanied by these signs from *heaven.* Some suggest that the words *he saw* indicate that only Jesus saw the opening of the heavens and the Spirit's descent. John, however, makes it clear that John the Baptist also "saw the Spirit come down from heaven" (John 1:32). Mark's word for the opening of heaven is a vivid term meaning "to rip open," as if it were some cosmic event (cf. Isaiah 64:1). Mark's description of the descent of the Spirit can be taken to mean either that the Spirit took the form of a dove and descended or that the Spirit's descending resembled the way a dove descends. Once again, a look at another Gospel account clears up the matter. This time it is Luke who helps us. He says specifically that "the Holy Spirit descended on him in bodily form like a dove" (Luke 3:22). Thus, these signs confirming the uniqueness of Jesus' baptism could be verified by objective witnesses.

The words *coming up out of the water* can hardly be understood without thinking of baptism by immersion. Nothing about other modes of baptism requires one to step down into the water. Jesus is immersed in the water just as believers later in the New Testament record are (see Acts 8:38; Romans 6:4).

11. And a voice came from heaven: "You are my Son, whom I love; with you I am well pleased."

With the *voice* from heaven it is clear that all three personalities of the Trinity—Father, Son, and Holy Spirit—are involved in this event. While the word Trinity is not found in the Bible, passages like this one imply the truth of the concept. The phrases *You are my Son, whom I love* and *well pleased* represent the Father's confirmation of Jesus. They also express his confidence in the work he sends Jesus to do (cf. Psalm 2:7; Isaiah 42:1).

WHAT DO YOU THINK?

What is significant to you about Jesus' desire to "fulfill all righteousness"? How does Jesus' submission to God's will motivate your own obedience?

"Thou art my beloved Son . . . in whom I am well pleased."

Post today's visual from the Adult Visuals Packet as you begin to discuss the lesson text (verse 9).

II. THE TEMPTATION OF JESUS (MARK 1:12, 13)

A. ACTION OF THE HOLY SPIRIT (v. 12)

12. At once the Spirit sent him out into the desert,

The words *at once* are an early indication of the urgency Mark sees in Jesus' actions. Mark uses this term more than forty times in his Gospel. The time is short!

No sooner has Jesus come up from the waters of baptism than the Holy *Spirit* forces him into *the desert* (or wilderness). The word *sent* is a mild translation of the original, which carries a more forceful quality. Jesus is now in the arena of temptation. He has moved without delay from exaltation to testing.

Perhaps the connection between these events is not so unusual. In our own lives, do occasions of high achievement sometimes lead us to our times of greatest vulnerability? Does praise open us up to temptation? Does hearing the expressions of congratulations bring us closer than at any other time to the devil's schemes?

WHAT DO YOU THINK?

Why is a transition from exaltation to temptation so common in the life of a Christian? What can we do about it?

B. ACTION OF SATAN (v. 13)

13. . . . and he was in the desert forty days, being tempted by Satan. He was with the wild animals, and angels attended him.

As much as Jesus' baptism represents the initiation of his ministry, so does this period of testing. Jesus does not present himself as God's Son without facing the temptations of *Satan*. Although Mark's account of Jesus' testing *in the desert* does not include details provided by the other gospel accounts, Hebrews 5:8 states that Jesus learned obedience by the things he suffered. In some sense this experience contributes to Jesus' right to carry the title of high priest appointed by God for every sinner in need of God's grace (Hebrews 4:15).

These *forty days* in the wilderness remind us of Moses who was with the Lord for forty days and nights without bread or water at the time of the giving of the law (Exodus 34:28). And as God sent an angel to minister to Old Testament Israel in the wilderness (Exodus 23:20, 23; 32:34), so he also puts *angels* at Jesus' disposal in this period of testing.

SURVIVOR

Just a few years ago, so-called "reality TV" was the hottest gimmick in TV programming. Complete strangers were forced into contrived circumstances that were exhaustively videotaped, then edited for the most sensational scenes. The archetype of these series was "Survivor," set on a deserted island. The contestants were divided into "tribes" that engaged in contests of strength, skill, or cunning and faced other challenges such as eating live earthworms or cooked rats.

The participants voted each other off the island one by one until only one remained to collect the $1 million prize—a scenario designed to bring out the worst in human nature. In the final episode, one of the last contestants said to another, who voted against her, "If I were ever to pass you along in life again and you were laying [sic] there dying of thirst, I would not get you a drink of water. I would let the vultures take you—with no ill regrets."

What a striking difference from Jesus' "survival" experience in our text! That was not "reality TV"; it *was* reality! Our Lord fought an enemy with a diabolical agenda, not just someone scheming to win a million dollars. If testing proves the worth of our character, Jesus set our example. Real "survivors" find their role model in Jesus, not in greedy television contestants!   —C. R. B.

III. THE MESSAGE OF JESUS (MARK 1:14-20)

A. THE REALITY (vv. 14, 15)

14. After John was put in prison, Jesus went into Galilee, proclaiming the good news of God.

VISUALS FOR THESE LESSONS

The small visual pictured in each lesson (e.g., page 232) is a small reproduction of a large, full-color poster included in the Adult Visuals packet for the Spring Quarter. The packet is available from your supplier. Order No. 392.

HOW TO SAY IT

Babylonian. Bab-ih-LOW-nee-un.

Boanerges. BO-uh-NUR-geez.

Capernaum. Kuh-PER-nay-um.

Galilee. GAL-uh-lee.

Herod Antipas. HAIR-ud AN-tih-pus.

Isaiah. Eye-ZAY-uh.

Jericho. JAIR-ih-co.

Nazareth. NAZ-uh-reth.

Nehemiah. NEE-huh-MY-uh.

synagogue. SIN-uh-gog.

Zebedee. ZEB-eh-dee.

WHAT DO YOU THINK?

At least four of Jesus' disciples were fishermen. Matthew was a tax collector. Simon (not Peter) was a political activist (a "zealot"). From what kinds of places do we see Jesus' disciples coming today? What is the significance of that?

John the Baptist's ministry ends sometime after Jesus' baptism. This end comes about because of John's imprisonment, an event mentioned by both Matthew (4:12) and Luke (3:19, 20).

But Jesus is not deterred from preaching about the kingdom, whatever the threat. Herod Antipas, who has imprisoned John, reigns *in Galilee.* But this is where Jesus goes in order to preach *the good news of God.*

15. "The time has come," he said. "The kingdom of God is near. Repent and believe the good news!"

Now Mark notes specifically the core of Jesus' message: he is preaching that *the time* is now and that *the kingdom of God* is very close—it is at hand. God's plans to usher in the kingdom are reaching their fulfillment. The message is urgent. There is no time for delay.

Although the exact phrase "the kingdom of God" cannot be found in the Old Testament, the concept is found in many places. Passages such as Exodus 15:18; Psalms 29:10; 145:13; Daniel 2:44; 4:3, 34; and 7:27 form the basis for Jesus' announcement of this kingdom. Many Jews of the first century hope for the arrival of this kingdom (see Acts 1:6). It is good news ("gospel") because God will establish this kingdom in righteousness. It will stand in contrast to the kingdoms founded by rulers like Herod Antipas where preachers of righteousness can be murdered (Matthew 14:1-12).

B. THE NECESSITY (vv. 16-20)

16, 17. As Jesus walked beside the Sea of Galilee, he saw Simon and his brother Andrew casting a net into the lake, for they were fishermen. "Come, follow me," Jesus said, "and I will make you fishers of men."

The *Sea of Galilee* is the beautiful fresh-water lake about seventy miles north of Jerusalem. Lying about seven hundred feet below sea level, it stretches some fourteen miles north to south and six miles east to west. Fishing is a primary industry of the region.

To make disciples, *Jesus* goes to places where people live their everyday lives. Mark does not pause to tell us whether *Simon* (Peter) *and his brother Andrew* have ever met Jesus (as John 1:35-42 tells us), but emphasizes the direct challenge issued by Jesus regarding discipleship. This challenge demands immediate response. Jesus' call is not to part-time discipleship but to a permanent adventure in the work of proclaiming the kingdom of God that is so close at hand.

The only promise the men have is that which Jesus includes in the call: the promise to make them fishers of men. Jesus uses their own experience in fishing to portray what is possible in the preaching of the kingdom. They can be disciples who know how to gather in people for the kingdom of God.

WHEN CELEBRITIES CALL

Turning off your telephone so you can enjoy an evening meal in peace no longer lets you escape from telemarketers. Whether the ringer on your phone is off or you are away from home, if you have an answering machine or service for your telephone, you still can get "phone spam." This is a computer-driven phone call in which your number is automatically dialed.

Telemarketers and politicians have found that a message can be sent to two hundred thousand answering machines per hour. They have also found that by using the voices of famous politicians, entertainment personalities, and sports stars, most people will listen to the message. It seems that many of us are happily deluded into thinking a celebrity is actually calling *us!*

But really, how significant is it when celebrities who care not at all about us as individuals send us a recorded phone call? Their only interest is in their political cause or their own pocketbooks! However, when the fishermen by the Sea of Galilee received their call from Jesus, it was a different story. Jesus was offering them a new life—one that would be filled with hardships, to be sure, but a new life, nevertheless—that would give them a key role in a movement that would change the world. It's exciting to think that Jesus offers us a similar call with the same amazing opportunities!   —C. R. B.

18. At once they left their nets and followed him.

Mark gives no details about the practical issues of the decision by Simon Peter and Andrew. Nothing is said concerning arrangements that would have to be made for their absence. Mark does not even describe a goodbye to their families. The urgency of Jesus' call is met with an instant response. The kingdom of God is too close to be bothered with earthly concerns. The Son of God has spoken.

19. When he had gone a little farther, he saw James son of Zebedee and his brother John in a boat, preparing their nets.

Jesus finds two more men as he walks along the shore of the lake. Jesus will later call *James* and *John* "Boanerges," which means "Sons of Thunder" (Mark 3:17). The four men now mentioned appear at the head of all the lists of the disciples of Jesus (Matthew 10:2-4; Mark 3:16-19; Luke 6:14-16; Acts 1:13).

20. Without delay he called them, and they left their father Zebedee in the boat with the hired men and followed him.

James and John answer the urgent summons without hesitation as the authority of Jesus is openly displayed. The picture of *their father Zebedee,* who is left alone *in the boat,* is softened somewhat by the mention of *the hired* hands he still has. When the Son of God calls people to become his followers, they respond in a hurry! (In a later instance, Jesus will not mince words with two men who want to delay their service because of practical concerns; see Luke 9:59-62.)

IV. THE AUTHORITY AND POWER OF JESUS (MARK 1:21-26)

A. AUTHORITY TO TEACH (vv. 21, 22)

21. Then they wen to Capernaum, and when the Sabbath came, Jesus went into the synagogue and began to teach.

Capernaum is a fishing town located on the northwest shore of the Sea of Galilee. Today the ruins of a *synagogue* are still visible, though the first-century structure lies underneath the present remains as foundation stones. Also visible are the ruins of a house thought to be that of the apostle Peter. This makes Capernaum a natural base for the ministry of *Jesus* (cf. Matthew 4:13).

The synagogue is the Jewish institution that grew up during the Babylonian captivity so that Jews would have a place to pray, read Scripture, and worship God while far from their homeland. Jesus and the apostles often begin their preaching efforts by finding the nearest synagogue (Luke 4:15; Acts 14:1; 17:1, 2) because most synagogues welcomed visiting rabbis to teach the lesson on the Sabbath Day.

22. The people were amazed at his teaching, because he taught them as one who had authority, not as the teachers of the law.

The astonishment of Jesus' audiences is well documented in Mark's Gospel (see 6:2; 7:37; 10:26; 11:18). Here he contrasts the authority in Jesus' *teaching* with the scribes who are the scholars of the day. On virtually any matter of doctrine the rabbis of the time fill their teaching with quotations of other rabbis, often indicating where they are at odds with one another.

But Jesus *has authority* as the Son of God. He speaks as the author of truth, proclaiming the very words of God. All Scripture, of course, should be interpreted

WHAT DO YOU THINK?

What can we learn from the consistent examples of urgency in Jesus' message, followed by a rapid, wholehearted response from his followers?

WHAT DO YOU THINK?

What was it that made Jesus' teaching so much more authoritative than that of the rabbis? Was it the content, the delivery, the corroborating miracles, or the combination of these? Or was it something else? How does it compare with teaching of our day?

DAILY BIBLE READINGS

Monday, Feb. 24—*Jesus Is Baptized, Tempted (Mark 1:1-13)*

Tuesday, Feb. 25—*Jesus Calls Four Fishermen (Mark 1:14-20)*

Wednesday, Feb. 26—*Follow Me (John 1:43-51)*

Thursday, Feb. 27—*You Will Catch People (Luke 5:1-11)*

Friday, Feb. 28—*Jesus Casts Out an Unclean Spirit (Mark 1:21-28)*

Saturday, Mar. 1—*Jesus Heals Many Sick Persons (Mark 1:29-38)*

Sunday, Mar. 2—*Jesus Preaches Throughout Galilee (Mark 1:39-45)*

PRAYER

Lord, help me to go about my service for Christ as if today will be the last day I have before seeing Him face to face. Through Christ and His authority I pray, amen.

THOUGHT TO REMEMBER

"Only one life, 'Twill soon be past.

Only what's done for Christ will last."

and explained so that people can understand. (The lessons in this book are examples; see also Nehemiah 8:7, 8.) But when teaching starts to embrace human tradition to the exclusion of God's explicit commands, danger looms (Mark 7:7, 8).

B. POWER TO HEAL (vv. 23-26)

23. Just then a man in their synagogue who was possessed by an evil spirit cried out,

An *evil spirit* is a demon. That this *man* is *in their synagogue* can either mean that he is a member of the assembly itself or that he is merely in the building that day. This is the first of four exorcisms recorded by Mark. (See 5:1-20; 7:24-30; 9:14-29.)

24. . . . "What do you want with us, Jesus of Nazareth? Have you come to destroy us? I know who you are—the Holy One of God!"

The words of the man are in reality those of the demon crying out, since Jesus responds specifically to the demon in the verse to follow. In referring to *us*, this demon is apparently speaking for all demons. Recognizing in Jesus the authority and power of God, they know that his mission is to *destroy* them (cf. 1 John 3:8). They must realize that they have made themselves enemies of God (see James 2:19). Many scholars see the demons' identification of Jesus of Nazareth by name and title to be a reflection of the belief that when demons name an individual it implies gaining some power over that person.

Ironically, though, even the confession of these demons acknowledges the major affirmations of Mark 1. Already truth about Jesus has been confessed by Mark himself, by the Father God, and (by implication) John the Baptist (1:7, 8). Now even the demons confess him.

25. "Be quiet!" said Jesus sternly. "Come out of him!"

No demon has greater power than *Jesus*. If the demon thinks he has gained some advantage by speaking Jesus' name, he soon learns better. Jesus does not need any of the chants or remedies often connected with driving out (exorcising) demons. All he needs to do is rebuke the demon and command him to leave the man. (For an instance where certain individuals attempt to use Jesus' name as a "magic formula," see Acts 19:13-16.) Christians do not need to fear the devil because the One who is in us is greater than he who is in the world (1 John 4:4).

26. The evil spirit shook the man violently and came out of him with a shriek.

With a last demonstration of loud demonic power, the *spirit* convulses the man and departs. As the following verse shows (not in our text for today), there is no doubt on the part of the onlookers that this is a supernatural event. The reaction of the synagogue audience repeats the theme of Mark 1:22. Their reaction also has a note of alarm. They had never seen anything quite like this. How could it be explained? Who is this man? That question will continue to be raised as the account of Mark moves forward. (See, for example, Mark 2:7; 3:22; 4:41; 8:29.) This opening salvo sets the stage for the battle that will rage between the Son of God and the forces of Satan throughout Jesus' earthly ministry.

CONCLUSION

"As the twig is bent" is an expression we sometimes use to speak about the direction a young life takes and how it shapes the end result. The phrase can be applied to Jesus' early ministry. His words and actions demonstrate the major theme of his entire mission. Our ministry for Jesus should be characterized by this urgency of the kingdom of God that is so obvious in Jesus.

Discovery Learning

*This page contains an alternative lesson plan emphasizing learning activities. Classes
desiring such student involvement will find these suggestions helpful. The next page
is a reproducible activity page to further enhance discovery learning.*

LEARNING GOALS

After participating in this lesson, each student will be able to:

1. Cite the significant details of Jesus' early ministry, including his baptism and teaching.

2. Explain the urgency of Jesus' ministry, both in his day and in ours.

3. Express a commitment to speak the good news of God's kingdom with boldness, knowing that Christ's own authority empowers us.

INTO THE LESSON

Before class arrange chairs so that class members will sit in groups of four. On a board, list the following roles: son, daughter, husband, wife, father, mother, brother, sister, employee, employer, tenant, landlord, landowner, church member, student, auto owner, small group member, stepparent, stepchild, other. When everyone is seated, say, "Each of us has many roles in life. Please indicate the roles that apply to you and that tell your group members about your life." (This activity is also found in *NIV® Bible Student*.)

After five minutes encourage learners in each group to tell which roles they like, which are challenging, which are frustrating, and which give them self-esteem.

After an additional five minutes call the groups to order. Then say, "Today as we study Mark's Gospel we will notice how Jesus also fulfilled different roles during his time on earth."

INTO THE WORD

LECTURE. Using the Lesson Background material (pages 231, 232), prepare a five-minute introduction on the book of Mark. Be sure to emphasize the urgency with which Jesus began his ministry.

Distribute copies of the reproducible activity "Wearing Many Hats" from the next page. Have the text read, and ask your students to fill in as many hats as they can in two minutes. Let the students report their entries, explaining any not immediately obvious to the group. Such entries as *baptismal candidate, Son, fisherman* can be expected.

STORY PANELS. Create groups of up to six students and give them the following assignment. Repeat assignments if necessary. You will need paper, pencils or pens, markers or art supplies, and Bibles for each student.

Group 1: Create a story panel of Jesus' baptism that includes all who were there. Depict the events as described in Mark 1:9-13.

Group 2: Create a story panel of the calling of the first disciples. These events are described in Mark 1:14-20.

Group 3: Create a story panel of Jesus driving out the unclean spirit. This event is described in Mark 1:21-28.

Explain that a story panel is a series of "snapshots" of the events described in the text. (A blank one is provided in the student book, *NIV® Bible Student*.)

Each group will present its storyboard after fifteen minutes. The lesson commentary will help you to answer students' questions.

ACROSTIC. Point out to students that there was a sense of urgency in Jesus' ministry. Then write the words "AT ONCE" vertically on a white board or overhead transparency. (A similar activity is also found in the student book.) Ask students to read Mark 1:9-26 and find words beginning with the vertical letters to describe Jesus' ministry. Words might include *amazing, teaching, obedient, newsworthy, captivating,* and *embracing.* Lead a short discussion using the following questions.

1. Which verses portray the urgency of Jesus' ministry? *(1:12, 18, 20, 38, 43.)*

2. Why does Jesus have this urgency? *(1:15.)*

3. Why should we have a sense of urgency today? *(The kingdom of God is still near!)*

INTO LIFE

Distribute copies of the reproducible activity "Following Jesus" from the next page. Have the students write on the net some of the things they have left behind or need to leave behind to follow Jesus. Then lead the group in a prayer for wisdom to leave behind the characteristics and behaviors identified.

Say, "Jesus called his disciples to speak the good news with boldness. Under the net of the 'Following Jesus' activity, add your personal response to proclaim this news to others. Use the verses given to make your answer."

Mark 1:15, 17   I will _____ *(follow him).*
Mark 1:27   I have _____
(Jesus' authority to speak).

Encourage the students to sign their copies of the activity. Then lead in a prayer for the students to have boldness in proclaiming the good news this week.

Wearing Many Hats

When someone serves in several roles, he or she is said to "wear many hats." Read Mark 1:9-45 and discern how many "hats" Jesus wore.

Following Jesus

Jesus called Simon, Andrew, James, and John from fishing nets. They had to leave the nets and family behind. On the net below, write some of the things you left behind or need to leave behind to follow Jesus. At the bottom, fill in your personal commitment.

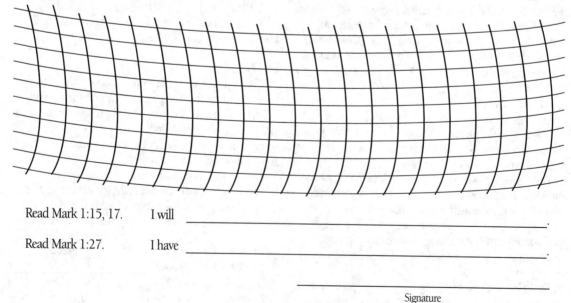

Read Mark 1:15, 17.   I will _____.

Read Mark 1:27.   I have _____.

_____
Signature

THE CONFLICT BEGINS

LESSON 2

WHY TEACH THIS LESSON?

We all have been cautioned, "Don't judge a book by its cover." On an intellectual level we know that is a valid warning against drawing conclusions from mere outward appearances. But on an emotional level we make such judgments anyway! Marketing people know it, publishing houses know it, and book retailers know it. That's the reason they spend so much time, effort, and money to create and display enticing covers on the books they're trying to sell.

In the pages of Scripture we never see God judging by outward appearances. Never. Jesus looks beyond people's appearances to see their true needs. And while we do not have Jesus' supernatural ability to see what is in a person's heart, we know that everyone needs the love of God. Some of your learners may need that reminder today, either to reassure themselves or to adjust their attitudes toward someone else. Today's lesson will remind them that everyone has worth in God's eyes. They can demonstrate that they believe that in the way they treat others this week.

INTRODUCTION

A. FORGIVE AND FORGET

Charlie Shedd tells a story about forgiveness in his book *Letters to My Grandchildren*. The evening began when little Philip came storming into the house, mad, mad, mad. To say that the word *angry* is the better choice would not work this time. This boy was mad, and it was all Ronnie's fault, again. Ronnie was Philip's buddy, and he lived across the street. But now things had changed. Ronnie was no longer his buddy. Not this time. Not forever! Whatever it was that Ronnie had done, he could never come into the house again! Never!

So Mom and Dad ate their meal with a certain sadness. They liked Ronnie a lot. Then suddenly the doorbell rang. As usual, Philip jumped up from the table to answer the door and back he came with, guess whom? It was Ronnie. "Hey, Mom, can Ronnie have some ice cream, too?"

"Of course he can, Philip. But what about all of those things you were saying? Did you mean them?"

"I meant them. But me and Ronnie, we got good forgetters!"

In today's lesson, Mark's account puts the emphasis on God's desire to forgive. He has sent His Son into the world for that very purpose. Jesus puts Himself in situations where He will have contact with sinners who need God's grace. He does this deliberately, even though there will be those who criticize Him for doing so. His ministry cannot succeed unless He associates with those who need His help.

B. LESSON BACKGROUND

For His ministry in Galilee, Jesus chose as His "headquarters" the fishing town of Capernaum, located on the northwest shore of the Sea of Galilee (cf. Mark 1:14, 21; 2:1). The convenience of this base of operations may have been assured by the fact that Capernaum was the home of Simon Peter and his brother Andrew (1:29). The ministry of Jesus already had gained notoriety in

DEVOTIONAL READING:
LUKE 15:1-7
BACKGROUND SCRIPTURE:
MARK 2:1–3:6
PRINTED TEXT:
MARK 2:3-17

LESSON AIMS

After participating in this lesson, each student will be able to:

1. Tell how today's texts illustrate that the heart of Jesus' mission was bringing the good news of God's grace to sinners.

2. Express appreciation for the grace that God offers and a sense of obligation to share that grace with others.

3. Tell what specific action he or she can take to show forgiveness to someone who is alienated from his or her fellowship.

KEY VERSE

Jesus said to them, "It is not the healthy who need a doctor, but the sick. I have not come to call the righteous, but sinners."
—Mark 2:17

the region of Galilee. He had driven out unclean spirits (1:25, 39), healed Peter's mother-in-law (1:31), preached in their synagogues (1:39), and healed a leper (1:41).

In 2:1–3:6, Mark turns his attention to five separate incidents in the vicinity of Capernaum. In each one Jesus' actions caused conflict with the religious leaders. Nothing in Mark's description of these events requires us to understand them as occurring in chronological sequence. They are simply incidents (perhaps typical kinds of incidents) where Jesus' actions resulted in controversy. We consider two of these five incidents today.

I. JESUS HEALS A PARALYZED MAN (MARK 2:3-12)

The scene to be described takes place in a Palestinian house in Capernaum (2:1). These houses are built with flat roofs, consisting of wooden beams and a mixture of sticks and mud filling in the gaps. Because of the heat, the rooftops are often used as places to relax at the end of the day. Outside steps lead up the side of the house to the roof. In this case, the teaching of Jesus has drawn such a crowd that the single room inside is full of people.

A. THE FAITH OF FRIENDS (vv. 3, 4)

3. Some men came, bringing to him a paralytic, carried by four of them.

Some kind of paralysis has taken away the man's ability to walk, and so he is carried by *four* of his friends. We might picture these men carefully transporting the paralyzed man on a mat, which they hold by the four corners as they walk along the dusty street leading to the house where Jesus can be found. Their faith is enabling this man to see Jesus.

4. Since they could not get him to Jesus because of the crowd, they made an opening in the roof above Jesus and, after digging through it, lowered the mat the paralyzed man was lying on.

Because the people are pressed into the room where Jesus is teaching, the four who carry the paralyzed man are unable to gain access to Jesus (cf. 2:2). But their determination will not allow them to be turned away. So they climb the outside stairway, hauling the paralyzed man on *the mat* to the roof. There they begin to dig through the hard-packed mud and thatch. The noise of this activity and the falling debris undoubtedly catch the attention of all inside.

UNWANTED VISITORS

Year after year, by far the biggest tourist event in the entire state of South Dakota is the week-long August gathering of "bikers" of every type imaginable in the town of Sturgis. Years ago, it was mostly "outlaw" bikers who came, brawling a bit and doing a lot of macho posturing. Many residents would leave town to avoid the trouble caused by the unwanted visitors. Renting out their houses for $2,500 or so per week made the inconvenience easier to take and also helped pay for repairs after the visitors were gone.

Nowadays, the "outlaws" are themselves complaining about unwanted visitors. "Rich Urban Bikers" (RUBs), the new breed of motorcyclists, have invaded Sturgis. They are dentists, lawyers, teachers, and other respectable citizens who have fantasies of a more exciting—and perhaps more perverse—lifestyle. They have changed the flavor of the event. There are fewer fights and arrests now that the RUBs have arrived.

The four men who tore up the roof and ceiling to lower their friend to Jesus were, no doubt, unwanted visitors. They upset the agenda of those already there; they messed up the house and got dirt on those sitting below them. But Jesus welcomed them and met their needs. What lesson might the church learn from how

Some striking characteristics of the paralytic's friends are their determination, their persistence, their resourcefulness, and their teamwork. How are the same characteristics necessary in our efforts to bring people to Jesus? What obstacles must be overcome by such qualities in order to bring people to the Lord?

Jesus handled these unwanted visitors? Would He welcome those whom we wish would go somewhere else?   —C. R. B.

B. THE AUTHORITY OF JESUS (v. 5)

5. When Jesus saw their faith, he said to the paralytic, "Son, your sins are forgiven."

The *faith* of the paralyzed man and his friends is clear to Jesus. Mark's Gospel frequently notes the faith of the people who come to Jesus for healing (5:34, 36; 9:23-34; 10:52). Jesus Himself often speaks about the role of faith in the healings that He performs, though the Gospels also present instances where Jesus heals without any evidence of faith on the part of the afflicted person (Luke 7:11-17; John 11:38-44). In pronouncing forgiveness of the man's sins, Jesus' words represent a claim about His own identity.

C. THE THOUGHTS OF ENEMIES (vv. 6-8)

6. Now some teachers of the law were sitting there, thinking to themselves,

The *teachers of the law* (or scribes) are the Bible scholars of the day. Mark already has mentioned them by noting the contrast people see between their teaching and that of Jesus (1:22). The teachers of the law will later become adversaries of Jesus (2:16), coming from all parts of Palestine to observe His teaching (cf. Luke 5:17).

7. . . . "Why does this fellow talk like that? He's blaspheming! Who can forgive sins but God alone?"

As interpreters of the Scripture, the teachers of the law are certainly correct in thinking that only *God* can *forgive sins* (cf. Exodus 34:6, 7; Isaiah 43:25; 44:22). For any mere mortal to assume the right to extend divine forgiveness of sins is to presume upon God. Thus the scribes conclude that Jesus is guilty of *blaspheming.*

The teachers of the law also know that the law makes blasphemy a capital offense (Leviticus 24:14-16). Since they think Jesus is now committing blasphemy, Jesus will have to pay with His life.

8. Immediately Jesus knew in his spirit that this was what they were thinking in their hearts, and he said to them, "Why are you thinking these things?

Jesus meets their unstated objections with a question. Like so many of Jesus' questions, this one probes the depths of their position (cf. Matthew 6:25, 26; Mark 3:33; 8:36, 37). This question, combined with another in the next verse, will demand that they consider how mistaken they are in their concept of Jesus' identity.

D. THE POWER OF JESUS (vv. 9-12)

9. "Which is easier: to say to the paralytic, 'Your sins are forgiven,' or to say, 'Get up, take your mat and walk'?

The teachers of the law refuse to believe that Jesus has power to forgive sins. Therefore, they reason, Jesus can pronounce forgiveness all he wants to, but it is without effect since only God can forgive sins. Anyone who takes on this divine right is trying to do the impossible and cannot be taken seriously!

But Jesus claims the authority to do both—to grant divine forgiveness of sins as well as to speak the powerful word of healing. Forgiveness can be faked; healing cannot. So if he speaks the word of healing so that his authority can be put to the test, then they must accept his authority to grant what cannot be seen.

In focusing on the sins of the paralyzed man, Jesus gives a powerful demonstration of the core of his preaching. The good news of the kingdom of God is that Jesus can provide forgiveness, that he came into the world not "to condemn the world" but that through him the world might be saved (John 3:17).

HOW TO SAY IT

Alphaeus. Al-FEE-us.
Antipas. AN-tih-pus.
blasphemy. BLAS-fuh-mee.
Capernaum. Kuh-PER-nay-um.
Decapolis. Dee-CAP-uh-lis.
Galilee. GAL-uh-lee.
Herod. HAIR-ud.
Isaiah. Eye-ZAY-uh.
Levi. LEE-vye.
Maccabean. Mack-uh-BE-un.
Messiah. Meh-SIGH-uh.
messianic. mess-ee-AN-ick.
Palestinian. Pal-uh-STEN-ee-un.
Pharisees. FAIR-ih-seez.
synagogue. SIN-uh-gog.

WHAT DO YOU THINK?

The lesson writer says that Jesus' focus on forgiving the paralytic's sin shows that forgiveness is the "core" of Jesus' ministry. How can we be sure that we share His concern on a personal level, that we are accepting of those who come to Christ and not condemning? How may recalling the time before we experienced God's grace help us in this?

10. "But that you may know that the Son of Man has authority on earth to forgive sins . . . . " He said to the paralytic,

Jesus obviously is moved with compassion to heal the ailing man, and he is impressed with the faith of the man and his friends. But Jesus has a more important reason for speaking the word of healing on this occasion. The phrase *that you may know* corresponds directly to the unspoken objections of His critics. They do not believe that Jesus has *authority* to grant divine forgiveness of *sins*. Now he will prove that he does have this authority by granting release from a malady that can be removed only by the power of God. The scribes will then be able to see the evidence of Jesus' authority and reconsider their opposition to him, since God obviously will not grant the power to heal to a blasphemer.

Jesus identifies Himself with the title *Son of Man* dozens of times in the Gospels. The title seems to come from Daniel 7:13, 14 where "one like a son of man" appears as a heavenly figure who receives authority, power, and glory from the Lord in the last days.

11. . . . "I tell you, get up, take your mat and go home."

Without any gimmickry Jesus simply gives the command to the paralyzed man. There is no magical formula. There is no chant or potions to drink. In this instance, there is not even a touch (cf. 7:33). Jesus simply speaks the word of healing as the One having full authority to do so. He does not even have to say anything like "by the power of God" or "through the anointing of the Spirit." He orders the man to arise as if the man's disease presents no challenge.

12. He got up, took his mat and walked out in full view of them all. This amazed everyone and they praised God, saying, "We have never seen anything like this!"

In this instance no series of treatments is necessary (cf. Mark 8:22-26). The paralyzed man simply gets up as any healthy man, rolls up his bed, and walks out of the room. Jesus has performed a miracle that speaks volumes about His identity. He has performed an act that is visible (physical healing) to prove that He can perform an act that is invisible (forgiveness of sins). The One who possesses the power to do so stands before them. He is the One they were questioning in their hearts.

The stunned crowd undoubtedly understands the connection Jesus is making between the forgiveness of sins and the healing of paralysis. Their amazement is a theme of Mark's Gospel (cf. 1:22; 5:20, 42; 6:2, 51; 7:37; 11:18).

II. JESUS ASSOCIATES WITH SINNERS (MARK 2:13-17)

The next incident in Mark 2:1–3:6 shows the kinds of controversies that swirl around Jesus. This particular incident relates to Jesus' contact with sinners.

A. INVITATION TO A "SINNER" (vv. 13, 14)

13. Once again Jesus went out beside the lake. A large crowd came to him, and he began to teach them.

The mention of *the lake* locates the event in the area of the Sea of Galilee, probably directly adjacent to Capernaum. Jesus' fame has been mentioned already in Mark 1:28, and we can imagine that at this stage in His ministry *Jesus* is attracting large audiences wherever he goes. Because he has come to proclaim the arrival of the kingdom of God, Jesus is always prepared *to teach* whenever a crowd gathers.

14. As he walked along, he saw Levi son of Alphaeus sitting at the tax collector's booth. "Follow me," Jesus told him, and Levi got up and followed him.

Levi is the same person identified as "Matthew" in Matthew 9:9; 10:3. Levi could be his given name, while Matthew may be a name given to him later, as

WHAT DO YOU THINK?

Those who saw Jesus heal the paralyzed man were "amazed" and "praised God." After reading the reports of Jesus' miracles so often, are we still "amazed" at Jesus' works? Why or why not? How can we praise God because of Jesus?

Jesus gave Simon the name Peter (Mark 3:16). As a tax collector, Levi is most likely employed by Herod Antipas. If Capernaum is the location of this incident, Levi may be sitting alongside the international road leading into Capernaum from the territory of Herod Philip or the Decapolis to the east. Levi's role is to collect the toll *tax* from travelers who might be moving goods for sale along the road.

Tax collectors in the first century are a despised lot. Jews are especially incensed at what they consider treason by their countrymen who collect money for the hated Roman occupational government. Besides that, most tax collectors are assumed to be cheats who extort more money than required by Rome and pocket the difference. Men such as Levi are not looked on with respect.

Nevertheless, *Jesus* says to Levi *follow me* just the way he had with Simon, Andrew, James, and John (Mark 1:16-20). For these four, responding to the call of Jesus meant leaving an occupation that would still be there if they went back to it. There is no such comfort for Levi, since he will not be welcomed back if he changes his mind later. Even with so much at stake, Levi responds exactly as did the four fishermen: leaving immediately to follow Jesus.

BEFRIENDING THE FRIENDLESS

Steven Kent, at age forty-five, was homeless, an alcoholic, and one of society's outcasts. Kent never committed any serious offenses, but he had been arrested seventy-five times for a host of minor ones. He had lived this way for twenty years when a wealthy relative died and left him $300,000. So he got on a bus heading from Long Beach, California, to Ohio to collect his inheritance. But the bus driver kicked him off because of his appearance (and possibly because of the way he smelled).

Then Ron Quarn, a police officer who had known Kent for years, found him. Quarn took him to jail and got him sober and cleaned up. Quarn paid for a haircut, bought Kent some new clothes and shoes, and once again put him on an Ohio-bound bus to collect his fortune and start a new life.

Levi and his friends were the kind of outcasts that "respectable" people thought would never change. But when Jesus befriended them, His actions said in a powerful, positive way, "You have worth in God's eyes and in mine. Let me help you make something new out of your life." Are we ever, like Jesus, God's agents of change for society's outcasts? —C. R. B.

B. MEAL WITH SINNERS (vv. 15, 16)

15. While Jesus was having dinner at Levi's house, many tax collectors and "sinners" were eating with him and his disciples, for there were many who followed him.

The issue that generates the controversy is now developed further. The call of Levi leads to a dinner party that includes many other *tax collectors*. The use of the word *sinners* here is not intended to suggest those participating in the dinner party are worse in Jesus' eyes than anyone else. Instead, it indicates that they are considered "sinners" by the religious authorities because they do not follow certain man-made rules of conduct. Tax collectors fall into this category, as do all Gentiles. The *dinner at Levi's house* is open to *many* friends of Levi whom the elite teachers of the law and Pharisees think of as unholy people.

Apparently Levi invited *Jesus* to attend this dinner and he accepted. This brings Jesus into contact with Levi's friends and acquaintances who have been invited as well. Here is the basis of the problem. Does the guest list of "sinners" include thieves, adulterers, and lawbreakers? Are they the kind of people with whom the Son of God should be sitting for dinner? Jesus' association with such people becomes an issue in other Gospel passages as well (see Matthew 11:19; Luke 15:1, 2).

WHAT DO YOU THINK?

What is the significance of Jesus' calling a tax collector (despised by most people) to him on the same terms as he had called four fishermen (whose trade was very popular in that region)?

What would be the modern-day equivalent of a tax collector? How can we be sure to welcome such a one into our fellowship?

DAILY BIBLE READINGS

Monday, Mar. 3—Your Sins Are Forgiven (Mark 2:1-12)

Tuesday, Mar. 4—Jesus Eats With Tax Collectors (Mark 2:13-17)

Wednesday, Mar. 5—Joy Over a Sinner Who Repents (Luke 15:1-7)

Thursday, Mar. 6—New Wine in Old Wineskins (Mark 2:18-22)

Friday, Mar. 7—Sabbath Was Made for Humankind (Mark 2:23-28)

Saturday, Mar. 8—Jesus Heals on the Sabbath (Mark 3:1-6)

Sunday, Mar. 9—You Are the Son of God! (Mark 3:7-12)

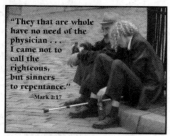

"They that are whole have no need of the physician . . . I came not to call the righteous, but sinners to repentance."
—Mark 2:17

Visual for lesson 2. Display this visual as you discuss verse 17. Ask, "What are we doing to call sinners to repentance?"

16. When the teachers of the law who were Pharisees saw him eating with the "sinners" and tax collectors, they asked his disciples: "Why does he eat with tax collectors and 'sinners'?"

According to the standards of the *Pharisees*, Jesus is committing a serious offense. To eat with people like this is to express personal friendship with them. When added to the messianic claims of Jesus, the Pharisees can point to a theological problem as well. The Messiah is going to institute the heavenly banquet where Abraham, Isaac, and Jacob will sit down with those who were coming from the east and the west. How can Jesus think that the Messiah will also sit down with sinners? (See Matthew 8:11.)

This is the first mention of Pharisees in Mark's Gospel. They are one of the major Jewish religious parties of the time, although their origin is shrouded in mystery. They are not found in the Old Testament. Most scholars trace their history to the Maccabean revolt of the second century B.C.

C. Ministry to Sinners (v. 17)

17. On hearing this, Jesus said to them, "It is not the healthy who need a doctor, but the sick. I have not come to call the righteous, but the sinners."

The Pharisees' attitude shows that they don't understand Jesus' mission at all. The Jewish leaders expect a Messiah who will vindicate *the righteous* and crack down on *the sinners*. Since Jesus isn't meeting that expectation, conflict results.

In responding to the implied criticism of the Pharisees, Jesus declares again the core of his mission. He intends to serve in the same way that a physician does. He will bring healing to those who are spiritually *sick*. His message of the arrival of the kingdom of God (Mark 1:15) is to be understood as a message of God's own initiative to restore those whose lives are ruined because of sin.

Jesus thus argues that he cannot accomplish this mission without coming into contact with those most in need of the truth of God. Of course, we know that there is no one who is truly righteous on his or her own because all are sinners (Romans 3:10, 23). In using the categories "the righteous" *vs.* "sinners," Jesus is arguing from the Pharisees' point of view. If the Pharisees continue to view themselves as "righteous" rather than as "sinners," they will not be included in Jesus' mission.

Jesus also understands that those who think they are spiritually *healthy* are fooling themselves. They, too, are more sick than they know. Yet they will be the ones in the end who mockingly look upon his suffering and say, "Physician, heal yourself" (Luke 4:23; cf. 23:35).

CONCLUSION

Jesus' early efforts to reach people with the truth of the gospel of forgiveness were met with resistance from those who could not understand His claims about himself or his habit of mixing with sinners. Nevertheless, he refused to back down. Jesus presented a message that highlighted the open door of God's forgiveness. He kept his guard up so that when criticized for his actions, he could articulate his approach as consistent with the mission of the Messiah.

Modern believers must not be handcuffed in their ministry to unbelievers. We are surrounded by people who need to experience the grace of God's forgiveness. We have in our hands the cure that the physician prescribes! How can we justify any lack of attention to those who need the cure? How can believers refuse to carry the good news of God's forgiveness to people whose lives are ruined by sin? Because Jesus extended divine forgiveness to sinners like us, we have the hope of eternal life. Now, through us, He extends that offer to others. We have the privilege of making sure someone else gets to hear about Jesus.

What Do You Think?

Jesus did not "come to call the righteous, but sinners" to repentance. Does our church reflect that priority? How much of our efforts are directed at the "righteous" (church members) and how much toward calling "sinners" (the unsaved)? How can we be sure we have the right balance?

Prayer

Lord, forgive us our trespasses as we forgive those who trespass against us. Then lead us to speak to someone today about God's good news of forgiveness. Because of Christ we pray, amen.

Thought to Remember

Jesus never met a sinner He didn't love.

Discovery Learning

This page contains an alternative lesson plan emphasizing learning activities. Classes desiring such student involvement will find these suggestions helpful. The next page is a reproducible activity page to further enhance discovery learning.

LEARNING GOALS

After this lesson each student will be able to:

1. Tell how today's texts illustrate that the heart of Jesus' mission was bringing the good news of God's grace to sinners.

2. Express appreciation for the grace that God offers and a sense of obligation to share that grace with others.

3. Tell what specific action he or she can take to show forgiveness to someone who is alienated from his or her fellowship.

INTO THE LESSON

Getting to know the heart of a person helps us to understand that person's actions. Introduce today's lesson by having students pair up, putting their chairs face to face. Each pair will alternate answering the questions from the reproducible activity "May I Introduce . . . ?" from the next page. Have the questions available to each person or written on a board or poster paper:

Encourage the pairs to answer quickly. If your class is small, have each person introduce his or her partner by completing the statement "The most interesting thing I learned about (partner's name) is _____." (For a larger class, report in groups of six.)

Say, "This activity was designed to get a glimpse into the heart of your partner. By asking a few questions and listening to answers, you have a better idea of the person and what he or she cares about. In today's text, we will discover the reason or heart of Jesus' mission."

INTO THE WORD

Recruit two individuals to research the settings of the two stories presented: one on the building and use of houses in Galilee and the other on the responsibilities of tax collectors in Jesus' day. Each report should be three or four minutes.

Divide your class into groups of four to six. Each group will need a copy of the following assignment and questions, as well as a heart shape cut from paper. (This activity is in the student book, *NIV® Bible Student*.)

GROUP 1: Read Mark 2:1-12.

GROUP 2: Read Mark 2:13-17.

QUESTIONS (same for both groups):

1. Who is present during this account?

2. What action does Jesus take?

3. What do the teachers think of Jesus?

4. What does Jesus say?

5. What does this indicate about Jesus' purpose? (*To bring the good news of God's grace to sinners.*)

Have the group members write on the heart the following: "The heart of Jesus' mission was _____."

(If you have a large class, you may want to add groups that will study Mark 2:18-22; 2:23-27; 3:1-6. Have them answer the same questions and write the heart of the mission just as described for the other two groups.)

Bring the groups together and discuss their findings. Display a large "heart" before the class. After each group has finished its report, summarize this section by saying, "We have seen the heart of Jesus' mission. In fact, let's write it here on this heart: 'Bring the good news of God's grace to sinners.' That is the reason Jesus came, and he brings that message to each of us."

INTO LIFE

Say, "Jesus entered the lives of those who were alienated from Jewish fellowship. Each was in need of forgiveness and restoration."

Ask, "Who entered your life to tell you about Jesus? How did it happen? What made you open to this person's claims about Jesus?" Distribute copies of the reproducible activity "What a Friend!" from the next page. Have students complete the assignment described there.

After a few minutes say, "Today many are alienated from Christ. We are called to reach them as Jesus' representatives. Distribute three-inch-by-five-inch index cards. Give these instructions: "Write the names of four friends who need a relationship with Jesus. (These might include some whom you noted in the previous activity.) At the bottom of your card write one or two ways you can reach out to them. Include a time frame for contacting them."

After the students have completed the above activity, have them turn their cards over and do the following: "Write a prayer of appreciation to God for the grace you have been offered. Many of you have received that grace and forgiveness in your submission to Christ's Lordship. If you have not yet received it, I'd be delighted to talk to you after class. As a part of your prayer ask God to give you the urgency to share grace with others, as well as the opportunity to do so."

After students have finished, close the class in prayer. Be prepared to show anyone who comes how to receive God's grace in Christ.

May I Introduce . . . ?

Work with one other person in your class to ask and answer the following questions. Be prepared to introduce your partner to the class by revealing some new piece of information you learn in this interview.

1. How did you get your name?

2. Where did you live when you were twelve, and what was your favorite springtime activity?

3. Describe a pet you had as a child (or wish you had).

4. What has been your favorite job?

5. Which of your possessions brings you most enjoyment?

6. What was your most memorable trip or vacation?

What a Friend!

Recall the time someone shared the gospel with you. Who told you about Jesus? What made you open to this person's claims about Jesus? Make a list below of the factors that made you most receptive to the gospel. Next to each factor that you can identify write the name of someone you know who might be influenced by the same factor to consider the claims of Christ.

_____   _____

_____   _____

_____   _____

_____   _____

_____   _____

JESUS DISPLAYS HIS AUTHORITY

LESSON 3

Mar
16

WHY TEACH THIS LESSON?

Fear is a God-given emotion, and it can save our lives in dangerous situations. But when we allow fear to rise when it is uncalled for, it can cause us to behave irrationally. U.S. President Franklin Delano Roosevelt recognized this fact in his first inaugural speech of March 4, 1933, when he said, "The only thing we have to fear is fear itself—nameless, unreasoning, unjustified terror which paralyzes needed efforts to convert retreat into advance."

The hard part, of course, is knowing when it is called for and when it is not. Even the closest disciples of Jesus sometimes gave in to fear, as we will see in today's lesson. Jesus called it a lack of faith. You and your learners have also given in to fear on occasion. Today's lesson will help you and your learners strengthen your faith, bolster your confidence, and banish your fears. The more specific you can be about the issues that cause fear, the more relevant will be your application of today's lesson. Don't be afraid to open up; you might just lead someone else to give to the Lord a long-standing fear and find relief.

INTRODUCTION

A. "YOUR FATHER KNOWS THE WAY"

James Hewett describes the fear of a small boy in terms that even adults can understand. He remembers his boyhood years, he says, when he was growing up in Pennsylvania. His family would often visit his grandparents, who lived nine miles away. One night a thick fog settled over the hilly countryside before they had started home. He remembers being terrified and asking if they shouldn't be going even slower than they were. Mother said gently, "Don't worry. Your father knows the way." James's father had walked that road during the war when there was no gasoline. He had ridden that blacktop on his bicycle to court James's mother. And for years he had made those weekly trips back to visit his own parents. "How often when I can't see the road of life and have felt that familiar panic rising in my heart I have heard the echo of my mother's voice: 'Don't worry. Your father knows the way.'"

Today's lesson speaks powerfully that same comforting reminder. Don't worry. Your Father knows the way. His Son brings us confidence to face our worst fears.

B. LESSON BACKGROUND

The Gospel of Mark begins with the declaration that Jesus Christ is the Son of God. Then Mark shows that the evidence of this fact is overwhelming. Jesus is proved to be the Son of God by the heavenly voice that was heard at his baptism (Mark 1:11), by the way he taught with authority (1:22), by his ability to cast out a demon from a man in the synagogue (1:27), and by his authority to grant divine forgiveness (2:10).

DEVOTIONAL READING:
JOHN 5:2-17
BACKGROUND SCRIPTURE:
MARK 4:35–5:20
PRINTED TEXT:
MARK 4:36-41; 5:2-13a

LESSON AIMS

After participating in this lesson, each student will be able to:

1. Recall the basic facts of Jesus' calming the storm and casting the demons out of the Gadarene demoniac.

2. Tell how these events provide evidence that Jesus is the Son of God.

3. Express a confidence that Jesus will help him or her to deal with a situation that previously has caused fear.

KEY VERSE

"Who is this? Even the wind and the waves obey him!"
—Mark 4:41

LESSON 3 NOTES

In spite of this evidence, opposition grew against Jesus. The teachers of the law thought Jesus to be committing blasphemy against God (2:7). The teachers of the law and Pharisees questioned Jesus' eating with sinners (2:16). The Pharisees and the Herodians looked for ways to destroy Jesus (3:6). With so much controversy swirling around him, Jesus withdrew once again to the lake (3:7).

At this point Mark begins another section of his Gospel. This section will offer some parables of Jesus (see Mark 4:1-34) along with some of the miracles he performed (4:35–5:43). Bracketing this material on the front side are Jesus' call of the Twelve (3:13-19) and Jesus' rejection by his family (3:20-35), and on the back side Jesus' rejection by his hometown (6:1-6a). Our lesson today focuses on two incidents in the middle portion of this section. In these verses the power and authority of Jesus are on display. But all of this is presented in the context of rejection by those who ought to understand by now that Jesus is the Son of God.

I. JESUS CALMS THE STORM (MARK 4:36-41)

After teaching the crowds in parables and explaining to his disciples what they meant, Jesus requested that they get into a boat and sail to the other side of the Sea of Galilee (Mark 4:35).

A. THE STORM ERUPTS (vv. 36, 37)

36. Leaving the crowd behind, they took him along, just as he was, in the boat. There were also other boats with him.

While *the crowd* sat on the shore, Jesus had been teaching from a *boat* (Mark 4:1). Now, for some reason, Jesus wants to leave and go directly to the other side. Is it because of some sense of danger? Is it just to retreat from the crowds for a time? (Later events suggest he was simply exhausted and needed a break. See v. 38.) Whatever the reason, the disciples are ready to grant his desire. That *they took him along, just as he was* implies that the disciples do not even take time to go ashore before heading on across the lake. At any rate, Jesus and the disciples begin making their way eastward across the Sea of Galilee. (See page 234 for a description of this lake.)

37. A furious squall came up, and the waves broke over the boat, so that it was nearly swamped.

Because of the cooler breezes that blow from the Mediterranean into the basin of the Sea of Galilee, a wind vortex can form that creates violent storms and waves. Mark's language here describes winds that force the waves into the fishing *boat*. The boat takes on water. The fear that it could be *swamped* is sweeping over the disciples. Such an experience would be especially frightening after dark.

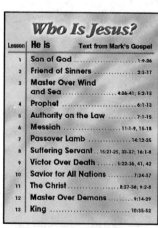

Who Is Jesus?

Lesson	He is	Text from Mark's Gospel
1	Son of God	1:9-26
2	Friend of Sinners	2:3-17
3	Master Over Wind and Sea	4:36-41; 5:2-13
4	Prophet	6:1-13
5	Authority on the Law	7:1-15
6	Messiah	11:1-9, 15-18
7	Passover Lamb	14:12-25
8	Suffering Servant	15:21-25, 33-37; 16:1-8
9	Victor Over Death	5:22-36, 41, 42
10	Savior for All Nations	7:24-37
11	The Christ	8:27-36; 9:2-8
12	Master Over Demons	9:14-29
13	King	10:35-52

Visual for lessons 3 and 11. Display this chart as you begin the lesson. It will be useful for this and other lessons in the quarter.

WHEN THINGS DON'T GO AS PLANNED

The event, scheduled for July 14, 2000, had been carefully planned: the decommissioned Royal Canadian Navy destroyer *Yukon* had had holes cut into its sides at strategic points, and it had been towed into place and anchored where it would be sunk the following day. It was to be part of an extravagant farewell to the ship. Speeches were planned, fireworks would explode, nearly five hundred people had paid thirty dollars each to watch from a nearby cruise ship, and the whole thing would be covered on live television.

It was all to begin with the detonation of on-board explosives that would send the ship to the bottom. There it would become part of an artificial reef off the coast of San Diego at a favorite spot of sport divers. But things didn't go as planned. About midnight, just hours before the celebration was to begin, the Yukon began taking on water. Within ninety minutes it was gone!

Things weren't going as planned for the disciples on the Sea of Galilee, either. They had no plans for sinking their boat, but the sudden storm made it look as if that was what would happen—and it seemed that Jesus didn't even care about their predicament! But when the right time came, he was there to help. There's an old saying, "God may not come when we call him, but he always comes on time." That's a good thing to remember when the storms of life threaten to sink our boats.   —C. R. B.

B. THE DISCIPLES PANIC (v. 38)

38. Jesus was in the stern, sleeping on a cushion. The disciples woke him and said to him, "Teacher, don't you care if we drown?"

After the weary day of teaching the crowds, Jesus has found a *cushion* to use for a pillow, and he has fallen asleep. Neither the rising winds and waves nor the rising fear of the disciples disturb his sleep.

The picture of the sleeping Jesus in the middle of the storm should not be overlooked. References in the Old Testament present sleep as the answer of a confident believer to the dangers of this world (see Job 11:18, 19; Psalm 3:5; 4:8). Jesus shows no fear because he truly has no reason to fear. His trust in his Father is complete.

To the disciples, however, the rolling boat and the relentless waves mean that they all are going to die a horrible death. For Jesus to be *sleeping* through the storm is incomprehensible to them. They do not yet seem to realize that Jesus is the Son of God. So in their fear they rebuke the One whose power and authority is limitless! Had they fully understood that Jesus is the Son of God, they would have realized how perfectly safe they were even in the face of danger.

C. THE LORD REBUKES (vv. 39-41)

39. He got up, rebuked the wind and said to the waves, "Quiet! Be still!" Then the wind died down and it was completely calm.

The New Testament makes clear that Jesus is the Creator. That the Creator is able to command his own creation in a miraculous way should not surprise us! (See John 1:1-4; Colossians 1:16.) The word *rebuked* echoes Jesus' earlier rebuke of the unclean spirit (Mark 1:25).

40. He said to his disciples, "Why are you so afraid? Do you still have no faith?"

After the storm calms down, Jesus turns to his *disciples* with two questions. The obvious contrast is between *faith* and fear. By this point in their experience with Jesus, the disciples should have been able to recognize that such dangers pose no real threat since the Messiah's work is not yet completed. This fact should have allowed them to show more courage when facing situations that bring fear and anxiety. This will not be the last time that Jesus will have to chastise them for a lack of faith (cf. Mark 7:18; 8:17-21).

41. They were terrified and asked each other, "Who is this? Even the wind and waves obey him!"

The disciples had brought their concern about the storm to Jesus, apparently with some kind of hazy idea that he could "do something" (v. 38). But now that Jesus has indeed done something, the disciples are *terrified*. This kind of fear can include the idea of being in awe, for Jesus has just displayed awe-inspiring power. But perhaps their fear is more than that because they have expressed doubt before One who is obviously able to control *the wind and the waves*.

So far Mark has selected certain events in the ministry of Jesus that prove that Jesus is the Son of God (1:1) and that he has a mission to perform (1:15). Jesus' calming of the stormy sea makes both points. The next incident does the same.

HOW TO SAY IT

Decapolis. Dee-CAP-uh-lis.
Fyodor. FEH-oh-door.
Fyodorovtsy. Feh-oh-door-OVT-
 see.
Gadarene. GAD-uh-reen.
Galilee. GAL-uh-lee.
Gentile. JEN-tile.
Gerasa. GUR-uh-suh.
Gerasenes. GUR-uh-seenz.
Gergesa. GUR-guh-suh.
Gergesenes. GUR-guh-seenz.
Herodians. Heh-ROE-dee-unz.
Pharisees. FAIR-ih-seez.
Rybalkin. Reh-BALL-kin.

WHAT DO YOU THINK?

Tornadoes, traffic, terrorism, tumors—our world is full of reasons to be fearful or anxious. How does (or how should) Jesus' authority over nature and circumstances affect the way we view such dangerous or fear-filled situations?

WHAT DO YOU THINK?

What is the problem with a person who claims to be a Christian yet is ruled by his or her fears? What can other, more mature believers do to help such a one to be more of a person of faith?

II. JESUS CASTS OUT DEMONS (MARK 5:2-13a)

This incident takes place after Jesus and the disciples have crossed from the western to the eastern shore of the Sea of Galilee (5:1). The western side of this lake is mainly populated by Jews. On the eastern side is the Decapolis ("ten cities"), which is primarily a Gentile area. Mark indicates the location is "the region of the Gerasenes" (5:1), though some ancient manuscripts have either *Gadarenes* or *Gergesenes*. Gerasa (or Gergesa) is located some thirty-five miles from the southeast shore of the Sea of Galilee, but this city apparently owned territory that joined the sea. In this area can be seen a fairly steep slope within forty yards of the water's edge.

A. DEGRADATION (vv. 2-5)

2. When Jesus got out of the boat, a man with an evil spirit came from the tombs to meet him.

A couple of miles from the site of a steep slope on the southeastern side of the Sea of Galilee is an area with cavern *tombs*, and this man lives among these tombs (v. 3). Only a social outcast would live this way (cf. Isaiah 65:1-7). The man has seen (even in the darkness) *the boat* moving in his direction (v. 6, below). (Matthew 8:28 notes that there actually were two demon-possessed men, so Mark is likely mentioning only the most prominent or the most vocal of these.)

LED BY WHAT KIND OF SPIRIT?

A small, persecuted Christian sect living in semi-exile in central Russia is known as the Fyodorovtsy. They believe Christ returned in the form of a Russian peasant named Fyodor Rybalkin sometime after World War I. According to some reports, Rybalkin went about teaching and performing miracles. Other reports say that he was sent to an asylum for the insane, or that he was arrested by the Communists. But whatever happened to him, the Fyodorovtsy believe he will soon resume his Second Coming and save them from their persecution.

In keeping with Jesus' words that in the kingdom of heaven there is no marriage, the sect's young people must make a spiritual commitment to be celibate all their lives. The sect has another strange belief: that God forbids them to make proselytes or evangelize. Thus, in their exile from the world, "the Fyodorovtsy" have declined in number from several thousand in the 1920s to only sixty today.

Like the Fyodorovtsy, the demon-possessed man in our text lived in exile. His strange behavior (which was also "spiritual" in its origins) caused others to force him away from them. Without doubting the sincerity of any who claim to follow Christ, we still must observe that various kinds of spirits make people do strange things—and not all of those spirits are the *Holy* Spirit.   —C. R. B.

3, 4. This man lived in the tombs, and no one could bind him any more, not even with a chain. For he had often been chained hand and foot, but he tore the chains apart and broke the irons on his feet.

This man does not suffer from a "mental illness," as some have alleged. This is supernatural demon possession. Because of his wild behavior, the people in the region naturally have looked for ways to control him. Apparently he has been driven away from society because efforts to control him with *chains* and leg *irons* have failed. His strength, most likely enhanced in a supernatural way by the forces of Satan, has made him impossible to subdue. Such an existence is degrading and is a mockery of the noble image of humanity that God intended in his creation of people.

5. Night and day among the tombs and in the hills he would cry out and cut himself with stones.

WHAT DO YOU THINK?

Compare and contrast the man in the tombs with Levi (Mark 2). What does Jesus' willingness and ability to deal with these people tell us about him, and what does his example mean for us today?

The man is isolated from society and apparently in great torment. With no family or friends to look after him, he spends his time in fearful shrieking among *the tombs*. The likelihood is that no one has enough courage to get close to him. His demonic condition makes every day a misery. Some associate his custom of cutting himself with stones with demonic worship (cf. 1 Kings 18:28). Others see it as erratic behavior by one whose mind is tormented beyond rational thought.

B. DIALOGUE (vv. 6-12)

6. When he saw Jesus from a distance, he ran and fell on his knees in front of him.

The respect the demon shows Jesus is born of fear. Mark's Gospel already has shown how the demons are inclined to acknowledge the truth of who Jesus is (cf. 1:24 from lesson 1). In 3:11 we read that unclean spirits who saw Jesus "fell down before him." The homage he pays to Jesus in this verse and the words he shrieks in the next certainly lead to this conclusion.

7. He shouted at the top of his voice, "What do you want with me, Jesus, Son of the Most High God? Swear to God that you won't torture me!"

The demon obviously is controlling the words of the man who comes to Jesus. The question *What do you want with me?* is another way of begging Jesus to leave him alone. Interestingly, the question the disciples asked in Mark 4:41 is correctly answered here by the demon! Although it is not true "worship," the demon's confession that Jesus is the *Son of the Most High God* is the highest tribute.

Even so, the demon's presumptuous posturing is evident. Claiming to know the identity of Jesus and then shouting his name is considered a means for gaining some control over an adversary (see discussion on page 236). Apparently the demon understands that God's judgment is coming on all unclean spirits, a sentiment reflected in the words of demons elsewhere in the Gospels (e.g., Mark 1:24). The punishment of which this demon speaks is that of the eternal torment that stands waiting at the final judgment (cf. Matthew 25:41; 2 Peter 2:4; Jude 6; Revelation 20:10). The spirit that torments the man now fears torment himself.

8. For Jesus had said to him, "Come out of this man, you evil spirit!"

This verse explains why the demon is so agitated: the bold words shouted by the demon (v. 7) came as a result of Jesus' command that he leave the man. The word *for* ("because") makes clear the cause-and-effect relationship of these words of *Jesus* and the demon. So mighty is the power of Jesus' position as the Son of God that the command for the demon to leave the man sends this spirit into a frenzy of trying to bargain for his survival.

9. Then Jesus asked him, "What is your name?"

"My name is Legion," he replied, "for we are many."

This is the first indication of the number of demons involved. The name *Legion* has reference to a Roman military force of six thousand soldiers—though the word was also used of any very large, often unspecific, number. The words of the demon may mean that this demon is speaking for thousands of other demons who are also opposed to God (cf. 1:24), or it may well mean the man is possessed by a very large number of demons.

Some take the Bible's references to demon possession as evidence that the first century was dominated by superstition and ignorance. To them, the idea of demon possession is a relic of an unscientific culture. But the New Testament writers are certainly able to speak about illness without referring to demons as the cause (cf. John 9:1-3; Philippians 2:26, 27). In fact, it distinguishes certain illnesses from demon possession in Matthew 4:23, 24.

Thus the people who hear Jesus teach do not necessarily conclude that every sickness is to be explained by demon possession. The modern scientific method

WHAT DO YOU THINK?

Today there are many people whose condition is as pitiable as that of the demon-possessed man. They are not necessarily possessed, but they may be homeless, mentally ill, wracked by guilt, physically disabled, or otherwise affected. What is our church doing to minister to such people, who dwell on the fringe of polite society? What more can we do?

WHAT DO YOU THINK?

The demons were afraid of being sent to their eternal torment (i.e., Hell). How much do we talk about Hell today? Is it enough, too much, or too little? What is the value of preaching and teaching about the reality of Hell?

DAILY BIBLE READINGS

Monday, Mar. 10—*Peace! Be Still! (Mark 4:35-41)*

Tuesday, Mar. 11—*Jesus Walks on Water (Mark 6:45-51)*

Wednesday, Mar. 12—*Jesus Confronts the Demoniac (Mark 5:1-10)*

Thursday, Mar. 13—*Everyone Is Amazed (Mark 5:11-20)*

Friday, Mar. 14—*Jesus Turns Water Into Wine (John 2:1-11)*

Saturday, Mar. 15—*The Son Gives Life (John 5:19-24)*

Sunday, Mar. 16—*He Taught as One With Authority (Matthew 7:24-29)*

PRAYER

Oh, Lord, may we remember today that with Jesus as our Creator, Redeemer, and King, we never have to fear our enemies, even if they are more powerful than we are. Through Jesus we pray, amen.

THOUGHT TO REMEMBER

"The one who is in you is greater than the one who is in the world."   *—1 John 4:4*

---

cannot be used to prove or disprove the spiritual realm because these are issues that are established by the evidence of history, and not by repeatable experiments in the laboratory.

What about demon possession today? If it was possible in the day of Jesus, then it cannot be ruled out as a possibility today. We would be foolish to try to explain every abnormality in life as a case of demon possession, but we would also be foolish to think that the devil of the Bible has ceased all of his activities!

10. And he begged Jesus again and again not to send them out of the area.

Previously *Jesus* had met and conquered a demon in a Jewish man in the synagogue (Mark 1:25, 26). Now Jesus must deal with not just one demon, but a legion of them—and from a wild-eyed Gentile living in the cavern tombs at that! The request that they not be sent *out of the area* may be a subtle way of asking that they not be thrown into their place of eternal punishment (Luke 8:31; Revelation 20:1-3).

11. A large herd of pigs was feeding on the nearby hillside.

For Jews, swine are just as unclean as tombs and evil spirits (see Leviticus 11:7, 8; Deuteronomy 14:8; Isaiah 65:4; 66:17). The presence of a herd of pigs in this location is another indication that Jesus is visiting a Gentile area.

12. The demons begged Jesus, "Send us among the pigs; allow us to go into them."

Since *the demons* recognize that they are powerless before Jesus, they ask for a lesser punishment. Rather than being thrown into eternal torment, could they not be thrown into (or among) the herd of *pigs*? With this request the demons perhaps hope also to create antagonism against Jesus—something we see in verse 17. In any case, they have no alternative but to do whatever the Son of God orders.

C. DELIVERANCE (v. 13a)

13a. He gave them permission.

Jesus' reason for permitting the demons to enter the herd of pigs is not easy to determine. Their action among the pigs is certainly dramatic (see v. 13b). Perhaps the drowning of the pigs makes clear to the man who was possessed not only the reality of demon possession, but also the power of the One who can throw them out. The need to verify the authority of Jesus is probably the best explanation.

We should also note, however, that Jesus does not appear eager to deal out the ultimate punishment that even the demons know is coming. The final punishment of the demonic powers seems to be set for a specific time (cf. Revelation 20:10).

This incident also reveals that human opposition to Jesus doesn't come from just his fellow Jews. As the rest of the account unfolds (vv. 13b-17, not in our text today), the inhabitants of the area will show that they value pigs over people.

CONCLUSION

Our faith is encouraged by the knowledge that Jesus as the Son of God has authority over every danger of life that we will face. Whether it is the storms of life that come suddenly to frighten us into doubting, or our worst fears rising to confront us about unseen spiritual powers—Jesus has the authority and power to keep us safe.

The power of Jesus is the best evidence of his authority. Not only did he teach with authority different from the teachers of the law (Mark 1:22), but when he spoke miraculous things happened. He spoke to the furious sea, and the waves fell silent. He commanded demons, and they instantly abandoned their operations. With this kind of authority and power, how wonderful to have Jesus as our Creator, Redeemer, and King!

Discovery Learning

This page contains an alternative lesson plan emphasizing learning activities. Classes desiring such student involvement will find these suggestions helpful. The next page is a reproducible activity page to further enhance discovery learning.

LEARNING GOALS

After this lesson each student will be able to:

1. Recall the basic facts of Jesus' calming the storm and casting the demons out of the Gadarene demoniac.

2. Tell how these events provide evidence that Jesus is the Son of God.

3. Express a confidence that Jesus will help him or her to deal with a situation that previously has caused fear.

INTO THE LESSON

As your students arrive, have the chairs arranged in groups of four. On each chair should be a half-sheet of letter-size paper on which are drawn four squares in a grid pattern. Outside the grid on the left side write "High Anxiety" beside the upper boxes, "Low Anxiety" beside the lower. Below the left boxes write "Can't Control"; below the right boxes "Can Control." (If you use the student book, *NIV® Bible Student*, you can refer the students to the appropriate page there for this activity.)

Ask the students to list in the appropriate quadrants several things that could cause anxiety in their lives, such as family, teens, world events, finances, work, marriage, stock market, illness, moving, bills, terrorism, death of a loved one. For instance, finances might fit the "High Anxiety/Can Control" quadrant. A parent of a "prodigal" child might list teens in the "High Anxiety/ Can't Control" quadrant. After about three minutes have volunteers tell some of the anxieties they listed and which quadrants they put them in.

Make the transition to the text saying, "Each of us wrote several anxieties we are facing. Our lesson features a time when the disciples were afraid and Jesus calmed their fears. Listen for ways Jesus calms our fears."

INTO THE WORD

Prior to class, recruit a student to prepare a short presentation on the purpose of Mark's Gospel with a chart showing Mark's proofs of Jesus being God's Son and the opposition he faced. Explain our text's place in the book.

After the presentation, divide your class into at least two groups. *Group 1* will develop a dramatic presentation of Mark 4:36-41 with sound effects and visual effects, as far as the classroom allows. Provide plenty of paper and broad-tip markers for creative scenery. Remind participants that they have only ten to fifteen minutes to make their preparations.

Group 2 will develop an interview of the man suffering from demon-possession, based on Mark 5:1-20. The group should think of ways to communicate clearly the events and the emotion of the passage. The interview can be taped (audio or video) and replayed for the class, or a live interview can be presented. This group will have ten to fifteen minutes to plan and prepare the presentation.

If your class is larger, assign these activities to the extra groups. Group 1 will need thirteen people; Group 2 will need six. If you have extra groups, be sure to have enough materials and a recorder. Choose a representative for each group.

After the presentation ask, "What aspects of these two events show Jesus to be in control?" (*You are looking for such answers as these: Jesus rebukes the wind and waves, and they become calm [4:38, 39]; Jesus speaks to the evil spirit, and the demon-possessed man is set free [5:8].*)

Say, "What about these texts shows Jesus to be God's Son?" Students should respond with answers based on 4:41 and 5:15. You may want to make clarifying comments based on the commentary and your own study.

Option: If you would rather not use drama, use the reproducible activity "Jesus in Control" from the next page to draw out this information.

INTO LIFE

Choose one or more of the following activities to help your students apply this lesson.

Option 1: Personal Testimony. Ask each learner to prepare a two-minute testimony on the topic, "How Jesus helps me deal with fear." Appropriate questions to be answered by the testimony are these: How do you know Jesus is more powerful than your fears? What ways have you tried to answer your fears without Christ? What differences has Jesus made in your life?

Option 2: Reflection on Anxieties. Have each student take his or her grid (from the opening activity) and briefly discuss one or two more areas with a neighbor. Ask each student to turn to 1 Peter 5:7. Ask each pair to pray together, asking God to take away the anxiety for things that can't be controlled, help in finding solutions in situations that can be controlled. As a final indication of surrender, students should write "1 Peter 5:7" across their grids.

Option 3: Reproducible Activity. Distribute copies of "What Great Things the Lord Has Done!" from the next page and have the students complete the activity.

Jesus in Control

Read Mark 4:36-41 and Mark 5:1-20. Then complete the chart below.

	Mark 4:36-41	Mark 5:1-20
1. What aspects of this event shows Jesus to be in control?		
2. What about this event shows Jesus to be God's Son?"		

What Great Things the Lord Has Done!

1. What is it that you are most concerned about in your "boat" today? Write it in the boat.

2. What is it that you are most concerned about outside your "boat" today? Write it on the water.

3. How does Jesus answer these concerns? Write your ideas in the space below.

Jesus: God's Power in Action

Unit 1: Jesus' Early Ministry
(Lessons 1-5)

REJECTION AND MISSION

LESSON 4

WHY TEACH THIS LESSON?

Rejection is painful. I remember this all too well from sixth grade. When it came time to play team sports at recess, the teacher would get things started by selecting two "captains." These captains would then alternate in picking class members to be on their respective teams. The best players naturally were picked first, but I was never one of them. The eyes and body language of the captain who finally picked me always said, "This guy will do our team more harm than good, but I guess we'll have to take him." That's rejection!

Your learners aren't choosing up teams to play games, but some of them are familiar with rejection nonetheless. For some it's a personality issue. For others it may be someone's cruel response to a physical or mental disability. And for many it's a matter of their faith. That's where today's lesson can give special help. Noting how Jesus himself was rejected by the people who had known him best will remind your learners that rejection "comes with the territory." In noting how Jesus dealt with rejection, you will find encouragement to do the same.

INTRODUCTION

A. "I AGREE WITH JESUS"

In May of 2000, a controversy broke out at a high school in the Columbus, Ohio, suburb of Upper Arlington. Many of the students, and for a while some of the teachers, began wearing bright yellow T-shirts emblazoned with the words, "I agree with Justin." The shirts expressed support for Justin Rule, one of the high school's very outspoken Christians, who had taken a public position regarding his faith. When the *Columbus Dispatch* interviewed some of the seniors about the story, one student expressed concern that too much of the focus would be directed toward Justin. Other students, however, considered wearing the T-shirts a good witnessing tool. One of them said putting "Jesus" in the slogan would have created a "bigger problem" for some people. She called the slogan "a more subtle way of exploring his beliefs."

In today's lesson Jesus demonstrates that sometimes the most difficult place to share one's faith is in the company of our friends and neighbors. Those who know us best are often those who least want to hear our testimony. But the example of Jesus challenges us to make God's message of truth available to every person who will listen to the gospel.

B. LESSON BACKGROUND

Mark's Gospel shows how Jesus was treated badly by his family and hometown (Mark 6:1-5). But Jesus took no time for self-pity. He moved on to other towns and villages to preach the good news (6:6). Then he prepared his disciples to begin a broader ministry to take in the whole region in an extended preaching tour (6:7-13).

In our previous lessons in Mark we have noted that Jesus' own works prove that he is the Son of God. The parables of Mark 4 tell how God's kingdom was being ushered in by Jesus. The powerful miracles of Jesus' calming the storm,

DEVOTIONAL READING:
JOHN 12:44-50

BACKGROUND SCRIPTURE:
MARK 6:1-13

PRINTED TEXT:
MARK 6:1-13

Mar
23

LESSON AIMS

After participating in this lesson, each student will be able to:

1. Tell how Jesus was rejected at Nazareth and how he responded with an expansion of ministry by sending out the Twelve to preach.

2. Compare the rejection of Jesus with the rejection of his messengers today.

3. Suggest at least one specific way to get involved in the effort to preach the gospel at home or around the world.

KEY VERSE

Jesus said to them, "Only in his hometown, among his relatives and in his own house is a prophet without honor."
—Mark 6:4

LESSON 4 NOTES

casting out demons, healing the sick, and raising the dead to life all testify to the fact that this Jesus must be God's Son (4:35–5:43). Bracketing this material are statements regarding Jesus' disciples and his family. In Mark 3:13-19, Jesus chose twelve followers who would become like family to him (cf. 3:31-34), and in 6:1-6 Jesus comments on the rejection he faced by his own hometown. But for all of the evidence that Jesus is God's Son, he still experienced hostility. Those who wanted to destroy him were finding his teaching objectionable (cf. 3:20-30).

Geographically, the focus of Jesus' ministry to this point in Mark's Gospel has been Galilee. Many of the incidents reported take place in Capernaum, on the northwest shore of the Sea of Galilee. But Jesus has also extended his ministry to Gentiles, as seen in last week's lesson. In Mark 6, the reader is again back in Galilee (cf. 5:21), this time at Nazareth, Jesus' hometown. The time is late in the second or early in the third year of Jesus' three-and-a-half year ministry.

I. JESUS PREACHES IN HIS HOMETOWN (MARK 6:1-6)

One might think that returning to his hometown will provide some grand opportunities for Jesus. He can be welcomed back by people who knew him from childhood. But his old friends from Nazareth are not ready for his message.

A. HOMECOMING (vv. 1, 2)

1. Jesus left there and went to his hometown, accompanied by his disciples.

The reference to Jesus' departure can be traced back to his raising of Jairus's daughter (reported in Mark 5:21-43), an event that probably took place in Capernaum. Now it is time for *Jesus* and *his disciples* to leave, so he travels twenty miles southwest, walking up into the hills to Nazareth. The journey takes about a day, and we can only imagine the teaching opportunities presented by this time together on the road.

2. When the Sabbath came, he began to teach in the synagogue, and many who heard him were amazed.

"Where did this man get these things?" they asked. "What's this wisdom that has been given him, that he even does miracles!

Mark alerts the reader to the purpose of Jesus' journey to Nazareth: he has come *to teach*. He is not there merely for a personal visit. His concern is for the kingdom of God to be preached and for his disciples to receive the kind of preparation needed to carry this work throughout Galilee.

The Jewish *Sabbath* Day is Saturday, the seventh day of the week. Jesus remains faithful in his Sabbath Day attendance at *the synagogue*. The custom of the synagogue is to invite guest rabbis to teach the lesson of the day (cf. Mark 1:21, 22; Luke 4:16). Jesus is ready when his opportunity comes. Whether these people had heard Jesus teach before is impossible to know. His fame already has spread far and wide in Galilee (1:28). At any rate they are astonished at what they hear.

The amazement of Jesus' audiences is a major theme in Mark's Gospel (cf. 1:22, 27; 2:12; 5:20, 42; 7:37; 11:18; 12:17). These crowds recognize in his teaching a stunning depth of *wisdom*, but they cannot determine the source of this wisdom. They know about the miracles that Jesus has performed, and they wonder where such power and wisdom have come from. Their two options are either God or Satan. They are trying to decide between the two (cf. Mark 3:22).

A PROPHET WITHOUT HONOR

Post this visual as you discuss verse 4. Note how rejection did not keep Jesus from his mission.

B. REJECTION (vv. 3, 4)

3. "Isn't this the carpenter? Isn't this Mary's son and the brother of James, Joseph, Judas and Simon? Aren't his sisters here with us?" And they took offense at him.

The questions now become more personal. The audience not only expresses difficulty with the origin of Jesus' teaching, but it is also reluctant to take him seriously.

Though elsewhere Jesus is called the "carpenter's son" (Matthew 13:55), here the occupation is connected with Jesus himself. A carpenter can be a skilled mason or smith, as well as a worker with wood. The term also applies to those who work in building construction, as well as with smaller tools. The questioners seem to express an opinion that Jesus, as a worker with his hands, is in no better position than they to understand the mysteries of God.

Usually, a Jewish man is described in relation to his father, not his mother. Some scholars see the phrase *Mary's son,* then, as hinting at some scandal regarding Jesus' birth. Perhaps there are some here who remember Joseph's original intention to divorce Mary when her pregnancy became known (Matthew 1:18, 19), and thus they know Jesus is Mary's son but not Joseph's. Other students, however, believe the phrase merely indicates that Joseph has already died.

From these questions it is clear that Jesus will not receive honor as the Son of God, or even as a great prophet, in Nazareth. As the crowd begins asking about Jesus' brothers and *sisters,* it is clear that the purpose of the questions is to argue that Jesus is a "commoner." These friends and neighbors know Jesus' family, his occupation, and his ordinary circumstances. They are offended at him in that they reject his teaching.

4. Jesus said to them, "Only in his hometown, among his relatives and in his own house is a prophet without honor."

Jesus is aware of the sentiments in Nazareth, and he puts their attitude into perspective by quoting a familiar proverb (cf. Matthew 13:57; Luke 4:24; John 4:44). Jesus' reference to *his own house* imply that he is not believed even among his own mother, brothers, and sisters (cf. Mark 3:21, 31, 32).

C. UNBELIEF (vv. 5, 6)

5. He could not do any miracles there, except lay his hands on a few sick people and heal them.

Mark's summary of the situation in Nazareth includes a negative element about the effectiveness of Jesus' work *there.* Their lack of faith creates an environment in which Jesus refuses to perform the kind of miraculous deeds that he has done elsewhere, such as in Capernaum (cf. Mark 1:23-28, 32-34). Nevertheless, he demonstrates that the lack of *miracles* is not due to his own weakness, since he does heal *a few sick people.* No doubt these few people perceive no limitations to his power.

The mention of the laying on of *hands* is also prominent in the healings recorded in Mark's Gospel (5:23; 7:32; 8:22, 25). This action by Jesus seems to set him apart from Jewish healers, who are not inclined to touch people with any disease.

6. And he was amazed at their lack of faith. Then Jesus went around teaching from village to village.

Thus far in Mark's Gospel it is always the crowd that is amazed at Jesus (cf. 1:22, 27; 2:12; 5:42). But now it is Jesus' turn to be *amazed.* In the case of these friends and neighbors from Nazareth, their stubborn refusal to see the truth is amazing indeed.

But Jesus does not permit this disappointment to keep him from his work. He continues traveling to villages to teach the gospel. Such a response to the disappointment of kingdom work should inspire modern believers not to give up when our witness is rejected.

WHAT DO YOU THINK?

What kinds of doubts, predictions, rejections, and questions are likely to come at us as Christians from those who know us best, or knew us once? How do we deal with them in both the short- and long-term?

WHAT DO YOU THINK?

What is the result for those who hear the gospel message yet refuse to take Jesus seriously? [Consider John 14:6; Acts 4:12; Hebrews 10:28, 29; 11:6 in your discussion.]

HOW TO SAY IT

Capernaum. Kuh-PER-nay-um.
Deuteronomy. Due-ter-AHN-uh-
me.
Ezekiel. Ee-ZEEK-ee-ul or
Ee-ZEEK-yul.
Galilee. GAL-uh-lee.
Gentiles. JEN-tyles.
Gomorrah. Guh-MORE-uh.
Jairus. JYE-rus or JAY-ih-rus.
Nazareth. NAZ-uh-reth.
shema (Hebrew). sheh-MA.
synagogue. SIN-uh-gog.

ACKNOWLEDGING THE POWER OF GOD

Alcoholics Anonymous (or "AA" as it is commonly known) has helped millions of people to overcome alcoholic addiction. A key feature of its program (and undoubtedly its most important) is its insistence that the person seeking recovery turn life over to a "Higher Power." While AA tries to broaden its appeal by saying the higher power can be anything you want it to be—even AA itself—most alcoholics who have gone through the program acknowledge that power to be God.

Non-believers, however, have turned to Secular Organizations for Sobriety, which denies the need for a spiritual component to recovery from alcoholism. Most of us will agree that this dislike for acknowledging God's reign over us is symptomatic of many of the problems our culture faces. Many people find it hard to admit the fact of God's presence in life.

It was much the same in Nazareth when Jesus returned to the village in which he had grown up. The residents could not deny the mighty works he had done elsewhere, but they couldn't bring themselves to admit that he was the Son of God. Hadn't they known him since he was a child? Their refusal to acknowledge the presence of God in their midst had tragic results: "He could not do any miracles there" (Mark 6:5) because of their lack of faith. None of us should be surprised if a lack of faith prevents God from doing great things in our lives.   —C. R. B.

II. JESUS SENDS THE TWELVE TO PREACH (MARK 6:7-13)

The ministry of Jesus now has reached a point for a broader proclamation of the good news. Mark's Gospel turns its attention to the way this ministry expands throughout Galilee and beyond its borders (6:7-13, 30–8:13), to the rising pressure from political authorities (6:14-29), and to the blindness of the disciples regarding the person and mission of Jesus (6:52; 8:14-21, 32).

A. A POWERFUL MISSION (v. 7)

7. Calling the Twelve to him, he sent them out two by two and gave them authority over evil spirits.

WHAT DO YOU THINK?

What different levels of sup-
port and involvement in world
missions exist at our church?
How can we increase our involve-
ment, both individually and for
the church as a whole?

After all of the preparation by Jesus of the disciples, it is now time for them to begin the process of calling Israel back to God. He has promised them that he would make them "fishers of men" (Mark 1:17), and they have been with him both in public and in private (cf. 3:7, 13; 4:10). They have witnessed his power at work in healings and in miracles of nature. From the very first, Jesus has prepared for this day (3:14, 15). The power that Jesus already has exercised over demons he now gives to his disciples (cf. 1:25, 39; 5:13). They serve in this capacity under his *authority.*

The significance of the number twelve should not be overlooked. Jesus' mission involves preaching the kingdom to the lost sheep of Israel (Matthew 15:24). His ministry involves the restoration of Israel (Acts 1:6, 7). It is natural, then, that this ministry make use of twelve disciples, just as Moses' ministry dealt with Israel's twelve tribes. The fact that they go *two by two* is a reflection of the Jewish priority for truthful witnesses (cf. Deuteronomy 17:6; 19:15; Matthew 18:16; Hebrews 10:28). The practice is still a good one for those church leaders who want to avoid the risks that can occur when one person travels alone in a ministry of visitation.

GOD AND CULTURE

Numerology has long fascinated the human mind. Ancient astrologers combined this fascination and the desire to control one's destiny with their readings of the stars and planets to offer advice that bordered on the fantastic. A trip to any New Age bookstore or a search of the Internet for "numerology" sites will prove that the ancient fascination is still very much alive.

In the middle of all of this is the Bible. Ancient Hebrews also paid attention to the significance of certain numbers. For example, the number one was symbolic of God as stated in the shema: "Hear, O Israel: The Lord our God is one Lord" (Deuteronomy 6:4). Twelve was the number of the sons of Jacob, and thus of the tribes of Israel. We should note that the Bible's use of numbers lacks the trust in the magical qualities of numbers found in other ancient cultures as well as in modern superstitions.

Nevertheless, it would have been significant to the Jewish mind that Jesus sent out the twelve disciples to preach the gospel of the kingdom to Israel, and that He sent them out two-by-two, as the law required for verification of the testimony of witnesses. It is an example of the fact that God, who stands above all human culture, desires that we present his message of salvation in ways that speak to each culture so that all may come to know him.   —C. R. B.

B. AN URGENT MISSION (vv. 8-12)

8. These were his instructions: "Take nothing for the journey except a staff—no bread, no bag, no money in your belts.

The prohibition of extra provisions makes the point that this preaching tour is urgent because time is short. In traveling so lightly the disciples will be demonstrating that they trust in God to provide hospitality from those who believed the good news. It will also set them apart from traveling preachers of the day who move about with *bread* and a *bag* for collecting money.

Matthew 10:9, 10 says that the disciples are not to take *a staff* for this tour. At first this prohibition seems curious since the verse before us says that they are to take a staff. But that the verb "take" in Matthew's account may indicate that the disciples already have at least one walking stick per team, and they are forbidden from getting any more. The walking stick that each team already has is the one Mark's account allows them to take along.

9. "Wear sandals but not an extra tunic.

The extra coat would be a benefit, because sleeping outside on chilly Galilean nights is easier for travelers if they can use a coat as a blanket. Matthew 10:10 forbids *sandals*, and the difference between the two accounts may be explained in the same way as that of the staff (v. 8, above). That is, they were not to take along an extra pair of sandals.

10. "Whenever you enter a house, stay there until you leave that town.

These directions are intended to keep the disciples from moving from *house* to house after arriving at a village. They are to exemplify gratitude by accepting the first offer of hospitality that comes to them, and then remaining in that house even if some better offer comes along. This strategy will prevent needless hard feelings against the mission and keep the disciples focused on the reason they are in any particular village in the first place.

11. "And if any place will not welcome you or listen to you, shake the dust off your feet when you leave, as a testimony against them."

Jesus anticipates that the disciples will face rejection. After all, if the Son of God has been rejected, why would the disciples expect anything less than rejection? The theme of rejection already has grown more prominent in Mark's Gospel. Beginning with the objections of the teachers of the law about Jesus' teaching about divine forgiveness (2:6, 7), the tension has been increasing, even reaching to the point where enemies are looking for ways to destroy Jesus (3:6), and claiming that he is allied with Satan (3:22). He has been rejected even in his own hometown of Nazareth (6:1-6).

When rejection comes, Jesus encourages the disciples to *shake the dust* from themselves. This practice seems to be connected with the Jewish custom of

DAILY BIBLE READINGS

Monday, Mar. 17—A Prophet Without Honor (Mark 6:1-6)

Tuesday, Mar. 18—People Question Jesus as Messiah (John 7:37-44)

Wednesday, Mar. 19—No Prophet Comes From Galilee (John 7:45-52)

Thursday, Mar. 20—The Kingdom of Heaven Is Near (Matthew 10:5-15)

Friday, Mar. 21—Be Wise Serpents, Innocent Doves (Matthew 10:16-26)

Saturday, Mar. 22—Whoever Welcomes You (Matthew 10:37-42)

Sunday, Mar. 23—Jesus Sends Out the Twelve (Mark 6:7-13)

WHAT DO YOU THINK?

How is the way we use our homes an indication of our stewardship and faith? What hospitality opportunities are available to all of us in the coming month?

shaking dust that had gathered on their clothing when they returned to the land of Israel from Gentile areas (cf. Acts 13:51; 18:5, 6). The Jews saw themselves as removing contaminated, pagan dust. Jesus turns this custom around, making Jewish dust the contaminant!

Since rejection of the Son of God is equal to the rejection of God, those who refuse to hear the news of the kingdom of God will be placing themselves under the judgment of God. Perhaps the greatest examples of cities that knew firsthand about the judgment of God were Sodom and Gomorrah (Genesis 19:23-29). In Matthew 10:15 (which is parallel to Mark's account), Jesus uses them for comparison of the divine judgment that will fall upon cities that will reject the message the disciples are bringing. The Old Testament uses those two cities as the proverbial "bad example" more than a dozen times. In the New Testament, see Romans 9:29; 2 Peter 2:6; Jude 7; and Revelation 11:8.

12. They went out and preached that people should repent.

At this point Mark summarizes the ministry carried out by the disciples. This message of repentance was the message of John the Baptist (1:4) and of Jesus himself (1:15). The preaching of the disciples is an extension of the preaching of Jesus.

The idea of repentance involves turning from sin to God. It is a message that was emphasized many times by the prophets of the Old Testament who called Israel back to the Lord (e.g., Ezekiel 14:6; 18:30). Jesus makes the matter of repentance the central theme of his preaching of God's kingdom.

C. A PREACHING MISSION (v. 13)
13. They drove out many demons and anointed many sick people with oil and healed them.

As Jesus ministers freely, so do his disciples. Repentance is the first element of their ministry (v. 12), and the exorcism of *demons* is the second. (Mark uses evil spirits and demons interchangeably.) Jesus has given them power to accomplish these exorcisms (6:7), and they use that power as needed. The third element of the disciples' ministry is healing of the sick. The New Testament connects oil with healing in Luke 10:34 and James 5:14. In Jesus' day, oil is considered to have medicinal value.

Today, every believer who wants to serve Christ can help to guarantee that the good news is heard in every city and town. Efforts of the church to witness in our communities always need willing believers. Missionary efforts around the globe need enthusiastic believers who hear the command of Jesus to take the good news to every village. As Jesus emphasized to the disciples, we cannot expect that everyone will respond positively. Even so, our duty is to preach and teach. God will give the harvest (1 Corinthians 3:6).

CONCLUSION
Mark's Gospel presents what we may consider the ultimate rejection of Jesus. To think that our own family—our spouse, our parents, our children—would turn their backs on us is a thought that we find too excruciating to bear.

But for Jesus the mission was too important to let it be stalled. Jesus counted the disciples as his new family (Mark 3:35). They were the ones who would enter into this mission with him. Their witness would make it possible for the kingdom of God to claim believers from every village. Jesus not only continued the mission in the face of rejection, he expanded it by including twelve missionaries in the effort. All of this should remind us how dedicated Jesus was (and is) to our salvation. His love compelled him to bypass every rejection so that he could bring it about.

Discovery Learning

This page contains an alternative lesson plan emphasizing learning activities. Classes desiring such student involvement will find these suggestions helpful. The next page is a reproducible activity page to further enhance discovery learning.

LEARNING GOALS

After this lesson each student will be able to:

1. Tell how Jesus was rejected at Nazareth and how he responded with an expansion of ministry by sending out the Twelve to preach.

2. Compare the rejection of Jesus with the rejection of his messengers today.

3. Suggest at least one specific way to get involved in the effort to preach the gospel at home or around the world.

INTO THE LESSON

As the students arrive, have the classroom as "homey" as you can make it. As people are getting comfortable, say, "Think of a story to share from your childhood that no one in this group knows: an accident, adventure, prank, or happy event. Keep your stories light." Start things by sharing a story from your own childhood. Then, if you have a large class, make this a "neighbor-nudge" activity, where students simply turn to someone next to them and share their stories.

Make transition to Bible study by saying, "Today's text focuses on a time Jesus was in his hometown. Townspeople knew him as a boy. Their responses to him are alarming. We will see how he reacts to their criticism."

INTO THE WORD

Have a volunteer read Mark 6:1-13. Introduce the study by saying, "Throughout Scripture we see people rejecting God's Word and his messengers. Today as we study, we will compare several biblical incidents with the story in Mark 6."

If you have a large class, use all the group activities. Divide the class into groups of four to six. Each group will write an interview from the assigned story. They are to pose questions and then find the answers in the text. (Questions might include, "What did you see happen here?" "What were the responses of the other participants?" "How did you feel while this was happening?" "What do you believe the outcome of these events will be?" These questions are in the student book.)

If the group writes questions without direct answers in the text, allow them to be creative in the answers. As leader, move between the groups to offer assistance.

Group 1: Interview Jesus and other participants in Mark 6:1-13.

Group 2: Read Acts 17:1-15. Interview Paul, members of his party, the opposition.

Group 3: Read 1 Kings 18:20-40. Interview Elijah, Ahab, the priests of Baal, bystanders, and others.

Allow fifteen minutes to prepare. Group One will present their interview to the whole group. If you used other projects, ask for a brief summary from each.

Lead a brief discussion with these questions:

1. What do these stories have in common? (*Believers have their message rejected.*)

2. Why do you think this opposition occurs? (*Critics find the teaching objectionable.*)

3. How does each event end? (*People believe God's message. More people speak the message. Jesus calls new messengers!*)

4. What do you conclude from these events? (*We, too, will face opposition but are to be faithful.*)

INTO LIFE

Distribute copies of the reproducible activity "Rejection in the News" from the next page. Ask the students to name the characteristics of rejection faced by Christ and have them write these on the "Nazareth News." Also ask for types of rejection faced by his followers today; these will be listed on the "Daily Press."

Ask students how the message of Christ has been rejected when they attempted to convey it to others. Read 1 Peter 4:12-19. Ask another volunteer to read Romans 10:12-15. Ask the class, "What should be our response to opposition?" (*Continue to carry the message!*)

This week, get a list of missionaries and the countries they serve from your church office or treasurer. Bring a map or globe to class to pinpoint locations.

Distribute copies of the reproducible activity "Risking Rejection" from the next page. Say, "As we close today, want us to be aware of those carrying the good news around the globe. What ways can we encourage then Distribute the list of missionaries and encourage stu to write the names of some of them on their hand.

Say, "Who are some people with whom you ar ing to share the gospel? Write their names on yo handout. How can you reach them more effecti-

Ask each learner to choose one or two of th re-tions that have have been made. Have them be veal their choices, and pray together that the faithful in completing their choices.

Rejection in the News

After reading today's text, list the characteristics of rejection faced by Jesus in "Nazareth News" and by people today in "Daily Press."

NAZARETH NEWS

Jesus Rejected

DAILY PRESS

Christians Rejected

Risking Rejection

Draw a map of the world or a country where you know a missionary is working to overcome rejection. Then draw a picture of your house and a person you are seeking to share Christ with. Read 1 Peter 4:12-19 and Romans 10:12-15.

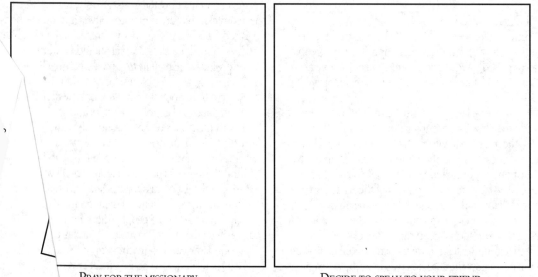

PRAY FOR THE MISSIONARY.

DECIDE TO SPEAK TO YOUR FRIEND.

Jesus: God's Power in Action
Unit 1: Jesus' Early Ministry
(Lessons 1-5)

WHAT REALLY DEFILES

LESSON 5

WHY TEACH THIS LESSON?

Recently, my wife overheard a conversation between two women in our church. When one began a sentence with the words, "It's our tradition here that . . . ," the other interrupted, "If I hear that word *tradition* one more time, I think I'll scream!"

With quick-thinking tact, the first woman replied, "Would it help if I used the word *heritage* instead of *tradition?*"

So—is tradition a good thing or a bad thing? Your learners probably have taken both sides on this issue, with some affirming tradition and some despising it. Today's lesson will provide at least one point for agreement. Even those who cherish tradition must agree that it must never come to replace or nullify God's Word. With eternity at stake, your learners must never forget this lesson!

INTRODUCTION

A. BETTER THAN SOAP

Warren Wiersbe has a story that illustrates how gutter talk has become a substitute for a comedy routine. A Christian woman attended an anniversary dinner in honor of a friend, not knowing that there would be a program of coarse-talking comedy following the meal. The so-called comedian tried to entertain the crowd with dirty jokes and humor that degraded everything that the Christian guest held to be sacred and honorable. At one point in the program, the comedian's throat became dry. "Please bring me a glass of water," he called to a waiter. At that point the Christian woman added, "And bring a toothbrush and a bar of soap with it!"

It would be nice if soap in the mouth could cure the problem of filthy speech, but unfortunately this cure is not strong enough. Something more is needed—a remedy that goes deeper than the tongue. Christians have the power of God's Word in their hearts (Colossians 3:16). They want their speech seasoned with salt (4:6) so that the words that they speak portray effectively the goodness of the Lord.

Today's lesson focuses on Jesus' instructions about purity. The incident recorded in Mark 7:1-15 offers contrasting views about what we have to do to acquire purity in life. The teachers of the day offered solutions to impurity that only made matters worse. Jesus challenges them and us to consider again whether the purity demanded by God is a high enough priority.

B. LESSON BACKGROUND

This section of Mark's Gospel highlights the expansion of Jesus' ministry beyond Galilee. While Jesus' ministry was expanding, however, trouble loomed on the horizon. Herod Antipas condemned John the Baptist to the executioner's sword (Mark 6:14-29). In addition, the disciples seemed incapable of understanding who Jesus was (8:14-21) even after he miraculously fed five thousand on the Jewish side of the Sea of Galilee (6:30-44), and the four thousand on the Gentile side (8:1-10). In today's lesson it becomes clear that the teachers of the law and Pharisees do not understand basic truths concerning Jesus' doctrine of pure living. More importantly, they do not understand that the law revolves around Jesus, and not the reverse.

DEVOTIONAL READING:
PSALM 51:10-17
BACKGROUND SCRIPTURE:
MARK 7:1-23
PRINTED TEXT:
MARK 7:1-15

Mar
30

LESSON AIMS

After participating in this lesson, each student will be able to:

1. Recall Jesus' answer to the Pharisees and teachers of the law about what really defiles those who try to live a pure life.

2. Contrast Jesus' method of purity with legalistic plans of achieving purity.

3. Confess specific sins that need to be eliminated from his or her lifestyle and pray to God for victory over them.

KEY VERSE

From within, out of men's hearts, come evil thoughts, sexual immorality, theft, murder, adultery.   —Mark 7:21

LESSON 5 NOTES

What must have been even more discouraging to Jesus was that even his own disciples could not grasp his message (Mark 7:17-23). If the disciples could not grasp his point about "unclean" foods, how would they ever be able to understand about reaching "unclean" Gentile people? If they could not understand that the gospel should be preached to Gentiles as well as Jews, then the kingdom of God would remain locked up in Palestine. There could be no Great Commission (Matthew 28:19, 20) to preach the gospel around the world. So much depended on Jesus' teaching in Mark 7:1-15! The lesson resulted from a question posed about the habits of Jesus' disciples. Once again, Jesus' enemies provided the perfect opportunity to reveal the truth of God.

I. RITUAL CLEANSING (MARK 7:1-5)

Jesus' ministry is now attracting the attention of the religious leaders from Jerusalem.

A. FAULTFINDING (vv. 1, 2)

1. The Pharisees and some of the teachers of the law who had come from Jerusalem gathered around Jesus and. . . .

This isn't the first time that religious officials have come to Galilee *from Jerusalem* to investigate *Jesus* (cf. Mark 3:22). The temple is located in Jerusalem, and that city is considered the holy city of God. Consequently, religious people among the Jews tend to hold the authority of those in Jerusalem in high regard. No doubt these officials are skeptical of Jesus and ready to find fault with his doctrine and activities. The report they will make regarding Jesus undoubtedly will be used to warn synagogues throughout Galilee that he is a dangerous force to be reckoned with.

2. . . . saw some of his disciples eating food with hands that were "unclean," that is, unwashed.

The religious officials have no trouble finding a "problem." Perhaps by attending some banquet where Jesus and the *disciples* are present, those officials discover that Jesus' disciples do not practice ceremonial cleansing of the *hands* before eating. The Pharisees' point is not that people should wash their hands to avoid picking up germs. These officials do not know anything about germs in the modern sense of the word. Their contention, rather, is that eating with *unwashed* hands means that the one eating the food is becoming defiled spiritually, because "*unclean*" hands contaminate the food in a spiritual way. The Jewish officials draw their concern from the law of Moses, which warns against touching things that are unclean (e.g., Leviticus 5:2; 11:8).

B. HANDWASHING (vv. 3, 4)

3. (The Pharisees and all the Jews do not eat unless they give their hands a ceremonial washing, holding to the tradition of the elders.

To prevent uncleanness during a meal, Jewish rabbis had developed a practice of *ceremonial* handwashing before meals. Jewish literature confirms the accuracy of this stress on ceremonial cleansing.

The Jews, of course, have the written law of Moses. But over the years the Pharisees also have developed their own "oral law." They hold the two to be almost equal in authority. By the year A.D. 200, their oral law becomes written down into a law code called the Mishnah. This code contains detailed instructions about when and how thoroughly the *hands* need to be washed before eating. Among some Jewish groups the *washing* of the hands was considered only a minimum. The strict Essenes, for example, took baths before meals.

DAILY BIBLE READINGS

Monday, Mar. 24—Holding to Human Tradition (Mark 7:1-8)

Tuesday, Mar. 25—What Comes Out Defiles (Mark 7:9-15)

Wednesday, Mar. 26—Evil Things Come From Within (Mark 7:17-23)

Thursday, Mar. 27—God Knows the Heart (Luke 16:10-15)

Friday, Mar. 28—Do Not Follow Human Tradition (Colossians 2:6-10)

Saturday, Mar. 29—Create in Me a Clean Heart (Psalm 51:10-17)

Sunday, Mar. 30—Take the Log From Your Eye (Luke 6:37-42)

Since Jesus' disciples are not abiding by the accepted regulations for cleansing their hands, the Pharisees conclude that they are defiled. And if Jesus as a teacher of God's law is not correcting his own disciples, then he must be a false teacher, to be dealt with accordingly.

It seems obvious to modern Bible students that the Pharisees' standard is man-made. Those who know the Old Testament realize that such regulations are given nowhere in the law of Moses. In other words, these Jewish religious officials are trying to hold Jesus and his disciples to a law that is not actually a law from God. It is a *tradition of the elders* that they consider binding. For the first-century resident of Galilee, however, that distinction is not so obvious. Copies of the Scripture are scarce, and most of the knowledge of them is passed on orally. If the religious leaders say this is binding, the average citizen assumes it must be Scriptural.

4. When they come from the marketplace they do not eat unless they wash. And they observe many other traditions, such as the washing of cups, pitchers and kettles.)

The Pharisees' concern about defilement extends also to kitchen utensils, which must be washed as well. Their requirements are directed at making these concerns into spiritual issues. Eating from an unwashed cup means that you could lose your standing before God. Eating with unwashed hands makes you no better than the Gentiles, who neither know God nor have a share in his blessing.

Mark's rather lengthy explanation of these Jewish customs leads us to believe that he is addressing a Gentile audience, who would need such an explanation. (Matthew, in his parallel account in chapter 15, does not include any such explanation.) Many scholars believe that Mark sent his Gospel to the church in Rome.

C. QUESTIONING (v. 5)

5. So the Pharisees and teachers of the law asked Jesus, "Why don't your disciples live according to the tradition of the elders instead of eating their food with 'unclean' hands?"

The Pharisees and teachers of the law are not asking this question for the purpose of gaining information. The question is designed to accuse Jesus of being careless about his obligation to the will of God in not correcting his disciples.

At this point, it should be apparent that the Pharisees are focused on outward purity rather than inward purity—thinking that the first automatically leads to the second. They do not pause in their criticisms to wonder if Jesus' heart is in the right place. They do not qualify their criticism by noting the actions of Jesus that do conform to the traditions of the elders: his synagogue attendance, his study of the Scriptures, or his prayer life. They do not pause to consider the evidence of the miracles that confirm his status as the Son of God. Rather, they spend their energies finding fault with his practices relating to questions of external cleanness.

II. HUMAN TRADITIONS (MARK 7:6-15)

For Jesus, spiritual purity is a deeper issue than whether the hands are cleansed. His response to the Pharisees is direct and caustic.

A. LIPS VS. HEART (v. 6)

6. He replied, "Isaiah was right when he prophesied about you hypocrites; as it is written:

"'These people honor me with their lips,
  but their hearts are far from me.

In answer to the Pharisees, Jesus quotes *Isaiah 29:13*. But he prefaces the quotation with a statement to make sure they know that the words of the prophet

WHAT DO YOU THINK?

Like the Pharisees, many today pay "lip service" to the Lord but do not wholeheartedly follow him. What are the dangers of such a practice, for those who do it and for those who see them?

WHAT DO YOU THINK?

Keeping in mind the importance and purpose of traditions, how can we be sure they do not override Scriptural doctrines and precedents?

point directly at their brand of religious hypocrisy. When he says that Isaiah had prophesied about them, Jesus does not mean that the prophet Isaiah originally had Pharisees and teachers of the law in mind. Rather, Jesus means that the same hypocrisy that Isaiah found prominent in eighth-century B.C. Israel could be seen among the religious leaders of Jesus' own day.

The condemnation Isaiah spoke about distinguished between the worship of God that is outward versus the inward devotion to God that is essential for true believers. The Pharisees, too, are demonstrating more interest in fulfilling man-made regulations than in honoring God. (See also Jeremiah 12:2.) This is the first time the Gospels record Jesus' use of the term *hypocrites* for these religious officials. It will not be the last.

B. MAN'S TEACHING VS. GOD'S COMMANDMENTS (vv. 7-12)

7. *"They worship me in vain;*
   their teachings are but rules taught by men.'

Jesus now finishes the quotation from Isaiah. In so doing, he calls attention to the crux of the problem: the Pharisees are substituting human authority for authority that belongs to God alone. They are holding people accountable for traditions that in some cases have no sign of God's approval. They are willing to judge people as unfit spiritually merely on the basis of human tradition.

8. *"You have let go of the commands of God and are holding on to the traditions of men."*

The mistake the religious leaders are making is not in merely adding traditions to the Word of God (as bad as that would be). They are creating traditions that actually overrule that Word! Jesus assumes a distinction between the Word of God and the words of the rabbis. Though many Jews apparently miss the distinction, Jesus makes clear that neglecting to separate the two leads to big problems. In Colossians 2:20-22 Paul also warns about keeping this distinction.

GOING BEYOND WHAT GOD HAS SAID

Men who have come to the West from other cultures usually dress like Westerners, but women from those cultures often choose to keep their traditional dress styles. However, in some parts of the world, there are very rigid strictures on women's clothing and behavior, usually the result of strict religious rules. Saudi Arabian women, for example, wear several veils so that their eyes are the only parts of their bodies visible to the public. An American envoy has complained that when Saudi women come into the U.S. Embassy to have their pictures taken for visas, all that can be seen is their eyes. All their pictures are, for all practical purposes, identical!

The laws go beyond dress: women are not allowed to socialize with men outside the family or home. One of the few places Saudi women are seen in public is in restaurants, but even there they are seated only with the men of their families in special family sections.

What is it about religion that tempts us to go beyond what God has said and impose our own ideas of spirituality on others? Jesus had no time for legalistic religion. He condemned the Jewish traditions that required more than God had demanded and actually nullified the purpose of God's commands. Do we as Christians have attitudes that parallel those that Jesus repudiated?   —C. R. B.

9. *And he said to them: "You have a fine way of setting aside the commands of God in order to observe your own traditions!*

Not only are the Pharisees willing to prefer man-made traditions over the Scripture, they are also willing to use traditions directly to violate the law of Moses.

10. "For Moses said, 'Honor your father and your mother,' and, 'Anyone who curses his father or mother must be put to death.'

Jesus assaults their hypocrisy by pointing to the Fifth Commandment (Exodus 20:12). The second reference is Exodus 21:17, which comes after the Ten Commandments but serves as a reinforcement of the Fifth Commandment.

To honor one's parents includes a commitment not to allow aging parents to become destitute. Jesus' concern here is not surprising. *Honor* of one's parents is basic to the will of God as expressed in the Old Testament.

11, 12. "But you say that if a man says to his father or mother: 'Whatever help you might otherwise have received from me is Corban' (that is, a gift devoted to God), then you no longer let him do anything for his father or mother.

Corban is a Hebrew term that refers to a religious *gift* that is reserved for God. The gift might take the form of an animal for sacrifice (Leviticus 1:2, 3, 10; 3:1; 27:9), a vegetable offering (Leviticus 2:1, 5), or a gift of precious metals (Numbers 7:13; 31:50). To declare any of these items to be "Corban" is to remove it from mundane uses. The Pharisees have supplanted the Fifth Commandment with an improper application of Corban.

Jesus is criticizing the practice of designating certain property as "Corban" in a deliberate attempt to withhold support from aging parents or to shame parents one is feuding with. Adults could thus use the declaration of "Corban" to keep money from going to their parents until their parents are safely dead. Then they could take advantage of the liberal "Corban" laws that allow for a reversal of their previous declaration. The money that was set aside for God while their parents were living could then be declared no longer set aside for God.

This trick allows Jewish adults to ignore their parents' needs in their old age and to feel justified that they are honoring God's law. Jesus' accusation is that the religious leaders are sponsoring a violation of the law while leaving the worshiper with no sense of wrongdoing.

C. IMPOTENCE VS. POWER (v. 13)

13. "Thus you nullify the word of God by your tradition that you have handed down. And you do many things like that."

Jesus concludes his criticisms of the practice of the Pharisees and teachers of the law by going to the heart of the danger. Rather than using *tradition* to help people understand and apply *the word of God*, their tradition actually nullifies that Word. Jesus ends his comments by noting that there are more traditions of this kind that he could list. But this one is sufficient to make the point.

D. FROM WITHOUT VS. FROM WITHIN (vv. 14, 15)

14. Again Jesus called the crowd to him and said, "Listen to me, everyone, and understand this.

Jesus has been addressing his words to the Pharisees and teachers of the law. But now he turns to the people to make sure that they hear the conclusion of the matter. He calls upon them to hear his words as if they represent the Word of God—words they must *understand* and obey!

15. "Nothing outside a man can make him 'unclean' by going into him. Rather, it is what comes out of a man that makes him 'unclean.'"

For Jewish listeners, this declaration is quite a shock. Not only is Jesus slapping down the authoritative traditions of the Pharisees, he is also pronouncing a certain Old Testament distinction to be no longer valid! The law clearly divided foods into clean and *unclean* categories (cf. Leviticus 11). Surely only God himself can change these regulations. But that's exactly what Jesus does (see Mark 7:19).

WHAT DO YOU THINK?

What do people do today that you find similar to the Pharisees' use of the "Corban" law to avoid caring for their parents? What can be done to right these modern wrongs?

Visual for lesson 5. Post today's visual as you conclude your discussion of verse 15. Discuss how one can receive a "spiritual heart transplant."

But the disciples do not yet grasp what is going on here (v. 18). It will take church leaders of the first century some time to let go of their food laws. A few years later, Peter will see a vision of a sheet being lowered from heaven with unclean animals on it. He will refuse to obey the command to eat any of the food, arguing that he has never eaten anything impure or unclean (Acts 10:14). Finally the heavenly voice convinces him not to call unclean anything that God has made clean. While the Christians in Rome are debating this matter of clean and unclean foods, Paul points out that no food is unclean of itself. Instead, it becomes unclean based on the conscience of the person eating it (Romans 14:14).

Today, Christians are not obligated to the dietary regulations of the Old Testament because Jesus declared all foods clean in Mark 7:19. These words of Jesus have changed our lifestyle forever. But more importantly, Jesus also clarified what it is that really defiles a person. The things that come *out of* a person in terms of attitudes, words, and expressions of thought—whether good or bad—reveal the content of the heart (see 7:20-23). Our words, therefore, serve as a kind of spiritual thermometer, revealing our true "temperature" as far as our devotion to God is concerned. What really defiles us is a sinful heart. The only way to get rid of that kind of defilement is to have our hearts cleansed from sin. The only cleansing agent strong enough to do that is the blood of Jesus Christ.

WHAT COMES FROM THE INSIDE

The largest flower blossom in the world is the *Amorphophallus titanum*. Ranging in color from crimson to purple, its grows to six feet in height and features a petal that is three feet wide. It has a striking, even beautiful, blossom that lasts only a couple of days and is rarely seen outside its native habitat, the jungles of Sumatra. The plant first flowered in "captivity" in 1937 at the New York Botanical Gardens and has done so only ten other times since then.

When a specimen blossomed in 1999 at the Huntington Gardens in San Marino, California, a record two-day crowd of twenty-two thousand people came to see this rare event in the world of horticulture. But they came more for another reason than for its beauty: the perfume of the blossom smells like rotting meat. A staff member at the Huntington Gardens described it as smelling like the decaying carcass of an opossum that had died under his house. What is seen on the outside is quite attractive; what emanates from within is loathsome.

This is what Jesus was saying to the people who had listened to his debate with the Pharisees: what comes from within us determines our purity or defilement, not external matters such as hands that are not ceremonially pure. The Pharisee's problem is sometimes ours as well; we so often judge people by external factors, don't we?

—C. R. B.

CONCLUSION

Today's lesson points to a ploy that comes from Satan himself: getting believers focused on human traditions instead of God's Word. Satan wins when believers assume they are serving God when they are really serving themselves. Satan wins when believers assume they have purified themselves from sin when they are really just ignoring sin. The danger is that human traditions can make Christians feel guiltless at just the wrong time.

Christ wants to remove our sins so that we have substantial reasons for being right with God. Human traditions deceive us into thinking that we can be right with God before the sin has been removed from our life. This is the reason that Jesus took so seriously this false security of the Pharisees. It is always better to allow the Word of God to affect us in the fullness of its power. With eternity at stake, it is always dangerous to allow human traditions to dilute this power.

Discovery Learning

*This page contains an alternative lesson plan emphasizing learning activities. Classes
desiring such student involvement will find these suggestions helpful. The next page
is a reproducible activity page to further enhance discovery learning.*

LEARNING GOALS

After participating in this lesson, each student will be able to:

1. Recall Jesus' answer to the Pharisees and teachers of the law about what really defiles those who try to live a pure life.

2. Contrast Jesus' method of purity with legalistic plans of achieving purity.

3. Confess specific sins that need to be eliminated from his or her lifestyle and pray to God for victory over them.

INTO THE LESSON

"Keeping up appearances" is a saying used by many when they make an effort to look all right on the outside but are falling apart on the inside. Group your students in threes. Each group member is to spend a few moments reflecting on, then responding to, the following: "Many people have joined the 'do-it-yourself' school of home decorating and repairs. Often this involves covering up previous defects or mistakes. Tell your group members of your worst experience with decorating or making repairs." Allow five minutes for the sharing. Call on volunteers to tell their stories.

Say, "In our text today Jesus encounters the teachers of Jewish law. The conflict is over what makes a person spiritually unclean. The teachers would talk about what happens on the outside of a person. We will see Jesus answer in a way very different from what they were expecting."

Option. Distribute copies of the reproducible activity "Hidden Defects" from the next page. Allow students about five minutes to reflect and write some ideas on their handouts. Then use the same transition as above.

INTO THE WORD

Create three groups of six among your class members. Each group will work on one of the following assignments. If you have more than eighteen students, create extra groups and repeat assignments. Each group needs at least four members.

Group 1: Research the Old Testament, particularly Leviticus, Numbers, and Deuteronomy, to create a quick chart containing some of the rules, regulations, and acts concerning "clean" and "unclean." Provide poster sheets or overhead transparencies and a projector.

Group 2: Write a short debate between Jesus and the Pharisees and teachers of the law. The topic will be Mark 7:15. One side will make points in support, as Jesus. The other side will make points negating the verse, as the Pharisees and teachers.

Group 3: Make a chart contrasting Jesus' method of purity with that of the Pharisees and teachers of the law. Students will need to read Mark 7:1-23 to develop the chart.

After fifteen minutes reconvene your groups for their reports.

INTO LIFE

Say, "How easily we can get caught up in the pace of life, trying to achieve spirituality by keeping ourselves 'looking clean.' Jesus teaches the Pharisees to pay attention to the 'inside' for maintaining purity."

Today's Scripture calls for a difficult application. You will be helping your students confess sin. As a teacher, your example will help students participate more readily.

Say, "There are three ground rules for this application. First, we will treat everyone here in a loving and gracious manner. Second, you may pass or keep your confession silent. Third, anything said is not to be repeated."

Option 1: Ask each member of the class to think quietly about what he or she needs to confess to God. After sixty to ninety seconds, lead the class in this prayer: "Father, forgive us for the ways we have sinned against you. In Jesus' name. Amen."

Then have volunteers read the following verses: Psalm 51:10-12; 1 John 1:9; Acts 2:38. Ask each class member to reflect on the verse that applies to him or her. Then close with this prayer: "Heavenly Father, thank you for forgiving us, for loving us, and for encouraging us to keep growing. In Jesus' name. Amen." (Use the reproducible activity "Prayer of Forgiveness" from the next page to help with this activity.)

Option 2: Prepare a three-inch-by-five-inch card for each member with the following printed on it: "My struggle with sin involves _____." Tell the group to use a category of sin, not a specific sin. After a few moments, call on volunteers to confess. If you do, be sure as the leader you go first to "model" the confession. After a short while, read the "forgiveness prayer" in Option 1. Ask for three volunteers to read the Scriptures above. Then have class members write the Scripture references on their three-by-five cards that best answers their need for forgiveness. Then pray the "prayer of thanksgiving" from above to close the class.

Hidden Defects

Walls, like lives, can look very good—even perfect. But both can hide many mistakes and defects. If this wall were to represent your "outward" life, what would be hidden behind it? Write those things here.

Prayer for Forgiveness

Read Psalm 51:10-12; Acts 2:38; and 1 John 1:9. After deciding the one Scripture that answers your need for forgiveness, write a prayer of confession below.

THE MESSIAH
CHALLENGES THE CORRUPT

LESSON 6

WHY TEACH THIS LESSON?

In some parts of the world practices including bribery and kickbacks are viewed as "the way we do business." While that seems scandalous to citizens in nations that have outlawed such unfair practices, the people who live in those countries are usually powerless to resist them.

Corruption is nothing new, of course, and it's not limited to "other countries." You may have read of a case in the morning newspaper. Perhaps a sports figure has been caught "shaving points"; or a corporate executive has been giving certain suppliers kickbacks; or an elected official has given undue aid to a wealthy supporter. It's easy for your learners to see such cases as someone else's problem. "They" are corrupt. Something should be done about "them."

Today's lesson is not about corporate or political corruption, but corruption in the religious realm. We will read about the corrupt practices of the ancient Jewish leaders in their "requirements" for proper worship in the temple. Your lesson will not be successful unless it challenges your learners to ask, "Do *we* impose certain standards and expectations on our worshipers that God does not? What can we do to make sure we are not corrupting the worship experience?"

INTRODUCTION

A. WHEN THE SECULAR INVADES THE SACRED

Several years ago the U.S. government took action to recover a million and a half dollars in back taxes that it claimed was due from a certain religious order. This particular order was engaged in the manufacture and sale of wine. Some of this wine was sold for sacramental purposes, but much of it was sold on the market in competition with regular commercial producers of wine. The religious order claimed exemption from the tax levied on commercial producers on the basis that their product was "subject to the control of the Pope," and thus was "exempt as a church" from taxation.

Compare the activities of this religious order with those of the money changers in the temple of Jesus' day. In both cases, people were using religion to justify a profit-making activity. There is nothing wrong with making a profit, of course, but in both cases the activities crossed the line into misconduct. In speaking to the money changers, Jesus said that they had made the temple into "a den of robbers." What would Jesus say today about the wine-making religious order?

B. LESSON BACKGROUND

The first five lessons in this quarter have given us thumbnail sketches of Jesus' early life and ministry. Beginning with his baptism and temptation, we have studied some of his early conflicts including his rejection at Nazareth and some of his ethical teachings. The three lessons of this unit bring his earthly life and ministry

DEVOTIONAL READING:
LUKE 19:28-40
BACKGROUND SCRIPTURE:
MARK 11:1–12:12
PRINTED TEXT:
MARK 11:1-9, 15-18

Apr
6

LESSON AIMS

After participating in this lesson, each student will be able to:

1. Summarize Mark's account of Jesus' triumphal entry into Jerusalem and the cleansing of the temple.

2. Explain how these events, which demonstrate Jesus' authority as the divine Son of God, challenge us to confront evil.

3. Suggest at least one specific way to detect and oppose corruption in society.

KEY VERSE

On reaching Jerusalem, Jesus entered the temple area and began driving out those who were buying and selling there. He overturned the tables of the money changers and the benches of those selling doves. —Mark 11:15

to its climax in his crucifixion and resurrection. Today's lesson begins what we have come to call the "Final Week."

Several months earlier Jesus had warned his disciples that he must go to Jerusalem and suffer many things, including his own death, at the hands of the elders, chief priests, and teachers of the law (Mark 8:31-33). Peter strongly resisted such an idea. He even rebuked Jesus. The idea of Jesus' dying was completely foreign to what Peter and the other disciples understood Jesus' mission to be. When Jesus entered Jerusalem, the disciples must have believed that their hopes of establishing Jesus as an earthly Messiah were about to be realized. By the next day, those hopes must have dimmed considerably.

I. THE KING'S PREPARATION (MARK 11:1-6)

A. RECEIVING THE INSTRUCTIONS (vv. 1-3)

1, 2. As they approached Jerusalem and came to Bethphage and Bethany at the Mount of Olives, Jesus sent two of his disciples, saying to them, "Go to the village ahead of you, and just as you enter it, you will find a colt tied there, which no one has ever ridden. Untie it and bring it here.

Just prior to this, Jesus had been in Jericho, where he had healed blind Bartimeus. Then Jesus and his disciples make the long, uphill walk to *Bethphage and Bethany*. While Bethphage (which means, "house of figs") has never been located, scholars believe that both villages were situated on the eastern slope of *the Mount of Olives*. This arduous trip of about sixteen miles takes the better part of the day. We may assume that they arrive at Bethany late in the afternoon just before the beginning of the Sabbath. Jesus is no stranger at Bethany. That is where Mary, Martha, and Lazarus live.

On Sunday morning after Jesus and the apostles had spent Saturday resting in observance of the Sabbath Day, Jesus sent *two of his disciples* on a special mission. They are to go to the nearby *village* of Bethphage, where at the entrance of the village they will *find a colt* that has never been *ridden*. This is the fulfillment of a prophecy found in Zechariah 9:9.

3. "If anyone asks you, 'Why are you doing this?' tell him, 'The Lord needs it and will send it back here shortly.'"

Jesus' knowledge of the availability of the colt may have come supernaturally. But, on the other hand, it is entirely possible that the Lord has made prior arrangements for the use of the animal. In either event, Jesus certainly has the owner's approval for its use.

B. BRINGING THE COLT (vv. 4-6)

4. They went and found a colt outside in the street, tied at a doorway. As they untied it, . . .

The two disciples follow Jesus' instructions and find *a colt* just as he has told them. Matthew's version of this account informs us that there were two animals—"a donkey tied there, with her colt by her" (Matthew 21:2). A colt that has never been ridden could be difficult to manage. Perhaps this is the reason that Jesus sends two disciples on this errand instead of one.

5. . . . some people standing there asked, "What are you doing, untying that colt?"

On the surface, this appears to be a case of good neighbors looking out for one another. Some villagers, noting that the two disciples are strangers, immediately challenge their action. In a small village where everyone knows everyone else, this is what we might expect. But Luke 19:33 reveals that the colt's owners are present. We would be very surprised if the owners did not say something when two strangers began *untying* their animals!

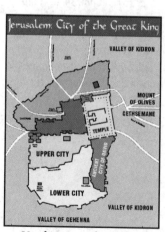

Use this map to locate sites in and around Jerusalem relevant to this and other lessons. You will find it in the Adult Visuals packet. (*See page 233 for ordering information.*)

6. They answered as Jesus had told them to, and the people let them go.

The disciples may be startled when they are questioned, but they respond as Jesus has instructed them, telling the villagers that "the Lord needs it" (v. 3). These words may be a prearranged password that establishes the identity of the disciples with the villagers. Many commentators believe that the owner of the colt is quietly making a contribution to Jesus' ministry in his own way. There may be thousands of such followers in Palestine at that time. The Lord needs some who serve publicly out in front, but he also uses many whose ministries are performed quietly behind the scenes.

II. THE KING'S ENTRY (MARK 11:7-9)

A. JESUS RIDES THE COLT (v. 7)

7. When they brought the colt to Jesus and threw their cloaks over it, he sat on it.

Saddles as we know them are not commonly used in the ancient Orient. Instead, the disciples lay some of their clothing on the back of the animal to cushion Jesus' ride. Without a saddle or stirrups, Jesus probably has to be lifted onto the back of the animal. Amazingly, the colt remains docile as Jesus begins to ride it. Apparently this animal recognizes Jesus for who he is and behaves accordingly.

B. PEOPLE PREPARE THE WAY (v. 8)

8. Many people spread their cloaks on the road, while others spread branches they had cut in the fields.

The spontaneous response of the *people* to Jesus' ride from the Mount of Olives to Jerusalem is remarkable. At least we assume that it was spontaneous, for we have nothing to indicate that Jesus made any effort in advance to encourage the people to respond in this fashion.

But even without the benefit of our modern electronic media, word passes from person to person with amazing speed. Jerusalem at the time is crowded with many visitors who have come to the city to celebrate the Passover. (The number of people in the city perhaps triples during this celebration!) No doubt some of these visitors, especially those from Galilee, already know of Jesus. Only a short time before, Jesus had raised Lazarus from the dead and this word spread among the visitors, increasing their excitement and their desire to see him.

As Jesus rides down the slope of the Mount of Olives, the people honor him by spreading tree *branches* and *their cloaks on the road*. John tells us that they also cut palm branches or fronds and wave these as they go out to meet him (John 12:13). Normally this behavior is reserved for nobility. Crowds of people had welcomed the Jewish hero Simon Maccabeus in a similar manner some 110 years before (see 1 Maccabees 13:51). The people are demonstrating their belief that Jesus is more than just another prophet or rabbi: he is the "Son of David" (Matthew 21:9.)

Since palm fronds grow at the very top of the trees, the people must have gone to considerable effort to cut them for this occasion. This action is the basis for observing the day of Jesus' triumphal entry as "Palm Sunday."

C. PEOPLE HAIL JESUS (v. 9)

9. Those who went ahead and those who followed shouted,
    "Hosanna!"
    "Blessed is he who comes in the name of the Lord!"

All four Gospel accounts record Jesus' triumphal entry into Jerusalem. However, these separate accounts present some interesting variations. Both Matthew and Mark indicate that two groups make up the crowd that accompanied Jesus:

WHAT DO YOU THINK?

Whether by divine foreknowledge or personal interview, Jesus knew the owner of the colt would allow him to use it on a moment's notice. What of your possessions (including time) would you find difficult to give up for the Lord's use? How can a believer release any and every possession to the Lord?

WHAT DO YOU THINK?

In Mark 11 many people exhibited an unplanned, uninhibited, unguarded response of praise to the lordship of Jesus. Why is it so hard for some of us to be spontaneous with our praise?

those who went ahead are those who come out from Jerusalem to meet him (cf. John 12:12, 13), while *those who followed* come from Bethany with him.

Both groups join in shouting their praise, and the two phrases they use catch our attention. *Hosanna* originally meant "save us," as in Psalm 118:25. Over the centuries, however, this word came to be used as an expression of acclamation rather than a cry for help. The phrase *blessed is he that comes in the name of the Lord* is found in Psalm 118:26. Verses 25 and 26 of that psalm are used in the formal worship services of the major Jewish feasts, indicating that the people attach great significance to Jesus' entry into Jerusalem. Matthew 23:39 notes that Jesus will use the second phrase himself a bit later.

John 12:13 records that the crowd also hails Jesus as "King of Israel." Luke also tells us that some of the religious leaders demand that Jesus silence the enthusiastic crowd. Jesus responds that "if they keep quiet, the stones will cry out" (Luke 19:40). Luke also informs us that Jesus stops before he enters the city and weeps as he predicts the tragic future that awaits Jerusalem (Luke 19:41-44).

Mark tells us in verse 11 that after Jesus enters the city, he goes into the temple area and observes some of the activities there. As events of the following day will show, Jesus is displeased with some of the things he sees. But since it is already late in the day, he chooses to wait until the next day to confront those who are corrupting God's house. And so he leaves and returns to Bethany with his disciples.

A LEADER, NOT A PUBLICITY HOUND

"Screaming Lord Sutch" was founder of Britain's Monster Raving Loony Party. When he died in June 1999, he was England's longest-serving political leader. He had run for parliament forty times without ever being elected. His campaign slogan was, "Vote for insanity—you know it makes sense!" His trademark "uniform" during his campaigns was an animal-skin print hat, gold lamé suit, and a gold megaphone.

Sutch was famed for such inane proposals as banning January and February in order to shorten winter, and forcing the unemployed to walk on a giant treadmill to generate cheap electricity. Appropriately, his countrymen saw his antics as publicity stunts more than efforts to bring positive change to the nation. However, he did have an effect on the British electoral process: the government drastically increased candidates' registration fees to keep people like him from running for office!

Skeptics may have seen Jesus' triumphal entry as a mere publicity stunt. However, unlike people's reaction to Screaming Lord Sutch and a multitude of his sort, the common people recognized that what Jesus said made sense, and they followed him gladly. We'll always have "Loonies" vying for our attention, urging us to join their parades. But the only leader really worthy of a devoted following is Jesus. Even at their best, all others pale in comparison.
—C. R. B.

III. THE KING'S ANGER (MARK 11:15-18)
A. THE SON OF GOD ACTS (vv. 15, 16)
15. On reaching Jerusalem, Jesus entered the temple area and began driving out those who were buying and selling there. He overturned the tables of the money changers and the benches of those selling doves,

The next morning Jesus returns to *the temple area* ready to confront the merchants and *money changers* in God's house. In the cleansing of the temple, Jesus challenges the corrupt practices of the religious leaders head on. At the beginning of his ministry Jesus had cleansed the temple in a similar manner (John 2:13-17), but in the three years that have passed since then, the merchants and money changers have returned to their lucrative practices.

At first glance, one might suppose that these merchants and money changers are rendering a service to those who come to the temple to worship. Worshipers

---

WHAT DO YOU THINK?

Jesus noted the situation in the temple, and then he left. It wasn't until the next day that he took action to clean things up. What value is there in assessing a situation before reacting? What dangers do we risk when we fail to do so?

HOW TO SAY IT

Bartimeus. BAR-tih-ME-us.
Bethany. BETH-uh-nee.
Bethphage. BETH-fuh-gee.
Galilee. GAL-uh-lee.
Jeremiah. Jair-uh-MY-uh.
Jericho. JAIR-ih-co.
Maccabeus. Mack-uh-BEE-us.
rabbi. RAB-eye.
Zechariah. ZEK-uh-RYE-uh.

are allowed to bring their own sacrificial animals for their offerings, but bringing a sheep or even a dove all the way from Galilee can be inconvenient. So many people prefer to purchase an animal from the vendors in the temple area.

Further, those bringing their own animals often run into another problem: sacrificial animals have to be without blemish (Leviticus 22:21). Those who bring their own animals often have them rejected by the temple inspectors. Thus the worshipers have to purchase approved animals at inflated prices. Then to avoid having to take their own "unacceptable" animal all the way back home, the worshipers sell them at greatly reduced prices to merchants in Jerusalem. These merchants have "inside connections" through which they can get these rejected animals approved for worship. Using this trick, the religious leaders are able to make a nice profit on the side.

But the corruption doesn't stop there. Worshipers often make contributions to the temple treasury, a practice that is quite acceptable to the religious leaders. However, those who bring coins from foreign lands will have those coins rejected because they bear images of their rulers, a violation of the second (and possibly the first) of the Ten Commandments (Exodus 20:3, 4). For this reason, worshipers have to trade those coins for the proper "temple currency" (cf. Matthew 17:24-27). There is little doubt that the religious leaders profited from a lopsided "exchange rate"!

Quite apart from the corruption involved in these temple activities, another issue is involved. Worship ought to be kept holy and sacred, but these religious leaders are squeezing out the sacred as they pursue their commercial venture. Today we are immersed in a secular world that uses every opportunity to intrude into the most sacred moments. These intrusions are often subtle and may go unnoticed. Sometimes they are blatant and obvious. Although the practices noted here are carried on in the outer courts of the temple (the area that surrounds the temple building) the smell and noise of livestock directly adjacent to a solemn place of prayer has to be a distraction. From time to time we need spiritual leaders with keen insights to call our attention to the compromises we are making. That's what Jesus is doing when he cleanses the temple.

A DIFFERENT KIND OF HOAX

Hoaxes have often been perpetrated on a gullible public, but the increasing use of E-mail has resulted in an increase of the number of people who can be duped by a given hoax. For example, an E-mail that purported to come from a law firm in the Washington, D.C. area warned a few years ago that a bill before Congress, 602P, would add a five-cent tax to each E-mail message a person received. Even worse, Republican Congressman Tony Schnell was trying to get an even higher tax passed in order to help the U.S. Postal Service fight its electronic competition.

However, the bill, the law firm, and the Congressman do not exist! A distrustful public's willingness to believe the worst about government's appetite for tax income conspired with its naïve acceptance of what it reads in E-mail messages. The result was the rapid spread of the hoax.

But hoaxes are nothing new. In Jesus' day, religious leaders conspired with greedy merchants and crooked money changers to force worshipers at the temple into believing that God required a specific kind of money and preapproved sacrificial animals for their worship. Jesus' actions in cleansing the temple should remind us to keep a watchful eye on those who, in claiming to be God's authorities, would fool us about God's requirements for pleasing him.   —C. R. B.

16. . . . and would not allow anyone to carry merchandise through the temple courts.

DAILY BIBLE READINGS

Monday, Mar. 31—Jesus Rides Into Jerusalem (Mark 11:1-11)

Tuesday, Apr. 1—The King Comes Riding a Donkey (Zechariah 9:9-12)

Wednesday, Apr. 2—The Stones Would Shout (Luke 19:28-40)

Thursday, Apr. 3—Jesus Cleanses the Temple (Mark 11:12-19)

Friday, Apr. 4—Have Faith in God (Mark 11:20-25)

Saturday, Apr. 5—By What Authority? (Mark 11:27-33)

Sunday, Apr. 6—The Story of Wicked Tenants (Mark 12:1-12)

PRAYER

We thank you, Father, that Jesus did not turn aside from the mission that brought him into the world. We pray that his example of facing corruption will serve as a model for us. Give us the wisdom to know how to oppose evil and defend the truth when your standards are rejected. In our Master's name we pray, amen.

The temple area covers most of the eastern side of the city of Jerusalem. Anyone wishing to travel to points east of the city has to go through the temple area or take a much longer route either north or south of that area. Jesus does not object to people taking a shortcut through the area, but he does condemn them for carrying *merchandise* with them. Because *merchandise* has such a broad meaning, a person carrying almost anything comes under Jesus' condemnation.

B. THE SON OF GOD EXPLAINS (v. 17)

17. *And as he taught them, he said, "Is it not written:*
 "'My house will be called
 a house of prayer for all nations'?
 But you have made it 'a den of robbers.'"

Certainly many who witness Jesus' actions are astonished, so he explains what he is doing and why. As he so often does when challenged, Jesus turns to the Scriptures for support. Here he quotes both Isaiah 56:7 and Jeremiah 7:11. What God intends to be a holy place has been turned into a site where profits are more important than *prayer*.

C. THE RELIGIOUS LEADERS REACT (v. 18)

18. *The chief priests and the teachers of the law heard this and began looking for a way to kill him, for they feared him, because the whole crowd was amazed at his teaching.*

Throughout much of his ministry Jesus has faced opposition from the religious leaders. Now the focused opposition is coming from *the chief priests and the teachers of the law,* who control both the temple and the policies concerning the nation's religious life. Even though the teachers of the law are the recognized scholars, they are at a loss in knowing how to challenge Jesus when he uses the Scripture. Probably they don't respond because they do not want to risk a humiliating defeat in front of the people, who are *amazed at his teaching*. His teaching amazes the people, not only because it contradicts what they have been taught by the religious leaders, but also because he has boldly entered the leaders' own territory to confront them. His is a voice of authority!

The religious leaders have good reason to fear him because he is a threat to their positions and their incomes (John 11:48). Thus they begin to look *for a way to kill him*. Jesus' earlier critics had sought to discredit him and to undermine his influence with the people. Realizing that these earlier efforts have only served to increase Jesus' popularity with the people, his enemies now resort to more drastic measures.

CONCLUSION

Unfortunately, corruption among religious leaders is not confined to the distant past. Moral disasters continue to confront us. Satan is always going about as a roaring lion, "looking for someone to devour" (1 Peter 5:8). He cleverly concentrates his attacks on our leaders because he knows that their fall will have widespread consequences. Notice how Satan influences Judas to have Jesus killed (Luke 22:3; John 13:27).

To thwart Satan in these matters, we need to take some important steps. We should choose our leaders carefully, seeking to ensure that they are sound in the faith and experienced enough to ward off Satan's attacks. We need to insist on their accountability. And we must lift them up in our prayers. And as we support our leaders in these ways, we also take the same steps to make sure that we ourselves do not fall into sin (cf. 1 Corinthians 9:27; Hebrews 4:1).

WHAT DO YOU THINK?

What social or religious injustices are opposed at our church? How do we decide whether one of our protests is shared by Jesus?

WHAT DO YOU THINK?

Being aware of the dire consequences of moral failure in church leadership, how can we contribute to the spiritual health and purity of our church's leaders?

THOUGHT TO REMEMBER

"Arm me with jealous care,
As in Thy sight to live,
And O, Thy servant, Lord,
prepare,
A strict account to give."
—Charles Wesley

Discovery Learning

*This page contains an alternative lesson plan emphasizing learning activities. Classes
desiring such student involvement will find these suggestions helpful. The next page
is a reproducible activity page to further enhance discovery learning.*

LEARNING GOALS

After participating in this lesson, each student will be
able to:

1. Summarize Mark's account of Jesus' triumphal
entry into Jerusalem and the cleansing of the temple.

2. Explain how these events, which demonstrate
Jesus' authority as the divine Son of God, challenge us
to confront evil.

3. Suggest at least one specific way to detect and oppose corruption in society.

INTO THE LESSON

Begin this lesson by grouping class members in sixes.
Each group is to plan a parade to celebrate a person or
event that normally gets overlooked. Distribute the following questions to each group:

1. What is the purpose of your parade?

2. What items or units will make up the parade?

3. What permits will be necessary?

4. Who will watch your parade?

Allow the groups six minutes to sketch an outline for
this task. When each group is finished let them tell the
others of their plans, the whys and the nature of their
parade.

Introduce today's lesson by saying, "Today we will
study a parade for Jesus. The response of the people
seems to be spontaneous as Jesus rides in on the donkey colt. As we study, look for how people respond to
Jesus and his authority."

INTO THE WORD

Option 1. One way to cover the details of today's text
is to contact some of the children's class teachers to prepare a skit for each of the text sections. One group will
do Mark 11:1-9, the second prepares Mark 11:15-18.

Option 2. Divide your class into three groups. Each
group should have four to six members. If your class is
larger, assign each of the following to multiple groups.
Provide Bible dictionaries, study Bibles, paper, markers,
and other materials necessary.

Group 1: Read Mark 11:1-9. Prepare a short dramatization of the events. Provide a narrator who can define
the word *Hosanna* and discuss the origin of Mark 11:9.
(The teacher's commentary is helpful here.)

Group 2: Develop a short report on "money changers" in the Jewish temple.

Group 3: Read Mark 11:15-18. Prepare a short
dramatization of the events. Provide a narrator to explain
some of the corruption which had entered into this
practice. (Use the commentary for help.)

Whichever options you use, call the class back together for reports or presentations on the projects. Lead
a discussion using the following questions (these are in
the student book):

1. How does the reaction of the people at Jesus' entry
remind us of who he is? (*They give adoration and quote
Psalm 118 to remind us.*)

2. How does Jesus react to their worship? (*He accepts
it.*)

3. What does Jesus' reaction to the money changers
signify about him? (*He has authority to confront activity
which does not honor God.*)

4. What does the response of the leaders tell us about
Jesus? (*He is powerful, he is feared, he is amazing.*)

5. What do the leaders seek to do? (*Kill him.*)

INTO LIFE

Pass out copies of the reproducible activity "The Triumphal Entry" from the next page. Use it to remind
your students of our daily need to praise God for sending Jesus.

Have the class move back to original groups. Distribute a variety of newspapers or news magazines that you
have collected over the past week. Also distribute poster
paper, markers, glue or tape, and scissors.

Ask each group to select stories from the newspaper
or magazines that reflect corruption in daily life. They
should paste or tape pictures or the story to the poster
paper. After ten minutes have each group explain the
poster. Ask each group the following questions (these
are in the student book):

1. How are Christians affected by these events?

2. What should be a Christian's response to these
events?

3. How can we be helpful to fellow Christians who
oppose these behaviors?

Finally, distribute copies of the reproducible activity
"Clearing the Tables" from the next page. Remind the students that societal change occurs one person at a time,
beginning with self changes. Then have them complete
this activity privately and to spend a moment in silent
prayer about the changes they need to make in their lives.

The Triumphal Entry

Read Mark 11:1-9, 15-18. What are some of the attributes of Jesus you praise God for? Write them on the palm fronds.

Clearing the Tables

What are some of the evils in our society that need to be "swept from the table"? What are some of the things you need to have "overturned" by Jesus in your life? Write them on the tables–society's on the one, your personal ones on the other.

In the box below write an action plan here that will help you to begin "overturning" these things in your life. Then clip the box and keep it with you as a reminder.

JESUS GIVES PASSOVER NEW MEANING

WHY TEACH THIS LESSON?

Sir Isaac Newton (1642–1727) was a brilliant mathematician who gave new direction to the study of physics. But then along came Albert Einstein (1879–1955). His "Special Theory of Relativity" came to displace long-held ideas about time and space that had been proposed by Newton. This radical change, or "paradigm shift," set the study of physics on a very new path!

Today, we will consider a paradigm shift of far greater significance. For more than fourteen centuries, the Jewish people were to observe the Passover to celebrate their deliverance from slavery in Egypt. But then the Son of God comes and gives this celebration a radically new meaning. The remembrance of "earthly" deliverance from Egypt now gives way to a remembrance of the Son's death to secure our eternal deliverance from sin and God's wrath. Could there be any lesson more important than this? From now on, every time your learners partake of the Lord's Supper, their participation in today's lesson will be made more significant.

INTRODUCTION

A. MEMORIES BRING RELIEF

S. S. Lappin, a well-known preacher of an earlier generation, told of his growing up in humble surroundings. Their house was scarcely more than a shack. There were large cracks in the wall, which the family kept filled with clay to keep the wind out. On one occasion after they had packed fresh clay into the cracks, a younger brother about two years old pressed his little hands into the clay, leaving the imprint of his hands. The clay soon hardened, leaving the handprints permanently etched into the clay.

Tragedy struck the following spring when the little brother suddenly became ill and died. Dr. Lappin told how for many months afterward his mother, who was losing her eyesight, would feel her way along the wall until she found the little handprints. Then she would gently caress them, thus bringing back fond memories of her son and finding relief in her soul for her painful loss.

In a way, this is our mindset when we come to the Lord's Supper. Saddened by the burden of our sins, we reach for the loaf and the cup as a reminder of our Lord. Although he is no longer with us in his physical body, we can find relief for our troubled souls in remembering what the Communion signifies.

B. LESSON BACKGROUND

The period between Jesus' triumphal entry and his resurrection the following Sunday is sometimes referred to as the "Final Week." This proved to be the busiest week in Jesus' ministry. In last week's lesson we studied his triumphal entry into Jerusalem and the cleansing of the temple. After that experience, Jesus left Jerusalem and spent the night in Bethany. On the following day (Tuesday) he

---

DEVOTIONAL READING:
MATTHEW 26:17-30
BACKGROUND SCRIPTURE:
MARK 14:1-25
PRINTED TEXT:
MARK 14:12-25

LESSON AIMS

After participating in this lesson, each student will be able to:

1. Describe the event that became the occasion for the institution of the Lord's Supper.

2. Explain the significance of the Lord's Supper both for the disciples and for Christians today.

3. Suggest some meditation thoughts that can help a participant have a more meaningful experience at the Lord's table.

Apr
13

KEY VERSE

This is my blood of the covenant, which is poured out for many.   —Mark 14:24

returned to Jerusalem, where his enemies challenged his authority in a series of bitter attacks. Jesus was able to turn aside these challenges, leaving the religious leaders more determined than ever to destroy him (Mark 11:27–12:34).

I. PREPARATIONS FOR THE PASSOVER (MARK 14:12-16)

A. THE DISCIPLES' QUERY (v. 12)

12. On the first day of the Feast of Unleavened Bread, when it was customary to sacrifice the Passover lamb, Jesus' disciples asked him, "Where do you want us to go and make preparations for you to eat the Passover?"

The *Feast of Unleavened Bread* was originally a festival of seven days beginning on the fifteenth day of the month of Nisan (formerly called "Abib"; see Exodus 23:15; 34:18; Leviticus 23:6). This corresponds to late March or early April. This feast became closely associated with the feast of *the Passover* (see Numbers 28:16, 17; 2 Chronicles 35:17), which commemorates the deliverance of the Israelites from Egypt (Exodus 12).

In preparation for this Passover, the group has to have a place large enough to accommodate Jesus and the twelve disciples. Extensive arrangements have to be made for the food that is needed for the meal. (See Exodus 12:3, 8, 43-47; Numbers 9:11.) With Jesus' enemies looking to arrest him (see Mark 14:1), the disciples may be concerned that meeting in a large room and the attendant preparations will draw unwanted attention to themselves. Yet even with security an obvious issue, their question is not *whether* they will observe the Passover, but *where.*

B. JESUS' INSTRUCTIONS (vv. 13-16)

13. So he sent two of his disciples, telling them, "Go into the city, and a man carrying a jar of water will meet you. Follow him.

As with the colt borrowed for his entry into Jerusalem, Jesus has either made prior arrangements or has used his supernatural abilities to know about the circumstances that will come together concerning his observance of the Passover. Just as he had sent *two of his disciples* to secure the colt, so he sends two to find the room and prepare it. (From Luke 22:8 we know that the two in this instance are Peter and John.)

Men normally carry *water* or wine in jugs or wineskin bottles. A Jewish woman, on the other hand, carries a pitcher or jar of water on her head. Even though the streets of Jerusalem are teeming with hundreds of visitors for this important feast, seeing a man carrying *a jar* in such a crowd will be certain to attract the disciples' attention.

14. "Say to the owner of the house he enters, 'The Teacher asks: Where is my guest room, where I may eat the Passover with my disciples?'

The disciples are to follow this man to a *house*, where they are to speak to *the owner.* In speaking to him, the disciples are to use certain words—*the Teacher asks*—to indicate to him that they come from Jesus.

15. "He will show you a large upper room, furnished and ready. Make preparations for us there."

Houses in this region often have a second story *room*, normally accessed by an outside stairway, that can be used for guests. The prophet Elijah had stayed in such a room when he was a guest of the widow of Zarephath (1 Kings 17:19; Luke 4:26). The fact that the room is *large* enough to accommodate the thirteen men indicates that the owner is a person of some means.

The room is *furnished*, but the furnishings are simple by today's standards— perhaps only a low table surrounded by pallets for reclining. Leonardo da Vinci's

---

WHAT DO YOU THINK?

The disciples were concerned for their safety, but they still wanted to observe the Passover as the law required. How different they are from the many today who abandon Scriptural precedents for the sake of convenience! How do we make sure that we, in attempting to be contemporary in our observance of Scriptural practices, do not change their essence?

HOW TO SAY IT

Abib. A-bib.

Bethany. BETH-uh-nee.

Deuteronomy. Due-ter-AHN-uh-me.

Elijah. Ee-LYE-juh.

Eucharist. YOO-kuh-rust.

Leonardo da Vinci. Lee-uh-NARD-oh duh VIN-chee.

Nisan. NYE-san.

Pentecost. PENT-ih-kost.

Renaissance. REH-nuh-SONTS.

Zarephath. ZAIR-uh-fath.

famous painting of *The Last Supper,* which shows Jesus and his disciples seated about a table, depicts a Renaissance Italian setting rather than the setting that would have been found in Jesus' day. The furnishings in the room do not include the food, which the disciples will have to provide.

16. The disciples left, went into the city and found things just as Jesus had told them. So they prepared the Passover.

The two *disciples* do as Jesus instructs them and find the situation exactly as he had said it would be. Making ready the *Passover* involves preparing or purchasing several things: the Passover lamb, which will take some time to kill and roast; unleavened bread—meaning bread made with no yeast—to remind them of the haste of the departure from Egypt; a bowl of salt water to remind them of the Red Sea; bitter herbs as a reminder of their bitter experience as slaves; a paste or sauce made of a mixture of fruit and nuts; and fruit of the vine to drink. All this preparation has to be finished on the fourteenth of Nisan within the space of just a few hours (see Exodus 12:6; Numbers 9:3; Deuteronomy 16:6).

II. PREDICTION OF BETRAYAL (MARK 14:17-21)

A. ASSEMBLY AND ANNOUNCEMENT (vv. 17, 18)

17. When evening came, Jesus arrived with the Twelve.

When evening comes, Jesus and the ten disciples who have remained with him walk from Bethany to join the other two in the upper room. Tradition holds that the upper room is in the western part of Jerusalem. Wherever this room is located, it must be somewhere within the walls of Jerusalem, since that is where the Passover meal must be eaten. A new day—the fifteenth of Nisan—begins in the evening at sundown, and the Passover meal can now begin.

18. While they were reclining at the table eating, he said, "I tell you the truth, one of you will betray me—one who is eating with me."

The Passover is a sacred and solemn occasion. But it is also a time to celebrate God's deliverance of the Jewish people from slavery in Egypt. As they eat the meal, however, Jesus makes an announcement that casts a pall over the celebration. These men had been together for three years, in all kinds of circumstances. That one of this number, his closest companions, *will betray* him is unthinkable.

B. SORROW AND RESPONSE (v. 19)

19. They were saddened, and one by one they said to him, "Surely not I?"

Jesus' announcement leads to a time of serious soul-searching. With sorrow, each in turn asks the same question: *Surely not I?* Except for Judas, each one is convinced that he will not knowingly betray the Master. Yet each harbors a lingering doubt that he might unwittingly or accidentally betray the Lord. If they know this in advance, they might take steps to avoid this possibility.

Matthew's version of this incident indicates that after the others have responded to Jesus in this way, Judas also asks, "Surely not I, Rabbi?" Jesus replies, "Yes, it is you" (Matthew 26:25). The other disciples apparently do not hear Jesus' response to Judas. Had the other disciples understood that Judas was to become the betrayer, they surely would have tried to stop him.

THE PRICE OF A GOOD (BAD) DEED

A couple of years ago, a professional musician left his 1673 Stradivarius cello in a New York City taxicab. The cab driver later realized his passenger had left something in the car and tried to return it where he had let the man off. However, the doorman would agree only to pass on the driver's phone number to the owner. The next day the musician picked up his cello and gave the cabbie a $75 check. The cabbie said it wasn't good enough so the offer was raised to $1,000. But the cab driver decided a "finder's fee" of 1 percent was more appropriate. Thus he should get $40,000 for returning a cello valued at $4,000,000. How much is a good deed worth? It seems it depends on the greed of the person doing it!

Many people have speculated about Judas's reason or motive for betraying Christ—and for a mere thirty pieces of silver at that! How much is a *bad* deed worth? A currently popular theory is that Judas was trying to do good by forcing Jesus to become king. On the other hand, it may well have been greed; it's a common human sin. In either case, Judas missed the point of what Jesus was trying to do. When Jesus announced that one of his disciples would betray him, the others asked, "Is it I?" We who follow Christ today must ask ourselves, "Would I betray my Lord for money, or even deny him for no tangible reward as the other disciples did?"

—C. R. B.

C. TREASON AND IMPLICATION (vv. 20, 21)

20. "It is one of the Twelve," he replied, "one who dips bread into the bowl with me.

In this meal it is a common practice for those participating to dip their *bread into the bowl* that contains the bitter herbs and fruit paste. Probably all of the disciples have dipped their bread into this dish at one time or another during the meal. In the ancient near East, sharing a meal with a host involves a sacred trust. It is considered most reprehensible for a person to violate that trust by harming the host in any way. This may have been Jesus' intent rather than an effort to identify Judas specifically as the traitor.

John's account of this event indicates that Jesus goes a step farther in identifying the traitor. When Peter presses John to ask Jesus specifically about the identity of the traitor, Jesus replies, "It is the one to whom I will give this piece of bread when I have dipped it in the dish." Then he *dips* a piece of bread and gives it to Judas (John 13:26). The other disciples miss even this clear signal, however, because they think Jesus is giving instructions to Judas about money (13:28, 29).

21. "The Son of Man will go just as it is written about him. But woe to that man who betrays the Son of Man! It would be better for him if he had not been born."

In referring to what *is written about him,* Jesus may have Psalm 41:9 in mind. This passage speaks explicitly of a person who betrays a friend, even after sharing bread. Other possible references are Isaiah 53:7-9 and Daniel 9:26.

Even though Jesus predicts his death, which is necessary in God's plan for human salvation, that does not make the guilt of the betrayer any less. Judas has the freedom to make a different choice. But from eternity past, God has known the path Judas would choose (cf. John 17:12; Acts 1:16-18). Surely to have *not been born* would be preferable to the eternal destruction that awaits Judas! (See Acts 1:25.)

III. INSTITUTION OF THE LORD'S SUPPER (MARK 14:22-25)

A. THE BREAD (v. 22)

22. While they were eating, Jesus took bread, gave thanks and broke it, and gave it to his disciples, saying, "Take it; this is my body."

Jesus injects a completely new element as the Passover meal approaches its conclusion. Taking some of the fruit of the vine and the *bread,* he gives them new meaning. With this new meaning in place, today we celebrate the Lord's Supper (or "Communion") rather than the Passover.

But exactly what the new meaning is has been a source of intense debate throughout church history. Various interpretations of the phrases *this is my body*

WHAT DO YOU THINK?

How can we follow Jesus' example of graciousness in the presence of someone who has betrayed, hurt, or disappointed us?

[See Colossians 3:13.]

and "this is my blood" (v. 24, below) have resulted in Christians' dividing themselves from one another. How sadly ironic this is: the Lord's Supper, which should bring Christians together, actually drives them apart! (See 1 Corinthians 10:17.)

Some teach that Jesus was speaking literally—that the bread and fruit of the vine in some miraculous way actually become his flesh and blood. But in his preaching and teaching Jesus often used figurative language to get his point across to his listeners. For example, in John 10:7 he said, "I am the gate." No one who heard him say these words supposed that he was actually a wooden gate that swung on iron hinges! Why then should anyone assume that the bread and fruit of the vine must actually be his flesh and blood? Even as Jesus breaks the bread and hands it to the disciples, he is still right there before them in the flesh. The disciples know that drinking actual blood is against the Old Testament law (cf. Leviticus 7:26, 27), but we see them raising no objection.

B. THE CUP (vv. 23, 24)

23. Then he took the cup, gave thanks and offered it to them, and they all drank from it.

Just as the bread Jesus uses is a part of the usual Passover observance, so also is fruit of the vine. Typically the Passover meal features four cups, each to be used at a particular point to correspond with the four promises of Exodus 6:6, 7.

The particular *cup* Jesus uses here is probably the third of the four cups, known as "the cup of blessing." But before he passes the cup around, he gives *thanks*. When the Greek letters of this word are pronounced in English, the result is the familiar word *Eucharist*, which in some churches is the term used to denote the Lord's Supper.

24. "This is my blood of the covenant, which is poured out for many," he said to them.

The word *covenant* is easy to understand as an agreement which is formal, solemn, and binding. This understanding allows us to compare more easily the "Old Covenant" with the "New Covenant" (cf. Jeremiah 31:31, 32; see also Hebrews 8:7-13). Sacrificial *blood* was an important part of the Old Covenant. When Moses initiated the people into God's covenant, he took the blood from the sacrificial animals and sprinkled it on the people (Exodus 24:8; Hebrews 9:18-22). This lent solemnity to the occasion and symbolically committed them to live according to the terms of that covenant. Now as Jesus passes the cup from which all drink, he points the disciples toward a New Covenant. This is a covenant that Jesus will seal with his own blood (cf. John 6:53-56; Hebrews 10:10-18).

A REMINDER OF A HEROIC SACRIFICE

The Arizona State Hospital cemetery contains some twenty-four hundred gravestones marked only with numbers. Beneath one of those stones lies Corporal Isaiah Mays. He was born in 1858 and after emancipation he became a member of the U.S. Army's Tenth Cavalry, an all-black unit. While guarding a payroll wagon near Tucson in 1889, his unit was attacked by thieves. Most of the soldiers were driven off, but Mays fought back valiantly. Although wounded in both legs, he crawled two miles to sound a warning.

Mays was awarded the Medal of Honor for his heroic deeds. But the government refused to give him a pension, and he died in poverty at the hospital in 1925. No relatives claimed the body, so Mays was buried under one of those numbered stones. However, a therapist at the hospital has taken on the task of trying to identify the remains of those twenty-four hundred soldiers. She was able to match Mays's numbered stone with hospital records. Finally, in 2001, Mays's grave

DAILY BIBLE READINGS

Monday, Apr. 7—A Woman Anoints Jesus (Mark 14:1-9)

Tuesday, Apr. 8—Plans Made for Passover (Mark 14:10-16)

Wednesday, Apr. 9—The Cup and the Bread (Mark 14:17-25)

Thursday, Apr. 10—Jesus Washes the Disciples' Feet (John 13:1-5)

Friday, Apr. 11—I Have Set You an Example (John 13:12-20)

Saturday, Apr. 12—Where I Go, You Cannot Come (John 13:31-35)

Sunday, Apr. 13—In Remembrance of Me (1 Corinthians 11:23-28)

"This is my blood of the new testament, which is shed for many." —Mark 14:24

Visual for Lesson 7. This classic illustration of the Lord's Supper is suitable for this lesson and for general use.

PRAYER

Gracious Father, as we participate in the Lord's Supper teach us to examine our hearts so that we may commune in a worthy manner. Let the Communion elements remind us of our Lord's suffering and death that purchased our eternal life. In Jesus' name we pray, amen.

WHAT DO YOU THINK?

What aspects of the Lord's Supper make it consistently meaningful for those of us who observe it frequently?

THOUGHT TO REMEMBER

"Do this in remembrance of me." —1 Corinthians 11:24

received a four-foot-high Medal of Honor headstone like those at Arlington National Cemetery.

The Lord's Supper is like that numbered gravestone. Both are such simple things, but both serve as reminders of courage and sacrifice. When we understand the nature of the Lord's Supper, this simple service beckons us to remember the heroic sacrifice that one Man made so long ago to pay sin's price.   —C. R. B.

C. THE FUTURE (v. 25)

25. *"I tell you the truth, I will not drink again of the fruit of the vine until that day when I drink it anew in the kingdom of God."*

Within six weeks of this meal, Jesus will return to his heavenly home (Acts 1:3, 9). There is no indication that he shares the Lord's Supper with the disciples during this period. The first indication we have that the disciples, along with other Christians, observe the Lord's Supper comes after the Day of Pentecost in Acts 2. Thus, many understand Jesus to be saying that he is looking forward to the consummation of his *kingdom* in Heaven (cf. Isaiah 25:6; Matthew 8:11).

Others take this to mean that Jesus will participate in Communion with Christians each time they assemble to worship and meet around his table. Of course, he will not be with them in the flesh, but he will be with them spiritually. "For where two or three come together in my name, there am I with them" (Matthew 18:20). Today when we participate in the Lord's Supper, Satan does his best to reduce this experience to a routine that becomes virtually meaningless. But when we realize that the Lord is present, our participation becomes a solemn, reverent experience that reminds us of whose we are.

CONCLUSION

Christianity can be viewed from four perspectives. Christianity is a *historic* religion with its roots deep in the past, but it is also a *futuristic* religion, looking to eternity beyond this world. Christianity is a *personal* religion, encouraging its adherents to examine their hearts, but it is also a *social* religion, looking outside the individual to the larger human family. Nowhere are these four aspects of Christianity better illustrated than in the Lord's Supper.

First of all, the participant is encouraged to look backward to the suffering and death of Christ. We are deeply humbled when we pause to consider what a great price our Lord paid for our sins.

The Lord's Supper is also a look forward. Jesus has promised that he will "drink it anew in the kingdom of God." Our hopes are not anchored permanently to the past or to the present but are free to reach out to eternity (cf. Ecclesiastes 3:11). Through his death Christians have the certain hope of eternal life.

Our participation in Communion challenges us to look inward. As we come together at his table, our thoughts are turned to our own failures. In those few moments we have the opportunity to examine our lives and compare them to the biblical standards. To that point, Paul writes, "A man ought to examine himself," before eating the bread and drinking of the cup (1 Corinthians 11:28). Paul goes on to warn of the dire consequences that will result when one does not conduct this self-examination.

Finally, the Lord's Supper is a look outward. The message of Christianity is a message for all humanity (Matthew 28:19, 20). In a way, Communion is this gospel message in a capsule form. Just as the Passover celebration had an important meaning to convey to future generations (Exodus 12:25-27), so also our observance of the Lord's Supper proclaims "the Lord's death until he comes" (1 Corinthians 11:26).

Discovery Learning

This page contains an alternative lesson plan emphasizing learning activities. Classes desiring such student involvement will find these suggestions helpful. The next page is a reproducible activity page to further enhance discovery learning.

LEARNING GOALS

After participating in this lesson, each student will be able to:

1. Describe the event that became the occasion for the institution of the Lord's Supper.

2. Explain the significance of the Lord's Supper both for the disciples and for Christians today.

3. Suggest some meditation thoughts that can help a participant have a more meaningful experience at the Lord's table.

INTO THE LESSON

As your students arrive today, put them in groups of four. Have the following materials ready (or you can use the student books for this activity): letter size paper, pens or pencils, markers, envelopes.

Say, "Today I want you to design an invitation to a class dinner. Determine the menu and the guest list. Make a list of what you will need for decorating the room."

Encourage class members to plan a meal that will be remembered by all. The invitation should include date and time, menu, and keynote speaker and subject (if any). This activity should take no more than six to eight minutes.

Call the class together by saying, "Keep your invitations and plans for later in the session. Today we are studying how Jesus prepared for and celebrated the Passover and then instituted the 'Lord's Supper.' As we study, think about how he has invited all his followers to his table."

INTO THE WORD

Use the commentary's Lesson Background to prepare a brief introduction of the events leading up to today's text.

Copy the following matching list for each student, putting the numbered column on the left and the lettered column on the right. Be sure each person has a Bible and a copy of the Scriptures. (This matching activity also appears in *NIV® Bible Student.*) Correct answers are: 1-d; 2-e; 3-g; 4-a; 5-c; 6-f; 7-b.

___ 1. Disciples wonder where Passover will be eaten.

___ 2. Jesus gives disciples specific instructions for preparation.

___ 3. The disciples find things as Jesus had told them.

___ 4. Jesus and the twelve eat the Passover.

___ 5. Jesus predicts his betrayal.

___ 6. Jesus institutes the Lord's Supper.

___ 7. The disciples sing a hymn and leave.

a. Mark 14:18a   e. Mark 14:13-15
b. Mark 14:26   f. Mark 14:22-25
c. Mark 14:18b-21   g. Mark 14:16
d. Mark 14:12

Give your class approximately five minutes to complete this activity. Review the correct answers and discuss the events. The text commentary contains helpful materials.

Emphasize to your class members the significance of the Lord's Supper for today by using the material in the commentary Conclusion (page 284) and the following questions:

How does the Lord's Supper help us to look backward?

How does the Lord's Supper help us to look forward?

How does the Lord's Supper help us to look inward? (See also 1 Corinthians 11:28.)

How does the Lord's Supper help us to look outward? (See also 1 Corinthians 11:26.)

From our text today, why did Jesus institute the supper? (*To solemnize the fact that the disciples were entering a covenant with Jesus.*)

INTO LIFE

Refer to the introductory exercise (or to the student book). Each student will complete an invitation to the Lord's Supper, a first-century guest list, and a twenty-first-century guest list. Help each student to realize that every Christian is invited to the Lord's table.

Use the reproducible page that follows to stimulate responses for the question: "How can a worship assembly be planned to emphasize the Lord's supper and the events of Jesus' death that it commemorates?"

Students may work in pairs as they plan. Ask volunteers to read elements of their finished version. Possibly class ideas can be passed along to those who plan your congregation's worship assemblies.

Close class with prayer and an appropriate hymn or song, perhaps one suggested in the planning for a worship assembly.

Plan a Worship Service

In today's text Jesus is shown making specific preparations for the Passover and then instituting the Lord's Supper. In the space below write a worship service plan emphasizing the Lord's Supper. Select elements and write them in the appropriate boxes.

HYMNS AND SONGS	SCRIPTURES TO BE READ

ELEMENTS OF PRAYERS	MEDITATIVE REMARKS

Now, how do you see the elements you have chosen becoming a unified time of worship, a time that truly reminds participants of the covenant Christians have entered into with Christ?

JESUS DIES AND LIVES AGAIN

LESSON 8

WHY TEACH THIS LESSON?

At some time or other, most of your learners have experienced the frustration of dealing with the expectations that other people have for their lives. Well-meaning friends and relatives can be very opinionated when it comes to how someone should dress, what career path they ought to choose, or which potential mate is right (or wrong). As they consider the pressure they have felt from such expectations, ask them to imagine the far-greater pressure Jesus was under—pressure to meet expectations to be the type of Messiah people thought he ought to be.

But God did not (and will not) change his plans. Even as Jesus was dying on the cross, he carried out his Father's plans right to the end—right to victory! Today's lesson will remind your learners that Jesus' obedience, even to death (Philippians 2:8), is what allows them to have the ultimate victory as well.

INTRODUCTION

A. "BOUGHT FOR ALL TIME"

Many years ago, a German nobleman determined to build a tomb that would stand against the ravages of time. Workmen fashioned the structure from huge blocks of granite that interlocked in such a way that once set in place they were almost impossible to move. When the nobleman died, his body was sealed in the tomb with this inscription on the outside: "This grave, bought for all time, must never be opened."

Within a few years a seed from a nearby tree fell into a small crevice between two of the stones. With the help of rain and sunshine, the seed germinated and sent its rootlets down into the microscopic cracks between the stones. The years passed and the seedling continued to grow. This growth, along with the freezing and thawing, eroded the granite and began to force apart the huge blocks. Eventually a large tree grew up through the middle of the tomb.

Those who thought that killing Jesus and placing him in a stone tomb "bought for all time" would eliminate him permanently didn't count on the power of God. If God, working through the forces of nature, could destroy a tomb of granite, what chance did a man-made tomb have of containing the body of Jesus against a far greater power? It is Jesus' *empty* tomb that is "bought for all time"!

B. LESSON BACKGROUND

When the meal in the upper room had been concluded, Jesus and his disciples sang a hymn and went out to the Garden of Gethsemane on the western slope of the Mount of Olives (Mark 14:26). Jesus, seeking privacy, left the disciples and went deeper into the garden. There he fervently poured out his heart in prayer to the Father: "Take this cup from me. Yet not what I will, but what you will" (14:36).

DEVOTIONAL READING:
JOHN 20:11-18
BACKGROUND SCRIPTURE:
MARK 15:1–16:8
PRINTED TEXT:
MARK 15:21-25, 33-37; 16:1-8

LESSON AIMS

After participating in this lesson, each student will be able to:

1. Cite the significant details concerning Jesus' crucifixion and resurrection.

2. Tell why the crucifixion and resurrection are vital to the Christian faith.

3. Prepare an answer for someone who might deny the resurrection.

Apr
20

KEY VERSE

"Don't be alarmed," he said. "You are looking for Jesus the Nazarene, who was crucified. He has risen! He is not here. See the place where they laid him."
— Mark 16:6

Shortly afterward, the forces of the religious leaders, led by Judas, seized Jesus. As Jesus was led away for trial, the disciples fled. In a series of trials before the Sanhedrin, Herod Antipas, and Pilate, Jesus was condemned to die on the cross. Today's lesson begins at this point.

I. JESUS' CRUCIFIXION (MARK 15:21-25)

A. THE HEAVINESS OF THE CROSS (v. 21)

21. A certain man from Cyrene, Simon, the father of Alexander and Rufus, was passing by on his way in from the country, and they forced him to carry the cross.

Crucifixions and other methods of capital punishment are conducted outside the city walls (cf. Leviticus 24:14; Numbers 15:35, 36; 1 Kings 21:13; Acts 7:58; Hebrews 13:12, 13). As Jesus is led to the place of the crucifixion (supposedly along the *Via Dolorosa*—the "Way of Sorrow"), he is *forced* to *carry* his own *cross* (John 19:17).

But Jesus has gone sleepless from the night before, probably has been denied food, and has been brutally tortured (Mark 15:16-20). It is little wonder that the weight of the cross becomes more than he can bear. Thus a certain *Simon*, from the province of *Cyrene*, is compelled to carry the cross as he comes into the city. Since Mark mentions this *man* by name along with the fact that he is *the father of Alexander and Rufus*, some propose that Simon is the father of the Rufus mentioned in Romans 16:13.

WHAT DO YOU THINK?

If Simon of Cyrene was the father of the Rufus mentioned in Romans 16:13, how much influence do you think carrying Jesus' cross had on Simon to lead him to become a Christian? Why? How can Christians today be good witnesses even when experiencing extreme circumstances?

B. THE PLACE OF THE SKULL (v. 22)

22. They brought Jesus to the place called Golgotha (which means The Place of the Skull).

Mark interprets the Aramaic term *Golgotha* for his Greek-speaking readers. Tourists today are shown a little mound north of Jerusalem's walls that does indeed resemble a *skull*. Another tradition holds that the crucifixion occurred near the modern site of the Church of the Holy Sepulchre. This *place* was near the city in the first century (John 19:20), but is located inside the city walls today. Of course, there is no way of knowing with certainty whether either of these spots is the actual location of the crucifixion.

C. THE ACTIVITIES OF THE SOLDIERS (vv. 23-25)

23. Then they offered him wine mixed with myrrh, but he did not take it.

Myrrh is a gum resin from trees that grow in Arabia and eastern Africa. It is highly prized as a perfume, as an embalming agent (cf. Matthew 2:11; John 19:39), and as a medicine. Some students think it was for this medicinal value that the soldiers offer the drink to Jesus—that it has some narcotic effect that will relieve some of Jesus' pain. They believe Jesus refuses it because he has committed himself to drink the full measure of the cup of suffering and he wants to have a clear mind when he speaks his last words.

Other students note, however, that myrrh is very bitter in taste. *Wine mixed with myrrh*, they say, would be undrinkable. The soldiers know that this mixture is too bitter to drink; they are merely adding to Jesus' torture by offering it (cf. Psalm 69:20, 21). We cannot say for certain which view is correct. However, it does seem more in keeping with the soldiers' hardened character that they would tease their victims with undrinkable wine than offer pain-relieving medicine.

24. And they crucified him. Dividing up his clothes, they cast lots to see what each would get.

To be *crucified* means to be either tied or nailed to a crossbeam, which is then fastened to an upright support. (In Jesus' case, he was nailed; see John 20:25.) In the Roman Empire, crucifixion is usually reserved for slaves or those who have committed the most heinous crimes. It is especially feared because it prolongs for hours (or even days) the agony of death, which eventually comes by exposure, infection, and/or asphyxiation. As in the case of those who are executed alongside Jesus, measures such as breaking the victim's legs are sometimes used to hasten death (cf. John 19:32).

The soldiers assigned to the execution are hardened to suffering. Once the condemned prisoners are on the crosses, the soldiers' interest turns to what personal gain they can get. And so *they cast lots*—using something like dice—to divide Jesus' meager earthly possessions among themselves. Jesus may have had an inner garment, an outer robe or tunic, a belt or sash, sandals, and perhaps a headpiece. This is a fulfillment of Psalm 22:18.

25. It was the third hour when they crucified him.

The ancient Jews count their days from sunrise to sunrise. Under this system, *the third hour* would be about 9:00 A.M. But John 19:14 indicates that the trial is still in progress at "the sixth hour." How could Jesus have been crucified at the "third" hour if the trial lasted past the "sixth" hour? There is more than one possible solution to this puzzle. One well-known suggestion holds that John, addressing a Roman audience, used a different means of counting time. In certain instances, the Romans count time from midnight rather than sunrise. Thus, John's "sixth hour" was 6:00 A.M., three hours before the crucifixion.

II. JESUS ON THE CROSS (MARK 15:33-37)

A. THE DARKNESS OF JUDGMENT (v. 33)

33. At the sixth hour darkness came over the whole land until the ninth hour.

The *darkness* that comes *over the whole land* at *the sixth hour* (noon) cannot be a normal eclipse. The moon is full during the Passover period. We can only conclude that this is a tremendous miracle, visible to thousands of people.

No doubt the darkness at midday strikes fear in the hearts of those watching the crucifixion. During this time, the veil in the temple is torn in two from top to bottom, the earth shakes, many godly people rise from their graves, and a pagan Roman centurion confesses that Jesus is indeed "the Son of God" (Matthew 27:51-54).

HISTORY'S DARKEST DAY

At 8:32 A.M. on May 18, 1980, volcanologist David A. Johnston yelled his last words as he radioed his colleagues: "Vancouver, Vancouver, this is it!" A fiery-hot cloud of gas was rolling toward him at three hundred miles per hour. Mount Saint Helens had just "blown its top." Johnston was camped five miles from the peak when the mountain erupted with the destructive force of a twenty-four-megaton nuclear bomb. Nearly four billion cubic yards of earth were blown off the north face of the mountain. Enough trees to build two hundred thousand homes were burned instantaneously by the 660-degree wind.

Some of the ash that roiled thousands of feet into the air came down as far away as Oklahoma. Closer to the scene, it darkened the earth as if it were night. Jay Thomas was a logger working in the forest more than twenty miles from the mountain that morning. He said, "It got quiet, eerie quiet—not a bird chirping, a frog croaking. And it got dark, midnight dark."

The afternoon Christ died must have been something like that: the silence of creation interrupted only by the terrified screams of people wondering if the end of their world had come. And the darkness that day—what an awesome symbol of God's judgment on sin! How terrifying the silence and blackness must have been when God bent creation to his will on the darkest day in human history!—C. R. B.

WHAT DO YOU THINK?

The soldiers' interest in the crucifixion was selfish: what could they get out of it? Who today displays an interest only in personal gain even in the midst of spiritually significant events? What can we do to change their focus?

HOW TO SAY IT

Aramaic. AIR-uh-**MAY**-ik.
Arimathea. AIR-uh-muh-**THEE**-uh.
Cyrene. Sigh-**REE**-nee.
Elijah. Ee-**LYE**-juh.
Eloi, Eloi, lama sabachthani (Aramaic). Ee-**LO**-eye, Ee-**LO**-eye, LAH-mah suh-**BACK**-thuh-nee.
Gethsemane. Geth-**SEM**-uh-nee.
Golgotha. **GAHL**-guh-thuh.
Herod Antipas. **HAIR**-ud **AN**-tih-pus.
Myrrh. mur.
Renaissance. REH-nuh-**SONTS**.
Sanhedrin. SAN-huh-drun or San-**HEED**-run.
sepulchre. **SEP**-ul-kur.
Via Dolorosa. **VYE**-uh (or VEE-uh) DOE-luh-**ROW**-suh.

WHAT DO YOU THINK?

Even as death arrived, Jesus still was able to utter a victory cry. Have you ever known some follower of Jesus who could see the "big picture" and have confidence of God's victory even in the face of what may have looked like defeat? How does one develop such overcoming faith?

B. THE CRY OF DESOLATION (vv. 34-36)

34. And at the ninth hour Jesus cried out in a loud voice, "Eloi, Eloi, lama sabachthani?"—which means, "My God, my God, why have you forsaken me?"

At the ninth hour, or about 3:00 P.M., Jesus raises his voice in a dramatic cry of desolation. The Aramaic words that Mark interprets for his readers come from the first part of Psalm 22:1.

This is one of the most difficult of all of Jesus' sayings. At first glance it may seem that the "human part" of Jesus is being critical of God because God has forsaken him. We are not capable with our mere human minds to comprehend fully how the human and the divine could be combined in the Christ. There seemed to be a struggle between Jesus' human and divine parts as he prayed in the Garden of Gethsemane—a struggle that reaches its climax on the cross.

Jesus' ordeal is physically painful beyond imagination. But the agony of bearing the weight of the sins of all humanity must be even more extreme than the physical torture. Suspended between Heaven and earth, he takes on the curse of God for our sake (Galatians 3:13). And yet, God is still present. If we read to the end of Psalm 22, we find the psalmist reaffirms God's presence and God's victory in his life. This, too, is prophetic of Jesus' experience on the cross.

35. When some of those standing near heard this, they said, "Listen, he's calling Elijah."

Because of his parched throat and tongue, Jesus may not be able to speak clearly. Apparently some people take *Eloi* for *Elijah*. Jewish tradition holds that Elijah will return someday to save his nation, and the people seem to make this connection. Malachi 4:5, 6 does predict the return of Elijah as a forerunner of the "great and dreadful day of the Lord," a prediction fulfilled in the ministry of John the Baptist (Matthew 17:10-13).

36. One man ran, filled a sponge with wine vinegar, put it on a stick, and offered it to Jesus to drink. "Now leave him alone. Let's see if Elijah comes to take him down," he said.

Jesus, suffering shock and the loss of blood, is undoubtedly quite thirsty. But whether this offer of a *drink* is an act of mercy or an act of mockery is hard to say. The *vinegar* mentioned here is a cheap, sour *wine* often drunk by laborers and foot soldiers. As with Mark 15:23 above, there is a tie-in to Psalm 69:21. The fact that the *sponge* soaked in wine has to be put *on a stick* in order for it to reach his mouth indicates that the cross that suspends him is some height above the ground.

If the offer of this drink is designed to prolong Jesus' life—and his agony—then it is not an act of mercy. With a morbid curiosity, the enemies of Christ want to wait and see if Elijah will come *to take him down* from the cross.

C. THE DEATH OF JESUS (v. 37)

37. With a loud cry, Jesus breathed his last.

Jesus still has enough strength to cry *with a loud cry.* Mark does not tell us the words he speaks, but Luke informs us that he says, "Father, into your hands I commit my spirit" (23:46). John tells us that just after he tastes the wine, he also utters, "It is finished" (19:30). These may have been his very last words. Jesus has now died as "a ransom for many" (Mark 10:45).

III. THE EMPTY TOMB (MARK 16:1-8)

A. THE WOMEN (vv. 1-4)

1, 2. When the Sabbath was over, Mary Magdalene, Mary the mother of James, and Salome bought spices so that they might go to anoint Jesus' body. Very early on the first day of the week, just after sunrise, they were on their way to the tomb. . . .

Joseph of Arimathea, "a prominent member of the Council" and follower of Jesus, has secured permission from Pilate to bury the body of Jesus (Mark 15:43). The burial place is a *tomb* cut out of rock (Mark 15:46), probably a tomb that Joseph has prepared for himself and members of his family. The tomb is conveniently close by (John 19:41), so they are able to bury Jesus before *the Sabbath* begins (Mark 15:42). After Jesus' burial, a large stone is rolled across the mouth of the tomb, a common practice in that day (15:46).

Some of the women followers of Jesus watched as Joseph and Nicodemus buried Jesus, so they know where the tomb is located (15:47; John 19:38-42). Early Sunday morning, after the Sabbath has past and there is enough sunlight to find their way in the retreating darkness (John 20:1), several women go to the tomb with *spices* to complete the burial process.

3. . . . and they asked each other, "Who will roll the stone away from the entrance of the tomb?"

As the women travel to *the tomb* with the sunlight just making its way over the horizon, it occurs to them that they have a problem. How will they be able to move *the stone* that covers the mouth of the tomb? Such a stone is usually quite large, round in shape, and resting in a channel. To move it will require several people equipped with poles for levers. The women also apparently do not know that Roman soldiers have been stationed at the tomb to guard it (Matthew 27:62-66).

4. But when they looked up, they saw that the stone, which was very large, had been rolled away.

As it turns out, however, they have no need to worry! There has been a "great earthquake" (Matthew 28:2) and an angel of the Lord has *rolled* the stone *away*.

B. THE ANGEL (vv. 5-8)

5. As they entered the tomb, they saw a young man dressed in a white robe sitting on the right side, and they were alarmed.

The entrance of a tomb in this era usually opens into a central room, making the tomb large enough to walk into. Bodies are placed in niches or shelves cut into the walls of this room. Several bodies—perhaps a whole family—can thus be buried in one tomb.

When they enter the tomb, the women receive a shock. The body of Jesus is missing, and *a young man dressed in a white robe* is sitting *on the right side* where the body formerly had been. Matthew tells us that he was an angel and that his "appearance was like lightning" (28:3-5). Luke informs us that there are two angels (24:4); Matthew and Mark apparently mention only the one who speaks.

6. "Don't be alarmed," he said. "You are looking for Jesus the Nazarene, who was crucified. He has risen! He is not here. See the place where they laid him.

It should come as no surprise that the women are frightened—so frightened that they bow their faces to the ground (Luke 24:5). But the angel quickly assures them that they have nothing to fear and gives them the good news that Jesus has *risen*. We can only imagine their conflicting emotions as they experience fear one moment and then unbelievably good news the next.

Visual for lesson 8. This poster is meant to spark some discussion. Ask, "How is the presence of Christ evident in our homes—and in our lives?"

A NEW REALITY

Some years ago, James Burke wrote a book entitled *The Day the Universe Changed*. In it he proposed that when our ideas about reality change, reality itself changes. Whether or not his thesis is true, Burke makes a case for the fact that the late Middle Ages was one of those critical points in history at which significant change took place in the way we understand the physical world about us. Because of the great minds of the Renaissance, who broke free from medieval notions, we

PRAYER

O Holy God, we thank you for sending your Son to die for our sins, unworthy though we are. We further thank you for the resurrection that offers us the hope we have for eternal life. In the name of the resurrected Lord we pray, amen.

WHAT DO YOU THINK?

What evidence of Jesus' resurrection in the first eight verses of Mark 16 give you confidence that the resurrection account is authentic and not manufactured?

WHAT DO YOU THINK?

The reality of Jesus' crucifixion and resurrection is absolutely essential to the Christian faith. How can we convince a "postmodern" culture, which values personal experience, of this great truth?

live in a world governed by physical laws rather than the world of ancient times in which superstition reigned supreme.

The day Jesus rose from the dead was a day unlike any other before or since. Because of what happened that day, there is a new reality in the universe. The power of Satan had been in control of human life from the time of the first sin, which we read about in Genesis 3. On the day of the crucifixion, Satan seemed to have taken complete control. Yet three days later that power was broken, and the world has been different ever since. The angel's words, "He has risen! He is not here," changed our way of looking at the world. Now the power of God is at work, redeeming and renewing the creation in anticipation of the day when Christ comes again to make all things new. It really is a new world since Christ arose! —C. R. B.

7. "But go, tell his disciples and Peter, 'He is going ahead of you into Galilee. There you will see him, just as he told you.'"

When God sends an angel to deliver a message to a person, that message is important. This case is certainly no exception. The women have seen the empty tomb and now it is their responsibility to carry that word to the *disciples*. There are good reasons for Jesus to meet his followers in *Galilee*. First of all, this fulfills a prophecy Jesus made before his death (see Mark 14:28). Further, the disciples will be safer there in case Jesus' enemies seek to follow up his killing by persecuting his followers. We know that Jesus does indeed visit Galilee after his resurrection (see John 21:1), but most of his recorded appearances are in and around Jerusalem.

8. Trembling and bewildered, the women went out and fled from the tomb. They said nothing to anyone, because they were afraid.

Torn between fear and hope, the women do not linger to discuss or debate what they have experienced. They do not stop to talk to anyone else as they hurry to find the disciples and report what they have witnessed. But Matthew tells us that Jesus meets them along the way. As they hold him by the feet and worship him, he repeats the instructions they had received from the angel at the tomb (Matthew 28:9, 10).

CONCLUSION

Mark 15:31 and 32 tell how the chief priests and the scribes mocked Jesus, saying, "He saved others . . . but he can't save himself!" They challenged him to come down from the cross—then they would believe in him. In the wilderness, Satan had challenged Jesus to perform miracles to prove that he was indeed the Son of God (Matthew 4:1-11). Even though the forty days in the wilderness left him hungry and weakened, Jesus consistently resisted the temptations to play by Satan's rules.

Now Jesus' enemies want him to play by their rules. They certainly have had every opportunity to know of his miraculous power. Surely some of them have witnessed at least a few of these miracles. But because Jesus doesn't meet their expectations of who they think the Messiah ought to be, they are not convinced that Jesus is the divine Son of God. Yet Jesus knew very well that even if he came down from the cross, they would still find a way to reject him. More importantly, coming down from the cross would thwart his very reason for coming to earth—to give his life as a ransom for our sins (Mark 10:45).

Modern skeptics are much like these religious leaders. God has ensured that sufficient evidence exists to establish the truth of Jesus' identity and the resurrection. When Jesus' enemies rejected his claims and that evidence, they eventually paid a terrible (eternal) price for their decision. In the same way, those today who reject Jesus' claims face an eternity of shame and contempt (Daniel 12:2).

Discovery Learning

This page contains an alternative lesson plan emphasizing learning activities. Classes desiring such student involvement will find these suggestions helpful. The next page is a reproducible activity page to further enhance discovery learning.

LEARNING GOALS

After participating in this lesson, each student will be able to:

1. Cite the significant details concerning Jesus' crucifixion and resurrection.

2. Tell why the crucifixion and resurrection are vital to the Christian faith.

3. Prepare an answer for someone who might deny the resurrection.

INTO THE LESSON

In the ancient world, roads were often marked by milestones, similar to the mile markers on federal interstate highways. They were used so the traveler could be aware of his direction and know where he was. Distribute to your class a piece of paper with several "milestones" on it. They can look like small stones or tablets. (This activity is in *NIV® Bible Student.*)

Students are to write on the "milestones" three or four significant events in their lives that help define who they are today. These events could be graduations, conversion to Christ, marriage, birth of children, career moves, or the like. They should write where they were and who observed the event.

In pairs, the students will share their milestones. Partners may ask questions for clarification. Call the class together and ask for two or three volunteers to share several of their significant milestones. Be sure to ask each one who their "witnesses" were.

Say, "When significant life-changing events happen in our lives, it is important that we have others who can corroborate the facts and enjoy them with us or comfort us in them. Most milestone events are very public and involve family, friends, and others. Today, as we study the greatest life-changing event ever, we will become aware of how many witnessed it."

INTO THE WORD

To set the stage and tie this week's lesson to last week, use the "Lesson Background" in a brief lecture.

Form groups of six. More than one group can work on an assignment.

Option 1. Group One will survey the relevant Bible texts to list five to seven details about the crucifixion. Write the following Scripture references on a chalkboard where all can see them: Matthew 27:11-61; Mark 15:2-47; Luke 23:1-56; John 18:28; 19:42. (This activity is in the student book.)

Group Two will survey the relevant Bible texts to list five to seven details about the resurrection. Write the following Scripture references on a board or individual sheets of paper: Matthew 28:2-20; Mark 16:1-20, Luke 24:1-53; John 20:1-31. (These are also in the student book.)

Option 2. Use the reproducible activity "Happy Ending" from the next page so that the whole class works together. When the "central truth" is identified, write it boldly where all can see it. (*He has risen.*)

Ask each group to report its conclusions. Compile a master list on a poster or chalkboard. Be prepared to clear up any misunderstandings by using the teacher commentary. Remind the class of how many witnessed the events. You may also refer to Acts 1:1-18 and 1 Corinthians 15:6, 7.

INTO LIFE

BRAINSTORM. Ask each group to brainstorm reasons why the crucifixion and resurrection are vital truths for the Christian faith. Each group should appoint a secretary to record the results. To discuss all the groups' suggestions, ask one of the students to record the answers on a large poster. Have each group call out one of their reasons. Go around the groups until all of the reasons are given. Keep this list up for the remainder of the class; it can be useful in following activities. Distribute copies of the "I Believe" section of the reproducible page and encourage students to write their own lists of reasons and to keep them.

STATEMENT OF FAITH. Keep the students in their small groups and ask each group to create a list of the most often used reasons for not believing in the resurrection of Jesus. This list might include, "It had never happened before," or, "He wasn't really dead." Then ask them to discuss why they do believe in the resurrection.

After a brief discussion, have each student write the name of one friend with whom they need to share the truth of the resurrection. Each person will write a one-paragraph defense of the resurrection using facts from today's study. (This activity is in the student book.)

Close with a prayer for boldness to confront those who deny the resurrection and strength to endure any opposition that arises.

Happy Ending

Though Jesus' followers were deeply saddened by the events around the crucifixion, one fact brought them to their senses and later into the streets. Fill in the blanks from Mark 15, 16 using the statements at the bottom. Check the letters in the highlighted column for our central truth.

1. ____ ____ ____ ____ ____ ____

2. ____ ____ ____ ____ ____

3. ____ ____ ____ ____ ____ ____

4. ____ ____ ____ ____ ____ ____

5. ____ ____ ____ ____ ____ ____

6. ____ ____ ____ ____ ____

7. ____ ____ ____ ____ ____

8. ____ ____ ____ ____ ____ ____

9. ____ ____ ____ ____ ____ ____

10. ____ ____ ____ ____ ____ ____

1. Simon was the ____ of Alexander and Rufus. (Mark 15:21)
2. Jesus was offered ____ to drink. (Mark 15:23)
3. They cast lots for his ____. (Mark 15:24)
4. At the sixth hour ____ came over the land. (Mark 15:33)
5. Jesus' words included "why have you ____ me?" (Mark 15:34)
6. Jesus made a loud ____ before he died. (Mark 15:37)
7. The women bought ____ to anoint Jesus' body. (Mark 16:1)
8. In order to enter the tomb the ____ must be rolled away. (Mark 16:3)
9. The young man in the tomb was ____ in a white robe. (Mark 16:5)
10. Because of their fear, the women said ____ to anyone. (Mark 16:8)

The fact that drives our message is _____ _____ _____!

I Believe

I believe in the resurrection of Christ for the following reasons:

FAITH CONQUERS FEAR

LESSON 9

WHY TEACH THIS LESSON?

When we step on an elevator, are we exercising faith? Of course, we are. Since we cannot see the future, we don't know with absolute certainty that the elevator will take us safely to the floor we want. But in faith we use elevators anyway because we know they have a good safety record.

But what if they didn't? What if more elevators plummeted to the basement than rose to the next floor? Who would get on one? Now suppose for some reason you must. The building is on fire; the stairway is blocked. The elevator is your only hope. Your condition is hopeless!

Your learners have been in tight spots on occasion. Perhaps their situation was not so hopeless as our elevator scenario, but desperate nonetheless. In that they can identify with two characters in today's text. The sick woman and Jairus had no hope. But like a firefighter on a rescue crane, Jesus gave them hope. He rescued them from their hopeless condition. He will give your learners hope, too!

INTRODUCTION

A. THE ACTION GOSPEL

All of our lessons this quarter have been from the Gospel of Mark. For the first five weeks we studied the opening chapters. Then for the resurrection season we studied the closing chapters, celebrating again the heart of the great good news: the King's entry into Jerusalem and his death and resurrection. Now we return to the central section of the Gospel record and the earlier days of Christ's ministry.

All along the way we are struck again by Mark's crisp style. his record doesn't start with the birth or early life of Jesus. It begins when Jesus started his ministry, when he began to "do" things. The Gospel of Luke, according to the opening verses of the book of Acts (Luke's other correspondence), reports what Jesus began to do and teach. Matthew spent a lot of time on the teaching part. John gives us his uniquely personal perspective on who Jesus was, as only "the disciple whom Jesus loved" might have understood. Mark majors on the "do." He launches right in to various encounters and healings after a very brief introduction.

It may be pure imagination, but some of us have wondered if Mark's approach had to do with his youthfulness. In the early years of school, it is hard to write a long paper, hard to think of "what else" there might be to say. Many of us, when we began to preach, finished a sermon in five minutes, and stretched it into ten by repeating ourselves—and we had gone from Genesis to Revelation! How much more could there be to say? Mark was younger than the others who presented Gospel records. Perhaps he listened to Peter's reports—it is generally believed that Mark recorded the apostle Peter's perspective on Jesus' life and teaching—pared away some of Peter's typical enthusiasm and tendency to talk, and acted rather like Sgt. Joe Friday of the old TV show *Dragnet*, who wanted "just the facts, Ma'am."

So Mark didn't waste any time getting to the heart of the matter. Jesus made a difference everywhere he went. Just watch what he did with people who were sick and dying. In the early chapters of Mark we see numerous encounters with

DEVOTIONAL READING:
HEBREWS 11:1-6

BACKGROUND SCRIPTURE:
MARK 5:21-43

PRINTED TEXT:
MARK 5:22-36, 41, 42

LESSON AIMS

After participating in this lesson, each student will be able to:

1. Recall the details of Jesus' healing of the woman with the bleeding problem and of Jairus's daughter.

2. Compare the anxiety of Jairus and the woman with the fears and uncertainties people bring to Jesus today.

3. In faith, give a specific fear to Jesus and allow him to give the victory.

Apr
27

KEY VERSE

Jesus told the synagogue ruler, "Don't be afraid; just believe."

— Mark 5:36

Jesus in which people were healed, but that just seems to scratch the surface. Early in the record the evangelist reports, "And Jesus healed many who had various diseases. He also drove out many demons" (Mark 1:34).

LESSON BACKGROUND

Jesus conducted much of the early part of his ministry around the Sea of Galilee. Specifically, much of the ministry was on the north end, in and around the village of Capernaum (Peter's hometown). And Jesus had begun to teach his lessons about life and about the kingdom of God in the rural areas and towns along the western side of the sea. It didn't take long for the crowds to follow him everywhere. His teaching was pointed. His spirit was magnetic. And having already healed so many people, his reputation had spread far and wide.

Jesus was building up his team of apostles, who gave up their occupations to follow him. He also was attracting a regular following of those who didn't believe in him and who wanted to find reasons to eliminate him. Everything he did was watched—either with loving appreciation or with suspicion.

In search of a little rest, and maybe in search of a new opportunity, Jesus had crossed to the eastern shore of the sea. There he cured a demon-possessed man who had been terrorizing the whole community. As a result, Jesus made some farmers who had lost their pigs very unhappy (Mark 5:2-17; see lesson 3). After certain people told Jesus that he was no longer welcome there, Jesus crossed back over into familiar territory. The news that he was coming had arrived ahead of him, and the crowds were waiting (Mark 5:21).

I. EXPECTANT FAITH (MARK 5:22-24)

A. A HUMBLE RULER (v. 22)

22. Then one of the synagogue rulers, named Jairus, came there. Seeing Jesus, he fell at his feet.

Jairus, as a synagogue ruler, is in a position of great influence (cf. Acts 13:15). Although he is not a priest, he is a religious leader—surely respected and counted on. But he is not arrogant or self-important to the point that he cannot go for help when he needs it. So he bows in respect before Jesus. Many of his contemporaries see the power of Jesus as a threat. Jairus sees the power of Jesus as a great hope, a potential blessing. It is evident that to him truth and life are more important than position and tradition. When your child is at the point of death, you go for genuine help. This is no time to posture or to play religious games.

B. A DYING CHILD (v. 23)

23. . . . and pleaded earnestly with him, "My little daughter is dying. Please come and put your hands on her so that she will be healed and live."

Clearly, Jairus has heard about Jesus. It is also clear that Jairus believes in Jesus' power to heal. Jairus is unlike some others in his position who are following Jesus as critics—watching for a lapse in his popularity or hoping that he will make a big mistake. Had Jairus been in need of healing himself, he might not have gone to the Master. Such an action surely would draw the ire of his fellow authorities. But when it is his little daughter, there is no hesitation. It is time for help, time for action. And he believes that Jesus can heal.

Jairus wants Jesus to touch his daughter. Ah! The healing power of touch! With Jesus it is something enormous. With us touch counts, too. It counts for a lot. Watch the eyes of the next person that you lovingly, respectfully touch.

And one teacher really hit a piece of truth squarely on the head when he said, "When Jesus is allowed to lay his hand on a family, it lives." That's a thought to

WHAT DO YOU THINK?

The critical illness of a child or other loved one has quite an impact on a person. How could such an illness change one's perspective of Jesus today? How can we enter the open door that such an occasion may provide?

give a lot of attention. Are the hand of Jesus, the heart of Jesus, and the manner of Jesus on your family?

C. THE RESPONSIVE CHRIST (v. 24)

24. So Jesus went with him.
 A large crowd followed and pressed around him.

Probably some of the friends of Jairus are certain that the Master will not go *with him*. But the great physician makes house calls. And, as usual, everywhere he goes a mob *followed*. It isn't only curiosity. It isn't always that they have someone who needs to be healed. They want to be part of the good things that are happening.

You may have heard that the chickens follow the one who is plowing up the worms. If your church is a place where good things are happening, where lives are being changed, where spiritual nourishment is being offered, then all kinds of people will want to take part.

II. EXCITED FAITH (MARK 5:25-33)

A. A SUFFERING WOMAN (vv. 25, 26)

25, 26. And a woman was there who had been subject to bleeding for twelve years. She had suffered a great deal under the care of many doctors and had spent all she had, yet instead of getting better she grew worse.

Along the way to Jairus's house, another need presents itself. But the need of this *woman* is not just medical. Her chronic *bleeding* has made her ceremonially "unclean" *for twelve years* (cf. Leviticus 15:25-33). This means she is ostracized from Jewish society, much like a leper. She is not supposed to be here with the crowd, since touching other people will make them "unclean" as well. If the bleeding is from her womb, which is likely, then she is probably barren as well—an added stigma for a woman in her day.

This woman has tried everything—doctor after doctor. But after the money is gone she is *worse*, not better. She is also desperate.

B. A HOPEFUL TOUCH (vv. 27, 28)

27, 28. When she heard about Jesus, she came up behind him in the crowd and touched his cloak, because she thought, "If I just touch his clothes, I will be healed."

Being ritually unclean, this woman cannot approach Jesus directly. Thus she attempts to slip in unnoticed. This is more than "I'll try just one more thing." She has heard of Jesus. She believes in his power. He doesn't even have to speak to her, see her, or touch her. She is confident that, if she can just *touch* him, or even the corner of *his clothes*, her hemorrhage will stop.

C. A POWER TRANSFER (vv. 29-33)

29. Immediately her bleeding stopped and she felt in her body that she was freed from her suffering.

Right away this woman can feel that she has been healed! (If you had hemorrhaged for a dozen years, you would know right away when it *stopped*, too.) If she expected Jesus' garment to have some magical power, then she was wrong about that. But she was absolutely right to believe. In a moment Jesus will clear up any possible misconception and make it clear that her faith in him has worked the healing. She has been healed because she believed in him. She expected to be healed, and she was. Just that quickly!

30. At once Jesus realized that power had gone out from him. He turned around in the crowd and asked, "Who touched my clothes?"

WHAT DO YOU THINK?

In the crowds that followed Jesus, there were some who were devoted disciples. Others were looking for entertainment—wanting to see what miracle Jesus would do next. Others were critics, looking for a way to throw cold water on the enthusiasm Jesus generated. How are the same three groups seen in the attendance of a vibrant church? What should we do about it?

WHAT DO YOU THINK?

Like the bleeding woman, many people have obstacles to overcome in trying to reach out to Jesus. What are some of them, and how can we eliminate such barriers?

HOW TO SAY IT

Capernaum. Kuh-PER-nay-um.
centurion. sen-TURE-ee-un.
Galilee. GAL-uh-lee.
Jairus. JYE-rus or JAY-ih-rus.
Nain. Nane.
nostrums. NAHS-trumz.
psychosomatic. SIGH-koe-suh-
  MA-tik.
Sepphoris. Sep-FOR-is.
synagogue. SIN-uh-gog.
Syrophoenician. SIGH-roe-fih-
  NISH-un.
Talitha koum. TAL-ih-thuh (or
  Tuh-LEE-thuh) KOOM.

DAILY BIBLE READINGS

This is the only place recorded in Scripture where Jesus feels an outflow of *power*. This is noteworthy, it seems, because he has not planned to do the healing, and he himself has "done" nothing. At other times he might very well have had the sense of power passing from him to another person. But in those cases he purposefully gives the gift. Here, the woman's faith taps into his power without Jesus' having initiated it.

But he knows when it happens. This proves that this is not some kind of "psychosomatic" healing. There is something more here than a woman having believed so strongly that she was going to be well that she actually "wills" herself to be well. Because Jesus feels the power go *out from him*, that possibility cannot be true. Her faith has facilitated the healing, but the healing power comes from outside her.

We sometimes call Jesus the "Great Physician." But he is more than a great doctor who knows how to treat and cure diseases. There is power in Jesus—power for life now and for eternity.

SEEKING REAL POWER

The New Age movement has brought some strange beliefs and practices with it. Many people have fantasized about the assumed mystical nature of crystals and are convinced that crystals have a magic power to heal. So it could be expected that someone would expand the theory a bit (not to mention make some money off of other people's gullibility).

In California, a musician who is a pet lover laminated some three-fourths-inch-long crystals to a copper heart and attached the devices to her two dogs and seven cats. She claims her animals are now in good health: the formerly lazy ones energetic and the previously excitable ones calm. So far her eleven turtles and nine-hundred-pound pig named Popcorn have escaped her ministrations, but she has plans to tape a crystal to a turtle that she says "has been acting kind of hectic lately." (Just how does a "hectic" turtle behave, anyway?) She is also offering her combination copper and crystal hearts to the public for only ten dollars apiece.

Although the woman who called on Jesus' healing power may have had a bit of superstition mixed in with her faith, she wasn't seeking New Age nostrums. She was looking for the real thing. For a long time she had been trying every type of help she could find, but to no avail. Now she saw in Jesus the person who had *real* power—power that would heal her at long last. He is *still* our greatest source of power.
    —C. R. B.

31. *"You see the people crowding against you," his disciples answered, "and yet you can ask, 'Who touched me?'"*
Dozens of people probably touch Jesus every few minutes with such a large crowd milling about. This fact makes the disciples' question seem very reasonable. Even so, the Twelve don't always seem to be as respectful or attentive as Jesus deserves for them to be. Every now and then it becomes apparent that they are a little slow and have not caught much of his spirit. The problem is usually that they have an agenda that doesn't match Jesus' own. In this case, the *disciples* apparently are focused on the urgency of the life-and-death situation that awaits them at Jairus's home. But Jesus has a spiritual sensitivity they do not have. Indeed, on a certain level, they are not able to have his sensitivity.
32, 33. *But Jesus kept looking around to see who had done it. Then the woman, knowing what had happened to her, came and fell at his feet and, trembling with fear, told him the whole truth.*
Jesus is not dissuaded by the disciples' question. When it becomes apparent to *the woman* that Jesus' searching eyes cannot be avoided, she comes forward, bows down, and tells her story.

Why is she afraid? And what is the connection between her *fear* and her decision to step forward? Is she afraid because she knows *what had happened to her*? That is reasonable. Her healing is evidence that Jesus acts with divine authority. There is always a sense of holy fear when the human meets the divine. Or is she afraid of the crowd? Is she still fearful of the stigma of her uncleanness? If so, her healing may be what emboldens her now to step forward. God has accepted her; he has healed her! Now she can face the hostile crowd.

III. REWARDED FAITH (MARK 5:34-36, 41, 42)

A. HEALING (v. 34)

34. He said to her, "Daughter, your faith has healed you. Go in peace and be freed from your suffering."

It is a faith lesson for the crowd! Trust Jesus, and be *freed from your suffering* and be *healed*. Interestingly, Jesus is repeating himself by using these two phrases. The woman's crippling physical disease had been cured. But surely this is not all that Jesus wants to say. If faith in Jesus guides her life, she will be free from spiritual, emotional, and social suffering, too—she will be a whole person. And the same thing is true of us, isn't it? In the case of the man carried to Jesus by four others and let down through the roof before Jesus, sinfulness was addressed first (see Mark 2:5; lesson 2). It is forgiveness that really makes us whole. Physical health is a bonus.

WHAT DO YOU THINK?

There is more to being a whole person than simply being free of disease. What is wholeness? What spiritual, mental, emotional, and physical traits are typical of one who is "whole"?

B. MESSAGE (vv. 35, 36)

35. While Jesus was still speaking, some men came from the house of Jairus, the synagogue ruler. "Your daughter is dead," they said. "Why bother the teacher any more?"

Apparently the healing encounter with the woman has delayed Jesus' arrival at the home of the synagogue *ruler*. Now, it appears, it is too late to continue the journey. But that is not an "unfortunate circumstance." There is no accident that has spoiled Jesus' intent. The delay actually offers him an even better opportunity to demonstrate his power. Rather than healing a little girl who is ill, he will bring her back from the *dead!*

36. Ignoring what they said, Jesus told the synagogue ruler, "Don't be afraid; just believe."

One writer suggests that the art of ignoring, here illustrated by Jesus, is one of the fine arts of faith. A human conclusion, even one that sounds reasonable and authoritative, is never the last word. God has the last word. Jesus' counsel to *just believe* is good advice yet today!

WHAT DO YOU THINK?

What beliefs or voices must we ignore today to have faith in Jesus?

C. RESURRECTION (vv. 41, 42)

41. He took her by the hand and said to her, "Talitha koum!" (which means, "Little girl, I say to you, get up!").

Not much drama! Jesus doesn't make a big show. He merely reaches down, takes her *hand*, and speaks to her. The Aramaic phrase *Talitha koum* is not a magic incantation of some kind. It is evident that Jesus speaks that language as his own. Including it for color and emphasis, Mark uses this forceful phrase to underline a significant moment. Even so, Mark is careful to translate Aramaic phrases for his readers. See Mark 7:34 and 15:34.

42. Immediately the girl stood up and walked around (she was twelve years old). At this they were completely astonished.

The witnesses in the room are Peter, James, and John, plus the child's parents (see vv. 37, 40, not in the printed text). Even though the disciples already had

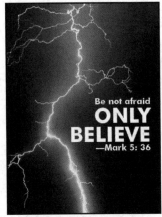

Be not afraid
ONLY
BELIEVE
—Mark 5: 36

Today's visual is an attractive illustration of the Key Verse— and a timely encouragement.

PRAYER

Father God, we are thankful above all for the sending of your Son and the eternal life he brings. Forgive our seasons of non-faith and of half-hearted discipleship. We rejoice in his power and in his love and are constantly amazed at his willingness to come to our house and heal. In Jesus' name, amen.

seen Jesus raise from the dead the widow's son at Nain (Luke 7:11-17), *they* are greatly *astonished* nonetheless.

The simplicity of Jesus' healing is striking. After Jesus' words and touch, this *twelve*-year-old immediately *stood up and walked*. Jesus didn't rage and shout, use dramatic props, or call attention to himself. When the power of life is there, all these other things are not necessary. And God is glorified.

THE MAN FOR ALL PEOPLE

The popular image of Jesus among many skeptics of the Bible is that he was a small-town, "backwoods hick" who appealed to his followers because they, too, were simple people. This view took a solid hit a few years ago when an archeological excavation at Sepphoris revealed something about the area in which Jesus grew up. Sepphoris was the Roman capital of Galilee for much of the first century A.D.

Eric Myers of Duke University, a leader of the Sepphoris excavation, says "Galilee [was] an enormously cosmopolitan urban area." Researchers have found that 80 percent of Jewish tombs in the area had inscriptions written in Greek. Other artifacts suggest that the Galilee of New Testament times was a very pluralistic society. These findings coincide with recent literary discoveries indicating the strong probability that Jesus was fluent in Greek, the cosmopolitan language of his day.

These discoveries offer us a partial explanation for why such a large variety of people were so at ease with Jesus and felt they could call upon him in their time of need. The poor woman and the ruler of the synagogue we read of in today's text, plus the Syrophoenician woman (Mark 7:24-30), the Roman centurion (Matthew 8:5-13), and a host of others we read about elsewhere all testify that Jesus was a man for all people. Today, he still is able to cure the ills of all societies and cultures, if only we will let him.

—C. R. B.

CONCLUSION

A. IT'S ABOUT FAITH

Faith is the one thing that stands out in today's text. The woman with the issue of blood believed in Jesus' power and was healed. The synagogue ruler also believed in Jesus' power, and his daughter came back to life.

But the faith in this passage is not the same as the common conception of faith today. It is much more than mere positive thinking, hope against hope, or petitioning the fates. We are concerned with faith in Jesus, the Son of the living God. Trust Jesus! Trust Jesus with your family! Trust Jesus with your destiny! Trust Jesus for your eternal wellness and wholeness! Sometimes he even will grant you physical wellness and emotional wholeness as an added blessing.

B. IT'S ABOUT JESUS' LOVE

In your Bible studies, surely you have noticed that the only "favorites" that Jesus has are those who love his Father and who respond to him. If we do that, we are his family (Matthew 12:50).

Jesus is eager to call men into service and to be in their company. He respects and expects many good things from women. Some were his financial supporters, and others were among his close friends. Jesus has a heart for children. His gospel is for all peoples. There are no first- and second-class citizens, as defined by age, gender, or race. Today, we have seen him respond to a father, raise a girl, heal a woman, and use a teachable moment to train his disciples. It is surely in the spirit of Jesus that Paul writes, "For all of you who were baptized into Christ have clothed yourselves with Christ. There is neither Jew nor Greek, slave nor free, male nor female, for you are all one in Christ Jesus" (Galatians 3:27, 28).

THOUGHT TO REMEMBER

Bring your fears to Jesus.

Discovery Learning

This page contains an alternative lesson plan emphasizing learning activities. Classes desiring such student involvement will find these suggestions helpful. The next page is a reproducible activity page to further enhance discovery learning.

LEARNING GOALS

After participating in this lesson, each student will be able to:

1. Recall the details of Jesus' healing of the woman with the bleeding problem and of Jairus's daughter.

2. Compare the anxiety of Jairus and the woman with the fears and uncertainties people bring to Jesus today.

3. In faith, give a specific fear to Jesus and allow him to give the victory.

INTO THE LESSON

Today's text deals with Jesus' ability to overcome the fears of sick people or those who had sick loved ones

Have your students in pairs answer the following: "Who is your favorite doctor? Why?" and, "What was your longest stay in the hospital?" Allow five minutes.

Say, "Some of us have experienced illness and physical difficulties. Some of us have been or are afraid of the future. In today's text we study how Jesus answered the requests of individuals and conquered their fears."

INTO THE WORD

Distribute the following true or false quiz based on today's text. In groups of two to four, students are to read Mark 5:22-43 and complete the quiz. Reasons for the answers are printed to help the teacher discuss the material further. (This is printed in *NIV® Bible Student*.)

1. The ruler ordered Jesus to come with him. (*False; he fell at Jesus' feet and begged, vv. 22, 23.*)

2. The ruler asked Jesus to touch his daughter. (*True, v. 23.*)

3. The woman with bleeding had been ill twelve years. (*True, v. 25.*)

4. The woman had never been to a doctor. (*False; she had seen many and had spent much money, v. 26.*)

5. Jesus touched the woman to heal her. (*False; the woman touched Jesus' cloak, vv. 27-29.*)

6. Jesus was unaware of what had happened. (*False; he realized he had been touched, v. 30.*)

7. Before Jesus arrived at the ruler's home, word came that the girl had died. (*True, v. 35.*)

8. Jesus told the man not to be afraid. (*True, v. 36.*)

9. Jesus only spoke to the girl; he did not touch her. (*False; he took her by the hand and spoke to her, v. 41.*)

10. Jesus accomplished both healings immediately. (*True, vv. 29, 42.*)

Some of your students will like the idea presented in the reproducible activity "Freedom From Fear" on the next page. Creating an imaginary letter to a friend describing the events of the Mark 5 text will be a good review of the facts of the incident.

INTO LIFE

Ask, "If you had been any of the participants or witnesses in these healings, how would you have felt? What would you have thought? How does this help you understand how Jesus conquers our fears?" Use the comments for Mark 5:29-33, 36, 41, 42 to address concerns.

Distribute to your groups newspaper and magazine articles concerning things people fear: sickness, financial problems, unemployment, and others. (You will need to have collected these during the week previous.) Ask the groups to identify the situations and the concerns raised. For example, you may have an article about a robbery and the natural concern for physical safety. Or you may have an article about a regional manufacturer with a major layoff of employees.

Distribute copies of the reproducible activity "Jesus Can Overcome Our Fears." Ask learners to use it to record the types of fears the articles highlight and other fears your class suggests. These might include an operation, a diagnosis, a family matter, personal employment. Then ask the class to say what they hear Jesus saying in response to each fear noted. (These can be actual quotes from Jesus or general truths from Scriptural teaching.) Record each one by the relevant fearful situation.

Ask each class member to put an asterisk by a situation in which he or she has a fear. Distribute a three-by-five card to each student. Each student is to write his or her fearful situation and compose a brief prayer asking Jesus to remove the fear and give victory to the student. (This activity is in the student book.)

Using the pairs originally formed for the Into the Lesson activity, ask the individuals to swap cards and have each person pray for the concerns of the other person. When the prayers are all completed, read 1 Peter 5:7 aloud, "Cast all your anxiety on him; because he cares for you." Suggest that each write the reference, "1 Peter 5:7" over the other words on the card. Then have a trash bag or waste basket available to be passed among the students so that they can literally "cast their cares away."

Freedom From Fear

Read Mark 5:22-43. Write a letter to a friend describing the events and how Jesus conquered the fears of those involved.

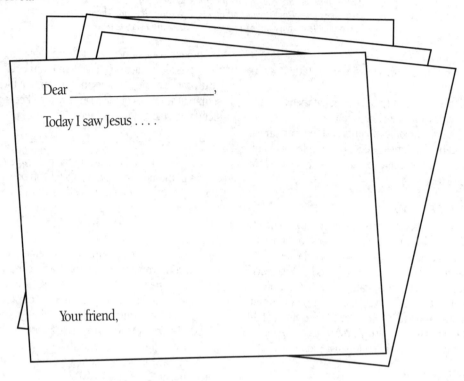

Dear _____,

Today I saw Jesus . . . .

Your friend,

Jesus Can Overcome Our Fears

Write below various situations where a person could be fearful. Next to each write how Jesus might answer and conquer the person's fear.

FEARFUL SITUATION	HOW JESUS MIGHT ANSWER

Jesus: God's Power in Action

Unit 3: Jesus' Responses to Faith
(Lessons 9-13)

JESUS HONORS BOLD FAITH

LESSON 10

WHY TEACH THIS LESSON?

Several years ago the International Disaster and Emergency Services (I.D.E.S.) was providing relief for war-torn Ethiopia. Their plan was to provide seed that the local residents could plant to raise wheat to feed their starving families. Shipping costs from the U.S. were prohibitive, however, so their representative went to Ethiopia with money that I.D.E.S. had raised and purchased the seed locally. When the Muslim dealer with whom he worked found out that foreign Christians were helping his own people, he was embarrassed. He agreed to match dollar for dollar the funds the American Christians had raised!

The Gentile woman in today's text must have embarrassed the disciples with her bold faith in Jesus. Not one to be rebuffed, she pressed her request because she was confident Jesus could help. Use this lesson to encourage your learners to be surprisingly bold in their own faith. Challenge them to a boldness in their faith they have never expressed before!

INTRODUCTION

A. TIME TO SPEAK—OR NOT

As you study this lesson, contrast it with a healing by Jesus from lesson 3. It took place on the eastern shore of the Sea of Galilee, where Jesus drove demons from a man who lived in the tombs and terrorized the people of the region. When the man was freed, clothed, and in his right mind, Jesus told him to go home to his friends and tell them what the Lord had done for him. In today's lesson, however, we will read about a healing where Jesus asked people *not* to tell anyone. Why the difference?

The Bible notes that there are times when people are supposed to be vocal and times when they are supposed to be quiet (see Ecclesiastes 3:7 and Amos 5:13). God gave the prophet Ezekiel specific times to speak out and to hold his tongue (cf. Ezekiel 3:26; 33:22). So when are we supposed to talk, and when are we supposed to be quiet?

Consider the demon-possessed man whom Jesus told to go home and tell his friends what had happened. Fewer people knew about Jesus in that region. The cured man could introduce the Master and draw others to his kingdom. Not only that, but Jesus really didn't have any enemies there yet who would try to find something negative in everything he did.

When Jesus told the deaf man (today's lesson) and the family of the little girl raised from the dead (last week's lesson) not to talk about their miracles, he had a good reason. By the time those two miracles occurred, Jesus' fame had spread to the north and west of the Sea of Galilee (cf. Matthew 4:24; Mark 1:28). With the fame came opposition, and people had even tried to kill him (Luke 4:29). Jesus knew that the building opposition eventually would result in his death—that was according to God's plan. But it was not yet God's time for that to happen. So it was important to slow down the mounting fame and the spreading visibility.

Followers of Jesus are to do what he says to do and stop what he says to stop. But knowing which is which can sometimes be a problem! However, if we read

DEVOTIONAL READING:
LUKE 7:1-10
BACKGROUND SCRIPTURE:
MARK 7:24-37
PRINTED TEXT:
MARK 7:24-37

LESSON AIMS

After participating in this lesson, each student will be able to:

1. Tell how Jesus rewarded the faith of two people in non-Jewish territory by healing disability and demon possession.

2. Tell how faith was more important than nationality, and remains so today.

3. Suggest one specific way to demonstrate boldness in his or her personal faith.

May
4

KEY VERSE

"[Jesus] has done everything well," they said. "He even makes the deaf hear and the mute speak."   —Mark 7:37

our Bibles carefully with a discerning spirit, it is usually not too difficult to know his will in this regard. The Bible is full of divine guidance. A failure to obey causes pain and trouble. A readiness to listen and to do what he says causes joy.

B. LESSON BACKGROUND

A lot of things happened between the time of the events that we studied last week and those of our current lesson. Jesus went to his hometown, where his ministry was discounted. He did some teaching and a little bit of healing; but they could hardly imagine that Mary's son, the local carpenter's boy, would have much to offer (Mark 6:1-6).

He sent out the Twelve to do several kinds of ministry: healing, teaching, and encouraging (6:7-13). He directed them to depend on the hospitality of the people they served. His cousin, John the Baptist, was beheaded by Herod, after Herod had made a rash and foolish promise to his stepdaughter (6:14-29). Jesus fed about five thousand men (plus families) with just five loaves and two fish (6:30-44) and then walked on the sea and calmed it (6:45-52). Landing in the area of Gennesaret, he was thronged by people seeking healing. After that he was confronted by some Pharisees from Jerusalem, and he chided them for their hypocrisy (7:1-13). He told the people that immorality defiles them, but that ceremonial matters are not nearly so important; and he taught them that right and wrong actions spring from right and wrong motives—things within us (7:14-23). Of course, that wasn't going to make him any more popular with the Pharisees, either. Tradition and ceremony were just about all there was to great religion, so far as they were concerned.

Now we follow Jesus into new territory, this time to the north.

I. THE FAITH OF A MOTHER (MARK 7:24-30)

As we have noted already, the popularity of Jesus is growing around Galilee. Everywhere he goes, the crowds follow. And most of them are looking for healing. He is glad to do that, but the healing dimension of his ministry is secondary. His primary concern is to introduce the kingdom of God, urging people to become part of it. His compassion makes him quite willing to give healing, which will bless and enrich lives for some years to come. But his passion is to offer spiritual healing, which is eternal! That speaks to the priorities of the church, doesn't it? "Seek first his kingdom and his righteousness" (Matthew 6:33). But we ensure people's physical needs are met as well (cf. Matthew 25:35, 36).

A. JESUS SEEKS REFUGE (v. 24)

24. *Jesus left that place and went to the vicinity of Tyre. He entered a house and did not want anyone to know it; yet he could not keep his presence secret.*

There are times when Jesus needs to slow down the aggressive adulation of the crowds and to find some time to renew himself. Here he goes into Gentile territory to separate from the crowds for a time. He travels to the northwest, from the regions around the Sea of Galilee up to the coastal cities of Tyre and Sidon.

Tyre is a city with a fine natural harbor (on the end of a land bridge) and is important for the commercial shipping business on the eastern end of the Mediterranean Sea. Sidon is another seacoast town about twenty-five miles farther north. God had condemned both cities centuries earlier (cf. Isaiah 23; Jeremiah 27:1-7; Ezekiel 28), but now Jesus considers them to be agreeable places for travel (cf. Matthew 11:21, 22). Somewhere in that region Jesus finds a receptive home and apparently he intends to spend some quiet time to plan and reflect. But since *he could not keep his presence secret*, it doesn't work exactly as he had hoped.

WHAT DO YOU THINK?

Jesus was looking to escape the crowds and to "renew himself." What can we do to renew ourselves for ministry? How can we be sure to allow our Christian leaders to have opportunities to renew themselves?

THE "GOLDFISH BOWL" SYNDROME

Public figures often pay a price for their high visibility. They sometimes become too visible, as if their lives are lived in a great "goldfish bowl" where everyone can observe them and there's no place to hide. Some revel in the publicity, but almost everyone wants some privacy at some time.

For entertainers, the problem is that everything they do is "news." What styles they wear, what they do with their hair, whom they see—the public wants to know all this. For political figures it's what they can offer. Private interests besiege them with requests for their support of, or opposition to, every item on the political agenda. And for religious figures, it's how they behave. And if they fall—committing the very sins they have publicly denounced—they lose their credibility. Sometimes they all just want to get out of the goldfish bowl and be "like other people."

Jesus also needed to get out of the goldfish bowl from time to time. So we find him in today's text trying to isolate himself so he could be at least somewhat "like other people" for a time. But he couldn't be, and we find him accepting the responsibility that comes with his position. Of course, this is the ultimate solution for all of us who are looked upon as role models.

—C. R. B.

B. FAITH CROSSES BARRIERS (vv. 25, 26)

25, 26. *In fact, as soon as she heard about him, a woman whose little daughter was possessed by an evil spirit came and fell at his feet. The woman was a Greek, born in Syrian Phoenicia. She begged Jesus to drive the demon out of her daughter.*

Greek is the same as "Gentile." *The woman* who finds Jesus is not Jewish. Her nationality is Phoenician. *Phoenicia* is the nation that occupies that part of the Mediterranean coast, part of the larger regional designation of Syria. So she is from *Syrian Phoenicia*. (There was a Libyo-Phoenicia in North Africa; that is probably the reason Mark uses both the *Syrian* and *Phoenician* labels.) The people who live in this area are ancient enemies of Israel (see Joel 3:4-6). But such issues are not important to her. Whatever barrier her nationality or background may have posed is shattered as she seeks help for her daughter. (Notice that *an evil spirit*, v. 25, is the same as a demon, v. 26.)

C. JESUS RESISTS (v. 27)

27. *"First let the children eat all they want," he told her, "for it is not right to take the children's bread and toss it to their dogs."*

Jesus' reply is startling to us. It sounds harsh. It sets us back a little bit to hear Jesus strongly implying that this anxious woman is one of the *dogs*. That simply doesn't sound like something that would come from the lips of Jesus! But he uses a word that describes a little dog, a puppy. That softens it somewhat for us. In the New Testament the word *dog* is used five times, and each time it is used in a negative fashion. But here, and in the parallel passage in Matthew 15 (just these two times), the word for "little dog" is used. Still, a puppy is a far cry from a child. We still puzzle over Jesus' choice of wording.

In our puzzling, however, let's not miss the "bigger picture." Jesus is using an illustration of *children* and dogs to teach a lesson in priority. The *bread* that he is talking about is his attention, his gracious healing, and his message. The children who are to come *first* are the children of Israel—the Jews (cf. Matthew 10:5, 6; John 4:22). Paul, the apostle to the Gentiles, later will express the same priority. The gospel of Christ, the power of God for salvation, is "first for the Jew, then for the Gentile" (Romans 1:16). However surprised or shocked we are by Jesus' words, they apparently do not surprise or offend the woman, as her reply shows.

HOW TO SAY IT

Decapolis. Dee-CAP-uh-lis.
Ecclesiastes. Ik-LEEZ-ee-AS-teez.
Ephphatha (Aramaic). EF-uh-thuh.
Ezekiel. Ee-ZEEK-ee-ul or Ee-ZEEK-yul.
Galilee. GAL-uh-lee.
Gennesaret. Geh-NESS-uh-ret (G as in GET).
Herod. HAIR-ud.
Mediterranean. MED-uh-tuh-RAY-nee-un.
Pharisees. FAIR-ih-seez.
Phoenicia. Fuh-NISH-uh.
Phoenician. Fuh-NISH-un.
Sidon. SIGH-dun.
Syrian. SEAR-ee-un.
Syrophoenician. SIGH-roe-fih-NISH-un.
Tyre. Tire.

WHAT DO YOU THINK?

Though Jesus' remark might seem "cold" to us, the woman did not take offense. How can we be sure we do not take offense at remarks that are not meant to be offensive but that some people might think are offensive?

D. FAITH PERSISTS (vv. 28-30)

28. "Yes, Lord," she replied, "but even the dogs under the table eat the children's crumbs."

If you have house dogs, you can visualize this very easily. You feed the children, but while you're at it you feed the *dogs*, too. And the first course of the dogs' meal often comes from the floor under the baby's booster seat. Homes in first-century Syria probably are more hospitable to animals and *crumbs* than are ours, but it is an easy picture for us to understand.

This woman recognizes the age-old distinction between Jew and Gentile. Even so, she believes that Jesus has enough love, power, and kindness to spare. After he feeds the needs of the children of Israel, the leftovers will be plenty for her. And Jesus honors her humility.

29, 30. Then he told her, "For such a reply, you may go; the demon has left your daughter."

She went home and found her child lying on the bed, and the demon gone.

Jesus admires her faith and her spunk. She is persistent, creative, quick thinking, courageous, and humble. Her faith does not even require Jesus' personal presence with her *daughter* (cf. Matthew 8:8). It is plain to him that she has the faith to accept his simple assurance. Unlike the long and involved "exorcisms" that one sees in the movies and on TV, Jesus merely says the word, and *the demon is gone.*

THE VALUE OF "SPUNK"

"Spunk" is that indefinable something that enables some people to attempt to do what others will not. When told, "It can't be done," or "No one will listen to you," they go ahead and try anyway.

That describes Nancy Wright. Her first motorcycle ride came when she was seventy-one. Shortly after that she bought one of her own. No doubt family and friends assured her of the dangers and (especially) the folly of someone her age trying to act like a kid again. Seven years later she had ridden her Honda Gold Wing all over the United States, even to the Yukon and Alaska and back! When she was seventy-seven she fell down some stairs. She got on her Gold Wing and rode twenty-five miles before she realized she had fractured her hip. Two months later she was out of the hospital and back on her motorcycle. Nancy Wright has spunk! She explains what drives her: "I lost my husband, and my kids are grown, so I found something interesting and challenging to do. . . . It's extended my life."

Another woman with spunk is the one in our lesson today. She was not a Jew, and people probably told her that Jesus wouldn't have time for her. She went looking for Jesus anyway, and when he challenged her faith, she replied with such spunkiness that Jesus admiringly granted her request. Do we possess the spiritual spunkiness that will bring us the spiritual blessings that God has waiting for us?

—C. R. B.

II. THE FAITH OF GOOD FRIENDS (MARK 7:31-37)

Jesus is now on the move again. Since he has just stressed the priority of Israel in receiving the gospel (7:27), we might expect him to return to Jewish territory. But he does not. He goes instead to the Gentile region known as the Decapolis. His decision to remain in Gentile territory may be a lesson in "balance" for the disciples: although Gentiles do not receive *priority*, they are not *excluded*.

A. A DISABLED MAN (vv. 31, 32)

31. Then Jesus left the vicinity of Tyre and went through Sidon, down to the Sea of Galilee and into the region of the Decapolis.

WHAT DO YOU THINK?

Jesus' remaining in Gentile territory may be a "lesson in 'balance' for the disciples." What do we today need to keep in "balance"? How do we do that?

Leaving *Tyre* and *Sidon* for the *Decapolis* means that Jesus is now back in the general area where he had healed the demon-possessed man earlier (Mark 5:1-20). The name *Decapolis* means "ten cities." East and southeast of the Sea of Galilee, ten cities had banded together, including the region surrounding them, to form what might be called a "league" of cities. Ancient lists of the ten cities that comprise the Decapolis vary, so the name applies more to the general area than to ten specific cities.

32. There some people brought to him a man who was deaf and could hardly talk, and they begged him to place his hand on the man.

A good English teacher might rebuke Mark for using the pronoun *they* without telling his readers who *they* are! We assume the reference is to growing crowds, which always seem to show up when Jesus is around.

The man they *brought* to Jesus is *deaf* and partially mute. We are not certain whether the impediment in his speech is due to the man's deafness or has a physical cause all its own.

B. A THOUGHTFUL MASTER (vv. 33-35)

33, 34. After he took him aside, away from the crowd, Jesus put his fingers into the man's ears. Then he spit and touched the man's tongue. He looked up to heaven and with a deep sigh said to him, "Ephphatha!" (which means, "Be opened!").

In taking *him aside*, perhaps Jesus wants to heal without calling unnecessary attention to the miracle. This is the same concern that we have noted before: avoiding the mounting visibility that draws mounting opposition. But some of us see it as a thoughtful gesture on the part of Jesus. This man may have had to endure the laughter of unthinking people who make fun of the unusual sounds he utters. He has endured enough of that unwanted attention. The next time the townspeople see him he will be different. They will meet a new man, able to hear and to speak clearly.

Jesus, of course, is able to heal without any touch whatsoever. But in this case he uses a bit of drama to communicate something to the deaf man. In pressing *his fingers into the man's ears* and touching his *tongue* with saliva, Jesus leaves no doubt as to the source of the healing. The same is true of his looking *up to Heaven* and his sigh, which could be part of a prayer.

As we have seen before, Mark translates Jesus' use of Aramaic for his readers. As Jesus speaks the word *Ephphatha*, the man being healed is unable to hear it since he does not regain his hearing until after the word is spoken. This means that Jesus is speaking for the benefit of the disciples and whatever witnesses happen to be close by.

35. At this, the man's ears were opened, his tongue was loosened and he began to speak plainly.

As before, the healed person needs no lengthy series of treatments to get better. This is a miracle by the power of God! Problems of both *ears* and *tongue* are solved immediately.

C. AN EXCITED PEOPLE (vv. 36, 37)

36, 37. Jesus commanded them not to tell anyone. But the more he did so, the more they kept talking about it. People were overwhelmed with amazement. "He has done everything well," they said. "He even makes the deaf hear and the mute speak."

Jesus tries again: "Please don't spread this word around!" But again, it doesn't work. Surely Jesus doesn't mind if people spread the news that "the kingdom of God is near" (Mark 1:15). It's the news of the miracles he wants kept quiet. *But*

WHAT DO YOU THINK?

It has been suggested that taking the deaf man aside privately was a "thoughtful gesture." How can we be sensitive to the feelings of those who have disabilities or special needs? How has our church planned for the presence and comfort of those with disabilities?

Visual for lesson 10. This hymn reminds us, who have received far more from the Lord than mere hearing and speech, to praise him.

the more he asks them to be quiet, the more they talk. It is just too good to keep to themselves, just too remarkable not to express. We might say it "blew their minds." That they would have a hard time keeping the news to themselves is easy to understand.

But Jesus' concern is also easy to see. Jesus has indeed *done* all things *well!* But the people (including the disciples) don't really understand who he is or the true nature of his mission. Like the crowds across the sea a few months earlier, these people would gladly make Jesus their earthly king (John 6:15). But were they ready to submit to a King whose kingdom is "not of this world" (John 18:36)? Are we?

CONCLUSION
A. WE'RE PRONE TO GET IT BACKWARD

Jesus asked these people to wait, to keep from spreading the information about his power to heal and to change their earthly lives. He is glad to address their physical needs. He cared about them. And it is not as though he didn't care about all of those other people—their friends and neighbors who had illnesses or who are near death. But the more they talked, the angrier his opponents became. And the angrier those religious authorities grew, the more active they would be in putting together whatever kind of coalition it would take to get rid of him.

But it just wasn't time for that yet. The people who had been healed or who had seen loved ones healed are well intentioned, but they are actually doing more harm than good. By broadcasting the fame of Jesus, they are potentially shortening the length and the breadth of his ministry. Consequently, he would be limited in where he could go and to whom he could speak. Fewer would hear about the kingdom, fewer would hear the message of repentance, and fewer, actually, would have access to him.

Today, Jesus commands us *not* to be quiet. The gospel is to be proclaimed "to the ends of the earth" (Acts 1:8). And some of his final words to his disciples are also his words to us: "Therefore go and make disciples of all nations, baptizing them in the name of the Father and of the Son and of the Holy Spirit, and teaching them to obey everything I have commanded you. And surely I am with you always, to the very end of the age" (Matthew 28:19, 20).

B. HE NEEDS OUR VOICE

What a remarkable thing that God has done! He does not send angels down to evangelize. He depends on his church instead. He does not address men and women caught in the bonds of sin—who are candidates for eternal death and Hell!—by using angels. The modern television drama *Touched by an Angel* has created a very positive sensitivity to spiritual things and has some great and encouraging moments. But what we see on that program is not the way it works in reality.

The gospel of Christ is, instead, spread by people: men and women who speak for Jesus. They are empowered by the Holy Spirit, who lives in and works with Christians. They are guided and instructed by the Bible, the Word of God, through which the Holy Spirit of God also works by inspiration. But the relationships are established, eternal life is demonstrated, and the words are spoken by everyday people. Those to whom they speak will respond to a reasonable message with a faith grounded in the evidence of history. It will not be confirmed by angelic beings who materialize, then disappear. As strange as it sounds, God needs our voices.

Discovery Learning

This page contains an alternative lesson plan emphasizing learning activities. Classes desiring such student involvement will find these suggestions helpful. The next page is a reproducible activity page to further enhance discovery learning.

LEARNING GOALS

After this lesson each student will be able to:

1. Tell how Jesus rewarded the faith of two people in non-Jewish territory by healing disability and demon possession.

2. Tell how faith was more important than nationality, and remains so today.

3. Suggest one specific way to demonstrate boldness in his or her personal faith.

INTO THE LESSON

As class members arrive, have them participate in an informal fellowship time, perhaps with coffee and pastries. During the week before this session ask a Christian of a different nationality to attend your class. Be sure you do not alert the class to this person's attendance. Observe how your class responds to the "outsider." (If you do not invite a person of another nationality, have someone "dress up" as an unkempt outsider and attend the class.)

After a few minutes call the class to order and ask the learners to sit in groups of four. Draw attention to your "outsider" and ask the person how he or she felt. Was this person welcomed by the group or treated as an outsider? Then say, "In today's text Jesus meets and deals with both a woman and a man who were outsiders to the Jewish religion. When have you felt like an outsider? What can you do to make visitors and new people feel more welcome and comfortable? Have you ever reached out to an 'outsider' in a situation where you saw uneasiness in the person? How did it make you feel?"

Make the transition to Bible study by saying, "In today's lesson we will see how Jesus treated outsiders and responded to them."

INTO THE WORD

Select someone earlier in the week to review the introductory remarks in today's commentary. This person will prepare a five-minute report on the events leading up to today's text and the differences in Jesus' instructions on speaking.

Distribute copies of the reproducible activity "Hurdles to Faith" from the next page. Ask a volunteer to Read Mark 7:24-37 and Matthew 15:21-31. While this person reads, have learners list some of the things that had to be overcome for the people in the text to hear the gospel.

Create three groups each with up to six students, and give them the following assignments. (If you have more students, create more groups and repeat assignments.) Each will make a short presentation to the class.

Group 1. Use Bible dictionaries, encyclopedias, and other helps to research the relationship of Jews to non-Jews. Look particularly at the differences of the Greeks and Jews and those of Decapolis and Jerusalem.

Group 2. Read Mark 7:24-37 and Matthew 15:21-31. Prepare a short drama on the events told here. Develop props and the characters a little more than the Scripture describes.

Group 3. Read Mark 7:24-37 and Matthew 15:21-31. Prepare a short drama putting these events in terms of a different nationality from your own and missionary work. Decide on what characters need to be present and what particular hurdles are present; then write the dialog.

After fifteen minutes call the groups together. Have Group 2 present its drama. If any questions arise from the presentation, refer to the commentary for answers.

Ask Group 1 to present the results of its research. Ask the class, "How easy is it for us to have groups with whom we do not share the gospel? Who might be some of those groups be?"

Then say, "With our biblical drama and our research, it is reasonable to assume that there were some large hurdles to overcome in carrying the gospel to other nations."

INTO LIFE

Ask Group 3 to present its drama, then ask, "How do you think most people feel when asked to talk about Jesus with someone of a different nationality? How would most people react if they had been the 'outcast'? What does this passage tell us about the need to carry the gospel to all 'people groups'? What are some examples of how faith transcends nationality lines?"

Provide stationery and envelopes for each student. The students are to write personal letters to themselves. In this letter they are to challenge themselves to share the gospel with others in a bold manner. Each should write specific goals for sharing over the next four weeks. After four weeks, return the letters, addressed by the student.

Give each student a copy of the reproducible activity "Personal Hurdles" from the next page. Have them complete these activities privately. Then close the session in a prayer for building personal faith.

Hurdles to Faith

Read Mark 7:24-37 and Matthew 15:21-31. List on the hurdles below some of the things that had to be overcome for these people to hear the gospel.

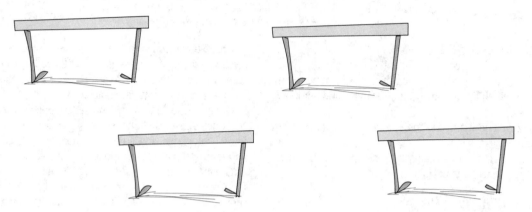

Personal Hurdles

Now list some of the things that keep you from being bold in your faith and sharing your faith boldly. Over these concerns write "Matthew 15:28," after you have read those verses.

PUTTING FAITH IN JESUS ALONE

LESSON 11

WHY TEACH THIS LESSON?

Postmodern thinking is "syncretistic." This means that postmoderns like to combine different, and sometimes even conflicting, ideas to come up with what they call truth. There is no room for absolutes or commitment to a single belief system.

Some of your learners are under special pressure to conform to this way of thinking. Educators are being forced to promote New Age concepts in the classroom and in extra-curricular activities. Business people are being pressured to treat homosexual couples and unmarried but cohabiting mixed couples the same way they treat married couples in terms of insurance benefits. Even newsmagazine readers are being chided that they must "develop a deep understanding and appreciation of at least one other religion" (*Newsweek*, Dec. 31, 2001/Jan. 7, 2002).

Today's lesson will remind them why they must resist such thinking. It will reaffirm the truth Jesus is the Christ (the Messiah). Beside him there is no other (John 14:6). It is only he who has "the words of eternal life" (John 6:68). In a culture that rejects absolute truth, this is a reminder we all need—absolutely!

INTRODUCTION

A. ABOUT SLOW (AND NON-) LEARNERS

Jesus' disciples were a rather unlikely team of followers. But Jesus was preparing them to step up and provide dynamic leadership for God's people when his own work on earth was finished. Peter, Andrew, James, and John were fishermen. Matthew had been a tax collector—considered a traitor by most Jewish people. Peter was clearly the leader—at least he said the most! James and John, Zebedee's sons, were rather impetuous (Luke 9:54). Simon the Zealot was part of a group of patriotic militants (Acts 1:13). Nathanael was prejudiced against people from Nazareth (John 1:46). All of them were slow to accept eyewitness testimony of the Lord's resurrection (Luke 24:11).

Some were outgoing; others were introverted. Of some we know very little. All of those personalities! But a blend like that can make a creative and productive team. They can balance and supplement each other.

That's the way it works in the church. Each member contributes the personality and spiritual gifts built in by God and developed by the Holy Spirit. Some have strengths in the areas where the others are weak. Together we are much more than any one of us would be without the others (see Ephesians 4:11, 12). Different personalities, perspectives, and gifts, when used together, can be a very good thing.

But the thing that puzzles us about the disciples is that even though they were right there and saw so many things that Jesus did, they often were slow to get the point. How could they watch him heal so many people and not know that there wasn't anyone else like him? How could they listen to his peerless teaching and miss the fact that he had divine insight? Why did they continue to fret about

DEVOTIONAL READING:
PHILIPPIANS 2:5-11
BACKGROUND SCRIPTURE:
MARK 8:27–9:8
PRINTED TEXT:
MARK 8:27-36; 9:2-8

LESSON AIMS

After participating in this lesson, each student will be able to:

1. Cite evidence from today's texts that Jesus is the Christ, the Son of God.

2. Compare people's wrong ideas about Jesus in his own day with modern misconceptions about him.

3. Make a statement of faith in Jesus Christ, and give a way to live out that faith.

May
11

KEY VERSE

"But what about you?" [Jesus] asked. *"Who do you say I am?"* Peter answered, *"You are the Christ."* —Mark 8:29

small things? In our look at the Lesson Background (below), we will see a perfect illustration of that blindness.

Another group that leaves us scratching our heads is that of the Pharisees and religious leaders who showed up so often to check on Jesus. No matter what Jesus did, they were never convinced. Mark 8:11, 12 says that he sighed deeply in his spirit to at least one of their requests for an additional sign. Such skeptics abound even today. Nothing is enough to satisfy them; they always seek another sign. When we are determined not to see, we just don't see, do we?

But the Christian faith is based on sufficient and reasonable evidence. God has done dramatic things in the world to illustrate his power. Jesus lived and did mighty works. The Bible, contemporary secular literature, and archaeology attest to these things. The faith that our salvation requires is a faith that trusts God to keep his promises for *the future* because of what he has done in *the past*.

B. LESSON BACKGROUND

Today we will see Jesus ask his disciples a very important question about his identity. But behind that question stands a prime illustration of just how slow they have been on the uptake. A short time before, they had been aboard a small ship, crossing from one side of the Sea of Galilee to the other (Mark 8:13). But the disciples had forgotten to bring along any lunch. Among them they just had one loaf of bread, and they were beginning to fret.

As Jesus listened to them, he asked them some questions. Do you remember when we fed the five thousand? How much food did we start with? Do you remember the twelve baskets of scraps left over? So how can you be worrying about having just one loaf of bread? "Do you still not understand?" (Mark 8:21). If they don't understand that, they don't understand him.

But now it's time for Jesus to clear up their confusion. It's not time for everyone in the country to understand yet; but it is time for the Twelve to know just who Jesus is.

I. JESUS THE CHRIST (MARK 8:27-33)

A. MISTAKEN IDENTITY (vv. 27, 28)

27, 28. Jesus and his disciples went on to the villages around Caesarea Philippi. On the way he asked them, "Who do people say I am?"

They replied, "Some say John the Baptist; others say Elijah; and still others, one of the prophets."

Jesus and *his disciples* will stay a little longer in Gentile territory. It is still time to keep a lower profile, time to train his disciples, time to spread his love a little farther. *Caesarea Philippi* is a city north of the land of Galilee. Herod Philip named it in honor of Caesar Augustus. This city is located near the modern Golan Heights.

The question Jesus asks marks a turning point in his ministry as he affirms to the disciples his identity and just what will soon happen to him. As a natural consequence, they will begin to understand the real meaning of faith and of discipleship. In asking who *people say I am,* Jesus is not requesting information from the disciples. He already knows the various beliefs the people hold about him. The question is intended to start a conversation.

The disciples' answer starts with Herod Antipas's frightened concern. He is nervous that this Jesus is *John the Baptist*—the man he had beheaded—back from the dead (Mark 6:16). That would have been a fairly logical conclusion for some people. Jesus has the same forceful personality that John had. The people turn out in droves to listen to him as well. So it must be John. Interestingly, some

Who is Jesus? Use this poster from the Adult Visuals *packet to note how this entire quarter has answered that question.*

had asked John if he were the Christ (John 1:19, 20). Now there are some who were thinking that the Christ was John. Jesus just doesn't fit the pattern of what they have come to expect from the Messiah. He shows no evidence that he is about to take charge of the empire.

Others thought that Jesus could be *Elijah*—or perhaps *one of the* other *prophets* who has been dead for many centuries (Mark 6:15). They remember that the Old Testament prophetic book of Malachi (4:5) predicts that Elijah will return to precede the arrival of the Messiah (cf. Matthew 17:10-13). The prophets, like Jesus, were wise men with powerful messages.

None of these guesses is unflattering. People think very highly of Jesus. But they do not recognize who he is.

B. THE EXPECTED ONE (vv. 29, 30)

29. *"But what about you?" he asked. "Who do you say I am?"*
Peter answered, "You are the Christ."

Jesus addresses his next question to the group as a whole. Peter answers for the group. He is always the first one to speak. Sometimes he speaks rashly, but here he speaks perfectly. Of course, he just barely knows what he is talking about, but he does say exactly the right thing. Now, every week, men and women who would be saved announce the same thing, in full faith. Jesus is *the Christ!*

The Christ! Messiah! The anointed one! The expected one! The one who has come from God! The only one in whom salvation can be found (Acts 4:12).

30. *Jesus warned them not to tell anyone about him.*

Jesus still does not want his identity broadcast. By saying what he does, it is clear that he is confirming Peter's statement. Now Jesus will accelerate his teaching schedule. He will bring the rest of the disciples to this same point. When the time comes for his death, his resurrection, and his ascension, these men will be equipped with the message and courage they need. But they are not ready yet. It is not yet God's time. But it is coming soon.

C. THE UNEXPECTED TRUTH (vv. 31, 32)

31. *He then began to teach them that the Son of Man must suffer many things and be rejected by the elders, chief priests and teachers of the law, and that he must be killed and after three days rise again.*

Son of Man seems to be Jesus' favorite designation for himself. He may be identifying his divine nature by drawing on a phrase that the prophet Daniel had used (see Daniel 7:13). Mark sometimes quotes Jesus' use of this phrase in such a way as to underline his divine nature (see Mark 8:38; 13:26; and 14:62).

The disciples must be shocked to hear these words. They are the exact opposite of what they expect for the Messiah. From this point on, Jesus gets increasingly clear about his future and about the nature of their discipleship (cf. Mark 9:31; 10:29-31, 33, 34, 45). He will not want them to carry on with him under false pretenses. His way will be a way of suffering. There is going to be a high cost to him, and there will be significant costs associated with following him.

The disciples know that *the elders, chief priests and teachers of the law* have opposed Jesus to this point. But they certainly don't expect things to turn out so grimly. Jesus will *suffer*? He will die? By the time Jesus gets to the part about *after three days rise again,* the disciples probably have stopped hearing, their minds numb from what he has just told them.

We might say that Jesus' prediction should not be such a big surprise. The prophet Isaiah had written about "a man of sorrows, and familiar with suffering" (Isaiah 53:3), and had said "he was pierced for our transgressions, he was

WHAT DO YOU THINK?

While it may be flattering that some people think highly of Jesus, what is the major problem with someone believing that he's simply some kind of prophet?

HOW TO SAY IT

Antipas. AN-tih-pus.
Augustus. Aw-GUS-tus.
Caesar. SEE-zur.
Caesarea Philippi. Sess-uh-REE-uh Fih-LIP-pie or FIL-ih-pie.
Elijah. Ee-LYE-juh.
Galilee. GAL-uh-lee.
Golan. GO-lahn.
Hermon. HER-mun.
Herod. HAIR-ud.
Messiah. Meh-SIGH-uh.
Nathanael. Nuh-THAN-yull (TH as in THIN).
Nazareth. NAZ-uh-reth.
Pharisees. FAIR-ih-seez.
Zealot. ZEL-ut.
Zebedee. ZEB-eh-dee.

WHAT DO YOU THINK?

The disciples had a blind spot about the Messiah, which kept them from understanding Isaiah's prophecy. How do we know whether our understanding of Scripture is blocked by a blind spot? How should we respond to "new" interpretations of Bible passages—interpretations that differ from our understanding?

crushed for our iniquities; the punishment that brought us peace was upon him, and by his wounds we are healed" (Isaiah 53:5). And the rest of the fifty-third chapter of Isaiah clearly describes what happened to Jesus. But most of the Jews of Jesus' day do not see the Messiah in Isaiah 53. A "suffering servant" is not the Christ they are anticipating. After Jesus' resurrection, the leaders of the first-century church will demonstrate that they have come to a profound understanding of Isaiah 53, as much of the New Testament shows.

32. He spoke plainly about this, and Peter took him aside and began to rebuke him.

Peter again speaks first, and his response is perfectly natural. It stands to reason that the One anointed by God to come to his people will not be abused and killed. What Jesus has just said doesn't seem to make sense!

D. GOD'S REALITY (v. 33)

33. But when Jesus turned and looked at his disciples, he rebuked Peter. "Get behind me, Satan!" he said. "You do not have in mind the things of God, but the things of men."

Peter's mistake is to think and talk from a worldly point of view. When he (or anyone else) doesn't embrace *the things of God,* he is automatically in league with *Satan.* Peter has stepped out of line. Jesus knows that if he takes the easy way— Peter's way, Satan's way, the way that the Jews have in mind—it will not be God's way. Satan had offered Jesus a kingship without suffering once before (Matthew 4:8, 9). Jesus had rejected that false path (4:10). Now he rejects it again: "Don't try to lead me, Peter. Follow me. *Get behind me.*"

II. THE FOLLOWERS OF CHRIST (MARK 8:34-36)

A. FOLLOWING AND SELF-DENIAL (v. 34)

34. Then he called the crowd to him along with his disciples and said: "If anyone would come after me, he must deny himself and take up his cross and follow me.

The concept of self-denial is rather easy to understand, although not many seem to practice it. Daily we are confronted with all kinds of enticements from others, and temptation to assert ourselves. When we begin to grow as Christians, we can also understand how foolish it is to say "no" to God and "yes" to ourselves.

Taking up the *cross* is a harder idea to grasp. Jews of the era know that being condemned to death by crucifixion also means carrying the burden of one's own cross on the way to the place of execution. So Jesus is talking about martyrdom as well as "death to self" (cf. John 12:24-26). Even if we are not called on to die because of our stand with Christ, Jesus still requires that we die to our old, sinful selves (Romans 6:6). Carrying a cross means more than merely "bucking up" when tough times come—enduring the normal challenges of life or working through personal failure. It means death to an old way, a way never to be followed again.

WHAT DO YOU THINK?

What has following Christ cost you? What "cross-bearing" experiences have you endured? What has been the result?

THE ORDEAL AHEAD

The annual Race Across America is a bicycle race of three thousand grueling miles, covered in about eleven days. Riders pedal through nighttime temperatures near freezing in eleven-thousand-foot mountain passes; daytime in the desert brings scorching temperatures well above one hundred degrees. Their strength will be sapped by the muggy heat of the Gulf states after they have gone nearly a week on two or three hours of sleep out of every twenty-four. Heat exhaustion, hallucinations, saddle sores, and the constant threat of accidents are all part of the ordeal.

Yet year after year, thirty to thirty-five men and women train rigorously for months, pay an entrance fee of several hundred dollars, and endure a week-and-a-half of agony with the prospect of a few thousand dollars as a reward *if they win!*

Half will drop out along the way with torn ligaments, strained muscles, and more severe physical problems.

Most people have no sense of what it means to endure such hardship. Perhaps that's the reason Jesus' announcement of what lay ahead caused such a strong reaction from Peter. But Jesus knew what he must face if he were to accomplish what he had been called to do. He also knew the hardships his disciples would face. When we answer his call to discipleship, none of us knows what lies ahead. Agonies of body and spirit may await us, but our Lord will help us to victory at the finish line.   —C. R. B.

B. LOSING TO WIN (vv. 35, 36)

35, 36. *"For whoever wants to save his life will lose it, but whoever loses his life for me and for the gospel will save it. What good is it for a man to gain the whole world, yet forfeit his soul?"*

Elsewhere in the Gospels, Jesus illustrates the folly of accumulating wealth at the cost of one's eternal *soul* (e.g., Luke 12:18-21). If I lose my soul I lose my very essence—all that I am. If I am in Christ, who I am will be his forever and ever. If I simply lose my life, I don't lose who I am. Many of the followers to whom Jesus is speaking will face this very choice.

III. THE TRANSFIGURED CHRIST (MARK 9:2-8)

A. THE BEST OF THE BEST (vv. 2-6)

2. *After six days Jesus took Peter, James and John with him and led them up a high mountain, where they were all alone. There he was transfigured before them.*

No one knows for sure exactly which *high mountain* this is. The fact that it is within a journey of *six days* doesn't help much in narrowing down the choices! A good candidate is Mount Hermon, which is about 9,166 feet high.

Peter, James, and John traditionally are referred to as "the inner circle" of disciples whose support and partnership Jesus wants and needs on certain occasions. James will be the first to be martyred (Acts 12:2), leaving the other two to be the clear leaders of the original Twelve.

The Greek verb for *transfigured* sounds like the word "metamorphosis" when pronounced in English. It means Jesus was changed in his outward form. This change underlines the most important point that has just been made by Peter's confession in verse 29.

3. *His clothes became dazzling white, whiter than anyone in the world could bleach them.*

Jesus' *clothes* appear to grow *whiter*, the whitest thing the disciples have ever seen (no *bleach* could ever get them that *white*). This dramatizes the character of the one who is wearing them. It gives these disciples a peek at the glory Jesus had before he came to earth as a man (cf. John 1:14; 17:5).

4. *And there appeared before them Elijah and Moses, who were talking with Jesus.*

God has brought back two important leaders from Israel's history for the three disciples to see. *Elijah* had lived over eight hundred years before the time of Jesus and was the foremost of the prophets. *Moses*, who lived some fourteen hundred years before Christ, was God's specially selected and prepared giver of the law—the law Jesus would fulfill. The apostles are dazed by all of this, but somehow they know who these men are (as Peter's next remark shows). The presence of Elijah and Moses with Jesus is powerful; but the point that God will make in taking them away (v. 8, below) is the far more powerful one.

5, 6. *Peter said to Jesus, "Rabbi, it is good for us to be here. Let us put up three shelters—one for you, one for Moses and one for Elijah." (He did not know what to say, they were so frightened.)*

DAILY BIBLE READINGS

Monday, May 5—*Who Do You Say I Am?* (Mark 8:27-33)

Tuesday, May 6—*Take Up Your Cross* (Mark 8:34—9:1)

Wednesday, May 7—*This Is My Son* (Mark 9:2-8)

Thursday, May 8—*You Have the Words of Life* (John 6:60-69)

Friday, May 9—*Zaccheus Sees Jesus* (Luke 19:1-10)

Saturday, May 10—*Every Tongue Shall Confess* (Philippians 2:5-11)

Sunday, May 11—*Confess That Jesus Is Lord* (Romans 10:5-13)

WHAT DO YOU THINK?

What do you do when you have spoken without thinking and made a foolish or even hurtful remark? What do you do when someone else does?

[See Proverbs 15:1; 26:4.]

PRAYER

Lord, our proper prayer today will be a heart-felt confession of your Son. Each of us individually, and all of us together as a church, make a commitment that Jesus' words will guide our minds and that Jesus' spirit will be the guide for our spirits. Jesus is Lord! And it is in his name we pray, amen.

WHAT DO YOU THINK?

What voices rival that of Jesus today? How can we be sure the message of Jesus prevails?

THOUGHT TO REMEMBER

No one comes to the Father except through Jesus.

In stressful situations, some people "clam up" while others run off at the mouth. Apparently, *Peter* is one of the latter, and is speaking out of fear. Before he stops to think, he suggests putting up *three shelters* (or tents), so that *Elijah* and *Moses* might stay awhile. It sounds like a good idea: he wants to freeze that moment in time. He wants to honor all three.

MONUMENTAL TRUTH

Paris has its Eiffel Tower, New York has the Statue of Liberty, St. Louis has the Gateway Arch, Kuala Lumpur has the Petronas Towers, Jerusalem has the Western Wall of the ancient temple mount, and London has Big Ben (although the London Bridge somehow escaped and ended up in Arizona!). Every major city in the world seems to have a piece of architecture that says, "This is _____" [insert city name].

Los Angeles's thirty-two-story City Hall was once recognized wherever its image was broadcast because it appeared in the old TV series *Dragnet*. But other, commercial buildings have long since surpassed it in prominence. So a few years ago, a grandiose scheme was hatched by an artist best known for his sculptures of Hollywood personalities. His $3.6 billion idea includes a 750-foot tower with a skeletal steel frame, topped by a winged angel. Skeptics derided the proposal as simply a ploy for fame and fortune. (Did someone say, "What else is new?")

Peter had no such grandiose concept in mind when he enthusiastically suggested that tabernacles or tents—memorials or monuments of sorts—be erected at the site of the transfiguration. But Jesus knew a monumental truth: such physical things have only a fleeting existence. Only spiritual realities will stand the test of time and eternity. Is that the testimony of our lives as well?   —C. R. B.

B. THE FIRST OF THE REST (VV. 7, 8)

7. Then a cloud appeared and enveloped them, and a voice came from the cloud: "This is my Son, whom I love. Listen to him!"

The *cloud* indicates the presence of God and that he has something to say (cf. Psalm 97:2; Isaiah 4:5). The disciples are privileged to hear God's direct *voice*. The message is similar to the one at the baptism of Jesus (Mark 1:11). It is a message of confirmation. God wants to make the message clear to the three apostles: the law (represented by Moses) and the prophets (represented by Elijah) point to his beloved *Son*, Jesus, and he is the One you now are to *listen to*. Jesus is primary!

8. Suddenly, when they looked around, they no longer saw anyone with them except Jesus.

The fact that Elijah and Moses now are gone is an important illustration in God's elaborate drama. The law and the prophets these two represent have done what they were supposed to do. They have prepared the way. Now Jesus is the fulfillment of everything. Acknowledge him and listen to him.

CONCLUSION

We can't improve on the declaration that Peter made. We can't improve on the drama that God orchestrated on the mountain. Jesus himself put it into the words that John, one of the primary observers to this scene, later recorded: "I am the way, the truth, and the life: no man cometh unto the Father, but by me" (John 14:6).

People will have wrong opinions about Jesus. Some will count him to be a fraud. Others will view him as no more than a nice, wise man. Some will consider him to be one of the prophets, along with other historic world leaders. But these ideas are all inadequate. Today, he confronts us with the truth of his identity as he asks us the same question he asked of Peter: "Who do you say that I am?"

Discovery Learning

This page contains an alternative lesson plan emphasizing learning activities. Classes desiring such student involvement will find these suggestions helpful. The next page is a reproducible activity page to further enhance discovery learning.

LEARNING GOALS

After participating in this lesson, each student will be able to:

1. Cite evidence from today's texts that Jesus is the Christ, the Son of God.

2. Compare people's wrong ideas about Jesus in his own day with modern misconceptions about him.

3. Make a statement of faith in Jesus Christ, and give a way to live out that faith.

INTO THE LESSON

As students enter the classroom have chairs arranged in groups of six. On each chair place these written instructions: "Take three things from your wallet or purse that will prove who you are. Arrange them in order from least convincing to most convincing."

Each group is to be sure all are introduced and the "proofs" given. Ask, "What was most convincing about the proof presented? Who gave the best proof? Why was it so?"

Ask, "What one word would your best friend use to define or describe you? Why?" Each person will need a few minutes to think and then share it with the group. Allow four minutes.

Say, "In today's lesson we will see how evidence is given of Jesus' true identity. We will see how clear the teaching is. This will help us grow in our faith in Jesus."

INTO THE WORD

Ask a volunteer to read Mark 8:27-36 and another to read Mark 9:2-8. Provide copies of the following questions and allow students several minutes to answer. Use these as a guide to discussion in studying the passage. (You will want to be familiar with the commentary material for difficult questions that may arise during the study.)

1. What is the most important thought in this passage?

2. What is the key verse in this passage?

3. How did Jesus teach this lesson?

4. What is the most practical teaching for you?

5. If you had been one of the disciples with Jesus, what would you have asked him?

After discussing the students' findings ask, "What do these two passages teach us about the identity of Jesus? Why is this important to us today?" Students will see

that Jesus' identity is central to his mission. Only the Son of God could accomplish the task of salvation.

For further study, distribute copies of the reproducible activity "Who Is Jesus?" from the next page. Have students work on the activity individually or in small groups.

INTO LIFE

Prepare a chart with the following three headings: "Opinions of Jesus–Then," "Opinions of Jesus–Now," and "Biblical Teachings of Who Jesus Is."

Say, "Suppose we are developing an evangelism program for our church. For it to be effective we need to be able to communicate who Jesus is. We want to be able to anticipate peoples' responses to 'Who is Jesus?' Using this chart what would you include?"

Discuss how this chart helps us to anticipate objections people might have to the teaching that Jesus is the Christ, the Son of God. Would it help a person recognize the biblical teaching concerning the identity of Jesus?

Provide paper and pencil for each student. Supply hymnals or songbooks also. Ask each individual to write a statement of belief. It can be a simple statement, such as the one Peter made in Mark 7:30 or more elaborate using other Scriptures and hymns or songs. As teacher you may need to help your students in this activity. Allow several minutes for completion. (A similar activity is in the student book.)

Have volunteers read their statements of faith to the class. After each statement, answer the student with Jesus' words in Matthew 16:17, "Blessed are you, (name), for this was not revealed to you by man, but by [the] Father in heaven."

If you have students in your class who are not believers, recognize that this may be difficult for them. Be sensitive to their situation, but encourage them to write what they presently believe.

Mark 9:7 reminds us that we are to listen to Jesus' teaching. Distribute copies of the reproducible activity "Listen to Jesus" from the next page. Have each student write the one or two things that keep him or her from listening to Jesus. Put the students into pairs and ask each one to share his or her answer with one other person in the group. Have the pairs close in prayer concerning their steadfastness in following Jesus.

Who Is Jesus?

"Who Is Jesus?" is a question asked many times through the centuries. Read Mark 8:1 and 9:13. Summarize the events that show Jesus is the Son of God.

Mark 8:1-13

Mark 8:11-21

Mark 8:22-26

Mark 8:27-30

Mark 8:31—9:1

Mark 9:2-13

Listen to Jesus

Mark 9:7 reminds us that we are to listen to Jesus' teaching. Write the one or two things that most often keep you from listening to Jesus. How can you tune these things out and listen more consistently to Jesus?

1.

2.

Unit 3: Jesus' Responses to Faith
(Lessons 9-13)

EXPRESSING HONEST FAITH

LESSON 12

WHY TEACH THIS LESSON?

I lived in "hurricane country" for about three years. Before a hurricane would hit, most trees in our town looked, by all outward appearances, to be quite solid and sturdy. But a hurricane would prove quickly which trees were healthy and which were rotten on the inside!

The soundness of our faith is tested by "the storms of life." The type of faith that Jesus wants us to have is a faith that shows itself to be unshakable when those storms strike. But the problem is that none of us seems to have a faith that never falters.

Your learners face their own storms in life. And they know they don't always respond with solid faith. They believe in the Lord, but unbelief creeps in as well. Some of the people who attend your class may feel discouraged about that. Guilt is added to their doubt, and they are pressed down. Today's lesson provides an opportunity to lift them up. They can identify with the grieving father who prays, "[Lord,] I do believe; help me overcome my unbelief!"

INTRODUCTION

A. Up THE Mountain . . . AND Down Again

A summer week at Christian service camp has always been a terrific time for a lot of the kids in the church. They love the team competition. Swimming and softball, funny new games, great music, and, in some places, even the old Bible drama nights are almost too exciting to bear. It's hard to settle down at night. Sleep deprivation is "the norm in the dorm."

One of the great things at camp is studying the Bible every day. In addition to Bible classes, there are vesper services and other worship times each night. Every camper has to examine his or her faith in the light of all that is being said. It is two months of Sunday school every day! And at week's end there are always young people ready to give their lives to Christ, eager to be baptized. It is a "mountaintop experience."

From the time we were children, a lot of us have heard about (and have had) mountaintop experiences. Frequently, adults used that description when talking to us as children about Christian service camp. They also cautioned us, however, to be aware that down in "the valley" (after leaving "the mountain") things wouldn't be the same as they had been during that glorious week. The idyllic experience of the songs and the swimming pool, thoughtful counselors and lots of laughter, God's Word and great hopes—these would not be much in evidence back in the old neighborhood. But on the mountaintop many wonderful things happened. And, properly embraced, they prepared us for the valley.

The "mountaintop experience" near Caesarea Philippi in last week's lesson is the model for that expression. There, three disciples began to understand Jesus' true nature. They had seen something of Jesus' heavenly glory. They had remembered how God worked through the law and the prophets. And God had confirmed that Jesus, their Master and Teacher, was his one and only Son. They were beginning to put the pieces together. And until Jesus' resurrection, this would be

DEVOTIONAL READING:
JOHN 16:25-33

BACKGROUND SCRIPTURE:
MARK 9:14-37

PRINTED TEXT:
MARK 9:14-29

LESSON AIMS

After participating in this lesson, each student will be able to:

1. Tell how Jesus healed the demon-possessed boy just after the transfiguration.

2. Compare and contrast modern levels of faith with that of the disciples, whom Jesus chided for their inability to cast out the demon, and of the boy's father, who believed but prayed for help with his unbelief.

3. Commit to Jesus one specific area of weak faith with the prayer, "I do believe; help me overcome my unbelief."

May
18

KEY VERSE

Immediately the boy's father exclaimed, "I do believe; help me overcome my unbelief!"
—Mark 9:24

Lesson 12 Notes

the crowning event that clinched their understanding. From that point onward, they would know who their Master was.

But then they came down from the mountain. As soon as they reached its foot, they heard an argument. They encountered illness. They heard about the failure of their colleagues. The harsh reality of everyday life in a sin-scarred world took about a minute to strike them. It was back to the grind. But they had new equipment, a new assurance. We rather suppose that as soon as things settled down that night, they told their fellow disciples all they had seen and heard. While Jesus had told them not to tell anyone (Mark 9:9), it seems reasonable that he meant no one outside the group of the Twelve.

B. Lesson Background

As they were coming down the mountain, Peter, James, and John, who comprised the inner circle of the disciples and who had just been treated to that majestic drama, were on sensory overload. They understood, but just barely. Jesus had told them not to broadcast the news of this event until after he "had risen from the dead" (Mark 9:9). This "rising from the dead" business troubled them (v. 10). And then there was the question of Elijah—wasn't he supposed to precede the Messiah (v. 11)? Jesus' explanation (vv. 12, 13) probably left them with even more questions, but with a measure of understanding as well. (See Matthew 17:13.)

So, with the experience on the mountaintop in their hearts and with these issues still in their minds, they came to the foot of the hill. Immediately they were in the midst of a squabble.

I. CRISIS ARISES (MARK 9:14-18)

A. A Religious Struggle (vv. 14-16)

14, 15. When they came to the other disciples, they saw a large crowd around them and the teachers of the law arguing with them. As soon as all the people saw Jesus, they were overwhelmed with wonder and ran to greet him.

The *disciples* mentioned here are the nine whom Jesus left behind when he went up on the mountain with Peter, James, and John. It is evident that there is some excitement surrounding them. And it is pretty clear that something is wrong. We can almost hear the confusion of near-Eastern voices debating with each other as *the teachers of the law* challenge the disciples. As we will see in verses 17 and 18 below, the debate is undoubtedly due to a certain failure on the disciples' part. The religious leaders, always alert for an opening, are quick to find fault.

The crowd plays a big part here. *The people* are listening to everything that is said—watching everything that happens. It seems as though they really don't expect to see Jesus; they are *overwhelmed with wonder* when he appears. While it seems natural and anything but amazing that Jesus would rejoin his disciples, there must be something in the timing of his arrival that seems more than coincidental. The people run to him immediately. If anyone can resolve this problem, he can.

16. "What are you arguing with them about?" he asked.

Jesus looks at the teachers of the law and challenges them to tell him why they are confronting his disciples. He knows that they have been *arguing*. With divine insight he also knows the issue at the heart of the argument. He wants to point up the foolishness of their dispute.

It's typical! It happens in the world; and more often than we like, it happens in the church. There is a child (or an adult or a family) in great need. And some who are unwilling or unable to meet the need go to war with others who are unable to meet the need. They discuss. They fight. They blame. And the need just sits there.

B. A FAILED ATTEMPT (vv. 17, 18)

17, 18. A man in the crowd answered, "Teacher, I brought you my son, who is possessed by a spirit that has robbed him of speech. Whenever it seizes him, it throws him to the ground. He foams at the mouth, gnashes his teeth and becomes rigid. I asked your disciples to drive out the spirit, but they could not."

The teachers of the law don't answer, but the father of a demon-possessed boy does. This is the most detailed description of a case of demon possession in the Gospels. This is unusual for Mark, whose record is usually more concise. Perhaps the event struck Peter with special significance. Jesus' unique authority, affirmed by the Father on the mountain, is now demonstrated. Mark picks up on it and is moved to write of the event fully.

Previously, Jesus had given his *disciples* power over such spirits (see Mark 6:7). But for some reason, the disciples could not release this demon's hold on the boy. The fierce demon, bent on destruction, lets its tenacious and angry actions speak for it as it tears at the boy and causes him to foam *at the mouth* and gnash *his teeth*.

One thing that strikes us is the controlled way that the father speaks to Jesus. He does not seem to be hostile about the fact that the disciples are unable to cure his son. He doesn't speak bitterly. But he is disappointed and discouraged. Even so, he still can come to Jesus in hope.

THE LIMITS OF HUMAN RESOURCES

Lloyd's of London was long a "rock solid" company. It started in 1688 as a coffeehouse where merchants and ship owners came to insure their cargoes and ships. Eventually Lloyd's became an insurer of many enterprises, from the risky to the mundane. Movie star Betty Grable even bought a Lloyd's insurance policy on her legs—legs that were as much a source of her celebrity status as was her acting ability!

But in 1987, Lloyd's began to lose money because of catastrophic losses on policies held by companies who suffered major disasters. In just two years' time, a petroleum drilling platform in the North Sea exploded; terrorists blew up Pan Am Flight 103 over Lockerbie, Scotland; the *Exxon Valdez* spilled its load of oil off the coast of Alaska; a refinery exploded in Texas; and the 1989 San Francisco earthquake struck—the one the world saw live during a World Series telecast. Lloyd's covered them all, and by the early 1990s it was questionable whether the fabled insurance company could survive.

The disciples seemed at one time to have everything they needed for a rock-solid ministry. After Jesus gave them power over demonic spirits earlier, it seemed the ministry of the disciples would be unstoppable. But like the disasters just mentioned, the demon in our text presented itself as an unrelenting disaster—wreaking havoc on its victim and pointing to the inadequacy of the disciples' resources for all to see. Whatever the source of evil, human power is often unable to solve our problems. God himself doesn't always make our problems go away, but ultimately only he can help us deal with them.   —C. R. B.

II. CRISIS MEETS THE CHRIST (MARK 9:19-27)

A. THE MASTER SHOWS IRRITATION (v. 19)

19. "O unbelieving generation," Jesus replied, "how long shall I stay with you? How long shall I put up with you? Bring the boy to me."

WHAT DO YOU THINK?

The disciples had failed in their attempts to minister. Of course, there were critics on hand to point the finger and blame. How should we respond to failure in our ministry efforts—and to those who criticize our failed efforts?

Jesus sounds almost angry. That may surprise us. There are not many times in his ministry when Jesus sounds this agitated. His strongest actions are directed against the cheats and profiteers who turn the temple into a thieves' market. His strongest words are directed toward the religious pretenders, teachers of the law, and Pharisees who twisted the laws and traditions to make life easy for themselves and hard for everyone else.

At first glance, we might think that Jesus is irritated with the father of the boy. Upon reflection, though, Jesus' primary frustration seems to be with his own disciples. They have reason to understand more about faith by now than they are giving evidence of using. *How long* is he going to have to *put up with* their slowness? How many illustrations is he going to have to give? How many miracles will they have to see? When will they understand and show evidence of that understanding? He could ask me the same things—and probably you, too!

Jesus teaches good lessons about anger. His anger is not out of control. It is controlled; it is directed. It has a purpose. He does not get angry about things that are done to him—such as rude slights or insults. He gets angry when his anger can make a difference. Here it makes a point about faith, whole-hearted faith; about trust, which depends on God for what is beyond ourselves. No, men, you can't handle this on your own. Why will you even try? Jesus had given them authority over unclean spirits (Mark 6:7), and already they had cast out demons (Mark 6:13). But when this tough one came along they did not believe enough, and they did not depend enough—on God's power.

B. THE DEMON REACTS TO THE MASTER (vv. 20-22)

20. So they brought him. When the spirit saw Jesus, it immediately threw the boy into a convulsion. He fell to the ground and rolled around, foaming at the mouth.

This is a resistant, insistent demon. He won't give up voluntarily, even when facing Jesus directly. This unholy *spirit* takes its rage out on *the boy* in very visible ways.

There has to be a lesson here, doesn't there? The devil won't give up on you either. He will scratch and tear and try to toss you around. Jesus scares him, but you don't. And it may be that you will not trust Jesus. He'll still get you.

21, 22. Jesus asked the boy's father, "How long has he been like this?"

"From childhood," he answered. "It has often thrown him into fire or water to kill him. But if you can do anything, take pity on us and help us."

Jesus, of course, does not need to ask any questions. As the Son of God, he is able to know the answer in advance. But in asking *how long* this problem has persisted, Jesus opens a way to test the man's faith.

The father's devotion to his son obviously is profound. He has had to keep an eye on his son continually since early *childhood* in order to be able to rescue him immediately any time the demon would throw the boy *into fire or water*. Notice the plural as the father asks Jesus to *take pity on us and help us*. This is not just the child's problem. It is a family problem.

The plea *if you can do anything* shows discouragement. The disciples have already tried and failed. But it is not an insult for the father to ask Jesus to help *if* he can. Everyone can see that this is the most awful kind of affliction that can be imagined. The father is aware that Jesus has done great things, but maybe this is too much. Anything that Jesus can do will be greatly appreciated.

C. THE MASTER SOLVES TWO PROBLEMS (vv. 23-27)

23. "'If you can'?" said Jesus. "Everything is possible for him who believes."

Jesus immediately responds to the father's "if" with an *if* of his own. The father's "if" in verse 22 has raised the issue of Jesus' power or ability. But Jesus

WHAT DO YOU THINK?

In what areas of the church might Jesus be wondering about us, "How long until they 'get it'?"

[If there are issues causing strife in your church, be careful with this question as it may provide an excuse to blast the "other side."]

WHAT DO YOU THINK?

The father said, "If you can." He wasn't sure Jesus could handle his son's problem. Which problems do we have trouble trusting Jesus to handle today?

turns the tables and says, in effect, that this isn't an issue of his own power, but of the father's faith. I can do it, if you can believe, Jesus answers. What Jesus is talking about, of course, is not just some general kind of belief, some hoping against hope, some power of positive thinking. Rather, it is an absolute trust in him. That's the only kind of faith that can yield results.

24. Immediately the boy's father exclaimed, "I do believe; help me overcome my unbelief!"

We understand! We *believe*, too, but imperfectly. We are a strange combination of believing and unbelieving. Please *help me*, despite my incomplete and imperfect faith, the man says. We know how that is. And probably we will pray that prayer to God as long as we live. *I do believe!* But my confidence and my follow-through are both flawed. Please accept my heart and my intentions, and help me.

25. When Jesus saw that a crowd was running to the scene, he rebuked the evil spirit. "You deaf and mute spirit," he said, "I command you, come out of him and never enter him again."

The crowd (v. 14) is growing, as more people are *running to the scene*. Before the commotion gets out of hand, Jesus decides to act. He does it from compassion for the boy. He does it in recognition of the faith of the father. He does it to underline for the crowd the fact that they can depend on him, and that he has that kind of power. He does it because he is not about to let demons have the last word against his disciples! So he rebukes the *evil spirit*—and it's over!

26. The spirit shrieked, convulsed him violently and came out. The boy looked so much like a corpse that many said, "He's dead."

One last surge! *The spirit* tears at the child again, a death-gasp this time. In the crowd, *many* jump to the logical (but wrong) conclusion that the boy is *dead*. Although Jesus has done his best, they think, this one was just too strong!

27. But Jesus took him by the hand and lifted him to his feet, and he stood up.

Jesus' healing of this boy certainly solves that young fellow's immediate problem. But more importantly, this healing demonstrates to the disciples, the father, and the crowd the importance of faith. Even so, the disciples won't really "get it" until they ask Jesus about it privately.

III. CHRIST EXPLAINS THE CRISIS (MARK 9:28, 29)

A. THE QUESTION (v. 28)

28. After Jesus had gone indoors, his disciples asked him privately, "Why couldn't we drive it out?"

The *disciples* had driven out demons before (Mark 6:13), but for some reason this one was different.

B. THE ANSWER (v. 29)

29. He replied, "This kind can come out only by prayer."

Jesus sometimes speaks to his disciples in public, but also instructs them in private, as now (cf. Mark 13:3; Luke 10:23).

Matthew's account of this event includes a gentle rebuke of the disciples. They could not cast out the demon "because you have so little faith" (Matthew 17:20). They suffer the same problem as the boy's father—they believe, but there is still unbelief. Both faith and *prayer* are vital to ministry. Apparently the disciples hadn't exercised much of either. Instead, they had drawn on their previous experience and depended on themselves. Perhaps they had tried to use their God-given power (Mark 6:7) as if it were some kind of "magic," requiring nothing but their own desires. (Later, the seven sons of Sceva would find out the hard way just how dangerous such a practice could be! See Acts 19:13-16.)

'Lord, I believe; help thou mine unbelief." — Mark 9:24

Today's visual powerfully illustrates the Key Verse and is an apt reminder of our need to pray.

WHAT DO YOU THINK?

In what extremely difficult areas of our society is it absolutely essential that serious, focused prayer be concentrated?

[Use Ephesians 6:12 in your discussion.]

But faith and prayer acknowledge that we are inadequate by ourselves. When we exercise them, we admit that we must depend on God. And the kind of prayer that Jesus is talking about is not a few words spoken with head bowed. It is a life of dependent communion with God, a life of sustained communication.

SPIRITUAL NAVIGATION

On a tiny island off the eastern coast of Africa in the Indian Ocean, archaeologists have found the remains of eight Islamic mosques, buried one on top of another. Islamic practice is to have mosques situated so that they point to Mecca, the Muslim holy city. Mecca is almost exactly due north of this small island.

The archaeologists discovered that as new mosques were built on top of older ones, the orientation changed. A mosque built in A.D. 780 pointed toward 310 degrees on the compass (roughly northwest); one built 120 years later was pointed at 329 degrees; and one built in A.D. 1000 was pointed at 342 degrees. (Mecca would be at 360 degrees from the island.) Apparently, Muslim navigators sailing the Gulf of Aden and the Indian Ocean gradually, over time, refined their ability to plot true directions. They used this improved knowledge in building each successive mosque.

Christians have no need to orient their church buildings toward Jerusalem (or any other city). But we are under obligation to orient our lives so that they point more and more toward Christ. Yet the process of increasingly accurate spiritual navigation is one that takes time, effort, and commitment on the part of the person who would serve God. We work through this process by deepening our levels of faith and prayer. This is an obligation each of us must take seriously as we plot a true direction for our life.

—C. R. B.

CONCLUSION

Jesus asked how long he was going to have to be with his disciples until they caught on, how long he was going to have to suffer with their obtuseness. How long would he have to teach before they learned the lessons?

Can't you hear him asking us the same kind of questions today? Some of us have studied in Sunday school for years. We have been through the International Sunday School Lesson series six or seven times. It's okay for us to continue to learn. It is understandable that every time we go through the Bible, we see things that we have not seen before. That's fine—we all overlook some things occasionally. But sadly, sometimes we choose not to see. As a result, we do not obey (cf. James 1:22-25).

PRAYER

Our Father, it is our prayer that we will have learned with the close disciples of Jesus the lessons in faith and prayer that he is eager to teach them. And we are thrilled to celebrate again the power of your Son, through whom we pray, amen!

We have so often missed the Spirit of Jesus. We have heard his words, but unlike the wise man who built his house on the rock, we have not put them into practice. How long is he going to have to wait for us to practice what he has preached?

Some of our debates over music styles in worship services have caught us not having listened. Those of us who have been longest in the church of Jesus seem to be the most frightened by any change. We are most resistant to some things to which other generations are responding—changing music style, levels of formality, and ways of addressing human need that are making them dynamic and enthusiastic Christians. They seem different from us. That seems to be most important. But are we, and are they, listening to the orders of Jesus and walking in his ways, copying his style? That's what is important. How long will he have to wait for us to understand that?

THOUGHT TO REMEMBER

"I do believe; help me overcome my unbelief!" —Mark 9:24

As long as we live, our faith will not be perfect. But to tax the patience and the grace of Jesus less and less as we grow will give the Father joy. When that happens, we are better able to become living sacrifices to him (cf. Romans 12:1).

Discovery Learning

This page contains an alternative lesson plan emphasizing learning activities. Classes desiring such student involvement will find these suggestions helpful. The next page is a reproducible activity page to further enhance discovery learning.

LEARNING GOALS

After participating in this lesson, each student will be able to:

1. Tell how Jesus healed the demon-possessed boy just after the transfiguration.

2. Compare and contrast modern levels of faith with that of the disciples, whom Jesus chided for their inability to cast out the demon, and of the boy's father, who believed but prayed for help with his unbelief.

3. Commit to Jesus one specific area of weak faith with the prayer, "I do believe; help me overcome my unbelief."

INTO THE LESSON

Decorate your classroom this week with a number of "snapshots": photos, newspaper or magazine pictures, or drawings. As the students arrive, give each a blank sheet of paper. (*NIV® Bible Student* has this activity.)

Ask the students to draw a picture of "mountaintop" experiences they have had in their spiritual lives. (Rather than drawing, they may write brief descriptions of the events.) Ask students to share their creations in groups of four.

Say, "Each of us has had 'mountaintop' experiences in the Lord. Today's lesson comes right after the disciples had experienced a special message from God. They struggled to obey him. As we study, we will see how we need to trust God more after the 'mountaintops.'"

INTO THE WORD

Use the introductory remarks of the commentary (pages 319, 320) for a brief lecture to remind students of what the disciples had experienced with Jesus.

Form two groups, each no larger than six. (If you have more people, assign the following to more than one group.) Give each group a twenty-four-inch by thirty-six-inch white poster board or an overhead transparency with markers. One person in each group serves as a secretary.

Group 1: Read Mark 9:14-29. Complete an acrostic of the word FAITH with as many words, phrases, or ideas that describe faith in the text. Examples would include *Focused on Christ, Accepts Christ's authority, Inspires action, Trusting, Heavenly-oriented.* (This activity is in the student's book.)

Group 2: Read Mark 9:14-29. List the major circumstances in this healing. Start with the crowd approaching Jesus. (*The list will include Jesus challenges the teachers of the law, the father approaches Jesus, Jesus rebukes the crowd for disbelief, the boy is brought to Jesus, Jesus questions the father, the father responds, Jesus teaches the father, the father believes, Jesus rebukes the evil spirit, the spirit departs leaving the boy in bad shape, Jesus helps the boy to his feet and answers the disciples' questions.*)

Call the groups together to present their findings. Discuss any difficult points using the lesson commentary for answers.

Distribute copies of the reproducible activity "Lessons to Learn" from the next page. Allow the students six to eight minutes to complete the activity; then review the results together.

1. What do we learn about Jesus? (*He is greater than evil spirits and seeks to encourage faith in himself.*)

2. What do we learn about the disciples? (*At times they were slow to understand Jesus' teaching. They often relied upon themselves and not upon Jesus.*)

3. What is faith? (*Believing and trusting Jesus to accomplish his will.*)

4. How does Jesus help the man in his unbelief? (*Jesus shows the man that he has the power to do God's will.*)

INTO LIFE

Ask the class to return to their original groups of six. Each group should discuss situations or examples of present-day individuals who exercised faith in Jesus' power. They may recall a missionary's presentation, a co-worker's challenge, a neighbor's friendly conversation, or a relative's concern. Encourage them to share some common denominators in each example. (*Examples may include trust in God, a willingness to admit personal frailty, or an openness to God's will.*) Ask, "How are these similar to the experiences of the disciples and the father in today's text? How are they different?"

Have the class form pairs. Give each class member a copy of the reproducible activity "Lord, Help Me!" Say, "Just as the man asked Jesus to help him in his unbelief, so we will ask Jesus to help us. Choose an area you believe yourself to be weak in faith. Write it on the 'business card' on the handout. Under that write, 'Lord, I believe. Help me in my unbelief.'

"Share the circumstance with your partner and pray together for strength."

Lessons to Learn

Read Mark 9:2-29. This passage describes a "mountaintop" experience for the disciples as well as a valley. The experience contains some valuable lessons for us to learn. Answer the questions below to explore some of these lessons.

1. What do you learn about Jesus?

2. What do you learn about the disciples?

3. What is faith?

4. How does Jesus help the man in his unbelief?

Lord, Help Me!

In the text today, Jesus is asked for help. He accomplishes the task. On the "business card" below, fill in how he can help you.

Help in Unbelief

JESUS' BUSINESS

"Just call me!"

Lord, I need your help in this area of my life:

Jesus: God's Power in Action
Unit 3: Jesus' Responses to Faith
(Lessons 9-13)

FAITH BECOMES SIGHT

LESSON 13

WHAT DO YOU THINK?

The familiar saying "There is none so blind as they that won't see" comes from the satirist Jonathan Swift (1667–1745). It is easy to uncover the truth of these words in the pages of the Gospels. Although Jesus performed miracle after miracle, for some these were never enough to convince them of Jesus' true identity (cf. Matthew 12:39). Their spiritual blindness was complete because they *chose* not to see (cf. Matthew 23:16-19).

Sometimes we call it having a "blind spot." It may seem obvious to everyone else, but for some reason we just can't see it. Somehow we have to get a new perspective, a new vantage point from which to view the situation.

Use this lesson to give that new perspective to your students. Let the blind man remind them that Jesus expects us to "live by faith, not by sight" (2 Corinthians 5:7), in anticipation of the time when faith actually will *become* sight.

INTRODUCTION

A. "WHEN E. F. HUTTON SPEAKS"

In the early 1980s, the large Wall Street brokerage firm of E. F. Hutton came to be identified with its series of clever TV commercials. These ten commercials featured people in various social situations talking about the status of their financial portfolios. At a certain point, someone would always say something like, "Well, my broker is E. F. Hutton, and E. F. Hutton says—" Immediately dead silence would fall, as everyone in the place turned his or her ears to the speaker to find out just *what* E. F. Hutton had to say! The commercial would then end with a hushed voice saying, "When E. F. Hutton speaks, people listen!"

By 1985, however, no one was listening to E. F. Hutton! That was the year that the company pleaded guilty to two thousand federal charges concerning manipulation of accounts. As a result of that plea, the firm agreed to pay two million dollars in fines and to reimburse defrauded banks as much as eight million dollars. In early 1988, E. F. Hutton ceased to exist when it was absorbed by another brokerage house.

Jesus is different. His timeless, living message never disappoints. But we must make sure that we are actually hearing *his* message. When we contaminate that message with our own expectations, disappointment will follow.

Today, we will see some disciples who allowed their own expectations to color what Jesus was saying. We will also see a crowd that tried to shout down a poor blind man because of their wrong understanding of Jesus and his message. As we examine their thinking, it will be a good time to examine our own!

B. LESSON BACKGROUND

Between the healing of the demon-possessed boy of last week's lesson and the events of today's text, a great deal has happened. Most of the intervening events are recorded in Luke 10–18 and John 7–11. These events include incidents of Jesus' later Judean ministry (e.g., the mission of the seventy) and of Jesus' later Perean ministry (e.g., the healing of ten lepers).

DEVOTIONAL READING:
JOHN 20:24-31

BACKGROUND SCRIPTURE:
MARK 10:32-52

PRINTED TEXT:
MARK 10:35-52

LESSON AIMS

After participating in this lesson, each student will be able to:

1. Summarize the story of James and John's asking for the chief seats of the kingdom as well as the account of the healing of Bartimaeus.

2. Tell why "blind" people sometimes see more clearly than others and why supposed leaders sometimes need to learn to follow.

3. Decide which "blind spot" he or she needs to work on most in order to follow the Lord more closely.

KEY VERSE

"Go," said Jesus, "your faith has healed you." Immediately he received his sight and followed Jesus along the road.
—Mark 10:52

May
25

Now Jesus and his disciples have started on the way to Jerusalem—the way to betrayal and the cross. Every day he was teaching. Every day the Pharisees were attacking. Not always were his followers learning. Sometimes it seemed they were not listening at all.

I. AN UNINFORMED FAITH (MARK 10:35-40)

A. The Questioners' Immaturity (vv. 35-37)

35. Then James and John, the sons of Zebedee, came to him. "Teacher," they said, "we want you to do for us whatever we ask."

In the two verses just before this one Jesus has again predicted his death—this time in very specific terms. Now Mark shows us that the disciples still "just don't get it." They have a plan of their own.

John's wisdom and maturity will be evident later in the five New Testament books he writes. We will see the spiritual maturity of his brother *James* in the martyrdom he will be willing to undergo (Acts 12:2). But right now both seem almost like children. This is the way a child speaks to his parents when he is about to ask something unreasonable. He seeks assurance first. "Tell me that you will give me *whatever I ask!*"

The parallel in Matthew 20:20 notes that it is their mother who asks the favor for them. Putting the two reports together, we can reasonably conclude that the two disciples have cooked up this idea, and their mother acts as the spokesperson. (Some students believe her to be Jesus' "mother's sister" of John 19:25. Perhaps the disciples believe Jesus will not refuse his own aunt!) Since the other ten disciples will be indignant with these two brothers (Matthew 20:24; Mark 10:41, below), the source of the problem is James and *John.*

36. "What do you want me to do for you?" he asked.

Jesus doesn't promise them, of course, that they can have whatever they want. But he is willing to listen to their request. Earlier, he had heard the disciples talking as they walked along the road. He knew that they were arguing among themselves about who was the best (Mark 9:33-37). It may be that he now just wants them to hear themselves make their selfish request out loud. This will be another opportunity to teach.

37. They replied, "Let one of us sit at your right and the other at your left in your glory."

The seats on the *right* and *left* sides of a king's throne are the places of highest honor, the places for the king's most trusted and respected aides. Despite all that Jesus has said about the nature of the spiritual kingdom over which he reigns, the disciples still think in terms of a physical and political kingdom. And here they are eager to have not only a reward for their partnership, but also position, rank, and preference.

That's so wrong! It's so selfish! And it proves they have not been listening to what Jesus has just recently been saying about his approaching death (Mark 9:31).

SWEET SEDUCTION

The search for love potions is a historic one: humans have long desired to find a magic substance that can arouse amorous passions in another person. Chocolate has found a place in Western culture as one such substance. That's the reason we see all those chocolate hearts for sale around Valentine's Day.

One story has it that the sixteenth-century Aztec emperor Montezuma daily drank fifty cups of a potion made from the cacao bean. It was called *chocoatl.* Rumors spread that this substance was what made the king a very virile man. From

What Do You Think?

Is it wrong for a Christian to seek advancement, leadership, and higher pay? Why or why not?

[Use passages such as Matthew 6:33; Mark 10:23; and 1 Timothy 6:6-11 to guide your discussion.]

the New World to Spain to England to Switzerland, the substance made its way, being refined with the addition of sugar and milk to the recipe as it went along. Today, chemists tell us Montezuma may have been on the right track: a chemical found in chocolate is also produced by the brain when one falls in love!

But there are other kinds of seduction as well. One that is perhaps subtler than that plied by the givers of chocolate is the seduction into which James and John had fallen: they wanted the glory of sitting on thrones beside Jesus in the glory of his kingdom. They could almost *taste* the sweetness of the honor. The temptation is with us yet. The glory of exalted positions still seduces many Christians who should know better.   —C. R. B.

B. THE QUESTIONERS QUESTIONED (vv. 38, 39a)
38. "You don't know what you are asking," Jesus said. "Can you drink the cup I drink or be baptized with the baptism I am baptized with?"

What Jesus really asks here is whether they can give their lives. The *cup* that he is talking about relates to judgment and suffering (cf. Psalm 75:8; Jeremiah 25:15-28). Later, in the garden as he prays to his Father, Jesus will ask that the cup (of suffering) be taken from him if possible. He knows that his death and the terrible things leading up to it are in God's design. But it will be very hard nonetheless. This suffering will come upon Jesus as a deluge, or *baptism*.
39a. "We can," they answered.

James and John surely are sincere. In their enthusiasm they are ready to commit to anything. They think they *can* do it. They know the result will be great because Jesus is great. They have already seen that the way is hard. But for one who could raise the dead and drive out demons, how hard could it really be?

C. THE QUESTIONERS INSTRUCTED (vv. 39b, 40)
39b. Jesus said to them, "You will drink the cup I drink and be baptized with the baptism I am baptized with, . . .

These two and the others *will* suffer for their discipleship. In the early days after Pentecost, Peter and John will be thrown into jail for preaching about the resurrection and healing (Acts 4:1-22). A few years later, Herod will have James executed. This will draw a good response from the Jewish leaders, so Herod will become more aggressive in pursuing and jailing other apostles (12:1-4). Tradition says that the enemies of Jesus tried once to boil John in oil, but failed. Subsequently, John is sent into exile on the tiny island of Patmos (Revelation 1:9).
40. . . . but to sit at my right or left is not for me to grant. These places belong to those for whom they have been prepared."

After sharing his cup and baptism of suffering, the disciples will indeed share in his kingdom. But it will be a kingdom different from the one they expect. Jesus cannot make a commitment to them about a place of prominence in his "court." God the Father has certain prerogatives that the Son does not have (Mark 13:32; John 14:28).

II. AN INFORMED FAITH (MARK 10:41-45)
A. THE WORLD'S WAY (vv. 41, 42)
41. When the ten heard about this, they became indignant with James and John.

The other *ten* are *indignant* because they are sorry that they hadn't thought of asking first! Their displeasure here is consistent with the adolescent conversation they recently had carried on along the road (Mark 9:33, 34). It is very unlikely that these ten have a better understanding of the Lord's way than do James and John.

WHAT DO YOU THINK?
James and John naïvely stated that they would be willing and able to drink from the same cup that Jesus would drink. How have you seen God transform the naïve overconfidence of a new believer into a mature faith that's truly willing to take up any cross for Jesus?

Visual for lesson 13. Use today's visual to summarize and review the lessons of the quarter. Note some relevant application of each lesson as well.

WHAT DO YOU THINK?

Jesus warned the Twelve against following the cultural pattern of leadership. What kinds of selfish values from our culture sometimes creep into the way that the church approaches leadership and greatness?

42. *Jesus called them together and said, "You know that those who are regarded as rulers of the Gentiles lord it over them, and their high officials exercise authority over them.*

Jesus understands. The Twelve are acting like products of what is around them. Greatness in the secular Gentile culture (the Romans in particular) means authority, superiority, the giving of orders. For the upper classes and those in positions of power, control, perks, and pomp are important. Such thinking still predominates today.

B. THE KINGDOM WAY (vv. 43-45)

43, 44. *"Not so with you. Instead, whoever wants to become great among you must be your servant, and whoever wants to be first must be slave of all.*

The world's way is not Christ's way. (Nor is it the church's way.) Greatness is related to service. The one who is in first place is like a lowly *servant*. Since the Greek word for *servant* here literally means *slave*, such thinking is undoubtedly a shock to the Twelve. But how many times have we heard Jesus turn human values on their head? His followers are in the world, but they don't belong there. We are not defined by the world. As Paul says, "the world has been crucified to me, and I to the world" (Galatians 6:14; cf. Colossians 2:8, 20).

The same is true of leadership in the church. Paul says that an elder must not be a novice, lest he succumb to pride (1 Timothy 3:6). There is a significant level of authority in the elder's task (Hebrews 13:17). A new Christian might not be able to handle such authority without its "going to his head." And Peter reminds the elders that they are not to act like lords over the flock, but rather to be examples to them (1 Peter 5:3).

45. *"For even the Son of Man did not come to be served, but to serve, and to give his life as a ransom for many."*

Jesus himself models the service he expects from his followers. And he models service and sacrifice to the point of giving *his life as a ransom for many*. The ultimate object of his life as a man is that very service: his death as ransom to recover prisoners and to free slaves. That's what Jesus' sacrifice does as it pays the price to release us from God's wrath (Romans 3:21-26). The price is paid for all who will accept it (Acts 2:38, 39).

III. A VICTORIOUS FAITH (MARK 10:46-52)

A. A BLIND MAN ASKS (vv. 46-48)

46. *Then they came to Jericho. As Jesus and his disciples, together with a large crowd, were leaving the city, a blind man, Bartimaeus (that is, the Son of Timaeus), was sitting by the roadside begging.*

Mark has one more healing encounter to tell us about before he reports the final week that ends with the cross and the empty tomb. Once more he wants to underscore a theme of his Gospel: Jesus is all-powerful. He rules over all illness, forces of nature, and spirits. He is able to protect us in every way. He is the Messiah, the Son of Man, the Son of David.

Jesus moves his base of operations for the final part of the ministry. Up north, his "headquarters" had been in Capernaum. Now to the south, he will spend valuable time teaching in Bethany (John 12:1-11). He and his disciples will travel the road from Jericho (about seventy miles south of Capernaum) to get there before entering Jerusalem. But right now, a poor, *blind man, the son of* a certain *Timaeus,* hears a crowd approach.

47. *When he heard that it was Jesus of Nazareth, he began to shout, "Jesus, Son of David, have mercy on me!"*

WHAT DO YOU THINK?

Can you think of someone who imitates Jesus' teaching on servanthood? How does following his pattern work out in "real life"?

Bartimaeus apparently has heard about *Jesus of Nazareth*. The reports of all of those healings, which caused the multitudes to follow him all over Galilee, have made their way to Jericho (about eighteen miles northeast of Jerusalem, where the Jordan River meets the Dead Sea). For a blind man, Bartimaeus can "see" with remarkable clarity.

We have noted already how slow Jesus' own disciples have been to understand Jesus' true identity. He has shown them many miracles. He has called their attention to Isaiah's description of the one who is coming, who would suffer. Peter eventually was able to put it into words: "You are the Christ" (Mark 8:29). Then three of the disciples had seen him transfigured on the mountain and had heard the voice of God expressing his approval (9:7). Now here is a blind man, who knows Jesus only by reputation, referring to Jesus by the messianic title Son of David (cf. Ezekiel 34:23, 24). Bartimaeus knows who Jesus is.

Seeing What God Wants to Show Us

The story is probably the same in every major city: thousands, perhaps millions of people hurry about their business unaware of places of beauty around them. In Long Beach, California, the El Dorado Park Nature Center is such a place. It is a 102-acre sanctuary of plants and wildlife right next to Interstate 605, one of the busiest freeways in the metropolitan Los Angeles area. Its meadows, brooks, and two lakes are home to a fascinating variety of flora and fauna. The garden is a quiet refuge in the midst of the noisy, teeming city. All it takes for anyone to enjoy it is the willingness to take the time to stroll, sit, look at, and listen to God's creation.

But from time immemorial, multitudes of people have considered themselves too busy (or perhaps too important) to take time out, stop, and appreciate the handiwork of God. This isn't a new problem. In Jesus' day, many were apparently too engrossed in their own plans and expectations to appreciate God's greatest piece of handiwork: the work his Son was doing in their very midst. But a certain blind man could "see" what so many others failed to notice: this Jesus was the messianic Son of David. Sometimes we have to stop the hurry of our lives and listen to God's voice and see what he is trying to show us. Bartimaeus can teach us a profound lesson if we are willing to learn!   —C. R. B.

48. Many rebuked him and told him to be quiet, but he shouted all the more, "Son of David, have mercy on me!"

Bartimaeus annoys *many* in the crowd. So they tell him to shut up. Jesus has better things to do than to deal with a pesky blind man. Obviously, these are people who have plans and expectations that are very different from those of Jesus. But this is nothing new! Even so, the blind man is persistent in crying out *all the more*.

B. A Blind Man Receives (vv. 49-52)

49. Jesus stopped and said, "Call him."

So they called to the blind man, "Cheer up! On your feet! He's calling you."

To *Jesus*, the *blind man* is not a hindrance to his mission, but a reason for it. Jesus always sees "little" people differently from the way others see them. Many in the crowd probably believe the man deserves to be blind because of sin (cf. John 9:1, 2). But Jesus stops and asks that the man be brought to him.

50. Throwing his cloak aside, he jumped to his feet and came to Jesus.

This report has an unusual amount of detail! Mark not only gives the man's name, but also the name of his father. Mark describes the persistence of his call. He relates the title that the blind man uses for Jesus and tells us that the man is a

What Do You Think?

How is Bartimaeus's cry to Jesus for mercy the basic prayer that every lost and blind person needs to pray before coming to Jesus?

How to Say It

Aztec. AZ-teck.
Bartimaeus. BAR-tih-ME-us.
Bethany. BETH-uh-nee.
cacao. Kuh-KAY-oh.
Capernaum. Kuh-PER-nay-um.
chocoatl. CHO-co-AHT-ul.
Gadarenes. Gad-uh-REENZ.
Galilee. GAL-uh-lee.
Gentile. JEN-tyle.
Herod. HAIR-ud.
Jericho. JAIR-ih-co.
Jordan. JOR-dun.
Judean. Joo-DEE-un.
messianic. mess-ee-AN-ick.
Montezuma. Mon-tuh-ZOO-muh.
Nazareth. NAZ-uh-reth.
Perean. Peh-REE-un.
Timaeus. Ty-ME-us.
Zebedee. ZEB-eh-dee.

DAILY BIBLE READINGS

Monday, May 19—*Can You Drink the Cup?* (Mark 10:32-40)

Tuesday, May 20—*The Great Must Become Servant* (Mark 10:41-45)

Wednesday, May 21—*Jesus Gives Bartimaeus Sight* (Mark 10:46-52)

Thursday, May 22—*Believing Without Seeing* (John 20:24-31)

Friday, May 23—*Abraham's Faith Did Not Weaken* (Romans 4:16-22)

Saturday, May 24—*Promises Seen From a Distance* (Hebrews 11:8-16)

Sunday, May 25—*Looking Ahead to the Reward* (Hebrews 11:23-28)

PRAYER

Lord, thank you for teaching us about faith and love this quarter, through the life of your Son and through the record of your servant Mark. Thank you for empowering Jesus to make such an eternal difference in so many lives. Through him we pray, amen.

THOUGHT TO REMEMBER

Blindness can be temporary— or eternal.

beggar. Now, Mark even describes the man's quick jump *to his feet* and the fact that he tosses *his cloak aside.*

Matthew 20:30 tells us there were actually two blind men. Mark mentions only one—apparently to focus on the spokesman. We saw the same thing with his description of Jesus' casting out the legion of demons from the man in the region of the Gadarenes (Mark 5, lesson 3). Matthew's account included a second man (Matthew 8:28).

51. "What do you want me to do for you?" Jesus asked him.
   The blind man said, "Rabbi, I want to see."

Jesus already knows, of course, what Bartimaeus wants. But Jesus doesn't provide the healing right away. He questions *the blind man* to give him a chance to express his hope and his trust. Here the word *Rabbi* that he uses means "my master." No beating around the bush! *"Rabbi, I want to see."*

52. "Go," said Jesus, "your faith has healed you." Immediately he received his sight and followed Jesus along the road.

He identifies Jesus. He asks for help. He believes that Jesus can give him his sight. Jesus doesn't waste any time. Bartimaeus receives *his sight.*

In an interesting conclusion to this healing encounter, Bartimaeus immediately becomes part of the crowd that *followed Jesus.* He doesn't take his healing for granted. He doesn't head off to use his newfound sight to do all of the things that he had always wanted to do, but couldn't. He uses his gift for the one who has given him the gift. That's a stewardship idea worth pursuing, isn't it?

This is unlike other healings in that Jesus does not forbid him from following as he has done elsewhere. For example, in Mark 5:18, 19 a man cured of demon possession was told instead to go tell his friends the good things that Jesus had done. But now, as the trip to the cross is very close, the crowds around him and all of the publicity that will relate to this healing will not matter. Let them talk. Let these throngs of people frustrate the Pharisees. It is time.

CONCLUSION

A. SEEING LIKE THE BLIND MAN

Maybe you know individuals who have been without one of their senses, particularly sight or hearing, who say that their other senses are sharpened. Such sharpening isn't automatic, however. Some people who suffer handicaps give up. Everything goes. They are not able to make much of a contribution. But others refuse to let one loss lead to many others. They make a remaining sense stand for two. That seems to be what this man did. Without his eyesight, his hearing sharpened. He listened. He processed what he heard. He understood. When Jesus came by, he was ready. He reached out. He trusted the Master.

Christians know that a loss doesn't have to be total or final. If one avenue is cut off, there are others to find. Christ is there. Sometimes he helps us be restored. Sometimes he helps us use very well what we have left.

B. SERVING LIKE THE GREAT MAN

Jesus also teaches us that greatness doesn't come from being the boss or exercising authority. It comes from being a servant—a slave. Jesus had time for people whom society ignored. He had time for blind men. He had time for people who recognized their need and put their trust in him.

In the days ahead, his disciples would watch him act out his service. He would make the ultimate sacrifice. They would soon understand how much they needed that sacrifice for their own sin. They would understand how much they needed to be servants themselves (cf. John 21:15-17). Is that true of you?

Discovery Learning

This page contains an alternative lesson plan emphasizing learning activities. Classes desiring such student involvement will find these suggestions helpful. The next page is a reproducible activity page to further enhance discovery learning.

LEARNING GOALS

After participating in this lesson, each student will be able to:

1. Summarize the story of James and John's asking for the chief seats of the kingdom and also the story of the healing of Bartimaeus.

2. Tell why "blind" people sometimes see more clearly than others and why supposed leaders sometimes need to learn to follow.

3. Decide which "blind spot" he or she needs to work on most in order to follow the Lord more closely.

INTO THE LESSON

Distribute copies of the following agree-disagree exercise. Ask your students to circle the response that best reflects their opinion for each statement. Place an "Agree" sign on one wall of the classroom, a "Disagree" sign on the opposite wall. Call for students to move to the side of the room which corresponds to their answer. (If your students don't like to move around, ask them to raise their hands if they agree.)

1. Leaders should be more highly paid than followers. Agree/Disagree

2. Leaders get more benefits than those whom they lead. Agree/Disagree

3. Leaders are more important than their followers. Agree/Disagree

4. Leaders should never do the tasks their followers do. Agree/Disagree

5. A servant's attitude is necessary for a good leader. Agree/Disagree

Discuss your students' responses. Tell the class that today's lesson deals with attitudes and actions which communicate a servant's heart as a leader. We will also "see" how things may be different than they appear.

INTO THE WORD

Prepare an eight-minute overview for today's lesson using the introductory remarks on page 327. This will set the stage for the important lesson Jesus will teach his disciples.

Option 1. Distribute copies of the reproducible activity "Again" and have the students complete these individually. After a few minutes, discuss the results.

Option 2. Divide your class into three groups of six each. More groups can be used if necessary. Copy the fol-lowing directions for groups and assign one to each group. If a group completes its exercise early, assign another. You will need poster paper, markers, blank paper, and pens or pencils.

Exercise 1: Read Mark 10:35-52. Develop a chart with column one titled "The Disciples" and column two titled "The Blind Man." Under each column write these categories: 1. Title Used for Jesus; 2. Persistence of Person(s); 3. Question Jesus Asked; 4. Request of Person(s); 5. Result of Encounter. Compare and contrast the encounters in your report to the class.

Exercise 2: Read Mark 10:35-45. Compose a summary of the encounter and the lesson Jesus taught the disciples. Present a summary to class.

Exercise 3: Read Mark 10:46-52. Compose a summary of the encounter and the lesson Jesus taught the blind man and the witnesses to the event. Present a summary to class.

Plan for this exercise to take about twenty minutes.

INTO LIFE

Distribute copies of the following to each class member. Allow each group to discuss and determine their best answer for each question. These questions are in the student book.

1. Compare Mark 9:35 and Mark 10:31 to this episode. Why are James and John's request and the reaction of the ten so amazing?

2. How does Jesus teach the concept again and what is his ultimate conclusion? (See Mark 10:45.)

3. Why do you think the apostles had to learn this lesson again?

4. How does Bartimaeus get Jesus' attention? How is this different from James and John?

5. Why do you think Jesus asked both James and John and Bartimaeus, "What do you want me to do for you?"

6. What do you think Bartimaeus "saw" that the apostles did not?

After some discussion, encourage class members to pick a partner. Give each student a copy of the reproducible activity "Help Me to See" from the next page. Allow time for the students to complete the activity; then ask them to share their responses with their partners.

After three minutes, close the class with your prayer for strength, asking God to answer class members' prayers.

Again?

Jesus often had to repeat his teaching in order for it to "sink in" to his followers. Today's text is an example of re-teaching. Jesus teaches this concept of "the greatest will be a servant" at least three times. Study the following passage to see how he teaches it, how he tests for it becoming a part of life, and how he re-teaches it. Write a summary of your findings on the chart below.

	Matthew 18:1-14 Mark 9:33-50 Luke 9:46-50	Matthew 19:13-30 Mark 10:13-31 Luke 18:15-30	Matthew 20:20-34 Mark 10:32-45
How he teaches it			
How he tests for it			
How he re-teaches it			

Help Me To See

If Jesus asked you, "What 'blind spot' would you like me to remove from your vision?" how would you answer?

If he asked, "What do you want me to do for you?" how would you answer him? Write a prayer of request below.

Summer Quarter, 2003

God Restores a Remnant
(Return From Exile)

Special Features

Lessons

About These Lessons

With this quarter we conclude the chronological study of the Old Testament begun in the summer of 1999. We have seen how God created the world and on that world blessed a special nation, Israel. We have seen how Israel was at times faithful to God, and how God blessed her in response. But we have seen sad times of disobedience, ultimately resulting in exile. Now we see the nation return and reestablished to be ready to bring about the ultimate fulfillment of God's promises—the coming of the Messiah. May we prepare our own hearts to receive Him as King of kings and Lord of our lives.

Jun 1

Jun 8

Jun 15

Jun 22

Jun 29

Jul 6

Jul 13

Jul 20

Jul 27

Aug 3

Aug 10

Aug 17

Aug 24

Aug 31

Return! Renewal! Repentance!

by Lloyd M. Pelfrey

The three words in the caption are the titles for the three units of study for the summer. Each represents the theme for one month in this quarter that has fourteen lessons. These studies bring to a close the history of Old Testament Israel as God's people return from exile to face the challenge of restoring their nation.

UNIT 1: RETURN

The king of Babylon destroyed Jerusalem in 586 B.C. In turn, Cyrus conquered Babylon in 539 B.C. and released all captives. Almost seventy years had passed since the first Jewish captives had arrived. The prophets were right: it had been a long stay. After becoming comfortable, would anyone want to "return"?

JUNE

Lesson 1: The Exiles Return. The Lord's prompting (through Cyrus) motivated about fifty thousand people to return, along with vessels of the temple.

Lesson 2: Beginning to Rebuild. The returnees wanted God's blessing, so one of their first acts was to rebuild the altar for burnt offerings.

Lesson 3: Returning to the Work. After the rebuilding stopped, God raised a prophet, Haggai, to challenge the people to evaluate their priorities. It worked.

Lesson 4: God Gives Hope for the Future. The prophet Zechariah then teamed with Haggai to assure the people of God's concern for them.

Lesson 5: The Exiles Dedicate the Temple. Under the prodding of prophets and decrees of kings, the people finally completed the temple. Celebration!

UNIT 2: RENEWAL

A seventy-year period elapsed between the completion of the temple and the rebuilding of Jerusalem's walls. God needed a man of prayer who was a capable leader, could motivate others, and persevere. That man was Nehemiah!

JULY

Lesson 6: Nehemiah Begins Work. Nehemiah was serving in the palace of the king of Persia when the distressing news came: Jerusalem needed walls!

Lesson 7: Nehemiah Completes the Wall. Every building project has those who oppose it. But Nehemiah prayed, resisted the enemies, and succeeded.

Lesson 8: Ezra Reads the Law. After dedicating the rebuilt temple, Ezra led in the reading of God's Word. The people's weeping turned into a joyful obedience.

Lesson 9: The People Renew the Covenant. A thousand years had passed since the Israelites had received God's covenant. They promised again to obey it.

UNIT 3: REPENTANCE

Exhortations to repent by four prophets conclude our lessons. Repentance involves examining the past and deciding again to keep God's Word.

AUGUST

Lesson 10: Message of Condemnation. Edom will be destroyed because of its sinful pride. The time to repent is always *now*.

Lesson 11. Call for Repentance. Joel portrays dreaded invasions of locusts as God's discipline. The underlying motive is God's love for his people.

Lesson 12: Promise to the Faithful. Ezra and Nehemiah receive support from Malachi's prophetic voice. Both judgment and blessings are in God's plans.

Lesson 13: Prophecy of an Eternal Kingdom. As a captive in Babylon, Daniel interpreted a dream involving four great earthly kingdoms. Only God's will last!

Lesson 14: Prediction of the End. God's sovereignty over history enables us to "return" for the "renewal" that only He can provide after our "repentance."

THE EXILES RETURN

LESSON 1

WHY TEACH THIS LESSON?

People become attached to where they grow up, not to where their parents grew up. This fact was reinforced to me a few years ago when a man I knew related that he had heard his young son declare proudly, "Daddy is Canadian and Mommy is British, but *I'm* an American!"

Today's lesson allows us to witness the struggles of ancient Israelites as they decide to leave a land in which most had been born to return to an ancestral homeland that only a minority had ever even seen. As we witness those struggles today let us not miss the far more important facts of God's guiding hand. Today's lesson is a needed reminder that that is the same hand guiding us in our journey from this temporary, earthly home—to which we can become very attached!—on toward our eternal home in Heaven.

INTRODUCTION

A. MOVING DAY!

The obituary revealed that she had had quite a past. Having been born in 1898 and dying in 2001, she had lived in three centuries. Her past included a six-hundred-mile move in a covered wagon when her parents decided to relocate to an area where there might be more opportunities.

The logistics of such a move are mind-boggling. Back then, there were no paved roads for travel. (In 1900, the United States had only 144 miles of such roads.) The arrangements for food and sanitation were far different from what is considered "normal" today. In addition, the time required for such a move stands in stark contrast to what the "now generation" expects. Such journeys took months, not one or two days. Obviously, one did not decide to undertake such a move lightly.

Today's lesson relates the circumstances behind the decision of many Israelites to make a nine-hundred-mile move from their settled situations in Babylon. This journey would take them back to Judah, the land of their roots.

B. LESSON BACKGROUND

Last November we concluded a three-month study that considered God's prophecies of judgment against Judah as well as the conquest of that country by the Babylonians. Nebuchadnezzar destroyed Jerusalem in the summer of 586 B.C. Before that, he already had taken captives from Jerusalem in 605 B.C. (including Daniel and his friends) and in 597 B.C. (including the prophet Ezekiel). The Babylonian Empire was a great empire, reaching its peak with King Nebuchadnezzar, who reigned from 605–562 B.C. It was just twenty-three years after Nebuchadnezzar's death that the troops of Cyrus, on October 29, 539 B.C., gained entrance to the city of Babylon and brought the Babylonian Empire to an end. As the Persian troops of Cyrus entered the city, Belshazzar was having a feast with a thousand of his nobles. He knew that the Persian troops were approaching, but he felt secure. Babylon was considered impregnable, and the city was ready for a long siege.

DEVOTIONAL READING:
ISAIAH 52:7-12

BACKGROUND SCRIPTURE:
EZRA 1

PRINTED TEXT:
EZRA 1

LESSON AIMS

After participating in this lesson, the students will be able to:

1. Narrate the highlights of the initial return of devout Jews from their Babylonian exile to their Judean homeland.

2. Explain the historical and spiritual significance of this return.

3. Develop a list of principles that can guide their reactions to new ventures or projects in the church.

KEY VERSE

Anyone of his people among you—may his God be with him, and let him go up to Jerusalem in Judah and build the temple of the Lord, the God of Israel, the God who is in Jerusalem. —Ezra 1:3

Then the appearance of fingers writing on the wall of his banquet hall petrified Belshazzar. The prophet Daniel was called to provide the meaning of the strange words. The ominous message that the kingdom would be given to the Medes and Persians was fulfilled that very night (see Daniel 5).

I. THE KING'S DECREE (EZRA 1:1-4)

The opening words of the book of Ezra are of great importance. God is ready to act again in a mighty way to bring his people to the promised land for a second time. The importance can be seen in the fact that the last two verses of the previous book, 2 Chronicles, match the first verses of Ezra almost verbatim. Regardless of which book is being read, the reader must know that the sovereign Lord was directing these historical actions.

In addition, the return of God's people to Judah was necessary to bring about the fulfillment of certain prophecies about the Messiah. For example, he would be born in Bethlehem (Micah 5:2), and it was imperative that David's descendants be in the right place.

A. DIVINE ASPECT (v. 1)

1. In the first year of Cyrus king of Persia, in order to fulfill the word of the LORD spoken by Jeremiah, the LORD moved the heart of Cyrus king of Persia to make a proclamation throughout his realm and to put it in writing:

Cyrus king of Persia is a special person in the plan of God. Approximately 150 years before Cyrus's birth, the prophet Isaiah recorded his name as one chosen by God (see Isaiah 44:28; 45:1, 13). Cyrus is God's "shepherd" and God's "anointed." Isaiah prophesied that Cyrus would speak the words that Jerusalem would be built and that the temple's foundations would be laid.

The prophecies about Cyrus are amazingly precise. Isaiah wrote that God would "subdue nations before him" and that gates would be opened to him. Cyrus had become a minor king within the nation of Media in 559 B.C. In a remarkable series of events, he became the ruler of all Media, conquering the nation of Lydia, Croeses its king, and his capital city of Sardis. The forces of Cyrus then marched on Babylon, ready for the long siege. To their amazement, the city's gates were opened by those who were unhappy with King Belshazzar. The siege never occurred.

Cyrus gives his "emancipation *proclamation*" in the spring of 538 B.C., in his first year of rule over Babylon. A possible reconstruction of the events indicates that he had left Babylon, turning it over to Darius the Mede (see Daniel 5:31), and later returned and issued this proclamation.

This act by Cyrus also fulfills prophecies that had been given by the prophet *Jeremiah*, who said that the desolation would last for seventy years (Jeremiah 25:1, 11, 12; 29:10; 2 Chronicles 36:21). Those same predictions also served as the background for one of Daniel's prayers (Daniel 9:2).

Daniel is in Babylon when the city falls to Cyrus (Daniel 1:21; 6:28; 10:1). Cyrus himself is about sixty years of age when he captures the city. He has been described as being a gentleman, not a tyrant, and his goodness is evident in the proclamation that he put in writing for the entire empire. Cyrus probably designed his decree to gain the support of conquered people, but it had larger purposes that Cyrus never knew.

FULFILLED PROPHECY

The Bible is filled with a pattern of fulfilled prophecies about people, cities, nations, and events. What are the odds of all this happening by accident?

WHAT DO YOU THINK?

The text says that God "moved" Cyrus—a pagan ruler—to a specific action. What significance, if any, do you find in that fact as you consider religious, political, and other leaders today? How should this affect us?

[Consider Acts 4:19; Romans 13:1; and 1 Peter 2:13-17 in your discussion.]

THE MEDO-PERSIAN EMPIRE

Visual for lessons 1 and 10. Use this map to locate the various places that relate to the events you will be studying this quarter.

Consider just the case of Cyrus. Isaiah made his prophecies concerning that ruler some 150 years before he was even born! In 1996, Dr. Hugh Ross calculated the probability of chance fulfillment of the prophecies of Isaiah 44:28; 45:1, 13 at one in one quadrillion! To get a perspective on how large a quadrillion really is, picture it this way: that many silver dollars would cover the entire surface of the state of Texas more than twice! Imagine having that many coins, marking one with a big X, and mixing it in. Then blindfold someone and put him in the middle of that twice-covered state with this instruction: "Go anywhere you wish, and pick a single coin." The odds of his picking the coin having the X on it are about the same as a chance fulfillment of the prophecy about Cyrus.

Cyrus, king of Persia, didn't know it, but he was God's errand boy for the fulfillment of Jeremiah's prophecy that the captivity of Judah would end after seventy years. The fulfilled prophecies of the Bible are testimony to God's sovereignty and the Bible's trustworthy nature as the Word of God. Fulfilled prophecy strengthens our faith.

—J. A. M.

B. ROYAL PROCLAMATION (vv. 2-4)

2. "This is what Cyrus king of Persia says:

"'The LORD, the God of heaven, has given me all the kingdoms of the earth and he has appointed me to build a temple for him at Jerusalem in Judah.

The expression *God of heaven* is popular among the writers of the closing days of the Old Testament. It emphasizes the sovereignty of God. He is the God who made the heavens and the earth. He is in the heavens directing the course of all history to his desired end. In fact, the phrase is used so often in Daniel 2 that many students believe Daniel may have been the one who actually penned the document on behalf of Cyrus.

The opening words of Cyrus's statement emphasize that it is *the Lord* who *has given* him *all the kingdoms of the earth,* and that it is he who has commissioned Cyrus to *build* the *temple for him at Jerusalem.* When Cyrus reflects on the ease by which he conquered Media, Lydia, and Babylon, he may conclude that it was not by his own might that he was able to do these things, but by God's. Interestingly, the first-century Jewish historian Josephus states that Cyrus actually read the prophecies of Isaiah about himself. This may only be a romantic embellishment, but the thought is intriguing nonetheless.

The rebuilding of the temple at Jerusalem is extremely important for Israel. Their worship is not considered complete without the temple and its facilities.

3. Anyone of his people among you—may his God be with him, and let him go up to Jerusalem in Judah and build the temple of the LORD, the God of Israel, the God who is in Jerusalem.

Cyrus is apparently impressed with the *God* of the Jews! This does not mean, however, that he has surrendered his pagan concepts about what "other" gods there may be. A famous archaeological find known as the "Cyrus Cylinder," a historical record written on baked clay in about 536 B.C., ends with this prayer of Cyrus: "May all the gods whom I have resettled in their sacred cities ask daily Bel and Nebo for a long life for me." (Bel and Nebo are Babylonian deities.) This inscription by itself does not clarify which god Cyrus considered his chief god. The mention of so many "gods" makes it clear that Cyrus is not a convert to the one true God. Cyrus is "pluralistic" in his thinking, and he would fit in very well with the popular views about religion that are held by many today.

According to the decree, each person is free to choose whether or not to make the nine-hundred-mile trip to Jerusalem. The time in Babylon has permitted the roots to grow deep. Pulling up those roots will demand a price that some will not want to pay.

VISUALS FOR THESE LESSONS

The small visual pictured in each lesson (e.g., page 338) is a small reproduction of a large, full-color poster included in the Adult Visuals packet for the Summer Quarter. The packet is available from your supplier. Order No. 492.

WHAT DO YOU THINK?

King Cyrus attributed his success to God. (Compare his reaction to that of other kings in Daniel 4:30 and Acts 12:21-23.) What does this say about the proper way to react to God's work in our own achievements?

DAILY BIBLE READINGS

Monday, May 26—Cyrus Is the Lord's Anointed (Isaiah 45: 1-5)

Tuesday, May 27—Cyrus Will Build God's City (Isaiah 45:7-13)

Wednesday, May 28—Israel Is Saved by the Lord (Isaiah 45:14-19)

Thursday, May 29—The Lord Will Go Before You (Isaiah 52:7-12)

Friday, May 30—The People Prepare to Return (Ezra 1:1-5)

Saturday, May 31—Their Neighbors Aid Them (Ezra 1:6–2:2)

Sunday, June 1—Freewill Offerings for God's House (Ezra 2:64-70)

Obviously, such a decision is monumental. Those who make that choice will never see certain of their family members again. There are no telephones for maintaining contact, and any postal deliveries depend on knowing someone who is planning to travel that direction.

Such a decision is similar to that made by those who decide to serve the Lord in foreign nations. While jet planes and E-mail have made it much easier to stay in contact with family back home, the separation is real and not always easy to endure. Wise churches will make special efforts to lessen the pain of separation for the missionaries they support.

4. And the people of any place where survivors may now be living are to provide him with silver and gold, with goods and livestock, and with freewill offerings for the temple of God in Jerusalem.'"

The final part of Cyrus's edict addresses the people who will choose not to return to Judah. Every Israelite can have a part in the rebuilding programs of Jerusalem and its *temple*. A project of this scope demands great resources, and each person must do his or her part, either by going or by giving *silver, gold,* and *goods,* plus *livestock* for sacrifices and food.

The sharing of provisions by those who stay behind invites comparison with the exodus from Egypt a thousand years before. On that occasion, the Israelites asked their neighbors for silver, gold, and clothing (Exodus 12:35). Those items were used in the building of the tabernacle (25:1-9; 35:4-9, 20-29).

II. THE PEOPLE'S DECISIONS (EZRA 1:5, 6)

The proclamation of the new king was made known throughout the land. It would be fascinating to know more about the discussions that were held by people of all ages. There was much to be considered. Would anyone be willing to return? Was the price too great to pay?

A. DECISIONS TO RETURN (v. 5)

5. Then the family heads of Judah and Benjamin, and the priests and Levites— everyone whose heart God had moved—prepared to go up and build the house of the LORD in Jerusalem.

As God had stirred the heart of Cyrus, so he prompts the leaders of three tribes—*Judah, Benjamin,* and *Levi—to go up* to *Jerusalem* in order *to build the house of the Lord.*

The mention of just three tribes is understandable. The Assyrians had taken the northern nation of Israel, with its ten tribal territories, into captivity in 722 B.C. The southern nation of Judah consisted primarily of just the two tribes of Judah and Benjamin. Many of the priestly *Levites* (who had no tribal territory) had lived in Judah where the temple was located. (See 2 Chronicles 11:13-17.) It will be imperative to have *priests* as a part of the group who will return; the priests are the ones who will officiate in offering sacrifices to God.

The number of people who decide to return totals nearly 50,000 (see Ezra 2:64, 65). While that seems small compared with the 603,550 adult males who came out of Egypt with Moses (Exodus 38:26), it still staggers the imagination when the factors such as transportation, food, and sanitation are considered. The emotions in the case at hand undoubtedly are quite mixed since the people are leaving their "home" in Babylon to return voluntarily to their "home" in Judah.

DECISIONS HAVE CONSEQUENCES

The 1981 Academy Award-winning film *Chariots of Fire* focused on decisions and their consequences. The film's main character, Eric Liddell, was a Scotch

WHAT DO YOU THINK?

Why was it right for the Jews who stayed in Babylon to give gifts to those who went to rebuild Jerusalem? How does their example apply to our practice of supporting missionaries who serve in distant places?

[Consider Matthew 28:19, 20 and 2 Corinthians 8:1-15; 9 in your discussion.]

WHAT DO YOU THINK?

How do we know when the promptings we feel are truly from the Lord and not just our own personal desires?

[Consider Jeremiah 23:26; Ezekiel 13:1-17; and 1 John 4:1-3 in your discussion.]

Presbyterian minister who believed that Sunday was the "Sabbath" and should not be used for any secular purpose. Liddell was also a gifted athlete who qualified to compete in the 1924 Olympics. For years he had set his heart on running in the games and winning a gold medal for England. He was considered the best sprinter in the world.

But Liddell was in for a surprise. For the first time in history, some Olympic events were scheduled on Sunday—including the sprint race in which he was to compete. Forced to choose between a potential medal and his principles, he decided to come down on the side of his faith.

In one of the film's decisive scenes, Harold Abrahams, a Jewish athlete friend, asked Liddell, "Do you have any regrets?" Eric Liddell responded, "Regrets, yes. Doubts, no."

Sometimes we shy away from making decisions, uncertain if we can handle the regrets and the consequences. Sometimes we stand at a crossroad and realize that each path leads to a different destination, but we aren't sure where. In either case, decision-making can be agonizing.

In Ezra's day, God's people faced a choice—stay in the security and certainty of the only home most had ever known, or follow the call of God and step into an uncertain tomorrow. What choice would you have made?   —J. A. M.

B. DECISIONS TO SHARE (v. 6)

6. All their neighbors assisted them with articles of silver and gold, with goods and livestock, and with valuable gifts, in addition to all the freewill offerings.

This outpouring of spiritual patriotism provides those returning with everything they need. They have resources for a temple (Ezra 2:68, 69), animals for sacrificing, and wealth to sustain them until they can establish themselves again in Judah. This is different from the conquest of Canaan in the days of Joshua some 950 years before. This time God moves his people to enter the promised land not as conquerors, but to reclaim what is still theirs.

III. THE VESSELS RETURNED (EZRA 1:7-11)

Nebuchadnezzar had taken items from the temple during each of the three major deportations: in 605 B.C. (Daniel 1:2), 597 B.C. (2 Kings 24:13), and 586 B.C. (25:14). The major articles of furniture for the temple were destroyed (25:13). These items were taken to Babylon to be stored in the house of Nebuchadnezzar's gods. Some have conjectured that they were in a temple that was built to honor the Babylonian god Marduk.

It was during this time that the famous ark of the covenant disappeared from history. Some believe it was destroyed by the Babylonians; others suggest that it was hidden by devout Jews. It is impossible to say which—if either—of these ideas is correct.

A. ENDOWED BY CYRUS (v. 7)

7. Moreover, King Cyrus brought out the articles belonging to the temple of the LORD, which Nebuchadnezzar had carried away from Jerusalem and had placed in the temple of his god.

Cyrus seems to want to be loved by his people, and this charitable deed will encourage a certain loyalty to him. Perhaps Daniel, who lives in Babylon, has a considerable influence on Cyrus and his decision.

B. ENTRUSTED TO SHESHBAZZAR (v. 8)

8. Cyrus king of Persia had them brought by Mithredath the treasurer, who counted them out to Sheshbazzar the prince of Judah.

HOW TO SAY IT

Assyrians. Uh-SEAR-e-unz.
Babylon. BAB-uh-lun.
Babylonian. Bab-ih-LOW-nee-un.
Belshazzar. Bel-SHAZZ-er.
Croeses. KREE-sus.
Cyrus. SIGH-russ.
Darius. Duh-RYE-us.
Ezekiel. Ee-ZEEK-ee-ul or Ee-ZEEK-yul.
Ezra. EZ-ruh.
Isaiah. Eye-ZAY-uh.
Jeremiah. Jair-uh-MY-uh.
Jerusalem. Juh-ROO-suh-lem.
Josephus. Joe-SEE-fuss.
Judah. JOO-duh.
Judean. Joo-DEE-un.
Levi. LEE-vye.
Levites. LEE-vites.
Lydia. LID-ee-uh.
Media. MEED-ee-uh.
Mede. Meed.
Mithredath. MITH-ree-dath.
Nebo. NEE-bo.
Nebuchadnezzar. NEB-yuh-kud-NEZ-er.
Persia. PER-zhuh.
Sardis. SAR-dis.
Shenazzar. Sheh-NAZ-ar.
Sheshbazzar. Shesh-BAZ-ar.
Zerubbabel. Zeh-RUB-uh-bul.

This is not a casual gift. It is carefully overseen by *Mithredath the treasurer.* (The name of this official is a frequent Persian name. The word for his title is also a Persian word, found nowhere else in the Bible.) As he looks on, the items are counted as they are given into the hands of a certain *Sheshbazzar, the prince of Judah.* The identity of Sheshbazzar has given rise to much speculation. His title could be translated as "leader," so he may or may not be an actual member of the royal family. Several possibilities have been put forth, but it is not certain that any of them is correct. Some believe he is a Persian official who is in charge of the entire project. Others think this is the Persian name for Zerubbabel (see Ezra 2:2) or that this is a variant name for Shenazzar, a member of the royal family (1 Chronicles 3:18)—who actually would be a prince. We also see Sheshbazzar mentioned in Ezra 1:11; 5:14, 16.

C. ENUMERATED BY EZRA (vv. 9-11)

9. This was the inventory:

gold dishes	30
silver dishes	1,000
silver pans	29
10. gold bowls	30
matching silver bowls	410
other articles	1,000

The content of the thousand *articles* is not specified, but the summary statement in the next verse indicates that all the returned items were *gold* or *silver.*

11. In all, there were 5,400 articles of gold and of silver. Sheshbazzar brought all these along when the exiles came up from Babylon to Jerusalem.

The number of items listed in the two previous verses total 2,499, not *5,400.* The most logical explanation for this difference is that many smaller items are not listed, but they are counted in with the grand total of 5,400. When the people return from their captivity, it will be in the context of returning items to place in the temple that they will rebuild. The important thing is that they make the trip! It will be a gigantic undertaking, and they will do it for the glory of God!

CONCLUSION

Many of the comments above are offered from the perspective that the decision to leave Babylon to return to Jerusalem was almost traumatic. While there must surely have been some trauma in the event, that must not be overstated.

Psalm 137 relates the emotions of a captive in Babylon, and the early verses indicate that the author longs for Jerusalem. For some, then, the decision to return may have been reached eagerly and quickly. They had been waiting for just such an opportunity. Those most eager to return were probably the older folks who had seen the temple before its destruction (Ezra 3:12).

The obvious question is this: for what do we long today? Where are our treasures and our hearts? Are we so attached to the familiar surroundings of our "earthly" home that we might say "maybe later" if Jesus offered us the option to go home with him today? On another level, do we have a longing or thirsting for the Word and things of God? If we were given the opportunity to serve God more completely, would we jump eagerly and quickly to take advantage of the opportunity, or would our decision entail a lengthy searching of the heart?

Jesus addressed this issue when he said, "But seek first his kingdom and his righteousness, and all these things will be given to you as well" (Matthew 6:33). These are words to live by—for eternity!

Discovery Learning

This page contains an alternative lesson plan emphasizing learning activities. Classes desiring such student involvement will find these suggestions helpful. The next page is a reproducible activity page to further enhance discovery learning.

LEARNING GOALS

After participating in this lesson, the students will be able to:

1. Narrate the highlights of the initial return of devout Jews from their Babylonian exile to their Judean homeland.

2. Explain the historical and spiritual significance of this return.

3. Develop a list of principles that can guide their reactions to new ventures or projects in the church.

INTO THE LESSON

Display these instructions: Think about a time when you have been homesick—for your home congregation or hometown or family or for a special period of time in your life. Turn to the person beside you and complete this sentence: "I wish I could go back to _____ because . . . ."

After pairs talk, ask for two or three volunteers to complete the sentence for the whole class. Say, "It is not unusual for us to want to return to a special time or place. The people in today's study decided whether they wanted to return to their homeland for a spiritual reason."

INTO THE WORD

ADVANCE PREPARATION. From the children's department borrow teaching pictures of people and events in this quarter's lessons. Post them as appropriate.

Lecture. Present a lecture that gives the historical and spiritual background for the quarter. Include the destruction of Jerusalem, relocation of the Jews, the captivity, and prophets of the time. Use the commentary, map (visual 1; see page 338), chart (visual 2; see page 346), and any teaching pictures that you have.

Group Study. Divide the class into small groups, giving each group one of the following assignments. (These are featured in *NIV® Bible Student* as individual study.)

GROUP 1. Read Psalm 137. Identify the emotions being expressed by the captives; suggest how these might motivate a person to return to the homeland.

GROUP 2. Read these prophetic passages and prepare a report of what the various prophets were saying: Isaiah 44:28–45:7; Jeremiah 25:1, 11, 12; 29:10-14).

GROUP 3. Read the following narrative passages about Cyrus king of Persia and prepare a report of the events: 2 Chronicles 36:22, 23; Ezra 1:1-8. What do you judge to be Cyrus's faith in God?

GROUP 4. Read Ezra 1:5, 6 and Ezra 2. What do these verses say about the ones returning? What of their character, lineage, and number? What of their generosity?

GROUP 5. Read Micah 5:2; Isaiah 9:1, 2; Zechariah 9:9. How does this return of Jews to their homeland relate to messianic prophecies?

Be ready to supplement their discoveries with insights from the commentary and your study.

Summarize their reports, pinpointing the historical events that fulfilled prophecy. Preview future lessons by saying, "Our study this summer will take us from the return of this first group of Jews to the completion of the building of the walls of Jerusalem, with a study of their leaders and two prophets. This period of history and spiritual pilgrimage concludes the Old Testament era and sets the foundation for the development of the nation of people from whom would come the Messiah. As Ezra and Nehemiah would say, we will see the 'hand of God' at work. Finally, we will look to the future return of Jesus."

INTO LIFE

Distribute copies of the reproducible activity "Journey to Jerusalem" from the next page. Say, "Imagine you are part of a family who hears about the plan to return to the homeland. What do you say to one another? What pros and cons will you list for making the trip? What might be the deciding factor why you would give up everything to go back? If you decide to remain in Babylon, what pros and cons are there for offering support to those going back?" Give the groups time to speculate, make notes, and discuss; then let the groups make their reports.

Use the reproducible activity "Church Project" from the next page, and make this assignment: "When church leaders today suggest a big project or new program to the congregation, what gets said by people in the hallways, the classrooms, and homes? What pros and cons are given? What is often the deciding factor? What could we learn from the Jews in Babylon that could help us step out with courage for God?" (If your leaders are contemplating a special project, apply the discussion to that project.)

List the suggestions and select those that class members think are appropriate to follow. Ask a volunteer to make a poster of the ideas for future reference. To conclude, read aloud the selected principles and ask God's help in carrying out such responses to church plans.

Journey to Jerusalem

You are a Jew living in Babylon. You hear about Cyrus's proclamation and a plan for a big return of Jews to Jerusalem. You have done a lot of thinking and reached your decision about whether to join the group for the nine-hundred-mile journey.

Write a letter to a friend. Describe Cyrus's proclamation and what you know about a return to Jerusalem. Tell whether you will join the group and why. If you are not going, tell how you will support the effort.

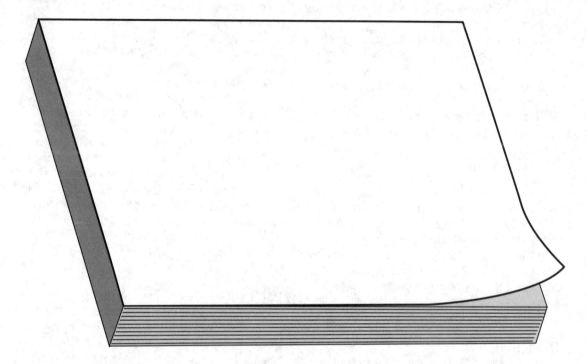

Church Project

Prepare a skit that allows your actors to portray Christians who are talking about a big project that has been announced by church leaders. (It might be remodeling a part of the building, updating the sound system, adding a staff person, sponsoring a trip by volunteers to a mission, or sponsoring an anniversary celebration for the congregation.) Let the conversation describe the emotions of such a venture, the values of the project, any hesitations, and ways that people in the congregation can be involved. Let your audience hear the people make their decisions about how they will be involved in the project. (Or, stop the skit at the decision point to let other class members decide how they think the people will finally respond and why.)

BEGINNING TO REBUILD

LESSON 2

WHY TEACH THIS LESSON?

When disaster strikes anywhere in the world, the media is quick to report it. Disasters come quickly and violently, creating captivating visual images and gripping story lines. It makes for powerful news. But the rebuilding after the disaster is much less newsworthy. The action is slow, tedious, and—in a word—"boring."

But if you are involved in the crisis, it's the rebuilding that is most significant. Some of your learners may be trying to rebuild after a disaster in their own lives: divorce, financial problems, prodigal children—the list could be endless. They don't need closeup looks at the disaster; they need a guide for rebuilding. They need some hope that rebuilding is possible.

That's what our lesson today has to offer. God shows us his providential care on a repentant people, a people ready to rebuild. God is not far from any of us (Acts 17:27), and he specializes in rebuilding! Those who need God's help in rebuilding their sin-shattered lives will find today's lesson particularly comforting.

INTRODUCTION

A. THE ARCHITECT

Somehow it seems fitting that the lesson for today involves building, because June 8 is the birthday of one of the premier architects of the twentieth century: Frank Lloyd Wright (1867–1959). The underlying philosophy that governed Wright's designs became known as "organic architecture." By this he meant that a building should seem to be a part of its natural surroundings. Houses and other buildings with his name attached often have become attractions for tourists.

On an infinitely grander scale, the name of the Ultimate Architect and Master Builder is attached to the universe itself (cf. Psalm 19:1). The writer of Hebrews describes Abraham as having "looking forward to the city with foundations, whose architect and builder is God" (Hebrews 11:10). Abraham was not looking for just any city. He was looking for the city that had been designed by God himself.

Abraham focused his attention on the heavenly Jerusalem, the final abode for all of God's people. In fact, the context of the word *looking* implies that Abraham continued to seek this city throughout his life. There may have been times when his attention was diverted briefly, but his focus always returned to the city that has God as its Architect and Builder.

Like Abraham, many other people in the Old Testament also maintained their faith and faithfulness. Today's lesson is about some of those people. We will see their faith as they return from their Babylonian captivity to the earthly Jerusalem, which gives its name to the heavenly city for which we long—the New Jerusalem (cf. Hebrews 12:22; Revelation 3:12; 21:2, 10).

B. LESSON BACKGROUND

The book of Ezra is divided into two major parts. In the first six chapters, Ezra describes the first return from captivity. That major event, occurring around 538 to 536 B.C., involved almost fifty thousand people. Ezra 7–10 tells of the return of

DEVOTIONAL READING:
PSALM 100:1-5

BACKGROUND SCRIPTURE:
EZRA 3, 4

PRINTED TEXT:
EZRA 3:1-3, 6, 7, 10-13

LESSON AIMS

After participating in this lesson, each student will be able to:

1. Give evidence of unity and worship in at least three distinct places in the text.

2. Understand that corporate worship is multi-dimensional and unifying.

3. Identify a new personal dimension of worship that will have a positive effect on the church body.

KEY VERSE

All the people gave a great shout of praise to the LORD, because the foundation of the house of the LORD was laid.
—Ezra 3:11

LESSON 2 NOTES

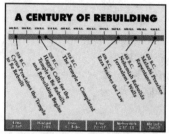

A CENTURY OF REBUILDING

Visual for lesson 2. This chart will help your students understand the chronology of this quarter's lessons.

a much smaller group. Ezra himself led that return about eighty years after the first, in 458 B.C.

Last week's lesson concluded by noting the first group's arrival in Jerusalem (Ezra 1:11). Ezra 2 lists the groups that were a part of that initial return. The final verses of the chapter reveal that the people wanted to rebuild the temple and that they gave generously to that end: about eleven hundred pounds of gold and three tons of silver!

I. REBUILDING THE ALTAR (EZRA 3:1-3)

Genuine worship at the central sanctuary ceased when the Babylonians destroyed the temple in 586 B.C. So it has been almost fifty years since any Israelite has been able to participate in worship that involves the continual offerings to God both morning and evening. The returnees desperately want to restore such worship.

A. GATHERING IN JERUSALEM (v. 1)

1. When the seventh month came and the Israelites had settled in their towns, the people assembled as one man in Jerusalem.

Some have conjectured that *the seventh month* refers to the seventh month since the exiles left Babylon or since they arrived in Judah. Since it is the custom for the Israelites to refer to the months of the year by numerical designations instead of the names of the months, however, it seems more likely that this refers to the seventh month on the ancient Israelite calendar. (This is the month "Tishri." In postbiblical Judaism, Tishri will remain the seventh month on the "religious calendar," but will become the first month of the "civil calendar.") This equates to late September and early October.

The seventh month is a special month in the Israelites' calendar. The first day of the month is the day the Feast of Trumpets begins (Leviticus 23:23-25). The high day of the entire year is the tenth day of this month. This is the Day of Atonement. While the tabernacle or temple stood, the Day of Atonement was the only day in the entire year when the high priest could enter the Holy of Holies. This day involves special sacrifices and the sending of the scapegoat into the wilderness (Leviticus 16; 23:26-32).

The Feast of Tabernacles (or Booths), one of Israel's major festivals, is also a part of the seventh month. This seven-day event starts on the fifteenth day of the month. Its purpose is to remind the Israelites of their forty years of camping during the wilderness wanderings (Leviticus 23:33-36). Ezra 3:4 (not in our text for today) notes that the Israelites observed this feast after rebuilding the altar of burnt offerings.

One of the outstanding features that Ezra cites is the unity of the returning Israelites: the people are *as one man!* If there is a time for "rugged individualism," this is not it. The sense of community overcomes negative attitudes that could have stifled or divided them. At last they are all together again in *Jerusalem,* the city of David, and they are ready to begin the work of restoration.

B. CONSTRUCTING THE ALTAR (vv. 2, 3a)

2. Then Jeshua son of Jozadak and his fellow priests and Zerubbabel son of Shealtiel and his associates began to build the altar of the God of Israel to sacrifice burnt offerings on it, in accordance with what is written in the Law of Moses the man of God.

Jeshua and *Zerubbabel* hold impressive credentials for leadership. Jeshua is in the lineage of the high *priests.* His grandfather Seraiah had been the chief priest

WHAT DO YOU THINK?

How important is a common vision to a group of people trying to complete a major project? Can you give an example of how a group has been moved to action by a compelling vision? Can you give an example where a project floundered because of an unclear vision?

and was executed by the Babylonians when Nebuchadnezzar destroyed Jerusalem (2 Kings 25:18, 21). *Jeshua* is spelled "Joshua" in Haggai 1:1, and there he is called the high priest. His father, *Jozadak*, apparently was high priest during most of the Babylonian captivity. (Jozadak is the same as "Jehozadak" in 1 Chronicles 6:14, 15 and Haggai 1:1.)

Zerubbabel is a grandson of Jehoiachin, one of the last kings of Judah. They are listed in the genealogy for the Messiah in Matthew 1:12, where Jehoiachin is called "Jeconiah." The returning captives thus have qualified leaders in two important areas: they have a religious leader who is a priest, and they had a civil leader who is of the Davidic line. (Zerubbabel may be another name for Sheshbazzar of Ezra 1:8, 11; 5:14, but this is not certain.)

The two leaders in view here are not left to do the work by themselves. Constructing *the altar of the God of Israel* is a community project. Undoubtedly, this new altar is built on the precise spot where the former altar for the temple had been. David had built an altar there even before it became the site for the temple (2 Samuel 24:25). Such sites were considered very sacred, and its location would have been easily determined.

We are not given the dimensions of the new altar, so we remain curious about its size. If Solomon's bronze altar is the pattern, then this altar is about fifteen feet in height and thirty feet in length and width (see 2 Chronicles 4:1). However, this was probably a more modest enterprise than the construction of Solomon's temple. The altar was probably smaller. The wooden altar constructed at Mt. Sinai was less than a third the size of Solomon's altar (cf. Exodus 27:1).

BE A LEADER

Those of you who are late-night channel surfers may have run across the 1952 black-and-white movie classic *Viva Zapata!* It is the story of one of Mexico's best-known political families. There is a dramatic deathbed scene in the film where the elderly Zapata is speaking his final words to his son. "Trouble is coming," the old man says. "Find a leader. If you cannot find a leader, be a leader." That challenge motivated his son to become one of Mexico's greatest and most colorful political leaders.

Zapata's insight that troubled times demand effective leaders rings true in every generation and nation. Be a leader! In ancient Jerusalem, Joshua and Zerubbabel recognized and responded to Israel's need for godly leaders. Centuries later, Jesus will look upon the multitude and have great compassion for them because he sees them as "sheep without a shepherd" (Matthew 9:36). There is still a tremendous leadership void in many churches today.

J. Oswald Sanders, in his book *Spiritual Leadership*, writes, "The overriding need of the church, if it is to discharge its obligation to the rising generation, is for a leadership that is authoritative, spiritual, and sacrificial." If you cannot find such a leader, be one!   —J. A. M.

3a. Despite their fear of the peoples around them, they built the altar on its foundation.

The Israelites' *fear* is understandable, as subsequent events demonstrate (Ezra 4). Some commentators suggest that *the altar* site has been used by others during the fifty years since the temple was destroyed. As the Israelites clear away all semblance of pagan worship, their religious neighbors resent the intrusion.

But those returning are convinced that there is only one God and that this altar is only for him. Their forefathers had attempted to blend the worship of God with pagan worship, and captivity was the result. This captivity accomplished one very important thing: it cured the Israelites of being tempted by idolatry. The Israelites now are convinced that there is only God. They will now have no other gods, just as the First Commandment instructs (Exodus 20:3; Deuteronomy 5:7).

C. USING THE ALTAR (v. 3b)

3b. . . . and sacrificed burnt offerings on it to the LORD, both the morning and evening sacrifices.

What a thrill it must be for these former exiles to see the smoke rise to heaven from the very first sacrifice on the new altar! The Mosaic Covenant decreed that *burnt offerings* are to be made each *morning and evening,* one animal each time. On the Sabbath Day, two animals are sacrificed in the morning and two in the evening (Numbers 28:1-10).

II. PREPARING FOR THE FOUNDATION (EZRA 3:6b, 7)

A. PROBLEM STATED (v. 6b)

6b. The foundation of the LORD's temple had not yet been laid.

With the construction of the altar, the Israelites have made a bold beginning. But those two little words *not yet* are a vivid reminder that there is more to be done. The old temple is gone. The fact that sacrifices now can be offered is a great thing, but some of the prescribed rituals cannot be carried out until a new *temple* is in place. This becomes the theme through Ezra 6.

The Israelites who have returned have many financial blessings (see page 341). But they cannot supply resources as did Solomon for the glorious temple that he constructed (2 Chronicles 2, 3). The new altar only starts the restoration. Can they complete it?

B. PROVISIONS MADE (v. 7)

7. Then they gave money to the masons and carpenters, and gave food and drink and oil to the people of Sidon and Tyre, so that they would bring cedar logs by sea from Lebanon to Joppa, as authorized by Cyrus king of Persia.

The organizing necessary to build the second temple now begins. Surely there are architects, planners, and an overall superintendent. Someone also has to be the treasurer in order to be able to distribute *money* to the stonemasons and *carpenters* who will do the work. Verses 8 and 9 (not in our text for today) offer at least a partial listing of those who lead in this endeavor. Undoubtedly many of the Israelites have acquired in Babylon the skills that they need for this undertaking.

Some of the stone necessary for the construction may be on the site already, depending on how thorough the Babylonians were in their destruction of the city and its temple. But all the wood of the previous temple had been burned when the temple was destroyed, so they need the *cedar* timbers that are available from the mountains of *Lebanon,* far to the north.

The similarities of this construction to that of Solomon some 430 years before are striking (see 1 Kings 5:1-11). In both instances the logs are taken from the mountains to the Mediterranean Sea, formed into giant rafts, and floated to *Joppa,* Israel's primary seaport. From there they are transported overland to the hills of Jerusalem, a distance of about forty miles. And in each case the workers in *Tyre* are paid with food.

This exchange between two nations has been pre-approved by *Cyrus king of Persia.* (See Ezra 6:3-5.) Cyrus's order suggests the method of construction. He surely has some input from Daniel or a knowledgeable Israelite about these matters.

What Do You Think?

For over fifty years it had been impossible for the Jews to offer sacrifices on the temple mount in Jerusalem. What are some religious privileges that we may take for granted, but that are denied to Christians in some places? What would you do if these privileges were prohibited in your own culture? What can we do for older or disabled members of our congregation who cannot assemble with us for worship?

III. CELEBRATING TOGETHER (EZRA 3:10-13)

A. PREPARATIONS (v. 10)

10. When the builders laid the foundation of the temple of the LORD, the priests in their vestments and with trumpets, and the Levites (the sons of Asaph) with cymbals, took their places to praise the LORD, as prescribed by David king of Israel.

Verse 8 (not in our text for today) notes that it is now the second month of the second year since the arrival from Babylon. This is late April or early May of 536 B.C. Interestingly, the building of Solomon's temple also began in "the second month" of the Jewish year (1 Kings 6:1).

The cultural climate for religion for the people of the Middle East lends itself to noise. The *priests* with their special garments use *trumpets* according to the law of Moses (Numbers 10:8). *Levites* who are *the sons of Asaph* provide percussion accompaniment (cf. Nehemiah 12:27).

The mention of Asaph and *David* has a certain significance: when David moved the ark of the covenant to Jerusalem, it was Asaph who sounded the *cymbals* (1 Chronicles 16:5). That was about 1000 B.C. It is now over 450 years later, and the sons of Asaph are still playing the cymbals! Twelve of the psalms have Asaph in the superscriptions as the author, so he must have been a capable musician.

The fact that they *laid the foundation* means that this is only the beginning of the building project. Unfortunately, the work will progress very slowly, as we will see in next week's lesson.

B. PRAISES (v. 11)

11. With praise and thanksgiving they sang to the LORD:

**"He is good;
    his love to Israel endures forever."**

And all the people gave a great shout of praise to the LORD, because the foundation of the house of the LORD was laid.

This is a day of great joy! The hopes, prayers, and dreams of the captives are being fulfilled before their very eyes. There is genuine worship again in Jerusalem, and it is a time to celebrate *to the Lord*. The language used indicates that the singing is antiphonal: two groups answering each other as *they sang*. The singing includes the important concepts of *praise* and thankfulness as the people recognize God's goodness and *mercy*. This event may be the fulfillment of a prophecy given by Jeremiah during the last days of Jerusalem before its destruction (see Jeremiah 33:11). Similar phrases are also seen in the book of Psalms (100:4, 5; 106:1; 107:1, etc.).

CELEBRATE!

C. S. Lewis once commented on the lack of emotion in the worship of his denomination. He said, "We have a terrible concern about good taste."

Too many are more concerned with what looks good to others than with what looks good to God. King David didn't make that mistake. On the day the ark of God returned to Jerusalem, King David was a man caught up in worship. His celebration included leaping and dancing and music and praise and joy (2 Samuel 6). Michal, David's wife, didn't like it, but God did.

I remember the first time I saw people raising their hands in worship. It shocked me. I wondered, "What are they doing? Is the roof leaking?" I felt a mild revulsion, but my revulsion had nothing to do with their worship. Since then I have learned the value of upraised hands in praise. This spirit of surrender and praise is something God encourages and desires. Don't be concerned with pleasing people. Please God.

HOW TO SAY IT

Abraham. AY-bruh-ham.
Asaph. AY-saff.
Babylonians. Bab-ih-LOW-nee-unz.
Cyrus. SIGH-russ.
Davidic. Duh-VID-ick.
Gerizim. GAIR-ih-zeem or Guh-RYE-zim.
Haggai. HAG-eye or HAG-ay-eye.
Israelite. IZ-ray-el-ite.
Jeconiah. JEK-o-NYE-uh.
Jehoiachin. Jeh-HOY-uh-kin.
Jehozadak. Jeh-HO-zuh-dak.
Jeremiah. Jair-uh-MY-uh.
Jeshua. JESH-you-uh.
Joppa. JOP-uh.
Joshua. JOSH-yew-uh.
Jozadak. JOZ-uh-dak.
Judaism. JOO-duh-izz-um or JOO-day-izz-um.
Lebanon. LEB-uh-nun.
Levites. LEE-vites.
Mediterranean. MED-uh-tuh-RAY-nee-un.
Michal. MY-kal.
Nebuchadnezzar. NEB-yuh-kud-NEZ-er.
Persia. PER-zhuh.
Seraiah. Seh-RAY-yuh or Seh-RYE-uh.
Shealtiel. She-AL-tee-el.
Sheshbazzar. Shesh-BAZ-er.
Sidon. SIGH-dun.
Tishri. TISH-ree.
Tyre. Tire.
Viva Zapata (Spanish). VEE-vuh Zuh-PAHT-uh.
Zerubbabel. Zeh-RUB-uh-bul.
Zion. ZYE-un.

THOUGHT TO REMEMBER

Whatever you do for the Lord, do it with all your heart, soul, mind, body, and strength.

WHAT DO YOU THINK?

The worship in our text included both shouts of joy and weeping. How does worship in our church give place to either expression?

DAILY BIBLE READINGS

Monday, June 2—The People Worship in Jerusalem (Ezra 3:1-5)

Tuesday, June 3—Worship the Lord With Gladness (Psalm 100:1-5)

Wednesday, June 4—The People Build the Foundation (Ezra 3:6-13)

Thursday, June 5—Adversaries Discourage the People (Ezra 4:1-5)

Friday, June 6—Adversaries Write to the Persian King (Ezra 4:6-16)

Saturday, June 7—The King Orders the Work Stopped (Ezra 4:17-24)

Sunday, June 8—Your Foundation Shall Be Laid (Isaiah 44:24-28)

David's attitude should be our own. When we worship we need to get our eyes off people and get our eyes on God. Our worship is not to be judged by people, but by the Master.

Ezra 3:11 records ancient Israel's return to the spirit and action of David in worship. Celebration was alive in the hearts of the people of God. Is that spirit of celebration alive in you? To come into his presence is to enter into joy. We are the beloved of the Father. He delights and takes pleasure in our praise. Let's celebrate!

—J. A. M.

C. EMOTIONS (v. 12)

12. But many of the older priests and Levites and family heads, who had seen the former temple, wept aloud when they saw the foundation of this temple being laid, while many others shouted for joy.

Men and women of all ages are present for this joyful dedication. Just as the ages vary, so do the emotions. Some of the older people had seen the temple of Solomon prior to its destruction some fifty years before. Now on this special occasion, they are the ones who *wept aloud*.

The text does not say why these older men are weeping, but it is likely that they are reflecting on the sin that caused the temple to be destroyed. Perhaps they are overwhelmed by the knowledge that there will be a temple again. They have painful memories of Jerusalem's destruction, of the deaths of loved ones, and of the long trek to Babylon when they were young. Now they have survived the journey back to Jerusalem, back to the places of their ancestral homes. Being able to worship at the temple site again makes for a very emotional moment.

D. SOUNDS (v. 13)

13. No one could distinguish the sound of the shouts of joy from the sound of weeping, because the people made so much noise. And the sound was heard far away.

So, which sound does God prefer, the *sound of joy* or *the sound of weeping?* The answer is simple: both! (See Psalm 126:5.) Sometimes God delights in the "sound" of a broken heart—broken in repentance as a person participates in the Lord's Supper and reflects on the agony of the Son of God on the cross. This type of "blended worship" is not a new thing. It is part of the fabric of the Old Testament, and it is relevant today. There is a time to weep and a time to laugh (Ecclesiastes 3:4). It is rather presumptuous for a worship leader to assume that everyone wants to jump for joy when a time of quiet sorrow may be appropriate for some.

On this occasion, the sound is so loud that people in the surrounding area know that something special is happening. Genuine worship does make an impact! Others are watching, and they can determine whether your worship is sincere.

CONCLUSION

There is a missionary message in today's lesson. Is Jerusalem the place to worship? Yes! Is it the only place? No! Jesus stated to the woman at the well that worship in the future would not be confined to Mt. Gerizim or Mt. Zion. What really matters is whether the worship is in spirit and in truth (John 4:21, 23).

The sounds of joy and the sounds of weeping may be heard throughout the entire planet whenever worshipers assemble to exalt God, examine themselves, exhort others, and determine to evangelize the lost. This type of "blended worship" is always pleasing to God.

Discovery Learning

*This page contains an alternative lesson plan emphasizing learning activities. Classes
desiring such student involvement will find these suggestions helpful. The next page
is a reproducible activity page to further enhance discovery learning.*

LEARNING GOALS

After participating in this lesson, each student will be able to:

1. Give evidence of unity and worship in at least three distinct places in the text.

2. Understand that corporate worship is both multidimensional and unifying.

3. Identify a new personal dimension of worship that will have a positive effect on the church body.

INTO THE LESSON

Before the class arrives write, "Major Events in This Church's History" on a board for all to see. As students arrive, ask them to write down, on their own or in pairs, what they think have been major events in the history of the congregation. Provide copies of the reproducible activity "A Review of Our Congregation's History" from the next page for the students to use. After a moment ask volunteers to tell what they have written, and write their ideas on the board. Draw attention to the relationship between what may be perceived as negative events and positive events. It is not unusual for a seemingly negative event to be followed by a positive event.

Say, "Often upheaval precedes change and growth in a church. The people in our text have just experienced significant upheaval in the exile, yet it resulted in a tremendous opportunity to enhance their worship."

INTO THE WORD

Ask a student to read Ezra 3:1-13. Divide the class into two groups of students. Ask one group to read through the text and record places they see *unity* demonstrated. Ask the other group to read through the text and record places they see *worship* demonstrated. After the groups have completed this task, ask a representative from each group to report on its findings.

Some places where *unity* is demonstrated are the assembling together (3:1), the building of the altar (3:3), the celebrating of the Feast of Tabernacles (3:4), the providing for the temple (3:7), the working on the temple (3:8-10), the praising of the Lord (3:11-13). Note the consistent use of the plural *they* throughout the text, indicating unified effort. Note that this text begins with an explicit reference to unity, in assembling "as one man," and ends with an explicit reference to unity, as different responses of the people are indistinguishable.

Places where *worship* is demonstrated are the assembling together in the seventh month (3:1; explain the significance of the seventh month in the people's worship life according to the commentary), the offering of sacrifices (3:2-6), the providing for the temple (3:7), the working on the temple (3:8-10), and the praising of the Lord (3:11-13). Help the students consider the work on the temple as a valid means of worship. Share this definition of worship to clarify the point: "to regard with great—even extravagant—respect, honor, or devotion."

Note that unity texts and worship texts are the same. Affirm: "Corporate worship and unity go together."

INTO LIFE

ADVANCE PREPARATION: Collect copies of your church newsletters from times significant to the history of the church. Ask long-time members for help with this, or consult someone in the church office for copies.

Have the students return to their groups. Distribute church newsletters from significant points in the church's history. Ask each group to write down ways they notice worship and unity as indicated in the church newsletters they view. (Provide copies of the reproducible activity "Worship and Unity" from the next page.) Direct the students to consider acts of service similar to those seen in the Ezra text. For example, a member who has consistently provided service through repair work may be seen as someone who regards God "with great, even extravagant respect, honor, or devotion" so that he or she gives time and effort dependably. Suggest learners fill in ideas for the "View to the Future" section of the reproducible page to be discussed with all.

Ask for volunteers to present the various ways worship and unity have been demonstrated throughout the history of the church. Discuss how many of the individual acts of service have facilitated worship and unity for the church. For example, you might ask, "How has the person who prepares the sanctuary each Sunday morning contributed to the worship experience?"

Ask the students to think of areas in their lives that can be considered worship, including specific acts not often considered to be. Have them list these. Finally, have each select an item from the list he or she will approach with an attitude of worship and will consider worshipful. Repeat the definition, "to regard with great, even extravagant respect, honor, or devotion."

A Review of Our Congregation's History

Significant points in our history   Approximate date

_____   _____

_____   _____

_____   _____

_____   _____

_____   _____

Worship and Unity

Worship has been demonstrated in our church by:

Unity has been demonstrated in our church by:

A View to the Future

List below some items you believe would enhance worship and unity in your congregation.

RETURNING TO THE WORK

LESSON 3

Jun
15

WHY TEACH THIS LESSON?

An acquaintance of mine once jokingly remarked, "I keep meaning to start a Procrastination Club, but I just can never seem to get around to it!" As amusing as that quip is, procrastination can have serious, eternal consequences when it comes to the Lord's work.

Procrastination is the problem we will see with the ancient Israelites in today's lesson. And it's a problem some of your learners wrestle with. Perhaps you do, too—how often is it Saturday night before you begin to prepare your Sunday school lesson? While delay seems harmless, procrastination often leads to a complete failure to do an important task. As you read how God chided the Israelites for their failure to complete his temple, listen carefully. Perhaps you will discover he is chiding you as well concerning some ministry that you have neglected.

INTRODUCTION

A. PRIORITIZE!

The student came home from the university with a new word that he learned sprinkled regularly into his conversations. The word was *prioritize*, and it really was a new word at the time. The dictionary indicates that the date for the earliest recorded use of the word *prioritize* is 1964, just thirty-nine years ago. It was easily recognized, for the noun form, *priority*, had been in use for a long time. Making a verb of the noun did sound strange at first, but it made good sense to use it, for it reduced to one word what had formerly been said in a phrase. A popular way of saying it was, "putting first things first." Illustrations of prioritizing are very familiar. Parents have often said, "Eat your spinach, and then you may have dessert," or "You cannot go out to play until your homework is done."

A man in a hospital was dying of cancer. Just a few days before he died, he uttered a five-word sentence that indicated that his priorities had been wrong: "I see it all now." He continued by saying that he had been determined that his children would not be deprived as he had been when he was a child. He worked two jobs, quit attending church (even though he had been baptized as a young person), and gave his children all that they wanted. He concluded by saying that if he had his life to live over, he would have put Jesus first and given his children what they really needed—salvation. His spoiling them had resulted in lives that embarrassed him and other family members.

The study for today is about priorities. The Israelites who had returned from Babylonian exile had started well, but then they found reasons to rearrange their priorities. They prioritized, but they put first things last!

B. LESSON BACKGROUND

The study from Ezra 3 last week ended with a tumultuous rejoicing. In the spring of 536 B.C., after the Jews returned from Babylon, they had laid the foundation of the temple. They had great resources. They had made arrangements for the material and the laborers to continue the task until the house of God was finished—but it wasn't.

DEVOTIONAL READING:
1 CORINTHIANS 3:10-17

BACKGROUND SCRIPTURE:
HAGGAI; EZRA 5:1, 2

PRINTED TEXT:
HAGGAI 1:2-14

LESSON AIMS

After participating in this lesson, each student will be able to:

1. Summarize the people's actions, God's actions, and the results of these actions in this text.

2. Recognize the ongoing interaction that God has with his people.

3. Prepare a godly response to an upcoming event by carefully considering the consequences of two previous events (one considered positive, one negative) in his or her life.

KEY VERSE

"Is it time for you yourselves to be living in your paneled houses, while this house remains a ruin?" —Haggai 1:4

LESSON 3 NOTES

What happened? The next five verses in the book of Ezra (4:1-5) reveal that the "fear" that gripped them because "of the peoples around them" (3:3) was based in reality. At first their enemies offered to help build, but the Jews were not about to risk mingling their worship with neighbors who served other gods. When the Jews rejected their neighbors' offer, those neighbors began active opposition, which lasted from about 536 to 520 B.C. In 520, when both Haggai and Zechariah received the word of the Lord and proclaimed it to the people of Jerusalem, they finally returned to the work.

Little is known about Haggai. He simply calls himself "the prophet." He uses that title five times—more than any other "minor" prophet (Haggai 1:1, 3, 12; 2:1, 10). He is mentioned also in the book of Ezra (5:1; 6:14) in connection with the historical record of the rebuilding and dedication of the temple.

Haggai was careful to date the four sermons that he gave. Each has a precise date, and it is therefore possible to provide the equivalent dates according to the calendar methods in use today.

I. THREE MESSAGES (HAGGAI 1:2-11)

The first date is August 29, 520 B.C. (1:1), and something amazing is about to happen: God is ready to break his silence. So far the people who have returned to Judah and Jerusalem have been responding on their own, armed only with a personal devotion to the Lord and his Word. This has led them from Babylon. It has inspired them to build the altar for the burnt offerings and to lay the foundation of the temple. Since their return in about 538 B.C., it almost has seemed that God has abandoned the Israelites. But now God speaks through Haggai.

A. TO THE LEADERS (v. 2)

2. This is what the LORD Almighty says: "These people say, 'The time has not yet come for the LORD's house to be built.'"

The verse just before this (not in our text for today) indicates that this message is addressed to Zerubbabel and Joshua, the governor and high priest respectively. Since their arrival, Zerubbabel evidently has been appointed as the governor by the Persian king (cf. Ezra 2:2).

The Lord Almighty begins his message with a stinging rebuke in the form of two words: *these people*. We can feel the sense of contempt here. At this particular time, the Israelites do not deserve to be called "my people," a phrase of endearment that God uses so often (see Hosea 2:23; Romans 9:25).

God reminds Zerubbabel and Joshua that the people are saying that it is not the right *time* to build *the Lord's house*. But God has a different opinion. The people undoubtedly have a variety of alibis to justify the sentiment that they express. If a person does not wish to perform a task, he or she can find many excuses not to do it. But it's now been sixteen years since the foundation was laid!

The context of the chapter provides various possibilities for the procrastination. "It's harvest time, and we are too busy." Or, "The crops are bad, and we cannot afford it" (vv. 10 and 11). They might have added that their neighbors would not like it, or that the new king, Darius, had not endorsed the project.

B. TO THE PEOPLE, PART 1 (vv. 3-6)

3, 4. Then the word of the LORD came through the prophet Haggai: "Is it a time for you yourselves to be living in your paneled houses, while this house remains a ruin?"

The Jews' *paneled houses* were probably lined with boards to cover the stone or other material used to form the walls.

WHAT DO YOU THINK?

What are some of the reasons that believers today give for postponing obedience to God? How do we guard our hearts against these?

[Use Luke 9:59-62; 14:15-24 in the course of your discussion.]

To live in comfort is not wrong in and of itself. To do so at the expense of the Lord's *house* that still lies in ruins, however, indicates that they have not prioritized correctly. Some commentators propose that cedar logs from Lebanon had been diverted to personal use, instead of being a part of the construction of the temple (Ezra 3:7). First Kings 7:7 notes that Solomon's palace had walls covered with cedar. That wood has a better appearance than bare stone, but it is costly, supposedly reserved for royalty and the wealthy.

Attitudes about such matters do make a difference spiritually. Many people buy only the top-of-the-line items for themselves, but think that the economy model is good enough for the Lord's work. When some folks buy a new microwave oven for their own house, they sometimes donate their old one to the church. But if the old one isn't good enough for them anymore, then why do they think it's good enough for the Lord? (See Malachi 1:8.)

5. Now this is what the LORD Almighty says: "Give careful thought to your ways.

The Israelites are commanded to examine their *ways*. Haggai likes to use the phrase *give careful thought*, and it appears four more times in his short book (1:7; 2:15; and twice in 2:18). The idea is that everyone should take a good, hard look at what they have been doing and what the results have been.

6. "You have planted much, but have harvested little. You eat, but never have enough. You drink, but never have your fill. You put on clothes, but are not warm. You earn wages, only to put them in a purse with holes in it."

Haggai lists five essential areas in which the people are lacking. The first has a certain irony to it. They are really trying to have good harvests in that they *planted much*, but ultimately they are able to harvest only *little*. Their expenditures of time, energy, and seed seem to be wasted.

The next three deal with the physical necessities of life: food, *drink*, and clothing. They *never* seem to *have enough* of any. To use familiar imagery, they go to bed hungry and cold every night. Keeping warm means putting on more clothing. But in their nicely furnished houses (Haggai 1:4), they never seem to be warm enough.

The final item of this five-fold observation is that their *wages* seemed to be going *in a purse with holes in it*. It takes all of their resources for what necessities they do have, and there is nothing left over (cf. Isaiah 28:20). The second part of the message that follows offers even more for the people to consider.

C. TO THE PEOPLE, PART 2 (vv. 7-11)

7. This is what the LORD Almighty says: "Give careful thought to your ways.

This repetition of the expression *Give careful thought to your ways* could mean that this is part of a new message, or it may be intended to capture the attention of the hearers who are allowing their minds to wander. Hope is a part of the message, and the next verse offers a positive note. It will comfort those who are seriously considering their ways.

8. "Go up into the mountains and bring down timber and build the house, so that I may take pleasure in it and be honored," says the LORD.

Three commands are given for the people: *go, bring,* and *build*. If the commands are obeyed, two results will follow. First, the Lord will *take pleasure* in obedience to his commands and in the restoration of the special worship that is possible only when the temple is completed. Second, the Lord will *be honored* in the sight of other peoples because of the obedience of the Israelites. This also will point to the glory that is in the future when the Messiah will come. In Jesus' final discourses to the apostles, he affirmed that the Holy Spirit would glorify him (John 16:14). Ultimately, God desires that all people glorify him.

WHAT DO YOU THINK?

Even though modern church buildings do not serve the same purpose as the temple did for the ancient Israelites, how can believers decide how much luxury to allow themselves relative to the needs and condition of their church building?

[Matthew 6:21 can start your thinking. Note also the poster pictured below. It is available in the Adult Visuals *packet. See page 339 for ordering information.*]

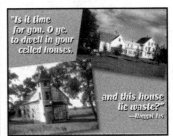

Use this visual to illustrate verse 4. Call attention to it also as you discuss the question above.

DAILY BIBLE READINGS

Monday, June 9—Time to Rebuild (Haggai 1:1-6)

Tuesday, June 10—God Stirs the People's Spirits (Haggai 1:7-15)

Wednesday, June 11—Take Courage; I Am With You (Haggai 2:1-9)

Thursday, June 12—They Did Not Stop (Ezra 5:1-5)

Friday, June 13—We Are the Servants of God (Ezra 5:6-12)

Saturday, June 14—From That Time Until Now (Ezra 5:13-17)

Sunday, June 15—From This Day I Will Bless (Haggai 2:13-23)

EXAMINE YOUR WAYS

Every June the National Basketball Association wraps up its playoffs by crowning a new champion. Years ago, a fan in Portland, Oregon, went to the airport to greet the Trailblazers following a victory over the Los Angeles Lakers.

At the airport this fan attempted to make some money by scalping two tickets to the next game. He spotted a well-dressed man and made his move.

"How much?" asked the gentleman.

"One hundred fifty," he replied. "Not a cent less."

"Sir, do you realize you're talking to a plain-clothes officer of the law?" the man asked the scalper. "I'm a detective. What you are doing is illegal and I'm going to turn you in."

Suddenly the seller began to backpedal. He talked about his large family and his financial need. He promised never to do it again.

Looking both ways the well-dressed man said, "Just hand over the tickets and we'll call it even." And he did. "Now get out of here and I better never catch you here again!"

What a close call! But that well-dressed man was no compassionate cop. He was just a quick-thinking opportunist who used imagination and guts to land two choice seats to the next playoff game. He anonymously admitted it in the local newspaper a few days later.

It hurts when others deceive us. But to live in the blindness of self-deception is even worse. God called Israel to examine their ways. Haggai 1:6 makes it clear that many in Israel were robbing themselves by their lack of self-examination. Take an honest look at your life. Any holes in your bag?   —J. A. M.

9. *"You expected much, but see, it turned out to be little. What you brought home, I blew away. Why?" declares the LORD Almighty. "Because of my house, which remains a ruin, while each of you is busy with his own house.*

Haggai now informs the people of the real reason behind their hardship. They are suffering because the Lord's *house* is still in ruins! Because each man *is busy with his own house,* God has withdrawn his blessings. *My house, which remains a ruin,* speaks of an unfinished building, an eyesore, and all that goes with such a situation.

We need a word of caution here. The doctrine of "divine retribution" is not absolute or universal in its earthly application. Often there is a cause-and-effect relationship between one's sin and subsequent suffering in his or her life. This may be simply a natural consequence of the behavior, as when an alcoholic develops liver disease. Or the penalty may be imposed by judgment. In the Old Testament, for example, famine, the sword, and/or captivity often came about because of the people's sin. The record of Job, however, establishes that humans may not be aware of all the circumstances. In a fallen world, bad things do happen to good people. It is important to remember the lesson from another Old Testament prophet: "the righteous will live by his faith" (Habakkuk 2:4; cf. Romans 1:17; Galatians 3:11). We must do this regardless of what happens.

10. *"Therefore, because of you the heavens have withheld their dew and the earth its crops.*

The dry season in Israel is from April to October. During this period, crops depend on heavy, overnight *dew* to be sustained in their growth. The prophet makes clear that the absence of the dew is not just a random weather condition. It actually is an act of God.

11. *"I called for a drought on the fields and the mountains, on the grain, the new wine, the oil and whatever the ground produces, on men and cattle, and on the labor of your hands."*

WHAT DO YOU THINK?

What is the outcome of being stingy with God? Do you believe that God withholds blessing today from those who put their own interests above his? Why or why not?

[Luke 6:38 may help you in this discussion.]

In Moses' farewell discourse, he warned the people of Israel that disobedience to God would bring about these kinds of disasters (Deuteronomy 28:23, 24, 38-40). As that nine-hundred-year-old warning has come true before, so now it is coming true again.

A drought affects everything. A bad crop of *grain* means that neither *men* nor *cattle* eat well. The three food items mentioned here—grain, *new wine,* and olive *oil*—are the foundation items in their diets. There is no prosperity without these three. Since the people are now at the end of their agricultural year, the results of the drought are impossible to miss.

II. TWO RESPONSES (HAGGAI 1:12, 13)

The combination of the catastrophes and the preaching of Haggai has gained the attention of the people. But after they gave "careful thought," what next?

A. THE PEOPLE'S RESOLVE (v. 12)

12. Then Zerubbabel son of Shealtiel, Joshua son of Jehozadak, the high priest, and the whole remnant of the people obeyed the voice of the LORD their God and the message of the prophet Haggai, because the LORD their God had sent him. And the people feared the LORD.

Haggai is a successful communicator. The backdrop of drought and famine allows him to preach a great, one-sermon revival with immediate results. The entire *remnant of the people obeyed the voice of the Lord their God.*

The use of the word *remnant* has special meaning. It tends to be reserved for the faithful few who are willing to serve the Lord, regardless of what the majority do. In this case, the reference is to the people who came back from captivity, as had been prophesied. In the New Testament, it is applied by Paul to those who are saved (Romans 9:27; 11:5).

The end of the verse introduces a very important concept: the people now have a proper reverence toward God that transcends any fear they have of their neighbors (cf. Ezra 4:4, 5). They now have a godly fear that produces godly living. Perhaps they realize that famine is only one of the punishments that God can bring about. Things could be worse! While they had not been bowing to any idols lately, and they may have been proud of themselves, they had their priorities all wrong.

TRULY FREE?

On December 18, 1865, the United States ratified the Thirteenth Amendment to its Constitution. With this amendment's adoption, slavery officially ended. What a wonderful day for America that was!

But then something strange happened: slaves were free to decide their own futures, but the vast majority voluntarily stayed in slavery. The war was over, blood had been shed, and the price of freedom had been paid. Yet little actual change took place as slavery continued to be the *de facto* practice. Yes, slaves were legally free, but to live out their new freedom in a practical way was something new and foreign. They had trouble living free lives.

Israel faced a similar challenge following years of captivity. When the people finally returned home, Haggai makes it clear that the Israelites had difficulty using their freedom to bless themselves and to serve God. They had trouble thinking in a new way. At Haggai's instruction, people finally learned to use their freedom to obey.

Christians today can identify with those slaves. Set free from sin—yes! Jesus is Savior. Transformed living? That can be a different story.

Galatians 5:1 says, "Stand fast therefore in the liberty wherewith Christ hath made us free" (*King James Version*). Second Corinthians 3:17 makes clear that

WHAT DO YOU THINK?

God called on the Israelites for obedience in building the temple. What is the obedience from believers today that would cause God the greatest pleasure and glory?

[Use John 15:9, 10 and Colossians 3:9, 10 to frame your answer.]

HOW TO SAY IT

Colossians. Kuh-LOSH-unz.
Darius. Duh-RYE-us.
Deuteronomy. Due-ter-AHN-uh-me.
Habakkuk. Huh-BACK-kuk.
Haggai. HAG-eye or HAG-ay-eye.
Jehozadak. Jeh-HO-zuh-dak.
Jeremiah. Jair-uh-MY-uh.
Joshua. JOSH-yew-uh.
Lebanon. LEB-uh-nun.
Persian. PER-zhun.
Shealtiel. Shee-AL-tee-el.
Zechariah. ZEK-uh-RYE-uh.
Zerubbabel. Zeh-RUB-uh-bul.

"where the Spirit of the Lord is, there is freedom." Have we learned what it means to live a life that is truly free to serve Christ as he wants?   —J. A. M.

B. THE PROPHET'S REASSURANCE (v. 13)

13. Then Haggai, the LORD's messenger, gave this message of the LORD to the people: "I am with you," declares the LORD.

The positive actions on the part of the people bring forth a *message* of assurance from the prophet. Here he is called *the Lord's messenger*, and that is a rare, special title in the Old Testament (cf. Malachi 2:7; Matthew 11:10).

His message is short but powerful: *I am with you!* Other faithful servants through the centuries who had that same assurance were Moses (Exodus 3:12), Gideon (Judges 6:16), and Jeremiah (Jeremiah 1:8). How much greater this same assurance is to us now that Christ—Immanuel—has come (Matthew 1:23)!

III. TWO POSITIVE ACTIONS (HAGGAI 1:14)

The last verse of chapter 1 gives us another precise date. Converted to modern reckoning, it is September 21, 520 B.C. The twenty-three-day interval allowed time for two things to happen.

A. THE LORD'S STIRRING (v. 14a)

14a. So the LORD stirred up the spirit of Zerubbabel son of Shealtiel, governor of Judah, and the spirit of Joshua son of Jehozadak, the high priest, and the spirit of the whole remnant of the people.

The spirits of the people and their leaders are bolstered by a divine stirring. Everyone now has to make changes in daily routines. When was the last time you saw God work at your church in such a way that the spirits of the people were stirred so that they started changing "the way we've always done things"?

B. THE PEOPLE'S WORKING (v. 14b)

14b. They came and began to work on the house of the LORD Almighty, their God.

Whereas the first temple in Solomon's day had been built by conscripted labor (2 Chronicles 2:2), the completion of the temple this time seems to have been by these eager volunteers. The three-week interval allows the people time to organize their *work* and gather the required material and tools. As the title for today's lesson says, they are "returning to the work."

CONCLUSION

A lesson on building the temple for worship in Israel lends itself to comparisons with the buildings used by churches today, but there are two major differences. First, the Lord commanded the construction of the tabernacle through Moses and the temple through David and Solomon, but there are no precepts that buildings must be constructed to use when Christians assemble. Second, the Old Testament temple was God's distinctive "holy place" on earth (2 Chronicles 5:13, 14; 33:7), but in New Testament times our bodies now are the temple of God's Spirit (1 Corinthians 3:16, 17; 6:19).

Is having a building wrong, because God did not command it? Absolutely not! The example of the early church is that the people met in different places. God left it up to each generation to determine the best way for a body of believers to come together. Changes in circumstances, cultures, and climates are to be considered when congregations make such decisions, but this is an area that is guided by principles, not by divine precepts. The most important thing to remember is that we are commanded to build his church—his holy people.

Discovery Learning

This page contains an alternative lesson plan emphasizing learning activities. Classes desiring such student involvement will find these suggestions helpful. The next page is a reproducible activity page to further enhance discovery learning.

LEARNING GOALS

After this lesson each student will be able to:

1. Summarize the people's actions, God's actions, and the results of these actions in this text.

2. Recognize the ongoing interaction that God has with his people.

3. Prepare a godly response to an upcoming event by carefully considering the consequences of two specific events (one considered positive, one negative) in his or her life.

INTO THE LESSON

After students arrive, hand them a copy of the reproducible activity "Consider Your Ways" from the next page. Say, "Think of two events in your life in which your actions had a direct impact on the outcome. One of these should be a positive event, one negative. One example of an event with a positive outcome might be the decision to attend Sunday school regularly. Examples of an event with a negative outcome might be an occasion of gossiping about a particular person or buying something on impulse and suffering the consequences." If it would make the students more comfortable, encourage them to think of situations that did not have a drastic outcome.

Say, "What sort of thoughts and actions contributed to the positive and negative outcomes of these two events? Consider your ways." Allow time for the students to ponder these past events. Then enter into the Word by saying, "The returning exiles started in a strong way, as we saw last week, but they soon began to fade. In today's passage God commands them to consider their ways and tells them the consequences of their actions or lack of action."

INTO THE WORD

Assemble the students into three small groups (or multiples of three). Assign one group to read the text and record the actions of the people. Assign another group to read the text and record the actions of God. Assign a third group to read the text and record the consequences of the actions of the people.

The people's actions are clearly seen in the Lord's rebuke of them in verses 4-6, 9. God's actions are seen again in verses 11, 13, 14. God's actions begin the assigned text by responding to the people's decision that the time has not come for them to build the Lord's house. (Note the commentary reference to God's attitude toward "these people," page 354.) Consequences of the people's actions may be found in verses 10, 11, and 13.

Have students report their findings. Make special note of the comforting, yet convicting, truth that God is with us (v. 13). This fact allows God's ongoing interaction with his people despite their fading spiritual lives. Emphasize that God's actions in verse 14 stirred the people to do the work he required. Say, "It is helpful to recognize God's involvement in the events and decisions of our lives. To see his hand in our daily lives builds faith."

INTO LIFE

Ask students to recall the events they were asked to consider when they entered the class. Have them write down the events, the decisions, and the actions made prior to and during the event.

Ask students to compare (and contrast) the decisions and actions of the event with a negative outcome with those of the event with a positive outcome. Ask students to share these comparisons and contrasts with a partner. They may include such determinations as making a selfish decision *versus* making a Christ-centered decision, listening to others *versus* listening to God's Word, thinking in a short-term way versus making long-term considerations.

On the board write any common themes you hear. Introduce the idea of God-focused decisions *versus* self-focused decisions, as this is evident in the text.

After completing this, have the students think of some future events in their lives. Provide copies of the reproducible activity "Future Event" from the next page. This event may be unique to each individual, or they may work in groups on an upcoming event in the church. Ask them to anticipate their ways and list what they will do in order to ensure a godly response to the upcoming event. If considering a church event, ask groups to work on the same event, then draw responses together in a single list at the end. If individual events are considered, allow time for each student to work through the task. Conclude by noting any similarities in the individual responses by asking for volunteers to tell their individual events and their plans for accomplishing it in a godly manner and with godly results.

Consider Your Ways!

Think of two events in your life in which your actions had a direct impact on the outcome. One of these should be a positive event, one negative.

EVENT WITH POSITIVE OUTCOME(S):	EVENT WITH NEGATIVE OUTCOME(S):
Decisions and actions that I took that are related to this event	Decisions and actions that I took that are related to this event

As I consider my ways, what are some of the differences in my decisions and actions that may have had an impact on whether the events had positive outcomes or negative outcomes?

Future Event

An event that will occur in my life in the future is:

Decisions I should make and actions I should take related to this event:

1. _____

2. _____

3. _____

4. _____

GOD GIVES HOPE FOR THE FUTURE

Jun
22

DEVOTIONAL READING:
PSALM 48:1-14
BACKGROUND SCRIPTURE:
ZECHARIAH 8
PRINTED TEXT:
ZECHARIAH 8:1-13

WHY TEACH THIS LESSON?

If you asked your learners, "What would your 'ideal future' be like?" most of the responses probably would be framed in terms of having enough money for something—quitting a job, sending the kids to the best schools, buying a certain house or car, travel, and the like. Perhaps something similar comes to your own mind. But God depicts the "ideal future" in terms of his presence with us. This is our ultimate hope! It is a hope God revealed dimly to his Old Testament people, in terms familiar to them. It is a hope that we understand with greater clarity now that Jesus has come. Today's lesson will be a time for you and your learners to be to refreshed at the fountain of this ideal future—a future promised by God himself!

INTRODUCTION

A. THE NEED FOR ENCOURAGEMENT

Someone has said that life may be compared to walking through a minefield, for disaster or death may come at any moment. We see this possibility in all the current fears that the media feels compelled to share in somber tones: air and water pollution, energy shortages, global warming, AIDS, cancer-causing products, heart diseases, overpopulation—not to mention threats of terror somewhere on the planet. The list seems to go on and on.

As we have noted previously, the biblical response to all these threats is to live by faith, regardless of what God allows to happen. However, the people around us often need to be encouraged and reminded of the hope that Christians have.

One Sunday school class has the right idea: it has designated itself *The Encouragers*. The teacher is taking the lead in providing encouragement to others. He may not be the official "greeter" for the congregation, but each Sunday he is at his post to welcome visitors and friends. His genuine interest in others is shared by his wife, who prepares a variety of cards to be sent through the class each week so that the members may sign them.

Behind acts of encouragement are the biblical concepts of thankfulness and the fruit of the Spirit as given in Galatians 5:22, 23. Every family, church, or other social group could benefit if its members would minimize the negatives and publicize the positives with encouragement.

B. LESSON BACKGROUND

God was speaking again through the prophets after the exile! It started with Haggai on August 29, 520 B.C. (last week's lesson). Slightly over two months later, the voice of Zechariah was also heard in Jerusalem (Zechariah 1:1). Both men provided encouragement to those who were building the temple (Ezra 5:1). The temple was finished and dedicated on March 12, 515 B.C., and the people prospered under the preaching of these two prophets.

LESSON AIMS

After participating in this lesson, each student will be able to:

1. Explain how God's jealousy for his people motivates him to provide hope for the future.

2. Understand the biblical concept of hope.

3. Develop a plan for providing one person eternal hope, which is in Christ.

KEY VERSE

"*I will return to Zion and dwell in Jerusalem. Then Jerusalem will be called the City of Truth, and the mountain of the LORD Almighty will be called the Holy Mountain.*"
—Zechariah 8:3

The name Zechariah means "Yahweh remembers" or "Yahweh has remembered." Combining the information in Zechariah 1:1 with Nehemiah 12:12 and 16, we conclude that this Zechariah was a priest, and that he was much younger than Haggai. Zechariah came to a tragic end (see Matthew 23:35).

The four messages in Zechariah 7 and 8 involve a delegation from Bethel, which is about twelve miles north of Jerusalem. The delegation arrived on December 7, 518 B.C., to pose some questions on the subject of fasting (7:1-3). The Jews had added days of fasting to their religious calendar to memorialize events associated with the fall of Jerusalem, which had occurred some sixty-eight years earlier. Specifically, the delegation was concerned about a fast in the fifth month (late July and early August) to remember the destruction of Jerusalem and a fast in the seventh month (late September and early October) to remind them of the murder of governor Gedaliah in a civil uprising after Jerusalem was destroyed (Zechariah 7:3, 5; Jeremiah 41:1, 2).

The Jews also had added two other fasts. One memorialized the month that the siege of Jerusalem had begun, and another was a reminder of when the Babylonians broke through the walls of the city (Zechariah 8:19). The Jews probably had been keeping these fast days during all the time that they were in Babylon (7:5). Now they wondered whether they should continue to observe these traditions (7:3).

The lesson today is from the first part of the third message that Zechariah gave to the men from Bethel. (The four messages begin at 7:4, 8; 8:1, and 18.) Zechariah's words were encouraging words for people who wondered about the future.

I. PROMISES FOR JERUSALEM (ZECHARIAH 8:1-8)

One hundred years ago, an English scholar wrote that Zechariah 8 contains a "decalogue of promises." These are messages of "hope," as the title for the lesson indicates. Our printed text covers several of these promises that concern Jerusalem.

A. THE LORD'S PASSION AND PRESENCE (vv. 1-3)

1, 2. Again the word of the LORD Almighty came to me. This is what the LORD Almighty says: "I am very jealous for Zion; I am burning with jealousy for her."

Throughout this chapter, Zechariah emphasizes that his words are from the Lord (cf. vv. 1 and 2, 3, 4, 6, 7, 9, 14, 18, 20, 23). All but one of the "ten promises" begins by stating that this is from *the Lord Almighty*. (The promise in v. 3 contains the phrase but does not begin with it.) There is no doubt that the message is from God himself!

Many centuries earlier, the Lord had stated in the Second Commandment that he is a *jealous* God (Exodus 20:5). *Jealousy* is a very strong emotion or passion. For humans, it can be good or bad; with God, however, this emotion is always for our benefit. To be *jealous for Zion* and to be *burning with jealousy for her* means that God is passionate about restoring his people (cf. Zechariah 1:14).

3. This is what the LORD says: "I will return to Zion and dwell in Jerusalem. Then Jerusalem will be called the City of Truth, and the mountain of the LORD Almighty will be called the Holy Mountain."

This promise involves the Lord's returning his presence to Jerusalem. *Zion* is one of the hills on which Jerusalem stands. The term became a synonym for Jerusalem itself and is used interchangeably with it.

When Solomon dedicated the temple in about 950 B.C. (1 Kings 6:38), a special glory prevented the priests from entering (see 2 Chronicles 7:2, 3). There is no record of any such event this time—just the assurance that God will *dwell in* his city (cf. Zechariah 1:16; 2:10). Before the city's destruction God's glory had withdrawn because of wickedness within her (see Ezekiel 9:3; 10:4, 18, 19; 11:23).

Two new descriptive names now are assigned to the city: *City of Truth* and *the Holy Mountain.* Before Jerusalem was destroyed by the Babylonians in 586 B.C., the city had become "full of injustice" (Ezekiel 9:9). Now it is to be holy, a city that is set apart for the Lord. Isaiah 62:4 prophesies still another name for Jerusalem: "Hephzibah," which means "my delight is in her."

B. THE LORD'S PEACE AND POWER (vv. 4-6)

4. This is what the LORD Almighty says: "Once again men and women of ripe old age will sit in the streets of Jerusalem, each with cane in hand because of his age.

This promise begins with assurance of a peaceful existence. Things are still difficult for the hardy remnant that has been back in their land and their city for less than twenty years. Although not describing their present situation, this verse gives them hope for the future. To have a time without the ravages of war, which had been so much a part of Jerusalem's past, will be a joy. *Jerusalem* will be a place where one can walk *the streets* in safety.

Our historical perspective teaches us that this type of tranquility for Jerusalem seems to come and go. Today, the threat of terrorism lurks around every corner in modern Jerusalem. Such uncertainty makes us look forward to the Heavenly Jerusalem, where perfect peace will exist (Revelation 3:12; 21:2, 10-27). Only there will this prophecy find ultimate fulfillment.

5. "The city streets will be filled with boys and girls playing there."

This verse depicts the other end of the age spectrum. In times of danger, *boys and girls* sometimes are compelled to play behind locked doors, with bars on the windows. That is not a pleasant childhood. (See Isaiah 65:19-25.) The imagery suggests that the children can play happily outside. Young people can grow old and not have their lives taken by the ravages of war, with dreams unfulfilled.

6. This is what the LORD Almighty says: "It may seem marvelous to the remnant of this people at that time, but will it seem marvelous to me?" declares the LORD Almighty.

The implied answer to the question *will it seem marvelous to me?* is to be a firm negative. To the people, that which seems marvelous to the point of being impossible is certainly not impossible with God. With God all things are possible (Matthew 19:26; Mark 10:27).

A similar question arose in the days of Abraham and Sarah. When the Lord promised that this aged woman would have Abraham's son the following year, her disbelief produced laughter. God then asked, "Is anything too hard for the Lord?" (Genesis 18:14). The implied answer is that the God who made the heavens and the earth could bring about this event. In Romans 4:18-22 the apostle Paul affirms that this is one of the events that demonstrated Abraham's faith.

In a similar hopeless situation Jeremiah the prophet expressed the same type of faith in a prayer. In his case, Jerusalem was under siege by the Babylonians, and he was instructed to buy a field. His symbolic act was intended to show that "Houses, fields and vineyards will again be bought in this land" (Jeremiah 32:15). He then voiced a prayer, and the opening words are the inspiration for a contemporary song: "Ah Sovereign Lord, you have made the heavens and the earth by your great power . . . Nothing is too hard for you" (32:17).

C. THE LORD'S PEOPLE (vv. 7, 8)

7. This is what the LORD Almighty says: "I will save my people from the countries of the east and the west.

WHAT DO YOU THINK?

What assurance do Christian believers have of God's presence? How do you experience that presence in your life?

[Passages such as Matthew 1:23; John 14:16, 17; Acts 2:38; Romans 8:9; and Galatians 5:16-26 can start your thinking.]

WHAT DO YOU THINK?

Recount a time in your life when God intervened in a situation that appeared hopeless.

"I . . . will dwell in the midst of Jerusalem . . . The holy mountain."

Zechariah 8:3

Use this poster to illustrate verse 8 of the text. Keep it on display for next week's lesson as well. You will find the poster in the Adult Visuals packet. See page 339 for ordering information.

This section concludes the brief messages of hope. The two opposite directions *east* and *west* express totality in signifying that God will regather his *people* from "the ends of the earth." Although this prediction is nothing new (see Isaiah 43:5-7 and Jeremiah 31:7, 8), it needs to be restated for a new generation.

8. "I will bring them back to live in Jerusalem; they will be my people, and I will be faithful and righteous to them as their God."

Isaiah 2:1-4 and Micah 4:1-3 prophesy that the journey to *Jerusalem* is for all of God's *people.* Most students agree that "Jerusalem" is not confined to the physical city. Rather, it includes all of spiritual Israel, all who are God's people in Christ (cf. Romans 9:24; 1 Peter 2:9, 10). The prophet foretold of a new covenant (Jeremiah 31:31-34), and the writer of Hebrews states that it is fulfilled in Christ now as he serves as the high priest for this new covenant (Hebrews 8:8-11). That writer adds that we already have come to the heavenly Jerusalem (Hebrews 12:22-24). The expression *my people* is a special concept in both Old and New Testaments (see last week's lesson).

II. PROMISES FOR THE PEOPLE (ZECHARIAH 8:9-13)

Zechariah again brings a message directly from the Lord. The people need encouragement as they continue to work on the temple in the year 518 B.C.

A. RETROSPECT (vv. 9, 10)

9. This is what the LORD Almighty says: "You who now hear these words spoken by the prophets who were there when the foundation was laid for the house of the LORD Almighty, let your hands be strong so that the temple may be built.

Encouragement comes from looking to the past. *The Lord Almighty* wants to remind the people of the way things were, but he prefaces the reminder with a strong admonition: *let your hands be strong.*

In an era before power tools, almost everything would be accomplished by the work of the hands. For this reason, "hands" frequently serves as a figure of speech in the Bible (e.g., 2 Samuel 16:21). Approximately seventy years after Zechariah's prophecy, Nehemiah will ask the Lord to strengthen his hands (Nehemiah 6:9) as he prepares to lead the work in rebuilding the walls of Jerusalem. (This will be a part of the study on July 13.) Zechariah will repeat this phrase in verse 13, below.

The prophet reminds the delegation from Bethel to look back to how the Lord has already blessed them. *The foundation was laid for the house of the Lord Almighty* in 536 B.C. (see Ezra 3:8-10). The work on the temple was resumed in 520 B.C., and both Haggai and Zechariah were eyewitnesses (Ezra 5:1, 2).

HARD WORK

Colonel Sanders, Kentucky's favorite son, said, "Hard work beats all the tonics and vitamins in the world." The chicken king knew the truth!

A good work ethic is not an American invention. It's biblical! Hard work pays. In Zechariah 8, the prophet challenged his hearers to have strong hands—to work hard! Hard work is God's high calling. God called Israel to work hard at rebuilding the temple. He calls us to greater energy in working for his kingdom.

Listen to the commands of God. "Whatever you do, work at it with all your heart" (Colossians 3:23). "Do your best to present yourself . . . a workman who does not need to be ashamed" (2 Timothy 2:15). "Never be lacking in zeal, but keep your spiritual fervor, serving the Lord" (Romans 12:11). These are verses that cut across every aspect and activity of our lives.

Years ago, doctors at New York's Montifiore Hospital advertised for volunteers to study the impact of complete bed rest. They were swamped with volunteers! A life without hard work seems the ambition of many. Is this a good thing? Not according to God.

Robert Frost said, "The world is full of willing people. Some willing to work, the rest willing to let them." Which category best describes you?   —J. A. M.

10. *"Before that time there were no wages for man or beast. No one could go about his business safely because of his enemy, for I had turned every man against his neighbor.*

Before that time is roughly the years 530–520 B.C. Haggai 1:6-11; 2:15-19 describe the economic conditions of that time period (see last week's lesson). The work on the temple had come to a halt. That happened in part because the economic situation did not provide for any extra funds for this major project. A certain physical and spiritual "slackness" on the part of the people also was a factor (see Haggai 1:9), as was opposition by their enemies (see Ezra 4:23, 24). The Lord has allowed the tensions to rise, which they do in such crises. It is God himself who has brought these conditions about in order to accomplish his larger purpose (cf. Haggai 2:17).

B. PROSPECT (vv. 11, 12)

11. *"But now I will not deal with the remnant of this people as I did in the past,"* declares the LORD Almighty.

The first two words *but now* offer a sharp contrast. The circumstances *in the past* are over. Those were the days between the laying of the foundation and the resumption of the work on the temple.

The prospect for the future will continue to be different for the *remnant of* the *people* who have returned from Babylon. The prophet Haggai already has confirmed this in his final sermon on December 18, 520 B.C. At that time (just about two years before Zechariah's message here) he had passed along the Lord's promise that "from this day on I will bless you" (Haggai 2:19c).

12. *"The seed will grow well, the vine will yield its fruit, the ground will produce its crops, and the heavens will drop their dew. I will give all these things as an inheritance to the remnant of this people.*

The future for Israel will include prosperity. All the necessary ingredients will come together to achieve it. These include *the heavens* (the atmosphere, to provide the *dew* during the dry season) and *the ground.* The ground would not be as hard as iron, but would provide the essential nutrients for growth (see Haggai 1:10, 11 in last week's lesson for the disastrous situation that the people had been experiencing).

One additional factor is necessary for such growth: peace, or freedom from conflict. The opening words in the Hebrew literally read, "For the seed of peace, the vine, will give its fruit." Scholars differ on whether it is *the vine* itself that is *the seed* of peace, or if this is a reference to the absence of conflict. Most translations ignore the issue and give the basic idea: the prospect for the faithful *remnant* is bright!

PEACE

People want peace. In the 1980s a retired couple was alarmed by the threat of war, so they undertook a serious study of all the inhabited places on the globe. Their goal: find the place in the world least likely to experience war, especially nuclear war.

They studied and traveled and finally found the *ideal* place. And on Christmas they sent their pastor a card from their new home, a little known and isolated place

---

HOW TO SAY IT

Abraham. AY-bruh-ham.
Babylonians. Bab-ih-LOW-nee-unz.
Bethel. BETH-ul.
Corinthians. Kor-IN-thee-unz.
decalogue. DEK-uh-log.
Ephesians. Ee-FEE-zhunz.
Ezekiel. Ee-ZEEK-ee-ul or Ee-ZEEK-yul.
Gedaliah. GED-uh-LYE-uh.
Yahweh (Hebrew). YAH-weh.
Haggai. HAG-eye or HAG-ay-eye.
Hephzibah. HEF-zih-bah.
Isaiah. Eye-ZAY-uh.
Jeremiah. Jair-uh-MY-uh.
Micah. MY-kuh.
Nehemiah. NEE-huh-MY-uh
Zechariah. ZEK-uh-RYE-uh.

PRAYER

Our Father in Heaven, you have no other hands but ours to use in taking your message to humanity. Today I resolve to strengthen my hands to do what I can to help give a bright hope for the future to others. In the name of your Son, amen.

WHAT DO YOU THINK?

What are some tasks or objectives for which God may call believers today to "strengthen their hands"? How much or how little attention do you consider that believers generally have given to those callings?

[Consider passages such as Matthew 5:16; 28:19, 20; Galatians 5:22-26; Ephesians 5:1, 2; and 1 Peter 1:13-16 in your discussion.]

THOUGHT TO REMEMBER

"According to his power that is at work within us, to him be glory" (Ephesians 3:20, 21).

called the Falkland Islands. But in just days their paradise became a battle zone as Great Britain and Argentina fought for control of those islands.

The Encyclopedia of Military History by Dupuy and Dupuy lists over four thousand battles and sieges since 3,500 B.C. The most destructive wars of the twentieth century were fought by the most "educated" countries in human history! Today, armed conflicts continue to pop up on every continent on the earth except Antarctica—and people would probably be fighting there if it weren't so cold! Our world still needs peace.

Peace isn't found in a property, no matter where it's located. Peace is found in a Person, Jesus Christ. Do you know him?

—J. A. M.

C. RESPECT (v. 13)

13. "As you have been an object of cursing among the nations, O Judah and Israel, so will I save you, and you will be a blessing. Do not be afraid, but let your hands be strong."

In the past the nation of *Judah* had suffered greatly by having its capital razed and its temple destroyed. People in other lands knew about these tragedies, so when they wanted to call down evil on a person or a nation—often using the name of a pagan deity in the expression—then either Judah or *Israel* could be an example in the curse or oath (cf. Jeremiah 26:6; 44:8, 22).

God's promises have an inclusive ring in mentioning both Judah and Israel. Two positive outcomes are stated for them: the Lord will *save* them, and they will *be a blessing*. That will be the opposite of their previous experiences when they had been used in curses. (Compare Jeremiah 31:1-31; Ezekiel 37:11-28; Romans 9–11.)

The conditional factor is in the final phrase *but let your hands be strong*. The Lord has the ability to do these things by himself, but he considers it essential for Judah to demonstrate her faith by cooperating with God in a genuine, sincere way. When people work with God, then "God gives hope for the future."

CONCLUSION

God in his compassion reaches out to help the helpless (e.g., Psalm 12:5). Even so, the final statement in the printed text, "but let your hands be strong," could well serve as the basis for the popular saying, "The Lord helps those who help themselves." That exact phrase is not in the Bible. (It has been variously attributed to Thomas Jefferson, Benjamin Franklin, and Algernon Sidney.) But although the exact words in that particular order may not be in the Bible, the concept is present in several places.

For example, Noah's righteous life enabled him to find favor in the eyes of the Lord. The Lord could have saved Noah from the flood in some other way than having him build the ark. Certainly that would have been much easier for Noah, for it was a major project for him and his sons with the primitive tools at their disposal. But the Lord did not choose some other way. He commanded Noah to build an ark. And Noah obeyed.

On the other hand, there are faithful Christians in some nations today who work diligently in many ways. Their hands indeed are "strong," but they will never experience prosperity in physical things.

We must conclude that the Lord really wants us to apply ourselves diligently to the spiritual aspects of life. This is expressed well in 2 Timothy 2:15: "Do your best to present yourself to God as one approved, a workman who does not need to be ashamed and who correctly handles the word of truth." When we are diligent for God, we will discover, as Paul did, that his grace is sufficient for us (2 Corinthians 12:9).

Discovery Learning

This page contains an alternative lesson plan emphasizing learning activities. Classes desiring such student involvement will find these suggestions helpful. The next page is a reproducible activity page to further enhance discovery learning.

LEARNING GOALS

After this lesson each student will be able to:

1. Explain how God's jealousy for his people motivates him to provide hope for the future.

2. Understand the biblical concept of hope.

3. Develop a plan for providing one person eternal hope, which is in Christ.

INTO THE LESSON

Distribute copies of the reproducible activity "Godly Jealousy" from the next page. Have learners fill these in as this discussion ensues. Some responses may make reference to a "jealous husband," "jealous of my neighbor's car," and others. Ask the students to read Zechariah 8:2. Note that the concept of *jealousy* with reference to God almost always involves people and very frequently occurs in the prophetic books. Have the students answer the question, "What is the first thing that comes to mind when you think of being jealous?" Then ask, "For whom are you jealous with a godly jealousy?" (*Likely responses will be anyone loved by the student: child, spouse, close friend, member of one's congregation of believers.*) Finally, ask, "How do you demonstrate this godly jealousy?" (*Possibilities may include being with the person often, providing growth opportunities for the person, praying diligently for the person's spiritual well being.*)

Say, "*Jealousy* is a word that, for some, carries a negative connotation. Equated, as some do, with envy, it is negative and destructive. However, as Paul says clearly in 2 Corinthians 11:2, godly jealousy is positive, not negative. Such jealousy has as its goal the blessing of God. In God's jealousy for his people we find hope."

INTO THE WORD

Read Zechariah 8:1-13 aloud to the students. After verse 2, stop and say, "These first two verses are unlike the rest of the text; they are not speaking of the future. As a result, these verses give the motivation (and a necessity) for the rest of the text." Emphasize God's jealousy for his people as a motivating force by saying, "Because of God's jealousy, he makes promises for the future in the remainder of the text." Continue reading the text and vocally emphasize the words *shall* and *will*.

At the conclusion of the reading, note that the word *hope* is not used in this text. Yet, it is difficult to miss the concept of hope. The future tense of the promises of the "This is what the Lord Almighty says" statements indicates God's distinct provision of hope.

Three different words are often translated *hope* in the Old Testament. These three carry meanings of both "waiting for with tension or confident expectation" and "being firmly rooted in a foundation." This biblical understanding of hope refers to that which transcends the temporary. Moreover, it is not based only in the future but on a sure foundation of trust and strength in the past and present. Here, God provides the foundation. Christ the Cornerstone transcends the temporary.

INTO LIFE

Say, "Some say hopelessness has become pervasive in much of the world." Ask the students to identify ways they encounter hopelessness. (*Responses may include suicide attempts, increasing violence, high rates of depression, and a lack of faith in various institutions.*)

William Dunn, in his book, *The Baby Bust*, pointed out that the lack of absolutes diminishes hope in people, especially children. Say, "There is a concept known as 'dying without death,' first named by Cecil Brown during World War II. It is a malady in which a person resigns himself to circumstances without any belief that he could possibly change those circumstances. This is the sense of hopelessness that many people feel today."

Say, "Yet, God's jealousy for his people moves him to provide them with hope. The hope he will provide is more than temporary. It is eternal." Ask the students to think of another person they are jealous "for,"not "of," reminding them of God's jealousy for them. This person should be someone in need of hope that goes beyond the temporary. It may mean a strengthening of faith for one with a terminal illness or salvation for a lost person or a renewal of hope for one who has become cynical.

Indicate that eternal hope is ultimately found in Jesus Christ. Provide copies of the reproducible activity "Eternal Hope" from the next page. Guide the students in developing a plan for providing hope to a person for whom they are jealous. The first step may be to strengthen the relationship by spending more time with the person. The second step may be to determine the person's core values.

Finish by having pairs pray for one another and the one for whom each is jealous. Focus on providing eternal hope to the "chosen" individuals.

Godly Jealousy

What is the first thing that comes to mind when you think of being jealous?

For whom are you jealous with a *godly* jealousy?

How do you demonstrate this jealousy?

Eternal Hope

Read Zechariah 8:1-13 and note any areas of hope by completing these sentences:

God's promise in verse 3 gives me hope because _____.

God's promise in verses 4, 5 gives me hope because _____.

God's promise in verses 7, 8 gives me hope because _____.

God's promise in verses 11-13 gives me hope because _____.

I am jealous for _____ with a godly jealousy.

Eternal hope is found in _____.

In order to provide _____ with eternal hope I will:

_____

_____

_____

_____

THE EXILES DEDICATE THE TEMPLE

LESSON 5

WHY TEACH THIS LESSON?

When we dedicate a building, we officially place it in service for a specific purpose. A building dedication is a time to celebrate a task completed and to recognize all the teamwork that was necessary to accomplish the goal. It is a transition point between anticipation and realization. It is also a time to prepare mentally to move on to other challenges.

As you and your learners note these elements in the dedication of the rebuilt temple in 515 B.C., be sure you focus on A.D. 2003, as well. Encourage your class members to follow this same pattern as they celebrate their own victories and accomplishments for the Lord. Challenge them to make every day a day of dedicating their own "temples" to the Lord's work (see 1 Corinthians 3:16, 17).

INTRODUCTION

A. SUMMER SOLDIER

On Friday, July fourth, the United States will celebrate another birthday. It will be 227 years since July 4, 1776.

But the winter of 1776–77 was very difficult for General George Washington and his men. The war was not going well. On December 23 of that year, Thomas Paine published the first chapter of his work *The Crisis*. After reading it, Washington gave orders that it be read to his discouraged men, especially the opening words: "These are the times that try men's souls. The summer soldier and the sunshine patriot will, in this crisis, shrink from the service of their country; but he that stands it now, deserves the love and thanks of man and woman." Those words had a positive effect on Washington's troops, and the rest is history.

Do you think that the final success in the War for American Independence had more meaning to the men who suffered through those cold winters? Did Joseph in Egypt have a greater appreciation for his position over all Egypt because of the trials he suffered? Was the dedication of the second temple in 515 B.C. more meaningful to the people who had lived through the exile and return?

What if everything had gone smoothly for the exiles after their return? What if they had been able to complete the temple without any interruptions or opposition? Would the dedication of the temple have become more of a ho-hum event? James, the brother of our Lord, has written thoughtful words that have application to these situations. "Consider it pure joy, my brothers, whenever you face trials of many kinds, because you know that the testing of your faith develops perseverance. Perseverance must finish its work so that you may be mature and complete, not lacking anything" (James 1:2-4).

Any faith that has been tested and has passed the test is a stronger, maturer faith. How's your faith today?

DEVOTIONAL READING:
PSALM 96:1-13

BACKGROUND SCRIPTURE:
EZRA 5, 6

PRINTED TEXT:
EZRA 6:13-22

Jun 29

LESSON AIMS

After participating in this lesson, each student will be able to:

1. Describe the special events that followed the completion and dedication of the temple.

2. Imagine the joy of people who worship God during a special event or religious holiday.

3. Select an event in the life of the class or church and help plan a celebration that will include all ages.

KEY VERSE

The people of Israel—the priests, the Levites and the rest of the exiles—celebrated the dedication of the house of God with joy.
—Ezra 6:16

B. LESSON BACKGROUND

The temple of Solomon, which had stood for over 360 years, had been burned by the troops of Nebuchadnezzar in 586 B.C. The Jews have been without their temple for over seventy years.

But that is just part of the story. The people who had returned from exile in Babylon had been back in Jerusalem for twenty years—since about 536 B.C. Enemies without and selfishness within have combined to delay the project. The people have provided well for their own homes, but the temple of God has been neglected (Haggai 1:4, 9).

Finally, the preaching of Haggai and Zechariah had motivated the people again to put first things first—to give first place to the things of God. As a result they resumed building on September 21, 520 B.C. (Ezra 5:1, 2; Haggai 1:14, 15).

That action brought questions from the Persian officials in the area. A project of such proportions could have subversive designs. The situation was explained to the regional governor, and he was told that permission for the construction had been received from Cyrus shortly after he conquered Babylon in 539 B.C. (Ezra 5:3-17).

The new king, Darius, upon hearing the report, ordered that a search be made for the original decree. It was located in the summer home of the Persian rulers in Ecbatana (cf. Ezra 6:2), in the mountains of Media, almost three hundred miles northeast of Babylon. Darius then ordered that the work must continue and that the royal revenues of the area be used to assist in the project (Ezra 6:6-12).

I. COMPLETING THE TEMPLE (EZRA 6:13-15)

A. COMPLIANCE (v. 13)

13. Then, because of the decree King Darius had sent, Tattenai, governor of Trans-Euphrates, and Shethar-Bozenai and their associates carried it out with diligence.

The identity of *Shethar-Bozenai* is unknown. He is probably an assistant to the *governor*. The rulers know how to do their part in the political system, so they comply with the king's order.

B. COMMANDS (v. 14)

14. So the elders of the Jews continued to build and prosper under the preaching of Haggai the prophet and Zechariah, a descendant of Iddo. They finished building the temple according to the command of the God of Israel and the decrees of Cyrus, Darius and Artaxerxes, kings of Persia.

As Ezra writes this account, perhaps up to eighty years after the events he is describing, he records the fact that many people are responsible for the rebuilding of the temple. It involved the work of *the elders of the Jews* as well as the forceful exhortations of *Haggai the prophet and Zechariah*, but behind them all was *the God of Israel*. Everything went *according to the* plan that he had revealed to Isaiah many years before.

The influence of three Persian kings is also cited. They include *Cyrus* (who gave the original decree for the project in 538 B.C.), *Darius* (who enforced the decree of Cyrus when it was found), and *Artaxerxes*. The mention of Artaxerxes is a surprise, for his reign is much later, from 464 to 424 B.C., in the time of Ezra and Nehemiah. Ezra, however, makes a very wise gesture by including the name of the king of his own time, for Artaxerxes provides significant assistance to the Jews (Ezra 7:11-28; Nehemiah 2:1-8). This also serves to introduce Artaxerxes in preparation for his part in the remainder of the book.

HOW TO SAY IT

Aaron. AIR-un.

Adar. AY-dar.

Artaxerxes. Are-tuh-ZERK-sees.

Assyria. Uh-SEAR-e-uh.

Babylon. BAB-uh-lun.

Cyrus. SIGH-russ.

Darius. Duh-RYE-us.

Ecbatana. Ek-buh-TAHN-uh.

Gentile. JEN-tyle.

Haggai. HAG-eye or HAG-ay-eye.

Hezekiah. Hez-ih-KYE-uh.

Iddo. ID-do.

Israelite. IZ-ray-el-ite.

Jeroboam. Jair-uh-BOE-um.

Josephus. Jo-SEE-fus.

Judaism. JOO-duh-izz-um or JOO-day-izz-um.

Levites. LEE-vites.

Nebuchadnezzar. NEB-yuh-kud-NEZ-er.

Nehemiah. NEE-huh-MY-uh.

Persia. PER-zhuh.

Shethar-Bozenai. SHE-thar-BOZ-nye.

Tattenai. TAT-eh-nye.

Zechariah. ZEK-uh-RYE-uh.

TEAMWORK

Herman Ostry, of Bruno, Nebraska moved a barn by hand! But, he didn't do it alone. Not long after he had bought a farm, a nearby creek swelled out of its banks and a barn on the property was flooded. Ostry half-jokingly said to his family, "I bet if we had enough people, we could pick up that barn and carry it to higher ground."

His remark prompted Ostry's son Mike to think. He counted the number of boards, timbers, and nails and estimated the barn's weight to be about nineteen thousand pounds. Mike figured 344 people would have to lift only about fifty-five pounds each to carry the barn to higher ground.

But how do that many people get a grip on the barn to lift it? Mike designed a grid of steel and attached it to the barn. This provided handles for the barn raisers. Herman Ostry then suggested a "barn raising" as part of the Bruno centennial celebration. Word of the "barn raising" spread far beyond Bruno. On July 30, 1988, nearly four hundred thousand people from eleven states showed up. When everything was ready, Herman gave the signal and 344 people lifted together. The barn rose like nothing at all! The crowd cheered as the nine-ton barn walked fifty yards up a hill in just three minutes.

How did it happen? Teamwork! When enough people work together with one heart, one mind, one purpose, and one direction, they can accomplish the impossible. Teamwork was necessary for rebuilding the temple, and teamwork is vital to build God's kingdom today. Are you part of a healthy team for God?   —J. A. M.

"I . . . will dwell in the midst of Jerusalem . . . The holy mountain."
— Zechariah 8:3

Display the same poster as was used last week. Use it to illustrate verse 15 of the text.

C. COMPLETION (v. 15)

15. The temple was completed on the third day of the month Adar, in the sixth year of the reign of King Darius.

The precise date is given for the completion of this lengthy project. *Adar* is the twelfth *month* of the year in the Jewish calendar. This date is equivalent to March 12, 515 B.C. The date given is actually a Sabbath Day, so the implication of the passage is that the new *temple* is used in the prescribed way for the very first time on a Sabbath. That is a special Sabbath in the history of the nation of Israel.

Now that the temple is *completed*, what is it like? Some other ancient works refer to the temple, but they give few details. They indicate that this temple is probably about the same size as the one Solomon built, but its furnishings are inferior. For example, the new temple has just one seven-branched candelabrum; Solomon's temple had ten. The ark of the covenant is missing from this temple. Josephus, the first-century Jewish historian, notes that in the Holy of Holies (where the ark of the covenant had been) "there was nothing at all."

II. CONSECRATING THE TEMPLE (EZRA 6:16-18)

A. DELIGHT OF THE REMNANT (v. 16)

16. Then the people of Israel—the priests, the Levites and the rest of the exiles—celebrated the dedication of the house of God with joy.

Everyone joins in the celebration. The work itself has been a cooperative effort, and *the dedication* is for all. Whenever new buildings for worship and service are dedicated, usually the *joy* is so contagious that even those who did not participate become enthusiastic supporters. Yet the purpose is not just to build, but to use the facility to fulfill its intended purposes. Continued support is therefore essential.

When the foundations of the temple were laid, two sounds had been heard: joy and weeping (Ezra 3:12, 13). This time only the emotion of joy is expressed. The entire nation is delighted that the temple is completed (cf. Nehemiah 8:12).

WHAT DO YOU THINK?

How do you respond when you hear a report of how vision, faith, and obedience led to a great accomplishment? How has others' success inspired you to greater endeavors for God?

WHAT DO YOU THINK?

What feelings come to mind when you recall successfully completing a large-group project? What nonmaterial rewards did you enjoy?

B. DETERMINATION OF THE SACRIFICES (v. 17)

17. For the dedication of this house of God they offered a hundred bulls, two hundred rams, four hundred male lambs and, as a sin offering for all Israel, twelve male goats, one for each of the tribes of Israel.

The celebration involves animal sacrifice. The *twelve goats* are noted as being sin offerings *for each of the tribes of Israel*. Most of the people present are from only the tribes of Judah and Benjamin. But Israel in its fullness has twelve tribes. No doubt many faithful Israelites relocated from the north to Judah when Jeroboam set up the idols in Bethel and Dan (1 Kings 12:25-33). (Luke 2:36 notes that Anna, the elderly woman present at the dedication of Jesus, was of the tribe of Asher; see also Acts 26:7.)

The other animals probably were offered for two purposes: as burnt offerings and as peace (fellowship) offerings. The latter type would have been the larger portion. Such offerings primarily are eaten by the people present. This is a very big picnic for the entire community!

In the dedication of Solomon's temple, 22,000 oxen and 120,000 sheep and goats were offered (1 Kings 8:63). The great difference in the numbers shows that there are fewer people in the nation when the second temple is dedicated.

Two additional differences are interesting. When Solomon finished his dedicatory prayer, fire descended from Heaven and consumed the portions of the animals on the altar, and the special glory of the Lord filled the area (2 Chronicles 7:1). Neither is recorded as recurring for the second dedication.

C. DELEGATION OF DUTIES (v. 18)

18. And they installed the priests in their divisions and the Levites in their groups for the service of God at Jerusalem, according to what is written in the Book of Moses.

The captivity had convinced the Israelites of one necessity: they must be obedient to the commands of God given through *Moses*. The consequences of experimentation with other gods and religions had led to disastrous results, just as the Lord had promised through Moses in one of his farewell addresses (Deuteronomy 28:15-68).

Moses, however, did not organize the *priests* into *divisions* in his own time, for the priests consisted of only his brother Aaron and two of Aaron's sons (Numbers 3:1-4). King David was the primary person who organized the priests and *Levites* into their groups (1 Chronicles 23–26). This became necessary in his time because of the major spiritual renewal that was a part of his reign. The Levites—the tribe from which the priests after Aaron would come—originally had been set apart and commissioned by God through Moses to meet the needs of Israel in the wilderness (Numbers 3:5-10; 8:5-14). The implications of worship at the temple demand that an organizational pattern now be employed again.

III. CELEBRATING THE FEASTS (EZRA 6:19-22)

A. PASSOVER OBSERVED (v. 19)

19. On the fourteenth day of the first month, the exiles celebrated the Passover.

The *Passover* is always a special event, but at this particular time it is even more meaningful to the Israelites. They must be feeling some of the same exhilaration as the devout Israelites did in the early years after the nation had achieved its independence from Egypt. It is a celebration in which they look to the past, to the time when the destroyer (Exodus 12:23) had gone through the land of Egypt. The firstborn of every household that did not have the blood of the lamb on the door frames was slain. The Israelite households, however, had an obedient faith that motivated them to apply the blood at the entrances of their homes and thus save them from that tragedy.

Moses had commanded all Israel to celebrate the Passover on the *fourteenth day of the first month* into the indefinite future (Exodus 12:24, 25). As the Passover is observed on April 21, 515 B.C., it now has been more than nine hundred years since that first Passover celebration.

B. PURIFICATION OF THE PRIESTS (v. 20)

20. The priests and Levites had purified themselves and were all ceremonially clean. The Levites slaughtered the Passover lamb for all the exiles, for their brothers the priests and for themselves.

The original specifications in Exodus were for the heads of families to sacrifice the prescribed animals. In the intervening years, *the priests and Levites* had assumed the task of slaying the animals for the worshipers.

The Passover in the time of Hezekiah (2 Chronicles 30) had to be deferred a month because too few of the priests had cleansed themselves ceremonially for the occasion. This time the Israelites were ready. Perhaps the people were being extra careful to do things properly. They had learned the consequences of careless, insincere worship.

We should note that the word *Passover* is used in two ways in verses 19, 20. In verse 19 it refers to the feast itself. But here in verse 20, it refers to the animals that are slain. Problems in interpretation may arise if that distinction is ignored.

C. PURIFICATION OF THE PEOPLE (v. 21)

21. So the Israelites who had returned from the exile ate it, together with all who had separated themselves from the unclean practices of their Gentile neighbors in order to seek the LORD, the God of Israel.

The identity of those *who had returned from the exile* is obvious. But who are the people *who had separated themselves* in order to be able to participate in the celebration? Two possibilities are usually given. The first is that it is a reference to Israelites who had been able to stay in the land (cf. Jeremiah 52:16). The other possibility is that it refers to Gentile converts to Judaism.

In either case, two definite actions are described for those people who had not come out of captivity. First, they separated and purified themselves from pagan filthiness in order to be able to join in the festive event. This uncleanness is mainly idol worship (cf. Ezekiel 22:4; 36:18, 25).

Their second action is *to seek the Lord.* In other words, they recognize that demands are made on those who would serve God. In some cases today, this message has been modified to say that the Lord requires no changes in the lives of those who decide to follow him. Such an idea suggests that such a person may believe or do whatever he or she wants, and still be a member of the community of the redeemed. The Bible certainly does not support this concept! (See John 14:15.)

PROJECT EXILE

The city of Richmond, Virginia, had a problem. For more than a decade, gun violence had plagued her streets to the point where she was usually among the top five U.S. cities having the worst per capita murder rates.

But all that began to change in 1997 when the U.S. Attorney's Office in Richmond developed and implemented a program called "Project Exile." Aggressive federal prosecution, stiffer bond rules, and tougher sentencing guidelines resulted in the imposition of mandatory minimum prison sentences for individuals convicted of firearm violations. In effect, these felons were sent "into exile." The resulting drop

DAILY BIBLE READINGS

Monday, June 23—A Decree to Rebuild (Ezra 6:1-5)

Tuesday, June 24—Adversaries Must Let the Work Alone (Ezra 6:6-12)

Wednesday, June 25—A Joyous Dedication (Ezra 6:13-18)

Thursday, June 26—Sing to the Lord (Psalm 96:1-6)

Friday, June 27—Ascribe to the Lord Glory (Psalm 96:7-13)

Saturday, June 28—God Has Done Marvelous Things (Psalm 98:1-6)

Sunday, June 29—Extol the Lord Our God (Psalm 99:1-5)

WHAT DO YOU THINK?

What would it take in today's world to separate oneself from "the unclean practices" of unbelieving neighbors? How important is that for Christians in preparation for worship?

[Passages such as Matthew 16:26; 1 Corinthians 10:14–11:34; and 1 John 2:15 may help guide your discussion.]

in Richmond's homicide rate was so impressive that one hundred fifty cities are expected to adopt similar "exile" programs by October 1, 2003.

The long-term effects on those who serve their sentences and return from this "exile," however, are unknown. Undoubtedly, they will all rejoice when they are released, but how will they choose to rebuild their shattered lives from then on? Will they resolve to separate themselves permanently from the filthiness of their sinful past? Will they devote themselves to seeking the Lord for the rest of their lives? Only time will tell for them—and for us.

—R. L. N.

D. PRAISES CONTINUED (v. 22)

22. For seven days they celebrated with joy the Feast of Unleavened Bread, because the LORD had filled them with joy by changing the attitude of the king of Assyria, so that he assisted them in the work on the house of God, the God of Israel.

The Feast of Unleavened Bread immediately follows the Passover (Leviticus 23:5, 6). It prolongs the festivities for another *seven days*. The two events are connected so closely that they are usually considered to be a part of the same celebration (cf. Mark 14:1).

The Feast of Unleavened Bread also has a distinctive purpose. Doing without leavened bread for seven days reminds the Lord's people of the exodus in the days of Moses. They had left Egypt quickly, so unleavened bread was standard fare as the Israelites fled. There was no time to leaven the bread and allow it to raise.

This celebration is therefore intended to remind the people that the generations in the past were compelled to experience self-denial and to be prepared for action before they were able to enjoy the blessings of freedom.

The reference to *the king of Assyria* is somewhat surprising at first. The Assyrian Empire had come to an end for all practical purposes in 612 B.C. (about a hundred years before this time) when it was conquered by the Babylonians. The Babylonian kingdom was followed in turn by the Persian kingdom. (The latter two kingdoms are found in the prophecies of Daniel 2 and 7.)

Many kings, however, prefer using different titles to show the greatness of their power. The Persians controlled the region that had been the heart of Assyria, and it is very likely that this is just one of the titles being used in the time of Darius (or in the time of Artaxerxes when the book is being written by Ezra). Note that Artaxerxes is also called "king of Babylon" in Nehemiah 13:6.

The word *joy* reveals to us that the spring of 515 B.C. is a time of great spiritual enthusiasm for the renewed nation of Israel. The same emotion was part of the dedication of the temple a few weeks before (Ezra 6:16), and its presence carried over to the first feasts of the New Year. There may be a time for sadness and remorse in worship, but it is joy that is a fruit of the Spirit (Galatians 5:22), not sadness.

CONCLUSION

This rebuilt, second temple stood for close to six hundred years. But its destruction by the Romans under Titus in A.D. 70 showed that it, too, was temporary. (It had a total refurbishing in the days of Herod the Great, but "Herod's Temple" was essentially the same structure.)

This brings up a question. When a congregation, a church building, a place of higher education, or a home is established in the name of Christ, how long will it retain its original purpose? The answer is always the same: it depends!

When a nation celebrates a birthday, and that nation clearly refers to divine providence in the document that called it into existence, the question must be asked again: how long will it remain in existence? The answer is still the same: it depends—and the choice is ours.

Discovery Learning

*This page contains an alternative lesson plan emphasizing learning activities. Classes
desiring such student involvement will find these suggestions helpful. The next page
is a reproducible activity page to further enhance discovery learning.*

LEARNING GOALS

After participating in this lesson, each student will be able to:

1. Describe the special events that followed the completion and dedication of the temple.

2. Imagine the joy of people who worship God during a special event or religious holiday.

3. Select an event in the life of the class or church and help plan a celebration that will include all ages.

INTO THE LESSON

Before class, think of a recent accomplishment or special event in the life of your church. To begin class ask, "When we celebrated the _____, what feelings did you hear people expressing?" After students answer, note the answers that reflect such emotions as joy, commitment, and bonding. "It is exciting and satisfying to celebrate accomplishments together. In today's text the people around Jerusalem—having made a significant accomplishment—enjoyed a celebration for over two months."

INTO THE WORD

From study of the Lesson Background material on page 370, present a lecture to review briefly the last four lessons and the chapters not studied in class. Fill in, as it were, the twenty years since the captives returned.

To prepare students for their reflection on the passage, describe the feasts of Passover and Unleavened Bread. If you have students who enjoy research, contact them and ask them to prepare lectures on the feasts.

Use a journaling technique to get your students to reflect on this lesson's events. (Use the reproducible activity "Just Imagine" from the next page to assist in this.) For an imaginary journal entry, students must "get inside the heads of the participants" to write from their perspective. To ensure a variety of entries, ask for volunteers for each group present: priest, Levite, elder, older person who came back from Babylon, young adult, parent, child. Let volunteers read their journal entries.

INTO LIFE

Ask, "As you listened to these journal entries, what common themes, attitudes, or emotions did you hear?"

As the students volunteer their answers, write them on the board. Mark and add anything you want to emphasize, like repentance for their delay in building the temple, satisfaction for getting priorities right, appreciation for the role of Darius the king, awareness of God's provision, or joy from being in the temple.

"Everyone was present for this special time of renewing obedience and purification. From your reflection as you wrote your journal entries, what impact do you think these three special events had on the various groups: priests, Levites, adults who returned from Babylon, adults who had always lived in Jerusalem, parents and children? How were they going to be different?"

"Sociologists have discovered that when people share in the same unifying event or activity, that event becomes a bonding experience. Faith development research is constantly confirming that the congregation in which children live contributes to their spiritual growth. Catherine Stonehouse writes, 'In the elementary school years, children begin to take ownership of the stories, beliefs, and religious rituals valued by those who belong to their faith communities. Their identity in the community grows as they learn the stories, recite some of the beliefs, and participate in the rituals—when they can say, "This is what we believe, what we do. This is our story"' (*Joining Children on the Spiritual Journey;* Grand Rapids: Baker Books, 1998, p. 162).

Say, "The events in Ezra 6 allowed Jews of all ages to experience joy and commitment together. They would be bonded with the children who were learning from the adults and rituals."

Your class could achieve something similar in one of several ways: support an intergenerational event already being planned; plan an event for class members and families; plan an event for the whole church. Guide class members to make a commitment to provide such an opportunity to help people of all ages to experience joy and commitment to God together.

Option for Individual Action: Give your learners a copy of these three questions as they ponder their own worship joy: (1) "What do I think and feel when I worship in God's house?" (2) "What can I do to begin to experience the joy of the people described in Ezra 6?" (3) "How can I express my joy in Christ to others, especially my children and/or grandchildren?"

Cut index cards lengthwise in half to distribute as bookmarks. Have students write the Key Verse from Ezra 6:16 on them as a reminder to worship God with joy. Close with prayer for more meaningful worship.

Just Imagine

Imagine that you are a participant at all of the special events in today's lesson. As you read each passage, put yourself into the event. What do you see around you? What sounds do you hear? What do you smell? What are you doing? What might you be thinking and feeling? Then write your observations, thoughts, and emotions about the event in your journal.

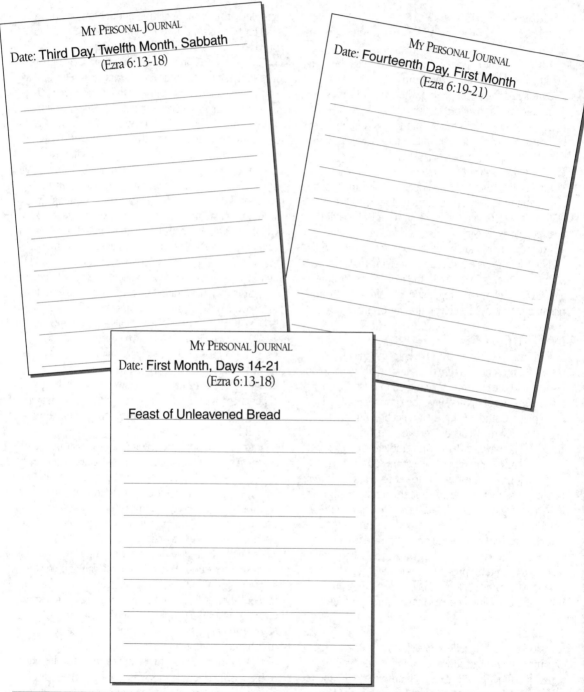

MY PERSONAL JOURNAL

Date: Third Day, Twelfth Month, Sabbath
(Ezra 6:13-18)

MY PERSONAL JOURNAL

Date: Fourteenth Day, First Month
(Ezra 6:19-21)

MY PERSONAL JOURNAL

Date: First Month, Days 14-21
(Ezra 6:13-18)

Feast of Unleavened Bread

NEHEMIAH BEGINS WORK

LESSON 6

WHY TEACH THIS LESSON?

Take a trip to the typical shopping-mall bookstore sometime and look at how many books there are on management and leadership. You will find dozens. But if you flip through those books looking for references to prayer, you won't find many. So most of these books are unsuitable for understanding godly leadership.

You may have some leaders in your class. Some may be leaders in business; others hold government leadership positions. Some of your class members may be elders or deacons or even hold staff positions at your church. They will find more guidance in your class today than in all of those secular leadership books at the mall! Nehemiah's example will be helpful to them as they exercise their leadership gifts. Nehemiah was successful because he had God's blessing, and a key to that blessing was his faithful exercise of prayer in his planning. Challenge the leaders in your class, including yourself, to follow the example of Nehemiah.

INTRODUCTION

According to the U.S. Census Bureau, about one in seven Americans changes residence each year. What a mobile society! But the challenges imposed by twenty-first century relocations pale in comparison to those of bygone years.

A. THE PIONEER LIFE

My grandfather and his bride moved to Nebraska when the Homestead Act of 1862 made land available there. Neighbors they left behind said those two were too young to have good sense, and perhaps they were right. In their new homeland it seemed that everything had to be done at once. The apple trees they had brought from Ohio had to be planted immediately. Their chickens needed a chicken house to keep them safe from coyotes at night. Humans, too, must have shelter before winter. They cut building blocks from the tough prairie sod and made a tiny house with a fireplace in one of its walls. No less urgent was the task of breaking up that tough sod and planting a little field of wheat that fall. This would supply them with bread when the flour barrel they had brought was empty. Naturally the Indians of that area resented the invasion of their hunting ground. Each night the settlers went to sleep wondering if they would have their scalps in the morning.

Similar problems faced the Jews when they returned from captivity in Babylon. They went to their ancient homeland, but they were like pioneers in a new country. They had to build houses, plant grapevines and fruit trees, wheat and barley, gardens of vegetables. They had to establish flocks of sheep and herds of cattle. They had to face the bitter opposition of people living nearby. In spite of all these problems, they wanted to build a fitting temple for the Lord.

Through the month of June, our lessons have focused on those pioneers in their homeland, their problems, and their successes. This week's lesson brings us first to the Eastern country, the land of captivity; but then it brings us back to that ancient homeland where the Jews are pioneers, where their troubles are not yet over.

DEVOTIONAL READING:
ISAIAH 26:1-9

BACKGROUND SCRIPTURE:
NEHEMIAH 1, 2

PRINTED TEXT:
NEHEMIAH 1:1-4; 2:4, 5, 13, 16-18

LESSON AIMS

Jul 6

After participating in this lesson, each student will be able to:

1. Retell the account of Nehemiah's conviction and commission.

2. Suggest actions and attitudes of Nehemiah that could help anyone carry out God's work.

3. Select a work project or ministry in which he or she will participate as an individual or with the rest of the class.

KEY VERSE

They replied, "Let us start rebuilding." So they began this good work. —Nehemiah 2:18

LESSON 6 NOTES

B. LESSON BACKGROUND

When Cyrus conquered Babylon and set the captives free in 538 B.C., the majority chose to stay right where they were. That is not surprising, for most had been born there. They had their work and their friends there. They had "put down roots." Even so, the Jews who stayed behind in the East had kinsmen and friends among the pioneers who moved back west to Palestine. They liked to hear from them. But the distance was long and travel was slow. News was hard to come by.

I. REQUEST FOR NEWS (NEHEMIAH 1:1-4)

Some of the Jews in the East became prominent there. Daniel is the most evident example. He was high in the government of Babylon (Daniel 2:48). Then when the Persians conquered Babylon, they promptly gave him a high place among them (6:1-3). Nehemiah had less power than Daniel had, but he was even closer to the king of Persia.

A. WHO, WHEN, WHERE, WHAT, AND WHY (vv. 1-3)

1. *The words of Nehemiah son of Hacaliah:*

In the month of Kislev in the twentieth year, while I was in the citadel of Susa.

The account of Nehemiah's life on the stage of world history begins as autumn is turning to winter, for *the month of Kislev* corresponds to the last part of November and the first part of December on our calendars. *The twentieth year* of Artaxerxes, king of Persia (2:1) means that this is either 445 or 444 B.C. As a personal cupbearer (1:11), *Nehemiah* has close access to this king. Nehemiah is in *Susa*, which is the winter capital of Persia.

More than ninety years have now passed since the Jews were released from captivity in Babylon. Seventy years have passed since the completion of the temple in Jerusalem (see last week's lesson).

2. *Hanani, one of my brothers, came from Judah with some other men, and I questioned them about the Jewish remnant that survived the exile, and also about Jerusalem.*

At some point, *Hanani, one of* Nehemiah's *brothers*, had chosen to make the nine-hundred-mile trip to Jerusalem and back again along with a few others. Nehemiah had chosen to stay in the East, and Hanani's return offers the opportunity to get some news *about Jerusalem*. Nehemiah is keenly interested in the progress of the Jewish pioneers there.

3. *They said to me, "Those who survived the exile and are back in the province are in great trouble and disgrace. The wall of Jerusalem is broken down, and its gates have been burned with fire."*

The answer Nehemiah receives is discouraging. The Jews, now in their old homeland, are *in great trouble*, affliction, and distress. They are a *disgrace* in the eyes of the peoples around them. God had promised this as part of their punishment (Jeremiah 24:9; 29:18), but he had also promised a time when such scorn would disappear (Ezekiel 36:15). But when would that promise be fulfilled?

Nebuchadnezzar's troops had destroyed the city *wall* nearly a century and a half earlier. Now it remains as they had left it: disorderly heaps and scattered stones. Nothing is left of the wooden *gates* that had been *burned*.

B. WEEPING AND WANTING (v. 4)

4. *When I heard these things, I sat down and wept. For some days I mourned and fasted and prayed before the God of heaven.*

Nehemiah's concern for the land of his forefathers is profound. Notice that his weeping, fasting, and mourning doesn't last for hours, but for *days!* Some believe

HOW TO SAY IT

Artaxerxes. Are-tuh-ZERK-seez.
Babylon. BAB-uh-lun.
Cyrus. SYE-russ.
Euphrates. You-FRAY-teez.
Ezekiel. Ee-ZEEK-ee-ul or Ee-ZEEK-yul.
Ezra. EZ-ruh.
Haggai. HAG-eye or HAG-ay-eye.
Hacaliah. Hack-uh-LYE-uh.
Hanani. Huh-NAY-nye.
Kidron. KID-ron.
Kislev. KIS-lef.
Nebuchadnezzar. NEB-yuh-kud-NEZ-er.
Nehemiah. NEE-huh-MY-uh.
Nisan. NYE-san.
Persia. PER-zhuh.
Sheshbazzar. Shesh-BAZ-ar.
Susa. SOO-suh.
Zerubbabel. Zeh-RUB-uh-bul.

that Nehemiah is ashamed because he has stayed in the East to live in the king's palace instead of going to help restore the ancient homeland. The text gives no hint of this, however. In fact, from his prayer for "favor in the presence of this man," (i.e., the king, v. 11), it could be assumed that the decision for Nehemiah to stay had not been his own.

II. REQUESTS FOR HELP (NEHEMIAH 2:4, 5)

Nehemiah's time of mourning, praying, and planning lasts four months, from the month Kislev to the month Nisan (1:1; 2:1). When the right time comes, he is ready to move decisively. His opportunity presents itself when the king notices his mournful countenance and asks the reason for it. Anyone in the presence of the king is expected to be happy to have that privilege. A man who displeases the king by looking sad might well lose his head! So Nehemiah was "very much afraid" (2:2) at the king's question, but he explained bravely that he was mourning over the plight of Jerusalem (2:3).

A. To GOD (v. 4)

4. The king said to me, "What is it you want?"
Then I prayed to the God of heaven.

Since Nehemiah is mourning over the poor condition of Jerusalem (v. 3), *the king* supposes he has some idea for improving that condition. But Nehemiah first prays *to the God of Heaven* before responding. No doubt it is a very short prayer and a silent one, but God values sincerity more than many loud words. Perhaps Nehemiah repeats the prayer that he might have mercy from the king (1:11). Nehemiah relies on prayer often (see 4:4, 9; 5:19; 6:9, 14; 13:14).

B. To THE KING (v. 5)

5. . . . and I answered the king, "If it pleases the king and if your servant has found favor in his sight, let him send me to the city in Judah where my fathers are buried so that I can rebuild it."

Nehemiah wants to go to Jerusalem, to go as the king's emissary with the king's authority to *rebuild* the ruined *city*. When *the king* asks how long that will take, Nehemiah makes an estimate and the king is pleased to send him (v. 6).

Then Nehemiah adds some details. He wants letters to the governors of provinces west of the Euphrates, ordering them to give him safe conduct (v. 7). He wants a letter ordering the "keeper of the king's forest" to supply the timber that will be needed (v. 8). Nehemiah obviously has thought all this out in advance, and in addition requests a military escort to ensure a safe journey (v. 9). The king grants all these requests and appoints Nehemiah as governor (5:14; 12:26).

Thus when Nehemiah comes to Jerusalem (v. 11), he comes as the highest official of the province. Clay seal impressions reveal that since the times of governors Sheshbazzar (538 B.C., Ezra 1:8; 5:14) and Zerubbabel (515 B.C., Haggai 1:1, 14), there have been three other governors before him. But Nehemiah does not behave as recent governors have behaved (see Nehemiah 5:14-18).

PLAN AND ACT

While heading Montgomery Ward & Company, Sewell Avery was responsible for leading Ward's to amass $607 million in cash. His plan? Avoid risk. Get all you can, can all you get, sit on the can!

Avery's cash accumulation plan was Montgomery Ward's most monumental mistake. This huge cash reserve earned the retailer a dubious Wall Street nickname:

WHAT DO YOU THINK?

What are some causes for which you would risk personal position, fortune, and comfort? What is the value of thinking about such situations ahead of time?

WHAT DO YOU THINK?

The response of the king to Nehemiah's request must have encouraged Nehemiah that he was doing the right thing. Give examples of times when God has confirmed plans by provision of resources or by opening doors of opportunity.

"the bank with the department store front." From 1941 to 1957, during his reign as CEO, Ward's failed to open a single new store.

Why didn't Avery join in the nation's postwar expansion by following Americans to the suburbs? He was afraid of uncertain circumstances. He believed that a depression had followed every major war since the time of Napoleon.

On the other side of Chicago, Ward's rival, Sears, Roebuck & Company, had a different idea. Sears took a risk and in 1946 began a costly expansion into suburbia. Sears' bold plan doubled its revenues. Sears never looked back and Ward's never caught up. In fact, in 1997 it went bankrupt.

Hearing of the situation in Jerusalem, Nehemiah had good reason to be cautious and to sit tight. The times were uncertain. But he was bold. He was willing to act in spite of uncertainty. He prayed long and hard, and determined a course of action, and then he went to the king. And the king granted him his desire, as Nehemiah himself put it, because "the gracious hand of my God was upon me" (Nehemiah 2:8). Make God your planning partner and count on him for success.   —J. A. M.

III. REQUEST FOR ACTION (NEHEMIAH 2:13, 16-18)

The trip to Jerusalem takes several weeks, giving Nehemiah time to think and pray about a plan of action. He does not announce his intention as soon as he arrives in Jerusalem. He first wants to examine the ruined city and estimate how big the job of rebuilding will be.

After arriving, Nehemiah takes three days to rest and otherwise "settle in" after the long journey (v. 11). He makes his investigation by night with a few trusted men, perhaps those who had come with him from Persia (v. 12). Nehemiah probably chooses a bright, moonlit night for his inspection tour.

A. SECRET SURVEY (vv. 13, 16)

13. By night I went out through the Valley Gate toward the Jackal Well and the Dung Gate, examining the walls of Jerusalem, which had been broken down, and its gates, which had been destroyed by fire.

This verse and the two that follow (not in our text for today) trace the course of Nehemiah's inspection trip. We cannot identify all the places that are named, but the direction of the trip is clear. Nehemiah and his few men go outside the city near the southwest corner. Outside the city they move eastward to the southeast corner, where they turn north in the Kidron Valley. The men then move on to the northeast corner of the city where they turn back (v. 15). Nehemiah does not make a complete circuit of the walls—he has seen enough!

What he sees is not encouraging. The former walls are *broken down*. Nothing is left of the wooden *gates* that had been *destroyed by fire*. More than two miles of rebuilt wall probably will be needed. This new wall will have to be high enough so it cannot be scaled easily. It will have to be strong enough to resist battering rams. The scattered stones of the former wall will provide at least part of the building material. But more stones, freshly quarried and unbroken probably will be needed as well. And there is no machinery to move or lift such stones. They will have to be moved and raised by muscles and rope. It looks like a hard job.

16. The officials did not know where I had gone or what I was doing, because as yet I had said nothing to the Jews or the priests or nobles or officials or any others who would be doing the work.

The moonlight survey is still secret. No one knows about it except Nehemiah and the few trusted men who have made the inspection with him. Perhaps Nehemiah wants a chance to contemplate without a lot of "Negative Nellies" constantly interrupting his train of thought!

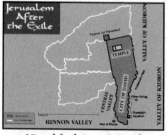

Visual for lesson 6. Use this map to trace Nehemiah's inspection tour of the walls of the city of Jerusalem (vv. 13-16).

B. PUBLIC RECOMMENDATION (vv. 17, 18a)

17, 18a. Then I said to them, "You see the trouble we are in: Jerusalem lies in ruins, and its gates have been burned with fire. Come, let us rebuild the wall of Jerusalem, and we will no longer be in disgrace." I also told them about the gracious hand of my God upon me and what the king had said to me.

Now is the time to end the secrecy. When Nehemiah speaks *to them*, he is addressing all the classes or groups named in verse 16, perhaps in a mass meeting.

His presentation is in three parts. First is the need: *You see the trouble we are in.* Until the rubble of the old wall is cleared away and a new wall is built, *Jerusalem* cannot have the dignity, respect, and protection of an important city. Second is the remedy: *Come, let us rebuild the wall of Jerusalem.* The Jews will not have a wall unless they go to work and build it. Third is the result of rebuilding: *we will no longer be in disgrace.* This will fulfill the promise of Ezekiel 36:15 and other prophecies.

Nehemiah cites two things to encourage the building: God's providential care and the favor of King Artaxerxes. If God and the king both want the people of Judah to build that wall, it would be dangerous not to build it, and quickly!

WHAT DO YOU THINK?

Nehemiah had impressive credentials for leadership. What qualities inspire you to follow a leader at work? in government? at church?

C. RIGHT RESPONSE (v. 18b)

18b. They replied, "Let us start rebuilding." So they began this good work.

The decision apparently is reached without a dissenting voice. Indeed, how could anyone of Judah dissent? God and the king are in favor of that wall. Building stone is already at the site, so the work can be started immediately. Timber is freely available in the king's forest. Nothing else is needed except a lot of "elbow grease" by the people who will benefit from the wall. With thinking like this, the people *strengthened their hands for this good work.*

WHAT DO YOU THINK?

Nehemiah's proposal met with strong agreement from the people. What are the projects or causes in your church or community that could be accomplished given a passionate and capable leader? What could be your role in pursuing one of those projects or causes?

COOPERATE!

The Kentucky state flag captures a Biblical principle when it shows two men clasping hands ringed by this motto: "United we stand. Divided we fall." Nehemiah cultivated cooperation to ensure success.

Cooperation lightens the load and increases effectiveness. Nehemiah 2:18 says the people of Jerusalem said, "Let us start rebuilding," and that "they began this good work." Nehemiah 3 lists seventy-nine leaders and contributors to the enterprise of rebuilding the walls and gates of Jerusalem. Seventy-nine are mentioned, but thousands shared in the work.

"Many hands make light work," the old saying goes. Rebuilding this city was an impossible task for Nehemiah alone. But, he wasn't alone. Nearly everyone cooperated. And because of the participation of all, the monumental task was completed in an amazing time. In fifty-two days the wall was completely rebuilt.

I cannot do the work of the church alone nor can you. No one person can meet every need and fill every role. Rather, the body grows as each part does its work.

Here is God's challenge: Cooperate! Let's each determine to do his or her part. When any one of us fails to cooperate and contribute, the load becomes a little heavier for all the rest. When we work together, everything is lighter.

Cooperation is essential for success in God's work. Does a harmonious, cooperative spirit always carry the day in your congregation? United we stand.   —J. A. M.

CONCLUSION

Nehemiah was a capable investigator, planner, politician, and man of prayer. He presented his plan to the people, along with encouragement to think it would work. The people accepted the plan enthusiastically, and with God's blessing it worked.

PRAYER

Thank You, Father, for entrusting some of your work to us. We want to see your church grow in size and goodness and influence, and we know its progress depends on us as well as you. For that progress we promise a worthy portion of our time, energy, and money. Grant us wisdom for our planning and strength for our doing. We pray in Jesus' name, amen.

THOUGHT TO REMEMBER

With God's help we can do what he wants us to do.

But today we are accustomed to democracy. Especially in a small congregation, we may prefer to have every member informed and involved in every step of investigation and planning. This can work, but is it always the best way?

A. NEHEMIAH'S WAY REPEATED

In Riverside, the church outgrew its building. The young married couples wanted a class of their own, but they had to meet in the auditorium along with the older adults. Both the high school and the college-career classes were put in that huge class with all the adults—and they were not happy about it. At the other end of the age scale, the keepers of the nursery were not happy to have toddlers in the nursery.

The elders of the congregation knew something had to be done. But like Nehemiah, they kept such thoughts to themselves while they investigated and planned. From those working with the children, the elders learned how much room was needed to accommodate the present attendance plus a 50 percent increase. With that information they sought out the architect who had designed their existing building. He now was retired, but he readily agreed to plan a new wing. One of the church members was a reputable builder. He looked at the architect's plan and estimated the cost. The elders consulted their banker. Finally, they examined the church's income. It would have to increase 8 percent to pay for the thirty-year loan on that addition.

Then it was time to end the secrecy. Everyone's help was needed. The elders summoned the entire congregation to a Sunday afternoon meeting to talk about enlarging the church house. All the members could see the need, and most of them came to the meeting.

The elders showed the architect's drawing of the proposed addition. They said it would accommodate a growing church and Sunday school for many years. They said each elder already had agreed to increase his contribution by 10 percent. They asked each member to follow the elders.

They did not ask for commitment that moment. They asked each member to think, pray, and remember that this was for God's church. Then they were to make their commitments to the future of the church. Nearly every member agreed to the 10 percent increase. Later, when the church gathered in the enlarged house for the first time, the feeling was pure joy. Not one grumble was heard.

B. OUR OWN NEEDS

What is the outstanding need in your church right now? A larger worship area? More parking? More people in the room you already have? More teachers in the Sunday school? More dedication and hard work among the people? A greater emphasis on prayer and spirituality? Exactly what is the most important "wall" in your church that needs to be built?

And how will you approach the need that is most pressing? Ask everyone for suggestions? Follow the elders? Appoint a committee? And where does prayer fit into the overall approach?

If it's facility improvements that your church needs, how will you pay for them? Hold bake sales, carnivals, and other such fund-raisers? Ask local businesses for donations? (Nehemiah, after all, solicited a pagan king!) Go door-to-door requesting contributions? Or will you and the people in your church sacrificially alter your spending and dig into personal bank accounts? Will there be a trust in God to help today as he helped the ancient Israelites to rebuild first their temple and then their wall? (See 3 John 7.)

Discovery Learning

This page contains an alternative lesson plan emphasizing learning activities. Classes desiring such student involvement will find these suggestions helpful. The next page is a reproducible activity page to further enhance discovery learning.

LEARNING GOALS

After participating in this lesson, each student will be able to:

1. Retell the account of Nehemiah's conviction and commission.

2. Suggest actions and attitudes of Nehemiah that could help anyone carry out God's work.

3. Select a work project or ministry in which he or she will participate as an individual or with the rest of the class.

INTO THE LESSON

ADVANCE PREPARATION: Investigate potential short-term projects and continuing ministries available in your church, ideas for both groups and individuals. Include projects for both active people and quieter people. Church staff may already have such a list. If not, such a handout could be a short-term project for someone in the class. Get enough details so that people will recognize tasks they want to investigate. Or ask someone who has done such a short-term project to prepare a testimony or report. These activities will be explained more in the "Into Life" section.

ADVANCE PREPARATION: Before class, ask two from the class or congregation to prepare a brief skit in which they are discouraged because no one will do anything.

To open the class session, let the actors present their skit. Then say, "Many of us have felt that way, haven't we? Today we are studying a man who heard about a sad situation in Jerusalem. It grieved him, but he took action to solve the problem."

INTO THE WORD

Read chapters 1 and 2 as students follow along. Ask students for their impressions of Nehemiah and write the descriptors on the board. Ask small groups to outline what happens from the time Nehemiah hears the need through the people's response.

If your students are not comfortable with outlining the passage, give them copies of the reproducible activity "Nehemiah the Leader" from the next page. Ask them to read Nehemiah 1 and 2 again and to fill in one or two details under each heading listed on their handouts. Allow a few minutes for the students to work; then ask for reports. (Students could work on this activity individually or in small groups.)

Option. Make a handout by scrambling the headings that are on the "Nehemiah the Leader" activity. Have the students place these in chronological order.

Ask, "What other words do you have to describe Nehemiah now?" Make additions to the list. "What else did you learn about Nehemiah and how he operated?" Add those insights. *(They will discover Nehemiah was prayerful, patient, persistent, a man of action with the right priority, realistic, a planner, sharp, willing to serve and lead, able to bring fresh perspective as an outsider, aware of God's hand, an effective presenter, a leader.)* Add concepts from your study that the class missed.

INTO LIFE

To make the lesson more personal, say, "We have good observations about Nehemiah. Let's list character qualities and principles that apply to all who want to serve God." Guide students in stating such principles. See the commentary and the list from "Into the Word."

Continue the discussion by saying, "How could developing such character traits or following such principles help prevent some frustrations in congregational life when it seems no one is willing to work?"

Direct the application to meet your students' needs. If you have leaders, talk about using these principles when they are leading. If you have potential leaders, challenge them to consider taking a leadership position and using the principles. Encourage people to consider how they can follow a leader in a short-term project or join an existing ministry (like teaching in the Bible school).

To encourage your students to get involved in serving, ask someone to give a testimony about the joys of serving. Distribute the handout(s) you obtained from a church staff member or copies of the list of projects you developed.

Distribute copies of the reproducible activity "A Call to Volunteer" from the next page. Encourage each student to give prayerful consideration to joining a ministry effort and to fill out the form accordingly. Collect the forms and forward the information to the appropriate ministry leaders.

Conclude the class by asking students to mark a short-term project or a continuing ministry that interests them. Suggest that they contact project leaders to get more information and then pray during the week about how they might serve God in such a short-term project.

Nehemiah the Leader

Nehemiah 1 and 2 reveal a man who uses his organizational skills to solve a serious problem for God's people. What subpoints or summaries would you add to the following outline?

A. Nehemiah learns of the condition of Jerusalem.

B. Nehemiah mourns, fasts, and prays for four months.

C. Nehemiah and the king talk.

D. Nehemiah returns to Jerusalem.

E. Nehemiah surveys the city at night.

F. Nehemiah presents the challenge to the Jews, priests, nobles, and rulers.

G. The people accept the challenge.

A Call to Volunteer

Like Nehemiah, I want to act upon a need, so I will . . .

Think some more about these projects or ministries:_____.

Make an appointment to talk to _____ to learn more.

Tell _____ I am interested in observing _____
to see if I could fit into that ministry.

Pray about _____.

Volunteer to _____.

God Restores a Remnant

Unit 2: Renewal
(Lessons 6-9)

NEHEMIAH COMPLETES THE WALL

LESSON 7

WHY TEACH THIS LESSON?

Question: Which leaders never have to face opposition? *Answer:* Those who never pose a threat to anyone! But great leaders and their projects always seem to pose a threat to *someone*.

Your learners who hold leadership positions already know that. Even if the only leadership title they hold is that of "parent," they have found out that opposition sometimes arises when unpopular decisions have to be made. How does the godly leader respond to opposition?

Nehemiah gives us the answer in today's lesson. Nehemiah always had his eyes focused on God and on the end result. He never let his enemies or the magnitude of the task at hand distract him from God's plan. With confidence that God was in control, Nehemiah forged ahead to accomplish the task God had called him to do. This is a lesson every leader in your class needs today.

INTRODUCTION

My great-uncle was an itinerant preacher on the American frontier. One day he and a friend were walking across the prairie when they spotted an Indian war party on the distant horizon. Cautiously the two hid in a buffalo wallow and waited for the danger to pass. But when they peeked out an hour later, the war party had not moved an inch. It was not a war party at all—just a clump of natural growth. Ashamed but relieved, the travelers went on their way.

A. REAL HOSTILITY

Hostile neighbors were real when the Jews went back to their homeland after their captivity in Babylon. More than a century before that captivity began, conquering Assyrians had deported most of the people of north Israel and had brought in immigrants to take their place (2 Kings 17:1-6, 24). Descendants of those immigrants quickly became enemies of the Jews who came back from captivity (Ezra 4:1-5). Those enemies were scornful when Nehemiah came and started to build a city wall (Nehemiah 2:19, 20). But the Jews organized their workers, and the wall began to rise (Nehemiah 3). The enemies then planned to stop the building by force (4:7, 8). But the Jews prayed and armed themselves for defense, and the enemies gave up that plan (4:9, 13-15).

B. LESSON BACKGROUND

The Jews went on with their work, but they did it without letting down their guard (Nehemiah 4:16-23). Since they were so well prepared to fight, and since they were now protected by a wall built to half its intended height (4:6), the enemies were afraid to launch a violent attack. Instead, they resorted to the strategy described in our text.

DEVOTIONAL READING:
ISAIAH 49:13-18

BACKGROUND SCRIPTURE:
NEHEMIAH 6

PRINTED TEXT:
NEHEMIAH 6:1-9, 15, 16

LESSON AIMS

Jul 13

After participating in this lesson, each student will be able to:

1. List the types of opposition Nehemiah and the people of Judah met while completing the wall.

2. Suggest some appropriate, godly ways to handle opposition.

3. Publicly commit to persevere dutifully in one area of his or her spiritual life in which he or she is experiencing opposition.

KEY VERSE

When all our enemies heard about this, all the surrounding nations were afraid and lost their self-confidence, because they realized that this work had been done with the help of our God.
—Nehemiah 6:16

I. CRAFTY OPPOSITION (NEHEMIAH 6:1-4)

Communication was so open and constant between the Jews and their enemies that neither could make a secret move. When the enemies were gathering their forces for a violent attack, they hoped it would be a surprise; but it was reported to the Jews (Nehemiah 4:11, 12). When the Jews then prepared to repel such an attack, that resolve was promptly told to the enemies (4:13-15). Then the enemy leaders thought it was time for a person-to-person talk with Nehemiah.

A. CALL ISSUED (vv. 1, 2)

1. When word came to Sanballat, Tobiah, Geshem the Arab and the rest of our enemies that I had rebuilt the wall and not a gap was left in it—though up to that time I had not set the doors in the gates—

These three leading *enemies* illustrate the fact that people of different nations now live in the area that once had belonged to Israel. Nehemiah 2:19 reveals a bit more information about the nationalities of these three. There, *Sanballat* is called "the Horonite." He is probably a native of Beth Horon, in the land from which northern tribes of Israel had been evicted (see Joshua 10:10; 16:3, 5). On the other hand, some students think that he comes from the city of Horonaim in Moab, a country east of the Dead Sea (see Jeremiah 48:34). *Tobiah* is from Ammon, east of the Jordan River. He is called "the Ammonite official" in Nehemiah 2:10. Many students think that Tobiah, like Nehemiah, is a servant of the king of Persia; perhaps he has been appointed to an official position in that western land. *Geshem the Arab* is the third enemy. He comes from the area that is still called Arabia today.

These three *and the rest of* Nehemiah's *enemies* are chagrined to learn that the wall now extends all the way around Jerusalem. It is only half as high as it eventually will be (4:6), but there is no *gap* through which armed forces might enter. The gateways are still open, but the enemies dare not attack through them when they know armed men are on guard there. So the enemies turn to diplomacy.

2. . . . Sanballat and Geshem sent me this message: "Come, let us meet together in one of the villages on the plain of Ono."

But they were scheming to harm me.

Ono lies on the coastal plain near Joppa, nearly thirty miles from Jerusalem (cf. 1 Chronicles 8:12). Some Jews returning from exile had settled there (Nehemiah 7:37; 11:35). The enemies pick this place to lure Nehemiah far away from the protection of his people who are working with their weapons at hand (4:16-18). No doubt the enemies are saying that they desire peaceful coexistence.

But Nehemiah records with full confidence that *they were scheming to harm me.* Considering the open communication between the enemy groups, we wonder if Nehemiah has learned this from some informant who has heard the plotting of the enemies. We know for certain that Nehemiah has enemy spies in his own midst (see 6:10-13, 17, 18), so the reverse probably is true as well.

We wonder what kind of mischief the enemies have in mind. Do they plan to assassinate Nehemiah? Will they hold him hostage to gain an advantage in negotiation with his people? Or are they thinking merely of slowing the work in Jerusalem by depriving the workers of their best leader? The Bible provides no answers to these questions.

B. CALL REJECTED (v. 3)

3. . . . so I sent messengers to them with this reply: "I am carrying on a great project and cannot go down. Why should the work stop while I leave it and go down to you?"

WHAT DO YOU THINK?

When is it appropriate to question the motives of someone who proposes negotiating resolution of a conflict?

Understanding the insincerity of the request, Nehemiah's answer is a flat refusal—he is just too busy. Accepting the invitation would be a waste of time at least, and a death trap at most. The *work* he is doing is so important that he cannot *leave it* at that time. Nehemiah does not even bother to suggest an alternative, "safer" location for the meeting.

C. CYCLE REPEATED (v. 4)

4. Four times they sent me the same message, and each time I gave them the same answer.

Nehemiah's reply does not discourage his enemies from repeating their "invitation." Perhaps they argue reasonably that it is important to avoid any hostility between their groups, that they want to be friendly neighbors, that it is better to talk than to fight. Whatever argument they use, Nehemiah is not fooled. He simply cannot take time for such a pointless conference.

PRIORITIES

Chris Spielman played middle linebacker for the Ohio State University and then in the NFL for the Buffalo Bills. He was tough, strong, smart, passionate, committed, and loyal. He played the entire 1995 season with a torn pectoral muscle sustained in the season opener. He was a leader.

But life took a different turn during the 1998 season. He didn't play at all—and that by choice. His priorities had shifted. Instead he cooked, took care of his kids, and cared for his wife. Stephanie Spielman was battling breast cancer. During her fight, Chris was at her side. He lived out his priorities—"family before job."

A reporter from the *Rochester Democrat and Chronicle* asked if he'd return to the Bills late in the season. Spielman said, "I'd play in a heartbeat, but what kind of man would I be if I backed out on my word to her? I wouldn't be a man at all."

Football fans saw Spielman as a man because of his aggressive toughness. But what really makes him a man? His priorities are in order. Personal sacrifice, unending commitment, and loyalty to his wife define him.

Nehemiah left behind the luxury, influence, and access to power that were his in Persia. In Jerusalem he faced challenge and uncertainty. But when tempted away from his work on the wall he replied, "Why should the work stop while I leave it and go down to you?" Nehemiah knew what was important and he invested his energy there.

Are your priorities in order? What are you doing that will last forever? —J. A. M.

II. OVERT THREAT (NEHEMIAH 6:5-9)

Four times the enemies have sent an apparently friendly invitation for a chat. Just as often Nehemiah has declined it. Still, Sanballat persists in inviting Nehemiah to join him for a talk. But the fifth invitation carries a clear threat of serious trouble if the request is declined again.

A. FALSE GOSSIP (vv. 5-7)

5. Then, the fifth time, Sanballat sent his aide to me with the same message, and in his hand was an unsealed letter.

To emphasize the serious nature of his request, Sanballat puts this communication in writing. Carrying an *unsealed* (open) *letter* is unusual; it may mean that Sanballat wants all the people to know of the letter's contents.

6. . . . in which was written:

"It is reported among the nations—and Geshem says it is true—that you and the Jews are plotting to revolt, and therefore you are building the wall. Moreover, according to these reports you are about to become their king.

Sanballat relates to Nehemiah what (supposedly) is being said *among the* peoples of the surrounding nations. Sanballat tries to improve the credibility of the rumor by attaching to it the name of a prominent pagan leader. This person, *Geshem,* is one of the leaders of the Jews' enemies (Nehemiah 2:19; 6:1, 2).

With mock concern, Sanballat passes along the anxiety that others supposedly have regarding Nehemiah's motives: fortifying *the wall* can mean only defense against the Persian troops that will soon come to put down the rebellion. A rumor of sedition could undo all of Nehemiah's work on the wall if such innuendo were credible and found its way back to the Persian king. We know already, of course, that Nehemiah is a loyal servant of that king. The king has authorized him to build the wall he is constructing.

7. "... and have even appointed prophets to make this proclamation about you in Jerusalem: 'There is a king in Judah!' Now this report will get back to the king; so come, let us confer together."

This verse falls naturally into three parts. First comes another accusation. The use of false prophets is nothing new in Jewish history. (See Jeremiah 14:14; 50:36.) Usually such "prophets" tell the leader what he wants to hear (e.g., 1 Kings 22:6). In this case, Nehemiah allegedly has *appointed prophets* to announce *in Jerusalem* that he is no longer a mere governor of a Persian province, but is now *king* of independent *Judah.*

Then comes the threat that *this report* will be given *to the king.* If Nehemiah does not agree to confer with Sanballat and his cronies, these enemies will tell the king that Nehemiah is proclaiming Judah's independence and is preparing to support that proclamation with a well-fortified city. If the king believes this report, overwhelming numbers of Persian troops soon will arrive to dispose of Nehemiah. So why go on building a wall that will just be battered down again anyway?

The last sentence of the verse is a repetition of the invitation already given and refused four times. But now that invitation is backed by the threat. This is nothing short of blackmail!

B. NEHEMIAH'S ANSWER (vv. 8, 9)

8. I sent him this reply: "Nothing like what you are saying is happening; you are just making it up out of your head."

Sometimes gossip contains truth, but it is spread maliciously nonetheless. Sanballat's report, however, is a pure fabrication, and Nehemiah knows it. He is not frightened enough to give in to the demand for a conference. The king has been his supporter. Nehemiah is doing exactly what the king has told him to do. Very likely, Nehemiah does not think the king now will accept such accusations at face value without an investigation. And any royal investigation will undoubtedly vindicate Nehemiah.

A previous king had promised death to anyone attempting to stop the rebuilding of the temple (cf. Ezra 6:11). The current king may not take kindly, either, to those who would spread false rumors to stop the rebuilding of the walls. Nehemiah, in effect, calls Sanballat's bluff.

9. They were all trying to frighten us, thinking, "Their hands will get too weak for the work, and it will not be completed."

[But I prayed,] "Now strengthen my hands."

Nehemiah is not frightened enough to give in (v. 8). Even so, it is sobering to think of the consequences that will follow if the king believes the lies the enemies said they would tell. But Nehemiah knows the solution to fear: he must trust in God. So Nehemiah prays for strength and keeps on working without a pause.

WHAT DO YOU THINK?

Why are leaders often targets for a charge of improper motives? How can they prepare for those attacks?

[Use 1 Peter 3:16 to stimulate discussion.]

III. ULTIMATE TRIUMPH (NEHEMIAH 6:15, 16)

Try to imagine the pressure that was on those builders of the wall. What would be the result if killers really would sneak in and murder Nehemiah as he slept (6:10)? What would happen if liars really could convince the Persian king that his trusted cupbearer was now a traitor, leading a rebellion? What would happen if the enemies plucked up enough courage to swarm into Jerusalem through the open gateways with swinging swords to slaughter the defenders? None of these things happened, and the people of Israel put their fears behind them and pressed on to a triumphant finish.

A. WALL COMPLETED (v. 15)

15. So the wall was completed on the twenty-fifth of Elul, in fifty-two days.

Now imagine the rejoicing among the people who had been toiling overtime for *fifty-two days!* Continuously haunted by the fear of what terrible thing the enemies might do, the job finally is done. And now the wise timing for the work is seen. It began in the middle of July. The busy, busy time of barley and wheat harvest is over. Some of the grain had been milled into flour; it is ready to be baked into bread for the hungry builders. And the wall is finished early in September, leaving time—though only a short time—for the ingathering of grapes and other fruit before the autumn festival, the Feast of Tabernacles. This is a harvest festival as well as a memorial of Israel's time in the wilderness as the nation was moving from Egypt to the promised land.

DON'T STOP!

Art Chen was a fighter pilot for the Chinese in the 1930s, when Japan was determined to conquer China. Duane Schultz records his story in his book *The Maverick War.*

On one occasion Chen "took on three Japanese fighters and shot one down before running out of ammunition. He deliberately rammed the second Japanese plane and then bailed out. He landed close to the wreckage of his plane and salvaged one of the machine guns, which he carried eight miles back to the airfield. Presenting the heavy gun to his commanding officer, Chen allegedly asked, 'Sir, can I have another airplane for my machine gun?'"

What spirit! What dedication to the cause! Art Chen is remembered because he refused to quit.

Nehemiah 4:6-23 reports a time of discouragement and intense opposition when the wall "reached half its height." The most difficult part of any project seems to be "halfway." The work is hard, the hours long, the obstacles are real and the outcome is uncertain. But victory comes to those who refuse to quit. The Jerusalem wall was completed because the workers didn't quit.

Are you halfway through some project? Sometimes success is achieved simply because of dogged determination, an unwillingness to quit. Someone said, "By determination the snail reached the ark!"

Are you ready to quit? To give up? To surrender? To resign? It's too soon to quit!

—J. A. M.

B. ENEMIES DISMAYED (v. 16)

16. When all our enemies heard about this, all the surrounding nations were afraid and lost their self-confidence, because they realized that this work had been done with the help of our God.

The *enemies* of the Jewish people feel disappointed, defeated, humiliated, and disgraced. The impudent immigrants from the East seem to be beyond the control of the earlier inhabitants. Short of all-out military action, there is nothing more

---

WHAT DO YOU THINK?

What do you think were the chief reasons that the rebuilding of the walls—delayed some ninety years—could be accomplished in just fifty-two days? What principles here can we apply to completing projects for the kingdom of God today?

In Spite of Enemies

"This Work Was Wrought of Our God." —from Nehemiah 6:16

Visual for lesson 7. Display this poster and discuss some of the victories God has "wrought" in your church.

What Do You Think?

It is hard to admit that you have been on the wrong side of an issue. What would have been the most constructive response of Nehemiah's enemies to the completion of the walls? What sometimes prevents us from seeking the most constructive response? How can we be more apt to do so?

Prayer

Thank you, gracious Father, for entrusting us with the greatest work in all the world—not the work of building a wall, but the work of building your church by leading the lost to salvation and leading the saved to understand your Word and obey it. For that work may we have consecration and courage and common sense and success in Jesus' name, amen.

Thought to Remember

Bring your plans before God, and listen carefully to his response.

those earlier inhabitants can do. Military action might be unsuccessful, for those Jews who have worked so hard probably would fight hard, too. And any attempt to exterminate the newcomers would likely be punished by the king of Persia.

Interestingly, the enemies give *God* credit for their defeat. They know the people of Israel have not been victorious by their own effort alone. Perhaps that was the main reason they *were afraid and lost their self-confidence:* they realize they have been fighting against God all along!

CONCLUSION

Jerusalem would have had no wall in that century if Nehemiah had chosen to live on in luxury in the king's palace in far-off Susa. But Nehemiah knew what needed to be done, he knew how to put a plan in motion, and he knew how to pray. He secured the support of the king in Susa, he secured the support of the people in Jerusalem, but most importantly he secured the support of God!

A. Fear and Leadership

In English-speaking countries where this book is read, people probably do not fear armed intervention to stop the work of Christianity. But our hands may be weakened by another kind of fear. When someone proposes a great, challenging work, voices may cry out, "No, no! We can't do it! It's too big!" We shall not accomplish anything very great for God unless we ignore such voices and press on with courage and determination.

But courage needs to be balanced with common sense. Sometimes the fear-mongers are right. Mistaking folly for faith, eager Christians may plunge into an enterprise far beyond their resources or with very little time spent in prayer. The result may be an unfinished church building standing through the years as a silent rebuke of their folly (cf. Luke 14:28-30). Wiser Christians may build a basement with a roof and simply meet in it until God grants them the resources to finish the interior. Such Christians have the faith to say, "If this is what God wants us to do, he will give us the ability to do it." No less true is the converse: "If God does not enable able us to undertake this project, then this is not what God wants us to do." When we prayerfully and fearlessly trim each dream to fit God's providence, we end up doing everything he wants us to do, and nothing that he doesn't.

B. Fear and Followership

Imagine what would have happened if the people of Jerusalem had answered Nehemiah's appeal by saying, "Forget it! We don't need a wall as much as we need to get along with our neighbors. If we build that wall, they will just see us as an even greater threat."

There are many reasons why people do not follow leaders who are worthy of being followed, but *fear* is one of the most damaging. Fear accepts "what is" because "what might be" *could* be even worse. This is paralysis at its worst! If the people had allowed themselves to be immobilized by fear, in effect they would have been saying, "The situation as it stands now is not ideal. But we've lived with it for quite some time, and we've adjusted. Things could be better, but we're getting by. Why rock the boat? Who knows what would happen after building that wall?!"

But the fear of earthly enemies has no place in God's program today any more than it did in Nehemiah's day. Our modern-day Nehemiahs cannot do it alone. They need thousands of godly followers. We follow our godly leaders today with full confidence that the gates of Hell shall not prevail against the church (Matthew 16:18).

Discovery Learning

This page contains an alternative lesson plan emphasizing learning activities. Classes desiring such student involvement will find these suggestions helpful. The next page is a reproducible activity page to further enhance discovery learning.

LEARNING GOALS

After this lesson each student will be able to:

1. List the types of opposition Nehemiah and the people of Judah met while completing the wall.

2. Suggest some appropriate, godly ways to handle opposition.

3. Publicly commit to persevere dutifully in one area of his or her spiritual life in which he or she is experiencing opposition.

INTO THE LESSON

Prior to the arrival of the students rearrange your classroom in a disorderly way. For example, place the chairs in ways that make it difficult to interact (back to back, for example), or turn a writing board around so that it faces away from students. The object is to place obstacles in the way of the students. As students arrive, they may take initiative to move items back to their usual places. Allow them to do this without comment. If they do not work to restore the room, make sure it is back to its usual appearance just before beginning the lesson. If some grumble that, "Someone left our room messed up," simply say, "Perhaps it was for a purpose."

Say, "Our room today was not set up as it usually is." Ask the students how the room's awkward setup could have affected learning. Help the students notice that certain elements were "in the way" of learning, a theme of opposition. Say, "In today's text, the Jews faced opposition to completing the wall. This was not violent opposition, but more covert and subtle."

INTO THE WORD

Ask for two volunteers to read. Assign the first one Nehemiah 4:1-3. Assign Nehemiah 6:1, 2 to the second. Ask the class to note similarities and differences in these two texts. Have the first volunteer read, followed immediately by the second. Let students list similarities (*Sanballat and Tobiah involved, the wall is the subject at hand*) and differences (*4:1-3–Sanballat ridicules; 6:1, 2–Sanballat seeks a meeting; 4:1-3–dismissal; 6:1, 2–scheming*).

Ask the first volunteer to read Nehemiah 4:7, 8, 11, 12. The second volunteer should read Nehemiah 6:2, 5, 9, and 13. Again, notice some similarities (*opposition*) and differences (*4:11, 12–violent opposition; 6:2, 9, 13–subtle opposition*). Ask the students to identify the different types of opposition Nehemiah and his associ-

ates faced while building the wall. (*These may be as simple as violence and covert or more specific including slander, killing the leader, entrapment, or others.*)

INTO LIFE

Say, "Having identified types of opposition faced by the people in rebuilding the wall, we will now consider types of opposition faced in our own spiritual lives." If your church is undertaking a major project, you might suggest that this be the "rebuilding of the wall" for your class. If this does not fit your church or if it is not an appropriate subject to discuss in class, have the students identify an individual "rebuilding-of-the-wall" spiritual life issue. These could include prayer life, Sunday school attendance, evangelism. Have the students identify a church issue or individual issue to address as the lesson continues. Provide copies of the reproducible activity "Facing Opposition" from the next page to give students response space.

Assemble the class into groups. Have half of the groups read Nehemiah 4:4, 5, 13, 14, 19-23. Have the other half read Nehemiah 6:3, 4, 8, 9b, 11-13. Ask each group to report what the people did in response to opposition. (*Answers include the following: 4:4, 5; 6:9b–pray; 4:13, 14–stand guard and protect one another; 4:19-23–remind one another of God's power, be diligent in the work; 6:3, 4–be steadfast; 6:8–identify the lie; 6:11-13–exhibit fearlessness, identify slander.*)

While the students are thinking about these, ask what specific opposition they have faced in personal life and ministry. Write these on a board. Ask, "What are typical responses to such opposition?" These may include appropriate (as seen in the text) and inappropriate responses (such as all of us have used to respond to opposition at times). Write these on the board also.

Remind the students that no type of opposition from the enemy dissuaded the people responsible for rebuilding the wall from their God-given task. Have each student publicly commit either to the entire class or to a partner to persevere dutifully in the "rebuilding-of-the-wall" spiritual life issue chosen earlier. This commitment should include an identification of a specific opposition and an appropriate response to such opposition. Give each student a copy of the reproducible activity "A Success Commitment" (bottom of page 392) to complete as a reminder of this commitment.

Facing Opposition

One spiritual life issue I want to address is:

Opposition I will face relating to this issue includes:

_____

_____

_____

_____

Rebuilding the Wall

I will face the opposition to this spiritual life issue by:

_____

_____

_____

_____

A Success Commitment

I promise not to be dissuaded from this "rebuilding of the wall" by any opposition.

Signed: _____

Date _____

EZRA READS THE LAW

LESSON 8

WHY TEACH THIS LESSON?

What is something that can bring tears to your eyes? For some, it might be a touching story of loss and healing. For others, it might be the playing of their national anthem. For still others, it might be reunion with a family member who hasn't been seen in years. One man I met years ago wept as he related to me his experiences during the attack on Pearl Harbor many decades previously.

But how many claim that a reading of the Word of God brings tears to their eyes? That's what happened in the days of Nehemiah and Ezra. People wept at the reading because the Word of God convicted them of their sin (cf. Hebrews 4:12). Today's lesson will challenge the casual attitude that you and your learners may have developed toward God's Word—and toward sin, for that matter. As with every lesson, do not allow this to be a mere academic exploration of what happened centuries ago. Let it speak to all who need greater conviction about what the Word has to say about sin—and a greater sense of joy for sin forgiven.

INTRODUCTION

A. BIBLE TEACHING?

Going to church was not easy when I was a boy on the farm. Church was more than six miles away. After the morning chores were done, there was not enough time to harness the team, dress in our best, and travel those miles in the old surrey.

Although we seldom went to church, we boys went to Sunday school every Sunday. Grandma saw to that. She subscribed to a children's weekly magazine that included a Sunday school lesson, and she led my brother and me through the lesson every week. Besides that, the children's books in our home had more Bible stories than fairy tales. That background forms a vitally important part of my Christian identity today.

B. LESSON BACKGROUND

When the Jews went back to their homeland after their captivity in Babylon, the grandmas among them had no magazines with Sunday school lessons. They had no children's books full of Bible stories. They did not even have Bibles in their homes. Jewish men were overworked with the tasks of building houses, tilling gardens, plowing, planting, and harvesting the fields, tending flocks of sheep and herds of cattle—not to mention the rebuilding of the temple and the city walls! It is not surprising to learn that Bible teaching was neglected.

About eighty years after the first Jews returned from Babylon, a priest, scribe, and scholar named Ezra (cf. Ezra 7:11) led a second group from the East back to Jerusalem in 458 B.C. Ezra was shocked to see how God's law was being ignored. Some men had even taken wives from among the pagans who lived nearby (Ezra 9). That was forbidden by God's law (Deuteronomy 7:3, 4). Ezra's first arrival and his teaching about the law had brought reform that was painful to those who agreed that they must give up the pagan wives whom they had cherished for years (Ezra 10:3, 14).

DEVOTIONAL READING:
PSALM 119:33-40

BACKGROUND SCRIPTURE:
NEHEMIAH 8

PRINTED TEXT:
NEHEMIAH 8:1-12

LESSON AIMS

After participating in this lesson, each student will be able to:

1. Explain the reverence that the people had for God's presence through the reading of his Word.

2. Show respect for the Bible as God's Word.

3. Implement one way in which respect for the Word of God might be increased.

Jul
20

KEY VERSE

They read from the Book of the Law of God, making it clear and giving the meaning so that the people could understand what was being read. —Nehemiah 8:8

LESSON 8 NOTES

Many students think Ezra soon must have gone back to the Eastern country, and injustice and lawbreaking increased while he was away. When Nehemiah came to rebuild Jerusalem's walls in 444 B.C., he found widespread injustice in the commercial life of the nation. He had to establish justice in Jerusalem even while he was building walls around the city (Nehemiah 5:1-13). After the walls were finished, however, Ezra was in Jerusalem again, and the people eagerly looked to him for more teaching about the law. It is to the credit of the people that they now wanted to learn more, though they must have suspected it would require further reforms that would be painful or costly. Today we see people who wanted to do God's will!

I. PURPOSEFUL MEETING (NEHEMIAH 8:1-3)

A. BY POPULAR DEMAND (vv. 1, 2)

1. All the people assembled as one man in the square before the Water Gate. They told Ezra the scribe to bring out the Book of the Law of Moses, which the LORD had commanded for Israel.

This isn't the first time *all the people* gather together *as one man* (see Ezra 3:1). The place where they meet, *the Water Gate,* is in the east wall of Jerusalem. It has that name because the people go through it to bring water from a spring outside the wall. The street leading to that gate widens into a *square* inside the wall. A great number of armed men can gather there to oppose enemies who might try to smash the gate with a battering ram. The same square provides space for a peaceful assembly when no enemy is in sight.

The people gather because they want *Ezra the scribe* to teach them more about the law. Literally, the word *scribe* means "writer." But when a writer painstakingly makes copies of the Scriptures by hand, naturally he comes to know those Scriptures very well and can teach them to others. Therefore the word *scribe* came to signify a scholar and teacher. That is what Ezra has proved himself to be, and now the people are eager to hear him teach the law.

The *Book of the Law* is not hundreds of flat pages bound between hard covers like a modern book. Rather, it is a long strip, probably of parchment, and perhaps about eighteen inches wide. It can be rolled up for storage and unrolled for reading. Moses had received the law from God and had written it down some one thousand years before. Although very old, that *which the Lord had commanded for Israel* is still mandatory in Ezra's day.

WATERGATE

On June 17, 1972, the word *Watergate* began to become part of the American psyche. That was the night that burglars broke into the offices of the Democratic National Committee, located in the Watergate office complex in Washington, DC.

The two-year investigation that followed uncovered a trail of corruption and abuse of power that pointed to the highest levels of the executive branch of government, and eventually to President Richard M. Nixon himself. Under threat of impeachment, President Nixon resigned from office on August 9, 1974.

Since that time, the very mention of the word *Watergate* has conjured up negative images of the arrogance of power and the dangers of having ethical blinders. For those who choose to look on the bright side, however, the outcome of the Watergate scandal reaffirms the concept of "the rule of law" upon which the United States of America was founded.

The gathering "before the Water Gate" in Jerusalem was a pivotal point in Israel's history. As the crowd of people heard the law read, negative thoughts and emotions swept through their minds concerning how the law had been broken so often, and they wept.

WHAT DO YOU THINK?

The people knew that hearing the law was important. How can we emphasize the importance of Scripture reading in our public worship and private devotions today?

DAILY BIBLE READINGS

Monday, July 14—The People Gather (Nehemiah 7:66–8:1)

Tuesday, July 15—Ezra Reads From the Law (Nehemiah 8:2-6)

Wednesday, July 16—This Day Is Holy (Nehemiah 8:7-12)

Thursday, July 17—The Study of the Law Continues (Nehemiah 8:13-18)

Friday, July 18—Teach Me Your Statutes (Psalm 119:33-40)

Saturday, July 19—Your Commandment Makes Me Wise (Psalm 119:97-104)

Sunday, July 20—I Long for Your Commandments (Psalm 119:129-136)

But Nehemiah and Ezra also made sure that the people had positive images because of the holiness of the day and the joy of forgiveness. From that day forward, any Israelites who had been there would only have to say, "Remember the water gate," and they would bring back both negative and positive emotions of recommitment. What causes you to renew your commitment to Christ each day?

—R. L. N.

2. *So on the first day of the seventh month Ezra the priest brought the Law before the assembly, which was made up of men and women and all who were able to understand.*

Now we see that *Ezra* is a *priest* as well as a scribe. The inclusion of *women and all who were able to understand* (i.e., older children) shows the seriousness of the occasion in that culture (see Deuteronomy 31:12, 13; Joshua 8:35; 2 Kings 23:2).

Last week we read that the city wall was finished on the twenty-fifth day of the sixth month (Nehemiah 6:15). If we now are reading of the same year, the assembly occurs only a few days after that big construction job ended. The timing of this gathering (Nehemiah 7:73b) coincides with the Feast of Trumpets (Leviticus 23:23-25; Numbers 29:1-6).

B. A LONG READING (v. 3)

3. *He read it aloud from daybreak till noon as he faced the square before the Water Gate in the presence of the men, women and others who could understand. And all the people listened attentively to the Book of the Law.*

This is no twenty-minute sermon! *From daybreak till noon* is at least five hours. Perhaps all the people are attentive because God is very prominent in their thoughts as they look around with amazement at their newly rebuilt walls.

II. WORSHIPFUL MEETING (NEHEMIAH 8:4-6)

A. IMPORTANT OCCASION (v. 4)

4. *Ezra the scribe stood on a high wooden platform built for the occasion. Beside him on his right stood Mattithiah, Shema, Anaiah, Uriah, Hilkiah and Maaseiah; and on his left were Pedaiah, Mishael, Malkijah, Hashum, Hashbaddanah, Zechariah and Meshullam.*

The biggest part of the preparation for this event probably is the building of *a high wooden platform.* It had to be big enough and strong enough to support Ezra and the other men listed in this chapter. We suppose the thirteen cited here are Ezra's fellow priests or other men of influence who take their place with Ezra to indicate their approval of what he is doing. With about half on *his right* and about half on *his left,* Ezra is the focal point of attention.

A huge supply of lumber had been procured to make the gates in the city wall. Probably enough of it was left over to build the big and sturdy stage on which Ezra and his companions are lifted so high that they can be seen by every person of that big throng in the square (v. 5). The appearance of so many leaders on that stage marks this as an important occasion.

B. REVERENT ATTENTION (v. 5)

5. *Ezra opened the book. All the people could see him because he was standing above them; and as he opened it, the people all stood up.*

Apparently most of the people have been sitting on the ground while Ezra and his companions assemble on the stage. Then Ezra holds the sacred scroll on which the law is written and starts to unroll it. *All the people* rise to their feet to show respect for the Word of God.

C. Emotional Worship (v. 6)

6. Ezra praised the Lord, the great God; and all the people lifted their hands and responded, "Amen! Amen!" Then they bowed down and worshiped the Lord with their faces to the ground.

To bless *the Lord* is to praise him. Often we open our own prayers in the way that Ezra does here. God is called *great* in other passages as well (see Deuteronomy 10:17; Nehemiah 9:32; Jeremiah 32:18; Daniel 9:4). Coupled with lifted *hands* and *bowed* heads, the people's response of *Amen! Amen!* shows intense emotion.

III. INSTRUCTIVE MEETING (NEHEMIAH 8:7, 8)

A. The Teachers (v. 7)

7. The Levites—Jeshua, Bani, Sherebiah, Jamin, Akkub, Shabbethai, Hodiah, Maaseiah, Kelita, Azariah, Jozabad, Hanan and Pelaiah—instructed the people in the Law while the people were standing there.

The meeting begins with worship that is united, fervent, and reverent. But the people have come primarily to listen to the Word of God and learn from it. Well might their opening prayer be that of the psalmist: "Open my eyes that I may see wonderful things in your law" (Psalm 119:18). That may well be our prayer, too.

In verse 4, we counted fourteen people on the stage. Now we see there are many more. (The phrase *the Levites* probably refers to those listed here; compare the names listed in Nehemiah 10:9-13.) The fact that they *instructed the people in the law* shows us the importance of the teaching function.

The English language changes rapidly, so some of the many new Bible translations that have come out can be very useful to us. Even so, all of us need additional help in understanding the Bible at one time or another. This was even more true in Ezra's situation. Moses wrote the law about a thousand years before Ezra read it to the people, so imagine how the Hebrew language has changed in that span of time! In fact, the Hebrew language is beginning to fade out of common use as Aramaic takes its place. The Jews need a lot of help understanding a book that is a thousand years old, and Ezra has a lot of help in explaining it. Do we do as well with the two-thousand-year-old phrases, terms, and concepts we use so freely in the church?

B. Their Method (v. 8)

8. They read from the Book of the Law of God, making it clear and giving the meaning so that the people could understand what was being read.

You may have noticed that some who read aloud are hard to understand because they do not read distinctly: they mumble, they slur short vowels, they run syllables together. The trained readers who help Ezra are easy to understand because they pronounce everything clearly. Perhaps these readers are also translating from Hebrew to Aramaic as they go.

The people *understand what was being read* not only because the words are distinct and clear, but also because the readers give *the meaning*. This is preaching and teaching at its finest! When we study and learn from godly teachers today and apply the Bible to our lives, then we are students who "correctly [handle] the word of truth" (2 Timothy 2:15).

Hearing and Knowing

Romans 10:17 teaches, "Faith comes from hearing the message, and the message is heard through the word of Christ." There ought to be in us an increasing desire to hear and know the Bible. However, most do not read the Bible regularly.

This poster illustrates verse 8. Discuss how the church can find new ways to help people understand the Bible.

Research confirms it. Billy Graham reported a survey indicating only 12 percent of people who say they believe the Bible read it every day.

Television confirms it. On *Jeopardy* "The Bible" is almost always the last category chosen.

Experience confirms it. Two ladies were overheard talking about the Bible. One asked the other if she knew about the epistles. She replied, "Of course. The epistles are the wives of the apostles."

Honors students in Newton, Massachusetts, high school gave these astounding replies on a quiz for a Bible as Literature course.

Sodom and Gomorrah were lovers.

Jezebel was Ahab's donkey.

The four horsemen appeared on the Acropolis.

The Gospel writers were Matthew, Mark, Luther, and John.

Eve was created from an apple.

Jesus was baptized by Moses.

Golgotha was the giant who slew the apostle David.

Can anybody dispute that Bible reading has fallen on hard times? Ezra, Nehemiah, Paul, and others knew the importance of hearing and knowing God's Word. Do you?
                                                                              —J. A. M.

IV. JOYOUS HOLY DAY (NEHEMIAH 8:9-12)

A. CALL TO JOY (vv. 9, 10)

9. Then Nehemiah the governor, Ezra the priest and scribe, and the Levites who were instructing the people said to them all, "This day is sacred to the LORD your God. Do not mourn or weep." For all the people had been weeping as they listened to the words of the Law.

The first *day* of any month is observed with special religious ceremonies (see Numbers 28:11-15). But the first day of the seventh month, known as Tishri (September-October), has added meaning because it marks the end of the agricultural and festival year. It eventually comes to be regarded as the "civil" New Year's Day, even after the Lord made Nisan (March-April) the first month of the "religious" year (Exodus 12:1, 2). Mourning is not appropriate for such a *sacred* day. The command to stop mourning and weeping comes from both civil and religious leaders, namely *Nehemiah* the *governor* and *Ezra the priest*.

When the law is made clear to the people, many know they have been violating it. They are overcome with shame, grief, and fear. The reading of the law has convicted the people of their sin. But this is a time to celebrate God's forgiveness. There is a proper time for grief and a proper time for joy, and we must know the difference (cf. Ezra 3:12; 10:1; Nehemiah 1:4; 2 Corinthians 2:5-11; James 4:9). The teachers instruct the people in a better way, and that is the climax of this great day of teaching.

10. Nehemiah said, "Go and enjoy choice food and sweet drinks, and send some to those who have nothing prepared. This day is sacred to our Lord. Do not grieve, for the joy of the LORD is your strength."

From daybreak until noon the people have been listening attentively, becoming increasingly convicted in their hearts (cf. Acts 2:37). Now *Nehemiah* dismisses them to go home and use the rest of the day in joyous celebration. But they are not to be selfish—the finest of *food* and *drinks* are to be shared with people too poor to prepare the best for themselves. And as the people resolve to leave sin behind, they are to remember that *the joy of the Lord* is their *strength* for avoiding future disobedience and its terrible consequences.

Our times of worship and fellowship today can be joyous for us as we draw upon the strength of the Lord through our fellow believers. Meeting around the

HOW TO SAY IT

Ahab. AY-hab.

Akkub. AK-ub.

Anaiah. Uh-NYE-uh.

Azariah. Az-uh-RYE-uh.

Bani. BAY-nye.

Golgotha. GAHL-guh-thuh.

Gomorrah. Guh-MORE-uh.

Hanan. HAY-nuhn.

Hashbaddanah. Hash-BAD-duh-nuh.

Hashum. HAY-shum.

Hilkiah. Hill-KYE-uh.

Hodiah. Ho-DYE-yuh.

Jamin. JAY-min.

Jeshua. JESH-you-uh.

Jezebel. JEZ-uh-bel.

Jozabad. JAWS-ah-bad.

Kelita. KEL-ih-tuh.

Maaseiah. May-uh-SEE-yuh.

Malkijah. Mal-KYE-juh.

Mattithiah. Mat-ih-THIGH-uh.

Meshullam. Me-SHUL-am.

Mishael. MISH-a-el.

Nehemiah. NEE-huh-MY-uh.

Nisan. NYE-san.

Pedaiah. Peh-DAY-yuh.

Pelaiah. Pe-LAY-yuh or Pe-LYE-uh.

Shabbethai. SHAB-ee-thigh.

Shema. SHE-muh.

Sherebiah. SHER-ee-BYE-uh.

Tirshatha. Tur-SHAY-thuh.

Tishri. TISH-ree.

Uriah. Yu-RYE-yuh.

Zechariah. ZEK-uh-RYE-uh.

WHAT DO YOU THINK?

In what ways has "the joy of the Lord" been your strength, both as an individual and as a part of the church?

Lord's Table on the Lord's Day, for example, can be a time of shared joy as we remember that Jesus indeed has paid the price that God demanded for sin.

B. END OF MOURNING (v. 11)

11. The Levites calmed all the people, saying, "Be still, for this is a sacred day. Do not grieve."

The Levites mentioned in verse 7 comfort *all the people.* Perhaps they do this by going out in the crowd to give personal messages of encouragement to those most distressed.

C. CELEBRATION OF LEARNING (v. 12)

12. Then all the people went away to eat and drink, to send portions of food and to celebrate with great joy, because they now understood the words that had been made known to them.

Now *the people* follow the instructions that we read in verse 10. The fact that they go off *to eat and drink* doesn't mean that their celebration was done in a frivolous, shallow, or profane manner (cf. Exodus 32:5, 6, 25). Rather, the idea is that they *celebrate* appropriately, *with great joy* for what God has done. How delightful it is to understand what God has *made known to them* in his book!

CONCLUSION

A. DO WE TEACH PROPERLY?

Karen was twelve years old when she made Peter's confession her own when she said, "I believe that Jesus is the Christ, the Son of the living God." Later, someone asked her what the word *Christ* means. Karen said, "It's Jesus' other name." But the word *Christ* really is a title rather than a name. It is the accepted English form of a Greek word that means "anointed." The Christ is the Anointed One.

In the centuries before Jesus came to earth, prophets, priests, and kings were anointed when they were appointed to those offices. (You can see some examples in Numbers 35:25 and 1 Samuel 16:13.) When we say that Jesus is the Christ, we are acknowledging that he is the supreme *Prophet* who makes God and his will known to us; we are saying he is the *Priest* who gave his own life as the only sacrifice that can win forgiveness for us by satisfying God's wrath; we are saying he is the eternal *King* whom we shall obey now and forever.

Should we have made all that plain to Karen before she made her confession?

B. DO WE MAKE THINGS PLAIN?

Ezra, Nehemiah, and the teaching Levites all gave the same advice, and that advice turned a day of mourning into a day of joy. The weeping people raised their heads, wiped their eyes, and went home to celebrate. For us, too, it is good to grieve for a while because we have sinned. But eventually it is better to stop sinning and be glad.

Today we understand this transformation from sorrow to joy better than did Ezra's hearers, better even than Ezra himself. We have sinned, yes, and the wages of sin is death (Romans 3:23; 6:23). But we escape death because Jesus died in our place. He took the punishment we deserved (Isaiah 53:4, 5), and we can live forever. In all the world there is no joy to compare with the joy of our salvation, and it is the Holy Spirit who grants us this joy (1 Thessalonians 1:6). Yet such great joy brings with it a great obligation. We ought to obey the Christ, our King, and we ought to be telling the good news of salvation far and wide. How can we not share our matchless joy?

Discovery Learning

This page contains an alternative lesson plan emphasizing learning activities. Classes desiring such student involvement will find these suggestions helpful. The next page is a reproducible activity page to further enhance discovery learning.

LEARNING GOALS

After participating in this lesson, each student will be able to:

1. Explain the reverence that the people had for God's presence through the reading of his Word.

2. Show respect for the Bible as God's Word.

3. Implement one way in which respect for the Word of God might be increased.

INTO THE LESSON

Prior to class time, read Nehemiah 8:1-12 to become familiar with it, practicing pronunciation of names (see the pronunciation guide on page 397) and noting phrases you want to emphasize vocally. After everyone has entered the room, read Nehemiah 8:1-5 while everyone remains seated. You, as the reader, should remain seated as well. Stumble through the names in verse 4. After concluding this first reading in a monotone, pause for a moment in silence. Then say, "Would everyone please stand for the reading of God's Word?" Stand and read the entire text (Nehemiah 8:1-12) with some intentional excitement, emphasizing the areas you planned in your preliminary reading.

Say, "You may be seated." Ask the students for their responses to the different presentations of the text. Listen for different thoughts and feelings. You may ask, "How did standing as opposed to sitting specifically affect your hearing of the Word of God?" Discuss the various responses. At the conclusion of this brief discussion say, "This text presents a clear reverence for God's Word. Let's study the passage today with reverence."

INTO THE WORD

Ask students to assemble into discussion groups of three to five. Each of these groups should read through the text again, writing down any elements that they see demonstrating reverence for the Word of God. (*These may include the following: publicly gathering as one, requesting the reading [8:1], the preparation for [see commentary on verse 3] and length of time of the reading [8:3—If this is raised, you may note that many people who have preached in cultures that do not have easy access to Scripture have asked preachers to continue to preach for hours], the building of a special platform [8:4], standing for the reading [8:5], and other obviously reverent behaviors such as responding to the reading with tears.*)

INTO LIFE

During the week, find articles showing respect or lack of respect for the Bible. *Christianity Today*™ is often a good source for these as are some *Focus on the Family*™ newsletters, local newspapers, and other such material.

To begin the activity say, "It is difficult to miss the respect the people in this text have and demonstrate for the Word of God." Distribute the various articles you have compiled to individuals or to small groups. Ask them to read through the articles to determine specific ways the Bible is shown to be either valued or disrespected. If you were unable to attain several articles, simply ask, "How does our culture demonstrate respect or lack of respect for God's Word?" Allow ample time for response. Responses may include such items as the Bible's continuing "best-seller" nature, and the presence of Bibles at weddings, funerals, and other special events.

In small groups ask students to write ways the Word of God could be treated with more respect in the culture at large. You may also ask them to share times when they have seen the Word treated respectfully. Have the groups share their responses with the class.

Next, have the students brainstorm ways in which the church can demonstrate greater value for the Word of God. Ask volunteers to share their responses. You might note that some people consider an effective way of doing this is to stand during the reading of Scripture prior to a sermon. In addition, one church in particular has a different person read Scripture each Sunday. The request to read is made by the preaching minister during the preceding week, and he communicates the honor and importance of the reading to the person asked. Comments about this process indicate that the people who read are considered to have a position of honor and that the people who hear while standing better recognize the reading as truly being God's Word.

Have the students agree on one way the congregation can better demonstrate value for God's Word, and have them make a plan toward implementing this. For individual application, distribute copies of the reproducible page that follows and have the learners complete it in a group discussion or individually. Ask each student to consider one way he or she can demonstrate greater respect for God's Word and commit to implementing this in daily life; point out the commitment line at the bottom of the page.

The Value of God's Word

Identify ways you could demonstrate the value of the Word of God in the following settings:

1. A worship service with your church

2. A conversation with a non-Christian friend

3. A small group Bible study

4. Personal Bible study

5. Sunday school lesson preparation

6. A gathering of people in the community

7. At your place of work

8. On vacation

Select one that you will make a commitment to accomplishing. Circle it and initial the circled statement.

THE PEOPLE RENEW THE COVENANT

LESSON 9

WHY TEACH THIS LESSON?

As a child, I had quite a sweet tooth. Sometimes I would search every nook and cranny of the kitchen trying to find some candy. Occasionally, all I could find would be Mom's bittersweet chocolate that she used for baking. I always had mixed feelings about eating that stuff. It was so great to get that chocolate taste on my tongue—but, oh, the bitterness that went with it!

The renewal of the covenant in ancient Judah was also a bittersweet experience. It was sweet to experience God's forgiveness, but it was bitter to realize that the covenant had to be renewed because it had been broken in the first place. That experience will speak to many of your learners today. Sensitive to the seriousness of their own shortcomings, they need to be assured of the sweetness of God's grace. Others, grateful for the grace of God, need to be reminded not to take it for granted. You can speak to both groups with today's lesson.

INTRODUCTION

A. THE VALUE OF YOUR PERSONAL HISTORY

Suppose you were to wake up tomorrow morning and couldn't remember anything about your past. Would you be able to function? I can safely predict that the answer would be a decisive *no*. It is your own personal history—with all its highs and lows, joys and sorrows, successes and failures—that will shape your today and all your tomorrows.

Each of us does indeed meet the world daily through our personal experiences of the past. If we are wise enough, we also meet the world daily through the past experiences of other people. Those other people certainly would include our own family members and loved ones. But the experiences—the histories—of those who lived at other times and in other places should not be overlooked. When we learn from such people, we avoid repeating their mistakes and their sins.

B. LESSON BACKGROUND

In several of our studies this summer, we have seen evidence that the returning exiles have truly "learned their lesson" concerning sin and punishment. That hard lesson comes from examining the experiences of their forefathers who neglected and violated God's law. Last week we saw the people of Judah assembled in a great mass meeting on the first day of the seventh month. They heard Ezra and others read and explain that law all morning long (Nehemiah 8:1-8).

The following day a group of leaders met for further study of the law. Among other things, they read about the Feast of Tabernacles (cf. Numbers 29:12-40). This feast, scheduled to begin in the middle of that very month, had not been celebrated as the law directed for a long time. So preparations were made, and the people again observed this ancient festival in the proper way (Nehemiah 8:13-18).

DEVOTIONAL READING:
PSALM 66:8-20
BACKGROUND SCRIPTURE:
NEHEMIAH 9:38–10:39
PRINTED TEXT:
NEHEMIAH 10:28-39

LESSON AIMS

After participating in this lesson, each student will be able to:

1. Describe the covenant made in Jerusalem under Ezra's leadership, identifying who signed it and who agreed to it.

2. Suggest aspects of the people's lives that were affected by the covenant and suggest how they might be worded today.

3. Begin a personal covenant with God.

Jul
27

KEY VERSE

"We are making a binding agreement, putting it in writing, and our leaders, our Levites and our priests are affixing their seals to it." —Nehemiah 9:38

LESSON 9 NOTES

When that happy festival was over, the people met again for a session that was not so joyous. They spent a quarter of the day in study of the law, and then a quarter of the day in mourning and confessing their disobedience (Nehemiah 9:1-3). The substance of their confession is recorded in 9:4-37. They said that they and their forefathers had often disobeyed the law, and that their disobedience had brought them many troubles. As a result, they had lost their national independence; because of disobedience they even then were subject to the Persians.

The climax of all this is recorded in our Key Verse. The people now would make a formal agreement to obey the law. They would put it in writing, and their leaders would make it official by putting their seals on it (Nehemiah 9:38).

Nehemiah 10:1-27 lists the leaders who sealed the covenant, and our printed text continues with what the rest of the people did.

I. OBEDIENCE PLEDGED (NEHEMIAH 10:28, 29)

In a single month, most of the people of Judah learned more about God's law than they had learned in all their lives before that time. After celebrating the Feast of Tabernacles, they are ready for commitment and action. They meant to honor that law!

A. ALL THE PEOPLE (v. 28)

28. *"The rest of the people—priests, Levites, gatekeepers, singers, temple servants and all who separated themselves from the neighboring peoples for the sake of the Law of God, together with their wives and all their sons and daughters who are able to understand—*

A covenant (or agreement) had been drawn up, a promise to obey the law. Leading citizens had affixed their seals to it (Nehemiah 9:38–10:27). Now the historian turns his attention to *the rest of the people,* and he names several different groups among them. The *priests* are in charge of public worship and teaching. The *Levites* (i.e., those of the historic tribe of Levi) are set apart to the service of God, and served in many ways, from janitor work to teaching and law enforcement. (All priests are Levites, but not all Levites are priests.) The *gatekeepers* work for the temple, and perhaps the city as well. The *singers* constitute the temple choir. The duties of the *temple servants* are not clearly described. Perhaps they did whatever the priests and Levites told them to do (cf. Ezra 8:20).

All who separated themselves from the neighboring peoples may mean pagans from the area who had converted to Judaism. They include whole families: men, women, and children old enough to understand the law that the people now intend to obey. This listing of different groups among *the rest of the people* seems intended to indicate that the people of Judah are unanimous in making the same promise that leading citizens had written in a covenant.

B. ALL THE LAW (v. 29)

29. *. . . all these now join their brothers the nobles, and bind themselves with a curse and an oath to follow the Law of God given through Moses the servant of God and to obey carefully all the commands, regulations and decrees of the LORD our Lord.*

All the people listed in verse 28 agree with the distinguished citizens who had put their seals on the contract. The distinguished ones are called *nobles* because they are specially honored as the heads of families or because they had won honor in some other way. Everyone takes *an oath* to keep the promise they make. They also place themselves under God's *curse* should they fail to keep it. (See similar promises in Ezra 10:5 and Nehemiah 5:12, 13.)

WHAT DO YOU THINK?

In what ways are God's people today to be separate and distinct from their neighbors?

[Use 1 John 2:15 to start the group's thinking.]

PLEDGES, SOLEMN AND OTHERWISE

Frivolous oaths and pledges seem to be common these days. A school principal makes the newspapers when he pledges to shave his head if his students read a certain number of books. When he actually carries through on his oath, the reporters and cameras turn out to cover the "news." College students "pledge" a fraternity or sorority through all kinds of inane activities. The list could go on.

The life-changing pledge made by Jonathan Edwards (1703–1758) could not have been more different. In his "Personal Narrative," Edwards relates that, "On January 12, 1723, I made a solemn dedication of myself to God, and wrote it down; giving up myself, and all that I had to God; to be for the future, in no respect, my own; to act as one that had no right to himself, in any respect. And solemnly vowed, to take God for my whole portion and felicity; looking on nothing else, as any part of my happiness, nor acting as if it were; and his law for the constant rule of my obedience: engaging to fight, with all my might, against the world, the flesh, and the devil, to the end of my life."

Jonathan Edwards went on to become one of the greatest revivalists in the history of New England. He also became a major figure in what came to be called Christianity's "Great Awakening" in the American colonies (1725–1760). Does anyone know what happened to that principal?   —R. L. N.

The terminology on today's poster comes from the Key Verse (King James Version). Discuss how Jesus' death has given us a "sure covenant"—that is, a "binding agreement."

II. BEHAVIORS CHANGED (NEHEMIAH 10:30, 31)

The general promise to do everything the law required may seem to be enough, but now some specific promises are added, promises to obey specific parts of the law. Perhaps these were parts that had been broken most frequently in the past.

A. HOLY PEOPLE (v. 30)

30. *"We promise not to give our daughters in marriage to the peoples around us or take their daughters for our sons.*

The law forbade Jews to marry pagans (Deuteronomy 7:1-4). That law had been broken in the past. When Ezra first came to Jerusalem, he found that more than a hundred Jewish men had foreign wives. Skilled teacher that he was, Ezra convinced the nation that all those wives, with their children, must be sent back to the homes from which they had come (Ezra 9, 10). Imagine how terrible it was for the husbands to give up the wives and children they loved. The consequences of sin can be truly heart-wrenching.

Now it is about thirteen years later. Remembering that traumatic time of parting, the men of Israel write into their covenant the specific promise that never again would any of them consent to such illegal marriages. Unfortunately, Nehemiah will have to correct this problem again a few years later (Nehemiah 13:23-28).

WHAT DO YOU THINK?

Where would you "draw the line" for yourself or your children about whom to marry?

[Note 2 Corinthians 6:14 in the course of your discussion.]

B. HOLY TIMES (v. 31)

31. *"When the neighboring peoples bring merchandise or grain to sell on the Sabbath, we will not buy from them on the Sabbath or on any holy day. Every seventh year we will forgo working the land and will cancel all debts.*

The Ten Commandments require that the seventh day of every week be holy. No regular work is to be done on that day (Exodus 20:9, 10). God takes this law seriously, prescribing the death penalty for its violation (31:15). *The Sabbath* is a memorial of the time when God finished his creation in six days and rested on the seventh (Genesis 2:1-3; Exodus 20:11). Failure to keep the Sabbath Day holy was one of the reasons for Jerusalem's destruction (see Jeremiah 17:19-27). When these Jews promise to obey the law, they go so far as to vow not even to *buy* food on the Sabbath or on any other *holy day*. But, as with the intermarriage problem, Nehemiah will have to provide more correction on this issue a few years later (see Nehemiah 13:15-22).

As every seventh day was to be a Sabbath, a time of rest, so also was *every seventh year.* In that year there was to be no sowing or reaping—the land was to lie fallow (Leviticus 25:1-5). In the harvest of the sixth year a little grain would be lost in the field. It would grow of itself in the seventh year, but it was not to be harvested by the landowner. It was for the poor and for animals (Exodus 23:10, 11). Frequent breaking of this law also was one of the reasons for the Babylonian captivity. (See 2 Chronicles 36:20, 21.) The land lay unused all the years of the captivity to make up for the Sabbath years that had been missed. But now the people rededicate themselves to keeping this ancient law and never again to sow and reap in the Sabbath year. The historical record in non-biblical sources suggests that the Jews did indeed keep this promise faithfully (cf. 1 Maccabees 6:49, 53).

Before the people promised to *cancel all debts,* wealthy moneylenders had been charging heavy interest, which was against the law (Exodus 22:25). They had been foreclosing on the property of debtors who could not pay, and even making them slaves in order to get back what had been lent. Nehemiah had insisted earlier that such heartless practices be stopped (Nehemiah 5:3-13). Now the people agree that a moneylender will take a loss rather than take away a poor man's means of livelihood or his children (cf. Deuteronomy 24:6; Proverbs 14:31).

III. OFFERINGS RENEWED (NEHEMIAH 10:32-39)

When we hear the word *offering,* we most often think of money or a check that can be put in the offering plate. But God's law for the Jews called for offerings of various kinds. Some of them are mentioned in our text.

A. TEMPLE TAX (v. 32)

32. *"We assume the responsibility for carrying out the commands to give a third of a shekel each year for the service of the house of our God:*

The men agree to pay an annual tax for the materials and manpower needed in the temple services. *A third of a shekel* is about one-eighth of an ounce of silver. What this equals in today's money is hard to say, but it is less than the half shekel required by the law (Exodus 30:11-16; 38:25, 26). The amount of money involved seems rather small for supporting *the service of the house of our God.* Perhaps the Persian government is still making generous contributions to the temple services (Ezra 6:8-10), or perhaps the financial situation of the people in Jerusalem justifies a reduced rate. In Jesus' day, the authorities ask about his payment of the "temple tax" (Matthew 17:24). This "temple tax" translates a term that literally means two drachmas, which is equal to half a shekel.

B. DAILY PERISHABLES (v. 33)

33. *. . . . for the bread set out on the table; for the regular grain offerings and burnt offerings; for the offerings on the Sabbaths, New Moon festivals and appointed feasts; for the holy offerings; for sin offerings to make atonement for Israel; and for all the duties of the house of our God.*

This verse lists some things involved in the temple services, and they are expensive. Some are provided by the tax mentioned in verse 32. Perhaps more are provided by the offerings mentioned in the following verses. If the Persian government is still making a contribution out of the tribute paid by its western provinces, that would be big help, too. (See Numbers 28:9-15.)

WHAT DO YOU THINK?

When the people reaffirmed their covenant with God, they pledged to change many areas of their lives, including their family structures, their schedules, their livelihood, and their personal finances. How should these areas of our lives be affected when we make a commitment to serving God? What significant lifestyle changes have you already made because of your faith?

WHAT DO YOU THINK?

To what extent is the Israelites' support of their temple a model of how Christians are to support the church today? Explain.

[Use 1 Corinthians 9:7-11 in your discussion.]

C. FIREWOOD (v. 34)

34. "We—the priests, the Levites and the people—have cast lots to determine when each of our families is to bring to the house of our God at set times each year a contribution of wood to burn on the altar of the LORD our God, as it is written in the Law.

Plenty of firewood is needed for the big altar that stands before the temple. When all the meat of an animal is burned in sacrifice, a big fire has to be maintained for some time, for meat does not *burn* easily. Sacrifices are burned every day (Exodus 29:38-42), and large numbers of them on feast days. Besides, the altar fire is kept burning continually, even in hours when no sacrifices are being made (Leviticus 6:8-13).

The priests, the Levites and the people all play a part in supplying needed *wood.* This even includes Nehemiah the governor (Nehemiah 13:31). The fact that *each* of the *families* brings wood at *set times* indicates that families take turns at this responsibility. It is not uncommon to see people *cast lots* in biblical times to make decisions (e.g., Numbers 26:55; Joshua 14:2; 18:10; 1 Chronicles 24:5; 25:8; 26:13; Luke 1:9; Acts 1:26).

D. FIRST PARTS (vv. 35-37a)

35. "We also assume responsibility for bringing to the house of the LORD each year the firstfruits of our crops and of every fruit tree.

The very first part of every harvest belongs to the Lord (Exodus 23:19a). Bringing that part *to the house of the Lord* means that these offerings are part of the support for the priests and Levites (Numbers 18:12, 13).

36. "As it is also written in the Law, we will bring the firstborn of our sons and of our cattle, of our herds and of our flocks to the house of our God, to the priests ministering there.

In Israel, *the firstborn* "whether man or animal" (Exodus 13:2) belongs to God; but fathers "buy back" their firstborn *sons* by paying five shekels (Numbers 18:15, 16). Suitable firstborn animals are sacrificed; the fat is burned, and the lean meat becomes food for *the priests* (18:17, 18). This agreement certainly will cost the people more than the third of a shekel of Nehemiah 10:32!

37a. "Moreover, we will bring to the storerooms of the house of our God, to the priests, the first of our ground meal, of our [grain] offerings, of the fruit of all our trees and of our new wine and oil.

Ground meal and *wine* and olive *oil* are manufactured products. Freewill offerings have already been noted in Ezra 8:28 and will be noted again in Nehemiah 10:39, below. The temple *storerooms* are the places where such things are held until *the priests* are ready to use them. Again, this attitude toward firstfruits means that the people promise to do just as the law directs them.

E. TITHES (v. 37b, 38)

37b. "And we will bring a tithe of our crops to the Levites, for it is the Levites who collect the tithes in all the towns where we work.

A *tithe* is 10 percent, or one-tenth. That part of each Israelite's income belongs to the Lord (Leviticus 27:30, 32). It is to be delivered to *the Levites* as payment for their services (Numbers 18:21, 24). We are not told just what their work is in the time of Ezra and Nehemiah. It seems reasonable to suppose that some of them are teachers of the law. But some are musicians and singers, and perhaps some even are carpenters and masons (cf. Nehemiah 10:28, above).

Whatever their duties are, the Levites are servants of God, and their pay comes from the tithes paid by other people of Israel.

WHAT DO YOU THINK?

In what specific ways can Christians offer the "firstfruits" of our families and of our livelihoods today? How does our attitude toward "firstfruits" help us remember that our lives and livelihoods depend first on God?

HOW TO SAY IT

Babylonian. Bab-ih-LOW-nee-
   un.
drachma (Greek). DROCK-muh.
Judaism. JOO-duh-izz-um or
   JOO-day-izz-um.
Levites. LEE-vites.
Maccabees. MACK-uh-bees.
Nehemiah. NEE-huh-MY-uh.
shekel. SHECK-ul.

PRAYER

How richly you have blessed
us, Father! How grateful we are
for a living in this world and
treasure in Heaven! Like those
Jews taught by Ezra, we who are
taught by Jesus promise an
earnest effort to do your will all
the days of our lives. In Jesus'
name, amen.

THOUGHT TO REMEMBER

Only our best is good enough.

38. "A priest descended from Aaron is to accompany the Levites when they receive the tithes, and the Levites are to bring a tenth of the tithes up to the house of our God, to the storerooms of the treasury.

The Levites receive tithes for their support, but do they pay tithes as well? Indeed they do! Their tithe of the tithes goes right back into the treasury for supporting the house of our God. Everyone must give something!

GIVING

Think about some of the important key words from the Bible. By one student's count the word believe (or some form of the word) is used 275 times. The word pray (including variations) is used 371 times. Some form of the word love is used 714 times.

For the word give (with variations) the student counted 2,162 uses!

Incredibly, Jesus taught more about money than any other topic. How we handle money is very important to God. Everything we have belongs to God and is a gift from him (1 Chronicles 29:10-14). As a response to God's generosity, we are called to be generous and cheerful givers of our financial resources. God loves a cheerful giver (2 Corinthians 9:7).

God commanded the Israelites to give tithes (10 percent) of everything they received, as well as additional gifts to maintain his temple, provide for the priests, and care for the poor (Leviticus 27:30; Numbers 18:26; Malachi 3:8-10). Israel recommitted themselves to that standard in Nehemiah 10.

In the New Testament Jesus taught about giving generously just as he gave generously. How much we give is a response to how God has given to us and changed our hearts.

Karl Menninger said giving "is a very good criterion of a person's mental health. Generous people are rarely mentally ill people." Have you discovered the joy of generous giving?

—J. A. M.

F. SUMMARY OF OFFERINGS (v. 39)

39. "The people of Israel, including the Levites, are to bring their contributions of grain, new wine and oil to the storerooms where the articles for the sanctuary are kept and where the ministering priests, the gatekeepers and the singers stay.

"We will not neglect the house of our God."

This verse summarizes all that the people of Israel, including the Levites, are to do to support the house of our God. All the Israelites, including the Levites, agree to bring to the temple all the offerings that were required by the law. The grain is mainly wheat and barley. The spacious storerooms in that facility are ready to receive the produce that is brought.

CONCLUSION

Christians are not under the law given at Sinai, as the Jews were. The work of Christ truly frees us from "the old way of the written code" (Romans 7:6); the Son of God has taken the old code "away, nailing it to the cross" (Colossians 2:14). Christ, in redeeming us "from the curse of the law" (Galatians 3:13), frees us to obey a better law (1 Corinthians 9:21; Galatians 6:2). This is "the perfect law that gives freedom" (James 1:25).

But this freedom is no excuse for doing wrong (Romans 6:15, 16). We are taught to do all that Jesus commanded (Matthew 28:20). We are to be holy, as God is holy (1 Peter 1:15, 16). Can that be any less than what the old law requires? The sacrifices we offer are not animals on an altar. They are our own bodies, living and serving God (Romans 12:1). What has your body been doing in the Lord's service this past week?

Discovery Learning

*This page contains an alternative lesson plan emphasizing learning activities. Classes
desiring such student involvement will find these suggestions helpful. The next page
is a reproducible activity page to further enhance discovery learning.*

LEARNING GOALS

After this lesson each student will be able to:

1. Describe the covenant made in Jerusalem under Ezra's leadership, identifying who signed it and who agreed to it.

2. Suggest aspects of the people's lives that were affected by the covenant and suggest how they might be worded today.

3. Begin a personal covenant with God.

INTO THE LESSON

Ask class members to brainstorm all the promises and contracts they can think of. (*They will name marriage, loan, business, employment, and possibly others.*) Then ask, "What does the contract accomplish?" Allow a few people to comment.

Say, "One dictionary says that a contract is 'an agreement that is usually formal, solemn, and intended as binding.' In today's study the Jews make such an agreement with God: formal, solemn, and binding."

INTO THE WORD

Raymond Brown in his book *The Message of Nehemiah* (Inter-Varsity Press, 1998, pp. 170, 171) describes the literary structure of political covenants made in the ancient Near East. An analysis of Nehemiah 9 and 10 reveals that the passage demonstrates just such a style. In our age of a general lack of commitment to any person or cause, it could provide a means for us to step outside our culture and make a commitment, a covenant with God.

Give students the outline of this literary style, as numbered in the following paragraph and enumerated on the reproducible page following, and let them find the features in the two chapters. If your students have the student book, they have the outline there also.

Such a covenant usually began by outlining the historical relationship between the two parties in the agreement, paying special attention to the generosity of the stronger party (the prayer). This was followed by a listing of the covenant's basic stipulations (10:29). Then there was a description of the specific and practical ways in which this more general commitment is to be applied (vv. 30-39). Fourth, the covenant required that a copy of the written agreement be deposited in the temple of the god and that the covenant's terms be declared publicly on given occasions. Those who signed (10:1-27) went

on to agree to blessings and cursings that would follow keeping or breaking the covenant (v. 29). The covenant concluded with a brief recapitulation of terms (v. 39).

INTO LIFE

"When we study this covenant, we see it was very specific and practical. Once people had heard God's law read again, they were willing to change their lifestyles. Their beliefs would change the way they lived. While Christians are not a legal part of this Old Covenant, we do find in it relevant principles for living in today's world."

Either as a whole class or in small groups, have students look again at the structure and glean principles to apply. The list will include such entries as these:

9:5-38—Remind ourselves of God's generosity.

10:29—Promise to obey God's Word.

10:30—Teach children to marry someone who is also committed to God.

10:31—Honor God's day; care for God's world.

10:32-39—Support God's work.

As the people in Jerusalem made a public commitment to obey God's law, challenge your learners to begin private covenants. Point out our need to make a conscious decision whether we are willing to make a commitment in a world where so few want to make commitments.

Suggest that the students may follow the full six-point pattern or concentrate on promises and commitments in a variety of areas, such as the authority of Scripture, family life, relationships, finances, ministry for God, and witness in the midst of so many different worldviews. Encourage the learners to add promises in the weeks and months ahead as they participate in Bible studies and hear sermons.

If you did not do so earlier, give a copy of the reproducible page to each learner and let people begin working on personal covenants. When the end of class time approaches, lead a prayer for commitments made and to be made.

Suggest that each person approach another to be the one who checks with him or her to confirm the status of covenant keeping after an agreed upon time frame.

Point out also the concluding recommendations at the bottom of the reproducible activity page: recommendations to add to and revise their covenants as opportunities and faith encourages.

My Covenant With God

A covenant usually includes the following elements. How would you state the nature of your covenant with God in each?

1. A description of the historical relationship between the two parties in the agreement, with special attention to the generosity of the stronger party

2. The covenant's basic stipulations

3. A description of the specific and practical ways in which this more general commitment is to be applied

4. A requirement that a copy of the written agreement be preserved and that the covenant's terms be declared publicly on given occasions

5. An agreement by the signers to blessings and cursings that would follow the keeping or breaking of the covenant

6. A brief recapitulation of the covenant's terms

You may fill out the whole covenant or concentrate on your promises and commitments in such areas as authority of Scripture, family life, relationships, finances, ministry for God, witness in the midst of so many different worldviews, or others. In the weeks (and months) ahead plan to add promises as you participate in various Bible studies and hear sermons.

God Restores a Remnant

Unit 3: Repentance
(Lessons 10-14)

MESSAGE OF CONDEMNATION

WHY TEACH THIS LESSON

At the time this book is being produced, tensions between Israel and its Arab neighbors are running high. Almost daily the news contains some story of a shooting, a suicide bombing, or a military retaliation in or around Israel. What an answer to prayer it will be if, by the time you teach this lesson, there has been some kind of resolution to the conflict and peace restored to the region!

There was conflict in Obadiah's time as well, as we'll see in today's lesson. It would be easy to try to make some connection between the ancient tensions and the modern. If that's all you do, you'll miss a good opportunity for personal application. The nations are addressed as "brothers" (see v. 10). More important to your learners this morning than the origins of Mideast conflict are their own interpersonal relationships. How are they treating their brothers and sisters?

INTRODUCTION

A. RED AND HEELCATCHER

Red and Heelcatcher were twins, and their rivalry began before they were born. Their prenatal struggles made their mother's pregnancy difficult (Genesis 25:22). To her the Lord revealed not only that she would have twins, but also that each twin would become the father of a nation and that the nation springing from the younger twin would be dominant (25:23).

The firstborn twin had so much body hair that he was named "Hairy" (or "Esau" in the language of his parents; 25:25). The second followed quickly, for his baby hand was grasping his brother's heel. Appropriately he was named "Heelcatcher," or "Jacob" in his parents' language.

When the boys grew up, Jacob turned out to be a homebody, while Esau became a roving hunter (25:27, 28). Then the younger twin began to dominate, using methods more shrewd than just or right.

One day Esau came home from his hunting, and he was very hungry. He found Jacob cooking a stew of red lentils. Naturally the hungry man wanted some of that savory food. Jacob was willing to sell it, but the price he asked was Esau's birthright. Reckless Esau accepted that deal. With a solemn oath he delivered his birthright. That meant that Jacob, not Esau, would become head of the family at the father's death and would inherit a double portion of the estate. All that for a bowl of stew (25:29-34)!

The father of those twins was Isaac, son of Abraham. In his old age he lost his eyesight. Then his wife conspired with Jacob to make him give to Jacob the blessing he intended for Esau. In that chosen family, a father's dying blessing was a real prophecy. It told what actually was going to happen later. So Isaac, thinking he was talking to Esau, promised to Jacob prosperity and dominion over nations (27:1-40). In later years, that promise was fulfilled.

DEVOTIONAL READING:
ISAIAH 43:1-7

BACKGROUND SCRIPTURE:
OBADIAH

PRINTED TEXT:
OBADIAH 1-4, 10, 11, 15, 21

LESSON AIMS

After participating in this lesson, each student will be able to:

1. Relate Obadiah's verbal portrait of a nation whose hatred carried it down the road to its own destruction.

2. Explain how hatred can cause us to put our pride in the wrong things.

3. Identify personal feelings of hatred and plan ways to begin removing those feelings.

Aug
3

KEY VERSE

As you have done, it will be done to you;

your deeds will return upon your own head.   —Obadiah 15

Because Esau was so eager for Jacob's red stew, he was given the nickname "Red" (25:30), or "Edom" in the language then spoken. That nickname clung so long that the nation descended from this man was called Edom as well as Esau. (See the two terms used interchangeably in Jeremiah 49:7, 8 and Obadiah 8.) In later years Jacob, "Heelcatcher," also received a new name. He was called "Israel," or God's contender (Genesis 32:28). So the nation descended from him was and is called Israel. This week our lesson brings us to those two nations at a time more than a twelve hundred years after the time of Esau and Jacob.

B. Lesson Background

The background to the book of Obadiah is a time of invasion and distress in Israel's history. But figuring out just which invasion Obadiah is referring to is a problem! There are at least six invasions or times of civil unrest between the breakup of Israel into two parts in 931 B.C. and the Babylonian exile in 586 B.C. Scholars have proposed as many theories for Obadiah as their were invasions!

Since the language of Obadiah 10-13 implies that the Jewish people have been carried off into captivity, it is most likely that Obadiah prophesies some time after 586 B.C. The first four verses of Obadiah look quite similar to Jeremiah 49:14-16, where the Babylonian exile has just become a reality. The condemnation of Edom in Lamentations 4:21, 22, which was written after the sobering events of 586 B.C., also supports this background for the book of Obadiah.

Before the Babylonian captivity, the Jewish people (descended from the younger twin Jacob) had lived in the country at the eastern end of the Mediterranean Sea. Edom (the nation descended from Esau) lived right next door, in the broad area south and east of the Dead Sea. As foretold in Genesis 25:23, the nation of the younger twin was stronger. King David subdued Edom in about 990 B.C. and added it to the Israelite empire (2 Samuel 8:14). After David's son Solomon died, that empire split apart in about 931 B.C. Edom eventually revolted in about 847 B.C. (2 Kings 8:20-22). For many years to follow there was more war than peace between Israel and Edom. In our text, we shall see the prophet Obadiah rebuking Edom for its enmity toward the nation God had chosen for his own.

I. WARNING TO EDOM (OBADIAH 1-4)

Obadiah means "servant of Yahweh." About this prophet we know only what we learn from this short book that bears his name. Nothing is said about his family, his home, or the time or method of his ministry. The prophet hides in the shadows; God's message stands in the spotlight.

A. Battle Is Coming (v. 1)

1. *The vision of Obadiah.*
> *This is what the Sovereign LORD says about Edom—*
> *We have heard a message from the LORD:*
> > *An envoy was sent to the nations to say,*
> *"Rise, and let us go against her for battle"—*

The phrase *the vision of Obadiah* stands out as the title of the book. The clause *this is what the Sovereign Lord says about Edom* may be called a subtitle. *We have heard* indicates that Obadiah is not alone as he prophesies. But exactly who the "we" are is uncertain. It may indicate that Obadiah is part of a group of prophets.

What Obadiah and the others have heard is very important, since it is *a message from the Lord.* The message is that of a coming *battle.* Just as God already has used pagan *nations* against Judah (e.g., Isaiah 8:1-10; Jeremiah 22:24-27), so he also promises to do against Edom (cf. Jeremiah 27:1-7).

Assyria. Uh-SEAR-ee-uh.
Babylon. BAB-uh-lun.
Babylonian. Bab-ih-LOW-nee-un.
Deuteronomy. Due-ter-AHN-uh-me.
Edom. EE-dum.
Edomites. EE-dum-ites.
Esau. EE-saw.
Ezekiel. Ee-ZEEK-ee-ul or Ee-ZEEK-yul.
Habakkuk. Huh-BACK-kuk.
Hasmoneans. HAZ-mow-NEE-unz.
Herod. HAIR-ud.
Idumeans. Id-you-ME-unz.
Isaac. EYE-zuk.
Isaiah. Eye-ZAY-uh.
Jeremiah. Jair-uh-MY-uh.
Maccabees. MACK-uh-bees.
Medes. Meeds.
Nabateans. NAB-uh-TEE-unz.
Nahum. NAY-hum.
Nineveh. NIN-uh-vuh.
Obadiah. O-buh-DYE-uh.
Persians. PER-zhunz.
Petra. PEH-trah.
Syrians. SEAR-ee-unz.
Yahweh (Hebrew). YAH-weh.

The *envoy* who is *sent* to the pagan nations perhaps is not literally a messenger walking from place to place. In some way not known to us, *the Lord* is stirring up the ungodly nations as instruments of destruction to attack Edom. Certainly those nations do not intend to serve the Lord. But God still uses them to punish people and nations that need punishment. Soon it will be Edom's turn on the chopping block.

B. Defeat Is Looming (v. 2)

2. "See, I will make you small among the nations;
   you will be utterly despised.

Edom does not know it yet, but God has made that nation too *small* to stand against the pagan *nations* he is stirring up for the attack. This smallness leads Edom to be *utterly despised* by those nations. When battle comes, defeat is certain.

C. Edom's Foolish Pride (v. 3)

3. "The pride of your heart has deceived you,
   you who live in the clefts of the rocks
   and make your home on the heights,
  you who say to yourself,
   'Who can bring me down to the ground?'

The Bible often warns of the dangers of *pride* and arrogance (e.g., Proverbs 16:18). Certainly the Edomites ought to be enthusiastic about their nation, their civilization, and their accomplishments. But that attachment becomes a self-deceiving pride; the Edomites think they are stronger, wiser, and better than they really are. As a result, they probably scorn Obadiah's warning. The Edomites have no fear of the nations around them.

The description of the Edomites' home as being *in the clefts of the rocks* and *on the heights* is both picturesque and accurate. Even today, visitors to that area are amazed at the rose-red city of Petra. It is not built of quarried stone; rather, it is carved out of the face of a towering cliff of solid rock. To approach it, one must go through a cleft of the rock too narrow for anything much wider than a single camel. It is small wonder that the inhabitants of such a place feel secure!

Only fifty miles from the Dead Sea, the mountain beside Petra rises a mile above that body of water. Edom's homeland is so high, so rough, and so difficult for the traveler, that the proud inhabitants feel immune to invasion. What natural defenses! *"Who can bring me down to the ground?"* they ask. But Edom reckons without God, and his viewpoint is different. See the next verse.

PRIDE

Five centuries ago in the city of Florence, a woman came day after day to worship and do homage before a statue of the Virgin Mary. "Look how she reverences the Virgin mother," said one priest to another.

"Don't be deceived by what you see," his colleague responded. "Many years ago an artist was commissioned to create a statue for the cathedral. He sought a young woman to pose as the model for his sculpture and found one who seemed to be the perfect subject. She was young, serenely lovely, and had a mystical quality to her face. The image of that young woman inspired his statue of Mary. The woman you now see worshiping the statue is the same one who served as its model years ago. Shortly after the statue was put in place, she began to visit it and has continued to worship there religiously ever since."

Pride is arrogant self-worship. Pride deludes its victims into believing that they have no peers and drives them to destroy anyone who takes recognition away from them. The proud are infatuated with themselves.

DAILY BIBLE READINGS

Monday, July 28—A Report From the Lord (Obadiah 1-9)

Tuesday, July 29—You Should Not Have Rejoiced (Obadiah 10-16)

Wednesday, July 30—Israel Shall Take Possession (Obadiah 17-21)

Thursday, July 31—I Will Say, "Give Them Up" (Isaiah 43:1-7)

Friday, Aug. 1—God Is Israel's Savior (Isaiah 43:8-13)

Saturday, Aug. 2—Israel Will Be the Lord's (Isaiah 44:1-8)

Sunday, Aug. 3—God Will Comfort Israel (Isaiah 66:10-14)

Visual for lessons 1 and 10. Locate Edom on a more detailed map; then point out for your students its general location on this wall map.

Centuries ago Edom was judged by God for a prideful heart and arrogant spirit (v. 3) Deceived by their own prideful illusions they became God's enemy.—J. A. M.

D. GOD'S CERTAIN VICTORY (v. 4)

4. *"Though you soar like the eagle*
and make your nest among the stars,
from there I will bring you down,"
    declares the LORD.

God is going to bring Edom *down.* Even if Edom could soar like an *eagle* far above those mile-high mountains, even if the Edomites could build their cities *among the stars* instead of carving them from the lofty rock, God still is going to bring that nation down. It won't be by an earthquake, to crumble the solid rocks where they dwell. Rather, the destruction will come at the hands of human invaders (v. 1). Edom's allies will become enemies (v. 7). They will be God's instrument to destroy both the wise leaders and the mighty soldiers of Edom, "and everyone in Esau's mountains will be cut down in the slaughter" (v. 9).

II. CHARGE AGAINST EDOM (OBADIAH 10, 11)

Edom would fall for the same reason that many nations had fallen before and since that time: Edom would fall because of wickedness. Next we see exactly what type of wickedness it is that condemns Edom.

A. VIOLENCE AGAINST ISRAEL (v. 10)

10. *"Because of the violence against your brother Jacob,*
you will be covered with shame;
you will be destroyed forever.

As we noted in the Introduction, Esau and *Jacob* were twin brothers many centuries earlier. Those two should have acted in brotherly fashion. But Jacob resorted to deceit to get the blessing their father meant to give to Esau as firstborn. To retaliate, Esau planned to kill Jacob, so Jacob had to flee the country to save his life (Genesis 27).

Likewise the two nations descended from those brothers should have maintained brotherly relations. Their people are blood relatives, and God expected civility between them (see Deuteronomy 2:1-8). But often they were hostile instead. Edom shall be humbled by being *destroyed forever.* In the next verse we see the Lord chose one example as a basis for his charge against Edom.

B. HELP TO ISRAEL'S ENEMIES (v. 11)

11. *"On the day you stood aloof*
while strangers carried off his wealth
and foreigners entered his gates
and cast lots for Jerusalem,
you were like one of them."

In the critical time when *foreigners* invaded Israelite territory and looted *Jerusalem,* Edom, Israel's kin, *stood aloof* and watched. The most disastrous of those invasions was that of the Babylonians, who destroyed Jerusalem and took most of its people into captivity. Therefore it is natural to suppose that the fall of Jerusalem to Babylon in 586 B.C. is in view here.

That destruction by the Babylonian forces was total. Those *strangers carried off his wealth.* The Babylonians completely eliminated Judah's military power and wealth—the Babylonians took it all! (See 2 Kings 25:11-21; 2 Chronicles 36:17-20; and Jeremiah 52:12-30.)

WHAT DO YOU THINK?

Edom stands condemned because of actions against "your brother Jacob." Family relationships are important to God; what can we do to strengthen our own family relationships?

WHAT DO YOU THINK?

How would you reconcile this passage with the Sermon on the Mount, in which Jesus tells us to pray for those who persecute us, bless our enemies, and turn the other cheek?
[See Romans 12:19; 13:1-4.]

WHAT DO YOU THINK?

God condemned Edom for standing "aloof" when Judah fell. How are we sometimes guilty of standing aloof when someone is in trouble? In what ways should we—as individuals, as churches, and as nations—help those we see in trouble?
[See Luke 10:25-37.]

After crashing through Jerusalem's walls, the invaders had *entered* into the city's *gates* and burned them (Nehemiah 1:3). Invading soldiers in the ancient world often divided up the loot with games of chance, such as casting lots (cf. Luke 23:34). This had happened both to Nineveh (Nahum 3:10) and Jerusalem (Joel 3:3). However this casting of lots was not for the purpose of showing favoritism or letting anyone "off the hook" (cf. Ezekiel 24:6). All of Jerusalem had suffered. And when it happened, Edom had shown no sympathy or compassion. Rather, the Edomites had stood on the sidelines and gloated (see Psalm 137:7).

Not merely content to gloat, Edom actively helped the invaders as verses 12-14 (not included in our text) make clear. Afterward, the Edomites started moving into Israelite territory themselves (cf. Ezekiel 25:12-14).

III. OVERTHROW OF EDOM (OBADIAH 15, 21)

The facts are stated clearly. First, God said proud Edom was to be brought low because of Edom's violence to Israel and help to Israel's enemies. Now the last two verses of our text relate the final outcome of all this.

A. DAY OF THE LORD (v. 15)

15. *"The day of the LORD is near*
   for all nations.
As you have done, it will be done to you;
   your deeds will return upon your own head."

The Bible speaks of *the day of the Lord* in many places. It is a foreboding phrase of judgment. It is a time of the Lord's victory and his enemies' defeat. That time is *near* for Edom. What Edom has *done* to others eventually is turned right back on that country's *own head*. Such is the ultimate fate of *all* nations that oppose God and his people.

MORAL COURT

In the late 1990s, televised legal proceedings became all the rage. It began in 1981 when Judge Joseph Wapner became the star of "The People's Court." By the year 2000, there were at least ten "courtroom" programs on TV. Televised legal proceedings today can feature the deadly serious. Who can forget the O. J. Simpson trial from 1995? But at the other end of the spectrum stands the downright trivial, as with one case on the show "Moral Court" that featured a mother "suing" her live-in daughter over how often the daughter should wash her hair!

As we read Obadiah's prophecy against Edom, we get the distinct impression that we are witnessing a courtroom scene there as well. The Judge, the evidence, the verdict, and the sentence are all easy to recognize. But when we realize that it is God himself who is the Judge, and that an entire nation is being condemned, we are reminded of how inconsequential many of today's "legal proceedings" really are.

The book of Obadiah also reminds us that a day is coming when we will be participants in God's "moral court." As John said, "I saw the dead, great and small, standing before the throne, and books were opened. . . . The dead were judged according to what they had done as recorded in the books" (Revelation 20:12). Will you be ready? —R. L. N.

B. TRIUMPH OF THE LORD (v. 21)

21. *Deliverers will go up on Mount Zion*
      to govern the mountains of Esau.
      And the kingdom will be the LORD's.

In the time between the Old and New Testaments, the eastern part of Edom (*Esau*) is taken by the Nabateans, an Arabian tribe. That happens in about 325 B.C.

WHAT DO YOU THINK?

Some people say the "God of the Old Testament" is vengeful and harsh, but the "God of the New Testament" is loving and merciful—that there are "two faces of God." How would you respond to such a statement?

[Passages such as Joel 2:13; Matthew 23, 24; and Revelation 6:15-17 may help you demonstrate a unifying theme.]

WHAT DO YOU THINK?

The Lord promised that one day the kingdom would be his. What is our part in this?

And although Obadiah's short book deals mostly with the sin and punishment of Edom, the people of Israel are sinners, too. They are punished by captivity in Babylon. When they are allowed to go back home, they are subjects of the Persian Empire. When Alexander the Great subdues that empire, the people of Israel are then in his realm. When Alexander dies, they are ruled by Syrian tyrants.

Then the *deliverers* (or "rescuers") come. They are a priestly family called Maccabees (or Hasmoneans), who lead a desperate revolt against the Syrians until Israel is independent again. Israel conquers the western part of Edom in a bloody campaign (2 Maccabees 10:14-23), and the Edomites (by then called Idumeans) are compelled to become Jews. (One of them, Herod the Great, even becomes a Jewish king.)

But then independent Israel is swallowed up by the growing Roman Empire. When the Romans destroy Jerusalem and scatter the Israelites in A.D. 70, Edom vanishes from the pages of history.

Yet it is also under Roman rule that the greater deliverer comes to *Mount Zion*. He is crucified as King of the Jews (Matthew 27:37), but his kingdom is not of this world (John 18:36). He is raised up to be King of kings (Revelation 19:16). His is the kingdom that "will crush all those kingdoms and bring them to an end, but it will itself endure forever" (Daniel 2:44; cf. Amos 9:12).

CONCLUSION

A. NATIONS USED AND PUNISHED

Perhaps it seem strange that the Lord used Babylon to punish Israel (Jeremiah 25:9), and then rebuked Edom for helping in that punishment. But this is just another example of God's customary way of working with evil nations. He will use one wicked nation to punish another, and then turn around and punish the first nation for its own wickedness. (This is a major theme of the book of Habakkuk.)

Isaiah 10:5-12 plainly shows God's way in this regard. There we see God using Assyria to punish northern Israel. But Assyria does not intend to be used by God. Assyria's motives are selfish and malicious. The Assyrian rulers are greedy for wealth and power (vv. 7-11). Therefore God punishes Assyria in her turn (v. 12). History reveals that God used Babylon to destroy Assyria; then used the Medes and Persians to destroy Babylon. Next, God used the Greek empire under Alexander the Great to destroy the empire of the Medes and Persians.

These are lessons for all nations of the twenty-first century! Read history and learn. The God of all history still casts a watchful eye over all nations today.

B. NATIONS AND PEOPLE

What makes a nation wicked? Wicked people do. What makes a nation good? Good people do. Do we want our nation to be better? If we do, we must help its people to be better. Two things are necessary for that to happen.

The first thing is *repentance*. A bad person will not become good unless he or she wants to reject evil. But no one can be good enough by personal effort alone. Something else is needed.

That something else is *forgiveness*. Forgiveness is God's doing, not ours. Forgiveness comes when a person believes in the Savior who long ago came up on Mount Zion and who gave his life at Calvary. A person who truly believes in the Savior will submit to Peter's instructions to "Repent and be baptized, every one of you, in the name of Jesus Christ for the forgiveness of your sins" (Acts 2:38). Jesus is the crucified King who now lives and rules forever. Forgiveness through him enrolls us in his kingdom, the "kingdom that will never be destroyed" (Daniel 2:44).

THOUGHT TO REMEMBER

Trust the Lord and do right.

Discovery Learning

This page contains an alternative lesson plan emphasizing learning activities. Classes desiring such student involvement will find these suggestions helpful. The next page is a reproducible activity page to further enhance discovery learning.

LEARNING GOALS

After this lesson each student will be able to:

1. Relate Obadiah's verbal portrait of a nation whose hatred carried it down the road to destruction.

2. Explain how hatred can cause us to put our pride in the wrong things.

3. Identify personal feelings of hatred and plan ways to begin removing those feelings.

INTO THE LESSON

ADVANCE PREPARATION: If you have the *Adult Visuals* that support these lessons, pull out this unit's map; get any pictures of the city of Petra that you can; and borrow appropriate teaching pictures from teachers of children's Bible classes. Recruit a good storyteller from the class to tell the historical background of Jacob and Esau from Genesis 25-33; provide the information from this lesson's commentary and other study sources.

Option 1: As students arrive say, "Have you ever noticed how many movies and television shows revolve around the theme of revenge? Can you identify some?" Write the titles and plot lines on the chalkboard or a poster sheet as they are suggested.

Option 2: Provide markers or watercolor paints and brushes and invite students to paint images of "hatred" on poster board or banner paper.

Whether you use option 1 or 2 (or both), make the transition to Bible study by saying, "Revenge is a strong motive for many people to act hatefully. Our study in the prophecy of Obadiah today will reveal how far such hatred ultimately can take people."

INTO THE WORD

An understanding of the historical background is imperative in order for your students to understand Obadiah's message. Using the unit map (or another map of Old Testament Palestine that clearly shows Edom) and teaching pictures, help your students understand the long legacy of hatred between the two nations and the false security that Petra's physical location gave.

With strong expression read the book of Obadiah to the class. Lecture on the contents of the commentary. You can use the outline given in it as your framework, or you can adapt the material to fit the following outline suggested by Loren Deckard (*Minor Prophets*; Cincinnati: Standard Publishing, 1999, p. 33):

I. Hateful thinking causes us to misunderstand who the enemy is (vv. 2, 4).

II. Hateful thinking causes us to overestimate our own power (vv. 3, 4).

III. Hateful thinking leads us to take joy and pride in the wrong things (vv. 12-14).

To get students to look closely at the text of Obadiah, divide the twenty-one verses equally among your class members. If you have more than twenty-one, repeat assignments. Indicate you are going to read "paraphrases" of verses and you want someone to identify and read the corresponding verse from the text. For example, "No one is so big that God can't make him small" (v. 2); "You can't get high enough above the ground to escape God's notice" (v. 4); "You should not stand across the street indifferent to a mugging going on on the other side" (v. 11). "Behavior is rewarded, whether good or bad" (v. 15); "One fire and then another, and all that's left of a field of golden grain is blackened stubble" (v. 18). Write and use others.

INTO LIFE

Guide students to make a comparison between the attitudes and actions of the people of Edom and that of people today. This can be done individually or in groups. Distribute copies of the reproducible activity "The Path to Destruction" from the next page. Allow time for the students to write some answers; then write their answers on the board or an overhead transparency as they report their findings.

After this analysis, challenge the students individually to examine their own lives to determine whether they are having feelings of anger or hatred. Provide copies of the reproducible activity "Anger Grid" from the next page. This will provide a space for the learner to do this analysis. It may also reveal the progression of anger to hatred (or show that hatred never forms when anger diminishes).

If your students are comfortable in being accountable to one another, let partners confess such feelings to each other and talk together about how each could begin removing those feelings this week. If your students are not that comfortable with such an exercise, let them write the first step down for their own eyes only, and then you follow with a prayer for God's strength and wisdom to be given in carrying out their plans.

The Path to Destruction

Obadiah traces how hatred caused the people of Edom to walk down the path to destruction. How might the path look today?

Edom hated Judah. Which groups express hatred today?

Edom's hatred caused the people to rejoice and boast when God's people suffered. What does hatred cause people to do?

The inhabitants of Petra felt secure in the city built into the face of a towering cliff. In what do we place our security today?

Edom's pride had deceived them. In what ways are we proud today? How could our pride be deceiving us?

Anger Grid

Think about a person with whom you are angry. Draw a line to show the ups and downs of your feelings toward this person. What does the direction of the line reveal? We know from Edom's experience that angry feelings and thoughts can grow into hatred that will bring eventual destruction.

		March 1	March 15	April 1	April 15	May 1	May 15	June 1	June 15	July 1	July 15	August 1
	3											
Very happy with the person	2											
	1											
Neither happy nor angry	0											
	-1											
Very angry with the person	-2											
	-3											

Write one step you will take to begin removing anger and hatred in your life.

CALL FOR REPENTANCE

LESSON 11

WHY TEACH THIS LESSON?

This is the time of year when people with vegetable gardens frequently share their harvest with friends and neighbors. Perhaps you have a gardener or two in your class who like to bring tomatoes and zucchini squash and other vegetables to the church house with them so others may have them.

If so, ask them about the work involved in raising such a crop. Particularly, ask them what do they do about weeds in the garden. Some may plant their rows wide enough to run a garden tiller through. A few may use chemical pesticides. But probably all of them have to get down on their hands and knees occasionally and uproot the weeds by hand. It's hard work, but it pays off.

Use this lesson as a challenge to uproot the weeds of sin in your learners' lives. Joel's call to repentance is a call to get the weeds out. Every garden has weeds; every life has sin. Both must be uprooted if there is to be a successful harvest!

INTRODUCTION

A. WHEN THE GRASSHOPPERS CAME

From my long-ago childhood on the farm, I carry a dim memory of the year the grasshoppers came. My brother and I picked our way with great care when we walked to the barn, for it was quite alarming to have a bare foot step on one of those squirming, scratching little creatures. On the wing, the insects would mindlessly smack us in the face, drop to the ground, and sit there looking stupefied. The chickens happily pounced on the invaders, but only for a time. When their gullets were full, they could only stand and watch the oversupply of food hopping around them.

We were all concerned with the crops, of course. So the county entomologist provided a recipe for poison bait, and the newspapers published it daily. We mixed bran with sorghum molasses to delight the grasshoppers' taste, and deadly poison to kill them. We spread the stuff in fields of corn and cotton, and the critters died by the millions.

We dared not poison the garden, however, lest we die with the bugs! So our growing beans and peas and turnips vanished. We ate the last of the vegetables Mom had canned the year before, and then we bought tin cans at the store.

The next year we watched with bated breath as "grasshopper time" approached, but the little pests came in their normal numbers. Only the chickens paid them any attention.

As bad as our grasshopper infestation had been, a plague of locusts in a Mediterranean country is worse. Exodus 10:12-15 provides a brief description of locusts as one of the famous ten plagues upon Egypt. Clouds of those insects blocked the sun and darkened the whole land. Those hordes devoured every green thing that grew.

The first chapter of Joel also describes a locust plague, but this description is not so short and literal as the one in Exodus 10. The locusts in Joel are "a nation, . . . powerful and without number; it has the teeth of a lion" (1:6). Vividly this account describes the devastation; poignantly it calls the people to mourn (vv. 7-20).

DEVOTIONAL READING:
ACTS 2:14-23, 32, 33

BACKGROUND SCRIPTURE:
JOEL 1, 2

PRINTED TEXT:
JOEL 2:1, 2, 12-14, 28, 29

LESSON AIMS

After participating in this lesson, each student will be able to:

1. Describe the message of Joel to the people in Israel's southern kingdom (Judah).

2. Make a list of sins and define repentance.

3. Identify a sin in his or her life and plan a private time to repent of it.

Aug
10

KEY VERSES

"Return to me with all your heart, with fasting and weeping and mourning."

Rend your heart and not your garments.

Return to the LORD your God, for he is gracious and compassionate, slow to anger and abounding in love, and he relents from sending calamity.

—Joel 2:12, 13

B. LESSON BACKGROUND

Other than his father's name (Joel 1:1), we know little about Joel himself. As with Obadiah from last week, the spotlight is on God's message. The dating of Joel's message is even more uncertain than that of Obadiah. Some think Joel to be among the earliest of the writing prophets; others think he was one of the latest. If we must guess about this, perhaps a date of about 780 B.C. would be good—during the time of Isaiah and King Uzziah. The prophet Amos, who definitely does live in the time of Uzziah (Amos 1:1), also speaks of locusts (4:9; 7:1-3).

That was a time of immorality and sloth in Israel's history. Here we use the name *Israel* to refer to the southern part of divided Israel—the part with its capital at Jerusalem, the part composed of the tribes of Judah and Benjamin, the part often called Judah. We use the name *Israel* to help us remember that this nation was descended from Jacob, whom God renamed Israel (cf. Joel 2:27; 3:2, 16). If our dating is correct, Joel was preaching heroically to a people so at ease in their "good times" that they paid little heed to the true meaning of that heritage or predictions of doom. God has decided to correct the problem.

I. WARNING OF DESOLATION (JOEL 2:1, 2)

Before we reach this point in Joel, the prophet already has painted a foreboding picture of locusts and great mourning. A call to repentance has been offered (1:13-20). Now the cycle repeats.

A. ANNOUNCING THE DAY OF THE LORD (v. 1)

1. Blow the trumpet in Zion;
     sound the alarm on my holy hill.
  Let all who live in the land tremble,
     for the day of the LORD is coming.
  It is close at hand—

Mount Zion is God's *holy hill*, the site of Jerusalem, the capital of God's holy people. Now *the day of the Lord is coming*, and soon. This is a day of "destruction" (Joel 1:15). It will be "dreadful" (2:11, 31), a day of "decision" (3:14). In Bible times, trumpets are used to *sound* alarms (e.g., Jeremiah 4:5, 19; 6:1, 17). Why would the announcement be an *alarm* to *all who live in the land*? Because the people supposed to be his were not his at all. By their sinning, they have made themselves his enemies: his victory will be their defeat.

The day of the Lord is any time when the Lord's victory and his enemies' defeat are clearly seen. The Lord's true people long for such a time; his enemies should dread it. In the Old Testament we see that God chose the people of Israel to be his people; but all too often they disobey him, and so they become his enemies by their sinning. Consequently, this is not good news for them, as the next verse will make clear.

INTELLIGENT ALARMS

People try various gadgets to keep their cars from being stolen. One of the most irritating is the car alarm. These things produce so many *false* alarms that people largely ignore them when they go off. The really irritating part comes when those devices awaken us at 3:00 A.M.!

But now enter the "intelligent" car alarm, announced in a story by the BBC March 7, 2001. When this alarm is installed, numerous sensors are placed within the car to detect break-in or towing. If the sensors notice questionable activity, the car's transceiver actually telephones the owner to warn of the theft in progress! The whole idea is to make car alarms viable again by overcoming the problem of "bystander apathy."

WHAT DO YOU THINK?

How has God used disasters ("natural" and otherwise) to communicate with people? Does he send disasters today to punish people for sin? Defend your answer.

[See Exodus 8; Luke 13:1-5.]

WHAT DO YOU THINK?

What emotions would you have if you knew that the ultimate "day of the Lord"—the final judgment—were tomorrow? How would you prepare yourself to let go of familiar though imperfect surroundings?

Throughout the history of his people, God has encountered a lot of human apathy in response to his alarms. This has been true regardless of how many alarms he has sounded. But no matter how "intelligent" he makes those alarms, they won't do any good if people are not discerning enough to hear them. Today, do we hear God's warning and take right action, or are we among those who are so apathetic that we cannot "interpret the signs of the times" (Matthew 16:3)?   —R. L. N.

B. DESCRIBING THE DAY OF THE LORD (v. 2)

2. . . . *a day of darkness and gloom,*
   a day of clouds and blackness.
Like dawn spreading across the mountains
   a large and mighty army comes,
such as never was of old
   nor ever will be in ages to come.

The *day* of the Lord will bring no bright joy to Israel. It will be a time of *darkness and gloom*—a time of loss, trouble, and sorrow. The imagery of *clouds* and *blackness* recalls Exodus 10:21, 22 and Deuteronomy 4:11. Most students agree that the imagery here describes the people's mood rather than the weather.

The reason for this gloominess is that the day of the Lord will bring upon Israel *a large and mighty army.* Joel may be using a double reference here. In addition to the literal locusts described in chapter 1, this "mighty army" may refer to an actual invading army of human soldiers. (Judges 6:5 and 7:12 use "grasshoppers" figuratively for "people.")

The description of these invaders—whether they are insects or human or even both—is continued in verses 3-11 (not included in our printed text). They spread like a wildfire, transforming fruitful land into "a desert waste" (v. 3). They seem to be unstoppable (v. 4). Their noise is deafening (v. 5). At their coming "nations are in anguish" (v. 6). No place is safe from them (vv. 7-9). They shake the earth and sky, darken the sun and moon. Perhaps this is a figurative way of saying the people are so shaken that nothing seems secure any more (v. 10; cf. Jeremiah 15:9). The Lord lets his voice be heard. Perhaps by this very prophet he lets it be known that people who persist in evil will have to face this "dreadful" day of the Lord (Joel 2:11).

II. CALLING FOR REPENTANCE (JOEL 2:12-14)

That dreadful day of the Lord, bringing an army of locusts and/or soldiers to punish the people of Israel for their stubborn sin—that day is near, not yet present (2:1). Could it be avoided if the people would repent and change their evil ways, and walk in a path of sincere obedience? (See 2 Chronicles 7:13, 14.) Or was that day too near to be avoided? (Compare Jeremiah 7:16-20; 11:14-17; 14:11, 12.) Must the people endure that coming judgment in order to be motivated to repent and avoid some worse catastrophe? Ultimately, we need not try to decide that question. In either case, God by his prophet is calling Israel to repent.

A. THE CALL (vv. 12, 13a)

12. "*Even now,*" declares the LORD,
   "*return to me with all your heart,*
with fasting and weeping and mourning."

Turning to God means turning away from disobedience and sin. It means humble and obedient service to the Lord. That is repentance. That is what it takes for a sinner to avoid judgment and punishment. No pretended repentance will do. People may be fooled by outward appearance and lying words, but God

HOW TO SAY IT

Amos. AY-mus.
Babylon. BAB-uh-lun.
Deuteronomy. Due-ter-AHN-uh-me.
entomologist. en-tuh-MAWL-uh-jist.
Ezekiel. Ee-ZEEK-ee-ul or Ee-ZEEK-yul.
Isaiah. Eye-ZAY-uh.
Jeremiah. Jair-uh-MY-uh.
Malachi. MAL-uh-kye.
Obadiah. O-buh-DYE-uh.
Pentecost. PENT-ih-kost.
Simeon. SIM-ee-un.
sorghum. SOR-gum.
Uzziah. Uh-ZYE-uh.
Zion. ZYE-un.

WHAT DO YOU THINK?

What happens when we "repent"? How do we demonstrate that we have done so?

[Matthew 5:23, 24 and Luke 19:8 can help stimulate the discussion.]

WHAT DO YOU THINK?

What effects do our prayers have on the will of God? Can we actually change his mind?

[Exodus 32:9-14 is an important example to consider.]

sees the heart (1 Samuel 16:7). Repentance may be expressed *with fasting and weeping and mourning;* but those things are worthless unless you repent sincerely, *with all your heart.* (See Isaiah 58:2-5.)

13a. Rend your heart
    and not your garments.

Tearing one's clothing is a time-honored way of expressing deep sorrow (e.g., Ezra 9:3-5; Esther 4:1-3). But such a visible sign can tell a lie as easily as words can. As David wrote, "a broken and contrite heart, O God, you will not despise" (Psalm 51:17; see also Isaiah 1:11-17; 58:3b-12; Amos 5:21-24; Micah 6:6-8).

B. THE LORD (v. 13b)

13b. Return to the LORD your God,
    for he is gracious and compassionate,
  slow to anger and abounding in love,
    and he relents from sending calamity.

The Bible stresses in several places that *the Lord* is *slow to anger* (e.g., Psalms 86:15; 103:8). He is never vindictive, never malicious. He has no pleasure in the death of one who dies in his or her own sin (Ezekiel 18:32). He cannot forgive a sinner who scorns his mercy and goes on stubbornly in willful sin, but he is eager to forgive one who truly repents. When true repentance takes place, the person turns away from doing evil, so God turns away from sending the punishment that he warned would come. That is how God *relents from sending calamity.*

C. THE HOPE (v. 14)

14. Who knows? He may turn and have pity
    and leave behind a blessing—
  grain offerings and drink offerings
    for the LORD your God.

If people will reject their sin and turn back to God with faith and obedience, perhaps the Lord will *leave behind a blessing* instead of the promised punishment. Instead of destroying the produce of the land, perhaps he will leave it so the people can make to him the offerings required by the law. (See also Exodus 32:14; 2 Samuel 24:16.)

REPENTANCE

Early in the 1989 basketball season, Michigan's Rumeal Robinson stepped to the foul line for two shots late in the fourth quarter. His team trailed Wisconsin by one point. With the game on the line, Rumeal could regain the lead for Michigan. He missed both shots. Michigan was defeated.

Robinson felt awful about costing his team the game, but his sorrow went beyond feelings. He changed his behavior, adding one hundred extra foul shots after each practice for the rest of the season.

Months later Rumeal Robinson stepped to the foul line again. There were just three seconds left in overtime in the game that would decide the national championship. This time he was ready. *Swish* went the first shot. *Swish* went the second. Two made free throws made Michigan the national champions!

Rumeal Robinson demonstrated an important element of genuine repentance. Repentance is not just regret. It is a change of mind and heart that leads to a change in behavior. Genuine sorrow motivated him to work so that he would never make that mistake again.

Paul wrote, "Godly sorrow brings repentance" (2 Corinthians 7:10). God's call to repentance in Joel 2:12, 13 involved both emotions and actions. God wants an internal transformation that is marked by an external reformation. Such repentance

Visual for lesson 11. Today's visual illustrates verse 13. Talk about the changes in one's life that are produced by such a rending of the heart.

opens the door to God's forgiveness and the presence and power of his Spirit. How has repentance changed your life?   —J. A. M.

III. ANTICIPATING THE FUTURE (JOEL 2:28, 29)

Verses 15-17, not in our printed text, continue the call to repent. The people should gather in solemn assembly to make their repentance known (vv. 15, 16). The priests should weep and pray fervently for mercy on the nation (v. 17). Verses 18-20 promise that the Lord then will bless his people with abundant harvests and protect them from enemies. Verses 21-27 call the people to rejoice and to praise the Lord. Prosperity could continue as long as the people would continue to obey the Lord, enjoy his blessing, and give him praise. Then the final verses of our text tell what would follow afterward, centuries later.

A. OUTPOURING OF GOD'S SPIRIT (v. 28)

28. "And afterward,
    I will pour out my Spirit on all people.
Your sons and daughters will prophesy,
    your old men will dream dreams,
    your young men will see visions.

The ideal conditions portrayed in verses 18-27 do not materialize in the time of Joel. Despite the warnings of prophets such as Isaiah and (later) Jeremiah, the Jewish people continue to slide down the slope to exile. A succession of bad kings and false prophets brings the people to such disobedience that God places them under the domination of Babylon for seventy years. When they return from captivity, again they waver between serving and rejecting God. Consequently he sometimes blesses them and sometimes punishes them. After the time of Malachi, it seems that there are no inspired prophets in Israel for about four hundred years. Our text points to a time *afterward*, a time when prophecy again will be abundant.

God's promise to *pour out* his *Spirit on all people* certainly does not mean that God will send his Spirit to make every person a prophet. But some people of every kind would be so gifted: both men and women, *your sons and daughters*, both *old men* and *young men*. Sometimes God used *dreams* and *visions* to convey truths (Obadiah 1; Matthew 1:20). Sometimes he imparted his messages using other methods (1 Kings 19:15; Daniel 5:5, 6; Joel 1:1; Luke 2:8-12). But now he promises a time when his people will be blessed by many prophets who will make his will and his truth known. Even so, Zechariah 13:1-6 also promises that there will come a time when there are no more prophets.

B. SERVANTS, TOO (v. 29)

29. "Even on my servants, both men and women,
    I will pour out my Spirit in those days."

When God pours out his *Spirit*, it will not be just on those of high position and power. The lowly servants and handmaids will receive this gift, too. This outpouring truly is for "all people" (v. 28). As history unfolds, this outpouring will not occur until some eight hundred years after Joel's time. But it will happen— on the Day of Pentecost.

CONCLUSION

A. PROPHETS IN THE NEW TESTAMENT

Very early in the New Testament we begin to read of prophets inspired by God. Before John the Baptist was born, his mother was "filled with the Holy Spirit" and inspired to pronounce on Mary the blessing that is recorded in Luke

WHAT DO YOU THINK?

   All Christians have the gift of the Holy Spirit. But not all believers have had "visions" or prophetic "dreams." So how can they participate in the fulfillment of Joel's prophecy?

PRAYER

Father in Heaven, what a gracious Father you are! How often you have healed our new sin with new forgiveness, that we may be your children still! Grateful for the Word you have given through your prophets, we promise a constant effort to obey it. Grateful for your Spirit living in us, we promise a constant effort to do your will, depending on his help. So in the last great and terrible day of the Lord, may we by your grace escape the everlasting fire and be gathered into your blessed garner forever. In Jesus' name, amen.

1:41-45. It is not stated that Mary's response was specially inspired by God, but who will doubt that it was? (See Luke 1:46-55.) After John was born, his father "was filled with the Holy Spirit and prophesied" as recorded in Luke 1:67-79. John the Baptist was a prophet, and more; he was the messenger foretold by Malachi 3:1, the one who would prepare the way for the Christ (Matthew 11:7-10). Simeon was an inspired prophet when he spoke at the infant Jesus' circumcision (Luke 2:25-35). Anna is plainly called a prophetess (Luke 2:36-38).

Perhaps the most notable record that the Spirit of God was poured out on people is the one recorded in Acts 2:1-12. God poured out his Spirit on the apostles of Jesus. They were under the Spirit's influence so completely that the Spirit used their voices to talk in human languages (Acts 2:8-11) that the apostles had not previously studied. Peter explained, "This is what was spoken by the prophet Joel"; and he quoted several verses from that prophet (Joel 2:28-32; Acts 2:16-21).

God poured out his spirit on others, too, and the Spirit guided them so fully that they spoke God's word, not their own. Read about some of them in Acts 11:27, 28; 15:32; 21:10, 11.

We can hardly conclude this lesson without a glance at the rest of those few words of Joel that are quoted by Simon Peter. Joel's prophecy sweeps past the centuries of the Christian era to "the great and dreadful day of the Lord," the day of final judgment (Joel 2:31; Acts 2:20). That day will be heralded by wonders in earth and sky (Joel 2:30, 31; Mark 13:24, 25; Acts 2:19, 20). Then people on earth will see Jesus "coming . . . with power and great glory" (Matthew 24:30). He will send his angels to reap the harvest of humanity (24:31). He will be "gathering his wheat into the barn and burning up the chaff with unquenchable fire" (3:12). And "everyone who calls on the name of the Lord will be saved" (Joel 2:32; Acts 2:21).

B. CALLING ON THE NAME OF THE LORD

Of course, calling on the name of the Lord includes more than just shouting for help. To the people of Joel's time the Lord said, "Return to me with all your heart, with fasting and weeping and mourning" (Joel 2:12). That means a change in the way of living, sorrow for past sins, and determination not to repeat them.

To the people of his time and ours, Simon Peter says, "Repent" (Acts 2:38). That means turning to God with the whole heart as the people of Joel's time were told to do. Peter also adds, "And be baptized, every one of you, in the name of Jesus Christ for the forgiveness of your sins." If one is sincere in repentance, his or her sins are washed away at the time of baptism (Acts 22:16). Those sins are not removed by water, of course, but by God's gracious forgiveness that is available to us because Christ has paid sin's penalty. From the water of baptism the sincere penitent rises to walk in a new way of life (Romans 6:4).

The result of repentance and baptism is that "you will receive the gift of the Holy Spirit" (Acts 2:38). Of course, God's Spirit does not make every baptized person a prophet like the apostles. But if one's baptism is accompanied by real repentance, the Holy Spirit comes to live within that person (1 Corinthians 3:16). With the Spirit's help he or she can overcome every temptation (1 Corinthians 10:13; James 4:7).

C. PROPHECY FOR TODAY

Do we have prophecy now? Indeed we do. We have the same prophecy the Christians had in New Testament times. We do not see the prophets of that era walking among us, but we hear their voices from the pages of the New Testament. The messages the New Testament writers give us are God's messages. Let's treasure them always, read them over and over, and obey them moment by moment.

THOUGHT TO REMEMBER

With the Holy Spirit helping me, I can do right today.

Discovery Learning

This page contains an alternative lesson plan emphasizing learning activities. Classes desiring such student involvement will find these suggestions helpful. The next page is a reproducible activity page to further enhance discovery learning.

LEARNING GOALS

After participating in this lesson, each student will be able to:

1. Describe the message of Joel to the people in Israel's southern kingdom (Judah).

2. Make a list of sins and define repentance.

3. Identify a sin in his or her life and plan a private time to repent of it.

INTO THE LESSON

ADVANCE PREPARATION: Gather the following supplies: roll of banner paper, markers, index cards, pencils, and pens. Put the key verse on a poster or transparency.

Describe a situation in which someone does something wrong (breaks something valuable, steals a parking place) and then says, "I'm sorry." Say, "Imagine that someone started a false rumor about you. When the person says, 'I'm sorry,' what do you think and feel?" Many students are probably frustrated by the ease with which people use this phrase without any remorse. Our culture has lost the concept of sin; saying "I'm sorry" is supposed to excuse one's mistake.

In today's lesson Joel the prophet calls the people of Israel to repent of their sins to avoid the calamity coming.

INTO THE WORD

Use the commentary to prepare a lecture on the background for this passage, Joel's call to repentance. Explain "the day of the Lord," Judah, Israel, southern kingdom, Zion, and repentance.

Say, "The call to repentance is strong and clear. The people had sinned. The corporate nature of the call reflects how widespread the sin was, and the actions required reflect the culture of Israel. How would a prophet state the call today?" Let students individually or in pairs paraphrase 1:13, 14; 2:12-14. (*They might write sentences such as, "Ministers and church leaders, put on dark clothing and cry to show your sadness. Call everyone to the church building where you will announce a time of fasting" [from Joel 1:13, 14]. "God says, 'Come back to me. Fast and cry. Looking sad or saying "I'm sorry" is not enough. Let your hearts break.' God is kind, merciful, slow to get angry, and loving. He would rather forgive than punish. Perhaps he will change his mind and you will be able to give an offering of thanksgiving" [from Joel 2:12-14].*)

Invite volunteers to read their paraphrases with prophet-like strong voices!

INTO LIFE

Say, "Israel and Judah comprised the chosen nation of God, yet they had turned away from him and were sinning so much they were being called to repent as a community. Joel is talking about national repentance for a nation that was a theocracy. Whether corporate or individual, the dynamics of repentance are the same. We twenty-first century Christians commit sins that could prompt someone to call for repentance with words you wrote as your paraphrase. Since our culture is no longer calling sin by that name, let's identify actions that God would call sin."

Distribute copies of the reproducible page that follows and direct attention to the activity "Modern-Day Sins." Form small groups and give each one Bibles and concordances. The familiar passages listed on the handout can help learners find both sins of commission and sins of omission. Add other passages that could be considered.

Now direct the group's attention to the "A Call to Repentance" section of the reproducible page. Say, "If you are like I am, you can select from our lists more than one sin with which you struggle." Tell students to write a sin on the sheet in the appropriate place. Display Joel 2:12, 13 as you point it out on their sheet: "'Even now,' declares the LORD, 'return to me with all your heart, with fasting and weeping and mourning.' Rend your heart and not your garments. Return to the LORD your God, for he is gracious and compassionate, slow to anger and abounding in love, and he relents from sending calamity." Ask your class to affirm the grand truths revealed in this text. Expect such declarations as the following: "God reveals himself to man"; "God invites wayward man to return to him"; "God is gracious"; "God fully understands our weakness"; "God expects (demands) repentance"; "God abounds in love."

Direct them also to write on the appropriate line of the reproducible page a time that they could and should go to God in repentance. Tell them that when they have repented of that sin and confessed it to God, they should erase or obliterate the sin from the sheet, as a symbol of what God has promised to do. Suggest that they keep and read the verse when they are tempted to commit that sin again.

Modern-Day Sins

Through his prophet Joel, God called the people of Israel to repent. We know from other writings in the Old Testament that the people often worshiped other gods, committed adultery, married people who did not worship God, drank too much, and committed many other sins. As readers in the twenty-first century, we often criticize them and wonder how they could have turned so far from God.

Yet, we also struggle with sin. What sins does God watch us commit today? Write some in the box below.

(Check all these passages: Matthew 5-7; Matthew 18:1-9; Matthew 22:34-40; Matthew 28:18-20; Luke 12:22-40; John 17:20-26; Romans 12; Romans 13; 1 Corinthians 13; 2 Corinthians 5:16-21; 2 Corinthians 5:14-18; Galatians 5:19-26; Galatians 6:1-10; Ephesians 4:17-32; Ephesians 5:1, 2; Philippians 2:1-4; Philippians 2:14-16; Colossians 3; 1 Thessalonians 5:12-22; Titus 2:1-10; Hebrews 10:19-31; Hebrews 13:1-6; James 1:19-27; 2:1-14; 3:9; 1 Peter 1:13-16.)

A Call to Repentance

Like the people of Israel, I too have sinned. I _____. I must remember that the Lord has said,

> "Even now," declares the LORD, "return to me with all your heart, with fasting and weeping and mourning." Rend your heart and not your garments. Return to the LORD your God, for he is gracious and compassionate, slow to anger and abounding in love, and he relents from sending calamity" (Joel 2:12, 13).

A good time for me to repent and confess my sin to God is

(Consider clipping the verse and using it as a Bible book mark.)

PROMISE TO THE FAITHFUL

LESSON 12

WHY TEACH THIS LESSON?

A few years ago a national newspaper carried a story of a man who was changing jobs to go to work for a competitor. The man's boss tried to persuade him not to leave by appealing to his sense of loyalty. The appeal didn't work. On his way out the door the man sneered, "If you want loyalty, get a dog!"

Probably there are some in your class who have been the victims of a lack of loyalty. Perhaps they have been laid off from their place of work after many years of service. Or maybe a friend has breached a confidence. No doubt there are some who have felt the sting of divorce. For them and those who have experienced other injustices, this lesson will give reassurance. How thankful we can be that God is always faithful and loyal to his people! Today's lesson provides a great opportunity to reflect on God's faithfulness and recommit to our own.

INTRODUCTION

A. WHOSE SIDE ARE YOU ON?

The story is told of an elderly gentleman who, in spite of failing health, did his best to attend Sunday morning services in his church. Regardless of how poorly he felt or how bad the weather was, he never missed a Sunday. Out of a concern for the man's health and safety, someone in the church told him one day, "People realize how hard it is for you to get out some Sunday mornings. They would understand if you missed worship occasionally."

The elderly man replied, "Perhaps they would. But I want to make it clear to everyone whose side I'm on."

God always has desired a relationship with humanity. Our sin has severed that relationship. It has put us on the wrong side. Malachi called the people of God back to God's side. His message calls to us with the same plea.

B. LESSON BACKGROUND

Unlike most of the other prophetic books in the Old Testament, the book of Malachi does not mention the name of any king at the beginning that would help us date the book. In order to arrive at the time of Malachi's ministry, it is necessary to search for clues within the book itself.

Those clues point to the days of Nehemiah, primarily because many of the sins highlighted in the book of Malachi are the same sins that Nehemiah had to confront. These include indifference toward the kind of sacrifices required by the Lord (Malachi 1:6-14; Nehemiah 10:37-39), disregard for the Lord's teaching concerning marriage (Malachi 2:14-16; Nehemiah 13:23-27), and the bringing of tithes and offerings to support the Lord's work (Malachi 3:8-10; Nehemiah 10:37-39; 13:10-13). In addition, the mention of a "governor" (Malachi 1:8) fits well with this time, since that was a title given to Nehemiah (Nehemiah 5:14).

From our studies so far this quarter we know that Nehemiah journeyed to Jerusalem in the twentieth year of Artaxerxes (445 B.C.). He came primarily to spearhead efforts to rebuild the wall of the city (Nehemiah 2:1-3, 11). This was almost one hundred years after the Jews had first returned from captivity in Babylon. After

DEVOTIONAL READING:
PSALM 90:1-17
BACKGROUND SCRIPTURE:
MALACHI 3, 4
PRINTED TEXT:
MALACHI 3:1-4, 16-18; 4:1-6

LESSON AIMS

After participating in this lesson, each student will be able to:

1. Explain the day of the Lord's coming, summarizing the outcomes for the evildoers and the outcomes for those who fear God's name.

2. Recognize the Messianic nature of this text.

3. Pray, throughout the week, for one person who is an evildoer and one person who is apathetic toward the future.

Aug
17

KEY VERSE

"You will again see the distinction between the righteous and the wicked, between those who serve God and those who do not." —Malachi 3:18

LESSON 12 NOTES

a twelve-year period of service, Nehemiah returned to Babylon (13:6). Following an unspecified length of time, he received permission to return to Jerusalem. Upon his arrival, he learned of the abuses noted above.

Exactly where Malachi's ministry fits with Nehemiah's is difficult to determine. Some believe that Malachi came forward to challenge the people during Nehemiah's absence when he had to return to Babylon. Others suggest that his ministry began during Nehemiah's second term as governor of Judah, and that Malachi's efforts served to support those of Nehemiah. Regardless of the specific time or number of years involved in Malachi's service, his ministry may be dated to approximately 430 B.C. This makes him the last of the Old Testament prophets. While he addressed the problems of his own day, Malachi, like other prophets, was used by the Spirit of God to foretell what God would bring to pass. This "promise to the faithful" is the heart of today's lesson.

I. THE LORD'S COMING (MALACHI 3:1-4)

A. WITH PREPARATION (v. 1)

1. *"See, I will send my messenger, who will prepare the way before me. Then suddenly the Lord you are seeking will come to his temple; the messenger of the covenant, whom you desire, will come," says the* LORD *Almighty.*

God's promise to *send* his *messenger* calls attention to the name *Malachi*, which in Hebrew means "my messenger." Thus, while Malachi serves as God's spokesman to communicate his will to his people, he is also pointing toward another messenger *who will prepare the way before* the Lord. The Christian cannot read these words without thinking of the ministry of John the Baptist, who called himself "A voice of one calling in the desert, 'Prepare the way for the Lord, make straight paths for him'" (Luke 3:4; cf. Isaiah 40:3).

This promise highlights the failure of certain contemporary "messengers" of the Lord to fulfill the task he has given them. Some of Malachi's sternest words are directed toward the priests of his day, who are supposed to be models of uprightness and holiness (Malachi 2:7). But what ought to have been and what really was are two different matters (2:8). So God planned to send another messenger, one who would not fail in accomplishing the task given him.

Once he had fulfilled his assigned role, the promised messenger would yield to the one for whose coming he had prepared. *Then suddenly the Lord you are seeking will come to his temple.* Nearly one hundred years earlier, the prophet Haggai had used similar language in his own prediction of the Messiah's coming (see Haggai 2:7). Those who had returned from captivity in Babylon had built the very temple that Jesus would enter when he came to Jerusalem (though by then it would be embellished significantly with the support of King Herod the Great). The word *suddenly* implies a time or manner that is unexpected and often accompanied by disastrous consequences for those caught unprepared (Mark 13:35, 36).

In addition, Malachi describes the Lord as *the messenger of the covenant.* Malachi is referring to two covenants made by the Lord. The first was with Levi (that is, the priesthood), a covenant that had been "violated" by the priests of Malachi's day (Malachi 2:8). The second is found in 2:10, where Malachi asks, "Why do we profane the covenant of our fathers by breaking faith with one another?" Apparently this refers to the covenant God had made with Israel at Mount Sinai, which was now being "profaned." Clearly a new covenant is in order.

Jesus came to usher in that New Covenant—one far superior to the old one. This is the theme of the book of Hebrews. Thus we are presented with a threefold "messenger" emphasis: the messenger Malachi, who announced the coming of the messenger John the Baptist, who in turn prepared the way for the messenger Jesus.

WHAT DO YOU THINK?

The Lord mentions his covenant several times in Malachi. What significance do you see in that?

B. WITH POWER (v. 2)

2. But who can endure the day of his coming? Who can stand when he appears? For he will be like a refiner's fire or a launderer's soap.

These questions are to be considered "rhetorical"—that is, they are more of a challenge to think than to give a verbal response. Those who have so flippantly asked, "Where is the God of justice?" (2:17) will see what it is like to have their question answered. The refining *fire* is used to burn away impurities from precious metals. *Soap*, at this time, is an alkaline lye used to bleach dirty garments white.

The message of these word pictures is that when the Lord comes, he will come to make changes in people's lives. (Compare Mark 9:3; Revelation 3:5.) He will want to purify and cleanse them, with the purpose of obtaining the results described in the next two verses.

C. WITH PURPOSE (vv. 3, 4)

3, 4. He will sit as a refiner and purifier of silver; he will purify the Levites and refine them like gold and silver. Then the LORD will have men who will bring offerings in righteousness, and the offerings of Judah and Jerusalem will be acceptable to the LORD, as in days gone by, as in former years.

The Lord's refining and cleansing ministry will focus primarily on *the Levites*. They already have been exposed as violators of the covenant that the Lord made with their ancestor Levi (Malachi 2:1-5). As noted in the Introduction, one of the concerns of both Nehemiah and Malachi was the abuses of the sacrificial system. Here the Lord cites the real problem: it is not just the offerings that are defective, it is also those who bring them!

An important characteristic of the New Covenant is that everyone who is part of the covenant has Levitical duties to fulfill. Everyone is considered a priest (1 Peter 2:9; Revelation 1:6). All Christians are called to offer the sacrifices of praise and of good works (Hebrews 13:15, 16). Participating in the New Covenant will make *the offerings of Judah and Jerusalem . . . acceptable to the Lord.* The situation will be radically different from Malachi's day, when God declared, "'I am not pleased with you,' says the Lord Almighty, 'and I will accept no offering from your hands.'" (Malachi 1:10). The term *Jerusalem* should be understood in its New Covenant sense; the "heavenly Jerusalem" is the "church of the first-born" (Hebrews 12:22, 23).

II. THE LORD'S PEOPLE (MALACHI 3:16-18)

A. SPEAKING TO EACH OTHER (v. 16)

16. Then those who feared the LORD talked with each other, and the LORD listened and heard. A scroll of remembrance was written in his presence concerning those who feared the LORD and honored his name.

Some of the people have spoken "harsh" words against God (Malachi 3:13). But there apparently are those among God's people who do not agree with those naysayers. The Lord always has had those among his people who have refused to bow to the spirit of negativity and pessimism, whether it be the seven thousand in Elijah's day (1 Kings 19:18) or those in Malachi's day. Here, those who *feared the Lord talked with each other,* perhaps offering words of mutual encouragement. As a result, *the Lord listened and heard* it.

The mention of *a scroll of remembrance* calls to mind the familiar book of life, which God is described as opening at the final judgment (Revelation 20:12, 15). Here it appears to be a way for those who fear the Lord to commemorate their commitment and express their loyalty to him. What joy this book must have brought to the Lord—and to his messenger Malachi!

WHAT DO YOU THINK?

What can we do to prepare for "the day of [the Lord's] coming"? What extremes should we avoid?

[Use Galatians 5:25; 1 Thessalonians 5:4-11; and 2 Peter 3:11, 12 to assist in the discussion.]

HOW TO SAY IT

Abraham. AY-bruh-ham.
Artaxerxes. Are-tuh-ZERK-sees.
Babylon. BAB-uh-lun.
Elijah. Ee-LYE-juh.
Haggai. HAG-eye or HAG-ay-eye.
Herod. HAIR-ud.
Horeb. HO-reb.
Jeremiah. Jair-uh-MY-uh.
Jerusalem. Juh-ROO-suh-lem.
Levi. LEE-vye.
Levites. LEE-vites.
Levitical. Leh-VIT-ih-kul.
Malachi. MAL-uh-kye.
Messianic. Mess-ee-AN-ick.
Nehemiah. NEE-huh-MY-uh.
Sinai. SIGH-nye or SIGH-nay-eye.
Zechariah. ZEK-uh-RYE-uh.

"Discern... between him that serveth God and him that serveth him not."
—Malachi 3:18

This visual illustrates Malachi 3:18. Challenge students to think of specific ways they "serve God."

B. SECURED BY THE LORD (v. 17)

17. "They will be mine," says the LORD Almighty, "in the day when I make up my treasured possession. I will spare them, just as in compassion a man spares his son who serves him.

God then gives a special promise to those who have chosen to honor his name: *they will be mine, . . . in the day when I make up my treasured possession.* God referred to his people in the same way when he spoke at Mount Sinai (Exodus 19:5). Those who are part of the Lord's "treasured possession" sparkle in the exemplary way that they serve and honor him (cf. Malachi 1:6). Judgment day will show that, in contrast to Malachi's pessimistic hearers, it is *not* "futile to serve God" (3:14). Here Malachi's words seem to anticipate the *day* of judgment when the Lord will make a clear distinction between the righteous and the wicked, as the next verse shows.

SECURING AN INFRASTRUCTURE

Following the terrorist attacks of September 11, 2001, *security* was something that everyone desperately wanted but nobody seemed to have. Suddenly, all of America seemed vulnerable. Even the parts that weren't attacked, such as the Internet, did not seem as secure as they once appeared to be.

In truth, America's computer networks have never been very secure. Yet the disruptions in air traffic control, delivery of electrical power, and financial services that could result from a successful "cyberterrorism" attack are massive! In 1997, the President's Commission on Critical Infrastructure Protection noted how much the world's economy increasingly depends on the Internet and its data lines.

So government and industry leaders are working hard to protect that vital infrastructure. But nothing in this world ever will be 100 percent "secure." By contrast, what a comfort it is to have God's secure promise, "they will be mine"! But this promise is only for those whose "spiritual infrastructure" is grounded in Jesus Christ.

Is yours?

—R. L. N.

C. SEPARATED FROM THE WICKED (v. 18)

18. "And you will again see the distinction between the righteous and the wicked, between those who serve God and those who do not."

One of Jesus' most striking images of the judgment day is that of a shepherd dividing the sheep from the goats (Matthew 25:31-46). There clearly is no middle ground; no "hybrids" will be found before God's judgment throne! Concerning that day, the task of Christians is clear: to prepare people for Jesus' second coming, just as John the Baptist prepared people for his first one.

III. THE LORD'S PLAN (MALACHI 4:1-6)

A. FOR THE WICKED (v. 1)

1. "Surely the day is coming; it will burn like a furnace. All the arrogant and every evildoer will be stubble, and that day that is coming will set them on fire," says the LORD Almighty. "Not a root or a branch will be left to them.

This verse elaborates on what will happen to the wicked who are mentioned in Malachi 3:18. Whereas God will spare those who have served him (3:17), the *arrogant* and *every evildoer* will be treated as *stubble* and will not be spared from the Lord's wrath (cf. Matthew 3:12).

Interestingly, previous judgments on God's people usually had left a "root" or a "branch," which became one of the names for the promised Messiah (Isaiah 4:2; 11:1; Jeremiah 23:5). But this judgment declared by Malachi will be so complete that *not a root or a branch will be left to them.*

WHAT DO YOU THINK?

How were God's people to distinguish between "righteous and wicked" in Old Testament times? How can we use this pattern in the New Testament era as we interact with non-Christians?

[Passages such as Leviticus 11:44, 45; Matthew 6:31, 32; 2 Corinthians 6:14; and 1 Peter 1:15, 16 can help guide your discussion.]

B. FOR THE RIGHTEOUS (vv. 2, 3)

2. *"But for you who revere my name, the sun of righteousness will rise with healing in its wings. And you will go out and leap like calves released from the stall.*

Many will recognize these words as part of one of the verses in the Christmas carol, "Hark! the Herald Angels Sing." Whereas the wicked will experience the burning heat associated with the Lord's wrath, the righteous will experience another kind of heat from Heaven: the warmth of God's *sun of righteousness*. Jesus is that "Sun" who *will rise with healing in its wings*. The term *wings* refers to the rays of the sun, as in Psalm 139:9.

Similar language is used by Zechariah, father of John the Baptist, when, in the Spirit-filled proclamation that followed the naming of his son, he speaks of the coming of the "rising sun . . . from heaven" (Luke 1:78). Like newborn *calves* just released from their *stall* into the bright sunlight, God's people will rejoice in all the Lord has done for them.

3. *"Then you will trample down the wicked; they will be ashes under the soles of your feet on the day when I do these things," says the LORD Almighty.*

Often in this fallen, sinful world it appears that *the wicked* are those who have the upper hand (or foot, in this case). They *trample down* the righteous with the utmost scorn. That situation will be reversed, however, in God's own time. In keeping with the image of fire and burning, the wicked are described as harmless *ashes under the soles* of the *feet* of the righteous. (Compare Micah 2:12, 13.)

C. FINAL CHALLENGE (vv. 4-6)

4. *"Remember the law of my servant Moses, the decrees and laws I gave him at Horeb for all Israel.*

While God's prophets in the Old Testament spoke of the glorious things that he would do for his people in the future, they also called their hearers to recall their historical roots as a people—to *remember the law* of God's *servant Moses*, given to him at Horeb (another name for Mount Sinai). The neglect of those roots—the failure to obey the *decrees and laws* received from God through Moses—had produced nothing but chaos and heartache for God's people. They do not need a new message from Heaven; they need to renew their allegiance to the one they have ignored.

5. *"See, I will send you the prophet Elijah before that great and dreadful day of the LORD comes.*

This promise is similar to the one of the "messenger" who would prepare the way for the Lord (cf. Malachi 3:1). Here that messenger is called *Elijah*. Jesus' words in Matthew 17:10-13 make it clear that this prophecy of Malachi was fulfilled in John the Baptist. The angel Gabriel told Zechariah that his son John would serve "in the spirit and power of Elijah" (Luke 1:17). This would take place *before that great and dreadful day of the Lord*. Malachi already has highlighted the judgment events associated with that day. Now he states that this day will not come without proper warning. However, it is the duty of God's people today (the church) to sound the warning and prepare sinners for the great and dreadful day that will surely come.

If we do not, who will?

6. *"He will turn the hearts of the fathers to their children, and the hearts of the children to their fathers; or else I will come and strike the land with a curse."*

Here Malachi describes what "Elijah" will achieve when he comes. Luke 1:17, previously mentioned, links these same words to the ministry of John the Baptist. There, however, the turning of *the hearts of the children to their fathers* is replaced with turning "the disobedient to the wisdom of the righteous."

WHAT DO YOU THINK?

Think about a situation that made you wonder whether God really cared about the righteous. How can people maintain their faith in God during such times? [Note Psalm 73.]

WHAT DO YOU THINK?

What things are we to "remember" in the New Testament era? Why?

[Two things, among many, are found in 1 Corinthians 11:24, 25 and 2 Timothy 2:8.]

DAILY BIBLE READINGS

Monday, Aug. 11—*A Priest Should Guard Knowledge (Malachi 2:1-9)*

Tuesday, Aug. 12—*The Lord's Messenger Will Refine (Malachi 3:1-5)*

Wednesday, Aug. 13—*Return to Me (Malachi 3:6-12)*

Thursday, Aug. 14—*The Lord's Special Possession (Malachi 3:13-18)*

Friday, Aug. 15—*The Sun of Righteousness Shall Rise (Malachi 4:1-6)*

Saturday, Aug. 16—*God's Steadfast Love (Psalm 89:19-29)*

Sunday, Aug. 17—*God Will Keep His Covenant (Psalm 89:30-37)*

PRAYER

Father, help us to make each day count in your service. May it be clear to all that we are on your side and that we have no regrets for having chosen to follow Jesus. In his name, amen.

THOUGHT TO REMEMBER

The best way to be ready for the day of the Lord is to be faithful to the Lord of that day.

While the term *fathers* may be used in a parental sense, it is also possible to see it as a reference to the forefathers or ancestors of Israel. There was a huge gap between these godly men and religious leaders in John the Baptist's day. Those leaders, while claiming to be children of Abraham, were really children of the devil (John 8:33, 39, 44). John came to appeal to such resistant hearts in order to prepare them for the coming of Jesus.

Many Bible students have called attention to the fact that the Old Testament ends with the word *curse*. This word well summarizes humanity's plight under the law of Moses. Although holy and just, that law was not able to provide salvation for sinners "in that it was weakened by the sinful nature" (Romans 8:3). Thus the conclusion of the Old Testament set the stage for the one who would come to deliver us from the curse of sin and death (cf. Galatians 3:10-13). Because of Jesus, the New Testament concludes, not with a curse, but with a blessing: "Blessed are those who wash their robes, that they may go through he gates into the city" (Revelation 22:14). True, there is a warning at the end of the New Testament as well (22:18, 19), but it is grace that has the final say.

PROPER FOCUS

Before he became what *Newsweek* called a "commercial supernova," John Grisham was an unknown, small-town lawyer. Then his novels *The Firm, Pelican Brief, The Client,* and others catapulted him to celebrity status. Grisham works to keep a proper focus on meaningful things, particularly his faith in God.

As a young law student Grisham was confronted with the inevitability of death. One of his best friends in college died of cancer at age twenty-five. Shortly before his death, Grisham's buddy took him to lunch and revealed his disease.

John Grisham asked his friend, "What do you do when you realize you are about to die?"

"It's real simple," he said. "You get things right with God, and you spend as much time with those you love as you can. Then you settle up with everybody else."

Finally he said, "You know, really, you ought to live every day like you have only a few more days to live." Those words were never forgotten.

Malachi's prophecy spells out several promises God makes to the faithful. His return and judgment are certain. How should we live in light of God's promises?

Death is a certainty. So is the return of Jesus. These realities call us to evaluate. Are you living your life with the proper focus? —J. A. M.

CONCLUSION

In thinking about how to apply today's lesson, "Promise to the Faithful," it may be helpful to reverse the words and think about the phrase "Faithful to the Promise." Do we, like the people in Malachi's day, need to return to our roots? Have we forgotten the promise we made when we first gave our lives to Christ? Have we lost the zeal we possessed when that happened? (If so, can we determine why that has happened?) Is it clear whose side we are on? As someone once asked, "If you were arrested and charged with being a Christian, would there be enough evidence to convict you?"

Skeptics sometimes have stated, rather defiantly, "If I had the chance to speak with God, here's what I would say to him." They then proceed to list all the complaints that they would lodge about various issues. It is far more profitable to consider what God will say to us when we face him at the Day of Judgment. We want to hear him say, "Well done, good and *faithful* servant" (Matthew 25:21).

Therefore, "Let us hold unswervingly to the hope we profess, for he who promised is faithful" (Hebrews 10:23).

Discovery Learning

This page contains an alternative lesson plan emphasizing learning activities. Classes desiring such student involvement will find these suggestions helpful. The next page is a reproducible activity page to further enhance discovery learning.

LEARNING GOALS

After participating in this lesson, each student will be able to:

1. Explain the day of the Lord's coming, summarizing the outcomes for the evildoers and the outcomes for those who fear God's name.

2. Recognize the Messianic nature of this text.

3. Pray, throughout the week, for one person who is an evildoer and one person who is apathetic toward the future.

INTO THE LESSON

Prior to the beginning of the lesson, ask a person who is not in this class to enter your class about five minutes after it starts. Have him dress as a contemporary courier (a bike messenger perhaps), an Old Testament prophet (Malachi), or even as John the Baptist.

During the first five minutes ask students to respond to the question, "What does the future hold for you?" Enter into a discussion that addresses many different time horizons (from the immediate future to the distant future) and social contexts (individual, family, community, national, and others).

When the "messenger" enters your class, he should read the assigned text, Malachi 3:1-4, 16-18; 4:1-4. Recalling lesson 8, the "messenger" may ask the students to stand for this important message.

INTO THE WORD

Direct students to read quickly through today's text. Ask a student to read Exodus 23:20-26. Have each student list on paper the similarities they see and hear between this text and the text being studied today (especially Malachi 3:1). The list will include such items as the fact that God will send a messenger or angel and that he will guard or prepare the way. Note that the language—very similar in Hebrew—ties these texts closely together. The Exodus passage promises a victory that God provides for his people. The Malachi text, by parallel, does the same thing. However, the Malachi text, clearly Messianic in nature, promises an eternal victory through Jesus.

Ask students to tell about the nature of Christ's coming and what will happen to those who do evil and those who fear God's name according to this text. Ask them to identify similar ideas in the Gospels.

INTO LIFE

Ask students to identify several high-profile people throughout history who can be identified as primarily good or evil in their actions. (*Some examples associated with evil behavior are Hitler, Stalin, Timothy McVeigh, Osama bin Laden. Examples of those associated with good behavior are Mother Theresa, Christian missionaries, and others.*) Write these on a display board. Next to the names, place three columns headed "short-term," "long-term," and "eternity."

Ask the students what consequences each of the people or groups listed have experienced as a result of their behaviors. (*Stalin lived a life of relative luxury and authority until his death; McVeigh died exactly as he wanted to; Mother Teresa suffered hardships during her life of service.*) Have learners read and compare these people's actions to Matthew 25:31-46.

Say, "It is common for evildoers to reap short-term benefits while God-fearers seem to suffer or at least not benefit from the world's perspective." Ask for personal examples at this point. Point out that we can judge the behaviors and some of the short- and long-term consequences but that we are not in a position to judge eternal consequences.

Use the reproducible page that follows as a way to get learners to summarize the discussions of good and evil people. When you get to the activity "The Appearance of Me," suggest that learners use this one day in the coming week as a meditation on personal righteousness and as a commitment to resemble more and more the righteousness of Christ.

Finally, prepare for a time of prayer. Ask each student to write down the name of someone he knows who is an evildoer and the name of someone who is apathetic or arrogant with regard to the eternal future. Provide a short time for the students to pray for these individuals silently. Close with a prayer for all who are behaving in such a way as to be outside God's kingdom for eternity.

At the close of the lesson ask the students to commit to praying for one week for the two people whom they chose. Remind the students that just as God protected the way of his people in Exodus and promised (in Malachi) to prepare the way for Christ, Jesus promised to prepare a place in his Father's house for those who trust in God (fear his name). Read John 14:1-6, emphasizing vv. 2, 3.

The Appearance of Evil

You may either draw a picture, paste a magazine picture, clip a newspaper article, or list characteristics to answer each of the questions below.

What does an evildoer look like?

The Appearance of Good

What does a God-fearer look like?

The Appearance of Me

What do I look like? In what ways do I resemble an evildoer? In what ways do I resemble a God-fearer? In what ways can and will I be changing my appearance to look more and more like Christ?

God Restores a Remnant

Unit 3: Repentance
(Lessons 10-14)

PROPHECY OF AN ETERNAL KINGDOM

LESSON 13

WHY TEACH THIS LESSON?

In less than three weeks the United States will mark the second anniversary of the terrorist attacks of September 11, 2001. On that day, terrorists hijacked four U.S. jetliners and crashed three of them into public buildings—two at the World Trade Center in New York and one at the Pentagon in Washington, DC. The fourth crashed in Pennsylvania when passengers overpowered the hijackers so that the plane would never reach its target. More than three thousand people died.

The attacks shocked Americans and left them with a foreboding sense of uncertainty. Safety seemed an illusion. The stock market plunged. Airport security procedures were overhauled. And America went to war to bring the terrorists to justice or to bring justice to the terrorists.

In many ways that uncertainty persists. As long as we depend on governments and other human institutions, it always will. Today's lesson will assure your learners that there is a source of real security. Our God is greater than any nation or its problems. He is God of time and eternity. The power of nations pales in comparison to him. Encourage your learners to put their confidence in the Lord.

INTRODUCTION

A. HOMESICKNESS

During a ministry with a church in Indiana, I served occasionally as dean for a "Beginner Week" at an area Christian service camp. This week was for children going into the third grade of school, and it lasted for only two-and-a-half days—from Sunday afternoon until Tuesday evening after dinner.

For some of the children, this experience was the first time they had ever been away from home for any length of time. Some had never spent even one night away from home. So there was always the possibility that some would begin to suffer pangs of homesickness—in some cases, even before it was time to go to bed on Sunday night. Camp counselors did their best to encourage the timid to "hang in there." We figured that if we could get a child past Sunday night and into Monday morning, we probably were "over the hump," because then we could assure them, "Tomorrow night you'll be home."

Just imagine a child (or anyone, for that matter) being taken from home and having to face the possibility of *never* returning! This was the bitter prospect faced by Daniel and his three companions as they were taken from their home in Judah to become captives in Babylon. True, they were probably older than third-graders (some believe they were around age fifteen or sixteen), but the ordeal they had to endure would have been nightmarish for anyone.

What kept these youths from giving in to despair and gloom? How were they able to rise above their circumstances? They knew that although they had been taken captive, their God could not be. He was still King, even in Babylon.

DEVOTIONAL READING:
REVELATION 21:1-7
BACKGROUND SCRIPTURE:
DANIEL 2
PRINTED TEXT:
DANIEL 2:26, 36-45

LESSON AIMS

After participating in this lesson, each student will be able to:

1. Retell Nebuchadnezzar's dream and its interpretation.

2. Explain God's eternal kingdom and his role in history.

3. Describe God's role in history to a non-Christian.

KEY VERSE

"In the time of those kings, the God of heaven will set up a kingdom that will never be destroyed, nor will it be left to another people. It will crush all those kingdoms and bring them to an end, but it will itself endure forever."
—Daniel 2:44

Aug
24

B. LESSON BACKGROUND

Last week's lesson was drawn from the book of the prophet Malachi, whom we suggested was serving as God's prophet during the time of Nehemiah (around 430 B.C.). The book of Daniel, from which the final two lessons in this quarter are taken, records events that took place before Malachi's time. The first date mentioned in the book is the "third year of the reign of Jehoiakim king of Judah," when King Nebuchadnezzar of Babylon came and besieged Jerusalem (Daniel 1:1). This would have been about 605 B.C.

We should note that *"the Lord* delivered Jehoiakim king of Judah into [Nebuchadnezzar's] hand" (1:2). From a purely secular standpoint, Nebuchadnezzar's efforts might be seen as a demonstration of Babylon's military superiority over the ill-equipped forces of Judah. But in truth, the Lord was bringing his promise of judgment to pass against a disobedient, rebellious people.

While the Babylonians were known for their brutal treatment of the peoples whom they overpowered, there was also a more rational or practical side to their conquests. This involved taking young men who had great potential for service in the Babylonian administration and "educating" them in the culture of the Babylonians. This was the position in which Daniel and his three friends found themselves.

Right from the start of their captivity, Daniel and his friends demonstrated exemplary faith in their God. Daniel 1:17 records God's special provision for them: "To these four young men God gave knowledge and understanding of all kinds of literature. And Daniel could understand visions and dreams of all kinds."

This unique ability to understand visions and dreams brought Daniel to prominence in a culture where dreams were thought to communicate significant messages. When King Nebuchadnezzar had a dream on one occasion, he first consulted his own "wise men" to get the interpretation. They requested that the king tell the contents of the dream so that they could concoct an "interpretation" of it (2:4). The king refused—he expected the "wise men" to give him the content of the dream as well as the interpretation (2:5-9).

When Daniel learned of the king's dilemma and of his intention to kill all the wise men (including Daniel and his friends), he spoke with his friends. Together they brought the matter to God in prayer. That night "the mystery was revealed to Daniel in a vision" (2:19). Armed with what the real King had shown him, Daniel requested an audience with Nebuchadnezzar.

I. A KING'S EXPECTATION (DANIEL 2:26)

26. The king asked Daniel (also called Belteshazzar), "Are you able to tell me what I saw in my dream and interpret it?"

Daniel received the Babylonian name *Belteshazzar* soon after his arrival in Babylon (1:7). It means, "O Bel, protect his life!" (Bel is one of the fictitious Babylonian gods.) *Belteshazzar* is not to be confused with *Belshazzar*, the king who saw the handwriting on the wall in Daniel 5.

King Nebuchadnezzar is troubled, and he wants to be sure that Daniel can address two issues. First, is Daniel able to know the content of the *dream*? Second, what does the dream mean?

Before giving the content and interpretation that God had revealed to him, Daniel wants the king to know about the source of the information about to be conveyed. Six times within verses 27-30, Daniel uses either a form of the word "reveal" or a form of *show* or *know* to emphasize that neither he nor any human being is responsible for what the king is about to hear. Only the "God in heaven who reveals secrets" (v. 28) can do what the king has asked.

WHAT DO YOU THINK?

Daniel was prepared to serve a pagan king in a pagan culture without compromising his faith. How is this an example for us today? How can we be "salt" and "light" (Matthew 5:13-16) without becoming "polluted by the world" (James 1:27)?

WHAT DO YOU THINK?

Daniel was careful to give God the credit for his ability to tell Nebuchadnezzar what the king wanted to know. How can we be more vocal about giving God credit for his role in our lives?

II. DANIEL'S EXPLANATION (DANIEL 2:36-45)

A. THE HEAD OF GOLD (vv. 36-38)

36. *"This was the dream, and now we will interpret it to the king.*

After describing *the dream* itself in verses 31-35, Daniel undoubtedly has the king's full attention. By saying *we will interpret it* Daniel makes clear that he is not performing a "solo" before *the king.* It is the one true God who has revealed both the contents of the king's dream and its interpretation.

37. *"You, O king, are the king of kings. The God of heaven has given you dominion and power and might and glory;*

The title *king of kings* is one that we normally give to Jesus (Revelation 19:16). Here Daniel uses it to call attention to Nebuchadnezzar's status as one of the most renowned rulers of the ancient world. Nebuchadnezzar's achievements in expanding Babylonian power and in enhancing the splendor of Babylon itself are impressive. Yet in spite of such credentials, this great man is only a steward. Whatever he has accomplished and whatever he has become have been *given* to him by *the God of Heaven*—the same God who has revealed to Daniel the content and the meaning of his dream.

38. *. . . in your hands he has placed mankind and the beasts of the field and the birds of the air. Wherever they live, he has made you ruler over them all. You are that head of gold.*

This verse calls to mind David's declaration of God's provisions for humanity in Psalm 8:6-8. The God of Heaven is the one who abundantly blesses Nebuchadnezzar, though often he sees himself as the primary reason for his power and success (see Daniel 4:30-37).

Nebuchadnezzar's dream consists of a "great image" (2:31) or statue. One can wonder at the king's reaction to find out that he himself is that statue's *head of gold.* Some suggest that Nebuchadnezzar's later construction of a golden image (3:1) is the result of his pride causing him to misapply the message of his dream.

B. TWO INFERIOR KINGDOMS (v. 39)

39. *"After you, another kingdom will rise, inferior to yours. Next, a third kingdom, one of bronze, will rule over the whole earth.*

Beside having a head of gold, the statue in the dream has a chest and arms made of silver (2:32) and a belly and thighs made of *bronze.* Instead of representing a king, as the head of gold had done, each of these metals stands for *another kingdom.* As silver and bronze are *inferior* metals to gold, so each of these kingdoms will be inferior to Nebuchadnezzar's.

The kingdom represented by the chest and arms of silver is the Medo-Persian empire, which took control from Babylon in 539 B.C. under Cyrus (cf. Isaiah 45:1). The two arms may represent the two major peoples who joined to form this empire: the Medes and the Persians (cf. Daniel 6:8, 12, 15). The territory controlled by Cyrus was far greater than what the Babylonians ruled. However, Nebuchadnezzar's empire was superior in terms of its lasting impact on history.

The bronze kingdom represents the Greco-Macedonian kingdom established by Alexander the Great (cf. 8:20, 21), who dies in 323 B.C. Through Alexander's relentless efforts, his empire expands *over the whole earth*—at least, as far as the earth is believed to extend at the time.

C. A KINGDOM STRONG AS IRON (v. 40)

40. *"Finally, there will be a fourth kingdom, strong as iron—for iron breaks and smashes everything—and as iron breaks things to pieces, so it will crush and break all the others.*

WHAT DO YOU THINK?

Nebuchadnezzar was a great king, and no one could doubt his accomplishments. Still, our lesson writer calls him a "steward" of what had been given to him by the God of Heaven. How can understanding that we are stewards help us to live as Christians today?

[See 1 Corinthians 3:6, 7; 4:2, 7; Philippians 2:12, 13.]

Legs of *iron* also are part of the statue in Nebuchadnezzar's dream (2:33). The *fourth kingdom* represented by this portion of the statue is the Roman Empire. Iron is an appropriate symbol for the might of Rome, which breaks *to pieces* all the existing kingdoms and ultimately incorporates them under Roman control.

Rome's "iron rule" perhaps is best illustrated by the actions of the Roman general Pompey, who conquered Jerusalem following a three-month siege in 63 B.C. After massacring Jewish priests during the performance of their duties, Pompey and his men defiantly entered the Most Holy Place. Such actions made Roman rule particularly loathsome to the Jews.

D. IRON MIXED WITH CLAY (vv. 41-43)

41. *"Just as you saw that the feet and toes were partly of baked clay and partly of iron, so this will be a divided kingdom; yet it will have some of the strength of iron in it, even as you saw iron mixed with clay.*

The *mixed* nature of *the feet and toes* means that the *kingdom* of iron described in verse 40—the kingdom of brute strength—will become *divided* and thus weakened significantly. Such a picture is an accurate representation of what happens to the seemingly invincible Roman Empire. The next verse elaborates on this thought.

42, 43. *"As the toes were partly iron and partly clay, so this kingdom will be partly strong and partly brittle. And just as you saw the iron mixed with baked clay, so the people will be a mixture and will not remain united, any more than iron mixes with clay.*

During the latter years of its existence, the Roman Empire expands by conquering peoples in lands that are now part of Europe. This may be the meaning of the phrase *the people will be a mixture and will not remain united.* At the same time this is occurring, the emperors grow increasingly self-serving and decadent, making it more and more difficult to maintain a strong, united empire. As is often noted, the Roman Empire does not collapse because it was overpowered by enemies from without; rather, it rots from within. (We still use the term "feet of clay" to call attention to an individual's weaknesses, primarily in the area of personal character.)

Just as the Old Covenant was shown to be weak and inadequate because of humanity's sinfulness (Romans 8:3), so it is with the kingdoms of this world. And just as that weakness of the Old Covenant demonstrated the need for a new and better way to God, the growing instability of the earthly kingdoms sets the stage for the special kingdom described in the next two verses.

"DO YOU SEE WHERE YOU'RE STANDING?"

In the 1983 movie *The Scarlet and the Black,* Gregory Peck plays the part of Vatican priest Hugh O'Flaherty. The setting is the city of Rome during the Nazi occupation of 1944. O'Flaherty is busy helping prisoners of war escape, and a German colonel is trying to put a stop to that activity.

But as the city is about to fall to the approaching American army, the German colonel believes that his own wife and children are in danger, so he contacts O'Flaherty for help. The two meet at night in the ruins of the Roman Coliseum, where the German begins bragging about the invincibility of Hitler's "Thousand Year Reich." Incredulous, O'Flaherty exclaims, "Do you see where you're standing?" What irony—there they were, surrounded by ruins that witnessed to the long-gone power of the Roman Empire, and the arrogant German officer couldn't "see" it!

There is only one kingdom that lasts. God's Word and the unfolding events of history will teach us about it, but only if we have the eyes to see (cf. Mark 8:18).

—R. L. N.

HOW TO SAY IT

Alexander. Al-ex-AN-der.
Babylon. BAB-uh-lun.
Babylonian. Bab-ih-LOW-nee-un.
Belshazzar. Bel-SHAZZ-er.
Belteshazzar. Bel-tih-SHAZZ-er.
Cyrus. SIGH-russ.
Greco-Macedonian. GRECK-oh-Mass-uh-DOE-nee-un.
Herod. HAIR-ud.
Jehoiakim. Jeh-HOY-uh-kim.
Malachi. MAL-uh-kye.
Medes. Meeds.
Medo-Persian. ME-doe-PER-zhun.
Nebuchadnezzar. NEB-yuh-kud-NEZ-er.
Nehemiah. NEE-huh-MY-uh.
Persian. PER-zhun.
Pompey. Pom-PAY.

E. A SUPERIOR KINGDOM (vv. 44, 45)

44. *"In the time of those kings, the God of heaven will set up a kingdom that will never be destroyed, nor will it be left to another people. It will crush all those kingdoms and bring them to an end, but it will itself endure forever.*

In contrast to the increasing weakness and instability of earthly *kingdoms*, the *kingdom* that *the God of heaven* sets up *will itself endure forever*. We may wonder why Daniel refers to *kings* in this verse when his emphasis thus far has been on a succession of kingdoms. Most likely Daniel wants to point out that the real King (the God of Heaven) will do something that earthly kings are incapable of doing.

During the era of Roman rule, just before Jesus begins his ministry, John the Baptist speaks of the kingdom that is "near" (Matthew 3:2). This is the kingdom that *will never be destroyed, nor will it be left to another people,* and *will crush* and *bring* an *end* to the earthly *kingdoms.* God's kingdom will outlast, and triumph over, all human governments, no matter how hostile to God and his purposes they may be. This is illustrated during the infancy of Jesus, when wicked King Herod attempted to kill this One whom he considered a rival. But his evil plot was foiled by God's intervention (Matthew 2:11-14). In the same way, those rulers who played a part in the crucifixion of Jesus were not exercising the real authority; their actions were used by the God of Heaven to bring about his kingdom—the kingdom of kingdoms.

The words *will itself endure forever* bring to mind the title of today's study, "Prophecy of an Eternal Kingdom." Throughout the history of the church, many rulers have attempted to silence forever the voice of Jesus and his followers. In every case it is the rulers who have been silenced. The voice of Jesus and his church remains strong. So it will be when he returns (see Revelation 11:15).

GET THE PICTURE

People long have been mystified by a series of strange and ancient lines (called "geoglyphs") made by the Nazca people in the high plains of Peru. In her 1968 book *Mystery on the Desert*, Maria Reiche (1903–1998) describes how these unusual markings were once assumed to be the remnants of ancient irrigation ditches.

All that changed in 1939 when Dr. Paul Kosok of Long Island University discovered that their true meaning could be discerned only from the air. When viewed from the higher perspective that an airplane provided, the seemingly random lines form enormous drawings of birds, insects, and animals. Ancient lines on a dry plain raise many interesting questions, but they also teach an important truth: you must have the right perspective, the correct viewpoint, to get the truth.

In Daniel 2, God gave Nebuchadnezzar a dream that left him mystified. He could see plainly the details of the dream, but he lacked the correct perspective to put those details together. He needed a higher vantage point, God's vantage point, to understand. God granted the correct perspective to Daniel, who relayed it to the king. The king responded by giving glory to God and promoting Daniel and his friends to positions of leadership in Babylon.

Sometimes people think of the Bible as a series of individual, unconnected stories. They see details, but miss the big picture. But seen from God's perspective—definitely a higher vantage point than our own!—the Bible tells a single great story of redemption. Get the picture and you'll see that the story of the Bible is the story of Daniel's little stone that crushes the kingdoms of this world and grows to fill the whole earth.

—J. A. M.

45. *"This is the meaning of the vision of the rock cut out of a mountain, but not by human hands—a rock that broke the iron, the bronze, the clay, the silver and the gold to pieces.*

DAILY BIBLE READINGS

Monday, Aug. 18—The King Has a Dream (Daniel 1:18–2:6)

Tuesday, Aug. 19—Daniel Agrees to Interpret (Daniel 2:7-16)

Wednesday, Aug. 20—Daniel Prays for Wisdom (Daniel 2:17-23)

Thursday, Aug. 21—God Reveals Mysteries (Daniel 2:24-28)

Friday, Aug. 22—Daniel Tells the Dream (Daniel 2:29-35)

Saturday, Aug. 23—This Kingdom Will Last Forever (Daniel 2:36-45)

Sunday, Aug. 24—The Alpha and Omega (Revelation 21:1-7)

"The God of heaven [shall] set up a kingdom, which shall never be destroyed." Daniel 2:44

Today's visual connects the prophecy of today's text with that of John in Revelation.

WHAT DO YOU THINK?

Suppose a fellow believer said to you, "If God is in control, what does he need me for?" How would you respond?

"The great God has shown the king what will take place in the future. The dream is true and the interpretation is trustworthy."

The phrase *not by human hands* highlights once more that this great kingdom is not of human origin (cf. v. 34). Human effort will have nothing to do with its establishment. (Human hands often wanted to prevent its establishment.) God is in control! See Psalm 118:23.

Like the kingdom Daniel has just described, his interpretation of the king's dream is not of human origin, either. God has *shown* the contents and the meaning of the dream to Daniel; he, in turn, has conveyed that knowledge to King Nebuchadnezzar. That information is not subject to the king's approval or disapproval. The God of Heaven has spoken; everything that Daniel has declared would (and did) happen. Without a doubt, *the dream is true and the interpretation is trustworthy.* It is to the king's credit that he falls upon his face before Daniel and confesses, "Surely your God is the God of gods and the Lord of kings and a revealer of mysteries, for you were able to reveal this mystery" (v. 47). True, "the king placed Daniel in a high position" (v. 48). But it is clear from our study that this is not really Nebuchadnezzar's doing. The real King had spoken.

STAND OR FALL

If you have ever participated in singing Handel's *Messiah*, you know that the climactic moment is the "Hallelujah Chorus" when everyone rises to their feet. King George II is the one who started that tradition in 1742 when he stood during the chorus's debut. Everyone stood when the king stood.

There are many theories about why King George stood at that particular point in the *Messiah.* One suggestion is that the king was so moved with the message of God's eternal kingdom and reign that he stood to honor the true King of kings and Lord of lords. Another is that King George merely was practicing his version of the seventh inning stretch.

I suspect the king stood up to honor a God who is far greater than himself. Many centuries earlier, Nebuchadnezzar had a similar reaction when he encountered God's awe-inspiring nature and power. When Daniel revealed and interpreted the king's dream, Nebuchadnezzar fell prostrate and honored God.

Whether you rise to your feet or fall on your face, when you encounter the wonder of God and his Kingdom you must react. Paul requires that "every knee should bow . . . and every tongue confess that Jesus Christ is Lord" (Philippians 2:10, 11). Do you do that now? When the Last Day comes, will you be in practice to do it then?

—J. A. M.

CONCLUSION

In the Introduction we thought about homesickness, using the example of children being away from home. Eventually most children become more comfortable with the idea of spending the night somewhere and are much less prone to homesickness. (Often the parents are the ones who wish their children didn't get quite so excited about being away from Mom and Dad!)

The term *homesickness* takes on a new meaning when one becomes a Christian and begins to see things from an eternal perspective. With the passing of time, we who are Christians find ourselves becoming "homesick for Heaven." This is especially so if we begin to experience physical ailments that are accompanied by constant pain or discomfort. How thankful we are that we belong to the eternal kingdom of which Daniel spoke! How encouraging to realize that each day that passes brings us one day closer to our arrival at our real home.

Let us press on faithfully in the Father's service, knowing that we are part of a "kingdom that cannot be shaken" (Hebrews 12:28).

WHAT DO YOU THINK?

Nebuchadnezzar seemed comforted by the interpretation Daniel gave. How does God's Word give you comfort today?

PRAYER

Father, we thank you for your kingdom and for the promise that it can never be destroyed. May we be faithful in doing the work you have for us to do, until the King himself, the Lord Jesus Christ, returns to take us home. In his name we ask, amen.

THOUGHT TO REMEMBER

Remember which kingdom you serve.

Discovery Learning

This page contains an alternative lesson plan emphasizing learning activities. Classes desiring such student involvement will find these suggestions helpful. The next page is a reproducible activity page to further enhance discovery learning.

LEARNING GOALS

After this lesson each student will be able to:

1. Retell Nebuchadnezzar's dream and Daniel's interpretation.

2. Explain God's eternal kingdom and his role in history.

3. Describe God's role in history to a non-Christian.

INTO THE LESSON

Begin class by asking, "Name a regime or kingdom that rose and fell during the twentieth century." (*Students will probably mention the Third Reich, the Soviet Union, Romania, Poland, some of the African countries, or revolutionary leaders.*) Say, "As we grew up, we learned about many kingdoms in our world, only to watch them fall. Only God's kingdom will stand forever."

INTO THE WORD

Make a handout with a sketch of a statue with five lines on either side of it, spaced to align with the different sections of the statue identified in the text. Reproduce this image on the board or an overhead transparency.

Briefly tell the background for today's passage. Then ask students to work individually or in small groups to explain the statue. On the lines to the left of the statue they should identify the parts of the statue (head of gold, chest and arms of silver, etc.). On the lines to the right they are to identify the interpretation (Nebuchadnezzar, Medo-Persian Empire, etc.).

Allow time for the groups to work; then ask for someone from each group to tell you what to write on the lines on the image on the chalkboard or overhead projection. Add a rock rolling toward the statue and ask what it is going to do. What does this rock represent?

Briefly contrast the earthly kingdoms of the statue and the kingdom of God, using commentary material for verse 44. Use the "God and Government" section of the reproducible page that follows to expand on this idea.

INTO LIFE

Say, "Daniel's interpretation reminds us that God's kingdom is eternal. God is in charge of history. No government is above God's control.

Find and play for your class the song "God Is in Control" by Twila Paris. Instruct students to listen carefully for phrases that demonstrate the truth of today's lesson.

The verses talk about God's ultimate purpose, which will not be stopped by culture or deception.

If you cannot get a recording of Twila Paris's song, use the song "Onward, Christian Soldiers." Distribute hymnals and direct students to the song. If you can, play a recording and let them do the same search described above. (If your hymnal does not include the following stanza, make a handout and distribute it. It expresses well the truth Daniel was telling.)

> Crowns and thrones may perish, kingdoms rise and wane,
> But the Church of Jesus, constant will remain;
> Gates of hell can never 'gainst that Church prevail;
> We have Christ's own promise, and that cannot fail.

Ask, "When we say, 'God is in control,' just what do we mean? How does that affect our own decision-making?" Observe that some people think that God wants them to marry only a specific person, take a specific job, work in a specific ministry, or buy a specific house. In other words, for every decision, there is only one right decision (God's will), and any other decision would be wrong. Others believe God's control is usually limited to what we might call the "big picture" of history.

In a big-picture sense God guides the general course of history, defining boundaries and times of nations, as Paul says in Acts 17. In the Bible when God intervened in a person's life, it was to bring about his big picture. For example, God's intervention in the Garden with Adam and Eve occurred because the whole world was affected. His interactions with Abraham, Isaac, and Jacob concerned the covenant that was part of God's plan for all mankind.

Distribute copies of the reproducible activity "If God Is in Control" from the next page. Give students time to write the case study called for. Have several students read their situations. Then ask the students to respond to the "your answer" segment of the activity. Again, after allowing time to complete the activity, ask several students to tell what they wrote. Add relevant explanations as needed.

Say, "It is not easy to remember everything we want to say when someone asks us questions, so we are going to practice explaining God's eternal kingdom and his role in history." Let partners practice with each other. Let two or three volunteers make their explanations for the class.

Play again the song you used, letting your students sing along as an expression of praise and thanksgiving to God.

God and Government

From each of the following Bible texts, state principles of God's plan for and expectation of human governments.

Acts 17:26

Romans 13:1-7

1 Timothy 2:1, 2

1 Peter 2:13-17

If God Is in Control . . .

Many nonbelievers cannot fathom why God would allow bad things to happen if he is truly in control. Write a short case study from such a worldview and mind-set.

"If God is in control, then why . . .

What is your answer to that "problem"? What Scripture texts can you bring to the issue?

PREDICTION OF THE END

WHY TEACH THIS LESSON?

Crystal balls, astrology, numerology—people foolishly use such things to try and see into the future. People want to find out in advance what the future holds! Even Christians sometimes get caught up in the speculation and guessing. But all that Christians really need to know about the future can be summed up in two words: God wins!

Perhaps some of your learners have been fretting about the future. They may have specific concerns or just a general anxiety. Either way, this lesson will provide reassurance that, when God wins, we share in the victory by his grace. That victory includes resurrection from the dead and eternal reward. If some of your learners are focused on the quagmire of their immediate personal circumstances, this lesson can lift their gaze to the bright hope and certainty of the Lord's reward. They will find today's lesson to be a blessing indeed!

INTRODUCTION

A. "THE END"

Whenever those two words appear on a movie screen, we know it's time to leave the theater. For many, however, "the end" is a topic of great fascination, particularly the topic of the end of the world. They sense that current events seem to be leading toward some kind of climax. Some have gone as far as attempting to attach specific dates to certain end-time events—despite Jesus' clear warning that such efforts are futile (Matthew 24:36, 42, 44).

Amid the current abundance of discussions and writings on the end times, it is easy to forget that ours is by no means the only generation to have a keen interest in such matters. Prior generations have interpreted certain wars, natural disasters, or other catastrophes as signs that "the end" was indeed at hand. There is a normal curiosity about these topics and a desire to possess some degree of understanding about them. Jesus' own disciples were very curious about such things (see Acts 1:6). Jesus' answer to them in Acts 1:7, 8 was not the answer they wanted, but it was certainly the answer they needed. Jesus clearly indicates that the study of "the end" should not distract us from doing the will of the one who is in charge of the end.

This same perspective can be seen in today's study from the book of Daniel. He was granted the opportunity to receive a revelation from God in the form of a "great vision" (Daniel 10:8). As a result, that prophet received a lengthy description of future events affecting God's people. When Daniel asks, "My Lord, what will the outcome of all this be?" (Daniel 12:8), the reply he received is similar to Jesus' response to his disciples' inquiry about restoring the kingdom (see Acts 1:7; Daniel 12:9).

Why does God seem to "dangle the carrot" in front of us and then withhold information that might prove useful in understanding what he is saying? Does he want to keep us guessing? No, but he does want to keep us *trusting* and fully assured that no matter how perplexing the circumstances of our lives or our times may be, he remains firmly in control—until "the end."

DEVOTIONAL READING:
REVELATION 7:9-17

BACKGROUND SCRIPTURE:
DANIEL 12

PRINTED TEXT:
DANIEL 12:1-9

LESSON AIMS

After participating in this lesson, each student will be able to:

1. Summarize the brief account of the end times found in Daniel 12.

2. Know that "everlasting" applies to both the saved and unsaved.

3. Write down and commit to changing one aspect of his or her life that would be different if Jesus were known to be returning within thirty days.

KEY VERSE

Multitudes who sleep in the dust of the earth will awake: some to everlasting life, others to shame and everlasting contempt.   —Daniel 12:2

LESSON 14 NOTES

B. LESSON BACKGROUND

The book of Daniel can be divided into two main sections, and they are very different from each other! Chapters 1–6 include some of the most familiar stories in the Bible. Chapters 7–12 consist of some of the more unfamiliar portions of Scripture, or, at least, portions that are among the most puzzling in the Bible. Unlike last week's lesson, which featured both a dream *and* its interpretation, today we consider part of a vision with very little aid in the way of interpretation.

The background for today's lesson takes us to Daniel 10. There we are told that in the third year of Cyrus king of Persia (536 B.C.), Daniel received a vision from the Lord, an experience that left the prophet terrified and unable to move (Daniel 10:7, 8). Then, in Daniel's words, "A hand touched me and set me trembling on my hands and knees" (10:10). The one who touched Daniel spoke and said, "I have come to explain to you what will happen to your people in the future, for the vision concerns a time yet to come" (10:14).

The description of future events begins with 11:2 and includes today's lesson text from 12:1-9. In order to have a better grasp of this text, a survey of the contents of Daniel 11 is useful.

Daniel 11:2-4 notes the appearance of four Persian kings. The first three Persian kings were most likely Cambyses (530–522 B.C.), Smerdis (522 B.C.), and Darius I (522–486 B.C.). The fourth king, Xerxes I (also known as Ahasuerus), reigns when the story of the book of Esther takes place. By reading that book and noting the lavishness of the banquets hosted by Xerxes, we can grasp how much "richer" (v. 2) he was than those who reigned before him. Xerxes tries to conquer Greece in 480 B.C., but fails.

The "mighty king" of verses 3 and 4 is Alexander the Great. Before his death in 323 B.C., his kingdom would be one of "great power" (v. 3), embracing an empire far more extensive than any in the history of the world to that point. After his death, his kingdom is the one that would be "broken up and parceled out toward the four winds of heaven" (11:3) after his death.

Daniel 11:5-20 traces the history of God's people from 323 B.C. until 175 B.C. following the division of Alexander's empire. The "king of the South" (Egypt) and the "king of the North" (Syria) had great significance for God's people (who were caught right in the middle).

Daniel 11:21-35 calls attention to a "contemptible person" (v. 21). This is most likely Antiochus Epiphanes, the Syrian ruler whose persecution of the people of God and abuses of their religious practices were particularly repulsive. He ruled from 175–163 B.C. (see 1 Maccabees 1–6).

Daniel 11:36-45 continues to chronicle the history of God's people during the time between the Old and New Testaments, also called the "Intertestamental Period." It begins with a description of a king who "will say unheard-of things against the God of gods" (v. 36). This is most likely Herod the Great, who sought to kill the infant Jesus. This brings us to today's lesson.

I. FUTURE EVENTS (DANIEL 12:1-4)

A. GREAT DISTRESS (v. 1a)

1a. "At that time Michael, the great prince who protects your people, will arise. There will be a time of distress such as has not happened from the beginning of nations until then.

Jude 9 refers to *Michael* as one of the archangels (apparently a designation of a higher rank of angel). Earlier in the book of Daniel, Michael's name is mentioned by the one who said that he had come to tell Daniel what would befall his people in the latter days (10:13, 14).

HOW TO SAY IT

Alexander. Al-ex-AN-der.

Ahasuerus. Uh-haz-you-EE-rus.

Antiochus Epiphanes. An-TIE-oh-kus Ih-PIFF-uh-neez.

Cambyses. Kam-BYE-seez.

Cyrus. SIGH-russ.

Darius. Duh-RYE-us.

Herod. HAIR-ud.

Josephus. Jo-SEE-fus.

Maccabees. MACK-uh-bees.

Michael. MIKE-ul.

Persia. PER-zhuh.

Smerdis. SMER-dis.

Syrian. SEAR-ee-un.

Tarot. TARE-oh.

Tigris. TIE-griss.

Xerxes. ZERK-seez.

In the verse before us, Michael's future action is linked with *a time of distress, such as has not happened from the beginning of nations until then.* The words of this verse are strikingly similar to what Jesus says in addressing his disciples' question about the destruction of the temple in Jerusalem (Matthew 24:1, 2, 21).

Great distress does indeed come in A.D. 70, when the city falls to the Romans. According to the Jewish historian Josephus, the atrocities the Romans commit upon the Jews on this occasion are unparalleled in history. In his work *Wars of the Jews,* Josephus vividly describes "the multitude of carcasses that lay in heaps one upon another" that "produced a pestilential stench." Daniel thus describes the next major event in the history of God's people (following the reign of Herod the Great, covered at the end of Daniel 11).

B. GREAT DELIVERANCE (v. 1b)

1b. *"But at that time your people—everyone whose name is found written in the book—will be delivered.*

There is, however, a ray of hope. Along with Jesus' warning of the disaster coming upon Jerusalem, he provides a way of escape to his followers: anyone who sees "'the abomination that causes desolation,' spoken of through the prophet Daniel" should flee to the mountains to escape the imminent destruction (Matthew 24:15, 16). Those Jewish Christians who take the words of their Master seriously (*everyone whose name is found written in the book*) will see the approaching Roman armies in A.D. 70 and leave the city. By doing so, they are spared the brutal treatment Josephus describes.

C. GREAT DRAMA (vv. 2, 3)

2. *"Multitudes who sleep in the dust of the earth will awake: some to everlasting life, others to shame and everlasting contempt.*

Many students see this as a prediction of the bodily resurrection to occur when Jesus returns, "a resurrection of both the righteous and the wicked" (Acts 24:15). Certainly that is part of what is described here. However, it is also possible to interpret these words in a more spiritual sense, as highlighting the abundant *life* (John 10:10) that Jesus came to bring us. Jesus spoke of passing from death to life in John 5:24. Those who oppose this message bring only *shame and everlasting contempt* upon themselves—a fact that will become especially clear at the resurrection and final judgment.

3. *"Those who are wise will shine like the brightness of the heavens, and those who lead many to righteousness, like the stars for ever and ever.*

Christians are to *"shine like* stars in the universe" as a testimony to the grace of God (Philippians 2:15; cf. Matthew 5:14). And when this present life is complete, they will shine even brighter (Matthew 13:43). The description of Christians as *stars* calls attention to this truth: no matter how dark death may seem to be, it only serves as a backdrop against which the Christian's hope shines ever more brightly.

UNSHAKEN

When hurricane Andrew hit south Florida in August, 1992, it was a time of distress. Many gathered at the South Dade Christian Church building for shelter from the storm. When the tempest hit, doors were ripped from the lobby and the wind blew open the sanctuary doors. Six men struggled to hold the doors together. Soon the windows began to blow apart and the very foundation of the building began to shake. Horrendous rain and wind swirled down through the baptistery.

Morning revealed a scene of terrible devastation. One worker began to clear the Communion Table covered with litter and debris. She discovered the Communion

WHAT DO YOU THINK?

Throughout history, God's people—either Israel or the church—often have had to endure special troubles because they were/are God's people. What gives you the determination to remain faithful in spite of troubles? How can you be sure your faith will hold up if the tribulation becomes intense? How do passages such as John 16:33; Romans 8:18; 2 Corinthians 4:16-18; James 1:2-4, 12; and 1 Peter 4:12 help?

WHAT DO YOU THINK?

How can our faith be strengthened by thinking about the end times? How can we be distracted or discouraged in our faith by thinking about the end times?

[Consider 2 Thessalonians 2:1-12; 3:6-12 and Hebrews 11:39, 40 in the course of your discussion.]

Many of them that sleep in the dust of the earth shall awake, some to everlasting life, and some to shame and everlasting contempt. —Daniel 12:2

Use today's visual to illustrate verse 2. Ask, "In what situations do you lean most heavily on this promise?"

still intact. Every cup was filled and the bread undisturbed. God seemed to be saying that what Christ purchased for us at the cost of his body and blood can never be taken away, no matter the storm.

Outside, the library wing was blown away. Only the north wall, covered with bookshelves, remained. All the books were blown away or destroyed except for one row with no water or wind damage: a row of Bibles. A coincidence? Yes. But also a reminder of Jesus' words, "Heaven and earth will pass away, but my words will never pass away" (Luke 21:33).

Daniel predicted a time of distress. But he also made it clear that there is security in the storm for those who trust the sacrifice of the Son and the unshakable truth of the Word. Those who do are wise and will shine (Daniel 12:3). —J. A. M.

D. COMMAND TO DANIEL (v. 4)

4. "But you, Daniel, close up and seal the words of the scroll until the time of the end. Many will go here and there to increase knowledge."

A document of the time is "sealed" by impressing upon a piece of wax the identifying mark of the person(s) responsible for its contents. Any text thus sealed is not to be tampered with. The command for Daniel to seal the words of the scroll may be symbolic of the fact that the events revealed to Daniel concerning the time of the end are unchangeable; they most certainly will come to pass. (Compare Revelation 5:1-5, where "the Lion of the tribe of Judah, the Root of David," is worthy and able "to open the scroll and its seven seals.")

There are two ways to understand the statement that many will go here and there to increase knowledge. From a positive standpoint, the "knowledge" may refer to the understanding of Daniel's message gained by God's faithful people as they go "here and there" in fulfillment of the Great Commission. Negatively, the verse may describe the efforts of people scurrying "here and there" to understand Daniel's message, yet having no success because they are relying on their own skill and insight, not God's. Either interpretation has merit.

II. FURTHER INFORMATION (DANIEL 12:5-7)

A. TWO BY A RIVER (v. 5)

5. Then I, Daniel, looked, and there before me stood two others, one on this bank of the river and one on the opposite bank.

Once again Daniel has the opportunity to participate in a celestial conversation, as the two individuals are apparently angels. This river is undoubtedly the river mentioned earlier in Daniel 10:4, identified as the Tigris River (located in modern Iraq). Thus, Daniel is standing by the Tigris River when he begins to receive the revelation recorded in chapters 10–12.

B. QUESTION RAISED (v. 6)

6. One of them said to the man clothed in linen, who was above the waters of the river, "How long will it be before these astonishing things are fulfilled?"

The man clothed in linen is first mentioned in Daniel 10:5, in connection with the beginning of Daniel's vision. The manner in which he is described in terms of chrysolite, lightning, bronze, fire, etc. (10:5, 6) brings to mind the description of the glory of God in Ezekiel 1:13-16 and the appearance of Jesus to the apostle John in Revelation 1:13-15.

One of the two individuals mentioned in verse 5 raises a question of the man in linen: How long will it be before these astonishing things are fulfilled? It appears that, just like human beings, these two angelic beings are curious as to the timetable for the events described previously.

WHAT DO YOU THINK?

Why do we have this urge to know the when of future events? What should we do about this desire?

C. ANSWER GIVEN (v. 7)

7. The man clothed in linen, who was above the waters of the river, lifted his right hand and his left hand toward heaven, and I heard him swear by him who lives forever, saying, "It will be for a time, times and half a time. When the power of the holy people has been finally broken, all these things will be completed."

Often in the Bible, if someone desires to state an oath, he raises one hand in a symbolic gesture, much as a person does in court today. (See Genesis 14:22-24 and Ezekiel 20:5, 6.) After stating the oath *by him who lives forever* (i.e., the Lord), the man utters the puzzling words in answer to the question that had been raised: *it will be for a time, times and half a time.*

The words "time, times and half a time" appear earlier in Daniel 7:25, where a period of oppression of God's people is described. (See also Revelation 12:14.) If the unit for measuring the time should be a year, then "time, times, and a half" would equal three and a half years. (This seems to be the most likely way to understand the word "times" in Daniel 4:25.)

Others take a more symbolic understanding, believing that the phrase designates simply a limited period of time (half the number seven, which generally symbolizes completeness in the Bible). If this understanding of the numbers is taken, then the message and its application are more general, being meant to speak to God's people in any situation where they are undergoing persecution. Such persecution is only temporary, it is never the final outcome for God's people. If they persevere and continue to be faithful to him, they will be blessed.

The power of the holy people (the Jews) is broken in A.D. 70 when the Romans destroy Jerusalem (Daniel 12:1; Matthew 24:2).

III. DANIEL'S RESPONSE (DANIEL 12:8, 9)

A. CONFUSION (v. 8)

8. I heard, but I did not understand. So I asked, "My lord, what will the outcome of all this be?"

Daniel *heard* the explanation given but does not *understand* it. His position is similar to ours as we try to understand certain prophetic passages in the Bible—such as the one before us now! Bible students continue to wrestle with the interpretation of this text. How can we possibly understand all the images and symbols that are both here and in the book of Revelation?

Daniel raises a question similar to the one asked of the man clothed in linen in verse 6: *what will the outcome of all this be?* The question in verse 6 seems to deal more with the time element concerning future events; Daniel wants to know about the consequences or the impact of these events.

INQUIRING MINDS WANT TO KNOW!

Several years ago, a supermarket tabloid popularized the phrase, "Inquiring minds want to know!" They used that phrase in their TV commercials to try to convince people of the need to buy the gossip sheet being promoted.

But think about how true the phrase itself is! Many today have an insatiable desire for more knowledge, especially knowledge about the future. Horoscopes, Tarot cards, and psychic readings abound. Even Christians can get obsessed with trying to figure out "Bible codes" and the precise meaning of the imagery in the books of Daniel and Revelation.

But God has given us just the amount of information that he knows we need concerning future events—more information than what Daniel had, but less than what we eventually will have when the Lord returns. How hard we push God for "more" information reveals something about our level of trust in him.   —R. L. N.

DAILY BIBLE READINGS

Monday, Aug. 25—*The Sealed Book (Daniel 12:1-7)*

Tuesday, Aug. 26—*Happy Are Those Who Persevere (Daniel 12:8-13)*

Wednesday, Aug. 27—*I Will Make You a Pillar (Revelation 3:7-13)*

Thursday, Aug. 28—*Inherit the Imperishable (1 Corinthians 15:50-56)*

Friday, Aug. 29—*The Multitude Before God's Throne (Revelation 7:9-17)*

Saturday, Aug. 30—*The Lord Will Be Their Light (Revelation 22:1-7)*

Sunday, Aug. 31—*Come, Inherit the Kingdom (Matthew 25:31-40)*

WHAT DO YOU THINK?

What would be different in your walk with Christ if you knew nothing about the end times?

B. CLOSED UP (v. 9)

9. He replied, "Go your way, Daniel, because the words are closed up and sealed until the time of the end."

Daniel is informed once more (cf. v. 4) that *the words are closed up and sealed until the time of the end.* He will have to trust the Lord. He will have to make certain that even though his understanding remains incomplete, he will determine to be the kind of person that God wants him to be—"purified, made spotless and refined" (v. 10).

This must be our attitude as well. We may not possess the detailed understanding we would like, but we know who holds the future and we must trust him to work out his purposes in his time. Both Daniel and Revelation conclude with a pronouncement of blessing upon a certain kind of person. It is not the person who has a complete understanding of all the contents in the books; rather, it is the one who waits for the end (Daniel 12:12) and who faithfully keeps the Lord's commandments (Revelation 22:14).

NO MORE MOCKING

There are those who mock God's kingdom. They say it doesn't amount to much. This mocking attitude is present throughout history. But mockers are often wrong.

When William Seward negotiated the U.S. purchase of Alaska from Russia, critics mocked and called the $7.2 million purchase "Seward's Folly." At about two cents an acre, Alaska has proved to be a real bargain!

George Washington Carver was mocked for his agricultural research on peanuts, which were not even recognized as a crop at the time. He later developed over 300 uses for the peanut and made the peanut the second largest cash crop for the Southern U.S.

Thomas Edison was called stupid by his teachers. Remember that the next time you turn on a light.

Walt Disney could not get financiers to invest in his idea for a theme park. They mocked while Disney raised the funds for Disneyland through his television program.

Albert Einstein was ridiculed because he could not speak until he was four and couldn't read until he was seven.

Human judgment is often wrong in assessing the ultimate outcome of individuals and groups. God's kingdom has always had its detractors. But all the detractors put together don't change our future, and it is glorious!

Daniel 12:10 says of this future, "Many will be purified, made spotless and refined, because the wicked will continue to be wicked. None of the wicked will understand." Verse 13 adds a wonderful promise to Daniel, and it applies to all of God's people: "At the end of the days you will rise to receive your allotted inheritance." Those who have ignored and mocked God's kingdom will be silent then.

—J. A. M.

CONCLUSION

Perseverance is a quality that God *always* has required of his people. Whether it is Noah building the ark, the children of Israel traveling toward the promised land, or Jesus who "endured" the cross (Hebrews 12:2), the standard has never changed. There is no room for the "faint-hearted" among those who follow Jesus—a point he often emphasized to would-be disciples (see Luke 9:57-62). Only the "faith-hearted" are "fit for service in the kingdom of God" (Luke 9:62). The language of Daniel and Revelation should not cause us to look at our calendars or at current world events, but at our hearts. If we are faithful, then it will not matter when "the end" comes—whether by our own deaths or with Jesus' return. Either way, we will be ready.

WHAT DO YOU THINK?

What are some ways we can "wait" in a way that pleases God?

[You may find the book of Proverbs and the Sermon on the Mount helpful in guiding your discussion.]

PRAYER

Father, help us to be faithful stewards of all we have so that when Jesus returns, his coming will be a time of joy for us, not embarrassment and dread. We are so thankful to know that the future, and the future of every Christian, is in your hands. In Jesus' name, amen.

THOUGHT TO REMEMBER

"I love thy kingdom, Lord."
—Timothy Dwight

Discovery Learning

This page contains an alternative lesson plan emphasizing learning activities. Classes desiring such student involvement will find these suggestions helpful. The next page is a reproducible activity page to further enhance discovery learning.

LEARNING GOALS

After participating in this lesson, each student will be able to:

1. Summarize the brief account of the end times found in Daniel 12.

2. Know that "everlasting" applies to both the saved and unsaved.

3. Write down and commit to changing one aspect of his or her life that would be different if Jesus were known to be returning within thirty days.

INTO THE LESSON

ADVANCE PREPARATION: Collect a variety of articles, books, and commentaries purporting to give details of the end times. These may be found in virtually any context, from a church library to a popular newsmagazine. Highlight segments of articles that tell the supposed details of the end times.

Prior to class, post a large sign that says, "The End" and scatter around the room the various articles, books, and commentaries you have gathered. Be sure to have enough of these to draw attention to them and to the subject matter. Tab appropriate segments with stick-on notes. As students arrive, ask them to pick up one of the items and skim through it (highlighted sections of articles, brief description on book jackets). Have a few students concisely report what the item they have says about the end times.

Say, "Throughout history there has been an abundance of speculation on the end times. Dates have been given. Specific events have been said to be the precursors to the last days. Appropriately, today's text concludes the quarter by addressing the matter of the end."

INTO THE WORD

Ask students to read Daniel 12:1-9 silently. At the conclusion of reading ask several students to provide their immediate impressions of the text, noting what it indicates about the end times. You should be familiar with the commentary material to enhance these reports. There will be different approaches to this text. Some will take the first verse as pointing to the end times; others may interpret it as referring to the destruction of Jerusalem in A.D. 70. Say, "It is often true that when, out of individual curiosity or intrigue, we get caught in the details of end times texts, we miss the basic point."

Ask students to work together in pairs to determine what the basic point of this text concerning the end times is. You may give the hint that the answer is alluded to in a phrase repeated in the text. Ask for volunteers to share their ideas. Direct the class to read Daniel 12:4, 9. Like many of us, Daniel asks a question concerning the details, and he is given the answer by God that they will not be known.

Draw attention to the consequences indicated in Daniel 12:2. (You may also recall the distinction between the righteous and the wicked seen in the lesson text in Malachi 3 and 4 two weeks ago.) Say, "There are many views of the afterlife today. Two of the primary ones are reincarnation and annihilation. Reincarnation presupposes an eternity that can get progressively better with each life. Annihilation assumes that death results in a person's ceasing to exist." Ask a student to read Acts 24:15. Then take time to compare this with the idea in Daniel 12:2. Say, "The idea of 'everlasting' applies to both the just and the unjust. The basic point of our text is that the end times will come with consequences, and we must be prepared regardless of how it comes to be."

INTO LIFE

Distribute copies of the reproducible activity "The Daily End Times" from the next page. Say, "Imagine that you know that Jesus will return within the next thirty days. Ignore any details about his coming. Just think about the fact that he is coming." Allow some quiet time for pondering this, and then ask the students to return to their pairs and reveal their "headlines." Ask them to describe the thoughts and emotions this exercise raised in each of them. Ask for volunteers to present their reactions to the class.

Say, "Dwight Moody was once asked what he would do if he knew Jesus was coming the next day. He replied that he would not change anything he does. It would be good if we were all able to say that honestly, but most of us would change something. Most of us would move something up our priority list." Have each student write down one thing that he would change if he knew Jesus would be coming in thirty days. Ask students to return to their earlier pairs, and direct the students to pray for one another in committing to this change. Now ask students to respond to the "Eternal News" section of the reproducible page.

The Daily End Times

Imagine that you know that Jesus will return within the next thirty days. Without focusing too intently on the details of his coming, think how you would respond to the simple fact that he is coming. Then write a banner headline announcing this grand fact. Below that write three story subheadings. (Do all your writing on the "newspaper" (*The Daily End Times*) below.

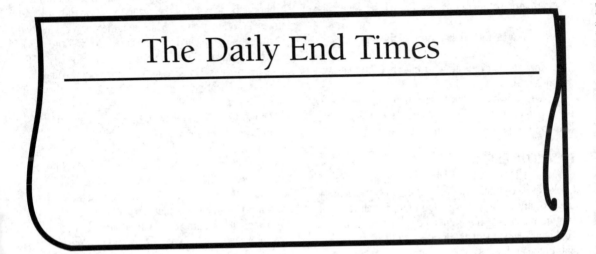

The Daily End Times

Eternal News

Now imagine that Heaven publishes a newspaper (*Eternal News*). Write a banner headline and three story subheadings on the newspaper below for the day *after* Jesus' Second Coming.

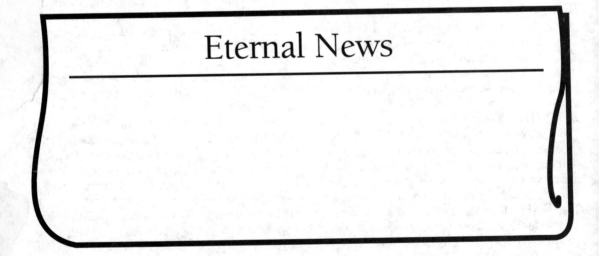

Eternal News